Moreton Morrell Site

THE *NEW*
STRATEGIC
BRAND
MANAGEMENT

'A real thought provoker for marketing and business people. *Strategic Brand Management* is an essential tool to develop strong marketing strategy.'

P Desaulles, Vice President, Du Pont de Nemours Europe

'A solid contribution written with depth and insight. I recommend it to all those who desire a further understanding of the various dimensions of brand management.'

David A Aaker, University of California at Berkeley, and author of *Managing Brand Equity*

'After reading Kapferer's book, you'll never again think of a brand as just a name. Several exciting new ideas and perspectives on brand building are offered that have been absent from our literature.'

Philip Kotler, Northwestern University

'The best book on brands yet. It is an invaluable reference for designers, marketing and brand managers.'

Design Magazine

'The treatment of brand-product strategies, brand extensions and financial evaluations are also strengths of the book.'

Journal of Marketing

'A "think book". It deals with the very essence and culture of branding.'

International Journal of Research in Marketing

'An authoritative analysis about establishing an identity and exploiting it.'

Daily Telegraph

'A full and highly informative text… well written and brought to life through numerous appropriate examples.'

Journal of the Market Research Society

'One of the best books on brand management. Kapferer is thought provoking and always able to create new insights on various brand related topics.'

Rik Riezebos, CEO Brand Capital and director of EURIB/European Institute for Brand Management

'One of the definitive resources on branding for marketing professionals worldwide.'

The Economic Times, India

'Jean Noel Kapferer's hierarchy of brands with six levels of brands is an extraordinary insight.'

Sam Hill and Chris Lederer, authors of *The Infinite Asset,* Harvard Business School Press

THE *NEW* STRATEGIC **BRAND** MANAGEMENT

Creating and Sustaining Brand Equity Long Term

JEAN-NOËL KAPFERER

KOGAN PAGE

London and Sterling, VA

Publisher's note

Every possible effort has been made to ensure that the information contained in this book is accurate at the time of going to press, and the publishers and authors cannot accept responsibility for any errors or omissions, however caused. No responsibility for loss or damage occasioned to any person acting, or refraining from action, as a result of the material in this publication can be accepted by the editor, the publisher or any of the authors.

First published in France in hardback in 1992 and in paperback in 1995 by Les Editions d'Organisation
Second edition published in Great Britain in 1997 by Kogan Page Limited
Third edition 2004

120 Pentonville Road
London N1 9JN
United Kingdom
www.kogan-page.co.uk

22883 Quicksilver Drive
Sterling VA 20166–2012
USA

© Les Editions d'Organisation, 1992, 1995, 1997, 2004

ISBN 0 7494 4283 2

British Library Cataloguing-in-Publication Data

A CIP record for this book is available from the British Library.

Library of Congress Cataloging-in-Publication Data

Kapferer, Jean-Noël.
  The new strategic brand management : creating and sustaining brand equity long term / Jean Noel Kapferer,--3rd ed.
    p. cm.
  Includes bibliographical references and index.
  ISBN 0-7494-4283-2
  1. Brand name products--Management. I. Kapferer, Jean-Noël. Strategic brand management. II. Title
HD69.B7K37 2004
658.8'343--dc22

2004011734

Typeset by Saxon Graphics Ltd, Derby
Printed and bound in Great Britain by Scotprint

Contents

Part Four: Brand valuation

List of figures

List of tables

Preface to the third edition

Integrating brand and business

This is a book on strategic brand management. It capitalises on the success of the former two editions. As far as we understand from our readers worldwide (marketers, advertisers, lawyers, MBA students and so on), this success was based on six attributes which we have of course maintained:

- **Originality**. *Strategic Brand Management* is quite different from all the other books on brand management. This is due to a unique balance between theory and first-hand cases, mostly taken from our consultancy work.
- **Relevance**. The cases and illustrations are new, unusual, and not over-exposed. They often represent business situations readers will relate to and understand more readily than examples using Coke, Starbucks, Cisco, Fedex, BMW and other great classics of most books and conferences on brands.
- **Breadth of scope**. We have tried to address most of the key issues faced by brands.
- **Depth of treatment**. Each facet of brand management receives a deep analysis, hence the bigger size of this edition.
- **Diversity**. Our examples cover the fast-moving consumer goods sector (FMCG) as well as commodities, business-to-business brands, pharmaceutical brands, luxury brands, service brands, e-brands, and distributors' brands – which are brands almost like the others.
- **International scope**, with examples from the United States, Europe and Asia.

This third edition is much more than a revision of the previous one. It is a whole new book for understanding today's brands and managing them efficiently in today's markets. Fifteen years after the first edition, so much change has happened in the world of brands! This is why this new edition has been thoroughly reorganised, transformed and enriched. Of course, our models and methodologies have not changed in essence, but they have been adapted to reflect current competition.

This edition concentrates much more than before on internationalisation and globalisation (how to implement these in practice), on portfolio concentration (managing brand transfers or switches), on the creation of megabrands through brand extensions, on the development of competitive advantage and dominant position through an adequate brand portfolio, and on the efficient management of the relationships between the brand, the corporation and the product (the issue of brand architectures).

There are many other significant new features in this edition, which reflect the new branding environment:

- Because distributors' brands (that is, the brands of major retailers) are everywhere and often hold a dominant market share, they need their own chapter. In addition, in each chapter we have addressed in depth how the recommendations do or do not apply to distributors' brands.

- Significantly, this edition includes a new section on innovation. Curiously, the topic of brands and innovation is almost totally absent from most books on branding. This seems at odds with the fact that innovation and branding has become the number one topic for companies. In fact, as we shall demonstrate, brands grow out of innovation, and innovation is the lifeblood of the brand. Furthermore, contrary to what is often said or thought, the issue of innovation is not merely about creativity. It is about reinventing the brand.

- This new edition is also sensitive to the fact that most modern markets are saturated. How can brands grow in such competitive environments? A full chapter on growth is included, starting with growth from the brand's existing customers.

- The issue of corporate brands and their increasing importance is also tackled, as is their relationship with classic brand management.

- We also stress much more than previously the implementation side: how to build interesting brand platforms that are able to stimulate powerful creative advertising that both sells and builds a salient brand; how to activate the brand; how to energise it at contact points; and how to create more bonding.

This book also reflects the evolution of the author's thought. Our perspective on brands has changed. We feel that the whole domain of branding is becoming a separate area, perhaps with a risk of being self-centered and narcissistic. Too often the history of a company's success or even failure is seen through the single perspective of the brand, without taking into account all the conditions of this success or failure. A brand is a tool for growing the business profitably. It has been created for that purpose, but business cannot be reduced to brands. The interrelationship between the business strategy and the brand strategy needs to be highlighted, because this is the way companies operate. As a consequence, we move away from the classic partitioning of brand equity into two separate approaches. One of these is customer-based, the other cash-flow-based. It is crucial to remember that a brand that produces no additional cash flow is of little value, whatever its image and the public awareness of it. In fact, it is time to think of the brand as a 'great shared idea supported by a viable economic equation'. In this third edition, we try regularly to relate brand decisions to the economic equation of the business.

Today, every business now wants to have its own brand, not for the sake of possessing it, as one possesses a painting or statue, but to grow the business profitably. We hope this book will help readers significantly, whether they are working in multinationals or in a small dynamic business, developing a global brand or a local one.

Introduction:
You can't build the brand
without building the business

It is surprising to see how brands continue to stimulate interest although so many prophets and experts have recently claimed they have no future. Today, all business managers are supposed to have attended conferences on CRM, ECR, loyalty programmes, relationship marketing, customer database management, e-relationships and proximity marketing: all these new tools criticise the old brand concept and focus on the most efficient techniques to serve the most profitable customers. They claim that conquering new clients is of no value any more: profitability will come from mastering one-to-one techniques. Despite this, managers keep on attending conferences on brand management. Why haven't they been convinced that brand management is an outdated tool? They have learnt that all these useful techniques soon lose their potential to create a lasting competitive advantage. The more they are diffused and shared, the more they become a standard, used by all competitors.

There are very few strategic assets available to a company that can provide a long-lasting competitive advantage, and even then the timespan of the advantage is getting shorter. Brands are one of them, along with R&D, a consumer orientation, an efficiency culture (cost cutting), employee involvement, and the capacity to change and react rapidly. This is the mantra of Wal-Mart and of Carlos Ghosn of Nissan.

Managers have also rediscovered that the best kind of loyalty is brand loyalty, not price loyalty or bargain loyalty, even though as a first step it is useful to create behavioral barriers to exit. Finally, A Ehrenberg (1972) has shown through 40 years of panel data analysis that product penetration is correlated with purchase frequency. In other words, big brands have both a high penetration rate and a high purchase frequency per buyer. Growth will necessarily take these two routes, and not only be triggered by customer loyalty.

In our materialistic societies, people want to give meaning to their consumption. Only brands that add value to the product and tell a story about its buyers, or situate their consumption in a ladder of immaterial values, can provide this meaning.

Pro logo?

Today, every organisation wants to have a brand. Beyond the natural brand world of producers and distributors of fast-moving consumer goods, whose brands are competing head to head, branding has become a strategic issue in all sectors: high tech, low tech, commodities, utilities, components, services, business-to-business (B2B), pharmaceutical laboratories, non-governmental organisations (NGOs) and non-profit organisations all see a use for branding.

Amazingly, all types of organisations or even persons now want to be managed like brands: David Beckham, the English soccer star, is an example. Real Madrid, a Spanish club, paid £24.5 million (approx. 41 million euros) to acquire this soccer hero. It expects to recoup this sum through the profits from licensed products using the name, face or signature of David Beckham, which are sold throughout the world. Everything David Beckham does is aimed at reinforcing his image and identity, and thus making sales and profits for the 'Beckham brand'.

Recently, the mayor of St Tropez, one of the most famous Riviera resorts, decided to define the town as a brand and to manage this brand for profit. The name was registered worldwide and a licensing policy created. Many others were to follow: Courchevel, Portofino in Italy and so on. Recently the author was asked to help Argentina work on its brand: countries do think of themselves in brand terms (Kotler *et al*, 2002). They are right to do so. Whether they want it or not, they act de facto as a brand, a summary of unique values and benefits. Argentina has a choice between allowing uncontrolled news and information to act (perhaps negatively) on world public opinion, or choosing to try to manage its image by promoting a common set of strategic values (its brand meaning), which might be differentiated by market. Countries compete in a number of markets, just as a conventional brand competes for profitable clients: in the private economic and financial investments market, various raw materials and agricultural markets, the tourism market, the immigration market and so on.

It takes more than branding to build a brand

Companies and organisations from all kinds of sectors ask whether or not a brand could consolidate their business or increase its profitability, and what they should do to create a brand, or become a corporate brand. What steps should be followed, with what investments and using what skills? What are realistic objectives and expectations? Having based their success on mastering production or logistics, they may feel they lack the methods and know-how to implement a brand creation plan. They also feel it is not simply a matter of communication. Although communication is necessary to create a brand, it is far from being sufficient. Certainly a brand encapsulates in its name and its visual symbol all the goodwill created by the positive experiences of clients or prospects with the organisation, its products, its channels, its stores, its communication and its people. However, this means that it is necessary to manage these points of contact (from product or service to channel management, to advertising, to Internet site, to word of mouth, the organisation's ethics, and so on) in an integrated and focused way. This is the core skill needed. This is why, in this third edition of *Strategic Brand Management*, while we look in depth at branding decisions as such, we also insist on the 'non-branding' facets of creating a brand. *Paradoxically, it takes more than branding to build a brand.*

Building both business and brand

Hit parades of the financial value of brands (brand equity) are regularly published in business, financial and economics magazines. Whatever doubts one may have on their validity (see page 468), they do at least stress the essentially financial intentions behind building a brand. Companies do not build brands to have authors write books on them, or to make the streets livelier thanks to billboard advertising. They do it to grow the business still more profitably. One does not make money by selling products, but brands: that is to say a unique set of values, both tangible and intangible.

Our feeling is that, little by little, branding has been constructed as a separate field. There is a risk however of the branding community falling in love with its own image: looking at the considerable number of books published on brands, and at the list of most recent brand equity values, one could think that brands are the one and only issue of importance. Indeed branding professionals may become infatuated and forget the sources of brand equity: production, servicing, staffing, distributing, innovating, pricing and advertising, all of which help to create value associations and effects which become embedded in clients' long-term memory.

Looking at one of the stars of this hit parade, Dell, whose brand is valued so highly, one question arises: is Dell's success due to its brand or to its business model? It could be argued that it is not the Dell brand but Dell activities in a broader sense that allowed the company to announce more price cuts in autumn 2003, putting Hewlett-Packard in a difficult position between two 'boa constrictors', Dell and IBM.

The brand is not all: it captures the fame but it is made possible by the business model. It is time to recreate a balance in accounting for success and failures. It is the end of fairy tales; let's introduce the time of fair accounts.

Throughout this new edition of *Strategic Brand Management*, we relate the brand to the business, for both are intimately intertwined. We regularly demonstrate how branding decisions are determined by the business model and cannot be understood without this perspective. In fact in a growing number of advanced companies, top managers' salaries are based on three critical criteria: sales, profitability and brand equity. They are determined in part by how fast these managers are building the strategic competitive asset called a brand. The goal of strategy is to build a sustainable advantage over competition, and brands are one of the very few ways of achieving this. The business model is another. This is why tracking brands, product or corporate, is so important.

Looking at brands as strategic assets

The 1980s marked a turning point in the conception of brands. Management came to realise that the principal asset of a company was in fact its brand names. Several articles in both the American and European press dealt with the discovery of 'brand equity', or the financial value of the brand. In fact, the emergence of brands in activities which previously had resisted or were foreign to such concepts (industry, banking, the service sector, etc) vouched for the new importance of brands. This is confirmed by the importance that so many distributors place on the promotion of their own brands.

For decades the value of a company was measured in terms of its buildings and land, and then its tangible assets (plant and equipment). It is only recently that we have realised that its real value lies outside, in the minds of potential customers. In July 1990, the man who bought the

Adidas company summarised his reasons in one sentence: after Coca-Cola and Marlboro, Adidas was the best-known brand in the world.

The truth contained in what many observers took simply to be a clever remark has become increasingly apparent since 1985. In a wave of mergers and acquisitions, triggered by attempts to take up advantageous positions in the future single European market, market transactions pushed prices way above what could have been expected. For example, Nestlé bought Rowntree for almost three times its stock market value and 26 times its earnings. The Buitoni group was sold for 35 times its earnings. Until then, prices had been on a scale of 8 to 10 times the earnings of the bought-out company.

Paradoxically, what justified these prices and these new standards was invisible, appearing nowhere in the companies' balance sheets. The only assets displayed on corporate balance sheets were fixed, tangible ones, such as machinery and inventory. There was no mention of the brands for which buyers offered sums much greater than the net value of the assets. The acquiring companies generally posted this extra value or goodwill in their consolidated accounts. The actual object of these gigantic and relentless takeovers was invisible, intangible and unwritten: they were aimed at acquiring brands.

What changed in the course of the 1980s was awareness. Before, in a takeover bid, merger or acquisition, the buyer acquired a pasta manufacturer, a chocolate manufacturer or a producer of microwave ovens or abrasives. Now companies want to buy Buitoni, Rowntree (that is, KitKat, After Eight), Moulinex or Orange. The strength of a company like Heineken is not solely in knowing how to brew beer; it is that people all over the world want to drink Heineken. The same logic applies for IBM, Sony, McDonald's, Barclays Bank or Dior.

By paying very high prices for companies with brands, buyers are actually purchasing positions in the minds of potential consumers. Brand awareness, image, trust and reputation, all painstakingly built up over the years, are the best guarantee of future earnings, thus justifying the prices paid. The value of a brand lies in its capacity to generate such cash flows.

Hardly had this management revolution been born than conflicting arguments arose regarding the reality and the durability of brand equity. With the systematic rise in distributors' own brands it was argued that the capacity of brands had been exaggerated. The fall in the price of Marlboro cigarettes in the USA in April 1993 created panic on Wall Street, with the share prices of all consumer goods firms falling. This mini-Pearl Harbor proved healthy. At the height of recession we realised that it was not the brand – registered trademark – as such that created value, but all the marketing and communication done by the firm. Consumers don't just buy the brand name, they buy branded products that promise tangible and intangible benefits created by the efforts of the company. Given time, the brand may evoke a number of associations, qualities and differences, but these alone do not comprise the whole offer. A map alone is not the underlying territory.

In the 1990s, because of recession and saturated markets, the emphasis shifted from brands to customer equity. New techniques, based on one-to-one targeting, replaced the emphasis on classic media advertising. They could prove their effectiveness and targeted heavy buyers.

Just as some have exaggerated the overwhelming power of brands, so the opposition to brands has been short-lived. The value of brands comes from their ability continuously to add value and deliver profits. Another question is, who is best placed to make use of brands? Is it the producer or the distributor?

You must be very wary as regards ideological preferences; for example, there are very few manufacturers' brands on the furniture market other than those of Italian designers, yet everybody talks about Habitat or Ikea, two distributors. They are seen as agents offering strong value-added style in the first case and competitive prices and youth appeal in the second.

In many sectors, brand management is still in its early stages even though brands are a business asset. At present, in many cases, the reality is to manage products that happen to have a name. Yet brand management involves different and specific reasoning and approaches. This will be the main focus of this book. Management books and marketing bibles have not yet assimilated the full implication of the brand revolution. Marketing books focus on the process of launching new products; the brand is considered merely as a tactical and final decision. Yet the reality of the situation is very different. From now on companies will be faced with the strategic issue of whether or not growth should come about through existing brands by stretching their sphere of activity or through new brands (either created or bought).

Classic strategic models talk about product portfolios, whereas in reality companies have to manage brand portfolios. Several companies have product managers but few have brand managers. This may cause problems in so far as brands are being extended to more and more differentiated categories, resulting in the delegation of the management of value to several business units. In the medium term this may diminish brand equity because individual decisions are taken without any integration of the brand meaning that is being created.

The brand is not the product but it gives the product meaning and defines its identity. Companies are discovering that brand equity has to be managed, nourished and controlled. Branding is raising new questions for managers: How many brands do you need? How do you manage your brand portfolio? What extensions can you give the brand and which products and services could and should these encompass? Or, on the other hand, into what areas should you not extend the brand even if you expect it to sell? Going too far may weaken brand equity. How do you manage brands over time and keep them up to date, as technology, products and customers change? How do you change while staying the same? How do you manage coherently and benefit from the synergy of a range of products sold under a single brand? How do you optimise the relationship between products and their brand? How far can a brand be extended geographically? Does it have the potential to become a homogeneous global brand in all countries? Or is this impossible or even undesirable? Several companies have the same name as their brand (eg Volkswagen, Nestlé, IBM, BT, etc), so what is the difference between managing a brand image, a corporate image and an institutional image? Finally, given that brands have a value, how can this be measured so as to survey and control it? Should it be included on the balance sheet to indicate its true economic value to shareholders, investors and financial partners?

These are all new questions, each one deserving a chapter to itself. For a long time the answers to these questions were found intuitively and the decisions made on a trial and error basis. The goal of this book is to provide the reader with a framework for comprehensive reflection and analysis and thus a rational means to finding answers. The models of analysis and decision-making presented here have grown out of research and have been tested in consulting situations and confirmed in practice. As demonstrated by the numerous case studies, the models offered concern brands ranging from industry to service, from luxury goods and fashion to consumer goods and distributors' own-brands from high-tech to utilities and commodities.

Too often brands are examined through their component parts: the brand name, its logo, design or packaging, advertising or sponsorship, the level of image and brand awareness or, more recently, in terms of financial valuation. Real brand management, however, begins much earlier, with a strategy and a consistent, integrated vision. Its central concept is brand identity, not brand image. This identity must be defined and managed and is at the heart of brand management. It calls for new ways of thinking and methods of investigation; they are presented here in depth.

Part One

Why is branding so strategic?

1

Brand equity in question

Brands have become a major player in modern society. In fact they are everywhere. They penetrate all spheres of our life: economic, social, cultural, sporting, even religion. Because of this pervasiveness they have come under growing criticism (Klein, 1999). As a major symbol of our economies and postmodern societies, they can and should be analysed through a number of perspectives: macroeconomics, microeconomics, sociology, psychology, anthropology, history, semiotics, philosophy and so on. In fact our first book on brands was a collection of essays by eminent scholars from all these disciplines (Kapferer and Thoenig, 1989).

This book focuses on the managerial perspective: how best to manage brands. Since brands are now recognised a part of a company's capital (hence the concept of brand equity), they should be exploited. Brands are intangible assets, assets that produce added benefits for the business. This is the domain of strategic brand management: how to create value with proper brand management. Before we proceed, we need however to clarify the brand concept.

What is a brand?

Curiously, one of the hottest points of disagreement between experts is the definition of a brand. Each expert comes up with his or her own definition, or nuance to the definition. The problem gets more acute when it comes to measurement: how should one measure the strength of a brand? What limited numbers of indicators should one use to evaluate what is commonly called *brand equity?* In addition there is a major schism between two paradigms. One is customer-based and focuses exclusively on the relationship customers have with the brand (from total indifference to attachment, loyalty, and willingness to buy and rebuy based on beliefs of superiority and evoked emotions). The other aims at producing measures in dollars, euros or yen. Both approaches have their own champions. It is the goal of this third edition of *Strategic Brand Management* to unify these two approaches.

Customer-based definitions

The financial approach measures brand value by isolating the net additional cash flows created by the brand. These additional cash flows are the result of customers' willingness to buy one brand more than its competitors, even when another brand is cheaper. Why then do customers want to pay more? Because of the beliefs and bonds that are created over time in their minds through the marketing of the brand. In brief, customer equity is the preamble of financial equity. Brands have financial value *because* they have created assets in the minds and hearts of customers, distributors, prescribers, opinion leaders. These assets are brand awareness, beliefs of exclusivity and superiority of some valued benefit, and emotional bonding. This is what is expressed in the now classic definition of a brand: 'a brand is a set of mental associations, held by the consumer, which add to the perceived value of a product or service' (Keller, 1998). These associations should be unique (exclusivity), strong (saliency) and positive (desirable).

This definition focuses on the gain in perceived value brought by the brand. How do consumers' evaluations of a car change when they know it is a Volkswagen, a Peugeot or a Toyota? Implicitly, in this definition the product itself is left out of the scope of the brand: 'brand' is the set of added perceptions. As a result brand management is seen as mostly a communication task. This is incorrect. Modern brand management starts with the product and service as the prime vector of perceived value, while communication is there to structure, to orient tangible perceptions and to add intangible ones.

Later we analyse the relationship between brand and product (see page 293). A second point to consider is that Keller's now-classic definition is focused on *cognitions* (mental associations). This is not enough: strong brands have an intense emotional component.

Brands as conditional asset

Financiers and accountants have realised the value of brands (see Chapter 17). How does the financial perspective help us in defining brands and brand equity?

▌ First, brands are *intangible assets*, posted eventually in the balance sheet as one of several types of intangible asset (a category that also includes patents, databases and the like).

▌ Second, brands are *conditional assets*. This is a key point so far overlooked. An asset is an element that is able to produce benefits over a long period of time. Why are brands conditional assets? Because in order to deliver their benefits, their financial value, they need to work in conjunction with other material assets such as production facilities. There are no brands without products or services to carry them. This will have great consequences for the method of measuring financial value (see Chapter 17, page 452). For now, this reminds us that some humility is required. Although many people claim that brands are all and every-thing, brands cannot exist without a support (product or service). This product and service becomes effectively an embodi-ment of the brand, that by which the brand becomes real. As such it is a main source of brand evaluation. Does it produce high or low satisfaction? Brand management starts with creating products, services and/or places that embody the brand. Interestingly, the legal approach to trademarks and brands also insists on their conditional nature. One should never use the brand name as a noun, but as an adjective attached to a name, as for instance with a Volvo car, not a Volvo.

▌ Third, *without benefits there is no brand value*. A brand unable to produce benefits has no financial value, whatever the level of its 'consumer-based assets' (brand awareness, brand image, brand attachment, brand pref-erence). As result, these assets are condi-tional in another way. To be held of value they need to be attached to a viable economic business model. If a business cannot profit from a brand, it is doubtful that the brand has any value. It may have great potential, as measured by the associations evoked in consumers' minds, but this potential needs a profitable economic equation to become reality.

The legal perspective

An internationally agreed legal definition for brands does exist: 'a sign or set of signs certifying the origin of a product or service and differentiating it from the competition'. Historically, brands were created to defend producers from theft. A cattle brand, a sign burned into the animal's hide, identified the owner and made it apparent if the animal had been stolen. 'Brands' or trademarks also identified the source of the olive oil or wine contained in ancient Greek amphoras, and created value in the eyes of the buyers by building a reputation for the producer or distributor of the oil or wine.

A key point in this legal definition is that brands have a 'birthday' – their registration day. From that day they become a property, which needs to be defended against infringements and counterfeiting (see page 201 for defence strategies). Brand rights disappear when they are not well enough defended, or if registration is not renewed. One of the sources of loss of rights is degenerescence. This occurs when a company has let a distinctive brand name become a generic term.

Although the legal approach is most useful for defending the company against copies of its products, it should not become the basis of brand management. Contrary to what the legal definition asserts, a brand is not born but made. It takes time to create a brand, even though we talk about launching brands. In fact this means launching a product or service. Eventually it may become a brand, and it can also cease to be one. What makes a brand recognisable? When do we know if a name has reached the status of a brand? For

us, in essence, *a brand is a name that influences buyers,* becoming a purchase criterion.

A brand is a name that influences buyers

This definition captures the essence of a brand: a name with power to influence buyers. Of course, it is not a question of the choice of the name itself. Certainly a good name helps: that is, one that is easily pronounceable around the world and spontaneously evokes desirable associations. But what really makes a name become a brand are the *saliency, differentiability, intensity* and *trust* attached to these associations. Are the benefits the name evokes (a) salient, (b) exclusive and (c) trusted?

We live in an attention economy: there is so much choice and opacity that consumers cannot spend their time comparing before they make a choice. They have no time and even if they did, they cannot be certain of being able to determine the right product or service for them. Brands must convey certitude, trust. They are a time and risk reducer. In fact where there is no risk there is no brand. We made this point in an earlier book (Kapferer and Laurent, 1995). The perceived risk could be economic (linked to price), functional (linked to performance), experiential, psychological (linked to our self-concept), or social (linked to our social image). This is why it takes time to build the saliency that is part of brand awareness, and this trust (trusted beliefs about the brand's unique benefits).

Brand power to influence buyers relies on representations and relationships. A representation is a *system* of mental associations. We stress the word 'system', for these associations are interconnected. They are in a network, so that acting on one impacts some others. These associations (also called brand image) cover the following aspects:

▌ What is the brand territory (perceived competence, typical products or services, specific know-how)?

- What is its level of quality (low, middle, premium, luxury)?

- What are its qualities?

- What is its most discriminating quality or benefit (also called perceived positioning)?

- What typical buyer does the brand evoke? What is the brand personality and brand imagery?

Beyond mental associations, the power of a name is also due to the specific nature of the emotional relationships it develops. A brand, it could be said, is an attitude of non-indifference knitted into consumers' hearts. This attitude goes from emotional resonance to liking, belonging to the evoked set or consideration set, preference, attachment, advocacy, to fanaticism. Finally, patents and rights are of course a key asset: they provide a competitive advantage over a period of time.

In short, *a brand exists when it has acquired power to influence the market*. This acquisition takes time. The timespan tends to be short in the case of online brands, fashion brands and brands for teenagers, but longer for, for example, car brands and corporate brands. This power can be lost, if the brand has been mismanaged in comparison with the competition. Even though the brand will still have brand awareness, image and market shares, it might not influence the market any more.

People and distributors may buy because of price only, not because they are conscious of any exclusive benefit from the brand.

What makes a name acquire the power of a brand is the product or service, together with the people at points of contact with the market, the price, the places, the communication – all the sources of cumulative brand experience. This is why one should speak of brands as *living systems made up of three poles*: products or services, name and concept. (See Figure 1.1.)

When talking of brands we are sometimes referring to a single aspect such as the name or logo, as do intellectual property lawyers. In brand management, however, we speak of the whole system, relating a concept with inherent value to products and services that are identified by a name and set of proprietary signs (that is, the logo and other symbols). This system reminds us of the conditional nature of the brand asset: it only exists if products and services also exist. Differentiation is summarised by the brand concept, a unique set of attributes (both tangible and intangible) that constitute the value proposition of the brand.

To gain market share and leadership, the brand must be:

- embodied in products, services and places;

- enacted by people at contact points;

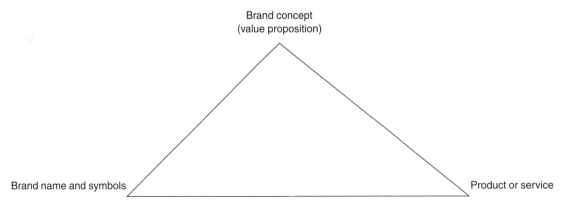

Figure 1.1   The brand system

activated by deeds and behaviours;

communicated;

distributed.

The brand triangle helps us to structure most of the issues of brand management:

What concept should one choose, with what balance of tangible and intangible benefits? This is the issue of identity and positioning. Should the brand concept evolve through time? Or across borders (the issue of globalisation)?

How should the brand concept be embodied in its products and services, and its places? How should a product or service of the brand be different, look different? What products can this brand concept encompass? This is the issue of brand extension or brand stretch.

How should the product and/or services be identified? And where? Should they be identified by the brand name, or by the logo only, as Nike does now? Should organisations create differentiated sets of logos and names as a means of indicating internal differences within their product or service lines?

What name or signs should one choose to convey the concept internationally?

How often should the brand symbols be changed, updated or modernised?

Should the brand name be changed (see chapter 14)?

Speaking of internationalisation, should one globalise the name (that is, use the same name around the world), or the logo, or the product (a standardised versus customised product), or the concept (aiming at the same global positioning)? Or all three pillars of the brand system, or only two of them?

Since a brand is a name with the power to influence the market, its power increases as more people know it, are convinced by it, and trust it. Brand management is about gaining power, by making the brand concept more known, more bought, more shared.

In summary, a brand is a shared desirable and exclusive idea embodied in products, services, places and/or experiences. The more this idea is shared by a larger number of people, the more power the brand has. It is because everyone knows 'BMW' and its idea – what it stands for – even those who will never buy a BMW car, that the brand BMW has a great deal of power.

The word 'idea' is important. Do we sell products and services, or values? Of course, the answer is values. For example, 'Volvo' is attached to an idea: cars with the highest possible safety levels. 'Absolut' conjures another idea: a fashionable vodka. Levi's used to be regarded as the rebel's jeans.

Differentiating between brand assets, strength and value

It is time to structure and organise the many terms related to brands and their strength, and to the measurement of brand equity. Some restrict the use of the phrase 'brand equity' to contexts that measure this by its impact on consumer mental associations (Keller, 1992). Others mention behaviour: for example this is included in Aaker's early measures (1991), which also consider brand loyalty. In his late writings Aaker includes market share, distribution and price premium in his 10 measures of brand equity (1996). The official Marketing Science definition of brand equity is 'the set of associations and behavior on the part of a brand's customers, channel members and parent corporation that permits the brand to earn greater volume or greater margins than it could without the brand name' (Leuthesser, 1988).

This definition is very interesting and has been forgotten all too quickly. It is all-encompassing, reminding us that channel members are very important in brand equity. It also specifically ties margins to brand associations and customers' behaviour. Does it mean that unless there is a higher volume or a higher margin as a result of the creation of a brand, there is no brand value? This is not clear, for the word 'margin' seems to refer to gross margin only, whereas brand financial value is measured at the level of earnings before interest and tax (EBIT).

To dispel the existing confusion around the phrase brand equity (Feldwick, 1996), created by the abundance of definitions, concepts, measurement tools and comments by experts, it is important to show how the consumer and financial approaches are connected, and to use clear terms with limited boundaries. Consumer research cannot live in a separate world: a brand is a tool for business. It exists only in so far as it creates a profitable business. As a consequence, *a brand that does not make it possible to create a profitable business has no value*. In short, it is time to link the brand and the economic equation. A brand is a strong idea supported by a profitable economic equation. Unless it has financial outcomes can one speak of brand equity? To clarify the issues, one needs to distinguish three levels of analysis (see Table 1.1):

- *Brand assets*. These are the sources of influence of the brand (awareness/saliency, image, type of relationship with consumers), and patents.

- *Brand strength* at a specific point in time as a result of these assets within a specific market and competitive environment. They are the 'brand equity outcomes' if one restricts the use of the phrase 'brand equity' to brand assets alone. Brand strength is captured by behavioural competitive indicators: market share, market leadership, loyalty rates and price premium (if one follows a price premium strategy).

- *Brand value* is the ability of brands to deliver profits. A brand has no value unless it can deliver profits. To say that lack of profit is not a brand problem but a business problem is to separate the brand from the business, an intellectual temptation. Certainly brands can be analysed from the standpoint of sociology, psychology, semiotics, anthropology, philosophy and so on, but historically they were created for business purposes and are managed with a view to producing profit.

Only by separating brand assets, strength and value will one end the confusion of the brand equity domain (Feldwick, 1996 takes a similar position). Brand value is the profit potential of the brand.

Table 1.1 From awareness to financial value

Brand assets ⟶	Brand strength ⟶	Brand value
Brand awareness	Market share	Net discounted cashflow attributable to
Brand reputation (attributes,	Market leadership	the brand after paying the cost of
benefits, competence,	Market penetration	capital invested to produce and run
know-how, etc)	Share of requirements	the business and the cost of marketing
Brand personality	Growth rate	
Brand deep values	Loyalty rate	
Brand imagery	Price premium	
Brand preference or attachment		
Patents and rights		

In Table 1.1, the arrows indicate not a direct but a conditional consequence. The same brand assets may produce different brand strength over time: this is a result of the amount of competitive or distributive pressure. The same assets can also have no value at all by this definition, if no business will ever succeed in making them deliver profits, through establishing a sufficient market share and price premium. For instance if the cost of marketing to sustain this market share and price premium is too high and leaves no residual profit, the brand has no value. Thus the Virgin name proved of little value in the cola business: despite the assets of this brand, the Virgin organisation did not succeed in establishing a durable and profitable business through selling Virgin Cola in the many countries where this was tried (see page 289).

Table 1.1 also shows an underlying time dimension behind these three concepts of assets, strength and value. Brand assets are learnt mental associations and affects. They are acquired through time, from past direct or vicarious, material or symbolic interactions with the brand. Brand strength is a measure of the present status of the brand: it is mostly behavioural (market share, leadership, loyalty, price premium). Not all of this brand stature is due to the brand assets. Some brands establish a leading market share without any noticeable brand awareness: their price is the primary driver of preference. There are also brands whose assets are superior to their market strength: that is, they have an image that is far stronger than their position in the market (this is the case with Michelin, for example). The obverse can also be true, for example of many retailer own-label brands.

Brand value is a projection into the future. Brand financial valuation aims to measure the brand's worth, that is to say, the profits it will create in the future. To have value, brands must produce economic value added (EVA), and part of this EVA must be attributable to the brand itself, and not to other intangibles

(such as patents, know-how or databases). This will depend very much on the ability of the business model to face the future. For instance, Nokia lost ground at the Stock Exchange in April 2004. The market had judged that the future of the world's number one mobile phone brand was dim. Everywhere in the developed countries, almost everyone had a mobile phone. How was the company still to make profits in this saturated market? If it tried to sell to emerging countries it would find that price was the first purchase criterion and delocalisation (that is, having the products manufactured in a country such as China or Singapore) compulsory. Up to that point, Nokia had based its growth on its production facilities in Finland. Nokia's present brand stature might be high, but what about its value?

It is time now to move to the topic of tracking brand equity for management purposes. What should managers regularly measure? Of course research data from customer panels can inform them about the brand strength amid that of its competitors, but to make a proper diagnosis of why this strength is going down or up, and how to make it improve, it is necessary to measure upstream: at the level of brand assets. Usage and attitude studies can capture the associations held by the market about brands and their competitors, but for the sake of efficiency it is necessary to use simplified tracking studies that can diagnose rapidly that something is changing, and prompt a rapid reaction. There are as many proposals for these studies as there are research institutes. We now turn to a proposal based on the synthesis of them.

Tracking brand equity

What is a brand? A name that influences buyers. What is the source of its influence? A set of mental associations and relationships built up over time among customers or distributors. Brand tracking should aim at measuring these sources of brand power. The role of managers is to build the brand and business. This is true of brand managers, but also of local or regional managers who are in charge of developing this competitive asset in addition to developing the business more generally. This is why advanced companies now link the level of variable salary not only to increments in sales and profits but also to brand equity. However, such a system presupposes that there is a tracking system for brand equity, so that year after year its progress can be assessed. This system must be valid, reliable, and not too complicated or too costly. What should one measure as a minimum to evaluate brand equity?

An interesting survey carried out by the agency DDB asked marketing directors what they considered to be the characteristics of a strong brand, a significant company asset. The following were the answers in order of importance:

▮ brand awareness (65 per cent);

▮ the strength of brand positioning, concept, personality, a precise and distinct image (39 per cent);

▮ the strength of signs of recognition by the consumer (logo, codes, packaging) (36 per cent);

▮ brand authority with consumers, brand esteem, perceived status of the brand and consumer loyalty (24 per cent).

Numerous types of survey exist on the measurement of brand value (brand equity). They usually provide a national or international hit parade based just on one component of brand equity: brand awareness (the method may be the first brand brought to mind, aided or unaided depending on the research institute), brand preference, quality image, prestige, first and second buying preferences when the favoured brand is not available, or liking.

Certain institutions may combine two of the components: for example, Landor published an indicator of the 'power of the brand' which was determined by combining brand-aided awareness and esteem, which is the emotional component of the brand–consumer relationship. The advertising agency Young & Rubicam carried out a study called 'Brand Asset Monitor' which positions the brand on two axes: the cognitive axis is a combination of salience and of the degree of perceived difference of the brand among consumers; the emotional axis is the combination of the measures of familiarity and esteem (see page 193). In France Sofres, in its study Megabrand System, uses six parameters to compare brands: brand awareness, stated use, stated preference, perceived quality, a mark for global opinion, and an item measuring the strength of the brand's imagery.

Certain institutions, which believe that the comparison of brands across all markets makes little sense, concentrate on a single market approach and measure, for example, the acceptable price differential for each brand. They proceed in either a global manner (what price difference can exist between an IBM PC and a Toshiba PC or a PC from Tandy?) or by using a method of trade-off which isolates the net added value of the brand name. Marketing directors are perplexed because so many different methods exist.

There is little more consensus among academic researchers. Sattler (1994) analysed 49 American and European studies on brand equity and listed no fewer than 26 different ways of measuring it. These methods vary according to several dimensions:

▮ Is the measure monetary or not? A large proportion of measures are classified in non-monetary terms (brand awareness, attitude, preference, etc).

▮ Does the measurement include the time factor – that is, the future of the brand on the market?

▌ Does the brand measure take the competition into account – that is, the perceived value in relation to other products on the market? Most of them do not.

▌ Does the measurement include the brand's marketing mix? When you measure brand value, do you only include the value attached to the brand name? Most measures do not include the marketing mix (past advertising expenditure, level of distribution, and so on).

▌ When estimating brand value do you include the profits that a user or a buyer could obtain due to the synergies that may exist with its own existing brand portfolio (synergies of distribution, production, logistics, etc)? The majority of them do not include this, even though it is a key factor. Seagram had bought Martell for FF 5 billion (about 1 billion euros) in order, among other things, to gain access to its distribution channels in Asia, which allowed it to develop its sales of other brands, such as Chivas, in this area.

▌ Does the measurement of brand equity include the possibility of brand extensions outside the brand's original market? In general, no.

▌ Finally, does the measure of brand equity take into account the possibility of geographical extension or globalisation? Again, most of the time the answer is no.

We recommend four indicators of brand assets (equity):

▌ *Aided brand awareness*. This measures whether the brand has a minimal resonance.

▌ *Spontaneous brand awareness*. This is a measure of saliency, of share of mind when cued by the product.

▌ *Evoked set*, also called *consideration set*. Does the brand belong to the shortlist of two or three brands one would surely consider buying?

▌ Has the brand been *already consumed* or not?

Some companies add other items like most preferred brand. Empirical research has shown that this item is very much correlated to spontaneous brand awareness, the latter being much more than a mere cognitive measure, but it also captures proximity to the person. Other companies add the item consumed most often. Of course this is typical of fast moving consumer goods; the item is irrelevant for durables. In addition, in empirical research the item is also correlated to evoked set. One should never forget that tracking studies dwell on the customer's memory. This memory is itself very much inferential. Do people really know what brand they bought last? They infer from their preferences, that logically it should have been brand X or Y.

Table 1.2 gives a typical result of a tracking study for a brand.

Table 1.2 Result of a brand tracking study

	Brand X	
	Japan	Mexico
Aided awareness	99%	97%
Unaided awareness	48%	85%
Evoked set	24%	74%
Consumed	5%	40%

There are two ways of looking at the brand equity figures in the table. One can compare the countries by line: although it has similar aided awareness levels, this brand has very different status in the two countries. The second mode is vertical, and focuses on the 'transformation ratios'. It is noticeable that in Japan, the evoked set is 50 per cent of spontaneous brand awareness, whereas it is 87 per cent in Mexico.

Although there is a regular pattern of decreasing figures, from the top line to the bottom line, this is not always the case. For instance in Europe, Pepsi Cola is not a strong brand: its market share is gained through push marketing and trade offers. As a result, Pepsi Cola certainly grows its business but not its intrinsic desirability. In tracking studies Pepsi Cola has a trial rate far higher than the brand's preference rate (evoked set). At the opposite end of the spectrum there are brands that have an equity far superior to their consumption rate. In Europe, Michelin has a clear edge over rival tyre brands as far as image is concerned. However, image does not transform itself into market share if people like the Michelin brand but deem that the use they make of their cars does not justify buying tyres of such a quality and at such a price.

Tracking studies are not simply tools for control. They are tools for diagnosis and action. Transformation ratios tell us where to act.

Goodwill: the convergence of finance and marketing

The 1980s witnessed a Copernican revolution in the understanding of the workings of brands. Before this, ratios of seven or eight were typical in mergers and acquisitions, meaning that the price paid for a company was seven to eight times its earnings. After 1980 these multiples increased considerably to reach their peak. For example, Groupe Danone paid $2.5 billion for Nabisco Europe, which was equivalent to a price:earnings ratio of 27. Nestlé bought Rowntree Macintosh for three times its stock market value and 26 times its earnings. It was becoming the norm to see multiples of 20 to 25. Even today when, because of the recession, financial valuations have become more prudent, the existence of strong brands still gives a real added value to companies. What happened between the beginning and the end of the 1980s? What explanations can be given for this sudden change in the methods of financial analysts? The prospect of a single European market certainly played a significant role, as can be seen by the fact that large companies were looking for brands that were ready to be European or, even better, global. This explains why Nestlé bought Buitoni, Lever bought Boursin, L'Oréal bought Lanvin, Seagram bought Martell, etc. The increase in the multiples can also be explained in part by the opposing bids of rival companies wishing to take over the few brand leaders that existed in their markets and which were for sale. Apart from the European factor, there was a marked change in the attitude towards the brands of the principal players. Prior to 1980, companies wished to buy a producer of chocolate or pasta: after 1980, they wanted to buy KitKat or Buitoni. This distinction is very important; in the first case firms wish to buy production capacity and in the second they want to buy a place in the mind of the consumer.

The vision has changed from one where only tangible assets had value to one where companies now believe that their most important asset is their brands, which are intangible and immaterial (see Table 1.3). These intangible assets account for 61 per cent of the value of Kellogg's, 57 per cent of Sara Lee and 52 per cent of General Mills. This explains the paradox that even though a company is making a loss it is bought for a very high price because of its well-known brands. Before 1980, if the value of the brand had been included in the company's earnings, it would have been bought for a penny. Nowadays brand value is determined independently of the firm's net value and thus can sometimes be hidden by the poor financial results of the company. The net income of a company is the sum of all the financial effects, be they positive or negative, and thus includes the effect of the brand. The reason why Apple lost money in 1996 was not because its brand was weak, but because its strategy was bad. Therefore it is not simply because a company is making a loss that its brand is not adding value. Just as the managers of Ebel-Jellinek, an American-Swiss group, said when they bought

Table 1.3   An estimate of the financial value of brands

Rank	Brand	Value (billion $)
1	Coca-Cola	69
2	Microsoft	64
3	IBM	51
4	GE	41
5	Intel	31
6	Nokia	30
7	Disney	29
8	McDonald's	26
9	Marlboro	24
10	Mercedes	21
11	Ford	20
12	Toyota	20
13	Citybank	18
14	Hewlett-Packard	17
15	American Express	16
16	Cisco	16
17	AT&T	16
18	Honda	15
19	Gillette	15

Source: Business Week/JP Morgan/Interbrand (2003)

the Look brand: the company is making a loss but the brand hasn't lost its potential. Balance sheets reflect bad management decisions in the past, whereas the brand is a potential source of future profits. This potential will become actual profit only if it can meet a viable economic equation.

It is important to realise that in accounting and finance, goodwill is in fact the difference between the price paid and the book value of the company. This difference is brought about by the psychological goodwill of consumers, distributors and all the actors in the channels: that is to say, favourable attitudes and predisposition. Thus, a close relationship exists between financial and marketing analyses of brands. Accounting goodwill is the monetary value of the psychological goodwill that the brand has created over time through communication investment and consistent focus on product satsifaction, both of which help build the reputation of the name.

What exactly are the effects of this customer and distributor goodwill?:

▮ The favourable attitude of distributors choosing the brand because of its expected rotation, even though they will still be demanding in terms of discounts, listing fees and other charges that have become customary. In fact a retailer may lose customers if it does not stock a well-known brand that by definition is present every-where; that is to say certain consumers will go elsewhere to look for the brand. This goodwill assures the presence of the brand at the point of sale, which is the key to selling for durable as well as consumer goods.

▮ The support of wholesalers and resellers in the market for slow-moving or industrial goods. This is especially true when they are seen as being an exclusive brand with which they are able to associate themselves in the eyes of their customers.

▮ The desire of consumers or end-users to buy the product. It is their favourable attitude and in certain cases the attachment or even loyalty to the brand that is the key to future sales. Brand loyalty may be reduced to a minimum as the price difference between the brand and its competitors increases but attachment to the brand does not vanish so fast; it resists time.

The brand is a focal point for all the positive and negative impressions created by the buyer over time as he or she comes into contact with the brand's products, distribution channel, personnel and communication. On top of this, by concentrating all its marketing effort on a single name, the latter acquires an aura of exclusivity. The brand continues to be, at least in the short term, a byword for quality even after the patent has expired. The life of the patent is extended thanks to the brand, thus explaining the importance of brands in the pharmaceutical or the chemical industry (see page 157).

The brand performs an economic function in the mind of the consumer and thus has a lasting and memorable effect on the company's activities, be it as distributor or owner of the brand. It is also because of this that it is seen as an asset from an accounting point of view: its economic effects extend far beyond the mere consumption of the product.

In order to understand in what way a strong brand (having acquired distribution, awareness and image) is a generator of growth and profitability it is first necessary to understand the functions that it performs with the consumers themselves, and which are the source of their valuable goodwill. If these functions have value, the consumer seeks out the brands and becomes attached, indeed loyal, to them and, in accordance with the valuation, is often prepared to pay more for the branded product. On the other hand, when these functions are either not fulfilled more than by rival brands or not valued by the public, the attraction of the branded product decreases and its premium price becomes unacceptable. Thus the market is dominated by retailers' own-brands or the discount products.

How brands create value for the customer

Although this book deals primarily with brands and their optimisation, it is important to clarify that brands do not necessarily exist in all markets. Even if brands exist in the legal sense they do not always play a role in the buying decision process of consumers. Other factors may be more important. For example, research on 'brand sensitivity' (Kapferer and Laurent, 1988) shows that in several product categories, buyers do not look at the brand when they are making their choice. Who is concerned about the brand when they are buying a writing pad, a rubber, felt-tip pens, markers or photocopy paper? Neither private individuals nor companies. There are no strong brands in such markets as sugar and socks. In Germany there is no national brand of flour. Even the beer brands are mostly regional.

Brands reduce perceived risk, and exist as soon as there is perceived risk. Once the risk perceived by the buyer disappears, the brand no longer has any benefit. It is only a name on a product, and it ceases to be a choice cue, a guide or a source of added value. The perceived risk is greater if the unit price is higher or the repercussions of a bad choice are more severe. Thus the purchase of durable goods is a long-term commitment. On top of this, because humans are social animals, we judge ourselves on certain choices that we make and this explains why a large part of our social identity is built around the logos and the brands that we wear. As far as food is concerned, there is a certain amount of intrinsic risk involved whenever we ingest something and allow it to enter our bodies. The brand's function is to overcome this anxiety, which explains, for example, the importance of brands in the market for spirits such as vodka and gin.

The importance of perceived risk as a generator of the legitimacy of a brand is highlighted by the categories within which distributors' own-brands (and perhaps tomorrow's discount products) dominate: canned vegetables, milk, orange juice, frozen pizzas, bottled water, kitchen roll, toilet paper and petrol. At the same time producers' brands still have a dominant position in the following categories: coffee, tea, cereals, toothpaste, deodorant, cold sauces, fresh pasta, baby food, beauty products, washing powder, etc. For these products the consumer has high involvement and does not want to take any risks, be they physical or psychological.

Nothing is ever acquired permanently, and the degree of perceived risk evolves over time. In certain sectors, as the technology becomes commonplace, all the products comply with standards of quality. Therefore we are moving from a situation where some products 'failed' whereas others 'passed', towards one where all competitors are excellent, but some are 'more excellent' than others. The degree of perceived risk will change depending on the situation. For example, there is less risk involved in buying rum or vodka for a cocktail than for a rum or vodka on the rocks. Lastly, all consumers do not have the same level of involvement. Those who have high involvement are those that worry about small differences between products or who wish to optimise their choice: they will talk for hours about the merits of such and such a computer or of a certain brand of coffee. Those who are less involved are satisfied with a basic product which isn't too expensive, such as a gin or a whisky which may be unknown but seems to be good value for money and is sold in their local shop. The problem for most buyers who feel a certain risk and fear making a mistake is that many products are opaque: we can only discover their inner qualities once we buy the products and consume them. However, many consumers are reluctant to take this step. Therefore it is imperative that the external signs highlight the internal qualities of these opaque products. A reputable brand is the most efficient of these external signals. Examples of other such external indicators are: price, quality marks, the retail outlet where the product is sold and which guarantees it, the style and design of the packaging.

How brand awareness means value

Recent marketing research shows that brand awareness is not a mere cognitive measure. It is in fact correlated with many valuable image dimensions. Awareness carries a reassuring message: although it is measured at the individual level, brand awareness is in fact a collective phenomenon. When a brand is known, each individual knows it is known. This leads to spontaneous inferences. As is shown in Table 1.4, awareness is mostly correlated with aspects such as high quality, trust, reliability, closeness to people, a good quality/price ratio, accessibility and traditional styling.

Table 1.4   How brand awareness creates value and image dimensions (correlations between awareness and image)

Good quality/price ratio	0.52
Trust	0.46
Reliable	0.44
Quality	0.43
Traditional	0.43
Best	0.40
Down to earth	0.37
Client oriented	0.37
Friendly	0.35
Accessible	0.32
Distinct	0.31
A leader	0.29
Popular	0.29
Fun	0.29
Original	0.27
Energetic	0.25
Friendly	0.25
Performing	0.22
Seductive	0.08
Innovative	0.02

(Base: 9,739 persons, 507 brands)
Source: Schuiling and Kapferer, 2004

However it has a zero correlation with innovativeness, superior class, style, seduction: if aspects such as these are key differentiation facets of the brand, they must be earned on their own merit.

Transparent and opaque products

At this stage it is interesting to remind ourselves of the classifications drawn up by Nelson (1970) and by Darby and Karni (1973). These authors make the distinction between three types of product characteristics:

- the qualities which are noticed by contact, before buying;

- the qualities which are noticed uniquely by experience, thus after buying;

- credence qualities which cannot be verified even after consumption and which you have to take on trust.

The first type of quality can be seen in the decision to buy a pair of men's socks. The choice is made according to the visible characteristics: the pattern, the style, the material, the feel, the elasticity and the price. There is hardly a need for brands in this market. In fact those that do exist only have a very small market share and target those people who are looking for proof of durability (difficult to tell before buying) or those who wish to be fashionable. This is how Burlington socks work as a hallmark of chic style. Producers' brands do exist but their differential advantage compared to distributors' brands (Marks & Spencer or C&A) is weak, especially if the latter have a good style department and offer a wide variety at a competitive price.

A good example of the second type of quality is the automobile market. Of course, performance, consumption and style can all be assessed before buying, as can the availability of options and the interior space. However, road-holding, the pleasure of driving, reliability and quality cannot be entirely appreciated during a test drive. The response comes from brand image; that is, the collective representation which is shaped over time by the accumulated experiences of oneself, of close relations, by word of mouth and advertising.

Finally, in the market for upmarket cars, the feeling that you have made it, that feeling of fulfilment and personal success through owning a BMW is typically the result of pure faith. It cannot be substantiated by any of the post-purchase driving experiences: it is a collective belief, which is more or less shared by the buyers and the non-buyers. The same logic applies to the feeling of authenticity and inner masculinity which is supposed to result from smoking Marlboro cigarettes.

The role of brands is made clearer by this classification of sought-after qualities. The brand is a sign (therefore external) whose function is to disclose the hidden qualities of the product which are inaccessible to contact (sight, touch, hearing, smell) and possibly those which are accessible through experience but where the consumer does not want to take the risk of trying the product. Lastly, a brand, when it is well known, adds an aura of make-believe when it is consumed, for example the authentic America and rebellious youth of Levi's, the rugged masculinity of Marlboro, the English style of Dunhill, the Californian myth of Apple.

The informational role of the brand varies according to the product or service, the consumption situation and the individual. Thus, a brand is not always useful. On the other hand, a brand becomes necessary once the consumer loses his or her traditional reference points. This is why there is an increase in the demand for branded wine. Consumers were put off by too many small chateaux which were rarely the same and had limited production of varying quality and which sometimes sprung some unpleasant surprises. This paved the way for brands such as Jacob's Creek and Gallo.

A brand provides not only a source of information (thus revealing its values) but performs certain other functions which justify its attractiveness and its monetary return (higher price) when they are valued by buyers. What are these functions? How does a brand create value in the eyes of the consumer? The eight functions of a brand are presented in Table 1.5. The first two are mechanical and concern the essence of the brand; that is, to function as a recognised symbol in order to facilitate choice and to gain time. The following three functions reduce the perceived risk. The last three have a more pleasurable side to them. Ethics show that buyers are expecting, more and more, responsible behaviour from their brands. Many Swedish consumers still refuse Nestlé's products because of the issue of selling Nestlé's baby milk to poor, uneducated African mothers.

These functions are neither laws nor dues, nor are they automatic; they must be defended at all times. Only a few brands are successful in each market thanks to their supporting investments in quality, R&D, productivity, communication and research in order to better understand foreseeable changes in demand. A priori, nothing confines these functions to producers' brands. Moreover, several producers' brands do not perform these functions. In Great Britain, Marks & Spencer (St Michael) is seen as an important brand and performs these functions, as do Migros in Switzerland, the Gap, Zara, Ikea and others.

The usefulness of these functions depends on the product category. There is less need for reference points or risk reducers when the product is transparent (ie its inner qualities are accessible through contact). The price premium is at its lowest and trial costs very little when there is low involvement and the purchase is seen as a chore, eg trying a new, cheaper roll of kitchen paper or aluminium foil. Certain kinds of shops aim primarily at fulfilling certain of these functions, for example hard discounters who have 650 lines with no brands, a product for every need, at the lowest prices and offering excellent quality for the price (thanks to the work on reducing all the costs which do not add value carried out in conjunction with suppliers). This formula offers another alternative to the first five functions: ease of identification on

Table 1.5 The functions of the brand for the consumer

Function	Consumer benefit
Identification	To be clearly seen, to make sense of the offer, to quickly identify the sought-after products.
Practicality	To allow savings of time and energy through identical repurchasing and loyalty.
Guarantee	To be sure of finding the same quality no matter where or when you buy the product or service.
Optimisation	To be sure of buying the best product in its category, the best performer for a particular purpose.
Badge	To have confirmation of your self-image or the image that you present to others.
Continuity	Satisfaction created by a relationship of familiarity and intimacy with the brand that you have been consuming for years.
Hedonistic	Enchantment linked to the attractiveness of the brand, to its logo, to its communication and its experiential rewards.
Ethical	Satisfaction linked to the responsible behaviour of the brand in its relationship with society (ecology, employment, citizenship, advertising which doesn't shock).

the shelf, practicality, guarantee, optimisation at the chosen price level and characterisation (refusal to be manipulated by marketing). The absence of other functions is compensated for by the very low price.

Functional analysis of brand role can facilitate the understanding of the rise of distributors' own brands. Whenever brands are just trademarks and operate merely as a recognition signal or as a mere guarantee of quality, distributors' brands can fulfil these functions as well and at a cheaper price.

Table 1.6 summarises the relationships between brand role and distributors' own-brands' market share.

How brands create value for the company

Why do financial analysts prefer companies with strong brands? Because they are less risky. Therefore, the brand works in the same way for the financial analyst as for the consumer: the brand removes the risk. The certainty, the guarantee and the removal of the risk are included in the price. By paying a high price for a company with brands the financial analyst is acquiring near certain future cashflows.

If the brand is strong it benefits from a high degree of loyalty and thus from stability of future sales. Ten per cent of the buyers of Volvic mineral water are regular and loyal and represent 50 per cent of the sales. The reputation of the brand is a source of demand and lasting attractiveness, the image of superior quality and added value justifies a premium price. A dominant brand is an entry barrier to competitors because it acts as a reference in its category. If it is prestigious or a trendsetter in terms of style it can generate substantial royalties by granting licences, for example, at its peak, Naf-Naf, a designer brand, earned over £6 million in net royalties. The brand can enter other markets when it is well known, is a symbol of quality and offers a certain promise which is valued by the market. The Palmolive brand name has become symbolic of mildness and has been extended to a number of markets besides that of soap, for example shampoo, shaving cream and washing-up liquid. This is known as brand extension (see Chapter 11) and saves on the need to create awareness if you had to launch a new product on each of these markets.

In determining the financial value of the brand, the expert must take into account the sources of any additional revenues which are generated by the presence of a strong brand. Additional buyers may be attracted to a product which appears identical to another but which has a brand name with a strong reputation. If such is the company's strategy

Table 1.6   Brand functions and distributor/manufacturer competition

Function or role of brand	Typical product category or brand	Power of manufacturers' brands
Recognition cue	Milk, salt, flour	Very weak
Practicality of choice	Socks	Weak
Guarantee of quality	Food, staples	Weak
Optimisation of choice, sign of high-quality performance	Cars, cosmetics, appliances, paint, services	Strong
Personalising one's choice	Perfumes, clothing	Strong but challenged
Permanence, bonding, familiarity relationship	Trust brands	Strong
Pleasure	Polysensual brands	Strong
Ethics and social responsibility	Reference brands, corporate brands	Strong but challenged

the brand may command a premium price in addition to providing an added margin due to economies of scale and market domination. Brand extensions into new markets can result in royalties and important leverage effects. To calculate this value, it is necessary to subtract the costs involved in brand management: the costs involved in quality control and in investing in R&D, the costs of a national, indeed international, sales force, advertising costs, the cost of a legal registration, the cost of capital invested, etc. The financial value of the brand is the difference between the extra revenue generated by the brand and the associated costs for the next few years, which are discounted back to today. The number of years is determined by the business plan of the valuer (the potential buyer, the auditors). The discount rate used to weigh these future cash flows is determined by the confidence or the lack of it that the investor has in his or her forecasts. However, a significant fact is that the stronger the brand, the smaller the risk. Thus, future net cash flows are considered more certain when brand strength is high.

Figure 1.2 shows the three generators of profit of the brand: the price premium, more attraction and loyalty, and higher margin. These effects work on the original market for the brand but they can be offered subsequently on other markets and in other product categories, either through direct brand extension (for example, Bic moved from ballpoint pens to lighters to disposable razors and recently to sailboards) or through licensing, from which the manufacturer benefits from royalties (for example all the luxury brands, and Caterpillar).

Once these levers are measured in euros, yen, dollars or any other currency they may serve as a base for evaluating the marginal profit which is attributable to the brand. They only emerge when the company wishes to strategically differentiate its products. This wish can come about through three types of investment:

▮ Investment in production, productivity and R&D. Thanks to these, the company can acquire specific know-how, a knack which cannot be imitated and which in accounting terms is also an intangible asset. Sometimes the company temporarily blocks new entrants by registering a patent. This is the basis of marketing in the pharmaceutical industry (a patent and a brand) but also of companies like Ferrero, whose products are not easily imitated despite their success. Patents are on their own an intangible asset: the activity of the company benefits from them in a lasting manner.

▮ Investment in research and marketing studies in order to get new insights, to anticipate the changes of consumers' tastes and lifestyles in order to define any important innovations which will match these evolutions. Chrysler's Minivan is an example of a product created in anticipation of the demands of baby boomers with tall children. An understanding of the expectations of distributors is also needed, as they are an essential component of the physical proximity of brands. Nowadays a key element of brand success is understanding and adapting to the logic of distributors, and developing good relations with the channels (even though it is still necessary when valuing a brand to make a distinction between what part of its sales is due to the power of the company and what part to the brand itself).

▮ Investment in listing allowances, in the sales force and merchandising, in trade marketing and, naturally, in communicating to consumers to promote the uniqueness of the brand and to endow it with saliency (awareness), perceived difference and esteem. The hidden intrinsic qualities or intangible values which are associated with consumption would be unknown without brand advertising.

The value of the brand, and thus the legitimacy of implementing a brand policy,

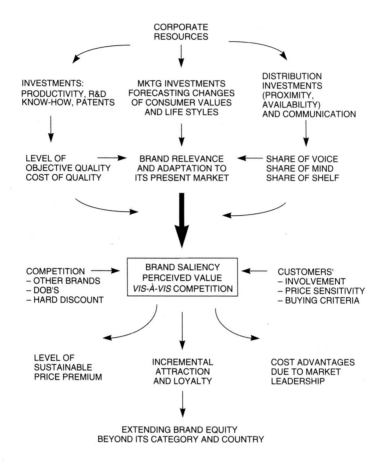

Figure 1.2   The levers of brand profitability

depends on the difference between the marginal revenues and the necessary marginal costs associated with brand management.

How brand reputation affects the impact of advertising

Brands are a form of capital that can slowly be built, while in the meantime one is growing business. Of course it is very possible to grow a business without creating such brand capital: a push strategy or a price strategy can deliver high sales and market share without building any brand equity. This is the case for many private labels or own-label brands, for instance. The volume leader in the market for Scotch whisky in France is not Johnny Walker or Ballantines or Famous Grouse but William Peel, a local brand that aimed all its efforts at the trade (hypermarkets) and sells at a low price. It has almost no saliency (spontaneous brand awareness).

Now managers are being asked to build both business and brand value. Their salary is indexed on these two yardsticks: sales and reputation. One should not see them as separate, leading to a kind of schizophrenia. Chaudhuri's very relevant research (2002) reminds us that advertising and marketing are the key levers of sales. However, their effects on market share and the ability to charge a premium price (two indicators of brand strength) are not direct but are mediated by brand reputation (or esteem). In fact, as shown by the path coefficients of Figure 1.3, brand reputation is created by familiarity (I know it well, I use it a lot) and by brand perceived uniqueness (this brand is unique, is different, there is no substitute). Advertising does play a key role in building sales, but it has no direct impact on gaining both market share and premium price. This is most interesting: in brief, it is only by building a reputational capital that both a higher market share and price premium can be obtained.

Reputation also adds to the impact of advertising on sales. It is well known from evaluations of past campaigns that the more a brand is known, the more its advertisements are noticed and remembered. It is high time to stop treating brands and commerce as opposing forces.

Case study: How branding affects medical prescription

Brands create value both for the company and to those that decide to use them. This is done by a dual quest of differentiation on tangible dimensions but also on intangible dimensions. This quest is often not simultaneous: most brands start as the mere name of a product innovation. Once they achieve success, they are copied and the intangible dimension created by the communication of brand identity creates a form of protection:

products may be similar but consumers choose one brand instead of another. This is the effect of habit, of proximity, of leadership and pioneering aura, and essentially of the need for reassurance. However, protections do not last: there is a need to recreate a material differentiation by innovation that delivers tangible benefits through improved products or services.

Very few sectors demonstrate the value of branding as much as the pharmaceutical sector. This sector is dominated by the ideology of progress through science. Those prescribing drugs are rational and make what they perceive as the best choice for the patient. Normally this should imply a product-driven market, in which brands are a forbidden word.

Recent research has shown however that medicines have a personality, as do all brands. By 'personality' we mean that both generalist doctors and specialists find it possible to attribute human personality traits to medicines. Not only did they not refuse to answer questions about brand personality, but statistical data analysis showed that some of the personality traits they ascribed to drugs were correlated with prescription levels (Kapferer, 1998).

When looking at Table 1.7, you will see that the anti-ulcer medicines that are most prescribed are described as more 'dynamic',

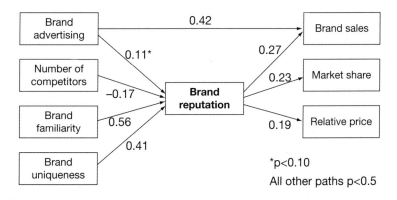

Figure 1.3 Branding and sales

Reprinted from the *Journal of Advertising Research*, copyright 2002, by the Advertising Research Foundation

Table 1.7   Brand personality is related to prescription levels

| | Personality score (1 to 3) of highly prescribed vs less prescribed medical brands | | | | | |
| | Anti-hypertension | | Antibiotics | | Anti-ulcer | |
	Low P	High P	Low P	High P	Low P	High P
Dynamic	2.01	2.20+++	2.17	2.37+++	2.10	2.46+++
Creative	1.87	1.92	1.81	1.93+	2.03	2.22+++
Optimistic	2.02	2.21+++	2.00	2.23+++	2.22	2.31
Prudent	2.13	2.11	2.08	1.98	2.08+++	1.90
Hard	1.58+++	1.39	1.70+++	1.45	1.56+++	1.31
Cold	1.67+++	1.45	1.72+++	1.40	1.60+++	1.33
Caring	2.04	2.11	2.01	2.09	2.03	2.09
Rational	2.28	2.23	2.38	2.27	2.23	2.15
Generous	1.85	1.95	1.87	2.02+++	1.93	2.02
Empathetic	1.88	2.09+++	1.90	2.02++	1.99	2.01
Close	2.06	2.09	2.16	2.25	2.08	2.13
Elegant	1.97	1.97	1.99	2.04	1.92	2.03
Class	2.01	2.04	1.87	1.94	1.93	2.20+++
Serene	2.10	2.12	2.12	2.25+	2.20	2.11
Calm	2.15	2.07	2.16+	2.04	2.12+++	1.90

Source: Kapferer (1998)

'warm' and 'close' than other forms of medication. A product, an active ingredient cannot be dynamic, warm or close; a brand can. Thus brands of drugs do have a mental existence and influence in the minds of the prescribers.

Interestingly too, statistical evidence shows that although they recognised the products themselves as being totally identical and saw two brands as fully similar in the functional benefits they delivered, respondents prescribed one three times more frequently than the other. However the chosen one was endowed with significantly more 'status' than the less chosen one. Status is an intangible dimension created by impressions of leadership. of presence, of proximity to the doctors, of intensity of communication. It is created by marketing once the drug has been developed. Once created, this serves as competitive edge against 'me too' products, at least before a new drug replaces the existing one as market leader.

This example illustrates the fact that even in the high-tech sector, brands are a psychological reality, which operate even in the context of rational decision makers who are disposed to make optimal rational decisions. Choice is always a risk: products increase the range of choice, and thus of perceived risk. Brands make choice easier by reducing the likelihood of choosing alternatives to the market leader.

The choice of the English word 'likelihood' here is interesting because it implies both a statistical concept (probability) and the mediating process by which alternatives are being more chosen (they are more 'likeable'). Branding is thus a consumer-oriented response to the problem of decision making in opaque and dense choice environments. Brand spontaneous awareness and positioning (linking to a need) are short cuts that are very helpful for decision making. Brands do create a decisional bias: as such they facilitate choice and reduce perceived risk (Kapferer and Laurent, 1988).

These examples illustrate the relationship between the product and the brand: there is a natural interaction between them. Brand mission determines what products or services should be created. These innovative products endowed with a value-adding identity create attractiveness, and encourage trials, repeat sales and loyalty despite incoming copies and low-cost alternatives. However, new disruptive innovations may shift clients' value curves, hence change their preferences. This means that the brand cannot be defended only through intangible values: even the much admired Jaguar brand went broke and had to be bought by Ford to enable it to regain the capacity to make high-quality and high-tech cars for today's exacting new affluent consumers.

Corporate reputation and the corporate brand

In 2003 Velux, which had become known as the number one brand for roof windows in the world, realised it needed to create a corporate brand. It felt that merely to compete through its product brand was not enough to protect it against the growing number of me-toos all over the world. In addition, its brand equity was stagnating. When any brand reaches a level of 80 per cent of top-of-mind

awareness in its category, part of its 'stagnation' is certainly due to a ceiling effect: there is not much room for improvement. However, the company felt that emotional bonding with its brand was not strong enough. Could the product brand alone improve the bond? The diagnosis was that it was high time to reveal 'the brand behind the brand' (Kapferer, 2000) and start building a corporate brand.

In fact many companies that based their success on product brands have now decided to create a corporate brand in order to make company actions, values and missions more salient and to diffuse specific added values. Unilever should soon develop some kind of corporate visibility, as Procter & Gamble does in Asia at this time and will probably do everywhere soon.

There is another reason that corporate brands are a new hot managerial topic: the defence of reputation. Companies have become very sensitive about their reputation. Formerly they used to be sensitive about their image. Why this change? Isn't image (perception) the basis on which global evaluations are formed (and thus reputation)? It is

Table 1.8 The brand influence in medical prescription

	Category: anti-ulcer	
	Brand A	Me-too
Product image		
Efficient	2.9	2.9
Rapid	2.7	2.7
Prevents recurrence	2.7	2.7
No side-effects	2.7	2.6
No anti-acid	2.6	2.6
Low cost	1.4	1.4
Brand reputation		
It is a reference product	3.7+++++	3.1-----
High reputation	3.8+++++	3.3-----
Superior quality	3.3	3.1
Major product	3.7+	3.6-
Prescription	6.7+++++	3.3-----

Source: Kapferer (1998)

likely that the term 'image' has lost its glamour. It seems to have fallen into disrepute precisely because there was too much publicity about 'image makers', as if image was an artificial construction. Reputation has more depth, is more involving: it is a judgement from the market which needs to be preserved. In any case reputation has become a byword, as witnessed by the annual surveys on the most respected companies that are now made in almost all countries, modelled on Fortune's 'America's most admired companies'. Reputation signals that although the company has many different stakeholders, each one reacting to a specific facet of the company (as employee, as supplier, as financial investor, as client), in fact they are all sensitive to the global ability of the company to meet the expectations of all its stakeholders. Reputation takes the company as a whole. It reunifies all stakeholders and all functions of the corporation.

Because changes in reputation affect all stakeholders, companies monitor and manage their reputation closely. Fombrun has diagnosed that global reputation is based on six factors or 'pillars' (Fombrun, Gardberg and Sever, 2000):

▧ emotional appeal (trust, admiration and respect);

▧ products and services (quality, innovativeness, value for money and so on);

▧ vision and leadership;

▧ workplace quality (well-managed, appealing workplace; employee talent);

▧ financial performance;

▧ social responsibility.

Since companies cannot grow without advocates and the support of their many stakeholders, they need to build a reputational capital among all of them; plus a global reputation, because even specialised stakeholders wish the company to be responsive to all

stakeholders. There is a link between reputation and share performance.

As a consequence of this growth of the reputational concept, companies have realised they cannot stay mute, invisible, opaque. They must manage their visibility and that of their actions in order to maximise their reputational capital – in fact their goodwill, to speak like financiers. The corporate brand will be more and more present and visible: through art sponsorship, foundations, charities, advertising. As such it addresses global targets. The corporate brand speaks on behalf of the company, signals the company's presence. Now companies are also developing specialised corporate brands such as 'You' (the recruiting brand of Unilever), or specialised campaigns (such as semi-annual financial road shows).

Corporate brands have therefore taken a new importance since they speak on behalf of the company, signal its presence and actions: in fact they draw the company's profile in the eyes of all those who do not have direct interactions with it. In our world people react more and more to names and reputations, to rumours and word of mouth. They do not see the headquarters or the factories any more. Often delocalised, corporations appear through the press, publicity, PR, advertising, financial reports, trade union reports, all sorts of communications, and of course their products and services. Managing the corporate brand and its communication means managing this profile. The methods to do so are not specific: they rely as do all brands on identity. They also rely on the markets.

What then is the difference between corporate brand methods and the product brand methods developed in this book? None. However. in practice, it must be realised that companies do have an internal identity, core values that bear on the profile they wish to, or can, express outwardly. Companies and corporations are bodies with a soul (from the Latin, *corpus*). Product brands are more imaginary constructions, relying on intangible values which have been invented to fulfil the needs of clients. Ralph Lauren's or Marlboro's intangible values are pure constructions. It cannot be the same for companies. Reality leaves fewer degrees of freedom.

Second, since brand management is both identity and market oriented, corporate brands must tailor their profile to meet the expectations of multiple publics. The core value must be tailored for this global audience, which symbolically has to 'buy' the company, as a supplier, an employee or an investor. Managing the reputation of the name, through (among other methods) the communication of the corporate brand, is aimed at making the company their first choice.

As to the very hot topic of the financial value of reputation, a conceptual distinction must be made: at the corporate level, this is called goodwill (the excess of stock value over book value). Now, the larger part of this goodwill is attributable to the financial value of the brand as commercial brand. This financial value is usually measured by the discounted cash-flow method. This shows that the financial value of the brand, be it product brand or corporate brand, can only be traced through prospective sales (see Chapter 17).

How do corporate brands relate to product brands? The latter are there to create client goodwill, build growth and profits. In modern mature markets, consumers do not make a complete distinction between the product brand and the corporation: what the corporation does impacts their evaluation of its brands, especially if they share the same name as the corporation or are visibly endorsed by the former. The issue of branding architectures with the four structural types of relationship (independence; umbrella; endorsement; source or branded house) will be covered in Chapter 12. It has strategic implications in terms of the spillover effects (Sullivan, 1988) the organisation might or might not want to capitalise on, and in terms of bolstering confidence in the product

(Brown and Dacin, 1997), if this is necessary, which is not always the case. For instance LVMH, the world's leading luxury group, remains separate from its 41 brands' communication and marketing: they look independent. GM endorses its brands: it reveals the powerful and respected corporation behind its car marques. GE follows an umbrella strategy: GE Capital Investment, GE Medical Services. A classic strategy, in our world of global communication and synergies, is to use for the corporation the same name as its best brand. This is how BSN became Danone – just as 50 years earlier, Tokyo Tsuhin Kogyo became Sony. As we shall see (page 294), there are strong benefits in doing this.

A conceptual issue arises when one speaks, say, of Canon or Nike or Sony or Citibank. Are they corporate brands? Are they commercial brands? Since the company and the brand share the same name it is difficult to say. The answer is that they are both: it depends on the context and objectives and target of communication. Naomi Klein's book *No Logo* (1999) criticises Nike as a company, for all it tries to hide behind the attractive images and sports stars of its commercial brand (for the sweatshops in Asia, the delocalisation of manufacturing to developing countries, the lack of reactiveness to critics). To make it clear who speaks, the corporation or the brand, some companies have chosen to differentiate the logo of each source of communication: Nestlé's corporate logo is not that of Nestlé as a commercial brand (which itself is differentiated by product category) (see page 79).

The case is more acute still for service companies: can one differentiate Barclay's Bank or Orange as a brand and as a corporate brand? Since both share the same employees this is more difficult, although looking at the objectives and target of the communication should help. This is why the issue of brand alignment (Ind, 2001) has become so important: the corporation has to align on its brand values. Its whole business should be brand driven.

2

Strategic implications of branding

Many companies have forgotten the fundamental purpose of their brands. A great deal of attention is devoted to the marketing activity itself, which involves designers, graphic artists, packaging and advertising agencies. This activity thus becomes an end in itself, receiving most of the attention. In so doing, we forget that it is just a means. Branding is seen as the exclusive prerogative of the marketing and communications staff. This undervalues the role played by the other parts of the company in ensuring a successful branding policy and business growth.

Yet the marketing phase, which we now consider indispensable, is the terminal phase of a process that involves the company's resources and all of its functions, focusing them on one strategic intent: creating a difference. Only by mobilising all of its internal sources of added value can a company set itself apart from its competitors.

What does branding really mean?

Branding means much more than just giving a brand name and signalling to the outside world that such a product or service has been stamped with the mark and imprint of an organisation. It requires a corporate long-term involvement, a high level of resources and skills.

Branding consists in transforming the product category

Brands are a direct consequence of the strategy of market segmentation and product differentiation. As companies seek to better fulfil the expectations of specific customers, they concentrate on providing the latter, consistently and repeatedly, with the ideal combination of attributes – both tangible and intangible, functional and hedonistic, visible and invisible – under viable economic conditions for their businesses. Companies want to stamp their mark on different sectors and set their imprint on their products. It is no wonder that the word 'brand' also refers to the act of burning a mark into the flesh of an animal as a means to claim ownership of it. The first task in brand analysis is to define precisely all that the brand injects into the product (or service) and how the brand transforms it:

- What attributes materialise?

- What advantages are created?

- What benefits emerge?

- What ideals does it represent?

This deep meaning of the brand concept is often forgotten or wilfully omitted. That is why certain distributors are often heard saying – as a criticism of many a manufacturer's brand whose added value lies only its name – 'For us, the brand is secondary, there is no need to put something on the product.' Hence, the brand is reduced to package surface and label. Branding, though, is not about being on top of something, but within something. The product or service thus enriched must stand out well if it is to be spotted by the potential buyer and if the company wants to reap the benefits of its strategy before being copied by others.

Furthermore, the fact that a delabelled item is worth more than a generic product confirms this understanding of branding. According to the 'brand is just a superficial label' theory, the delabelled product supposedly becomes worthless when it no longer carries a brand name, unless it continues to bear the brand within. In passing, the brand has intrinsically altered it: hence the value of Lacostes without 'Lacoste', Adidases without 'Adidas'. They are worth more than imitations because the brand, though invisible, still prevails. Conversely, the brand on counterfeits, though visible, is in effect absent. This is why counterfeits are sold so cheaply.

Some brands have succeeded in proving with their slogans that they know and understand what their fundamental task is: to transform the product category. A brand not only acts on the market, it organises the market, driven by a vision, a calling and a clear idea of what the category should become. Too many brands wish only to identify fully with the product category,

thereby expecting to control it. In fact they often end up disappearing within it: Polaroid, Xerox, Caddy, Scotch, Kleenex have thus become generic terms.

According to the objective the brand sets itself; transforming the category implies endowing the product with its own separate identity. In concrete terms, that means that the brand is weak when the product is 'transparent'. Talking about 'Greek olive oil, first cold pressing' for example, makes the product transparent, almost entirely defined and epitomised by those sole attributes, yet there are dozens of brands capable of marketing that type of oil. Going from bulk to packaging is also symptomatic of this phenomenon. The weakness of fresh vacuum-packed food brands is partially due to the fact that their packaging, though designed to reassure the buyer – such as with sauerkraut in film-wrapped containers – only recreates transparency. Significantly, Findus and l'Eggs or Hoses do not just show their products, they *show* them *off*. This is the structural cause of Essilor's brand weakness, as perceived by the customers. They do not perceive how Essilor, the world leader in optical glass, transforms the product, nor its input, its added value. To them, glass is just glass to which various options can be added (anti-reflecting, unbreakable, etc). The added value seems to be created solely by the style of the rims (hence the boom in licensing) or the service, both of which are palpable and in the store. What is invisible is not perceived and thus does not exist in their eyes. However, the example of Evian reminds us that it is always possible to make a transparent product become opaque. The major mineral water brands have been able to exist, grow and prosper only because they have made the invisible visible. We can no longer choose our water haphazardly: good health and purity are associated with Evian, fitness with Contrex, vitality with Vittel. These various positionings were justified by the invisible differences in water contents. Generally speaking, anything adding to the complexity of ingredients also contributes to creating distance *vis-à-vis* the product. In this respect, Coca-Cola is doing the right thing by keeping its recipe secret. When Orangina was taken over by Pernod-Ricard, its concentrate was remixed into something even more complex. Antoine Riboud, the former CEO of Danone worldwide, expressed a similar concern when declaring: 'It is not yoghurts that I make, but Danones.'

A brand is a long-term vision

The brand should have its own specific point of view on the product category. Major brands have more than just a specific or dominating position in the market: they hold certain positions within the product category. This position and conception both energise the brand and feed the transformations that are implemented for matching the brand's products with its ideals. It is this conception that justifies the brand's existence, its reason for being on the market, and provides it with a guideline for its life cycle. How many brands are capable today of answering the following crucial question: 'What would the market lack if we did not exist?' The company's ultimate goal is undoubtedly to generate profit and jobs. But brand purpose is something else. Brand strategy is too often mistaken for company strategy. The latter most often results in truisms such as 'increase customer satisfaction'. Specifying brand purpose consists in (re)defining its *raison d'être*, its absolute necessity. The notion of brand purpose is missing in most marketing textbooks. It is a recent idea and conveys the emerging conception of the brand, seen as exerting a creative and powerful influence on a given market. If there is power, there is energy. Naturally, a brand draws its strength from the company's financial and human means, but it derives its energy from its specific niche, vision and ideals. If it does not feel driven by an intense internal necessity, it

will not carry the potential for leadership. The analytical notion of brand image does not clearly capture this dynamic dimension, which is demanded by modern brand management.

Thus, many banks put forward the following image of themselves: close to their clients, modern, offering high-performing products and customer service. These features are, of course, useful to market researchers in charge of measuring the perceptions sent back by the market and the level of consumer satisfaction. But from which dynamic programme do they emanate, which vision do they embody?

Certain banks have specified what their purpose is: for some it is 'to change people's relationship to money', while for others it is to remind us that money is just a 'means towards personal development'. Several banks have recently worked at redefining their singular reason for existence. All of them will have to do so in the future. The Amex vision of money is not that of Visa.

More than most, multi-segment brands need to redetermine their own purpose. Cars are a typical example. A multi-segment brand (also called a generalist brand) wants to cover all market segments. Each model spawns multiple versions, thereby theoretically maximising the number of potential buyers: diesel, gas, three or five doors, estate, coupé, cabriolet, etc. The problem is that by having to constantly satisfy the key criteria of each segment (bottom range, lower mid-range, upper mid-range and top range), ie to churn out many different versions and to avoid over-typifying a model in order to please everyone, companies tend to create chameleon brands. Apart from the symbol on the car hood or the similarities in the car designs, we no longer perceive an overall plan guiding the creative and productive forces of the company in the conception of these cars. Thus, competitors fight their battles either over the price or the options offered for that price. No longer brands, they become mere names on a hood or on a dealer's office walls. The word has thus lost most of its meaning. What does Opel or Ford mean?

What unifies the products of a brand is not their marque or common external signs, it is their 'religion': what common spirit, vision and ideals are embodied in them.

Major brands can be compared to a pyramid (see Figure 2.1). The top states the brand's vision and purpose – its conception of automobiles, for instance, its idea of the types of cars it wants, and has always wanted, to create, as well as its very own values which either can or cannot be expressed by a slogan. This level leads to the next one down, which shows the general brand style of communication. Indeed, brand personality and style are conveyed less by words than by a way of being and communicating. These codes should not be exclusively submitted to the fluctuating inspiration of the creative team: they must be defined so as to reflect the brand's unique character. The next level presents the brand's strategic image features: amounting to four or five, they result from the overall vision and materialise in the brand's products, communication and actions. This refers, for example, to the positioning of Volvo as a secure, reliable and robust brand, or of BMW as a dynamic, classy prestigious one. Lastly, the product level, at the bottom of the pyramid, consists of each model's positioning in its respective segment.

The problem is that consumers look at the pyramid from the bottom up. They start with what is real and tangible. The wider the

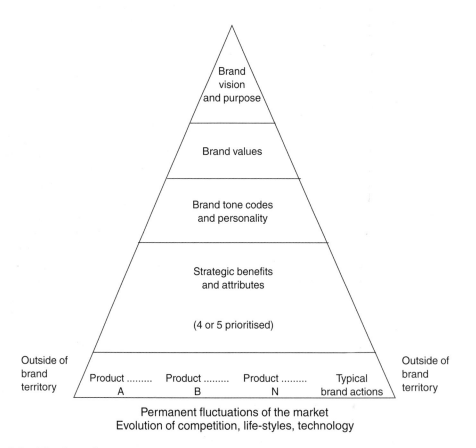

Figure 2.1   The brand system

pyramid base is, the more the customers doubt that all these cars do indeed emanate from the same automobile concept, that they carry the same brand essence and bear the stamp of the same automobile project. Brand management consists, for its part, in starting from the top and defining the way the car is conceived by the brand, in order to determine exactly when a car is deserving of the brand name and when it no longer is – in which case, the car should logically no longer bear the brand name, as it then slips out of its brand territory.

As automobile history is made of great successes followed by bitter failures, major multi-segment brands regularly question their vision. Thus, after its smash hit models, the 205 and 405, Peugeot was somewhat perturbed, both internally and externally, by the series of set-backs with the 605 and the slow take-off of the 106 and 306. A basic question was then asked: 'Are Peugeots still Peugeots?' Answering it implied redefining the long-term meaning of the statement 'It's a Peugeot', ie the brand's long-lasting automobile concept.

Internal hesitation about brand identity is often revealed when searching for slogans. There is no longer a trend toward obvious and meaningless slogans such as 'the automobile spirit', which neither tell us anything about the brand's automobile ideal, nor help to guide inventors, creators, developers or producers in making concrete choices between mutually exclusive features: comfort and road adherence, aerodynamism and feeling of sturdiness, etc.

Permanently nurturing the difference

Our era is one of temporary advantages. It is often argued that certain products of different brands are identical. Some observers thus infer that, under these circumstances, a brand

is nothing but a 'bluff', a gimmick used to try to stand out in a market flooded with barely differentiated products.

This view fails to take into account both the time factor and the rules of dynamic competition. Brands draw attention through the new products they create and bring onto the market. Any brand innovation necessarily generates plagiarism. Any progress made quickly becomes a standard to which buyers grow accustomed: competing brands must then adopt it themselves if they do not want to fall short of market expectations. For a while, the innovative brand will thus be able to enjoy a fragile monopoly, which is bound to be quickly challenged unless the innovation is or can be patented. The role of the brand name is precisely to protect the innovation: it acts as a mental patent, by becoming the prototype of the new segment it creates – advantage of being a pioneer.

If it is true that a snapshot of a given market often shows similar products, a dynamic view of it reveals in turn who innovated first, and who has simply followed the leader: brands protect innovators, granting them momentary exclusiveness and rewarding them for their risk-taking attitude. Thus, the accumulation of these momentary differences over time serves to reveal the meaning and purpose of a brand and to justify its economic function, hence its price premium.

Brands cannot, therefore, be reduced to a mere sign on a product, a mere graphic cosmetic touch: they guide a creative process, which yields the new product A today, the new products B and C tomorrow, and so on. Products come to life, live and disappear, but brands endure. The permanent factors of this creative process are what gives a brand its meaning and purpose, its content and attributes. A brand requires time in order for this accumulation of innovations to yield a meaning and a purpose.

As shown in Figure 2.2, brand management alternates between phases of product differentiation and brand image differentiation. The

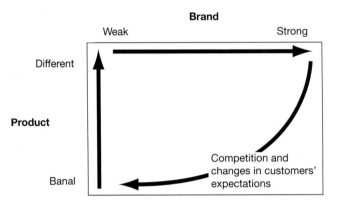

Figure 2.2   The cycle of brand management

typical example is Sony, whose advertising focuses on innovations when they exist, and on image in between.

What you do first is most important

A brand does in fact act as a genetic programme. What is done at birth exerts a long-lasting influence on market perceptions. Indeed revitalising a brand often starts with re-identifying its forgotten genetic programme (see page 387).

Table 2.1 shows how brands are built and exert a long-term influence on customers' memories, which in turn influence their expectations, attitudes and degree of satisfaction.

In the life of a brand, although they may have been forgotten, the early acts have a very

structuring influence. In fact they mould the first and long-lasting meaning of this new word that designates Brand X or Brand Y. Once learnt, this meaning gets reinforced and stored in long-term memory. Then a number of selective processes reinforce the meaning: selective attention, selective perception, selective memory.

This is why brand images are hard to change: they act like fast-setting concrete.

This process has many important managerial consequences. When going international, each country reproduces it. It is of prime importance to define the products to be launched in relationship with the image one wants to create in the long term. Too often they are chosen by local agents just because they will sell very well. They must do both: build the business and build the brand. Brand management introduces long-term effects as criteria for evaluating the relevance of short-term decisions.

Table 2.1   The brand as genetic programme

Early founding acts (past)	Memory (present)	Expectations (future)
First product	Brand prototype	Legitimate extensions for the future
First channel of distribution	Associated benefits	(what other areas of new products)
First positioning	Brand identity	
First campaign		
First events		
First CEO		
Corporate visions and values		

New generations discover the brand at different points in time. Some discovered Ford through the Model T, others through the Mustang, others through the Mondeo, others through the Focus. No wonder brand images differ from one generation to another.

The memory factor also partly explains why individual preferences endure: within a given generation, people continue, even 20 years later, to prefer the brands they liked between the ages of 7 and 18 (Guest, 1964; Fry *et al*, 1973; Jacoby and Chestnut, 1978).

It is precisely because a brand is the memory of the products that it can act as a long-lasting and stable reference. Unlike advertising, in which the last message seen is often the only one that truly registers and is best recalled, the first actions and message of a brand are the ones bound to leave the deepest impression, thereby structuring long-term perception. In this respect, brands create a cognitive filter: dissonant and atypical aspects are declared unrepresentative, thus discounted and forgotten. That is why failures in brand extensions on atypical products do not harm the brand in the end even though they do unsettle the investors' trust in the company (Loken and Roedder-John, 1993). Bic's failure in perfume is a good example. Making perfumes is not typical of the know-how of Bic as perceived by consumers: sales of ball pens, lighters and razors kept on increasing.

Ridding itself of atypical, dissonant elements, a brand acts as a selective memory, hence endowing people's perceptions with an illusion of permanence and coherence. That is why a brand is less elastic than its products. Once created, like fast-setting concrete it is hard to change. Hence the critical importance of defining the brand platform. What brand meaning does one want to create?

A brand is both the memory and the future of its products. The analogy with the genetic programme is central to understanding how brands function and should be managed. Indeed, the brand memory that develops contains the programme for all future evolution, the characteristics of upcoming models and their common traits, as well as the family resemblances transcending their diverse personalities. By understanding a brand's programme, we can not only trace its legitimate territory but also the area in which it will be able to grow beyond the products that initially gave birth to it. The brand's underlying programme indicates the purpose and meaning of both former and future products. How then can one identify this programme?

If it exists, this programme can be discovered by analysing the brand's founding acts: products, communication and the most significant actions since its inception. If a guideline or an implicit permanence exists, then it must show through. Research on brand identity has a double purpose: to analyse the brand's most typical production on the one hand and to analyse the reception, ie the image sent back by the market, on the other. The image is indeed a memory in itself, so stable that it is difficult to modify it in the short run. This stability results from the selective perception described above. It also has a function: to create long-lasting refer-ences guiding consumers among the abundant supply of consumer goods. That is the reason a company should never turn away from its identity, which alone has managed to attract buyers. Customer loyalty is created by respecting the brand features that initially seduced the buyers. If the products slacken off, weaken or show a lack of investment and thus no longer meet customer expectations, better try to meet them again than to change expectations. In order to build customer loyalty and capitalise on it, brands must stay true to themselves. This is called a return to the future.

Questioning the past, trying to detect the brand's underlying programme, does not mean ignoring the future: on the contrary, it is a way of better preparing for it by giving it roots, legit-imacy and continuity. The mistake is to embalm the brand and to merely repeat in the present what it produced in the past, like the new VW Beetle and other retro-innovations. In fighting competition, a brand's products must always belong intrinsically to their time, but in their very own way. Rejuvenating Burberrys or Helena Rubenstein means connecting them to modernity, not mummifying them in deference to a past splendour that we might wish to revive.

The brand is really a contract

Brands become credible only through the persistence and repetition of their value proposition. Through time they become a quasi contract, unwritten but most effective. This contract binds both parties. The brand must keep its identity, but permanently increase its relevance. It must be loyal to itself, to its mission and to its clients. Each brand is free to choose its values and positioning, but once chosen and advertised, they become the benchmark for customer satisfaction. It is well known that the prime determinant of customer satisfaction is the gap between customers' experiences and their expectations. The brand's positioning sets up these expectations.

On the other side, customers should be loyal to such a brand.

This mutual commitment explains why brands, whose products have temporarily declined in popularity, do not necessarily disappear. A brand is to be judged over the long term: a deficiency can always occur. Brand support gives products a chance to recover. If not, Jaguar would have disappeared long ago: no other brand could have withstood the detrimental effect of the decreasing quality of its cars during the 1970s. That is a good illustration of one of the benefits a brand brings to a company, besides the capitalisation and patent effects referred to earlier.

The brand contract is economic, not legal. Brands differ in this way from other signs of quality such as quality seals and certification. Quality seals officially and legally testify that a given product meets a set of specific characteristics, previously defined (in conjunction with public authorities, producers/manufacturers and consumers) so as to guarantee a higher level of quality and distinguishing it from similar products. A quality seal is a collective brand controlled by a certification agency which certifies a given product only if it complies with certain specifications. Such certification is thus never definitive and can be withdrawn (like ISO).

Brands do not legally testify that a product meets a set of characteristics. However, through consistent and repeated experience of these characteristics, a brand becomes synonymous with the latter.

A contract implies constraints. The brand contract assumes first of all that the various functions in the organization all converge: R&D, production, methods, logistics, marketing, finance. The same is true of service brands: as the R&D and production aspects are obviously irrelevant in this case, the responsibility for ensuring the brand's continuity and cohesion pass to the management and staff, who play an essential role in clientele relationships.

The brand contract requires internal as well as external marketing. Unlike quality seals, brands set their own ever-increasing standards. Therefore, they must not only meet the latter but also continuously try to improve all their products, even the most basic ones, especially if they represent most of their sales and hence act as the major vehicle of brand image; in so doing, they will be able to satisfy the expectations of clients who will demand that the products keep pace with technological change. They must also communicate and make themselves known to the outside world in order to become the prototype of a segment, a value or a benefit. This is a lonely task for brands, yet they must do it to get the uniqueness and lack of substitutability they need. The brand will have to support its internal and external costs all on its own. These are generated by the brand requirements, which are to:

▪ Closely forecast the needs and expectations of potential buyers. This is the purpose of market research: both to optimise existing products and to discover needs and expectations that have yet to be fulfilled.

▪ React to technical and technological progress as soon as it can to create a competitive edge both in terms of cost and performance.

▪ Provide both product (or service) volume and quality at the same time, since those are the only means of ensuring repeat purchases.

▪ Control supply quantity and quality.

▪ Deliver products or services to intermediaries (distributors), both consistently over time and in accordance with their requirements in terms of delivery, packaging and overall conditions.

▪ Give meaning to the brand and communicate its meaning to the target market, thereby using the brand as both a signal and reference for the product's (or service's) identity and exclusivity. That is what advertising budgets are for.

▪ Increase the experiential rewards of consumption or interaction.

▪ Remain ethical and ecology-conscious.

Strong brands thus bring about both internal mobilisation and external federalisation. They create their company's panache and impetus. That is why some companies switch their own name for that of one of their star brands: BSN thus became Danone, CGE became Alcatel. In this respect, the impact of strong brands extends far beyond most corporate strategies. These only last while they are in the making, after which they

either vanish or wind up as pompous phrases ('a passion for excellence') posted in hallways. In any case, the corporate brand is the organisation's external voice and, as such, it remains both demanding and determined to constantly outdo itself, to aim ever higher.

Becoming aware that the brand is a contract also means taking up many other responsibilities that are all too often ignored. In the fashion market, even if creators wish to change after a while, they cannot entirely forget about their brand contract, which helped them to get known initially, then recognised and eventually praised. This can indeed cause serious problems for international brand management, as different countries tend to perceive brands in different ways. Thus, in Europe, Polo by Ralph Lauren typifies the Bostonian preppie style. Meanwhile, in the United States, the Ralph Lauren brand has changed its image significantly by launching the Safari fragrance, which is radically different from the previous style of its products.

In theory, both the brand's slogan and signature are meant to embody the brand contract. A good slogan is therefore often rejected by managing directors because it means too much commitment for the company and may backfire if the products/ services do not match the expectations the brand has created so far. In too many cases brands are seen as mere names: this is very evident in some innovations committee meetings, where new products are reallocated to different brands of the portfolio many times in the same meeting. One brand name or another is perceived as making no difference. Taking the brand seriously, as it is (that is, as a contract) is much more demanding. It also provides higher returns.

The product and the brand

Since the early theorisation on the brand, there has been much discussion on the relationship of brands to products. How do the concepts differ? How are they mutually interrelated? On the one hand, many a CEO repeats to his or her staff that there is no brand without a great product (or service), in order to stimulate their innovativeness and make them think of the product as a prime lever of brand competitiveness. On the other hand, there is ample evidence that market leaders are not the best product in their market. To be the 'best product' in a category means to compete in the premium tier, which is rarely a large segment. Certainly within the laundry detergent category, market leaders such as Tide, Ariel and Skip are those delivering the best performance for heavy-duty laundry, but in other cases it is the brand with the best quality/price ratio that is market leader. Dell is a case in point. Are Dell's computers the best? Surely not. But who really needs a 'best computer'? What would be the criterion for evaluation? 'Best' is a relative concept, depending on the value criteria used to establish comparisons and identify the 'best'. In fact the market is segmented: the largest proportion of the public, and even most of the B2B segment, wants a modern, reliable, cheap computer. Thanks to its build-to-order business model, Dell was able to innovate and become the leader of that segment. Co-branded 'Intel inside', it reassures buyers and surprises them by its astonishing price and one-to-one customisation: each person makes his or her own computer. Is Swatch the best watch? Surely not either. But in any case this is not what is asked by Swatch buyers: they buy convenience and style, not long-lasting superior 'performance', whatever this may mean.

It is time to look deeper into the brand–product relationship. Finance and accounting remind us that a brand is a conditional asset. It can deliver future cash flows only if it is carried by a product or service. There is no brand valuation without a product or service to transform a name and its mental associations and affect into cash flows.

Looking at history, most brands are born out of a product or service innovation which outperformed its competitors. A superior product/service was the determining factor of the launch campaign. Later, as the product name evolves into a brand, customers' reasons for purchase may still be the brand's 'superior performance image', although in reality that performance has been matched by new competitors. This has been the basis of Volkswagen's leadership and price premium: a majority of consumers keeps on believing that Volkswagen cars are the most reliable ones. The new Golf Five, launched in September 2003, 30 years after the first Golf, is 10 per cent more expensive than its two European rivals, the Peugeot 307 and the Renault Megane. This quality reputation is crucial for Golf and for Volkswagen itself: this model used to represent 28 per cent of its sales and almost half its operating profit. When Golf 4 sales fell by 17.9 per cent over 12 months, Volkswagen's operating profit fell too, by 56 per cent.

As all tests and garage repair records demonstrate, Volkswagen quality has now been matched and even bypassed by its competitors; but for buyers, perception is reality. Brand assets are made of what people believe. As for rumours (Kapferer, 2004), the more people believe a rumour, the more strongly their belief is held. Why would so many people be completely wrong? It took 20 years for Toyota to shake the belief among US consumers that Volkswagen cars are the most reliable: it takes time to prove one's reliability. Often, to go faster it is best to target a new generation of drivers with an open mind.

Looking at competitive behaviour, it seems that brands alternate in their focus. They capitalise on their image, then innovate to recreate or nurture the belief of product superiority (on some consumer benefit), then recapitalise on their image, and so on (Figure 2.2). Sony's advertising is very typical of this pendulum behaviour: it alternates ads that introduce new products and pure image ads with no specific material content or superiority content. These latter ads maintain brand saliency (Ehrenberg et al, 2002).

Figure 2.3 summarises the product–brand relationship.

Suppose a consumer wants to buy a new car because of the birth of his or her fourth child. This major event creates a new set of expectations, some tangible, some intangible. The consumer wishes to buy a minivan, with two sliding doors, high flexibility within the cabin, and of course a reliable, secure brand, with credentials and some status. By looking at Internet sites, at magazines and visiting dealers, it is possible to identify those models with the requested visible attributes (size, flexibility, sliding doors). Now what about the invisible attributes, like the experiential ones (driving pleasure) or those one has to believe on faith, such as reliability? Obviously, these attributes do or do not belong to the brand's reputational capital. They cannot be observed. This is one of the key roles of brands: to guarantee, to reassure customers about desired benefits which constitute the exclusive strength of the brand, also called its positioning.

Psychologists have also identified the halo effect as a major source of value created by the brand: the fact that knowing the name of the brand does influence consumer's perception of the product advantages beyond what the visible cues had themselves indicated, not to speak of the invisible advantages.

Finally, attached to the brand there are pure intangible associations, which stem from the brand's values, vision, philosophy, its typical buyer, its brand personality and so on. These associations are the source of emotional ties, beyond product satisfaction. In fact, in the car industry, they are the locus of consumers' desire to possess a brand. Some brands sell very good products at fair price but lack thrill or desire: they cannot command a price premium in their segment. Their dealers will have to give more rebates (which undermine brand value and business profitability).

Figure 2.3 reminds us of the double nature of brands. People buy branded products or services, but branding is a not a substitute for marketing. Both are needed. Marketing aims at forecasting the needs of specific consumer segments, and drives the organisation to tailor products and services to these needs. This is a skill: some car marques offer minivans with sliding doors, some do not. However, part of the willingness to pay is based on a personal tie with the brand. Uninvolved consumers will bargain a lot. Brand-involved consumers will bargain less. Brand image is directly linked to profitability. In fact, in the Euromonitor car brand tracking study, measuring the image of all automobile brands operating in Europe, it has been said that a positive shift of one unit on the global opinion scale means there is 1 per cent less bargaining by customers.

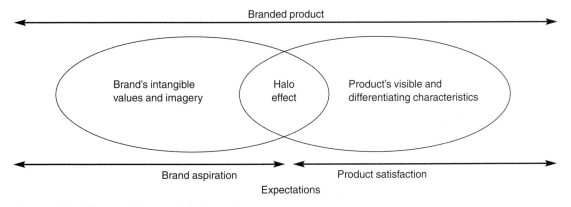

Figure 2.3   The product and the brand

Each brand needs a flagship product

A given brand will not be jeopardised by competitors offering similar products, unless there are large quantities of the latter. It is indeed inevitable for certain models to be duplicated in the product lines of different brands. Suppose that brand A pursues durability, brand B practicality and brand C innovation: the spirit of each brand will be especially noticeable in certain specific products, those most representative or typical of the brand meaning. They are the brand's 'prototype' products. Each product range thus must contain products demonstrating the brand's guiding value and obsession, flagships for the brand's meaning and purpose. Citroën, for instance, is best epitomised by its top-range cars, Nina Ricci by its entrancing evening gowns, Lacoste by its shirts, Sony by its Walkmans and digital pocket cameras.

However, there are some products within a given line that do not manage to clearly express the brand's intent and attributes. In the television industry, the cost constraints at the low end of the range are such that trying to manufacture a model radically different from the next-door neighbour's is quite difficult. But, for economic reasons, brands are sometimes forced to take a stake in this very large and overall highly competitive market. Likewise, each bank has had to offer its own savings plan, identical to that of all other banks. All these similar products, though, should only represent a limited aspect of each brand's offer (see Figure 2.4). All in all, each brand stays in focus and progresses in its own direction to make original products. That is why communicating about such products is so important, as they reveal the brand's meaning and purpose.

The problem arises when brands within the same group overlap too much, with one preventing the other from asserting its identity. Using the same motors in Peugeots and Citroëns would harm Peugeot, built on the 'dynamic car' image. It is when several brands sell the same product that a brand can become a caricature of itself. In order to compete against Renault's Espace and Chrysler's Voyager, neither Peugeot or Citroën, Fiat or Lancia could take the economic risk of building a manufacturing plant on their own; neither could Ford or Volkswagen. A single minivan was made for the first four brands. Similarly, a Ford–Volkswagen plant in Portugal

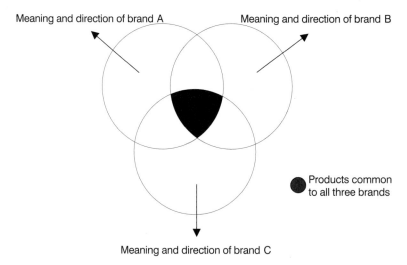

Figure 2.4   Product line overlap among brands

was set to produce a common car. The outcome, however, is that in producing a common vehicle, the brand becomes reduced to a mere external gadget. The identity message was simply relegated to the shell. So each brand has had to exaggerate its outward appearance in order to be easily recognised.

Advertising products through the brand prism

Products are mute: the brand gives them meaning and purpose, telling us how a product should be read. A brand is a both a prism and a magnifying glass through which products can be decoded. BMW invites us to perceive its models as 'cars for man's pleasure'. On the one hand, brands guide our perception of products. On the other hand, products send back a signal that brands use to underwrite and build their identity. The automobile industry is a case in point, as most technical innovations quickly spread among all brands. Thus the ABS system is offered by Volvo as well as by BMW, yet it cannot be said that they share the same identity. Is this a case of brand inconsistency? Not at all: ABS has simply become a must for all.

However, brands can only develop through long-term consistency, which is both the source and reflection of its identity. Hence the same ABS will not bear the same meaning for two different car-makers. For Volvo, which epitomises total safety, ABS is an utter necessity serving the brand's values and obsessions: it encapsulates the brand's essence. BMW, which symbolises high-performance, cannot speak of ABS in these terms: it would amount to denying the BMW ideology and value system which has inspired the whole organisation and helped generate the famous models of the Munich brand. BMW introduced ABS as a way to go faster. Likewise, how did the safety-conscious brand, Volvo, justify its participation in the European leisure car championships? By saying 'We *really* test our products so that they last longer.'

The minivans that Peugeot, Citroën, Fiat and Lancia have in common has left only one role for the respective brands to play: to enhance its association with the intrinsic values of the respective's brand – imagination and escape for Citroën, quality driving and reliability for Peugeot, high class and flair for Lancia, practicality for Fiat. (See Figure 2.5.)

Thus brand identity never results from a detail, yet a detail can, once interpreted, serve to express a broader strategy. Details can only have an impact on a brand's identity if they are in synergy with it, echoing and amplifying the brand's values. That is why weak brands

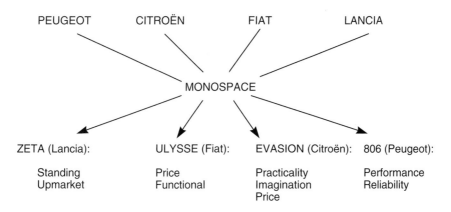

Figure 2.5   Brands give innovations meaning and purpose

do not succeed in capitalizing on their innovations: they do not manage either to
enhance the brand's meaning or create that
all-important resonance.

A brand is thus a prism helping us to
decipher products. It defines what and how
much to expect from the products bearing its
name. An innovation which would be
considered very original for a Fiat, for
instance, will be considered commonplace
for a Ford. However, though insufficient
engine power may scarcely have been an
issue for many car-makers, for Peugeot it is a
major problem. It disavows Peugeot's deeply-
rooted identity and frustrates the expectations that have been raised. It would be at
odds with what should be called Peugeot's
'brand obligations'.

In fact, consumers rarely evaluate innovations in an isolated way, but in relation to a
specific brand. Once a brand has chosen a
specific positioning or meaning, it has to
assume all of its implications and fulfil its
promises. Brands should respect the contract
that made them successful by attracting
customers. They owe it to them.

Brands and other signs of quality

In many sectors, brands coexist with other
quality signs. The food industry, for instance,
is also filled, with quality seals, certificates of
norm compliance and controlled origin and
guarantees. The proliferation of these other
signs results from a double objective: to
promote and to protect.

Certifications of origin (eg real Scotch
whisky) are intended to protect a branch of
agriculture and products whose quality is
deeply rooted in a specific location and
know-how. The controlled origin guarantee
capitalises on a subjective and cultural
conception of quality, coupled with a touch
of mystery and of the area's unique character.
It segments the market by refusing the certification of origin to any goods that have not

been produced within a certain area or raised
in the traditional way. Thus in Europe since
2003, Feta cheese has been a name tied to a
controlled Greek origin. Even if Danish or
French cheese-makers were to produce a 'feta'
cheese elsewhere that buyers were unable to
tell apart from the feta cheese made in Greece
in the traditional way, their products can no
longer lay claim to the name 'feta'.

Quality seals are promotional tools. They
convey a different concept of quality, which is
both more industrial and scientific. In this
respect, a given type of cheese, for example,
involves objective know-how, using a certain
kind of milk mixed with selected bacteria, etc.
Quality seals create a vertical segmentation,
consisting of different levels of objective
quality. The issue here is not so much to
present typical characteristics as to satisfy a
stringent set of objective criteria.

The legal guarantee of typicality brought by
a 'certified origin' seal means more than a
simple designation of origin, a mere label
indicating where a product comes from, in
that the latter implies no natural or social
specificity – although it may mislead the
buyer into thinking that there is one.
Moreover, several modern cheese-makers
deliberately mix up what is genuine and what
is not, inventing foreign names for their new
products that are reminiscent of places or
villages in an effort to build their own rustic,
parochial imagery.

It is interesting to see how European countries tried to reassure consumers during the
'mad cow crisis' in order to redress the 40 per
cent drop in beef consumption:

▮ Although it is not legal under EU regulations, they reinstated designations of origin
referring to a country (ie French beef). This
did not prove fully reassuring since it was
soon heard that French cattle could have
eaten not only local grass but also contami-
nated organic extracts imported from the
UK.

▌ Certifications of origin (ie Charolais beef) add typicality but cannot guarantee a 100 per cent safe meat.

▌ Seals of quality did not exist and had to be created but it would take years to promote them: however, unless full control of the entire cattle raising process is guaranteed, the output itself cannot be guaranteed.

▌ The crisis highlighted the need for meat brands. Since 1989, alerted by early warnings, McDonald's had indeed sought new suppliers in Europe, scrutinising the way in which each and every one raised and fed their cattle.

▌ Retailers like Carrefour have promoted their own signed contract with farmers.

Whether or not official indications of quality in Europe should still exist in 2010 is a bitter issue that is still being discussed among northern countries (United Kingdom, Denmark, etc) who believe that only brands should prevail, and southern countries (France, Spain, Italy) who support the idea of having official collective signs of quality coexist with brands (Feral, 1989).

The northern European countries claim that brands alone should be allowed to segment the market and thus build a reputation for excellence around their names, thanks to their products and to their distribution and marketing efforts. These countries tend to favour an objective concept of quality: it does not matter that the feta cheese that the Greeks prefer is made in Holland or that Smirnoff vodka is neither Russian nor Polish. The southern European countries believe for their part that collective signs enable small companies to use their ranking and/or their typical characteristics as promotional tools, since they do not have their own brands. As their products do not speak for themselves, their market positioning is ensured by quality or certified origin seals. Clearly, behind the European debate on whether or not brands that have built their reputation on their own should coexist with official collective signs of quality lies another more fundamental debate between the proponents of a liberal economy on the one hand, and the partisans of government intervention to regulate it on the other.

From the corporate point of view, choosing between brand policy and collective signs is a matter of strategy and of available resource allocation.

Often, quality certificates reduce perceived difference. Distributors' brands can also receive them. Brands define their own standards: legally, they guarantee nothing, but empirically they convey clusters of attributes and values. In doing so, they seek to become a reference in themselves, if not the one and only reference (as is the case with Bacardi, the epitome of rum). Thus, in essence, brands differentiate and share very little. Brands distinguish their products. Strong brands are those that diffuse values and manage to segment the market with their own means.

In handling the 'mad cow' crisis, McDonald's wondered whether they should rely on their own brand only or also on the collective signs and certificates of origin.

On an operational level, let us once again underline the fact that brands do not boil down to a mere act of advertising. They contain recommendations regarding the long-term specificities of the products bearing their name, such as attractive prices, efficient distribution and merchandising, as well as identity building through advertising. It is easier for a small company to earn a quality seal for one of its products through strict efforts on quality, than it is to undertake the gruelling task of creating a brand, which requires so many financial, human, technical and commercial resources. Even without an identity, the small company's product can thus step out of the ordinary, thanks in part to the legal indicators of quality.

Obstacles to the implications of branding

Within the same company, brand policy often conflicts with other policies. As these are unwritten and implicit, they may seem innocuous, when in fact they are a hindrance to a true brand policy.

Current corporate accounting, as such, is unfavourable towards brands. Accounting is ruled by the prudence principle: consequently, any outlay for which payback is uncertain is counted as an expense rather than valued as an asset. This is the case of investments made in communications in order to inform the general public about the brand's identity. Because it is impossible to measure exactly what share of the annual communications budget generates returns immediately, or within a specified number of years, the whole sum is taken as an operating expense which is subtracted from the financial year's profits. Yet advertising, like investments in machinery, talented staff and R&D, also helps build brand capital. Accounting thus creates a bias that handicaps brand companies because it projects an under-valued image of them. Take the case of company A, which invests heavily to develop the awareness and renown of its brand name. Having to write off this investment as an expense results in low annual profits and a small asset value on the balance sheet. This usually occurs during a critical period in the company's growth, when it could actually use some help from outside investors and bankers. Now compare A to company B, which invests the same amounts in machines and production and nothing whatsoever in either name, image or renown. As it is allowed to value these tangible investments as fixed assets and to depreciate them gradually over several years, B can announce higher profits and its balance sheet, displaying bigger assets, will project a more flattering image. B will thus look better in terms of accounting, when,

in fact, A is in a better position to differentiate its products.

The principle of annual accounting also hinders brand policy. Every product manager is judged on his yearly results and on the net contribution generated by his product. This leads to 'short-termism' in decision making: those decisions which produce fast, measurable results are favoured over those that build up brand capital, slowly no doubt, but more reliably in the long term. Moreover, product-based accounting discourages product managers from putting out any additional advertising effort that would serve essentially to bolster the brand as a whole, when the latter serves as an umbrella and sign for other products. Managers thus only focus on one thing: any new expenditure in the general interest will be charged to their own account statement. For example, Palmolive is a brand covering several products: liquid detergent, shampoo, shaving cream, etc. The brand could decide to communicate only one of these products singled out as a prominent image leader, capitalising on image spill-over reciprocal effects (Balachander, 2003). But the investment made would certainly be higher than could be justified solely by the sales forecast of that product. This new expenditure will in fact always be on the given product, even though its ultimate purpose is to collectively benefit all products under the umbrella brand.

In order to react against the short-term bias caused by accounting practices and the under-estimation of (corporate) value as shown in the balance sheets, some British companies have begun to list their own brands as assets on their balance sheets. This has triggered a discussion on the fundamental validity of accounting practices that emerged in the 'age of commodities', when the essential part of capital consisted of real estate and equipment. Today, on the contrary, intangible assets (know-how, patents, reputation) are what make the difference in the long run. Beyond the need for an open debate in Europe and the

United States on how to capitalise brands, it has become just as important to find a way for companies to account for the long-term pros and cons of short-term brand decisions in their books. It is all the more compelling as brand decision-makers themselves rotate often, perhaps too often.

Even the way in which the various types of communication agencies are organised fails to comply with the requirements of sound brand policy. Even if an advertising agency has its own network of partner companies – in charge of proximity marketing, CRM, e-business and so on – and can thus promote itself as an integrated communications group, it remains the crux of the network. Furthermore, advertising agencies think only in terms of campaigns, operating in a short, one-year time frame. Brand policy is different: it develops over a long period and requires that all means be considered at once, in a fully integrated way.

It is clear that a company rarely finds contacts inside so-called communications groups who are actually in charge of strategic thinking and of providing overall recommendations rather than merely focusing on advertising or on the necessity to sell campaigns. Moreover, advertising agencies are not in a position to address strategic issues, such as what should be the optimal number of brands in a portfolio. As these affect the survival of the brands that are under their advertising responsibility, the agencies find themselves in the awkward position of being judge and jury. That is why a new profession has been created: strategic brand management consulting. The time had indeed come for companies to meet professionals with a mid-term vision who are capable of providing consistent, integrated guidelines for the development of brand portfolios without focusing on one single technique.

A high personnel turnover disrupts the continuity a brand needs. Yet companies today actually plan for their personnel to rotate on different brands! Thus, brands are often entrusted to young graduates with impressive degrees but little experience and the promotion they expect often consists of being assigned to yet another brand! Thus, product managers must achieve visible results in the short term. This helps to explain why there are so many changes in advertising strategy and implementation as well as in decisions on brand extension, promotion or discounts. These are in fact caused by changes in personnel.

It is significant that brands that have maintained a continuous and homogeneous image belong to companies with stable brand decision makers. This is the case for luxury brands: the long-lasting presence of the creator or founder allows for sound, long-term management. The same is true of major retailers where senior managers often handle the communication themselves or at least make the final decisions. As a means to alleviate the effects of excessive brand manager rotation, companies aim not only at incorporating brand value into their accounts, but also at creating a long-term brand image charter. The latter represents both a vital safeguard and an instrument of continuity.

Business organisation is sometimes an obstacle to building the brand. In 2001, the very high-profile Toshiba Corporation created a new and hitherto non-existent vice-president post: VP Brand. Significantly, the appointee was the existing VP of Research and Development. The fact that the world number one in laptops and a major player in the television, hi-fi and lo-fi sectors should create such a post demonstrates a strong awareness of an unfilled gap. Toshiba's products are undeniably excellent, and until now this been the key to the success of Japanese companies in general, and Toshiba in particular. This is a company that enjoys a dominant position in a sector as cut-throat as the laptop industry. So what was it missing?

Worldwide studies had revealed that there was no 'magic' to the Toshiba brand. It could be compared to a colleague at the office whom you would regularly consult for advice, but would never invite home for dinner. It was a brand based on a single pillar: there was a strong rational component, but little by way of emotional appeal, intangible values and 'magic'. In short, it was no Sony, and could not command Sony's higher margins. A company can become a leader in the Toshiba mould through excellent products and prices, or a leader like Dell by dint of a distribution system with levels of efficiency that remain head and shoulders above any (known) competitor. But since the effect of competition is to erode perceived difference, other instruments are needed to attract customers and keep them loyal; to ensure that they remain customers of the brand. This desire is based on the need for security, and on intangible factors.

Up until 2001, there was no management of the Toshiba brand. The company's organisation was based on a branched structure, and thus no one was responsible for the cross-company resource that is the brand. The medical branch had one view of Toshiba, while the computer branch had another, and so on. There was no coordination or global brand platform, to say nothing of joint promotions between branches, of course. Horizontal initiatives (such as sponsorship) were rare, and commercial necessity dictated that the power lay with the distribution subsidiaries: the name of the game was to sell imported products, not to build a brand reputation. Local managers' remuneration packages were calculated on sales, not brand equity.

Another syndrome pertains to the relationship between production and sales. In the Electrolux group, for instance, production units are specialised according to product. Both mono-product and multi-market, they sell their product to the sales units who are, on the contrary, mono-market and multi-product (grouped under an umbrella brand). The problem is that these autonomous sales divisions, who each have their own brand, all want to benefit from the latest product inno-vation so as to maximise their division's turnover. What is missing is a structure for managing and allocating innovations in accordance with a consistent and global vision of the brand portfolio. As we will see later, there is no point in entrusting a strong innovation to a weak brand. Moreover, this undermines the very basis of the brand concept: differentiation.

Lastly, if words mean anything at all, communications managers should have the power to prevent actions that go against the brand's interest. Thus, Philips never succeeded in fully taking advantage of its former brand baseline: 'Philips, tomorrow is already here'. In order to do so, they would have needed to ban all advertising on batteries or electric light bulbs that either trivialised the assertion, contradicted it, or reduced it to mere advertising hype. It would also have been possible to communicate only about future bulb types rather than about the best current sales. Unfortunately, nobody in the organisation had the power (or the desire) to impose these kinds of constraints. When the Whirlpool brand appeared, however, the managers from Philips actually created the organisation they needed for implementing a real brand policy: as it was directly linked to general management, the communications department was able to ensure the optimal circumstances for launching the Whirlpool brand, by banning over a three-year period any communication about a commonplace product or even a best-selling product.

Failing to manage innovations has a very negative impact on brand equity. Even though sales people go up in arms when they are not given the responsibility of a strong innovation, it is a mistake to assign the latter to a weak brand, especially in multi-brand groups. When dealing with a weak brand, attractive pricing must indeed be offered to distributors as an incentive to include the latter in their reference listing. But since the brand's consumers do not expect this inno-vation (each brand defines its type and level of consumer expectations), the product turnover is insufficient. As for the non-buyers, such a brand is not reassuring. If the innovation is launched a few weeks later under a leading brand name, distributors will refuse to pay for the price premium due to a leader because they purchased it at a lower price just a while back from the same company. Thus, even with the strong brand, the sales price eventually has to be cut.

Breeding many strong brands, L'Oréal allocates its inventions to its various businesses according to brand potency. Innovation is thus first entrusted to prestigious brands sold in selective channels as the products' high prices will help cancel out the high research cost incurred. Thus, liposomes were first commercialised by Lancôme, the new sun filter Mexoryl SX by Vichy. Innovation is then diffused to the other channels and eventually to the large retailers. By then, the selective channel brands are already likely to have launched another differentiating novelty.

However, this process is affected by the fact that innovation is not exclusively owned by any one company; it quickly spreads to competitors, which calls for immediate reaction. That is why Plénitude (a brand dedicated to hypermarkets) was quick to market liposomes. When two competing brands within the same group share the same innovation, they must nonetheless capitalise on it in their own specific way. Thus, L'Oréal was not the first company to market AHAs (alpha hydroxy acids), which are cosmetic copies of acid vitamin A, prescribed by dermatologists to smooth out wrinkles. Estée Lauder was the innovator. L'Oréal did not wish to react by using Lancôme because AHAs are aggressive, and so do not express the softness symbolised by the star brand. Instead, L'Oréal marketed in pharmacies and under the Vichy brand name an AHA version called Novactia, focusing the message on the new product's purity, in keeping with Vichy's brand identity. At the same time, L'Oréal did not hesitate to offer an AHA-based cream under the Plénitude brand name in large stores. This weakens Vichy's uniqueness somewhat, but also Lauder's. As we see, the competitive system impacts on the brand equity system.

Along the same lines, when a producer supplies a distributor's brand with the same product it sells under its own brand, it will eventually erode its brand equity and, more generally, the very respectability of the concept of a brand. This simply means that what customers pay more for in a brand is the name and nothing else. When the brand is dissociated from the product it enhances and represents, it becomes merely superficial and artificial, devoid of any rational legitimacy. Ultimately, companies pay a price for this as sales decrease and distributors seize the opportunity to declare in their advertising that national brands alienate consumers, but that consumers can resist by purchasing distributors' own-brands. This also justifies the sluggishness of public authorities regarding the increasing amount of counterfeit products among distributors' own-brands. Finally, such practices foster a false collective understanding of what brands are, even among opinion leaders, which contributes to the rumour that nowadays all products are just the same!

Service brands

There is no legal difference between product, trade or service brands. These are economic distinctions, not legal ones. By focusing only on branding *per se*, ie on signs only, the law does not help us much to understand either how brands and the branding process work or what the specific characteristics among the various players are.

Service brands do exist: Europcar, Hertz, Ecco, Manpower, Visa, Club Med, Marriott's, Méridien, HEC, Harvard, BT, etc. Each one represents a specific cluster of attributes embodied in a quite concrete, though intangible, type of service: car rental, temporary work, computer services, leisure activities, hotel business or higher education. However, some service sectors seem to be just entering the brand age. They either do not consider themselves as being a part of it yet or have just started becoming aware that they are. This evolution is fascinating to watch, as it highlights all that the brand approach involves and reveals the specificities of branding an intangible service.

The banking industry is a fine example. If bank customers were asked what bank brands they knew, they probably would not know or understand what to answer. They know the names of banks, but not bank brands. This is significant: for the public, these names are not brands, identifying a specific service, but corporate names or business signs linked to a specific place.

Until recently, bank names designated either the owner of the corporation entrusted with the customers' funds (Morgan, Rothschild) or a specific place (Citibank) or a particular customer group. Name contraction often signals that a brand concept is in formation. Thus, for example, Banque Nationale de Paris has become BNP. Some observers consider this as just a desire to simplify the name, as per the advertising principle 'what's easy to say is easy to remember', as short signatures make it easier to identify the signer. Such abbreviations have definitely had an impact; however, they seem to reduce the whole branding concept to a mere part of the writing and printing process solely within the realm of communication.

As they are contracted, these bank names come to represent some kind of relationship instead of a mere person or place. In order to become visible, this relationship may take the form of specific 'bank products' (or standard policies in the insurance industry). But these visible and easy-to-imitate products are not the explanation and justification for why they have decided to build a true brand. They are merely the brand's external manifestation. Banks and insurance companies have understood the key to what makes them different: the relationships that develop between a

customer and a banker under the auspices of the brand.

Finally, one aspect of service brands that contrasts with product brands is that service is invisible (Levitt, 1981; Eiglier and Langeard, 1990). What does a bank have to show, except customers or consultants? Structurally, service brands are handicapped in that they cannot be easily illustrated. That is why service brands use slogans. No wonder: slogans are indeed vocal, they are the brand's *vocatio*, ie the brand's vocation or calling. Slogans are a commandment for both internal and external relations. Through a slogan, the brand defines its behavioural guidelines, and these guidelines give the customer the right to be dissatisfied if they are transgressed. Claiming to be the bank with a smile or the bank who cares is not enough. These attributes must be fully internalised by the people who offer and deliver the service. The fact that humans are intrinsically and unavoidably variable is definitely a challenge for the brand approach in service industries.

This is why brand alignment has become so important if the whole organisation is to 'live the brand' (Ind, 2001). Brand alignment is the process by which organisations think of themselves as brands. The brand experience in the service sector is totally driven by what happens at points of contact, where customers meet the company's staff, salespeople and so on. This is true of Starbucks as well as of Citibank or HSBC. It is also crucial at Dell. This company is actually not a computer manufacturer but a service company, identifying each client's need and assembling the product to fit it. There is hardly any R&D investment at Dell. All the efforts are concentrated on the customers and organising the company by customer segment to better listen and react. People are essential in this process, not machines.

Branding in the service sector entails a double recognition. Within the company, people must recognise the brand values as their own. The internalisation process is crucial. It means explaining and justifying these values to each cell within the company. It also means stimulating the self-discovery of how these values might modify everyday behaviour. At the client level it also means that clients recognise these values as those to which they are attracted.

One point must not be overlooked. Brand management in the service sector means not only delivering a differentiated experience but ensuring that the resulting satisfaction will be attributed to the right brand. This is why the design and branding of all contact points are so important. Places of business, call centers, Web sites and the like must all follow the brand. Just posting one's logo on the front door is not enough.

3

Brand and business building

How do companies grow both the brand and business? What does it take to build a brand? What are the necessary steps and phases? In this chapter we address these questions with a particular emphasis on integration of efforts. Brand building is not done apart, it is the result of a clear strategy and of excellence in implementation at the product, price, place, people and communication levels. There are prerequisites before a brand can be built, and they need to be understood.

Are brands for all companies?

The brand is not an end in itself. It needs to be managed for what it is – an instrument for company growth and profitability, a business tool. Does branding affect all companies? Yes. Are all companies aware of this? No. For many industrial companies or commodity sellers, the concept of the brand applies only to mass markets, high-consumption products and the fast-moving consumer goods (FMCG) sector. This is a misconception. A brand is a name that influences buyers and prescribers alike. Industrial brands have their own markets: Air

Liquide sells to industry, Somfy sells its tubular motors to window-blind installers and fitters, BPB (British Plaster Board) and Lafarge sell to companies and craftspeople in the construction and public works sectors, and the William Pitters company is famous among retailers for the quality of its trade relationships.

Nevertheless, these companies are affected by brands in a variety of ways:

▌ Stock-exchange-listed groups have to manage the widened recognition for their products. Their corporate brand is the vehicle for this recognition. Stock exchanges operate on anticipation. By definition an anticipation is not rational, but can be influenced by emotive factors. Consider, for example, the Internet boom, Eurotunnel and Euro Disney. Thousands were persuaded to buy stock through the mirage of the so-called 'New Economy', the historical link between UK and Europe and the value of the Disney name. The management of corporate brand visibility and content has now become a strategic concern.

■ Worldwide groups should be asking themselves whether it might not be time to complete their transformation into worldwide buyers and distributors in order to consolidate their local operators under a single name.

■ Chinese or Indian groups should be asking themselves how to get rid of the status of low cost supplies and take a larger part of the high margin segments in developed countries: to do so they need a global brand.

■ Producers should be asking themselves whether the brand is a differentiating factor in any sector threatened by commoditisation. For this reason, it is noteworthy that BPB chose to retain the Placoplatre product brand – a local brand which had become synonymous with the product itself, and indeed a leader in its own markets. Similarly, it is significant that the industrial Air Liquide company asked Mr Lindsay Owen-Jones, the CEO of l'Oréal, to sit on its board of directors. Having worked its way through hundreds of product names and legal trademarks for these names, Air Liquide realised that it had still failed to create any real value. What it needed was to restructure its range of high-tech products under several megabrands, as l'Oréal had done.

■ Producers of intermediary goods should be asking themselves whether it might not be time to sell to their clients' customers, not through direct sales, but by instilling a brand awareness in these customers. In this way, Lafarge – a world leader in construction materials – invested several million euros on informing the general public about the advances made possible by its innovations, in order to create a demand for its products among people who would live in the flats or work in the offices built by its clients. In relationships with intermediaries and distributors, the brand

is an instrument of power. Another typical example is Somfy, a world leader in motors for window blinds and openings for home use: this leadership has been earned through changing its OEM business model and refocusing the brand on the end user, just as Intel, Lycra, Woolmark and others have successfully done. After all, what do you say to a window-blind dealer for whom the Somfy motor makes up 35 per cent of the product cost and who is threatening to source the part from China at half the price? Somfy fears being relegated to the role of a mere OEM player: hence its increasingly high-profile public 'Somfy powered' strategy.

Many companies continue to underestimate the brand as a motor of growth. The fear of the negative effects of recognition is one reason stated for this. Bureau Veritas, a company with a sufficiently long pedigree to have been mentioned by Jules Verne, has not yet decided to make its name the world standard for compliance and certification. Instead, its ISO 9000 certification is conducted by BVQI, while the compliance of Asian-manufactured toys is assessed by ACTS, a recently purchased company.

What concerns Bureau Veritas is the possibility of an accident that receives media coverage: what company was responsible for inspecting the Erika, the Prestige, the Amoco Cadiz and the Torrey Canyon? Each of these oil tankers caused ecological disasters when they foundered on beaches or rocks, spilling their toxic cargoes. In such circumstances there is a need to find a scapegoat, and the certifier of the vessel could arguably fill this role, since the aim of the certification process is to check that a certain number of international, regional or national standards have been met at the time of inspection. That this was done before the accident does not necessarily mean that the certifier was at fault. By analogy, a guarantee might be given that a manufacturing process complies with standards, but this is not the same as guaranteeing the goods that are produced by the process. Will this subtlety be understood by the media, the general public and even the industrial clients themselves? The management of this highly profitable company is not convinced that it will.

However, by using this tactic it is missing an opportunity to become a world leader on the weight of its reputation. Bureau Veritas, 'the name for quality assessment', supported by a strong logo, has the potential to become an object of value for its corporate clients (following the example of 'Intel inside').

The better known the brand, the more sought after it becomes by companies looking for a recognised certification body, as the brand increases their perceived value. It creates value for clients through their capacity to bid, reassurance of their own clients, and so on. The result is a 'virtuous circle' of repu- tation and quality in terms of prospecting, sales and building loyalty – which would enable Bureau Veritas to move from a reactive to a proactive stance.

CGEA Transport is an interesting example of a group that for a century grew without fanfare, an unknown company with an unpronounceable name, to become a market leader in public transport concessions. However, in 2000 this cautious, highly prag- matic group decided to create a world brand for itself: Connex. Its targets are city mayors and councils that need to delegate management of public transport services to outside operators. To meet them, CGEA Transport devised a business model based on extreme localisation and networking. In each city, a local joint organisation was created with the city authority and CGEA Transport as its two founders. The core competence of CGEA Transport is managerial: it knows how to bring productivity and efficiency. Its key resource in each country is networking: word of mouth and lobbying did the sales. The organisation remained unknown and prof- itable. The bus lines were given names, but

these were local brands, and in addition they were owned by the cities themselves.

How to adapt to a changing world? More and more cities and countries want to pull out of some facets of what used to be considered as public service, including the former communist countries, cities like Shanghaï in China, and countries that have deregulated part or all of their public transport systems (as happened with the breaking up of British Rail in the UK). However, CGEA Transport found that its networking tactic was of little use in these new countries and markets: the company had to become more visible. Soon the question of the brand was raised. The organisation needed to back up its status as market leader by adopting a global brand, which would be not only a corporate brand, but also a commercial brand. Thus it made Connex (the chosen name) the first ground transportation brand in the world.

To adapt to the new situation, the company had to modify part of its business model, although surely its expertise and know-how are the same as before. However, its anonymity had become a barrier preventing it from reaching the invisible college of people taking part in the decision-making process whenever a public service must be allocated to a private operator. Brand awareness is source of value: not only does it help in reaching unknown people with influence on the buying process, but it creates a source effect: it gives credibility to the company.

Within an organisation, branding creates the need to align the organisation with the brand's implicit or explicit promises.

It would be unreasonable to pretend that brands are accessible to any company. In the FMCG sector there are three prerequisites.

The first function of a brand is to guarantee a constant quality through time and space, so the first prerequisite is that the product be of consistent quality. Not being able to deliver a constant product and service quality when production increases is a clear handicap of many companies in emerging countries or in the former communist ones. This is also a risk in small companies.

Second, there is no brand without communication. A lack of marketing and communication resources is also a major barrier to branding, although as will be shown below one can build a market leader without advertising. However, one then needs to be excellent in promotion and trade relationships.

Finally, being able to create and launch successfully a flow of relevant innovations through time is essential to all brands.

Building a market leader without advertising

What does it take to build a brand? Brand definitions are innumerable (see the discussion on page 9), and almost every author in the field has his or her own. Although they can be useful, definitions tell us very little about how to build a brand. Definitions are static: they take the brand for granted. Building the brand is dynamic.

In general, in our executive seminars, when we ask attendees how to build a market-leading brand, typical answers include advertise, create an image, and develop awareness. They are mostly answers that focus on communication. The best answer is, by developing the business in a particular way. Which way?

Instead of answering that question frontally, we shall look at an interesting case: how did an unknown Australian company, Orlando Wyndham, build the UK's leading bottled wine brand, Jacob's Creek? This brand is now the leader in volume and the leader in spontaneous brand awareness, with a very strong image. All that was achieved without mass-market advertising before 2000. It is most interesting also to note that between 1984 and 2000, the UK wine market doubled in size. What then was needed to create a successful wine brand in the UK mass market?:

■ The first condition is to have enough volume. Addressing the mass market means being able to fulfil trade expectations. Multiple retailers hate to deal with companies that cannot provide sufficient supply if a product is a success. For a wine maker this means being able to rely on a very large supply source.

■ The second condition is to secure a stable quality. The first role of any brand is to reduce perceived risk: the consumer experience must be the same whenever and wherever the product is bought. (This is why branding services is tougher than branding tangible products: human variability works against this stability.) For a wine maker, it means mastering the art of blending, to make sure consumer expectations are not betrayed. Once consumers discover they like a specific wine taste, their repurchase indicates a willingness to reduce risk and re-find the same taste, the same pleasure.

■ For a mass-market brand, price is key: it must be mainstream. Everything must be done, at the back office level, to ensure higher productivity, and hence a lower production cost, while not altering the quality and taste.

■ It is essential to be end-user driven, and find the right taste for the particular market. Many UK consumers are not long-practised wine drinkers. Their tastes have been shaped by cold soft drinks and beer. This means that they prefer wines with a specific taste and in-mouth profile. In addition, if an organisation hits the right local expectations it can expect to obtain good publicity, medals and press coverage, thus reinforcing the trade support.

■ Another requirement is a national sales force. Wine is mostly chosen at the point of purchase. On-shelf visibility and point-of-purchase advertising are success factors. It is important to draw up national agreements with the major multiple retailers (in this case Sainsbury, Asda, Tesco and a few others) to achieve this, but even when these are in place a day-to-day check needs to be carried out, store by store, to make sure everything is in place. Only a national sales force can achieve this. In addition, an intensive wet trial phase is needed, to encourage customers to pause in wandering up and down the store aisles and taste the product. This too requires a national sales force.

These five tactics to build a brand in the market may seem straightforward and easy to follow. Actually they are not. French wines could not meet the conditions, while New World wines, and Australian wines in particular, could. Let us examine why, for each condition.

Old World wines are based on one principle. The quality of the wine is totally dependent on natural factors: the specific type of soil, the sun, the climate, the air. As a consequence, hundreds of wines have been created, differentiated by the wine-growing area, or even specific vineyard, from which they come, and its unique characteristics. Each vineyard claims its soil is better than that of competitors, for example. As a consequence, the product is fragmented. For example, behind many of the 5,000 sub-brands of Bordeaux wine there is a single grower, usually rather small. This prevents suppliers from responding to the first condition for building a brand: enough volume.

Old World wines have tried to secure their market leadership by transforming their wine-producing practices into laws. Producing a Burgundy or a Bordeaux wine means obeying these laws. What was intended as a quality control system has become a major block against innovating to address the competition from emerging growing areas.

If a wine is to be called a Pauillac, a Graves or whatever (these are sub-regions within Bordeaux), its producers are not permitted to mix the grapes from this region with grapes grown anywhere else, or only at a very small

level. If one season is dry they cannot irrigate; nor can they add chemicals to moderate the differences in quality caused by differences in climate from year to year. Because they respect these laws, Old World wines have an inherent variability: they are the true produce of nature, more than the produce of man. There is much more variety of soils and variance in climate from year to year in Europe than in Australia, California or Argentina, and this too leads to differences between one Old World wine and another.

Branding means suppressing this variability: to secure the same taste from year to year, one must master the art of blending grapes coming from very different soils – and regions, if one of them is under-producing. Australia, as a relatively newly settled country without a long wine-growing tradition, had few laws governing wine producing; it could do it. It was not so for wine makers from Bordeaux or Burgundy.

The same holds true for getting the right quality at low production costs. French wine makers are not allowed to use mechanised harvesting: they are required to harvest by hand. They cannot irrigate, and so radically increase the productivity of their soils; they cannot make use of chemical additives. In France too, wine is stored in barrels as a rule. In Australia wine is kept in huge aluminium tanks, and wood cuttings are put in the wine: there is more wood surface in contact with the wine, which accelerates the process of giving the wine the right 'woody' taste. Time being money, this reduces production costs.

Point four concerns getting the right taste to appeal to the target market. New World wines have no tradition to respect: they started from the customer. They adapted their product to the taste of customers in emerging markets, used to drinking soft drinks and beer. Their wine had to be fruit-driven, very soft, very smooth, easy to drink for all occasions. Some varietals (types of grape) such as Chardonnay and Semillon Chardonnay could deliver such a taste. These were not the varieties that made the reputation of Bordeaux or Burgundy wines.

One other dimension of being client-driven is language. Marketing research showed that the English were still broadly an 'island race': many of them are not well versed in European languages and the cultural traditions of Continental Europe. Unlike the maze of thousands of hard-to-pronounce wine names from Europe, Jacob's Creek is an English name, and the wording on the wine labels is written in English. Until recently French wines rarely provided any labelling information in English. Furthermore, Australia is part of the Commonwealth, and some English people identify more closely with it than with France.

In addition, each New World country has become associated with a small number of grape varieties. This means that consumers find it easier to forecast the taste of an Australian wine than of a French wine. The country of origin adds its own risk-reducing role to the brand.

Last but not least, the industry's organization in the Old World is too fragmented. Individual growers cannot afford a dedicated sales force even in their homeland. Even when the wine is produced by cooperatives of growers, the coops tend to want to remain independent and refuse to join larger organisations, the only viable path to reaching the critical size to create a brand.

As a result, in the 16 years to 2001, Australian wines, led by Jacob's Creek, went from zero to a 16.9 per cent share by volume and a 20.1 per cent share by value of the British market. Meanwhile the market doubled in size. Interestingly, as is shown by the value share being higher than the volume share, price is not the main reason consumers choose Australian wines. The New World growers have succeeded in persuading customers to trade up, by offering higher quality brand extensions designed to appeal to former novice wine drinkers who are now willing to explore more complex wines.

Can Old World wines come back and stop their sharp decline? As long as they do not suppress their internally based regulations, their production laws, and do not encourage supplier concentration, they will not be able to fulfill the five conditions for building brands. Bordeaux and Burgundy cannot do it. However, the Languedoc wine-growing region is the biggest in the world. As such it fulfils the first condition. In this region, which historically produced lower-status wine than Bordeaux and Burgundy, there are very few production rules to obey. The future is in the hands of Languedoc's growers if they can concentrate and meet customers' requirements, not only in the UK but also in Japan, Korea and other countries with a growing market for wine. They might also export their know-how and build brands where the future market is: China. This is why so many players are signing joint ventures with Chinese companies and authorities, to grow grapes in China and develop brands that have none of the Old World wine industry's self-imposed limitations.

What lessons can be drawn and generalised? New World wine brands have succeeded because they innovated, breaking with the competition's conventions for consumer profit. They have not stopped innovating and disrupting conventions. In Australia, Jacob's Creek recently introduced screw cap closures on its Riesling varieties, abandoning a sacred cow: cork closure. Riesling is more likely than wines from some other grape varieties to be affected by problems of cork quality, and half-bottles are especially vulnerable. Both consumers and the trade reacted favourably to this small but revolutionary innovation.

A second lesson is that a part of Jacob's Creek appeal was based on one enduring weakness of competition: it was not an elitist brand, and it had no snob value. It was approachable for everybody.

The product's quality–price ratio was excellent, attracting praise from experts and taste makers. This an endless race: each year the brand continues to improve the quality, thus winning continuous publicity. Since it was the first of the major Australian wine exporters, Jacob's Creek benefited from the 'pioneer advantage', and became the symbol of Australian wine. Interestingly, Orlando Wyndham, the company that owns the brand, is far smaller than some of its Australian competitors such as Hardy's, but all its energy and efforts were focused on this one single brand.

Brand building: from product to values, and vice versa

It takes time to build a really strong brand. There are two routes, two models for doing so: from product advantage to intangible values, or from values to product. However, with time, this two-way movement becomes the essence of brand management: brands have two legs.

Most brands did not start as such: their founders just wanted to create a business. They needed a very specific product or service: an innovation, a good idea to start their business and open the distributors' closed doors. Through time, their name or the name of the product became a brand: well known and endowed with market power (the ability to influence buyers). It did not simply designate a product or a person, but little by little came to be associated with imagery, with intangible benefits, with brand personality and so on. Perception had moved from objects to benefits, from tangible to intangible values.

As is shown by the upward-pointing arrow in Figure 3.1, most brands start not as brands but as a name on an innovative product or service. Nike started out as a meaningless name on a pair of innovative running shoes: if they had not been innovative no distributor would have paid attention to Phil Knight in the first place. With time, that name acquired awareness, status and trust, if not respect or liking. This is the result of all the communication and stars which accompanied the business building. Little by little an inversion takes place in the process: instead of the product building the brand awareness and reputation (the bottom-up arrow of influence), it is the brand that differentiates and endows the product/service with its unique values (the top-down dotted arrow). In fact at this time the brand determines which new products match its desired image. Nike is now in the phase of brand extensions: the brand has stretched from running shoes to sports apparel and now golf clubs.

Through time, brand associations typically move up a ladder (the vertical axis of Figure 3.1), from ingredient (Dove with hydrating cream) to attribute (softening), to benefit (protection), to brand personality, brand values and even mission (Apple or Virgin have a mission), at the very top intangible end.

Now this does not mean that, with time, brand management should not be concerned with material issues and differentiation any more. Brands are two-legged. Even luxury brands, bought for the sake of show, must give their buyers the feeling that they have bought a great product and that the price difference is

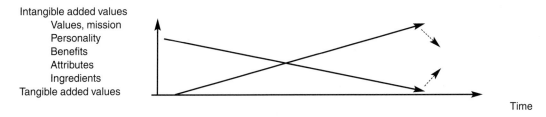

Figure 3.1 The two models of brand building through time

legitimate. But material differentiation is a never-ending race: competitors copy your best ideas. Attaching the brand to an intangible value adds value and prevents substitutability. The Mercedes price premium is permanently explained by product-based advertising copy, but also by PR operations that accentuate the unique status of the brand.

This first model concerns brands that started as a product. There exists a second model of brand building: many brands start as concepts or ideas. This is true of all licensed brands (Paloma Picasso perfume, Harry Potter products and so on) and of many fashion brands, spirits or cigarette brands, as with a cigarette called News to capture the spirit of the news, of world journalism. Obviously in this case, the brand starts at an intangible level of meaning. This is the source of the brand benefit: it sells a symbolic participation in this world. Although it is conceived at an intangible level, one very basic question arises concerning the physical product: what features or attributes should substantiate or embody these values and benefits? Brands need a product/service to live and convey their benefits (as shown by the top-down arrow).

This model also provides a reminder that that even when launching a product brand (that is, a brand based on a product advantage) it is important to incorporate from the start the higher levels of meaning that are intended to attach to the brand in the longer term. The brand should not simply acquire them, by accumulation or sedimentation; they should be planned from the start and incorporated at birth. Incorporating this perspective from the start accelerates the process by which products become brands. This is why product launch and brand launch are not the same.

This is also why brand names should never be descriptive of the product. The first reason is that what is descriptive soon becomes generic, when competitors come into the market with the same product. Second, clients will soon learn what the business is about. Names should better aim at telling an intangible story. Amazon speaks of newness, force and abundance (like the River Amazon), and Orange says 'definitely non-technical', just as AppleComputers did 25 years earlier.

Finally, as is illustrated by the two dotted arrows of the graph, brand management consists of a permanent coming and going between tangible and intangible values. Brands are two-legged value producing systems. This means is that having an excellent product is not enough in modern competition. (See for instance the Toshiba case, page 50). However, neither luxury nor image brands can afford to forget the functional realities of products (see page 69).

Are leading brands the best products?

To create a brand is much more than simply marking a product or service, the necessary first step of brand differentiation. It is about owning a value.

It is often held to be a paradox that the number one brands are not the best products. Was the original IBM PC the best PC available at the time? No. Is Pentium the best chip? Who knows? Are Dell computers the best computers?

The paradox stems from the word 'best': best for whom, and at what? Let's take the analogy of a school class. Academic gradings are determined according to well-understood criteria: students who do well display qualities such as excellent memory, the ability to solve problems fast, to work accurately and to present their work well. These are the values of the schoolroom; and similarly, each market has values. To become number one in any market it is necessary to understand what the market values are. Of course, one cannot succeed without a good product or service. Those who try the product must like it enough to make repeat purchases, to refer others to it; the product must build brand loyalty. In the truck tyre market, Michelin is certainly the number one: it holds 66 per cent of the original tyre market (that is, the tyres the manufacturer supplies with the truck). But in the replacement market, the so-called 'after market', although Michelin is still the market leader, its share falls to 29 per cent. It looks as if Michelin is not as well oriented to the values of the buyers in this after-market, fleet owners and those who maintain their trucks.

In the spirits market, Bacardi is world number one; is it the best spirit? One could certainly argue that it is nothing of the kind: it has no taste, and in all blind testings it fares very poorly. So why does it sell in such volume? The source of its business is not experts deliberating over its taste, but casual drinkers and partygoers. They generally want a spirit that will blend well in a cocktail, and an ideal mixer should have a very neutral taste. This is exactly what Carta Blanca delivers; it provides 90 per cent of Bacardi's sales.

Branding starts from the customer, and asks, what does he or she value? Bacardi is certainly not the 'better', but it could be called the 'batter'. One of its key intangible added values is its personality, epitomized by its symbol: a bat. The first Bacardi factory in Cuba was full of bats. This became the brand's symbol, adding an enduring halo of mystery to it.

Another example can be found in the educational market. The Master's degree in Business Administration (MBA) is a visa to success. It was first introduced in US universities. To get their MBA, students at US universities need two years of intense work: one year to learn the fundamentals, and one year to specialise in a major field.

Insead is now a respected brand in the MBA market, and Europe's best-known MBA. However its MBA course lasts less than a year (10 and a half months). This is the strength of branding: a strong brand awareness acts as a quality cue. Because it created the MBA

category in Europe, Insead soon benefited from the pioneer advantage: its qualification effectively became the local standard, because of the lack of competition. When competition came in, it was too late to change the standard. The French management school HEC created its MBA in 1969, while Insead had started in 1957. HEC and some other late entrants made another mistake: they delivered a genuine American-type MBA. The HEC MBA, which lasted two years, was arguably of too high quality for the European recruitment market.

Understanding the value curve of the target

Insead became Europe's most renowned MBA by understanding the value curve of European human resources directors who hire young executives. In delivering an MBA based on the US model, premium schools such as HEC showed that they did not understand the value curve of this market. In Europe, recruiters do not really care how much time students have spent on campus: the extra salary one gets after having spent two years at Harvard, Stanford or Northwestern instead of less than a year at Insead is very small. One thing recruiters do value, however, is an intensive immersion in a truly international programme, in which students learn to work with 10 different nationalities. This mirrors the working context for which they are being hired. European companies tend to consider that they will really teach their recruits how to do business in-house, and that an academic introduction lasting less than one year will suffice. Finally, companies prefer to rely on continuing education, providing a regular stream of specialised company seminars, throughout their managers' working lives.

Since not all clients are alike, different brands can coexist in the same sector, because they address the value curve of different segments. This is why groups build brand portfolios. GM has a portfolio of car marques, as does the Volkswagen Group.

Breaking the rule and acting fast

The Insead example also illustrates another issue: to build a brand one must quickly reach the critical size to create barriers to entry (such as top-of-mind awareness). By breaking the two-year rule, Insead was able to deliver twice as many graduates as an US school of the same size, and so to reach the critical size of alumni who act as its referees within companies in half the time. Recently it made a strategic move by doubling the number of graduates per year from 350 to 750, thus accentuating its market share and increasing its productivity (the number of students per professor). It also decided to capitalize on its now well-known brand to open a branch in Asia. The success of this move will depend at least partly on Asian companies' value curves being the same as those of European companies.

Many lessons should be drawn from the above examples:

▊ The first is that all brands start by being non-brands, with zero awareness and image. However, they were based on an innovation that succeeded. Starting a brand means finding a valuable innovation.

▊ Second, creating a market is the best way to lead it. This is the well-known pioneer advantage. However, to be able to create a market, one must break free from the conventions and codes that create herdism in the marketplace.

▊ Third, time is an essential ingredient of success. The winners start first and move fast so as to rapidly create a gap from the incoming competition.

▊ Fourth, it is important to reach the critical size rapidly, to reinforce that gap from the competition. This creates more resources for advertising, communication and word of mouth.

▊ Fifth, a brand is not a producer's brand or a retailer's, as is often heard in marketing circles: it is the customer's brand. A brand epitomize values, but as we know, value lies in the eyes of the beholder, the customer. It is essential to be market focused and ask, what is the value curve of the target? Then comes the question how to address this value curve better than the existing competition. The best way is to create a disruption (Dru, 2002), to break the conventions of the market.

Comparing brand and business models: cola drinks

It is interesting to compare a number of brand and business models within the same category. This illustrates how one cannot understand market leadership simply in terms of brand image. Structural factors such as production costs, the type of competition, and the trading structure of the sector need to be incorporated into the analysis. Why not take as a field for analysis the very symbolic one of colas? Colas as a commodity have succeeded remarkably in 'decommoditisation', unlike other soft drinks. They are also the market in which the largest brand in the world, Coca-Cola, operates.

What is a soft drink? In a material sense it consists of water, flavourings, a sweetening agent and carbonate. In the fruit juice market, brands are having a hard time: in Germany, hard-discount labels hold more than 50 per cent of the market. The same process is taking place in UK and all over Europe, where unlike in the United States, distribution is very concentrated and discount labels do not mean poor-quality products. The problem faced by brands is how to differentiate a product like orange juice that seems generic. In addition, the raw cost of orange juice is high: this creates pressure on the margins, and as a consequence on the level of advertising budget affordable, when selling prices are under pressure from retailer own-labels and unbranded generic products.

In the fruit juice market, there are not many ways of finding a favorable economic equation. Tropicana follows a premium price strategy, based on permanent product innovations (freshly collected oranges for instance) and a premium image. These are value innovations, increasing the price paid by consumers per litre. It is the premium market leader, and a global brand, but in each country it is a small player in volume.

As always, Procter & Gamble followed a high-tech approach to differentiate its product. It introduced Sunny Delight as a competitor in the fruit juice market although it has almost totally artificial ingredients (there is only 5 per cent orange in it, for legal reasons). These created a taste and texture that beat all the competitors using natural fruit juice. It also added vitamins to appeal to mothers. Thanks to its name, its colour (orange, and variants for the different flavours) and logo (a round sun), Procter & Gamble created an innovative product, which was reminiscent of orange juice and was certainly thought by some consumers to be orange-based. Its artificial chemical formula is patentable, which creates a barrier to entry and prevents it from being directly copied. Most important, it is priced high, whereas its raw material cost is far lower than that of natural orange juice.

Coca-Cola is an opaque product: almost black, mysterious, with a secret formula, it created from the start the conditions, both real and psychological, of a product that is not fully substitutable. Also, since it is an invented rather than natural product, the brand became associated with the product, which can be described by no other name. It has since become the reference product for an entire genre of cola drinks. Benefiting from

Table 3.1 Consumer price (in euros/litre) of various orange-flavour drinks

Brand	Price
Hard discount Carrefour	0.25
Orange juice	0.70
National brand	0.84
Sunny Delight	1.08
Tropicana	2.45

the pioneer advantage, throughout more than a century the Coca-Cola brand has pursued one single objective, now on a worldwide scale: to continue to grow the cola category. It was in competition first with sodas in America, then with other soft drinks, and now with virtually all other types of drink, including water in Europe or tea in Asia.

Coke's brand essence is 'the refreshing bond between people everywhere'. In making its brand the number one drink in the world, it benefited from being made from a syrup that is easy to transport at low cost, with high efficiency (that is, it can be highly concentrated, so many litres of Coca-Cola are produced from a single litre of concentrate) and remarkably high resistance to temperature and time (it can be stored for a long time, anywhere, unlike most fruit-based soft drinks). It is definitively a great physical product. In addition, the tuning of its acidity/sweetness ratio is optimal so customers can drink many glasses or cans in a row without being satiated. The cola syrup itself is very cheap to produce, thus allowing high margins and as a consequence high marketing budgets to reinforce its top-of-mind position (a key competitive advantage in this low-involvement category, where the buying decision is based on impulse). It is resold to bottlers at five times its production price, so profit can be located at the company level and pressure can be exerted on bottlers/ distributors to pursue a high-volume strategy if they want to be profitable.

To grow the business through the expansion of the category, the strategy rests on three facets, which are always the same: availability, accessibility, attractiveness, in that order. Most people focus on communication, but the key of Coke's domination is in these three levers:

▌ Availability, the distributive lever, comes first. 'Put Coke at arms' reach'. The aim is for people to find Coke everywhere: bars, fast-food restaurants, canteens, retailers, vending machines in streets and public places, refrigerators in offices, classrooms soon.... An essential point to appreciate is that building both the business and the brand image is tied to the active presence on premises. On-premise presence gives status to a drink, and creates consumption habits. In addition, unlike multiple retailers (Wal-Mart, Asda, Ika, Carrefour, Aldi and the like), which do not sell one brand exclusively, but their clients have the choice, on-premise customers do give exclusive rights, thereby granting a local monopoly to the brand. This is why Coke makes global alliances with McDonald's and other synergistic organisations. One condition of this type of exclusive deal is that the supplier provides, and the outlet agrees to stock, its full portfolio of soft drink brands. The goal is to create a barrier to entry to any soft drink competitor.

As part of competing on availability, one should not forget access to the bottlers: in many countries there are few good bottlers, and eventually one only. Controlling this bottler is a sure way to prevent competition entering the country. Conversely, it is a way to push competition out, as when the Venezuelan bottler that had formerly handled Pepsi decided to work for Coke. Within a day, Pepsi operations in Venezuela were closed.

▌ Accessibility is the price factor: 'In China, in India, sell Coke at the price of tea'. This is made possible by the low cost of syrup production, its easy transportability, and also the volume-based strategy. Economies of scale create another pressure on the competition, if not a total barrier to entry. Having located the profit at the company level (exactly as Disney Corporation does through licensing royalties, while some of its foreign entertainment parks are not profitable), the Coca-Cola Corporation can afford to have its local companies lose money for the sake of rapidly growing a high per capita consumption rate. In addition, to push competition out of the market (whether it is defined as cola drinks or more widely), the company exerts a high-price pressure on the whole market. For instance, it seems that specific prices on Coke are granted to trade distributors if they give preference to the company's other brands, such as Fanta, Minute Maid and Aquarius. This is why the Coca-Cola Company is now being sued by the European authorities on charges of anti-competitive manoeuvres.

▌ Attractiveness is the third factor: it is the communication issue. Although Coke's advertising is conspicuous, non-media communication (relationship, proximity, music and sports sponsorship, and on-premise communications) it represents the main part of the budget. Share-of-mind domination is made possible, let us remind, by the low production cost. Last but not least, Coke's image is not that of a product but of a bond: it delivers both tangible promises (refreshment) and intangible ones (modernity, dynamism, energy, American-ness, feeling part of the world) which make it so special, much more now than its secret formula.

Coca-Cola's main challenger worldwide, Pepsi-Cola, is following exactly the same brand and business model. Its differentiation is based on the fact that it was introduced more recently than Coke, and did not create the category. As a challenger, its brand image and market grip are lower. It challenges the leader on three facets: price, product and image:

▌ Price: it is a dime cheaper than Coke, at consumer level, but this creates a higher pressure profitability.

▌ Product: since it is not the referent, Pepsi is more daring and permanently works on the product to beat Coke on palatability and taste (the 'Pepsi challenge'). Its formula is actually preferred to Coke in most blind tests. It pushed Coca-Cola Corporation to make the 'marketing blunder of the century' launching New Coke in 1985 to replace the classic Coke, the water of the United States. More innovating by necessity, it practised line extensions such as Diet Pepsi well before Coke.

▌ Image: Pepsi is younger than Coke. Capitalising on the only durable weakness of Coke, its advertising positioning makes Pepsi the choice of the new generation. Pepsi's essence is 'the soft drink for today's taste and experiences'.

To secure a presence for Pepsi-Cola on premises and circumvent the barriers to entry created by Coke, the Pepsico Company had to diversify into restaurants and fast-food chains.

Other rivals to Coke have had an even harder time. In February 2000, Richard Branson of Virgin admitted defeat in its war against Coca-Cola and Pepsi in the United States, less than two years after he rode into New York's Times Square in a tank to launch his challenge. On reviewing the brand and business model that is common to both Coke and Pepsi, it is easy to understand why Virgin Cola failed everywhere but in the UK, its domestic base. Even there it won less than 5 per cent of the market. Brand is not enough.

Virgin Cola bought the Canadian company Cott's, which was able to make a very good syrup: it makes the cola sold under Loblaw's President's Choice private label. It proposed a cheaper price than Coke or Pepsi. But Virgin Cola never got the distribution, it never accessed the consumer. Branson's whole idea was to save on advertising and thus make a cheaper price possible by taking advantage of the Virgin umbrella brand. Unlike the two world-leading carbonated soft drink companies, which both follow a product brand policy (one brand per type of flavour), Virgin's only brand asset is its core brand, which has been extended to all types of category (see page 289), and in the process gained extensive worldwide awareness. As well as a low volume of advertising and selling a large volume on promotion, Virgin had a small sales force, a sure handicap for trade marketing and store-by-store direct relationships. Finally, Virgin Cola was not able to work in the market without a full portfolio of soft drinks to support it. This is necessary to access the on-premise consumption sector, and is also the only way to make a true national sales force economically possible.

As a rule, extension failures are immediately attributed to some image-based reason that it is impossible for the brand to extend to the new category. The brand and business perspective shows us that this explanation is superficial. It was not the Virgin brand that was the source of the failure, but the fact that Virgin could not compete on the same brand and business model as its two Goliath competitors. Fairy tales are one thing, but most of the time David gets killed.

Virgin Cola failed to get enough distribution: in Europe, for instance, it never entered the main multiple retailers. It was not sold sufficiently in the fashionable bars and restaurants. To do better in distribution terms it would have needed a real sales force and a real portfolio of brands and products. Arguably it should have looked for alliances with soft drink manufacturers looking for a branded cola.

Without advertising, the cola was mostly sold on a promotional basis. It is questionable whether that creates the basis for a long-term preference. Also, Virgin wanted to be perceived as the anti-Coke cola. However throughout the worldwide market this role already belonged to Pepsi. Finally, is the Virgin brand image that strong among the young generation outside the UK?

What other brand and business model could exist in this sector? At this time, two alternative models are surviving: ethnic colas and colas dedicated to trade. In its edition of Sunday 12 January 2003, the *New York Times* published an article, 'Ire at America helps create the Anti-Coke'. This announced the creation of Mecca Cola by a young Tunisian-born entrepreneur. He targeted it at the Muslims of France and soon of other countries. This brand had two strengths. The first was immediate goodwill in the Muslim community: its identity is based on a real feeling of community and resentment against what is felt as an imperialist drink and brand. The second was an immediate presence in the specific channel of distribution held by this community, innumerable small convenience stores that open long hours.

It is too early to judge its success, since this will only be evidenced by long-term durability. However, sales are skyrocketing. Interestingly, other colas have burgeoned, based on the same approach: they capitalise on religious, ethnic or geographical feelings of community and identity. For instance there are Corsica Cola and Breiz'h Cola (sold in Brittany), aimed at two regions with strong identity and even independentist movements. This model can be reproduced elsewhere: Irish cola? Scottish cola? In the era of globalization, regional identities are revived to resist what is perceived as a loss of essence, soul, and quality of life. Such attempts access local distribution or the local stores of national multiple retailers. No store owner or manager wants to take the risk of hurting the local feelings of the community living around its store.

Monarch Beverage Company has created an interesting alternative brand and business model. It is totally trade oriented, thereby securing access to modern distribution, worldwide. However it is not simply providing cola for retailers own labels. This is a true branding approach.

The problem for multiple retailers is to get free from the grip of Coke and Pepsi. Unfortunately, with some exceptions (Sainsbury's Cola in the UK, President's Choice Cola in Canada), market shares of own labels remain very small. This is probably because compared with the real thing, private labels look like faked cola. Parents who buy own-label colas to save money risk being criticized by their children. Private labels have no image in a category that has been decommoditised by brand image. Coke's identity encapsulates the American dream, authenticity and pleasure. Pepsi has the same associations, although to a lesser extent, and also means youth. Own-labels create no such value in the eyes of the young heavy consumers. They create bad will.

The Monarch Beverage Company was created in Atlanta, USA, by two former Coca-Cola marketing VPs. With the help of a former Coca-Cola chemist, it knew how to produce a good cola syrup. Most important, instead of focusing on the end-consumer (the mistake of Virgin) and running the risk of having no access to mass distribution, it focused on the customer problem: to increase the share of its own label with profit. Even if they were given away free, own-label colas would not be consumed: they lack authenticity, a reassurance on quality and taste, and fail to deliver the right intangible values. Monarch has created a portfolio of brands, all looking American (like 'American Cola'), and coming from a true American company based in the Mecca of colas, Atlanta, close to Coca-Cola's own headquarters. These brands, owned by Monarch, are granted under licence to multiple retailers. Each mass multiple retailer therefore has its own brand, different from its competitors', for its operations worldwide. Carrefour for instance has American Cola. The syrup is made by Monarch to match each retailer's specifications. The company provides the brand and the product; it leaves its customers totally free to manage their own bottlers, prices and promotion. No national sales force is needed: negotiations are carried out at the corporate level, with the category global manager.

This in-depth comparison of alternative brand and business models has illustrated the benefits of enlarging the perspective on competitive strategies, beyond communication and brand image. Brand leadership is gained through the synergy of multiple levers within a viable economic equation. Thus is the true condition of brand equity.

Two different approaches to luxury brand building

The only real success is commercial, yet there are many roads to this destination. An examination of 'new luxury' brands such as Ralph Lauren, Calvin Klein and DKNY proves that it is possible to become an overnight success in the luxury market without the long pedigree of a Christian Dior, Chanel or Givenchy. True, these newer brands have not yet demonstrated their ability to endure and survive beyond the death of their founders, but their commercial success is evidence of their attractiveness to customers the world over. We need to distinguish between two different business models for brands. The first includes brands with a 'history' behind them, while the second covers brands that, lacking such a history of their own, have invented a 'story' for themselves. It comes as no surprise that these companies are US-based: this young, modern country is a past master in the art of weaving dreams from stories. After all, both Hollywood and Disneyland are American inventions.

Furthermore, the European luxury brands – rooted as they are in a craftsperson-based tradition predicated upon rare, unique pieces of work – place considerable emphasis on the actual product as a factor in their success, while the US brands concentrate much more on merchandising, and the atmosphere and image created by the outlets dedicated to their brand, in the realm of customer contact and distribution. What we see is the creation of a dichotomy between 'history' and the product on the one hand, and 'stories' and distribution on the other. Let us examine and compare these two brand and business models in more detail.

The first brand and business model may be represented by the luxury pyramid (see Figure 3.2). At the top of the pyramid, there is the

Figure 3.2 The pyramid brand and business model in the luxury market

griffe – the creator's signature engraved on a unique work. This explains what it fears most: copies. Brands, on the other hand, particularly fear fakes or counterfeits. The second level is that of luxury brands produced in small series within a workshop: a 'manufacture' in its etymological sense, which is seen as the sole warrant of a 'good-facture'. Examples include Hermès, Rolls-Royce and Cartier. The third level is that of streamlined mass production: here we find Dior and Yves Saint Laurent cosmetics, and YSL Diffusion clothes. At this level of industrialisation, the brand's fame generates an aura of intangible added values for expensive and prime quality products, which nonetheless gradually tend to look more and more like the rest of the market. Hence its name equals mass prestige.

In this model, luxury management is based on the interactions between the three levels. The perpetuation of *griffes* depends on their integration in financial groups that are able to provide the necessary resources for the first level, and on their licensing to industrial groups able to create, launch and distribute worldwide products at the third level (such as P&G, Unilever and l'Oréal). Profit accrues at this level, and is the only means to make the huge investments on the *griffe* pay off. These investments are necessary to recreate the dream around the brand. Reality consumes dreams: the more we buy a luxury brand, the less we dream of it. Hence, somewhat paradoxically, the more a luxury brand gets purchased, the more its aura needs to be permanently recreated.

This is exactly how the LVMH group operates. The model is best explained in the actual words of Bernard Arnault, the CEO of LVMH, the world's leading luxury group, which owns 41 luxury brands. What are the key factors in the success of its brands? Arnault (2000: p 65) lists them in the following order:

- product quality;
- creativity;
- image;
- company spirit;
- a drive to reinvent oneself and to be the best.

Writing earlier in his book with reference to Dior, the ultimate luxury brand, he notes, 'Behind Dior, there is a legitimacy … roots … an exceptional evocative power … a genuine magic, to say nothing of its potential for economic growth' (p 26).

As we can see, in this pyramid model, with its base which expands to feed the brand's overall cash flow (through licensing, extensions and a less elective distribution system), there must be a constant regeneration of value at the tip. This is where creativity, signature and creator come in, supplying the brand with its artistic inventiveness. Here we are in the realm of art, not mere styling. Each show is a pure artistic event. Unlike the second brand and business model (as we shall see), it is not a question of presenting clothing which will be worn in a year's time. As Arnault puts it, 'One does not invite a thousand guests to watch a procession of dresses which could be seen on a coat hanger or in a show room' (p 70); 'most competitors prefer to show off mass-produced clothing on their catwalks, or indulge in American-style marketing. We are not interested in working this way' (p 73); and 'Marc Jacobs, John Galliano and Alexander McQueen are innovators; fashion inventors; artists who create' (p 75).

The creativity of the signature label, at the tip of the pyramid, is at the heart of the business model: within a few years of the arrival of John Galliano at Dior, sales had increased fourfold. Never before had Dior been talked about so much worldwide. Dior was back at the centre of world artistic creation for women.

The disadvantage of this model – and after all, every model has a disadvantage – is that the more accessible secondary lines are entrusted to other designers, and the further away you move from the tip of the pyramid, the less creativity there is. In this model, there is a strong danger that brand extensions will show little of the creativity of the brand itself: they will merely exploit its name.

The second brand and business model may have originated in the United States, but we should also include the likes of Armani and Boss in this category, which is characterised by its flat, circular, constellation-like model. At the centre is the brand ideal, while all manifestations of the brand (its extensions, licences, and so on) are around the edge, at a more or less equal distance from the centre. Consequently, these extensions are all treated with equal care, since each of them brings its own individual expression of this ideal to its target market. Each portrays the brand in an equally important way, and plays its own part in shaping it. For example, Ralph Lauren's home textile extension (bed sheets, blankets, tablecloths, bath towels and so on) is a complete expression of the patrician East Coast ideal and its values: indeed, the tactic of merchandising the range in the corners of department stores aims to create an idealized reconstruction of a room in a house.

This second model can include brand 'places' such as The House of Ralph Lauren – superstores which not only stock the entire brand range and its various collections and extensions, but are also specifically designed to give flesh, structure and meaning to the brand ideal. Ralph Lifshitz, Ralph Lauren's founder, built his brand on an ideal: that of American aristocracy, symbolised by Boston high society. Ralph Lauren's flagship stores are three-dimensional recreations of this fanciful illusion (Figure 3.3).

The same model is also used by brands such as Lacoste, created in 1933 in the days of tennis champion René Lacoste, a Davis Cup winner along with his friends 'Les Mousquetaires', and nicknamed 'The Crocodile' for his tenacity. Ever since then, the brand's values, which are encapsulated in his famous *chemise* (meaning 'shirt': the word itself is important), have been upheld by the Lacoste family and a collection of partners, their licensed producers and distributors. Lacoste thus has a certain authenticity and a genuine history, yet at the same time follows this second business model.

Indeed, the creation of this model has nothing to do with chance: it is an economic necessity for any brand which continues to be sold at an accessible price point. There is no way of sustaining an exclusive distribution network with an average till price of around 65 dollars or euros – that is, the price of a Lacoste shirt – or 50 dollars, the price of a Ralph Lauren polo shirt. The economics only become feasible with multiple extensions. Following our model, this can be done in two

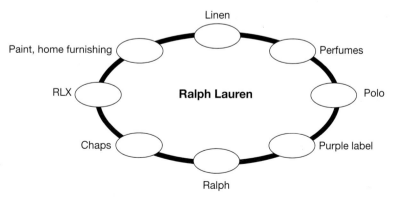

Figure 3.3   The constellation model of luxury brands

ways. The first is horizontal product extension to increase brand recognition, providing that elusive access to large-scale advertising budgets, and breaking into different distribution channels or different locations inside the same department store. This increases the perceived presence and status of the brand.

The second is vertical product extension to increase average till prices. Today, for example, Lacoste has segmented its product range into three groups – sport, sportswear and Club – yet has steered clear of formal wear, which is outside the brand's sphere of legitimacy. This segmentation makes it possible for customers to wear Lacoste in a variety of situations: sport, leisure and 'dress-down Friday wear'. At the same time, the average product price is increasing according to the particular segment: the high-quality materials used in a Club jacket explain why. Of course, the product ranges of all Lacoste's extensions are arranged around this same segmentation.

Ralph Lauren uses a similar model: its recent Purple Collection features Italian-made outfits produced from quality materials, and a price tag to match: 6,000 euros per outfit.

This brand extension policy makes matters easier for distributors, who have come to understand that the rate of return increases as the physical sales area expands. Each store can now offer a rich assortment of products which are no longer mere accessories, but extensions in their own right – and in so doing, can increase the value of the average shopping trip.

It should be noted that 'pyramid-based' brands face a rather perverse problem. If they create too many accessible extensions, they reduce the profitability of the sales outlets. In a Chanel boutique, it makes more sense to spend 10 minutes selling a customer a Chanel bag – given the margin it offers – rather than a perfume or a product from the Chanel Precision range. Clearly, the extension policy is inseparable from the distribution policy.

Part Two

The challenges of modern markets

4

The new rules of brand management

Is brand management in 2005 to be the same as it was in 1995? For the sake of rhetorical effects, it is useful to say that everything has changed, and to contrast the new decade with the former one, urging brand managers to update their thinking, concepts, skills, methods and strategies. We shall not fall into this stereotypical type of address.

Of course it is difficult to generalise when a book is aimed at managers throughout the world: what is true in Chicago may not be true in Mumbai, Buenos Aires or Stockholm. If we focus on the developed markets, a number of points characterise the new and sustainable environment of brands, which in turn commands a new type of management.

The new challenges of modern markets

What are the key characteristics of our modern markets that have a significant impact on management style?

Markets are mature. We shall regularly analyse the considerable implications of this structural factor throughout the analysis of brand deci-

sions. What it means is that needs are satisfied, and many product categories are not growing any more. They are saturated. Certainly there have been new areas like mobile phones, Internet broadband and digital or plasma televisions, technological disruptions that led consumers to feel that their former technology was obsolete. But in the context of FMCG, most categories no longer grow in volume.

That these markets are saturated is a problem for the growth and return on investment (ROI) figures expected by the financial markets. The first consequence is that brands must now move from a focus on needs to desires, and fulfil consumers' emotional aspirations much more than before. The winning formula for brand management of tomorrow is:

- to seduce through shared values (putting the brand in the consideration set);

- to attract customers regularly and repeatedly with innovations that are consistent with these values;

- to develop customer loyalty by quality and price that need to be continually justified for mature consumers.

New facets such as ethics, sustainable growth and equitable commerce will be sources of strengthening for brands, not as a basis of their positioning (as The Body Shop made it), but as added values, showing the brand is responsible and is more than a commercial artefact.

Another consequence is that to stimulate markets, innovations will have to be surprising, enticing. To surprise consumers, one should break free from the rampant herdism of marketing. Sharing the same methods, analysing the same datas and questionnaires, finding the same insights into consumer behaviour, companies invent lookalikes. Forecasting and trend-spotting will become more important in the quest for innovations that succeed and give a reasonably durable competitive advantage to the brand.

A final consequence is that direct relationships will increase in importance. Brands will have to be activated at contact much more than before, if they want to overcome their handicap of being distant (a reality only on television and on store shelves). Stores are a living reality. They must become a living, exciting experience for saturated consumers. Brands will have to be 'enacted', to make their values more real, beyond the products themselves.

Retailer own-brands are now the main competitors to manufacturer brands in a growing number of sectors. This is well known. But retailer brands are becoming more sophisticated, and are now positioned in all three tiers of any market: low-cost economy products, mainstream products, premium products, and even niche products. Retailer brands are there to position the store itself, to create store differentiation in markets where all the concentration of commerce has left only the best and biggest to compete.

Even worse, we have seen the rise of hard-discount brands in European countries such as the Netherlands, France, Spain and Italy, not to speak of Germany where it is the dominant form of commerce, and now is being exported on an ample scale even to the United States. Hard discount is a form of commerce that is aimed not just at the less well-off, but at mature consumers. This has led regular multiple retailers to accentuate their own pressure on prices, and therefore on the margins of their suppliers, who in turn are obliged to reduce their operating costs and therefore to cut their marketing expenditure.

The only answer to the pressure of price is again to recreate desire through innovation, and nurture loyalty by emotional bonding and shared values (although stores also fight on these values). The search for efficiencies is also vital: this is why brands have to become bigger. The key word 'mega-brand' refers to capitalising on one single name to support a wider range of products under one umbrella or endorsing brand.

Stores want to own customers. If they do so they will influence their choices. Customer relationship management (CRM) becomes a necessity for all brands, not only because this will increase the loyalty rate of clients who encounter often identical product and service propositions elsewhere, but also to communicate the brand values, deliver services and stimulate the brand community, be it real or virtual. More than before the brand must become 'mediactive' (Kapferer, 2001) and see its role also as a medium between the members of its community.

Modern markets are also those in which customers have access to pricing information and market intelligence. The Internet creates the ability to access all kinds of botshops (shopping robots) or price comparison search engines. A simple click creates market transparency, a challenge for brands that thrive on market opacity (created by the excess of supply). Brands will have to justify their price differential much more than they used to do. This will be done by a flow of information on the material added values (that is, the product or service quality) but also through the creation of intrinsic desire (by means of immaterial values). Brands are two-legged: as such they must manage both sources of added value, tangibles and intangibles, in parallel.

Over time, customers get older. Brands will also have to manage in parallel both their existing customers and their prospective future customers, who may have a very different preference or value curve. This requires a dual method of management: it is impossible to target only one of these two groups. Existing customers are the source of cash flow and profitability, while future customers are the source of survival and long-term adaptation to changing values.

Finally, *globalisation is everywhere.* It now concerns all forms of companies operating in mature markets, even small ones, because their main source of growth is outside their domestic market. Local companies and brands face global competition. One of the strategies open to them is to go international themselves, and deal with the mass of new questions this perspective creates. Should they adapt their product or export it as it is? Should they pursue a global marketing strategy, and to what extent? Is it time to change the brand architecture to better compete in the foreign markets? Which of their portfolio of brands should be international, and which should not be? How can the local brands in the brand portfolio be grown?

The challenge of ethics

Many brands and corporations have discovered they have a new stakeholder: non-governmental organisations (NGOs). These groups keep on watching the acts of these companies and brands, wherever in the world they operate, and they spread the word instantaneously on a global scale as soon as they identify an ethical problem. The globalisation of claims of unethical corporate or brand behaviour is a definite new factor of the economic and media environment. Shell and Nike are among those that have learnt this to their cost.

From the viewpoint of investors, it is noticeable that pension funds are now inter-ested in knowing more about the social, environmental and ethical behaviour of the companies in which they consider investing. Finally, more and more producers, retailers and brands now communicate their concern for the environment, for sustainable development, fair trade and so on.

The challenge is high: can we reconcile business objectives and ethics? This is a subject large enough to fill a whole book, and it is preposterous to try to summarise it in a few lines. But the question must be addressed: can a brand prove sustainable in modern markets, if it does not care about sustainable development, for instance?

One thing is certain: in our communication society rumours travel fast. True or false (Kapferer, 1991), they are a menace to reputations. The problem is that in our mediated virtual world, words and images may have more effect than true facts. For instance, although Total, the fourth largest petroleum company in the world, is regularly claimed to practise unethical behavior in Burma and to have close relationships with the military dictatorship, recent investigations by Amnesty International, one of the most efficient NGOs, have revealed no trace of such misbehaviour. But the rumours keep going round, with their emotional charge and energy.

Why will the ethical dimension become a necessary one for respected brands? It will, because being respected is a prerequisite for sustainable company growth. In fact, in Fortune's Most Respected Corporations Annual Survey, respect for the environment is growing in importance as a lever of perception.

The introduction of ethics into corporate governance and brand management typically takes four forms:

- The first one is reactive. For example, Shell was attacked on the Brent Spar case, then on its involvement with the Nigerian crisis. The company reacted by creating a Directorate of Sustainable Development, and holding up transparency as one of its key new values. After Nike was shown to be outsourcing its production to sweatshops in Asia, it was forced to participate in setting up a new NGO, the Global Alliance for Workers and Communities.

▌ The second one is imitative: companies follow the trend, so as not to be outdistanced by competitors.

▌ The third one is based on compliance with the new standards and expectations of stock rating agencies, opinion leaders and the public itself. Companies' motivation here is preventive: they want to avoid a crisis of reputation. To the same end they also invest increasing sums of money in monitoring the press and the world's Internet chatrooms. The technology for doing this has become remarkably efficient. Companies' perspective is here short-term and image-oriented: all they do or say is based on the objectives of not making waves and leaving intact their reputational capital.

▌ The fourth one sees an opportunity to create a competitive advantage by going beyond what is expected from all stakeholders, through these new standards. Companies realise that in our modern materialistic world, consumers and customers will expect more from companies and big brands: they do not want bigger brands, but better brands.

The more deeply we become involved in an ethos of materialist consumption, the more there is a felt need for meaning. It is hard to live in a purely materialistic world. For the same price, in our oversupplied markets, consumers will expect more from their brands: they expect them to be respectable. When they consider a product, the first question consumers ask is, what is it? Then they ask, what does it do for me (that is, what are its tangible or intangible benefits)? Now consumers also ask, what does it mean to me?

Of course this moral sensitivity is not evenly spread through the population. As ever, it is the activist groups that take the lead: youth groups, wired through the Internet, are prompt to spread the alarm. They have ideals, morals and expectations; they care for the environment. They now care for the global inequalities created by the increasing gap between rich and poor countries. As an effect of globalisation, things that take place (and are intended to be kept hidden) say in Nigeria, are rapidly whispered in the Netherlands, in the UK, then everywhere. These active groups are also very attached to the notion of cultural diversity and to the respect of local communities, a dimension so far overlooked by the global brands. Tomorrow, business and brand intelligence will have to be moral: their sustainable growth depends on it.

Key principles of competitive branding

How do these challenges impact brand management in practice? How do they require companies to modify some of their current practices?

Brands do not belong any more to marketing

Since the concept of brand equity began to be promoted, the first noticeable change was that management itself began to pay close attention to the organisation's portfolio of brands. In the beginning, brands were considered as a mere communications issue, then as the sole prerogative of the marketing managers; nowadays, CEOs themselves consider brands to be their responsibility. Y. Barbieux, formerly CEO of Nestlé Thailand, France and then of Italy, declared: 'Brands can no longer be entrusted to the marketing people only.' They have thus been disowned in a certain way, as they are no longer the only ones in charge of brand policy. Nowadays, financial, accounting, technical and legal managers, and of course managing directors, are all participating in this task. This new situation has also led multi-brand groups to redefine the position held by their communications managers. No longer serving the marketing departments, they now directly report to general management. This is the case at Whirlpool Europe: thanks to their new position, communications managers are now able to fund major brand events independently from market share constraints.

In terms of organisation, companies have become aware that their structures are often too ephemeral for efficient brand management. A company must have people who ensure continuity in and respect for the brand's intangible attributes once they have been defined. On the other hand, companies have become aware that a given brand can be linked to several different technologies. Buitoni, for instance, is a brand that sells frozen, canned and vacuum-packed foods, all produced by different business units and marketed by different sales teams. It became necessary to create a new profession: brand management across business units. Finally, the typical pyramid-shaped marketing structures have caused responsibilities to be diluted and managers to specialise more and more in only one particular facet of the brand. That is why the Danone group has flattened its hierarchy down from four to three tiers, thus leaving a brand marketer, a brand marketing manager in charge of the brand's overall management and a marketing director in charge of coordination and, more specifically, of the 'mega-brands'.

Capitalising on 'mega-brands'

Apart from the brand's new internal environment, the notion of brand equity means it is essential to manage the value of this equity. In doing so, the key word is 'capitalisation'. Yet it seems impossible to capitalise on several brands at the same time, unless the company is a powerful multinational. Most companies therefore reduce their brand portfolios and focus only a few so-called 'mega-brands'. As a matter of fact, brand portfolios are often overloaded, due more to successive acquisitions than to thorough planning of what each brand needs to do, both for its consumers (through their specific positioning) or for its distribution channels (in order to avoid conflicts). This tendency is even stronger in the industrial sector: as many companies pursued their growth through buy-outs, they now have to cope with a stack of local brands, product or product-line brands and company brands, as well as with a set of problems for which they are not prepared.

Reducing the brand portfolios has a corollary effect: fewer brands now encompass more products. Products whose brands no longer exist must be transferred to existing ones. Danone, for instance, covers more than 100 product lines. It has therefore become necessary to create intermediate brands in order to structure Danone's overall product range, such as Taillefine for waist-conscious consumers, Charles Gervais for gourmet adults, Kid for children, Bio for the health-conscious, etc. Each product-line brand has its own target market and its own positioning. In order to ensure that the structure benefits Danone and does not represent a mere patchwork, each product-line brand sets its own brand image objective, yet all of them share two benefits inherent to Danone's identity: proximity and health. In a similar way, the Nestlé company has selected a limited number of master brands (Nescafé, Maggi, Buitoni, Nestlé, and so on), each of them acting as a mega-brand for a wide range of products and sub-brands.

The end of new brand proliferation

This urge to capitalise has thus put an end to the proliferation of brands and product names which has so far worked against all major groups. It is true that any product manager in charge of launching a new product is tempted to give it a name of its own: its own brand name. This is especially true in industry where the naming process is practically the only way both for the manager and the new product to gain instant recognition from all. That is why companies registered bucket-loads of brand names for their new products, encouraged by the classical Procterian ideology of the product brand. Those times are over. Not only did it prove expensive (Du Pont Agricultural Products has almost 800 brand names to manage, which costs a lot of money) but also inefficient: most of the names remained unknown, legally defined as brands, but meaning nothing whatsoever to buyers. It would have been wiser just to retain the best-known names and to transform them into umbrella brands. That is the only way to capitalise.

Having experienced the same syndrome, Nestlé decided to create a brand management department in their headquarters in Vevey, Switerland, uniquely entitled to create new brands all over the world. The results were radical: in 1991, Nestlé launched nearly 101 new products worldwide, but only created five new brands. Thus 96 innovations were launched either under the umbrella or the endorsement of existing brands! For example, chocolate-flavoured cereals were launched under the Nesquik brand name because they serve the same purpose: to provide mothers with a means of coaxing their children into drinking milk. In order to prevent itself being perceived as a censor and arbitrary ruler, 3M distributed worldwide an internal booklet specifying both the market conditions under which creating new brands would be authorised (eg Post-it) and the most prevalent ones under which innovations must bear one of three existing name possibilities: a generic one plus the 3M brand name (3M cassettes or overhead projectors); its own surname within an existing product-line brand (Magic Tape by Scotch); a generic name plus the product-line brand (video cassettes by Scotch). This document, entitled *'Brand Asset Management'*,

made it possible to internalise some basic management principles. This explains why requests for new brands at 3M dropped from 244 ten years earlier to 70. In 1991 only 4 were accepted, versus 73 in 1989: this is how 3M managed to reduce its portfolio from 1,500 to only 700 brands! At 3M, all brands are intrinsically global and international, hence creating local brands is now strictly forbidden. The only time the creation of a new brand can be envisaged is when a new primary need is discovered: such was the case for Post-it. Creating new sub-brands such as Scotch's 'Magic' can be done only if using the brand name (Scotch in this case) does not allow sufficient differentiation among products (see page 309).

Sustaining brands with innovations

All too often, brand management is equated with communication management. In fact brands are created by innovations and thrive by a continuous flow of innovations. Because innovations recreate a temporary competitive advantage, it is their flow that is important. It fosters the perception that the brand is really a leading one, addressing the needs of consumers more effectively than do rivals. Every time a brand's share is shrinking, the diagnosis is the same: the brand's innovation rate has declined. The marketing teams have nothing ready for the future. In contrast, whenever a brand's share leaps, one should look at its innovation rate. In February 2003, PSA Peugeot Citroen became the European co-leader in the automobile market, with 16.87 per cent of the market against 16.64 per cent for the Volkswagen Group as a whole. There was no miracle: it had launched 28 new and attractive models between 1998 and 2002 (Folz, 2003).

Seen from a distance, these rules may seem to limit and restrict the creative drive. From within, though, they have proven to be the only means of renewing existing brands, enhancing both their value and their worldwide impact. Brands manage to grow only if they constantly renew themselves and if the new products end up accounting for a significant part of their turnover. Today in many sectors this part varies between 25 and 33 per cent. Brands demonstrate their contemporary relevance by showing their ability to market new products that satisfy new needs and meet modern expectations. Yet most of the time product managers would prefer to launch innovations under a new brand name. This amounts to depriving existing brands of the aura of modernity conveyed by new products. When naming their new instant mashed potatoes Mousline instead of Maggi, one of the corporation's mega brands, the Nestlé managers tarnished the latter's image by slightly outdating it. Thinking in terms of capitalisation thus requires addressing the issues in the reverse order: choosing a name for a new product no longer matters as much as deciding which new products should be launched under the existing brand name. Brands are rejuvenated by new products matching new needs, not by advertising. That is why Cadbury-Schweppes did not allow a new soft-drink to be launched as 'Wipps': instead, it became 'Dry' by Schweppes and subsequently 'Schweppes Dry'. For young people, 'Wipps' would have caused Schweppes to lose contact with youth and to become a brand associated with their parents. 'Dry' by Schweppes at least aimed to connect the new brand with the new consumers, and thus ensured a better future for the Schweppes brand equity. Today, Coca-Cola would never have launched its light version as 'Tab' (1964), but immediately as Diet Coke – without waiting until 1981 to do so. Meanwhile, Pepsi-Cola reacted to Tab by launching Diet Pepsi, which gave the brand an upbeat, health-conscious image.

Addressing diversity

One of the most dramatic changes in the environment of brands is the fragmentation of markets. Consumers are no longer seen as a monolithic mass. They have become situational: their brand choices vary, for they are guided by the purchase and consumption situation. They have also become more eclectic, and do not hesitate to mix products from different brands. In clothing for instance, we have seen the end of the 'total look'.

Media are also much more fragmented. Not only do people spend more time on the Web, thus having less time for classic media, but the latter have never been so diversified, through cable and satellite access.

As a result markets have changed. A simple look at the automobile market shows that the classic sedan car is now an endangered species. People choose cars that look like them, or the way they would like to live. Hence the booming demand for pick-up cars, coupés, convertibles, minivans, four-wheel drives, roadsters, and all types of car that did not exist before. It is not so much the technology that did not exist, rather the concept of the different varieties of car.

The era of a product that represents 90 per cent of a company's sales is completely gone in many sectors. Instead, brand sales represent an aggregate of demands. In fact in the automobile industry, cars are launched from the start with a number of widely differing versions to capture both publicity and the attention of involved consumers. In another sector, that of fashion apparel, Ralph Lauren has no less than 15 labels or sub-brands, from the expensive Purple Label to RLX, Chaps and Polo Jeans. Nike multiplies the lines of its sneakers for the same reason, and gives them the names of famous sportspeople. Retailer brands themselves have understood that they are much more likely to create a buzz and attract people in-store if they fragment themselves, addressing new product lines with new trendy behaviours as soon as they emerge. Unlike the multinational producers, where each new product launch takes at least a year to be approved and tested worldwide, retailers can be much more reactive and adaptive: their risk level is low. They invest time, not money.

Of course this concern for addressing diversity in the brand's product lines is all the more valid for global brands: they must integrate cultural diversity in their global range from the start. In fact, evidence shows that products aimed at the requirements of a specific country can be exported elsewhere. Multinational corporations have become globalisers of diversity.

Managing innovation allocation

The capitalisation concept also impacts on the way in which innovations are allocated in a company with a multi-brand portfolio. As already mentioned, when companies do not properly allocate their innovations, they actually undermine the strong brand's premium while failing to increase the weaker brand's sales.

It is, therefore, not up to the brand managers to decide whether their brand needs an innovation or not. The marketing manager, who has a clear vision of each brand's territory and boundaries, must alone determine innovation allocation, according to the respective contract and positionings of each brand. This helps clarify both the consumers' and the distributors' perception of each brand's function on the market. It also increases profitability. The problem is that many brands no longer know why they even exist, as they get handed down from one generation to another, often inherited from mergers and acquisitions. They do project a more or less clearly defined image, but neither their positioning nor the role they are supposed to play on the market have ever been specifically stated. Capitalising on a brand can only be done if it is clear where it is headed and what it is fighting for. That is why all headquarters elaborate brand charters, which aim at defining once and for all the brand's values and its specific benefits and attributes, its uniqueness and core business (see page 149).

Identity prevails over image

Up to now, brand management has been governed by brand image. The brand's main concern is to know how it is perceived. Today, marketing considers the notion of identity as the core concept of brand management: before knowing how we are perceived, we must know who we are. Only identity can provide the right framework for ensuring brand consistency and continuity (multi-product, multi-country) and for making capitalisation possible. It is not up to the consumer to define the brand and its content, it is up to the company to do so. Certainly it will make use of market data and consumers' opinions. However, the latter have no feelings about the long-term interest of the brand and its owner and about coherence within brand portfolios. Today there are too many people, both internally and externally, taking part in the management of each brand. The more participants there are, the more distortions, personal interpretations and variations in style there are. Even though brands act democratically by bringing progress onto the market, they should be managed by an enlightened despot, not by a democrat. Someone has to be both the boss and the guarantor of its continuity and identity. This guardian, as mentioned above, is to be found high up in the hierarchy nowadays. He/she is thus in the perfect position to resist different sorts of daily pressure, which can be tempting in terms of short-term turnover but damaging in the medium term. One must be capable, for instance, of refusing attractive proposals of brand extension under licensing, if these do not fit the brand's intrinsic identity. The latter can only build up with time and continuity. That is why the current turnover of marketing managers goes against brand interests. It is therefore necessary to have a brand charter that serves as a guarantor for brand identity, perpetuity and consistency, and that encompasses all of the countries, managers and products that it endorses. Knowing the brand project intimately is the best way of sharing it both internally and externally and, thus, of leaping into the future.

Exploiting brand equity

Capitalising is a good thing, of course, but brands are a tool for growing business more profitably. It is also legitimate to take advantage of the return yielded by the brand's equity. This is what brand extension is all about. For decades, marketing managers just adopted Procter & Gamble's brand management model. Those days are over. Reducing a brand to only one product often means shrinking brand equity. This can jeopardise the brand since according to the product life cycle all products eventually die out – and often their brands, too. That is what nearly happened to VW: as VW was exclusively associated with the famous 'Beetle' for too long, the destiny of its brand became too dependent on the car's life cycle. All products enter a downward phase at some time. Likewise, the French cigarette brand, Gauloises, knew when to pull out of the declining market for brown-tobacco cigarettes and transfer its image to that of light, blond-tobacco cigarettes. Brand extension is now a must. Nivea is a good example: it would have been a mistake to associate Nivea exclusively with its well-known multi-purpose basic product (its moisturising cream). Nivea has now created a full range of products. The values attributed to a brand often help segment categories other than that in which the brand was born. Thus Bic symbolises 'cheap, relaxed lifestyle, simple and practical product'. These values were first embodied in the famous ball-point pen; thereafter, they proved relevant for disposable lighters and razors. This brand extension was legitimate, as it was reinforced by the fact that the disparate products used similar distribution channels. However, these values are less relevant for body perfume. Thus that extension failed, though it would have worked for air fresh-

eners. Hence, brand extension uses awareness and image assets in order to gain significant market share at minimal entry costs. That is why Essilor has now become threatened by two unexpected newcomers to the market for corrective glasses: Seiko and Nikon. The values of precision, detail and high technology conveyed worldwide by Seiko justify its presence on the huge international market hithero dominated by Essilor. As we see, brand values generate brand financial value and price justification.

Brand equity and price war

As the economic crisis has reached a climax, it has become quite common to talk about brand chaos and crash. Such alarming statements pertain above all to consumer goods but also to services and industrial goods. They address the general issue of brand value. In effect, distributors' own brands and low-priced goods (hard-discount products) now occupy about 40 per cent of large retailers' shelf space. As this trend is bound to last, the survival of many producer brands is a matter of concern. Why are brands, or at least certain renowned brands, becoming less attractive?

The main reason for this is the discrepancy between price and value, which is actually caused by the producers themselves. Too many of them have indeed taken brand equity for a guaranteed source of income. They have thus neglected to work on maintaining the perceived difference and have systematically raised the selling prices. This remained unnoticed during times of inflation. Neither decreases in VAT nor increases in productivity were passed on to consumers; instead they went to retailers, which grew richer and richer. All in all, prices kept on rising so that even the more classical, quality-focused distributors' own-brands had to follow the upward price trend. In doing so, producers actually gave way to a new, hitherto undeveloped, segment of buyers: those wanting to buy the cheapest possible and those who do not care enough about the product class to want to pay more. Unconditional brand loyalty does not exist any more. Marlboro's repeated price increases were bound to reach a limit some day. Price perception is definitely a relative concept: as new producers entered the market with cigarettes 40 per cent cheaper, the price perception of that brand, and of many other consumer good brands, became totally exaggerated. In fact, lowest price products no longer mean worst quality products. The price difference no longer corresponds to a perceived difference in quality: the brand is no longer in equilibrium. Price increases due to sole intangible values no longer prevail. The price gap must still be explained rationally to consumer.

After 40 years of economic growth, managers have inherited a false idea about price. During these years, market growth and inflation compensated for most pricing mistakes. For many executives, to lower prices is to give in. This is no longer true: price competitiveness has become the sign of performing companies. Dell's growing market share is due to the price pressure it exerts on HP and other rivals.

What brand strategies, then, should be implemented? They differ according to two main brand types. Those based on technology (cosmetics, hygiene, beauty, detergents, etc) must invest in R&D in order to recreate a difference in performance which advertising should help sell. The other type of brand has no better option than to maintain volume levels in order to cover fixed costs. In this case, the only solution is to cut prices in order to come back and compete in the mainstream market.

However, some brands are making risky moves. They think that they should drop their prices to the level of the lowest priced competitors. But such a decrease in prices is bound to undermine the brand's long-term credibility as far as its loyal customers are concerned, who might, in which case, start wondering about the brand's true value.

Moreover, it would not be well-grounded, nor would its purpose be clear. The market mechanism can indeed be compared to a trammel-hook (Degon, 1994). There is a hierarchy of tiers or segments in every market. Real competition first takes place within the segment itself. The cheapest product of each segment is often the most attractive. As a matter of fact, they are the only ones with increasing volumes. The strategy thus consists in assessing a realistic price difference, taking into consideration both brand image and awareness, and the segment the brand competes in.

Brand equity and producing distributors' own brands

The brand equity concept directly impacts on the way in which producers address the following key issue: should we produce the distributors' own-brands?

First of all, both the low price and the DOB segments often represent an important share of the market (40 to 50 per cent), which can no longer be neglected. These are bound to last and to develop. Thus, it would be unreasonable for many corporations not to produce for those two segments. However brand defence calls for precautions, as mentioned below:

- Brands based on technology have no reason to concede their technology. In this respect, L'Oréal does not supply distributors' own-brands. The competitive advantage of L'Oréal's brands is entirely generated by R&D and advertising. It is thus legitimate to want to preserve it exclusively. L'Oréal actually discourages the entry of DOBs by means of its brand portfolio, which contains a brand for each level of consumer involvement. In fact, for L'Oréal, the equivalent of DOBs in functional terms is Nivea or Oil of Ulay.

- Well-known producers should not invest to produce distributors' own-brands. Indeed, distributors' choice of producers is often changing so quickly that it would be risky to make any specific industrial investment.

▮ Producers should not concede their best technology but the one that is almost, or entirely, the same as that produced by their competitors.

▮ DOB activity must be intrinsically profitable. It is thus necessary to stop reasoning in terms of marginal cost, given the increasing volumes such activity generates. Resulting cash flow can then be used to defend the brands and preserve their competitiveness. However, financial data show that companies that do not produce own-label brands are more profitable.

These are some aspects of the management revolution resulting from the realisation that companies must create, preserve and use that precious brand equity of theirs. This revolution is just starting. The obsession now is capitalising on the best brands. This is still contrary to current practice. Many companies still spend a lot more time on their weak than on their strong brands, which should be the ones guiding them into the future. In this respect, it is quite revealing that Edwyn Artzt, former CEO of Procter & Gamble, was nicknamed 'Terminator' for having terminated many brands incapable of yielding added value: Citrus Hill orange juice, Solo laundry detergent, White Cloud paper. Whenever the price differential barely covers the marketing and advertising costs needed for brand upkeep, there is no good reason for the brand to live on.

The enlarged scope of brand management

Brand management itself is much influenced by the revolution that has shaken marketing theory and practice: a shift from a mere transactional perspective to a relational perspective.

This has led theorists to ask new questions, and propose new working methods, new modes of thinking, new tools, which often claiming to be substitutes for the former 'old' ones.

From transaction to relationships

Traditionally marketing focused on consumer behaviour: it aimed at influencing choice. Its focus was on understanding purchase, and the choice criteria that prompted it, whether they were tangible or intangible, product-based or image-based. Its tool for influencing demand was the marketing mix, with its sacred four Ps: product, price, place and publicity. Marketing research aimed at identifying the attributes that predict purchase, and its typical statistical tool was a multi-attribute model. Segmentation is another key concept of transactional marketing: recognising that transactions are facilitated when expectations are higher, and the mass market has been segmented into groups, or types with similar expectations. Then brands could be profiled and created to meet each set of expectations.

Because competition is fierce, imitation rapid, and consumers sometimes seemed overwhelmed by these very tightly tailored proposals and brands, the focus of marketing has moved from conquering clients to keeping them, from brand capital to customer capital. The new buzz words of good efficient brand management are share of requirements, shared loyalty and CRM. The focus is on building lasting relationships through time, and on post-purchase activities, all of which is subsumed under the term 'relationship marketing'. The focus of research has moved from predicting choice to classifying the different types of relationships consumers have with brands (Fournier, 2000), or the different types of interactions companies engage in with their clients, beyond selling a product or service (Rapp and Collins, 1994; Peppers, 1993).

It should be noted that relationship marketing is a financially driven concept. Customers are still segmented, but the distinctions are behavioural. In traditional marketing, segmentation aimed at maximising the value created by the brand or company for its customers. In relationship marketing, segmentation is based on the value a customer brings to the company: only profitable customers should receive repeated attention. Hence the concept of lifelong customer value. Internet technology has created the means to meet this demand for more and more efficiency in tracking, analysing, servicing and selling to each one of these important customers.

Of course, these two approaches are complementary. The best loyalties are not based on mere calculus and loyalty cards: they are internalised as voluntary loyalty, as brand commitment. On the other hand, weak brands need to start somewhere. Behavioural loyalty programmes create the conditions for deepening the customer–brand relationship, and create emotional connections between consumers and the brand.

From purchase to satisfaction and experiential rewards

Another consequence of this shift towards post-purchase phenomena is the focus on product/service satisfaction. How does what the product/service delivers match the expectations of the consumer? How can this satisfaction be raised, improved relentlessly? In this process the conditions of the consumption situation need to be taken into consideration. A product is always consumed in a context. The nature of this context affects the degree of satisfaction that the customer reports, through the notion of a 'rewarding experience'. In fact all marketers have known for a long time that food served in a pleasant atmosphere is judged to taste better than food eaten in unpleasant surroundings. Philip Kotler (1973) has coined the term 'atmospherics' to point out this facet

of consumption, the experiential facet. Today, stores as such Niketown and the House of Ralph Lauren are typical applications of this experiential concept (Kozinets *et al*, 2002). As early as 1982, a pioneering paper by Holbrook and Hirschman insisted on the necessity of providing modern consumers with fantasies, feelings and fun in their experiential consumption. Schmitt (1999) has coined the term 'experiential marketing' to refer to 'how to get customers to sense, feel, think, act and relate to your company and brands'.

Bonding through aspirational values

Beyond functional and experiential rewards, brands must now also be aspirational. It is through their intangible values that they help consumers to forge their identities, at a time when inherited identities are weaker. The famous and elusive 'customer bonding' is based on product satisfaction, on a rewarding consumption experience (which includes the tailoring of proactive services even for products). It cannot exist if the brand values do not fit the consumers' values. All brands have to be somehow aspirational. Beyond materialistic and hedonistic satisfactions, they say, 'We understand each other, we share the same values, the same spirit.' This is why it is so important to specify these non-product-based values. Visions and missions are the typical source of these values.

It is therefore possible to plot the extension of the scope of brand management on a two-dimensional matrix (Figure 4.1). The horizontal axis refers to the time perspective of the relationship sought (from immediate transaction to repeat purchase to long-term commitment), while the vertical axis refers to the depth of customer bonding. It has three tiers: product satisfaction, experiential enchantment and aspirational intimacy, or the sharing of deep values. At the intercept, it is possible to position the new tools and behaviours of modern brand management.

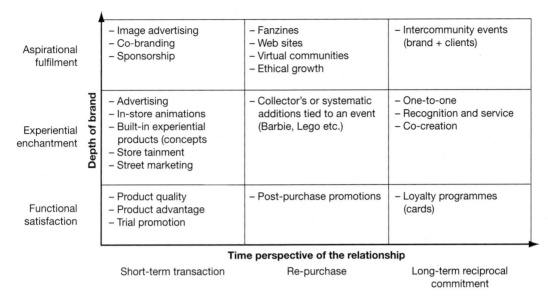

Figure 4.1 The extension of brand management

The importance of communities

How many fans does the Manchester United football team have all around the world? Five million in the UK and 50 million elsewhere in the world? Most of these will never see the team play in the flesh, but they watch real-time television showings or connect to webcasts of the team's matches on the Internet. They consume merchandise such as T-shirts. In the Old Trafford stadium, UK fans drink only Manchester United Cola. This is a real community; thanks to it, the team can hire the most expensive players, such as David Beckham. The income from the merchandise sold by association with the most famous players virtually covers their enormous wages and transfer fees.

Traditionally, in consumer research consumers were seen as individuals, who were eventually aggregated into market segments. Most multi-attribute models aiming at predicting purchase made that implicit assumption, for they were based on individual responses. One could argue that consumers are not isolated individuals: they belong to groups, tribes or communities, either stable or transient, durable or situational. In fact, the brand acquires meaning not through a summation of individual evaluations, but after a collective screening made of conversations within the reference groups, the community, where opinion leaders can play a determining role.

Along with advertising, new forms of behaviour have emerged through which brands are *enacted*, that is, they eventually 'live' their values with consumer communities in a non-commercial environment. Classical examples of this are the Michelin-sponsored races around the world, or the Harley-Davidson rally where management and bikers meet once a year. The modern brand also animates communities created around itself or a topic (parenthood for Pampers, rock music for Jack Daniel's). Internet sites, 'fanzines', hotlines, brand clubs and events, are the classic tools to implement this new attitude and share the brand values through servicing or animations. The brand becomes 'mediactive', it helps its customers get in touch with each other, on the Net or in reality through specific events. Building *brand communities* is now part of the scope of brand management (Hagel, 1999). For consumers, getting together and sharing experiences is another form of reward. Feather (2000) has identified four drivers of e-communities: they can be interest-based, transaction-based, relationship-based or fantasy-based. Each one determines a specific type of site, of content, of interaction between the brand and this very involved public; it goes beyond mere purchasing and looks for inter-actions with the brand and other customers. The customers are driven by the rewards of community interaction and transaction.

Activating the brand at contact

Most of our thinking about the role of adver-tising in supporting brands is based on the *'big bang model'* (Kapferer, 2001). At a time when there were few channels available, the core media could really be called mass media. But attention is scarce and fragmented now, because there is such a diversity of available media channels, not to mention the Internet. The power and energy of the massive gross rating point (GRP) campaigns is fragmented. Down in the marketing channels, this energy arrives weakened. This is why it is necessary to recreate energy at contact. All brands must be concerned with the energisation of their value-transmitting chain, including prescribers, VIPs, opinion leaders, profes-sionals, early triers, involved consumers and of course distributors. A brand that existed only on shelves and on television would seem remote and lack depth. One does not create relationships at a distance.

As a consequence, all brands now must think of their activation plan:

▌ Acting within communities (like Vittel mineral water, which has developed part-nerships with local sports clubs where consumers train).

▌ Acting on premises, at the point of the consumption, creating memorable collective experiences.

▌ Acting with prescribers (that is, those who recommend the brand to an user further down the channel), to foster their cause.

▌ Acting with virtual communities created around the brand. The brand must become a medium between the people in the community, real or virtual, and provide more than products. It must provide real services.

Licensing: a strategic lever

Licences are a rapidly growing phenomenon (Warin and Tubiana, 2003), demonstrating an awareness of two facts. First, although brands are a form of capital, they still have to produce revenue. Second, this type of partnership enables the brand to acquire abilities or distri-bution that it had previously lacked, and so to be extended yet further. However, there is still an image problem with licences, which explains why they have experienced slower growth in some countries than others. English-speaking countries, for example, have extensively exploited this concept. Yet in numerous other countries, licences are still restricted only to the luxury sector, sport and so-called 'derivative' products – knick-knacks from every sector that this pejorative name implies. Furthermore, the current trend among luxury brands for announcing – as Gucci has done – that they are to cut the number of their licences has served to strengthen this negative aura around the licence. For some brands, such action has merely been a case of correcting the licensing excesses into which they had fallen, as part of a drive to recreate the rarity (and perhaps even quality) of their brand. Gucci was a typical example of this.

In reality, licences have now become a truly magnificent opportunity for improving business volume, brand capital and profitability. Why was this not the case before?

First, brand managers have now realised they need to focus on relationships. Beyond the product itself, the brand must forge links with its customers – and its best customers in particular – which are based on a rapport and mutual understanding. The products we currently refer to as 'derived' should really be renamed as 'customer relationship products'. For example, one initiative taken by Orangina has been to rebuild its relationship with the young people and teenagers who had increasingly been abandoning the product in the face of Coca-Cola's relentless encroachment.

Second, today's brand is community focused, as in, 'Tell me which community you belong to, and I'll tell you who you are.' In other words, the choices the brand makes in terms of promotional agreements reveal the community to which it belongs and whose tastes it shares. The decision by the Suze apéritif company to launch an annual limited edition, teaming up with J-C de Castelbajac in 2001 and Christian Lacroix in 2002, is an illustration of this principle, and has positioned Suze as the drink for lovers of arts and literature, revitalising a fundamental aspect of the product which this character brand had ignored for too long.

Third, the brand builds its status through its extensions. The one-product brand has had its day, and the brand is viewed no longer as a product, but rather as a concept. Once created, a concept develops and strengthens itself via extensions. Under this approach, the company acknowledges that the brand extension calls for industrial, logistical or commercial skills that the company itself probably does not possess in the short term. However, there are many other companies that do have the required resources, and can place them at the immediate disposal of the brand.

The strength of the brand is also linked to its geographical extension. Production and distribution licences are necessary in order to understand and penetrate continent-sized countries such as China and India. The product range of a luxury ready-to-wear brand such as Lacoste in Japan or Korea has to take into consideration the physical size of its customers and the specific sports they play. The local licensee is in the best position to develop an extension to the collection which improves the brand's local relevance, while creative and quality control remain in the hands of the talented licence holder.

In sectors eroded by the dictates of concentrated large-scale distribution, the licence provides an opportunity to release some of the pressure. This applies to any sector in which companies have failed to create brands based on strong, intangible values, for this is the one thing that the distributor brands are incapable of copying. The principle operates across the most diverse categories, from spectacle frames to men's footwear. It also applies to SMEs that, lacking the finances to create their own brand, manufacture and distribute under licence. This is how Weight Watchers has expanded its world distribution.

However, it would be a mistake to see licences as nothing more than a godsend to SMEs crushed by the excessive demands of concentrated large-scale distribution. They also represent an opportunity for multinationals making a late entry into a marketplace already dominated by other firms. Creating a new brand makes the risk of competition too great. A better strategy is to use a ready-made one, thus circumventing the barriers to entry. This is what l'Oréal did with Ushuaia, a shampoo brand that has taken the name of a very famous French television programme on Channel 1 based on the Earth, the environment and its preservation. The licence owned by Channel 1 enabled l'Oréal to compete with Unilever and Henkel in the shower gels market, in which it had previously had no presence.

Lastly, the case of the J Dessanges hairdressing and beauty chain provides an illustration of a remarkable use of licensing in its strategy to increase its prestige, status and desirability still further. By using l'Oréal as its licensee to distribute a full range of large-scale distribution products, this upper range or even luxury chain not only created an exceptional source of profits, but also strengthened its brand via the licence. The whole of France is familiar with, and is now able to buy, products from the J Dessange Professional Range (which are, it should be said, the most expensive on hypermarket and supermarket shelves), while at the same time dreaming of one day being able to afford visits to the hairdressing salons, whose spiralling prices are driven by their luxury strategy. After all, in the West, luxury derives its desirability from being well known to all, yet affordable by very few; and Dessange would not have been as desirable without this licence. It is worth pointing out that the company has launched a second, cheaper hairdressing salon brand (Camille Albane) at the same time as releasing a line of large-scale distribution products named 'Camille Albane'. Here, the licence will serve as a motor to accelerate recognition and image, since the number of Camille Albane salons is still small. Hence its low profile.

Ultimately, the very nature of a brand can change as a result of its licences. Cacharel is an example of a licence that went on to become the true centre of gravity of a brand. Cacharel started out as a woman's ready-to-wear brand in the 1970s, positioned to appeal to romantic women. A perfume licence was subsequently granted to l'Oréal, with the launch of Anaïs Anaïs, a worldwide best-seller, followed by Loulou and Eden. In the last five years, four perfumes have been launched to appeal to today's young clientèle: Noa, Nemo, Gloria and Amor Amor. For l'Oréal, the problem with the Cacharel licence is that it is built on nothing: the ready-to-wear business has since vanished into obscurity. This is precisely the opposite of the Armani and Ralph Lauren licences. However, for Cacharel, the situation is very different: thanks to the recognition generated by advertising and the worldwide

distribution of its perfumes, the company is in a position to consider other licences for its brand. In this way, it plans to increase its royalties from 7.6 million euros to 12 million euros over five years (*Les Echos*, 7 July 2003). Cacharel has become a de facto perfume brand and is exploited through various other licences (household linen, lingerie, sunglasses, fine leather goods, scarves): an original business model.

As we can see, the licence can take many forms in the question of how to manage the brand over time: at launch, or during the growth, reinforcement, maturity or relaunch phases. It provides a source of accessible, creative solutions, taking competitors by surprise. It is truly a tool for increasing brand competitiveness.

No such discussion would be complete without considering the fiscal element of the licence, by which many multinationals have shifted profits from their local subsidiaries back to the head office through the mechanism of royalties paid in remuneration for the use of brands, logos, artwork and so on. For example, it is common knowledge that Disneyland Paris is a commercial success but a financial disaster. More than 12 million visitors a year queue up to get into the park, yet given the scale of the initial investment and interest rates, and thus the venture's current liabilities, the project could only start to turn in a profit if the banks were to write off their debts. Despite this, Disney Corporation still draws annual royalties for the concession of its brands and trademarks (all of the Disney characters) to Disneyland Paris.

Yet good fiscal administration knows that licensing may be a way to siphon profit out of a country and pay less taxes: it demands proof that a genuine service is being provided. If royalties are being paid, they should reflect real and tangible added value. Thus a holding that requires its subsidiaries in other countries to pay royalties for the use of a company name and logo may find itself required to produce evidence of the value of the service provided to the subsidiary through the use of this name and logo. Paradoxically, it may be the holding itself that ought to pay for such a service. The holding's name is often unknown to consumers; yet if it is listed on a stock exchange, a visible profile is essential. Unless the holding chooses to produce its own advertising (such as the LVMH group's sponsorship programme), such visibility can only be created further downstream, by appending its name to all its subsidiaries' products.

The logic of co-branding

With increasing frequency, companies today are undertaking joint marketing projects. That is, two different companies pair their respective brands in a collaborative marketing effort (see Table 4.1):

▪ New product launches clearly identify the brands that cooperated to create and market them. Thus Danone and Motta introduced 'Yolka', a yogurt ice cream with packaging that uses both brands to endorse it. Similarly, M&Ms and Pilsbury invented a new cookie concept, and Compaq and Mattel combined their respective expertise to bring out a line of high-tech, interactive toys.

▪ Many line extensions capitalise on a partner brand's equity. Häagen Dazs, for example, launched a Bailey's-flavoured ice cream. In the same vein, Delicious brand cookies now includes a Chiquita banana taste in its line, Yoplait sells a Côte d'Or chocolate cream, and new Doritos ads tout 'the great taste of Taco Bell' or 'Pizza Hut'.

▪ To maximise their brand extension success rates, many companies seek help from other companies' brands, whose established reputation in the new market might prove decisive. Hence Kellogg's co-branded its cereals for health-oriented adults with Healthy Choice.

▪ Co-branding may help usage extension. In Europe, for instance, Bacardi and Coke advertise together. This helps Bacardi's market penetration strategy because the ads demonstrate another way to drink Bacardi. Moreover, Bacardi's status is a powerful endorsement for Coke as the ideal mixer. Thus the pairing also benefits Coke, which wants to remain the number one adult soft drink.

▪ Ingredient co-branding has now become commonplace. Nutrasweet, for example, wanted to bolster its image, so it encouraged and co-financed advertising campaigns by its client brands. In turn, these client brands endorsed Nutrasweet and endowed it with connotations of pleasure and affective values, until now sugar's exclusive domain. The same holds true for Lycra, Woolmark and Intel: these ingredient brands are eager to promote co-branding, both on the product itself and in advertising and promotion.

▪ Image reinforcement may also be an objective of co-branding. In the detergent industry, for instance, famous white goods brands endorse particular detergents, and vice versa. Thus, Ariel and Whirlpool recently launched a co-branded advertising campaign, whose claim is 'The art of washing,' illustrated by a famous 1914 Renoir painting. By these means, Ariel seeks to reinforce its market leader status and gain a more affective image. As for Whirlpool, the campaign bolsters its European launching strategy, and creates a caring image. Orangina and Renault provide two more examples. To get closer to the youth market, Orangina launched specially designed cans, co-branded with famous youth brands (eg Lee Cooper). For its part, Renault launched limited series of its Twingo car, endowing them with famous designer names – Twingo Kenzo, Twingo Easy (Kickers).

▪ Co-branding appears in sales promotions too. Whirlpool, for instance, includes Findus or Bird's Eye coupons in its refrigerator owner's manuals. Similarly, companies find that prizes, such as Club Med vacations, work better than cash awards in promotional consumer contests or sweepstakes.

- Loyalty programmes, increasingly, include co-branding arrangements. Although co-branded loyalty programmes are not new (GM initiated the concept, with co-branded credit cards), a new twist has appeared. That is, corporations are sharing the cost of loyalty programmes between their own brands. For example, Nestlé issued a collector's booklet that includes all of its brands (from KitKat to Buitoni, Perrier and Findus).

- Co-branding may signal a trade marketing operation. For instance, the product may be designed specifically for a distributor and signed by both manufacturer and retailer. Thus, Danone created a special yogurt for Quick, the European fast-food chain that competes against McDonald's. Yoplait did the same for McDonald's.

- Capitalising on synergies among a number of brands is another co-branding objective. Nestlé is a case in point, and it has a number of brands that could gain from a joint marketing action (eg Nestlé's yoghurts, Nescafé, Nesquik, Herta's pork and bacon). To compete against Kellogg's and increase its market share in the breakfast market, therefore, Nestlé launched joint advertising campaigns, showcasing all these brands around a 'healthy breakfast' theme.

Is co-branding new? No. There are the early classics – detergents endorsed by white goods brands, and oil brands endorsed by car manufacturers. Later, in the 1960s, Kellogg's began making Pop Tarts with Smucker's fruits, and in 1967 General Mills' Betty Crocker added Sunkist lemon cake as a line extension. Finally, Grand Marnier flavoured ice creams are well known.

What is new is today's corporate awareness that strategic alliances are essential to acquiring and maintaining a competitive edge. 'Coopetition', a new word coined by Brandenburger and Nalebuff (1996), illustrates this new attitude. The idea: sometimes corporations may have to cooperate with and compete against the same company. From this standpoint, co-branding is an alliance made visible. Furthermore, co-branding involves recognising that the public's knowledge of an alliance is added value.

Even though co-branding has become fashionable, not all alliances should be made visible:

- In the photocopy market, many products sold by, say, Canon are actually made by Ricoh.

- In the car industry, although the Rover company is now owned by BMW, at the product level Rover cars show no BMW insignia. Mercedes and Swatch have created a joint venture to produce and market a revolutionary new car, called Smart, to which each company will add its specific expertise. However, Mercedes is unlikely to put its trademark on the Smart!

- To conquer the iced tea market (despite late entry), Nestlé and Coca-Cola decided to unite against Unilever's Lipton range. Nestlé would create and market the product, and Coca-Cola would distribute it. The product, called Nestea, is not co-branded, though – the Coca-Cola Company gets only a small mention on the back of the packaging.

Table 4.1   Strategic uses of co-branding

| How | Sources of growth | | | |
	Increasing frequency per client	Enhancing proximity to a target	Enhancing perceived quality	Creating a new market
Same product	Co-branded loyalty cards – Air France Amex – Smiles	Image strategy – Orangina Lee Cooper cans – Orangina–Kokaï	Component advertising – Collective (Intel) – Proprietary (Damart)	
Line extension		Limited series – Peugeot 205 Lacoste – Renault Clio Kenzo	Endorsement – Weight Watchers by Fleury Michon – Smart distributed by Mercedes	
New full line		Co-creation – T-Fal Line designed by/for Jamie Oliver – Philips–Alessi		
Value innovation				Co-creation – Danoe (Minute Maid–Danone) – Mattel–Sega

5

Brand identity and positioning

Few brands actually know who they are, what they stand for and what makes them so unique. Classic marketing tools do not help answer such questions. Every advertising campaign is, of course, based on a copy strategy, which varies from one campaign to the other. However, very few brands actually have a brand charter defining the brand's long-term identity and uniqueness. Nor can the answers be found in any graphic guidelines, which often focus only on the brand's outward appearance. Yet understanding what the brand truly represents is not just a graphic exercise. It is an investigation of the brand's innermost substance and of the different facets of its identity. This chapter aims to explore these facets and to suggest the basis for a brand charter.

Modern competition calls for two essential tools of brand management: 'brand identity', specifying the facets of brands' uniqueness and value, and 'brand positioning', the main difference creating preference in a specific market at a specific time.

For existing brands, identity is the source of brand positioning. Brand positioning specifies the angle used by the brand to attack a market in order to grow its market share at the expense of competition.

Defining what a brand is made of helps answer many questions that are asked every day, such as: Can the brand sponsor such and such event or sport? Does the advertising campaign suit the brand? Is the opportunity for launching a new product inside the brand's boundaries or outside? How can the brand change its communication style, yet remain true to itself? How can decision making in communications be decentralised regionally or internationally, without jeopardising brand congruence? All such decisions pose the problem of brand identity and definition – which are essential prerequisites for efficient brand management.

Brand identity: a necessary concept

Like the ideas of brand vision and purpose, the concept of brand identity is recent. It started in Europe (Kapferer, 1986).The perception of its paramount importance has slowly gained worldwide recognition; in the most widely read American book on brand equity (Aaker, 1991), the word 'identity' is in fact totally absent, as is the concept.

Today, most advanced marketing companies have specified the identity of their brand through proprietary models such as 'brand key' (Unilever), 'footprint' (Johnson & Johnson), 'bulls' eyes' and 'brand stewardship', which organise in a specific form a list of concepts related to brand identity. However, they are rather checklists. Is identity a sheer linguistic novelty, or is it essential to understanding what brand are?

What is identity?

To appreciate the meaning of this significant concept in brand management, we shall begin by considering the many ways in which the word is used today.

For example, we speak of 'identity cards' – a personal, non-transferable document that tells in a few words who we are, what our name is and what distinguishable features we have that can be instantly recognised. We also hear of 'identity of opinion' between several people, meaning that they have an identical point of view. In terms of communication, this second interpretation of the word suggests brand identity is the common element sending a single message amid the wide variety of its products, actions and communications. This is important since the more the brand expands and diversifies, the more customers are inclined to feel that they are, in fact, dealing with several different brands rather than a single one. If products and communication go their separate ways, how can customers possibly perceive these different routes as converging towards common vision and brand?

Speaking of identical points of view also raises the question of permanence and continuity. As civil status and physical appearance change, identity cards get updated, yet the fingerprint of their holders always remains the same. The identity concept questions how

time will affect the unique and permanent quality of the sender, the brand or the retailer. In this respect, psychologists speak of the 'identity crisis' which adolescents often go through. When their identity structure is still weak, teenagers tend to move from one role model to another. These constant shifts create a gap and force the basic question: 'What is the real me?'

Finally, in studies on social groups or minorities, we often speak of 'cultural identity'. In seeking an identity, they are in fact seeking a pivotal basis on which to hinge not only their inherent difference but also their membership of a specific cultural entity.

Brand identity may be a recent notion, but many researchers have already delved into the organisational identity of companies (Schwebig, 1988; Moingeon et al, 2003). There, the simplest verbal expression of identity often consists in saying: 'Oh, yes, I see, but it's not the same in our company!' In other words, corporate identity is what helps an organisation, or a part of it, feel that it truly exists and that it is a coherent and unique being, with a history and a place of its own, different from others.

From these various meanings, we can infer that having an identity means being your true self, driven by a personal goal that is both different from others' and resistant to change. Thus, brand identity will be clearly defined once the following questions are answered:

- What is the brand's particular vision and aim?
- What makes it different?
- What need is the brand fulfilling?
- What is its permanent nature?
- What are its value or values?
- What is its field of competence? Of legitimacy?
- What are the signs which make the brand recognisable?

These questions could indeed constitute the brand's charter. This type of official document would help better brand management in the medium term, both in terms of form and content, and so better address future communication and extension issues. Communication tools such as the copy strategy are essentially linked to advertising campaigns, and so are only committed to the short term. There must be specific guidelines to ensure that there is indeed only one brand forming a solid and coherent entity.

Brand identity and graphic identity charters

Many readers will make the point that their firms already make use of graphic identity 'bibles', either for corporate or specific brand purposes. We do indeed find many graphic identity charters, books of standards and visual identity guides. Urged on by graphic identity agencies, companies have rightly sought to harmonise the messages conveyed by their brands. Such charters therefore define the norms for visual recognition of the brand, ie the brand's colours, graphic design and type of print.

Although this may be a necessary first step, it isn't the be all and end all. Moreover, it puts the cart before the horse. What really matters is the key message that we want to communicate. Formal aspects, outward appearance and overall looks result from the brand's core substance and intrinsic identity. Choosing symbols requires a clear definition of what the brand means. However, while graphic manuals are quite easy to find nowadays, explicit definitions of brand identity *per se* are still very rare. Yet, the essential questions above (ie the nature of the identity to be conveyed) must be properly answered before we begin discussing and defining what the communication means and what the codes of outward recognition should be. The brand's deepest values must be reflected in the external signs of recognition, and these must

be apparent at first glance. The family resemblance between the various models of BMW conveys a strong identity, yet it is not *the* identity. This brand's identity and essence can actually be defined by addressing the issue of its difference, its permanence, its value and its personal view on automobiles.

Many firms have unnecessarily constrained their brand because they formulated a graphic charter before defining their identity. Not knowing who they really are, they merely perpetuate purely formal codes by, for example, using a certain photographic style that may not be the most suitable. Thus Nina Ricci's identity did not necessarily relate to the company's systematic adherence to English photographer David Hamilton's style.

Knowing brand identity paradoxically gives extra freedom of expression, since it emphasises the pre-eminence of substance over strictly formal features. Brand identity defines what must stay and what is free to change. Brands are living systems. They must have degrees of freedom to match modern market diversity.

Identity: a contemporary concept

That a new concept – identity – has emerged in the field of management, already well versed in brand image and positioning, is really no great surprise. Today's problems are more complex than those of 10 or 20 years ago and so there is now a need for more refined concepts that allow a closer connection with reality.

First of all, we cannot over-emphasise the fact that we are currently living in a society saturated in communications. Everybody wants to communicate these days. If needed, proof is available: there have been huge increases in advertising budgets, not only in the major media but also in the growing number of professional magazines. It has become very difficult to survive in the hurly-burly thus created, let alone to thrive and successfully convey one's identity. For communication means two things: sending out messages and making sure that they are received. Communicating nowadays is no longer just a technique, it is a feat in itself.

The second factor explaining the urgent need to understand brand identity is the pressure constantly put on brands. We have now entered an age of marketing similarities. When a brand innovates, it creates a new standard. The other brands must then catch up if they want to stay in the race, hence the increasing number of 'me-too' products with similar attributes, not to mention the copies produced by distributors. Regulations also cause similarities to spread. Bank operations, for example, have become so much alike that banks are now unable to fully express their individuality and identity. Market research also generates herdism within a given sector. As all companies base themselves on the same lifestyle studies, the conclusions they reach are bound to be similar as are the products and advertising campaigns they launch, in which sometimes even the same words are used.

Finally, technology is responsible for growing similarity. Why do cars increasingly look alike, in spite of their different makes? Because car makers are all equally concerned about fluidity, inner car space constraints, motorisation and economy, and these problems cannot be solved in all that many different ways. Moreover, when the models of four car brands (Audi, Volkswagen, Seat and Skoda) share many identical parts (eg chassis, engine, gearbox), for either productivity or competitiveness purposes, it is mainly brand identity, along with, to a lesser extent, what's left of each car, which will distinguish the makes from one another.

Diversification calls for knowing the brand's identity. Brands launch new products, penetrate new markets and reach new targets. This may cause both fragmented communications and patchwork images. Though we are still able to discern bits and pieces of the brand here and there, we are certainly unable to perceive its global and coherent identity.

Why speak of identity rather than image?

What does the notion of identity have to offer that the image of a brand or a company or a retailer doesn't have? After all, firms spend large amounts of money measuring image.

Brand image is on the receiver's side. Image research focuses on the way in which certain groups perceive a product, a brand, a politician, a company or a country. The image refers to the way in which these groups decode all of the signals emanating from the

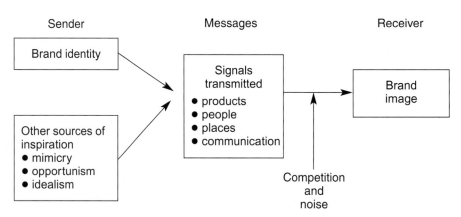

Figure 5.1   Identity and image

products, services and communication covered by the brand.

Identity is on the sender's side. The purpose, in this case, is to specify the brand's meaning, aim and self-image. Image is both the result and interpretation thereof. In terms of brand management, identity precedes image. Before projecting an image to the public, we must know exactly what we want to project. Before it is received, we must know what to send and how to send it. As shown in Figure 5.1, an image is a synthesis made by the public of all the various brand messages, eg brand name, visual symbols, products, advertisements, sponsoring, patronage, articles. An image results from decoding a message, extracting meaning, interpreting signs.

Where do all these signs come from? There are two possible sources: brand identity of course, but also extraneous factors ('noise') that speak in the brand's name and thus produce meaning, however disconnected they may actually be from it. What are these extraneous factors?

First, there are companies that choose to imitate competitors, as they have no clear idea of what their own brand identity is. They focus on their competitors and imitate their marketing communication.

Second, there are companies that are obsessed with the willingness to build an appealing image that will be favourably perceived by all. So they focus on meeting every one of the public's expectations. That is how the brand gets caught in the game of always having to please the consumer and ends up surfing on the changing waves of social and cultural fads. Yesterday, brands were into glamour, today, they are into 'cocooning'; so what's next? The brand can appear opportunistic and popularity seeking, and thus devoid of any meaningful substance. It becomes a mere façade, a meaningless cosmetic camouflage.

The third source of 'noise' is that of fantasised identity: the brand as one would ideally like to see it, but not as it actually is. As a result, we notice, albeit too late, that the advertisements do not help people remember the brand because they are either too remotely connected to it or so radically disconnected from it that they cause perplexity or rejection.

Since brand identity has now been recognised as the prevailing concept, these three potential communication glitches can be prevented.

The identity concept thus serves to emphasise the fact that, with time, brands do eventually gain their independence and their own meaning, even though they may start out as mere product names. As living memories of past products and advertisements, brands do not simply fade away: they define their own area of competence, potential and legitimacy. Yet they also know when to stay out of other areas. We cannot expect a brand to be anything other than itself.

Obviously, brands should not curl up in a shell and cut themselves off from the public and from market evolutions. However, an obsession with image can lead them to capitalise too much on appearance and not enough on essence.

Identity and positioning

It is also common to distinguish brands according to their positioning. Positioning a brand means emphasising the distinctive characteristics that make it different from its competitors and appealing to the public. It results from an analytical process based on the four following questions:

▪ A brand for what? This refers to the brand promise and consumer benefit aspect: Orangina has real orange pulp, The Body Shop is environment friendly, Twix gets rid of hunger, Volkswagen is reliable.

▪ A brand for whom? This refers to the target aspect. For a long time, Schweppes was the drink of the refined, Snapple the soft drink for adults, Tango or Yoohoo the drink for teenagers.

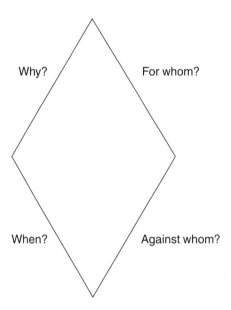

Figure 5.2   Positioning a brand

- A brand for when? This refers to the occasion when the product will be consumed. When a brand says 'we try harder', for instance, it caters to customers with pressing requests; J&B whisky caters to night owls.

- A brand against whom? In today's competitive context, this question defines the main competitor(s), ie those whose clientele we think we can partly capture. Tuborg and other expensive imported beers thus also compete against whisky, gin and vodka.

Positioning is a crucial concept (Figure 5.2). It reminds us that all consumer choices are made on the basis of comparison. Thus, a product will only be considered if it is clearly part of a selection process. Hence the four questions that help position the new product or brand and make its contribution immediately obvious to the customer. Positioning is a two-stage process:

- First, indicate to what category the brand should be associated and compared.

- Second, indicate what the brand's essential difference and *raison d'être* is in comparison to the other products and brands of that category.

Choosing the category to which the product belongs is essential. While this may be quite easy to do for a new toothpaste, it is not so for very original and unique products. The Gaines burger launched by the Gaines company, for instance, was a new dog food, a semi-dehydrated product presented as red ground meat in a round shape like a hamburger. Unlike normal canned pet foods, moreover, it did not need to be refrigerated, nor did it exude that normal open-can smell.

Given these characteristics, the product could be positioned in several different ways, for example by:

- Attacking the canned pet food market by appealing to well-to-do dog owners. The gist of the message would then be 'the can without the can', in other words, the benefits of meat without its inconveniences (smell, freshness constraints, etc).

▌ Attacking the dehydrated pet food segment (dried pellets) by offering a product that would help the owner not to feel guilty for not giving meat to the dog on the basis that it is just not practical. The fresh-ground, round look could justify this positioning.

▌ Targeting owners who feed leftovers to their dogs by presenting Gaines as a complete, nutritious supplement (and no longer as a main meal as in the two former strategies).

▌ Targeting all dog owners by presenting this product as a nutritious treat, a kind of doggy Mars bar.

The choice between these four strategies was made by assessing each one against certain measurable criteria (Table 5.1).

The firm ended up choosing the first positioning and launched this product as the 'Gaines burger'.

What does the identity concept add to that of positioning? Why do we even need another concept?

In the first place, because positioning focuses more on the product itself. What then does positioning mean in the case of a multi-product brand? How can these four questions on positioning be answered if we are not focusing on one particular product category? We know how to position the various Scotch-brite scrubbing pads as well as the Scotch video tapes, but what does the positioning concept mean for the Scotch brand as a whole, not to mention the 3M corporate brand? This is precisely where the concept of brand identity comes in handy.

Secondly, positioning does not reveal all the brand's richness of meaning nor reflect all of its potential. The brand is restricted once reduced to four questions. Positioning does not help fully differentiate Coca-Cola from Pepsi-Cola. The four positioning questions thus fail to encapsulate such nuances. They do not allow us to fully explore the identity and singularity of the brand.

Worse still, positioning allows communication to be entirely dictated by creative whims and current fads. Positioning does not say a word about communication style, form or spirit. This is a major deficiency since brands have the gift of speech: they state both the objective and subjective qualities of a given product. The speech they deliver – in these days of multimedia supremacy – is made of words, of course, but even more of pictures, sounds, colours, movement and style. Positioning controls the words only, leaving the rest up to the unpredictable outcome of creative hunches and pre-tests. Yet brand language should never result from creativity only. It expresses the brand's personality and values.

Table 5.1 How to evaluate and choose a brand positioning

▌ Are the product's current looks and ingredients compatible with this positioning?

▌ How strong is the assumed consumer motivation behind this positioning? (what insight?)

▌ What size of market is involved by such a positioning?

▌ Is this positioning credible?

▌ Does it capitalise on a competitor's actual or latent durable weakness?

▌ What financial means are required by such a positioning?

▌ Is this positioning specific and distinctive?

▌ Is this a sustainable positioning which cannot be imitated by competitors?

▌ Does this positioning leave any possibility for an alternative solution in case of failure?

▌ Does this positioning justify a price premium?

Creative hunches are only useful if they are consistent with the brand's legitimate territory. Furthermore, though pre-test evaluations are needed to verify that the brand's message is well received, the public should not be allowed to dictate brand language: its style needs to be found within itself. Brand uniqueness often tends to get eroded by consumer expectations and thus starts regressing to a level at which it risks losing its identity.

A brand's message is the outward expression of the brand's inner substance. Thus we can longer dissociate brand substance from brand style, ie from its verbal, visual and musical attributes. Brand identity provides the framework for overall brand coherence. It is a concept that serves to offset the limitations of positioning and to monitor the means of expression, the unity and durability of a brand.

Why brands need identity and positioning?

A brand's positioning is a key concept in its management. It is based on one fundamental principle: all choices are comparative. Remember that identity expresses the brand's tangible and intangible characteristics – everything that makes the brand what it is, and without which it would be something different. Identity draws upon the brand's roots and heritage – everything that gives it its unique authority and legitimacy within a realm of precise values and benefits. Positioning is competitive: when it comes to brands, customers make a choice, but with products, they make a comparison. This raises two questions. First, what do they compare it with? For this, we need to look at the field of competition: what area do we want to be considered as part of? Second, what are we offering the customer as a key decision-making factor?

A brand that does not position itself leaves these two questions unanswered. It is a mistake to suppose that customers will find answers themselves: there are too many choices

available today for customers to make the effort to work out what makes a particular brand specific. Communicating this information is the responsibility of the brand. Remember, products increase customer choice; brands simplify it. This is why a brand that does not want to stand for something stands for nothing.

The aim of positioning is to identify, and take possession of, a strong purchasing rationale that gives us a real or perceived advantage. It implies a desire to take up a long-term position and defend it. Positioning is competition-oriented: it specifies the best way to attack competitors' market share. It may change through time: one grows by expanding the field of competition. Identity is more stable and long-lasting, for it is tied to the brand roots and fixed parameters. Thus Coke's positioning was 'the original' as long as it competed against other colas. To grow the business, it now competes against all soft drinks: its positioning is 'the most refreshing bond between people of the world', whereas its identity remains 'the symbol of America, the essence of American way of life'.

How is positioning achieved? The standard positioning formula is as follows:

> For ... (definition of target market)
> Brand X is ... (definition of frame of reference and subjective category)
> Which gives the most ... (promise or consumer benefit)
> Because of ... (reason to believe).

Let us look at these points in detail.

The target specifies the nature and psychological or sociological profile of the individuals to be influenced, that is, buyers or potential consumers.

The frame of reference is the subjective definition of the category, which will specify the nature of the competition. What other brands or products effectively serve the same purpose? This is a strategic decision: it marks out the 'field of battle'. It must not under any circumstances be confused with the objective description of the product or category. For example, there is no real rum market in the UK, yet Bacardi is very popular. This is because it is perfectly possible to drink Bacardi without realising that it *is* a rum: it is the party mixer *par excellence*.

Another example illustrates the strategic importance of defining the frame of reference. Objectively speaking, Perrier is fizzy mineral water. Subjectively, however, it is also a drink for adults. Seen in the light of this field of reference, it acquires its strongest competitive advantage: a slight natural quirkiness. As we can see, the choice of the field of competition should be informed by the strategic value of that field: how big, how fast growing, how profitable? But it also lends the brand a competitive advantage through its identity and potential. Perceived as water for the table, Perrier has no significant competitive advantage over other fizzy mineral waters, even though this market is a very large one. However, when viewed in relation to a field of competition defined as 'drinks for adults', Perrier becomes competitive again: it has strong differentiating advantages. What are its competitors? They include alcoholic drinks, Diet Coke, Schweppes and tomato juice.

The third point specifies the aspect of difference which creates the preference and the choice of a decisive competitive advantage: it may be expressed in terms of a promise (for instance, Volvo is the strongest of all cars) or a benefit (such as, Volvo is the 'safety' brand).

The fourth point reinforces the promise or benefit, and is known as the 'reason to believe'. For example, in the case of the Dove brand, which promises to be the most mois-turising, the reason is that all of its products contain 25 per cent of moisturising cream.

Positioning is a necessary concept, first because all choices are comparative, and so it makes sense to start off by stating the area in which we are strongest; and second because in marketing, perception is reality. Positioning is a concept which starts with customers, by putting ourselves in their place: faced with a

plethora of brands, are consumers able to identify the strong point of each, the factor that distinguishes it from the rest? This is why, ideally, a customer should be capable of para-phrasing a brand's positioning: 'Only Brand X will do this for me, because it has, or it is ...'

No instrument is entirely neutral. The above formula was created by companies such as Kraft–General Foods, Procter & Gamble, and Unilever. It is designed for businesses that base competitive advantage on their products, and works perfectly for the l'Oréal Group which, with its 2,500 researchers worldwide, only ever launches new products if they are of demonstrably superior performance. This fact is then promoted through advertising.

There are cases where the brand makes no promise, or where the benefit it brings could sound trivial. For example, how would you define the positioning of a perfume such as Obsession by Calvin Klein in a way that clearly represented its true nature and origi-nality? It would be wrong to claim that Obsession makes any specific promise to its customers, or that they will obtain any particular benefit from the product apart from feeling good (a property which is common to all perfumes). In reality, Obsession's attrac-tiveness stems from its imagery, the imaginary world of subversive androgyny which it embodies. In the same way, Mugler appeals to young people through its inherently neo-futuristic world, and Chanel stands for timeless elegance.

What actually sells these perfumes is the satisfaction derived from participating in the symbolic world of the brand. The same is true of alcohol and spirits: Jack Daniel's is selling a symbolic participation in an eternal, authentic untamed America. To say that Jack Daniel's is selling the satisfaction of being the finest choice would be a mere commonplace, like the tired old cliché that customers are satisfied at having made a choice that set them apart from the masses (a classic benefit stated by small brands attempting to emphasise their advantage over large ones).

Faced with this conceptual dilemma, there are three possible approaches. The first of these is to define positioning as the sum of every point that differentiates the brand. This has been Unilever's approach: the 60-page mini-opus known as the Brand Key, which explains how to define a brand across the entire world, starts with the phrase: 'Brand Key builds on and replaces the brand positioning statement ...'. There are eight headings to Brand Key:

1. The competitive environment.

2. The target.

3. The consumer insight on which the brand is based.

4. The benefits brought by the brand.

5. Brand values and personality.

6. The reasons to believe.

7. The discriminator (single most compelling reason to choose).

8. The brand essence.

Fundamentally, therefore, this collection forms the positioning of a brand. However, the concept that most closely resembles positioning in the strict sense of the word is referred to here as the 'discriminator'. McDonald's also adopts a similar reasoning (see Figure 5.3). Larry Light defends the idea that positioning is defined when this chain of means–ends is completed (this is a parallel concept to the 'ladder' – moving from the tangible to the intangible):

Our own position is that two tools are needed to manage the brand. One defines the brand's identity, while the other is competitive and specifies the competitive proposition made at any given time in any given market. This is the brand's unique compelling competitive proposition (UCCP). Thus the tool called 'brand platform' will comprise, first, the 'brand identity', that is to say, brand uniqueness and singularity throughout the world and whatever the product. Brand identity has six facets, and is therefore larger than the mere positioning. It is represented by the identity prism. At its centre one finds the brand essence, the central value it symbolises.

Second, the brand platform comprises 'brand positioning': choosing a market means choosing a specific angle to attack it. Brand positioning must be based on a customer insight relevant to this market. Brand positioning exploits one of the brand identity facets. Positioning can be summed up in four key questions: for whom, why, when and against whom? It can be represented in the form of a diamond, the 'positioning diamond' (see Figure 5.2, page 100).

In positioning, the brand/product makes a proposition, plus (necessarily) a promise. The proposition may additionally be supported by a 'reason to believe', but this is not essential.

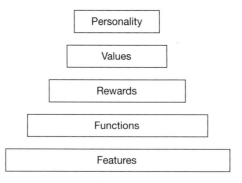

Figure 5.3   The McDonald's positioning ladder
Source: L Light

Marlboro presents its smoker as a man – a real man, symbolised by the untamed cowboy of the Wild West. No support is offered for this proposition; no proof is necessary. It is true because the brand says so. And the more often it is repeated, the more credible it becomes.

In this way the brand's proposition, which forms the basis of the chosen positioning at a given moment in a particular market, may be fuelled by various 'rough edges' contained within the brand's identity:

- a differentiating attribute (25 per cent moisturising cream in Dove, the smoothness and bite of Mars bars, the bubbles of Perrier);

- an objective benefit: an iMac is user-friendly, Dell offers unbeatable value for money;

- a subjective benefit: you feel secure with IBM;

- an aspect of the brand's personality: the mystery of the Bacardi bat, Jack Daniel's is macho, Axe/Lynx is cool;

- the realm of the imaginary, of imagery and meaning (the American Wild West for Marlboro, Old New England for Ralph Lauren);

- a reflection of a consumer type: successful people for Amex;

- 'deep' values (Nike's sports mentality, Nestlé's maternal love), or even a mission (The Body Shop, Virgin and so on).

A few introductory remarks should be made at this juncture.

What is the connection between identity, essence and positioning? Clearly, for existing brands, positioning derives from identity. But it exploits a specific aspect of identity at a given point in time in a given market and against a precise set of competitors. Consequently, at the level of global brands, a unified identity can generate various angles of attack for different markets. For example, Bacardi favours its Carta Blanca white rum product in Northern Europe – a market that consumes very little rum – and thus places its confidence in the party spirit that surrounds the Cuba Libre cocktail drink. However, in its Southern European market it chiefly promotes its mature brown rums, with an almost gastronomic promise.

For 50 years, Mars was little more than a chocolate bar. The essence of Mars is energy; its positioning is as a meal substitute in the UK and as a revitalising snack in Europe.

It is this degree of freedom between identity, essence and positioning that enables a brand to change over time while still remaining itself. Thus, over time (40 years), Evian has changed its slogan and baseline on several occasions, symbolising a change in its angle of market attack: for indeed, the market itself has changed. It has become increasingly saturated with competing brands, the original consumers have aged, and low-cost brands have carved out a significant share. On each occasion, these changes have led to a re-examination of the most compelling advantage, the angle of market attack. There has thus been a shift from 'water for babies' to the purest of waters, water from the Alps, well-balanced water, and now the water of youth (this time round, the campaign is worldwide). However, each positioning has remained true to the essence of the Evian brand, which is more than any other water distinguished by its origins, its composition, its first campaign (babies) and so on. Evian is about life itself.

What is the connection between the positioning of the brand and the positioning of its products? It is true that today's brands are increasingly based on multiple products: Dove was born as a soap in the United States, but now encompasses shampoos, shower gels, moisturising cream, deodorants and so on. The essence of Dove is 'Femininity restored'. But Dove is being launched in a market via one or more products that have to fight for their own space amid a host of competitors:

hence when Dove soap was launched, its positioning was: 'Dove is a premium beauty bar for the mature women, worried about their skin, which won't dry your skin like soap because it contains one quarter moisturising cream.'

This example is a good illustration of how the product's positioning promotes a consumer attribute or benefit, while the parent brand specifies the 'terminal value' that this attribute and benefit enables the consumer to reach. When a brand consists of multiple products, care should be taken to ensure that their respective positioning converges on attaining the same core value (that of the parent brand). If this is not the case, either the product requires repositioning, or the question should be asked whether it is part of the right brand at all.

Table 5.2 illustrates the link between the essence of the l'Oréal Paris parent brand and the positioning of its products such as Elsève and Studio Line.

The six facets of brand identity

A specific set of concepts and tools is needed for tackling the new type of market we are in. When products were rare, the USP (unique selling proposition) was the key concept. As we leave brand image, positioning and personality behind, we enter the modern age

of brand identity and positioning, the former being the source of the latter.

In order to become, or to stay, strong, brands must be true to their identity. The notion of brand image is both volatile and changing: it focuses too much on brand appearance and not enough on brand essence. The notion of brand (or retailer) identity shows that managers are now willing to look beyond the surface for the brand's innermost substance. The identity concept is crucial for three reasons: a brand needs to be durable, to send out coherent signs and products, and to be realistic. It is thus a defence against the risks of an idealised, fickle or opportunistic brand image.

What is brand identity made of? Many ad hoc lists have been proposed in the brand literature, with varying items. One of the sources of this diversity is their lack of theoretical basis. By being too analytical, some of these tools get their users into a muddle.

In fact, leaving the classical stimulus–response paradigm, modern brand communication theory reminds us that when one communicates, one builds representations of who speaks (source re-presentation), of who is the addressee (recipient re-presentation), and what specific relationship the communication builds between them. This is the constructivist school of theorising about communications. Since brands speak about the product, and are perceived as sources of products,

Table 5.2 Product and parent brand positioning

	Elsève Nutri-céramides	Revitalift	Studio Line	l'Oréal
Target market	Women with dry and brittle hair	Women aged over 45	Men and women under 35	All adults, men and women
Market segment	Shampoo	Skin care products	Hair styling products	Beauty and hygiene products
Positioning	Nourishes and repairs damaged hair (consequence)	Reduces wrinkles and firms the skin (consequence)	Enables you to create the hairstyle of your choice (consequence)	Enhances consumers' self image

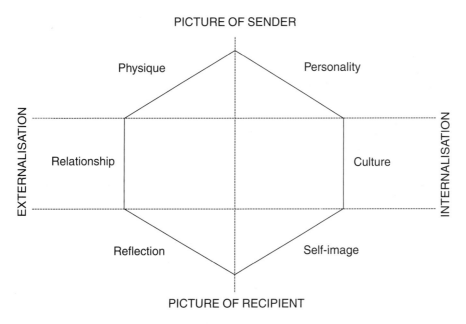

Figure 5.4 Brand identity prism

services and satisfactions, communication theory is directly relevant. As such it reminds us that brand identity has six facets. We call this the 'brand identity prism'.

The identity prism

Brand identity should be represented by a hexagonal prism (see Figure 5.4):

1. A brand, first of all, has physical specificities and qualities – its 'physique'. It is made of a combination of either salient objective features (which immediately come to mind when the brand is quoted in a survey) or emerging ones.

   Physique is both the brand's backbone and its tangible added value. If the brand is a flower, its physique is the stem. Without the stem, the flower dies: it is the flower's objective and tangible basis. This is how branding traditionally works: focusing on know-how and classic positioning, relying on certain key product and brand attributes and benefits. Physical

appearance is important but it is not all. Nevertheless, the first step in developing a brand is to define its physical aspect: What is it concretely? What does it do? What does it look like? The physical facet also comprises the brand's prototype: the flagship product that is representative of the brand's qualities.

That is why the small round bottle is so important each time Orangina is launched in a new country. The bottle used today is the same as it has always been. From the beginning, it has served to position Orangina, thanks to its unique shape and to the orange pulp that we can actually see. Only later was it marketed in standard family-size PET bottles and in cans. In this respect, it is also quite significant that there used to be a picture of the famous Coca-Cola bottle on all Coke cans. It is true that modern packaging tends to standardise brands, making them all clones of one another. Thus, in using the image of its traditional bottle, Coca-Cola aims to remind us of its roots.

There are several delicate issues regarding Coke's physical facet. For example, is the dark colour part of its identity? It is certainly a key contributor to the mystery of the brand. If it belongs to the brand's kernel, key identity traits, then there could never be any such thing as colourless Crystal Coke, even though there is such a thing as Crystal Pepsi. Likewise, would grapefruit Orangina in the classic round bottle be possible?

Many brands have problems with their physical facet because their functional added value is weak. Even an image-based brand must deliver material benefits. Brands are two-legged value-adding systems.

2. A brand has a personality. By communicating, it gradually builds up character. The way in which it speaks of its products or services shows what kind of person it would be if it were human.

'Brand personality' has been the main focus of brand advertising since 1970. Numerous American agencies have made it a prerequisite for any type of communication. Ted Bates had to come up with a new USP (now, the unique selling personality), while Grey had to define brand personality. This explains why the idea of having a famous character represent the brand has become so widespread. The easiest way of creating instant personality is to give the brand a spokesperson or a figurehead, whether real or symbolic. Pepsi-Cola often uses this method, as do all perfume or ready-to-wear brands.

In the prism, brand identity is the personality facet of the source. It should not be confused with the customer reflected image, which is a portrayal of the ideal receiver.

Thus, brand personality is described and measured by those human personality traits that are relevant for brands (see page 28 for an application). Since 1996,

academic research has focused on brand personality, after Aaker's (1995) creation of a so-called 'brand personality scale'. However, despite its wide diffusion among scholars, this scale does not measure brand personality in the strict sense, but a number of intangible and tangible dimensions that are more or less related to it, and that correspond in fact to other facets of a brand's identity (Azoulay and Kapferer, 2003). Recent empirical research (Romaniuk and Ehrenberg, 2003) has corroborated this. For instance, computers or electronic equipment were the categories most associated with the 'up to date' trait, as ice creams were associated with the 'sensuous' trait, and energiser drinks with 'energising'. These data demonstrate that this scale is not measuring personality: a lot of its traits instead measure a physical facet of the brand, while some others relate to the cultural facet of the identity prism, thus creating conceptual confusion in the field. This is because Aaker's conceptualisation of brand personality is inherited from the old habit of advertising agencies of describing as 'brand personality' in their creative briefing and copy strategy everything that was not related to the product's tangible benefits.

3. A brand is a culture. A brand has its own culture, from which every product derives. The product is not only a concrete representation of this culture, but also a means of communication. Here culture means the set of values feeding the brand's inspiration. It is the source of the brand's aspirational power. The cultural facet refers to the basic principles governing the brand in its outward signs (products and communication). This essential aspect is at the core of the brand. Apple was the product of Californian culture in the sense that this state will forever symbolise the new frontier. Apple

was not interested in expanding geographically but in changing society, unlike the brands of Boston and the East Coast. Even in the absence of Apple's founders, everything carried on as if Apple still had some revolutionary plan to offer to companies and to humankind. This fruit symbol is a source of inspiration which is manifested not only in Apple's original products and services, but also in its way of communicating.

Major brands are certainly driven by a culture but, in turn, they also convey this culture (eg Benetton, Coca-Cola, IBM, etc). The cultural facet is the key to understanding the difference between Adidas, Nike and Reebok or between American Express and Visa. In focusing too heavily on brand personality, research and advertising have neglected this essential facet (we will also notice this with retailers: the leading ones are those who not only have a personality, but also a culture). Mercedes embodies German values: order prevails. Even at 260 km/h, a Mercedes has perfect handling. Even though the surrounding landscape may be whizzing by, the Mercedes remains stable and unperturbed. Symmetry governs this brand: the three-box bodywork is a strong physical characteristic of Mercedes. The brand symbol set at the nose-tip of every Mercedes further epitomises this spirit of order.

Countries of origin are also great cultural reservoirs for brands: Coca-Cola stands for America, as does IBM, Nike or Levi's. In other cases, however, they are ignored: thus, Mars is a worldwide brand like Shell. Canon and Technics deny their Japanese origin whereas Mitsubishi, Toyota and Nissan emphasise it. One of the bonuses for Evian exports is that it actually represents a part of French culture. However, this is not the only factor adding to their value. When Americans buy Evian, they are not just paying for the cultural facet but for all six

aspects of these brands, starting with the basic consumer benefit: Evian quenches thirst and promotes health. American style food is McCain's cultural and symbolic reference; for Jack Daniel's, it is the authentic untamed America.

Culture is what links the brand to the firm, especially when the two bear the same name. Because of its culture, Nestlé has not succeeded in conveying the image of a fun and enjoyable food brand. Indeed, its image cannot be fully dissociated from that of the corporation, which is overall perceived as austere and puritan. The degree of freedom of a brand is often reduced by the corporate culture, of which it becomes the most visible outward sign.

Brand culture plays an essential role in differentiating brands. It indicates the ethos whose values are embodied in the products and services of the brand. Ralph Lauren is WASP; Calvin Klein's minimalism expresses a different set of values.

This facet is the one that helps differentiate luxury brands the most because it refers to their sources, to their fundamental ideals and to their sets of values. Culture is also the basis for most bank brands: choosing a bank means choosing the kind of relationship with money one wishes to have. Even though their services are identical (physical facet), the Visa Premier and the American Express Gold cards do not belong to the same cultural system. The American Express Gold card symbolises dynamic, triumphant capitalism. Money is shown, or even flashed about. Visa Premier, on the contrary, represents another type of capitalism, such as the German kind, making steady, quiet progress. Money is handled discreetly yet efficiently, neither gingerly nor flamboyantly.

4. A brand is a relationship. Indeed, brands are often at the crux of transactions and

exchanges between people. This is particularly true of brands in the service sector and also of retailers, as we shall see later. The Yves Saint Laurent brand functions with charm: the underlying idea of a love affair permeates both its products and its advertising (even when no man is shown). Dior's symbolises another type of relationship: one that is grandiose and ostentatious (not in the negative sense), flaunting the desire to shine like gold.

Nike bears a Greek name that relates it to specific cultural values, to the Olympic Games and to the glorification of the human body. Nike suggests also a peculiar relationship, based on provocation: it encourages us to let loose ('just do it'). IBM symbolises orderliness, whereas Apple conveys friendliness. Moulinex defines itself as 'the friend of women'. The Laughing Cow is at the heart of a mother–child relationship. The relationship aspect is crucial for banks, banking brands and services in general. Service is by definition a relationship. This facet defines the mode of conduct that most identifies the brand. This has a number of implications for the way the brand acts, delivers services, relates to its customers.

5. A brand is a customer reflection. When asked for their views on certain car brands, people immediately answer in terms of the brand's perceived client type: that's a brand for young people! for fathers! for show-offs! for old folks! Because its communication and its most striking products build up over time, a brand will always tend to build a reflection or an image of the buyer or user which it seems to be addressing

Reflection and target often get mixed up. The target describes the brand's potential purchasers or users. Reflecting the customer is not describing the target; rather, the customer should be reflected as he/she wishes to be seen as a result of

using a brand. It provides a model with which to identify. Coca-Cola, for instance, has a much wider clientele than suggested by the narrow segment it reflects (15- to 18-year-olds). How can such a paradox be explained? For the younger segment (8- to 13-year-olds), the Coca-Cola protagonists embody their dream, what they want to become and do later on when they get older (and thus freed from the strong parental relationship), ie an independent life full of fun, sports and friends will then become true. Youth identifies with those heroes. As for adults, they perceive them as representatives of a certain way of life and of certain values rather than of a narrowly defined age group. Thus, the brand also succeeds in bringing 30- or 40-year-old consumers to identify with this special way of life. Many dairy brands positioned on lightness or fitness and based on low fat products project a sporty young female customer reflection: yet they are actually purchased in the main by older people.

The confusion between reflection and target is quite frequent and causes problems. So many managers continue to require advertising to show the targeted buyers as they really are, ignoring the fact that they do not want to be portrayed as such, but rather as they wish to be – as a result of purchasing a given brand (or shopping at a given retailer's). Consumers indeed use brands to build their own identity. In the ready-to-wear industry, the obsession to look younger should concern the brands' reflection, not necessarily their target.

All brands must control their customer reflection. By constantly reiterating that Porsche is made for show-offs, the brand has weakened.

6. Finally, a brand speaks to our self-image. If reflection is the target's outward mirror (they are ...), self-image is the target's own

internal mirror (I feel, I am ...). Through our attitude towards certain brands, we indeed develop a certain type of inner relationship with ourselves.

In buying a Porsche, for example, many Porsche owners simply want to prove to themselves that have the ability to buy such a car. In fact, this purchase might be premature in terms of career prospects and to some extent a gamble on their materialisation. In this sense, Porsche is constantly forcing to push beyond one's limits (hence its slogan: 'Try racing against yourself, it's the only race that will never have an end'). As we can see, Porsche's reflection is different from its consumers' self-image: having let the brand develop such a negative reflection is a major problem.

Even if they do not practise any sports, Lacoste clients inwardly picture themselves (so the studies show) as members of an elegant sports club – an open club with no race, sex or age discrimination, but which endows its members with distinction. This works because sport is universal. One of the characteristics of people who eat Gayelord Hauser health and diet products is that they picture themselves not just as consumers, but as proselytes. When two Gayelord Hauser fans meet, they can strike up a conversation immediately as if they were of the same religious obedience. In promoting a brand, one pledges allegiance, demonstrating both a community of thought and of self-image, which facilitates or even stimulates communication.

These are the six facets which define the identity of a brand as well as the boundaries within which it is free to change or to develop. The brand identity prism demonstrates that these facets are all interrelated and form a well-structured entity. The content of one facet echoes that of another. The identity prism derives from one basic concept – that brands have the gift of speech. Brands can

only exist if they communicate. As a matter of fact, they grow obsolete if they remain silent or unused for too long. Since a brand is a speech in itself (as it speaks of the products it creates and endorses the products which epitomise it), it can thus be analysed like any other speech or form of communication.

Semiologists have taught us that behind any type of communication there is a sender, either real or made up. Even when dealing with products or retailers, communication builds an image of its speaker or sender and conveys it to us. It is truly a building process in the sense that brands have no real, concrete senders (unlike corporate communication). Nevertheless, customers, when asked through projective techniques, do not hesitate to describe the brand's sender, ie the person bearing the brand name. Both the physique and personality help define the sender thus built for that purpose.

Every form of communication also builds a recipient: when we speak, everything seems as if we were addressing a certain type of person or audience. Both the reflection and self-image facets help define this recipient, who, thus built, also belongs to the brand's identity. The last two facets, relationship and culture, bridge the gap between sender and recipient.

The brand identity prism also includes a vertical division (see Figure 5.4). The facets to the left – physique, relationship and reflection – are the social facets which give the brand its outward expression. All three are visible facets. The facets to the right – personality, culture and self-image – are those incorporated within the brand itself, within its spirit. This prism helps us to understand the essence of both brand and retailer identities (Virgin, K-Mart, Talbott's).

Clues for strong identity prisms

Identity reflects the different facets of brand long-term singularity and attractiveness. As such it must be concise, sharp and interesting. Let us remember that brand charters are management tools: they are necessary for decentralised

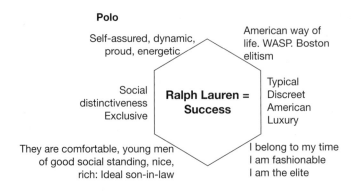

Figure 5.5 Sample brand identity prisms

decision making. They must help all the people working on the brand to understand how the brand is special, in all its dimensions. They must also stimulate creative ideas: they are a springboard for brand activation. Finally, they must help us to decide when an action falls within the brand territory and when it does not.

As a consequence, a good identity prism is recognisable by the following formal characteristics:

▌ There are few words to each facet.

▌ The words are not the same on different facets.

▌ All words have strength and are not lukewarm: identity is what makes a brand stand out.

Too often, in our consulting activity, we notice just the opposite:

▌ Facets are filled up with image traits that derive from the last usage and attitude study. Let us remember that identity is not the same as image. The question is, which of these very many image items does the brand want to identify with?

▌ There is a lot of redundancy between facets, the same words being used many times. This should not be possible. Although related, each facet addresses a different dimension of brand uniqueness.

▌ Most of the words are looking for consensus, instead of looking for sharpness. Consumers do not see the strategies, nor do they see the brand platforms. They do experience the brand by its creations, or at contact, or in its places. To produce ideas, creative people need flesh: an identity with soul, body, forms, a real profile, not an average excellent profile, where nothing really stands out.

Sources of identity

How can we define a brand's identity? How can we define its boundaries, its areas of strength and of weakness? Anyone in charge of managing a well-established brand is perfectly aware that the brand has little by little gained its independence and a meaning of its own. At birth, a brand is all potential: it can develop in any possible way. With time, however, it tends to lose some degree of freedom; while gaining in conviction, its facets take shape, delineating the brand's legitimate territory. Tests confirm this progression: certain product or communication concepts now seem foreign to the brand. Other concepts, on the contrary, seem to be perfectly in tune with the brand, as it both endorses and empowers them, by giving them greater credibility.

Brand image research does not provide any satisfactory answer to these questions. Neither do the purchasers when asked to say what they expect from the brand. Generally, they haven't a clue. At best, they answer in terms of the brand's current positioning. Thus, in the USA, and the UK, there are only very few purchasers of Saab cars: the brand is not widespread though it is expanding its market distribution network. That is why English or American owners see their Saab as unusual rather than foreign. When asked what they expect from the brand, they are, indeed, likely to answer that Saab must continue to design unusual, unique cars. In doing so, they expect that the brand will reinforce their own unusuality and uniqueness which they, as the only few marginal Saab buyers, most definitely

want to demonstrate. Obviously, however, if Saab focused exclusively on such self-centred expectations, its market share would most certainly remain restricted: the economic future of the Saab automotive division would then be under threat.

Consumers and prospects are often asked what their ideal brand would be and what attributes it would need in order to get universally approved. This approach fails to segment properly the expectations and thus to produce any definition other than the average brand ideal. It is typical for consumers to expect banks to provide expertise and attention, availability and competence, proximity and know-how. These expectations are also ideal in the sense that they are often incompatible. In pursuing them, such brands may lose their identity and regress to the average level. In seeking at all costs to resemble the ideal brand described by the consumers (or industrial buyers), brands thus often begin to downplay their differences and look average.

The mistake is to pursue this market 'ideal': it's up to each brand to pursue an ideal of its own. Commercial pressure naturally requires a firm to stay attuned to the market. Of course no brand envies the destiny of Van Gogh, who lived a life of misery and became famous only after he died. Nonetheless, present brand management policy must be reappraised, because unfortunately it still assumes that consumers are the masters of brand identity and strategy. Consumers are actually quite incapable of carrying out such functions. Firms should, therefore, begin to focus more on the sending side of brand marketing and less on the receiving side.

Trying to define the specifics of a brand's substance and intrinsic values naturally requires an understanding of what a real brand is all about. A brand is a plan, a vision, a project. This plan is hardly ever written down (except for the few brands which have a brand charter). It can therefore only be inferred from the marks left by the brand, ie the products it has chosen to endorse and the symbols by which it is represented. Discovering the essence of brand identity, ie of the brand's specific and unique attributes, is the best way to understand what the brand means overall. That is why identity research must start from the typical products (or services) endorsed by the brand as well as on the brand name itself, the brand symbol if there is one, the logo, the country of origin, the advertisements and the packaging. The purpose of all this is to semiologically analyse the sending process by trying to discover the original plan underlying the brand's objectives, products and symbols. Generally, this plan is simply unconscious, neither written anywhere, nor explicitly described. It is simply enacted in daily decisions. Even creators of famous brand names (Christian Lacroix, Yves Saint Laurent, Calvin Klein or Liz Claiborne) are not conscious of it: when asked about the general plan, they are indeed unable to explain it clearly, yet they can easily say what their brand encompasses and what it does not. Brand and creator merge. We have shown (p 120) that, paradoxically, a brand does not really begin to exist until its creator dies. It then shifts from body and instinct to plan and programme.

In conducting research on brand identity, it may well be that we discover several underlying plans. The history of a brand indeed reflects a certain discontinuity in the decisions made by different brand managers over time. Thus Citroen changed when it was purchased by Michelin, and later by Peugeot. A lot of its cars have left no print, although they reached a high level of sales. Rather than attempt the impossible task of making sense of all its products, brand managers must choose the sense that will best serve the brand in its targeted market and focus only on that one. Finally, when dealing with a weak brand, we might not discover any consistent plan at all: in this case, the brand is more like a name stuck on a product than a real player in the field. This situation is very similar to the initial stage of brand creation: the brand has great latitude and almost infinite possibilities, even though it

has already planted the seeds of its potential identity in the memory of the market.

The brand's typical products

The product is the first source of brand identity. A brand indeed reveals its plan and its uniqueness through the products (or services) it chooses to endorse. A genuine brand does not usually remain a mere name printed on a product, ie a mere graphic accessory added on at the end of a production or distribution process. The brand actually injects its values in the production and distribution process as well as in the corollary services offered at the point of sale. The brand's values must therefore be embodied in the brand's most highly symbolic products. This last sentence calls for some attention. Cognitive psychology (Kleiber, 1990; Rosch, 1978; Lakoff, 1987) has taught us that it is easier to define certain categories by simply showing their most typical members than by specifying what product features are required to be considered a member of those categories. As stated in this example, it is difficult to define the 'game' concept, ie to specify the characteristics which could help us identify when we are in a game situation and when we are not. For abstract categories, made of heterogeneous products, the difficulty is even greater. In this case, brands can serve as examples only if they are not exclusively attached to one specific product. What is Danone? When does a product deserve to be named Danone and when does it not? The same holds true for Philips or Whirlpool (see p 262).

Consumers can easily answer this question: they are indeed able to group products in terms of their capacity to typically represent and perfectly exemplify a large spectrum brand. This is shown in Table 5.3, which ranks Danone's most typical products against Yoplait's, according to the consumers' point of view. The most representative product is called the 'brand prototype', not in the sense of an airplane or car prototype, but rather in that of the best exemplar of the brand's meaning. In this respect, in Europe Danone has two prototypical products: plain yoghurt (natural) and the refrigerated dessert cream, Danette. The cognitive psychologists around Rosch (1978) claim that prototypes actually transfer some of their features to the product category (Kleiber, 1990). In other words, if there were no definition of Danone, the public would probably be able to come up with one anyway, by taking a close look at the features of Danone's most representative products. This is what we call prototype semantics. It is true that each brand spontaneously brings to mind certain products – some more than others – and actions as well as a certain style of communication. These prototype products are representative of the various facets of brand identity. According to some cognitive psychologists, such products may convey brand identity, but above all they generate it. In fact, when questioned on Danone's brand image, consumers are more likely to answer in terms of Danone's prototype products.

Historically, it is quite significant that Danone became famous with its plain yoghurt, a product which had previously been sold in pharmacies as natural medication. That is where Danone's health image origi-

nated. And it is now revived by the creation of the Danone Foundation. But the duality of prototypes has also contributed to soften Danone's image: Danette cream dessert signifies hedonism, pleasure and opulence. Danone's brand identity is thus dual: both health and pleasure (Table 5.3). As such it captures the largest share of the market. It leaves the smallest shares to brands that do not provide this balance to consumers: they offer either diet brands or sweet confectionery brands.

If this theory holds, another question comes to mind: just what is it, in a typical product, that conveys meaning? A brand's values only convey meaning if they are at the core of the product. Brand intangible and tangible realities go hand in hand: values drive reality, and reality manifests these values.

For example, the essence of Benetton's brand identity is tolerance and friendship. Colour is more than an advertising theme. It is both the symbolic and industrial basis of the brand. Using a technical innovation, dyeing sweaters at the last minute, Benetton could stay ahead of its competitors through its capacity to meet the latest fashion requirements, ie the new colours of the season. Saying it is not enough though: the toughest part is doing it, and they did. Unlike their

Table 5.3 The most typical products of two mega-brands

Products	Danone	Yoplait
Danette – dessert cream	9.33(1)	4.04
Plain yoghurt (natural)	9.16(2)	8.93(1)
Fruit yoghurt	8.64(3)	8.39(5)
Whole milk yoghurt	8.55(4)	8.88(2)
Liquid yoghurt	8.54(4)	8.51(4)
Whipped yoghurt	8.44(6)	6.76
Petit fromage frais	8.13(7)	7.98
Fromage frais	8.11(8)	8.66(3)
Chocolate/coffee delight with whipped cream	8.07(9)	7.6

Key: grading from 0 to 10 (rank in parentheses if grade >8)

Source: Kapferer and Laurent (1996)

competitors, Benetton innovated by dyeing pullovers after they were made and not before, which helped save lots of precious time. By delaying their decision on the final colours, they were indeed better prepared for the whims of fashion and last-minute changes. If summer turned out to be magenta, Benetton could immediately react and fulfil expectations. However, although it is an essential physical facet of Benetton's brand identity, colour is not just a question of physique (in the identity prism): the colour element also impacts on the other facets of the prism, especially the cultural (which has sometimes made brands look like religions), a key facet when a brand markets to youth.

Colour does not merely serve to position the brand (the colourful brand); it is the outward sign of an ideology, a set of values and a brand culture. In its very slogan 'United Colours of Benetton', as in its posters showing a blond and a black baby, the brand expresses its inspiration and its idealistic vision of a united world in which all colours and races live together in harmony. Colour then ceases to be a mere feature distinguishing the manufacturer. It is a banner, a sign of allegiance. Colour is celebrated by the youth who wears it. Brotherhood and cultural tolerance are the brand's values. That is why the provocative style of Benetton's recent advertising was so disturbing: it was at odds with the brand's past identity.

Orangina is the case of a brand in search of identity, substance and psychological depth. For years Orangina has been represented by both a certain physique and a unique product: a fizzy orange soft drink. What makes it really stand out is that the orange pulp is purposely left in the liquid. This feature was so crucial to the product that an orange-shaped bottle was designed especially for it and its advertising focused on the need to shake the bottle well in order to disperse the pulp and experience the unique and best-tasting flavour of Orangina. The brand further developed its own personality through its TV advertising, which was done in a jumpy, video-clip style so popular among young people. The last stage in this process consisted of conveying the full meaning of the brand and, to do this, the brand/product relationship had to be reversed. Until then, Orangina was merely the name of a soft drink containing orange pulp. Thus, adopting a modern style does not change the structure of this relationship. Today, the basic question is asked the other way around: what are the values that a soft drink containing orange pulp could serve to embody? Coca-Cola's leadership among 13- to 18-year-olds cannot be understood on the basis of physique and personality only. Coca-Cola is a brand that vows an allegiance to the all-American cultural model. Pepsi-Cola embodies the values of the new generation, as does Virgin in the UK, hence its ability to challenge Pepsi's second place in terms of cola market share with its own Virgin Cola. Orangina must find its own source of inspiration as well as the set of values that its product will embody. This search for identity is based on our fundamental axiom of brand management: the truth of a brand lies within itself. It is not by interviewing consumers or consulting oracles of socio-cultural trends that the brand will discover itself. Roots last, trends don't. They indicate the present direction of the wind, the energy that pushes consumption.

The values that Orangina has conveyed since the beginning are: spontaneity, humour and friendliness. Orangina is a healthy, natural drink, a mixture of pulp and water. It symbolises sunshine, life, warmth and energy. All combine latently to give a typical taste and feeling of the South (underlying it all, there is a common model: the Southern model). The word 'model' reminds us that a strong brand is always the product of a certain culture, hence of a set of values which it chooses to represent. In the case of Orangina, Southern values seem to be a potent alternative to the North. Living in the South means both looking at the world and experiencing it in a different way.

The Lacoste shirt now only represents 30 per cent of the company's world sales. It is nonetheless a core product, since it conveys the brand's original values. This shirt was indeed designed at a time when tennis was still being played in long trousers and shirts with rolled-up sleeves. One day (Kapferer *et al* 2002), René Lacoste asked his friend André Gilliet to make a 'false' shirt: something that would look like a shirt (so as not to shock the Queen at Wimbledon), yet would be more practical, ie airy (hence the cotton knit), sturdy and with straight sleeves. Thus right from the beginning, and by accident, René Lacoste's shirt came to embody the individualistic and aristocratic ideal of living both courageously and elegantly. Whatever the occasion, a Lacoste is always appropriate: perfectly suited to the person who, overall, cares to respect proper dress codes, but not in very minute detail. Lacoste is neither trendy nor stuffy: it is simply always appropriate.

All major brands thus have a core product in charge of conveying the brand's meaning. Chanel has its gold chain, Chaumet its pearls and Van Cleef a patented technique of setting stones in invisible slots. These features do not merely characterise the products, they actually embody the brands' values. Dupont, on the other hand, does not seem to have much at stake: it certainly endorses superb lighters, but beyond them is there any dynamic brand concept in evidence? In terms of ready-to-wear clothing, 501 jeans are at the heart of the Levi's brand and of the carefree and unconventional ideology it represents. (On this point, it is significant that the product most frequently worn with a Lacoste

shirt is a pair of jeans.) Conversely, brands such as Newman suffer from never having created a real core product, one exclusive to the brand which conveys its very identity.

These examples serve to illustrate a key principle for brand credibility and durability: all facets of brand identity must be closely linked. Moreover, the brand's intangible facets must necessarily be reflected in its products' physique. This 'laddering' process is illustrated by the Benetton case (Table 5.4). Likewise, Lacoste's identity prism can neither be dissociated from the story behind its famous shirt nor from the values of its emblematic sport, tennis.

The power of brand names

The brand's name is often revealing of the brand's intentions. This is obviously the case for brand names which, from the start, are specifically chosen to convey certain objective or subjective characteristics of the brand (Steelcase or Pampers). But it is also true of other brand names which were chosen for subjective reasons rather than for any apparent objective or rational ones: they too have the capacity to mark the brand's legitimate territory. Why did Steve Jobs and Steve Wozniak choose Apple as their brand name? Surely, this name neither popped out of any creative research nor of any computer software for brand name creation. It is simply the name that seemed plainly obvious to the two creative geniuses. In one word, the Apple brand name conveyed the exact same values as those which had driven them to revolutionise computer science.

Table 5.4   Brand laddering process: the Benetton case

- Physical attribute: colour and price.
- Objective advantage: the latest fashion.
- Subjective advantage: the brand for young people who want to be 'in'.
- Value: tolerance and brotherhood.

What must be explained is why they did not go for the leading name style of that period, ie International Computers, Micro Computers Corporation or even Iris. The majority of entrepreneurs would have chosen this type of name. In deciding to call it Apple, Jobs and Wozniak wanted to emphasise the unconventional nature of this new brand: in using the name of a fruit (and the visual symbol of a munched apple), was it taking itself seriously? With this choice, the brand demonstrated its values: in refusing to idolise computer science, Apple was in fact preparing to completely overturn the traditional human/machine relationship. The machine had, indeed, to become something to enjoy rather than to revere or to fear. Clearly, the brand name had in itself all the necessary ingredients to produce a major breakthrough and establish a new norm (which all seems so obvious to us now). What worked for Apple also worked for Orange. This name reflected the founders' values, which materialised into user-friendly mobile phone services. Similarly Amazon conveys strength, power, richness and permanent flow.

The brand name is thus one of the most powerful sources of identity. When a brand questions its identity, the best answer is therefore to thoroughly examine its name and so try to understand the reasoning behind its creation. In so doing, we can discover the brand's intentions and programme. As the Latin saying goes: *nomen est omen* – a name is an omen. Examining the brand name thus amounts to decoding this omen, ie the brand's programme, its area of legitimacy and know-how as well as its scope of competence.

Many brands make every effort to acquire qualities which their brand name fails to reflect or simply excludes altogether. 'Apple' sounds fun, not serious.

Other brands simply proceed by ignoring their name. The temptation for a brand to just forget about its name is caused by a rash interpretation of the principle of brand autonomy. Experience indeed shows that brands become autonomous as they start to give words specific meanings other than those in the dictionary. Thus when hearing of 'Bird's Eye', no one thinks of a bird. The same is true of Nike. Mercedes is a Spanish Christian name, yet the brand has made it a symbol of Germany. This ability is not only characteristic of brands but also of proper nouns: we do not think of roofing when talking of Mrs Thatcher. Thus, strong brands force their own lexical definitions into the glossaries: they give words another meaning. There is no doubt that this process takes place, but the time it requires varies according to its complexity.

A name – like an identity – has to be managed. Certain names may have a double meaning. The purpose of communication then is to select one and drop the other. Thus, Shell naturally chose to emphasise the sea-shell meaning (as represented in its logo) rather than the bomb-shell one! Likewise, the international temporary employment agency, Ecco, has never chosen to exploit the potential link with economy suggested in its name. On the other hand, it does use its name as a natural means to reinforce its positioning in the segment of high quality service: its advertising cleverly plays upon the theme of duplication – those stepping in from Ecco will of course perfectly duplicate and echo those stepping out of the company.

Generally speaking, it is best to follow the brand's overall direction as well as its underlying identity, whenever possible. All Hugo Boss is entirely contained in that one short, yet international, name – Boss: it conveys aggressive success, professional achievement, conformity and city life. Rexona is a harsh name all over the world because of its abrupt R and its sharp X: thus it implicity promises efficiency.

Brand characters

Just as brands are a company's capital, emblems are a brand's capital equity. An emblem serves to symbolise brand identity through a visual figure other than the brand name. It has many functions such as:

- To help identify and recognise the brand. Emblems must identify something before they signify anything. They are particularly useful when marketing to children, since the latter favour pictures over text, or when marketing worldwide (every whisky has its own emblem).

- To guarantee the brand.

- To give the brand durability – since emblems are permanent signs – thereby enabling the company to capitalise on it. Thus Hermès' legendary horse is the common emblem of 'Equipage', 'Amazone' and 'Calèche'.

- To help differentiate and personalise: an emblem transfers its personality to the brand. In doing so, it enhances brand value. But it also facilitates the identification process in which consumers are involved.

Animal emblems are often used to perform this last function. Animals symbolise the brand's personality. It is quite significant, in this respect, that both the Chinese and Western horoscopes represent human characters by animals. The Greek veneration of animals reflected their conception of a certain spiritual mystery. The animal is not only allegorical of the brand's personality but also of the psychological characteristics of the targeted public. Wild Turkey symbolises the independent mind and free spirit of the drinker of this particular bourbon. The red grouse, symbol of Scotland and a rare bird, has been chosen as the emblem of Famous Grouse whisky in order to reflect the aesthetic ideal of its consumers.

Emblems epitomise more than one facet of brand identity; that is why they play such a crucial role in building identity capital. The world of whisky is filled with wild, rare, untameable animals that symbolise the natural, pure and authentic character of this alcohol. The associated risk perceived by the customer is thus reduced. They also demonstrate, as we saw above, the brand's personality: the red grouse is known for its noble gait and carriage; the wild turkey is a stubborn and clever bird symbolising independence in the US. These animals also represent the brand's value and culture facet, either because they are geographical symbols (the grouse for Scotland, the wild turkey for the USA) or because they refer to the brand's essence itself.

Many other brands have chosen to be represented by a character. A character can, for example, be either the brand's creator and endorser (Richard Branson for Virgin) or an endorser other than the creator (Tiger Woods for Nike). It can also be a direct symbol of the brand's qualities (Nestlé's bunny rabbit, Mr Clean, the Michelin bibendum). Some characters serve to build a certain relationship and an emotional, prescriptive link between the brand and its public (Smack's frog, Esso's tiger). Others, finally, serve as brand ambassadors: though Italian, Isabella Rossellini embodied the type of French beauty that Lancôme promises to all women.

Such characters say a lot about brand identity. They were indeed chosen as brand portraits, ie as the brand's traits, in the etymological sense. They do not make the brand, yet they define the way in which the brand brings to reality its traits and features.

Visual symbols and logotypes

Everybody knows Mercedes' emblem, Renault's diamond, Nike's swoosh, Adidas' three stripes, Nestlé's nest, Yoplait's little flower and Bacardi's bat. These symbols help us to understand the brand's culture and personality. They are actually chosen as such: the corporate specifications handed over to graphic identity and design agencies mainly pertain to the brand's personality traits and values.

What is important about these symbols and logos is not so much that they help identify the brand but that the brand identifies with them. When companies change logos, it usually means that either they or their brands are about to be transformed: as soon as they no longer identify with their past style, they want to start modifying it. Some companies proceed otherwise: to revitalise their brands and recover their identity, they milk their forlorn brand emblems for the energy and aggressiveness they need in order to be able to change. Just as human personality can be reflected in a signature, brand essence and self-image can be reflected in symbols.

Geographical and historical roots

Identity is born out of the early founding acts of a brand. Among these one finds products, channels, communications and also places.

The identity of Swissair is intimately associated with that of Switzerland. The same is true of Air France abroad or of Barclay's Bank. Outside of the United States, the Chrysler brand represents the cars of the New World. Certain brands naturally convey the identity of their country of origin. Others are totally international (Ford, Opel, Mars, Nuts). Others still have made every possible effort to hide their national identity: Canon never refers to Japan, while Technics has adopted an Anglo-Saxon identity though the company is Japanese.

Some brands draw their identity and uniqueness from their geographical roots. It is a deliberate choice on their part. What advantage did Finlandia expect to gain, for example, by launching a premium vodka? As its name suggests, Finland is the country where the earth ends – a cold, austere, unspoilt, remote land, where the sun scrapes the ground. This spontaneous vision both feeds and supports the creation of an extremely pure water and vodka.

Brands can benefit from the values of their native soil. Apple has thus adopted the Californian values of both social and technological progress and innovation. There is a touch of alternative culture in this Californian brand (which is not true of all Silicon valley brands, such as Atari). IBM epitomises East coast order, power and conservatism. Evian's symbolism is linked to the Alps, or rather to the image of the Alps, as projected by the company. Roots are crucial for alcoholic drinks too: Glenfiddich means Deer Valley, Grouse is the fetish bird of Scotland. The Malibu drink, on the contrary, has never defined its origin: only recently has its advertising specified that its home was the Caribbean.

The brand's creator

Brand identity cannot be dissociated from the creator's identity. There is still a lot of Richard Branson in Virgin's brand identity. Inspired by its creator, Yves Saint Laurent's brand identity is that of a feminine, self-assured and strong-minded 30-year-old woman. The YSL brand celebrates the beauty of body, of charm, of surrender to romance, and is flavoured with a hint of ostentatious indecency. Paloma Picasso's flaming Mediterranean looks permeate her perfume products and explain why she is so successful in South America, in the US Sun Belt (Florida, Texas, California) and in Europe (Spain, France, Germany). The relationship between a brand and its creator can last far beyond the death of the creator. Chanel is a good example of this: Karl Lagerfeld does not try to imitate the Chanel style, but to interpret it in a modern way. The world is changing: the brand's values must be respected, yet adapted to modern times. The same holds true for John Galliano and Dior, or Tom Ford for Gucci.

When its creator passes away, the brand becomes autonomous. The brand is the creator's name woven into a set of values and a pattern of inspiration. Thus, it cannot be used by another member of the creator's family. This was confirmed in court in 1984 when Olivier Lapidus, son of the founder of the Ted Lapidus ready-to-wear brand, was refused the right to use the word 'Lapidus'. Even blood kinship thus does not entitle one to use brand name equity in the same sector.

Advertising: content and form

Let us not forget that it is advertising which writes the history of a brand, retailer or company. Volkswagen can no longer be dissociated from the advertising saga that helped it develop. The same is true of Budweiser and Nike. This is only logical: brands have the gift of speech and they can only exist by communicating. Since they are responsible for announcing their products or services, they need to speak up at all times.

When communicating, we always end up saying a lot more than we think we do. Any type of communication implicitly says something about the sender, the source (who is speaking?), about the recipient we are apparently addressing and the relationship we are trying to build between the two. The brand identity prism is based on this hard fact.

How is this implicit message slipped between the lines and conveyed to us? Simply through style. In these times of audio-visual media, a 30-second TV ad says just as much about the style of the brand sending the message and of the recipient apparently being targeted as about the benefits of the product being announced. Whether or not they are managed, planned or wanted, all brands acquire a history, a culture, a personality and a reflection through their cumulative communications. To manage a brand is to proactively channel this gradual accumulation of attributes towards a given objective rather than just to sit and wait to inherit a given brand image.

Yet what is inherited can also be a boon. Volkswagen tightly controls its marketing, but entirely delegates its communications to its agency. Thus all Volkswagen cars are launched under the same name, no matter what the country. However, the Volkswagen style is

definitely a legacy of the advertising genius, Bill Bernbach: indeed, he succeeded in making the entire DDB network follow the stylistic guidelines which he had defined. It is thus through the memorable VW Beetle campaigns that both the brand's specific style and scope of communication began to take shape.

Both in its advertising films and spots, the VW brand has always freely played with the motifs of both the cars and the logo. The brand's style of expression is one of humour and humour only, as shown in its attitude of self-derision, false modesty and impertinence towards competitors as well as in the use of paradox. Volkswagen's advertisements have thus built a powerfully intimate relationship with the public. They appeal to consumers' intelligence, reflecting the image of the pragmatic people who prefer functional features to fancy ones.

The paradox of Volkswagen is that it has always managed to speak of a quite prosaic product in an almost elitist, yet friendly and humorous style. This has enabled Volkswagen to introduce minor modifications as major developments. The selling points put across in the adverts are based on facts and on certain values, which the brand has always conveyed, such as product quality, durability, weather-resistance, reliability, reasonable prices and good trade-in value.

But this advertising style, though created outside the Volkswagen company, was not just artificially added to the brand. Who could possibly have created such a monstrous car with an insect name (the Beetle), which so completely defied the trends in the US automobile world at the time? It could only have been an extremely genuine, honest creator, with a long-term vision. To encourage its own customers to buy, the brand had not only to flatter their ego and intelligence but also to acknowledge them for breaking away – if only this one time – from the stylistic clichés of North American cars. In a tongue-in-cheek style, the brand manages to convey its values and its culture. The Volkswagen style *is* Volkswagen, even though it was created by Bernbach.

Brand essence

Many companies and advertising agencies use the phrase 'brand essence'. The analysis of this practice reveals that it stems from a desire to summarise the identity and/or the positioning. Some would say that the essence of Volvo is security (its positioning), others would say that the essence of Volvo is 'social responsibility' (a high-order typical Scandinavian value), from which is derived the desire to build the most secure as well as recyclable cars. Similarly, some speak of Mars' essence as 'bite and smoothness, with caramel and chocolate', others as 'vitality and energy'. In essence, the concept of 'brand essence' asks in an atemporal and global way: what do you sell? What *key value* does the brand propose, stand for?

Part of the discussion lies in the notion of value: some speak of benefit, others of higher order ideals, such as those revealed in a classical means–ends questionnaire called 'laddering' (see the Benetton example, page 117). In fact it is possible that for some brands, essence is intimately tied to the product experience, whereas it is not true for others.

Let us look at an example. What is Nivea's essence? To answer one needs to first specify Nivea's identity. As we have seen in this chapter, we should look to the prototype to find the key values of any brand. In Nivea's case, this is Nivea cream and its characteristic blue box – the means via which the brand gains entry to each country, and thus the brand's underpinning factor. More than a mere product, Nivea cream in its round box constitutes one of the first acts of love and protection that a mother performs for a baby. After all, doesn't everyone remember the typical scent, feel, softness and sensuality of this white cream, reinforced by the Nivea

blue? The blue box is thus the brand's true foundation in all senses:

▌ It is the first Nivea product people encounter in their life, from the age of four.

▌ It bears the Nivea values.

▌ It constitutes the first sales of Nivea in every country where the brand is established.

So what is the significance of this blue colour and this flagship moisturising cream, the cornerstones of the whole edifice?

Remember that blue is the favourite colour of more than half the population of the western world, including the United States and Canada. It is the colour of dreams (the sky), calm (the night), faithful, pure love (the Virgin Mary has been depicted in blue since the 12th century), peace (UN peacekeepers) and the simple, universal appeal of blue jeans (Pastoureau, 1992). The cream's whiteness is the white of purity, health, discretion, simplicity and peace (a white flag). As for the moisturising cream itself, it adds water to the skin, an essential injection of a human aspect to one's natural environment.

This reveals the values of the brand. Nivea's philosophy penetrates to its very core: a view of life founded on human coexistence, and containing strong moral values such as confidence, generosity, responsibility, honesty, harmony and love. In terms of competence, it stands for safety, nature, softness and innovation. Lastly, it sells itself as timeless, simple and accessible, at a fair price. And this is the way in which the Nivea brand itself is identified worldwide. Even if at any given moment, within a particular group, segment or country, these values are not perceived, they remain the values that form the basic identity of the brand. What does Nivea sell in essence? Pure love and care.

Other examples of brand essence directly derived from the early prototype of the brand are:

▌ masculine attractiveness (Axe/Lynx dual brand);

▌ untamed America (Jack Daniel's);

▌ family preservation (Kodak);

▌ love and nutrition (Nestlé);

▌ sign of personal success (Amex).

Do we need the brand essence concept? It has a managerial utility: trying to summarise the richness of an identity. As such it is easier to convey. Its inconvenience is that the meaning of words is highly culturally specific. Thus a word as simple as 'natural' does not evoke the same things in Asia and in Europe, and within Europe there are huge differences between southern countries and northern countries. As such, to understand a brand one really needs the full identity prism, where words acquire their meaning in relationship with others.

Practically, the brand essence can be written in the middle of the brand identity prism or on the top of the brand pyramid, relating essence, values, personality and attributes (see page 112).

6

The logic of retail brands

Distributors' or retailers' own-label brands are on the rise everywhere. Having been restricted for so long to the mass consumption sector, they now form part of the competitive environment in all sectors: automobile equipment, agricultural cooperatives, pharmacy groups and so on. For so long merely the cheapest products, they have now become innovators which are quick to offer consumers products that keep pace with the latest trends in society (organic foods, sustainable growth, fair trade, balanced diets, luxury foods, adventure and so on), following in the footsteps of the Monoprix and Sainsbury's brands. In many cases, these have become inseparable from the distributor itself. The Body Shop sells only under a distributor's brand, just like Gap, whose success began with the establishment of a 100 per cent Gap products range, making it move from being Levi's number one client to its number one competitor. Decathlon, Ikea, Habitat, Roche, Bobois are both stores and brands; in fact since they do much more than distribution, they invent the product concepts and design, so they are full store brands. In the office furnishings business to business sector, Office Depot and Guilbert (direct sales and delivery) have built their success on a distributor's brand. And is there not something paradoxical about the way that the same big companies that complain about the rise of distributors' brands then buy the Niceday brand from their Guibert supplier instead of opting for products branded 3M, Esselte Dymo, Stabilo, Pentel, Bic and so on? In short, they are criticising consumers for doing what they are themselves doing: managing their spending.

The changing nature of retail brands

Academic studies have long failed to pay sufficient attention to distributors' brands. With the producer's brand being considered as the only point of reference, distributors' brands were thought of as 'non-brands', attracting price-sensitive customers. Furthermore, the scale of the problem was different in Europe from the United States where, with the exception of Wal-Mart, no single retailer/ distributor dominated: distribution is regional, and the national brands still have power in the distribution channel. This is why distributors' brands have long been perceived in the United States as low-cost, low-quality alternatives, an assessment that failed to take the full measure of the phenomenon. However, this situation too has recently changed, as can be seen from the recent interview with Russ Klein, the Executive Director of 7-Eleven, the store that invented the convenience store concept some 76 years ago: 'Private label has changed to the point where retailers are using it as the premium brand in some cases' (*Marketing Management*, Jul–Aug 2003, p 19).

Throughout the world, the distributor's brand is often becoming the only true competitor to the producer's brand. Hypermarket or supermarket shelves are divided into three parts, holding producers' brands, the store brand and the lowest-price products. This further heightens the urgency to act (Quelch and Harding, 1996), and positions the producer's brand firmly and squarely on its pillars of differentiation: innovation and quality on the one side, emotive added value on the other.

Distributors' brands are found in the richest, most developed countries, and are thus not a phenomenon linked to low income. In Switzerland – which has one of the highest per capita incomes in the world – the leading food brand is Migros, well ahead of Nestlé. This is hardly surprising, as Migros is a dominant multiple retailer: every village has its own Migros store, and Migros – without exception – sells only Migros products. The citizens of Germany, Europe's most powerful country, enjoy their luxury cars, but they buy most of their food from the Aldi and Lidl hard-discounters, which also – without exception – sell only exclusive private-label products. It is hard to imagine that Germans would buy low-quality goods. Loblaw's, a Canadian chain, has built its reputation on its President's Choice brand. The story is the

same at Carrefour, Albert Heijn in the Netherlands and Ika in Scandinavia.

Distributors now manage their brand portfolios as part of an overall vision for the category and for the store. They have to choose their 'brand mix' for each category segment, and make a decision for each of them with regard to the type of brand to offer: producer's or distributor's brand? The latter may offer either ranges of economical products, a value-for-money line (sometimes under the name of the distributor itself), or own brands (private labels) offering more flexibility in terms of positioning – perhaps even genuinely premium positioning.

From a managerial point of view, distributors' brands are, broadly speaking, brands like any other. They have all the features of a brand, but in addition they have to find their place within the marketing mix of a distributor, to whom they now represent a key component of identity, differentiation and loyalty generation (although their effect on customers' loyalty to the store has not yet been proven – Corstjens and Lal, 2000). They generally use price as the driving force behind their own marketing mix, even when they are positioned in a premium segment.

For consumers in mature countries, distributors' brands are perceived as genuine brands, with their attributes of high profile and image always combined with an attractive price. Over time, some distributors' brands are able to generate the typical brand effect, as shown by Table 6.1, which looks at the UK, for many years a leader in this field. According to the Brandz study, the consumer's proximity to the brand moves from a feeling of presence (recognition, familiarity) to a feeling of relevance ('it's for me') to the perception of performance and a clear advantage, and ultimately to a genuine affective attachment. It is interesting to note that two distributors' brands have made it into the top ten UK brands studied by Brandz: Marks & Spencer and Boots.

Table 6.1   Brand attachment: distributors' and producers' brands

1	Gillette	57	7	Nescafé	39
2	BT	56	8	Heinz	39
3	Pampers	53	9	Kellogg's	39
4	Marks & Spencer	42	10	Boots	37
5	McDonald's	42	11	Colgate	32
6	BBC	40	12	Royal Mail	32

Source: Brandz (UK)

Why have a retail brand?

For an answer to the question, 'Why have distributor's brands?', we should look not to the consumer, but to the industry: the distributors and producers themselves.

In the mass consumption sector, the early distributors' brands are almost always born of a conflict between the distributor and the producer; dissatisfied with the poor treatment it receives, the distributor has its goods produced elsewhere, either under its own name or as a private label. The atmosphere of conflict persists, particularly since – in Europe, for example – brands now depend on a very small number of distributor clients (four) for 60 per cent of their sales. In some sections, the concentration is even higher: Decathlon, as we have seen, accounts for more than 10 per cent of Nike's sales in Europe. Furthermore, the rise of these distributor's brands parallels the worldwide growth of distributors, leading them to encounter the expectations of quality products at lower prices that are prevalent in emerging countries (Brazil, Eastern Europe, Russia, India and so on).

Naturally, it is up to consumers to decide in which categories they are the most tempted to buy distributors' brands: those in which they have a low degree of involvement (Kapferer and Laurent, 1995). Remember that brands exist wherever customers perceive a high risk in purchasing; conversely, where they see no risk, they are tempted by the distributor's brand product, particularly if they consider that distributor to have a good reputation and

an image of quality and service. For example, the butter category is now dominated by distributors' brands, but not the new low-fat butters – as though that particular product development were a source of concern, and customers need the reassurance of a well-known brand name. In all cases where the consumer expects superior performance (for example, cosmetics), the producer brand wins out. The same is true wherever the product has assumed the status of a symbol or 'badge'; again, the distributor's brand fails to make an impression unless the store bag itself is a badge (like Abercrombie & Fitch).

Now, emboldened by satisfactory past experiences, consumers are taking the plunge: distributors' brands exist for PCs, 120-euro bicycles, hi-fi units and domestic appliances. Consumers may want a Sony or Thomson television for their living room, but in the kitchen or a child's bedroom they are less involved: they may opt for a First Line (the hi-fi brand from Carrefour). The same is true in home computing. Dell is a product assembler, and sells under its distributor's brand. However, its products are guaranteed 'Intel inside'.

In reality, the distributor's brand phenomenon is based on supply, not demand. Whenever distribution is concentrated, there is no other way of increasing ROI (return on investment) but to integrate the supply vertically.

On the one hand, in the previously independent retail sector, as trade concentration progresses, the first step is to buy in bulk to reduce purchasing costs. Next, a collective commercial store name is applied. But if there is to be a collective name, there must also be a collective range: this forms the heart of the stores' product range. The logical last step is to create a distributor's brand to name this kernel product range.

On the other hand, bear in mind that over time, distribution becomes concentrated as competing channels or types of business are absorbed, followed by competitors themselves. In this way, in Europe, small traders have vanished altogether in many categories, having been swamped by the hypermarkets and discounters; this was how the distributors first started to grow. Having reached the end of this path, distributors have turned to the international market and cost reductions: hence the fashion for cost-cutting techniques such as ECR (efficient consumer response), trade marketing and so on. The final stage is the distributor's brand as a way of improving ROI:

▎ because distributor's-brand products give the distributor a better margin;

▎ because the fear of seeing the distributor's brand increasing its in-store presence leads producers to assign even bigger margins in selling their own brands in the stores, increasing the distributor's bargaining power, as the recent study by Pauwels and Srinivasan (2002) confirms.

▎ because, if managed correctly, it is a key long-term method of obtaining differentiation and customer loyalty (once short-term techniques such as reduced-price coupons and tickets have been adopted by all competitors and parity has thus been established) (Corstjens and Lal, 2000).

The business logic of retail brands

In a competitive market, the distributor's brand is a logical stage in the growth of a distributor. It satisfies the need to maintain ROI once all other approaches have been

exhausted. Alternatively, it may have been the key differentiating component from the outset (as in the case of Gap, Decathlon and so on). Let us look again at the principle of ROI in order to understand why the distributor's brand is an advisable step at a certain stage in a distributor's growth.

$$\text{ROI} = \frac{\text{Net margin} = \text{Gross margin} - \text{Costs}}{\text{Stock rotation} = \text{Sales per square metre/}} \times$$
$$\text{Investment per square metre}$$

What does a distributor do when it wants to increase ROI from 20 per cent to 22 per cent (an increase of 10 per cent)? Suppose that the distributor in question is a hypermarket, with a net margin of 2 per cent and a rotation of 10. Two possible options are available: either to increase sales by 10 per cent per square metre of sales area (giving a rotation of 11), or to increase net margin by 2 per cent to 2.2 per cent through selling private labels and demanding even more price concessions from brand producers, or a share of the profits from their promotional campaigns (which ultimately amounts to the same thing).

This second option is a much easier way of increasing ROI: everyone knows how hard it is in a mature market to increase turnover per square metre. This is why all distributors are choosing, or will choose, the distributor's brand if they wish to make optimal profits.

How retail brands grow

Once the decision has been taken, there are two identifiable stages in the process of creating a mature distributor's brand business:

The first stage: imitating the leading brand

The first stage is to take market share from the big brands by allocating more space to one's own distributor's brand and increasing the average price of the major brands to attract consumers to the distributor's brand (Pauwels and Srinivasan, 2002). The range is constructed reactively: gaps are identified in the brand producers' ranges, and then filled. The distributor also examines its competitors' distributor's brand ranges and sets about imitating them, producing the same products typically supplied by its other competitors. By means of this emulative method, a distributor's brand core offer is constructed. We should add that this is also typically a phase during which the distributor chooses to imitate, trait for trait, the packaging of the brand products (generally the category leaders) that it is targeting: this so-called 'copycat' approach borders on trademark infringement, and sometimes gives rise to court cases brought by producers complaining of either an infringement of their brand copyright or unfair competition (see page 139). In most cases, however, disputes – arising from the over-zealousness of the designers – are resolved amicably. Furthermore, the distributor takes refuge in the fact that the issue is not brand codes, but rather category codes established by the category leading brand.

The aim of this approach (the imitation of the essential attributes of branded product packaging) is to confuse inattentive consumers into choosing the distributor's brand product instead of the big-brand product – and then, once the consumers have

hopefully been convinced that the distributor's product is a good one, to retain their loyalty.

It has actually been calculated that for mass-consumption products sold in hypermarkets, consumers spend seven seconds on each purchase: speed matters to them. When there is a strong resemblance between packaging, a hurried buyer with an average attention span can be confused. Our research into the imitation of brand packaging (trade dress) by distributors' products (Kapferer and Thoenig, 1992) has shown that confusion rates could reach 42 per cent. The factors of confusion were, in decreasing order of importance:

1. Colour (half of the confusion effect).

2. Packaging shape.

3. Key designs.

4. Name, typography and so on.

As demonstrated by the results in Table 6.2, in tests where pairs of products are arranged in decreasing order of resemblance, the stronger the perceived resemblance in trade dress, the more the consumer infers that the producer is one and the same – and the more confidence the copy inspires.

Another study has shown that that the discovery of a quality distributor's brand created a less positive attitude towards the leading brand. Zaichkowsky and Simpson (1996) conducted consumer trials with Lora

Table 6.2   How distributors' copycat brands influence quality perceptions

Percentage of consumers who think: Original/copycat (product):	They are made by the same manufacturer			I trust the private label
	Surely	Probably	Total	Yes
1 Panzani/ Padori (pastas)	39	41	80	78
2 Martini/Fortini (spirit)	30	31	61	56
3 Amora/Mama (ketchup)	21	46	67	62
4 Ricore/Incore (coffee)	16	17	33	38

Source: Kapferer, 1995

Cola, a distributor's brand imitating Coca-Cola. The taste of the product was manipulated in such a way as to ensure that one section of consumers would find it very good, while others would find it bad. Among the latter group, the Coca-Cola evaluation, measured twice (before and after trying Lora Cola) did not change (5.41 versus 5.71). However, it did fall significantly in the case where consumers liked the taste of the copy (falling from 5.67 to 5.22, or a drop of –0.45).

The second stage

In the second stage, the goal of the distributor's brand is to capture market share from competitors. It becomes a genuine instrument of strategic differentiation, expressing the identity, values and positioning of the store itself. It should generate loyalty not just to itself (through its effect on the share of requirements), but also – more challengingly – to the store.

During this stage, the brand's power and management is no longer in the hands of the purchaser alone. The purchaser strives for an optimal mix of purchase and resale conditions. Making the brand into an instrument for shaping identity and positioning presupposes a genuine marketing strategy, and also the construction of a range that reflects the brand's ability to communicate the distributor's own values and identity. Here, the trick is to effect the shift from a purchase driven by confusion to one driven by preference.

In this situation, the distributor's brand holds key positioning importance, as its contents – its products – express the values of the (distributor's) brand. This is the way in which it is advertised, and it must itself innovate if it is to communicate a message about more than just a low price. It is no longer simply a way of filling a price gap in the market; it offers one or more components of added value based on its ingredients, packaging, traceability, concept and so on.

This is generally the point at which brands appear whose price is no longer the sales argument, but the concept itself. Often they have no equivalent among the branded producers, and for one simple reason: producers specialise in particular categories, products or business areas. For example, what producer could construct an umbrella brand around the concept of 'Pleasures of yesterday' – bringing together more than 100 of the best products from every region in the country, with rediscovered recipes and methods of manufacture? Nestlé would be incapable of doing this, as it does not produce oils, jams, biscuits and the like. The same is true of Unilever, Philip Morris and Danone. Carrefour, however, can: all it needs to do is promote the concept among small regional companies in each country where it operates.

Success factors of retail brands

As always, the rise of a new brand is also the result of the actions (or lack of action) taken by the competition. For example, distributors' brands have strong market share in the cosmetics sector in Germany. The reverse is true in France, and yet both are among the more highly developed countries. Setting aside any possible differences between the two countries' relative conceptions of beauty, one explanation lies in an analysis of the competition. In France, l'Oréal has dragged all other brands into a war fought on scientifically proven performance, supported by colossal advertising budgets. In Germany, the leading national brand is Nivea, which relies much more on empathy, softness and a close relationship than on the rational approach of proven results. We believe this explains why the distributor's brand has found it easier to make inroads there: consumers have not perceived it to be all that different from Nivea.

Hoch and Banerji (1993) have analysed the factors behind distributor's brands' market share.

These are:

- the size of the potential market: the distributor opts for long production runs;

- the high margin in the sector;

- the low advertising expenditure;

- the ability to achieve quality;

- price sensitivity.

However, these authors also maintain that market fragmentation does not appear to constitute a barrier to the growth of distributor's brands: it offers opportunities for de-segmented 'all in one' products. Conversely, it is known that a factor that does affect the penetration of distributors' brands is the rate of innovation in a sector: it forces product ranges to be continually renewed, and is associated with a large amount of advertising.

As has been observed, most of these factors are linked to management deficiencies among the producers: insufficient rate of innovation, high margins, low advertising. When a brand is treated as a 'cash cow', the door is opened to distributor's brands. Meanwhile, many branded companies agree to produce products under distributors' brands. For example, tyres from Norauto (a chain of stores selling spare parts and services to the motorist) are actually manufactured by the Michelin group: it is inconceivable that they should be low-quality products.

In this way, the success of distributors' brands is linked to a supply effect (by strong promotion on distributors' shelves and the creation of 'me-toos' that ape big-brand products), but also by a lack of competitiveness from high-profile brands which are too accustomed to high margins and do not innovate, or reduce their cost.

Lastly – and obviously – this penetration depends on the specific range and category. It is strong in basic products, but no longer unique to them. Kapferer and Laurent (1995)

linked the attractiveness of distributors' brands to consumers' degree of involvement, either in an enduring sense (their interest in the product) or as a temporary feeling at the time of purchase (Is the purchase a risky one? Does it have badge value? Will it give me pleasure?). A framework was then constructed covering eight purchasing situations, cross-linked to 20 product categories (such as food, hygiene and beauty, clothing and consumer durables) which explained the penetration of the distributor's brands. These purchasing situations were ranked from low involvement to high involvement, with intermediate levels of involvement that were more or less rational. This approach also helps to guide the distributor's choice of brand types: range by range, price point by price point, should the distributor's brand bear the store name or not? After all, there are several types of distributor's brands:

- Low-price lines, to stop customers from defecting to the hard-discounters (50 per cent cheaper than producer brands).

- The 'store brand' (generally 15–20 per cent cheaper than producer brands).

- Lastly, the private labels, each of which has its own separate name and packaging. With their (unlimited) numbers, they provide a practical solution to the distributor's need for flexibility and segmentation. For example, a range can contain several private labels, depending on price points or segments. Alternatively, the aim may be to capitalise on one single brand bearing the store's own name (Carrefour), or a separate name (President's Choice); but the need for coherent positioning dictates that one brand cannot be used to cover all segments and all price points.

We should add that the three types of distributor's brands above can spawn hybrids: for example, there is nothing preventing the endorsement of an individual brand by the store name, or even a low-price product line (the tactic used by Tesco Value).

These are strategic decisions in the sense that different distributors will make different decisions: they stem not only from differences in the competitive environment and the power of their name, but also from their identity and strategic positioning. Consumers also have a view on these subjects and brand types, which we will now examine.

Optimising the retail brand marketing mix

Distributors' brands are not a homogeneous reality. They differ according to their objectives and their strategy. This leads to visible differences in their marketing mix and branding approach on such key facets as:

- the level of product quality (low, same as the leader, premium);

- the naming strategy (should they use the name of the store or not ?);

- the style of packaging (should it be differentiated or copy the market leader?);

- the pricing level in comparison with both the market leader and the hard discount products in the sector;

- the position and size of shelf placement;

- the display position in relation to competitors.

It has become unrealistic to tackle these issues by talking of a generic distributor own brand (DOB). These hark back to a heterogeneous sector and a concept that is not analysed in detail. It is rather necessary to research how the specific marketing mix of a DOB influences consumer preferences. Some types of DOB pose more of a threat to market leaders than do others.

One recent piece of research (Lewi and Kapferer, 1996) examines the impact of types of DOB that are differentiated according to four criteria:

- The product quality, as shown through blind tests. Two quality levels were used in the research: equivalent to the market leader, and markedly inferior to the market leader.

- The price level compared with the market leader. Three levels were used (20 per cent, 35 per cent and 50 per cent cheaper).

- The naming strategy. Does the DOB use the store name or is it a private label?

- The degree of packaging similarity to the market leader: whether the brand is a copycat or clearly differentiated, as has already been discussed. Our research has established that a copycat brand can cause up to 42 per cent of consumers to confuse it with the market leader.

The research led to the following main conclusions:

- The objective quality of the DOB has an impact on customer preference, as shown in Table 6.3. In some markets it is possible for small suppliers to provide a product that is equivalent in quality to the market leader. Sometimes, of course, the market leader itself agrees to supply its competitor (the DOB product), and frequently there is little or no difference in specification between the market leader and the own-brand product.

- The brand name strategy also affects consumer preferences. As shown in Table 6.4, the store name tends to be more attractive to consumers than a private label.

- Each type of distributor's brand has its own price elasticity. As the research results show, the impact of the price differential from the

Table 6.3   Customer choice depends on the quality of the distributor own-brand

	Quality of distributor brand	
	Equal to the leader	Markedly inferior
Consumer intention to buy the distributor brand	34%	16%

Notes:
p < 0.01
Quality based on blind tests.

Table 6.4   How brand naming affects consumer intention to buy

	Brand uses store name	Brand uses private label (not based on store name)
Consumer intention to buy a retailer brand	30%	20%

Note: p < 0.05
Source: Lewi and Kapferer, 1998

market leader varies depending on other branding decisions (the choice of brand name, the packaging and so on). Some decisions enable a price closer to the brand leader, others do not. The most significant conclusion of the triple interaction (see Table 6.5) is that acting like a real brand enables DOBs to maximise both their sales and profits. Clearly it is no longer possible to treat distributor brands as homogeneous. After all, customers too are not homogeneous.

In summary, to use a distributor brand can be a winning strategy if the correct decisions are taken about the marketing mix (the quality, differentiation from the market leader and so on). It is also clear that it is not always true that a large price differential from the market leader is necessary in order to prompt a preference for the distributor brand.

Changing the brand and business model: Decathlon

Decathlon's first store was created some 25 years ago. In 2000 it was the fifth largest sports

retailer in the world, with a sales turnover of US $2.5 billion, after Intersport, Wal-Mart, Venator (Foot Locker and Champs) and Sport 2000. The concept is to present all major sports (70 in total) in a single megastore (from 5,000 to 10,000 square metres), with 35,000 products. Decathlon's mission is to increase the pleasure of sport for the general public. It does it through an obsession: providing the best choice of the best quality/price ratio products on the market. To achieve this goal, it is a discount store with its own brand. A store brand was rapidly seen as the only way to be able to deliver to the market that expected quality/price ratio that most well-known sport brands fail to deliver: their price is largely based on intangible values, marketing-based, not on the true technical value of the products.

Little by little the Decathlon store brand grew from 23 per cent of in-store sales in 1987 to 52 per cent in 2000. It is one of the main reasons for Decathlon's success: the products made by Decathlon itself (it was the 14th largest producer of sports goods in the world in 2000) were rapidly perceived not as typical cheap products from a discount store, but as

Table 6.5   How the distributor's brand marketing mix impacts consumer purchase intentions

Brand and packaging	Price gap	Percentage of consumers who intend to buy the distributor/retailer brand		
		−20%	−35%	−50%
Store brand (not copycat)		38	38	28
Store brand (copycat)		17	28	38
Private label (copycat)		26	31	27
Private label (not copycat)		21	24	31

offering the best value/technicality/price ratio on the market. They create a high level of satisfaction and the desire to repurchase the brand.

This is not a surprise: there are 100 product managers at Decathlon. They define the products to be created or improved. To reduce production costs, Decathlon itself buys the raw materials, makes all the production plans and provides them to the OEM manufacturer it has selected for the item, on the basis of the targeted production price.

In addition to the prices, there is a large choice and a friendly atmosphere at Decathlon, largely influenced by the youth, expertise and service orientation of the sales staff. After-sales service is friendly: products are exchanged without question.

In addition to its store brand, there is a limited discount range called 'best price technical', intended to convey that although there are cheaper products on the market, these are the cheapest that conform to Decathlon's standards. Even a very cheap product has to be technically competent. This is how Decathlon differentiates itself from other pure hard-discounters. In Europe, Decathlon is Nike's largest client, representing close to 20 per cent of Nike's sales. Nike however provides only 7 per cent of Decathlon's sales.

Decathlon's objective is to operate 500 fully owned megastores in the world by 2005. It recently created a beachhead in the United States by purchasing a discount chain based around Boston, to test its concept and operations in the competitive US environment. Due to less than satisfactory results, it closed all the poorly located stores and kept the best stores to test the validity of the brand and business model in the United States.

In 2000, however, a key signal turned red. For the first time since Decathlon started up, the number of consumers saying they would visit a Decathlon store first when considering purchasing their next sports item, although very high, dropped a little. This very reactive company and organisation analysed the reasons for this drop, and found the main one to be a perceived lack of choice. When a retailer becomes dominant in a country, a single store brand strategy creates feelings of a lack of freedom, or of massification of choice: everybody is forced to buy the same brand as other consumers. The answer was not, of course, to increase the number of international brands, because of their structurally poor quality/price ratio. Instead, Decathlon changed the branding model that had accompanied its growth for 25 years. It decided to create instead a portfolio of seven private labels, named 'passion brands', to differentiate them from classical private labels which in fact are simply a name.

There were originally planned to be 15 of these passion brands. However, they had to be concentrated into a smaller number in order to respect Decathlon's mission statement. Only fewer but larger brands would allow the masses to practise sport with passion. In addition, if these brands had all been set up as narrowly upmarket brands, it would have created a problem in naming the low end of the range. If the Decathlon name had been used for the low-end products only, this might have endangered the equity attached to it. Instead, it was decided that each passion brand would carry an eco-technical 'first price' line.

Very few examples demonstrate as clearly as Decathlon the implications of a change of branding model for the business and organisation as a whole. First, worldwide there would be one single policy. As a consequence, Decathlon stores in new countries would launch with the seven passion brands. A new experience had to be invented, unlike that of the domestic market where synergy was maximised between the store name and the store brand name were the same. If Decathlon was to achieve one of its goals (relieving the impression of lack of choice and of massification), it needed the passion brands to look independent. The Decathlon name itself would no longer be visible on the products (but only inside, on the labels).

Second, if the new brands were to become real brands, with emotion – with passion – they needed to be close to the opinion leaders of each sport, working intimately in co-creation. This had radical consequences on the type of organisation Decathlon had established over its 25 years. Up to that point Decathlon had been very centralised, with its store brand being managed from its headquarters. If Quechua was to become a leading winter sports brand, for example, it needed to be based in the mountains: in this case in the Alps, with all the brand's staff – its marketing staff, product managers, designers and so on – working closely with professionals and amateur enthusiasts to test ideas, concepts and products. The same held for Tribord, the

marine sports brand, and for the rest of the passion brands. Only cycles were to be managed from the headquarters, (The store name had been retained only for cycling, because this technical and popular product had become very symbolic of Decathlon's values and positioning).

This was a real challenge for the whole business model. Decathlon embraced it boldly.

How manufacturers compete against retail brands

A key year in the history of Coca-Cola, a paragon of brand culture, was 1994. For the first time, in Sainsbury's retail outlets the sales of own-brand cola surpassed those of Coca-Cola (see Table 6.6), a demonstration of sorts that loyalty at any price no longer exists. An important fall in price, the guarantee of the Canadian company Cott (for the concentrate quality and taste), similarities in packaging bordering on counterfeiting and a product of sufficient quality are dissuading occasional buyers of the brand. What happened to the world's number one brand had already struck many well-known brands. The generators of profitability examined above seem to have been put to bad use in many sectors. The recession has certainly changed consumer behaviour, leading to more price sensitivity, but the lessons learnt through the purchase of distributors' brands will not easily be forgotten by consumers and distributors. In fact, the principles explaining the sources of profitability generated by the brand also explain the loss

Table 6.6 The effects of Sainsbury's Cola launch on Coke's market share

	Before launch	After launch
Coca-Cola	60%	33%
Own-label	18%	60%
Other brands	22%	7%
(Index) category volume	100	150

of affection which brands can create in several markets.

If it is true that the three principal generators of brand profitability are:

▪ the price differential allowed compared to a non-branded product;

▪ the differential of attraction and loyalty;

▪ the differential of the margin coming from the economies of scale and the consequences of being market leader when such is the case;

then most brands have chosen to benefit only from the price differential. This explains the following acknowledgement of the directors of Danone: 'Fuelled by consumption growth and concealed by high inflation, producers tend sometimes to increase the price too much in an attempt to maintain their margins' (IREP, 1994, p 35). In the USA, the consequence of the sudden fall in the price of Marlboro, known as the famous Marlboro Friday, was to bring to an end the continued rise in price of this brand. Once a company is lucky enough to have this differential in price, it is necessary either to have a clearly superior product due to investment in R&D (in the case of computers, cosmetics or washing powders) or to invest heavily in advertising in order to create intangibility. However, the equilibrium between tangible and intangible added value depends on the product category. As we have already seen, little emphasis is placed on intangible value in the men's sock market, so this product does not create psychological involvement. On the other hand, Nike, Adidas and Reebok aim to appeal to young people by using iconic figures such as Michael Jordan, Tiger Woods and Eric Cantona. Many managers have placed disproportionate faith in intangible values. Perhaps influenced by their success in the leisure goods market, they have extended the logic of intangibility too far. However, mass market brands are not born from the stars of the sports world; they

democratise technical progress. Strong brands were historically created when the mass producers could create products in large quantities of similar quality and cheaper than the craft industry. This progress was announced to as many people as possible through advertising. If it is true that the brand is an intangible asset, it is wrong to believe that its image has to concentrate on the intangible. Everyday products with low involvement leave very little to the imagination. If you decide to invest exclusively in advertising for these brands you risk weakening the brand because you will have to sell a product for £1.20 even though it is only worth £1 in the eyes of the consumer, with the extra 20p corresponding to the price of the advertising. This is where the disequilibrium comes from, which the image cannot overcome. This is why Procter & Gamble also decided to follow an everyday low price (EDLP) policy.

All brands do not build on a price premium: KitKat, Swatch and even Coca-Cola have always seen to it that they are within as many people's reach as possible in terms of price. As the CEO of Coca-Cola, R. Goizetta, said, Coke must be the same price as tea in China. Which, in fact, it is. Swatch, faced with Japanese and Asian competitors, decided deliberately on a low-price strategy. Thanks to its design, variety, fashion appeal and Swiss quality, Swatch has succeeded in maximising the price/quality relationship in its favour, thus creating considerable value attraction with its consumers.

The producers' brand crisis started when we tried too hard to be semioticians and forgot industrial logic. Did we not limit the brand to its legal definition: a sign which distinguishes the goods of a company from those of other entrepreneurs while guaranteeing its origin? Many people believed that the sign alone – stimulated through advertising – would, from now on, not only distinguish products but also, miraculously, legitimise a price premium.

This theory was thrown into disarray when products that were functionally as good and cheaper than branded versions appeared on the market. When you find imported Italian spaghetti from an unknown but authentically Italian producer selling for 42p a kilo, whereas the same product by the market leader costs 72p a kilo on promotion, the price differential widens – not through the fault of management but because of the arrival of external actors on the market who are capable of supplying the same quality at a substantially lower price. The functions of practicality, identification, guarantee and permanence which make up the leading brand are perhaps worth a differential of 10p per kilo but not 30p. The difference in price is no longer explained by the added value: it has become an exorbitant sacrifice in the consumer's eyes.

In truth, due to the fact that distributors are not aiming to create dreams, they have concentrated their attention and efforts on the reality, on the products. If the early own-labels were of average quality, own-brand products have constantly improved in quality. Closely focused on the national brands, they have thus followed their price increases, but have maintained a price differential of 20 per cent. The shock came from German hard-discounters like Aldi and Lidl. This type of distribution was created in 1948 during the reconstruction of Germany and is, therefore, a form of distribution typical of a rich country. Spreading throughout Europe because of the recession, it should continue to develop even when the economy starts improving. However, the products of German hard discounters are 50 per cent cheaper than those of national brands: but is this at the expense of quality? No. Aldi's instant coffee is made by Nestlé. Long-established partnerships with large producers, the search for maximum economies of scale and the reduction of any costs which fail to add value throughout the value chain have led to the launching of 600 unbeatable products in terms of price/quality relationship. In a recent comparison of the technical characteristics and quality of 50 consumer products, the Nielsen group found that in 25 per cent of the cases the national brands were superior, in 20 per cent of the cases the products of German hard-discounters were better and in 36 per cent of the cases the quality was identical. Discount products launched by retail outlets to defend themselves were found, in 55 per cent of the cases, to be of inferior quality. A blind tasting test by Nielsen revealed identical results (see Table 6.7). If products which cost half the price come second in a quality test, the extra price of the national brand is an extra cost

Table 6.7 Quality ranking of top brands and their competitors

Type of brand or product	Average ranking	Main advantage
International brands	First overall, but fourth in 25% of the cases	Flavour and design
Products of German hard-discounters	Second overall, but first in 20% of the cases	Colour and texture
Distributors' own brand	Third overall, but second in 45% of the cases	Texture and flavour
Products of local discounters	Fourth overall, but fifth in 25% of the cases	Smell and colour
Discount products of hypermarkets and supermarkets	Fifth overall, but second in 20% of the cases	Smell

Source: Nielsen

rather than extra value. Admittedly there are always intangible aspects to the image of food products because everything that enters our body poses a certain amount of risk, but this can be overcome by buying from a well-known retailer that guarantees its own brand.

The long-term problem is that hard-discounters' products may become tomorrow's references for consumers in terms of both quality and price once this type of shop is present throughout the country and can operate as a nearby shop for everyday products (600 products per outlet). Then you will have to justify paying twice as much for a man's shirt than for a quality Tex, Carrefour's brand of clothes.

In Germany, more than half of the national sales of orange drinks are made by Aldi and Lidl. Brands will cease to exist unless they are able to offer added value due to an exceptional product or a unique taste and a strong image (like Tango or Orangina, for instance). Certainly, Tropicana thrives: but it is a niche brand. The whole category has become a price-led commodity.

This change in competition will result in the price differential on the shelves noticed by consumers increasing from 20 per cent (compared to a classic brand) to 45 or 50 per cent. Thus, it is inevitable that there will be a fall in demand.

The threat also comes from the fact that less and less shelf space will be given to national brands. These two phenomena will rapidly reduce the gains due to margins which are created by the economies of scale, the experience curve and the leadership advantages which have been lost.

In several markets the future of producers' brands is precarious. There are only two strategies possible for manufacturers of branded mass market goods:

- First, invest in creativity, innovations, quality and R&D in order to recreate differential advantage, while at the same time communicating to a wide range of people to maximise the exclusiveness and the image of quality associated with the brand. This has been the successful strategy of, among others, L'Oréal, Procter & Gamble, Michelin, Gillette, Sony, Ferrero, 3M, Philips.

- Alternatively, reduce costs through improving productivity in an attempt to maintain the pressure on prices. Pepsi-Cola, Bic, Benetton and Dell try to reduce costs by economies of scale or by their business model. They keep prices low to discourage the entry of own-brands while reinforcing their image thanks to a policy of umbrella brands and brand extensions.

Throughout this chapter, several conclusions have emerged. From now on it will become more difficult, more costly and more demanding to remain a big brand, a buyer's reference. Only large companies who have the resources to invest in R&D, productivity and total quality control, who are able to foresee the future through market research and who invest in visibility and proximity on distributors' shelves and in communication in order to consolidate the strong product image and the exclusivity of their brands will benefit from the new environment. The strength of a brand will depend directly on the strength of the company who owns it.

On the other hand the price premium is definitely going to fall if the big brands wish to stay at the heart of the market and not be sidelined in the premium segment, as nowadays it is the distributors who set the prices. Everybody is concerned with this, from FMCG manufacturers to the makers of office equipment, electrical domestic appliances or desk-top computers. This explains why, coming back to the financial valuation of brands, the multiples which had reached their peak (25 or 30) are returning to more acceptable levels. The result of this is that brand assets have no longer the same value as they did in 1990. The gearing effect is less, as can be seen in Figure 6.1. (Chapter 13, which deals with financial evaluation and accounting procedures for brands, will examine this point in detail.)

Let us take an example. Yesterday, the third or fourth brand on the market was very proud of its performance. Today, such a brand would have a hard time getting shelf space in a store. The marked increase in the leader's advantage is clear from the PIMS (Profit Impact of Market Strategy) database. On average, market leaders generate a profit of 12.1 per cent from their sales, those who are second generate 8.3 per cent and those who are third only 3.5 per cent.

Thus the producer brand is under threat in several markets, but for a company a brand is still the best way to become profitable. This explains why distributors are themselves becoming more interested in brand thinking. However, as we have seen, to be a brand is not to be a name on a product: rather it is, through constant investment in know-how, to become and remain the reference of quality at an acceptable price, implying the promise of tangible and also intangible benefits. Certain distributors' own-brands are already on the right track and certain manufacturers' brands have deviated from it. For consumers

there are only two types of brand: those which justify their price, and those which don't. This new competitive situation has strongly influenced the new rules of brand management.

Defending against imitation by retail brands

In developed countries, brands fall victim to unfair competition in the form of imitation. This is where competitors increase their 'me-too' product's chances of success by closely imitating – albeit with a few differences – the characteristics of the target brand product, as well as its distinctive marks. To be considered as an unfair threat, the imitation must be likely to cause confusion to a consumer of average attentiveness.

Imitations can come either from competing producers or from the product's own distributors – and the response must vary depending on the individual case. Most big companies would in fact be reluctant to take action against their distributor if they believed that one of its distributor's brand products, placed alongside one of their own brand's products, was imitating it too closely and constituting

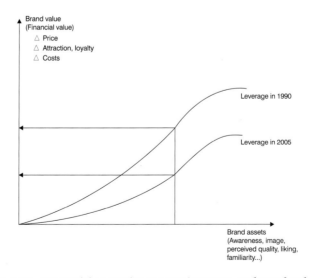

Figure 6.1   How the new competitive environment impacts on brand valuation

an act of unfair competition. It is true that the first phase in the implementation of a distributor's brand policy is generally to imitate the targeted market leader on a product by product basis. It can even be the case that distributor's brands within a given group copy each other. Bicycles sold by the Auchan hypermarket have borne an extremely close resemblance to a best-seller at Decathlon (the 'be-twin') – the two stores are part of the same group.

Actual legal proceedings against the distributor are rarer still. Big companies, many of whose products are stocked by the distributor, fear a Pyrrhic victory and prefer to draw up a dossier with the aim of avoiding legal action and resolving disputes amicably. The dossier consists of a form of proof that could be produced as legal evidence if required, for it is in fact possible to devise a scientific approach to prove illegal imitation. Two methods exist.

The first works on a legal definition: an imitation is illegal if it is likely to confuse a consumer of average attentiveness. There are two techniques capable of demonstrating such a risk of confusion, without actually asking customers directly if they would be confused by the copycat (an invalid method). The first is the use of a tachystoscope, which 'flashes' a picture of the copy product at consumers, first at high speed, then at slower speeds. They are then simply asked what they have seen (Kapferer, 1995). The second method is to start with a computer-degraded picture of the copy and to build it up, step by step, using computer software. Consumers state what they think they can see on the computer screen. These two methods produce a working imitation of consumers of average attentiveness, either by limiting the length of their exposure to the product (the tachystoscope) or by presenting low-resolution pictures (the computer method).

The second approach ignores the legal concept of confusion. Indeed, although they pay lip service to the notion in their rulings, judges do not truly use the concept of confusion. Rather, they concentrate on excessive manifest resemblance. They pay more attention to resemblances and less to differences (as advanced by the imitator's lawyer). Objective proof of an excessive resemblance can be obtained by asking one group of consumers to describe the original, and then asking an identical group of consumers to describe the copy. An analysis is made of which aspects are stated first, second, third and so on, for each of the two products, and of the level of agreement between the aspects stated first by each group.

Contact with the distributor must be made at a high managerial level in order to emphasise the seriousness of the matter. Furthermore, this is the level at which long-term interests are best appreciated. On the one hand, the distributor needs big brands, a dynamic aspect to its store shelves, the value innovations the brands bring to the category and the margins they give the distributor. On the other, the manufacturer needs the distributor to gain access to the customer. At lower managerial levels, the producer–distributor relationship is more antagonistic. The outcome of such contact is the modification of the trade dress or packaging of the distributor's disputed products.

In general terms, brand management must plan for these phenomena and put the brand in a position to be able to defend itself strongly. Thus, in order for it to be possible to protect a brand colour, the brand must itself protect it internally against the dilution of its proprietary codes. For example, the brand's product lines are very often segmented: this leads to the use of different colours to identify each segment. In this way, the ability to claim that the brand is characterised by a particular colour is reduced. Thus, if a Coke label is red and a Coke Light label is silver, red is no longer the colour of the Coca-Cola brand; after all, when producing their own colas, distributors always start by producing red packaging.

In general terms, the brand must make itself a 'moving target' through innovation and regular modifications to its packaging and its characteristic components. However, it must be always remembered that the aim of these modifications is to bring more value to the consumer. The difficulty that this permanent movement creates for copies is a secondary effect, a by-product.

On the design front, the brand must accentuate and radicalise the signs of its own individuality in order to be able to defend them better, and at the same time make them recognisable to consumers of average attentiveness. It is significant that the often-imitated Baileys goes as far as to print the word 'Original' twice on its front label: 'Original Irish Cream' and 'Baileys the Original'.

Facing the low-cost revolution

It would be hard to underestimate the rise of hard-discount as a fundamental phenomenon in mature societies. Offering a reduced range or a pared-back service at an unbeatable price, hard-discount is more than just a price – it is a business model. It also represents a new attitude towards consumption, and heralds a crisis for added value. It throws marketing itself into question, and thus brands too. This is why no organisations should consider themselves safe from this phenomenon.

Even in the country that invented the hypermarket, and where this form of commerce is now dominant, hard-discount has succeeded in capturing nearly 12 per cent of market share by value in the last 15 years. Given that in the food products business, the price gap between discounters and the leading brands varies between 50 per cent and 70 per cent, it can be seen that this represents between 18 per cent and 24 per cent by volume. And of course – depending on the category – these figures may be even higher. For example, in the pre-packed cold meats (ham) market, the hard-discounters' market

share by value is of the order of 16.5 per cent.

Hard-discount is more than just a price. It is a new way of doing business, with its own specific retailers: German (Lidl and Aldi) or French (Ed, Leader Price) or Spanish (Dia). At present, the most recent European panel figures suggest that 62 per cent of households shop at a hard-discount food store, but the phenomenon continues to expand: in the food market, the figure of 20 per cent of market share by value should soon be reached. In the DIY sector, the major retailers have created separate, hard-discount-style retail brands. The phenomenon now also extends to textiles: the traditional discount stores were well known, but now genuine hard discount retailers are emerging.

All these figures show that hard-discount cannot simply be categorised as a phenomenon that targets lower-income groups. Hard-discount is a necessity for the poorest in society, but also an opportunity for the better-off. It offers an alternative way of living: consumers can do the daily shop, in a store close to their home, in 10 minutes thanks to the simplification offered by a reduced range of goods, freeing buyers from the torments of too much choice. This is a genuine challenge for the major brands, as this growing form of distribution excludes them in favour of the discounters' own products. For the major brands, this further erosion of their accessibility on store shelves compounds the problem created by the amount of space already set aside for distributors' brands in the hypermarkets and supermarkets. Indeed, even retailers' brands are coming under threat from this increasingly cut-price competition. which attracts clients to a different store.

What do Ryanair, Virgin Express, Asda and Aldi have in common? They are all what is known as 'low cost' companies. How has the traditional competition responded? By means of 'lowest price' products. The difference in terminology here relates to scale: low cost is a business model, while low price is an outcome in the range which can be achieved by putting further pressure on manufacturers, cutting corners with the product or buying in bulk. Over 50 years of supplying a quality product at the lowest prices, Aldi and Lidl have devised an efficient business model based on eliminating all costs deemed to be unnecessary, and on a vision: long-term agreements with manufacturers, dedicated use of these manufacturers' factories and cooperative product design, not to mention a no-frills store concept with an ultra-reduced range. However, the fact that Aldi fruit juice is the market leader in Germany is proof of its quality: it represents unbeatable value.

By contrast, the lowest-price product from Carrefour, put together in haste to stem the haemorrhage of clients, was first obtained through heavy pressure on suppliers, and qualified as fruit juice only in a strict legal sense. This is why customer loyalty is being won by the hard discounters and not by the low-price hypermarket products.

The same is true of the airlines. It is simply not possible to offer London–Paris flights for £30 without a business model that breaks completely with the major airlines' traditional *modus operandi*.

The hard-discount phenomenon is set to spread. Everyone will look for a way to increase their purchasing power in an ultimately painless way, by making shrewder purchasing decisions in respect of a portion of their consumption. This will affect telephone communications, the Internet, transport, petrol, clothing and other areas. No company is immune to this phenomenon, because the competition has changed: consumers have become highly versatile, situation-driven and pragmatic. They are quite capable of shopping both at a hard discounter and at Harrods on the same day.

Modern competition is thus expanded competition: it is no longer restricted to peers, identical brands or similar channels. Like the modern consumer, it is open and all-embracing. In the process of experimenting with new channels, consumer are bound to find themselves re-evaluating brands and their added value.

Does this mean that a certain type of marketing is under threat? First of all, we should remain calm and avoid scaremongering: books heralding 'the death of the brand' or some similar disaster are constantly appearing. Yet it has to be acknowledged that while hard-discount is making inroads in 'old Europe', entire countries dream of becoming consumer societies: one need only visit Shanghai for proof of this. However, all modern marketing is a response to the problem of saturated markets. Since a household's shampoo budget cannot be expanded infinitely, the perceived value of new shampoos must be increased – hence the hyper-segmentation of ranges and new products. The range of shampoos on store shelves continues to multiply, divide and fragment. This is a source of complexity and of cost to the manufacturer, distributor and consumer. But do these enforced costs of complexity really create value? Many customers have found that the answer is 'no'. They want to be able to exercise their right to added value at times and places of their own choosing. This choice had vanished. It does not take a Ryanair devotee to appreciate that the gap between its prices and those of British Airways or Air France calls into question the true added value of the latter companies. They may be two or three times more expensive, but do they offer a service that is two or three times better? The answer is no.

Hard-discount represents a return not to asceticism, but to reality. For consumers who have the option of shopping elsewhere, it speaks of a desire for simplification, a less complex life and the recovery of control. It will put heavy pressure on brands with low added value: brands of average quality, which have not made themselves sufficiently aspirational. Hard-discount preaches a form of intangible value, the return to a certain simplicity for those who have not already been forced down this path through a lack of resources. Hard-discount is the pursuit of purification and 'detoxification' in lifestyle terms: freedom from imposed constraints.

What should our answer to this be? Heeding the implicit message but remaining true to itself, the brand should retaliate with a different intangible factor and value system: its own. Hypermarkets have no choice either: their own brands exist only in relation to the producer brands which innovate, create and nurture markets, reveal tendencies and also participate in the consumer society.

Remember that a brand can justify its existence only through the innovations it offers. Most brands are born of innovation, and innovation continues to be the brand's oxygen: it has a stimulating, euphoric effect in promoting a sense of well-being, pleasure, *joie de vivre* and hedonism. However, this intangible factor will have to start earning its keep. The first step is respect for the customer. An intangible benefit that is not rooted in a tangible superior quality will be weakened, and contribute to the brand's excess. There are plenty of expensive polo shirts, but only one Lacoste; this point has to be reinforced repeatedly. Also, most FMCG companies are not cost conscious enough: they use innovations to repeatedly raise prices, without asking when the gap will become too big between their products and the DOBs, not to speak of the hard-discounters. It is a matter of economics and also of ethics.

Today, consumers do not need bigger brands but better brands: the brand must adopt ethical principles and demonstrate that consumption is not a synonym for inefficient waste, pollution and exploitation – themes to which society is becoming increasingly sensitive. Even Nike has had to make changes in the wake of the revelations in Naomi Klein's book *No Logo* (1999). This mega-brand, with its iconic status among the young, may have invented concept upon concept, but its social conscience left much to be desired, a fact that is particularly unacceptable in a flourishing company.

It would be a mistake to believe that hard-discount will become the norm. However, it will grow – and in so doing, it may lead to a re-evaluation of attitudes and behaviour. As is always the case in our modern society, contradictory tendencies appear, coexist, and learn to live together – but what they cannot do is ignore one another.

Part Three

Creating and sustaining brand equity

7

Launching the brand

When they came into being, all the major brands examined so far – Nike, Lacoste, Amazon, Orange, l'Oréal, Nivea, Ariel – were of course also new brands. Over the years, and often by intuition, chance or accident, they became major brands, leading brands, powerful brands.

Since at one point they were all necessarily new, we might ask ourselves what the established brands have or have done that the others don't have or have not done. In the previous chapters, we carried out an in-depth examination of major brands from both producers and retailers. Each had a strong identity: a well-identified core activity, a genuine performance, a defined brand personality and a set of values, ie an authentic brand culture, etc. Every one of these established brands seemed both to have a specific meaning – ie to be driven by a specific source of inspiration – and to know where they were heading in terms of products and services which they would not hesitate to endorse.

Here we have all the key requirements for launching a new brand. To paraphrase King (1973), the best way for a new brand to succeed is to act like an old brand! In other

words, instead of worrying about how to launch new brands, we had better think about how we might invent an established brand. Looking at things in this way, though, is not at all common practice at present: launching a new product is still confused with launching a new brand.

Launching a brand and launching a product are not the same

Marketing books devote chapters to the definition of new products, but none to the launching of new brands, except for an occasional word or two on how to choose the name of a new product. This confusion between product and brand is an enduring problem. Most famous brands, rich in meaning and values, started out as the ordinary names of innovative products or services, different from those of competitors. These names were generally randomly chosen, without any prior study or analysis: Coca-Cola reflected the contents of the new product; Mercedes was the name of Mr Daimler's daughter; Citroën was a family name; Adidas is a spin-off of Adolphe Dassler; likewise Lip of Lippman and Harpic of Harry Picman. The new product had to be given a new name so that it could be advertised. Advertising was then put in charge of presenting the advantages of the new product as well as the benefits which consumers could expect from it.

After some time, new products usually get copied by competitors. They then get replaced by new, higher quality products, which often benefit from the fame of the existing product name. However, although products change, brands stay. In the beginning then, advertisements will boast the merits of the new, initial product, say X. But, since all products naturally become obsolete over time, X will soon come to announce that it's about to update and upgrade itself by lending its name to a higher quality product. And that's how a new brand comes to life. From then on, it is no longer advertising that will sell the products, but the brand itself.

Over time, the brand will gain greater autonomy and part with its original meaning (often the name of the company founder or of a specific feature of the product) by developing its own way of communicating (about the products), of addressing the public and of behaving. Few British people think of 'clean' when saying 'Kleenex' and few French think of the lotus leaf when saying 'Lotus'. The product name has become a proper noun, meaningless in itself, yet loaded with associations that have built up through experience (of the products and services), word-of-mouth and advertising. Advertising gives us hints of who the X who is now communicating really is: what is its core activity, its project, its cultural reference, its set of values, its personality, and whom is it addressing? Over time, the meaning of X has changed: it is no longer the mere name of a product, it is the very meaning of all products X, present and yet to come. The famous brand, X, is now the purveyor of values, from which its own endorsed products can benefit (as soon as they enter production).

In terms of brand creation, there is only one simple lesson to be learnt from this: if the new brand does not convey its values from the very start, ie as soon as it is created and launched, it is quite unlikely that it will manage to become a major brand.

On an operational level, this means that in launching a new brand, knowing its intangible values is just as important as deciding on the product advantage. Why was Atari not ranked as a major brand when Apple was? It is not due to their products or software. The 520 ST, the 1040, the Portfolio, the Mega and the Transputer were very good products. They concretely represented a manufacturing philosophy that was literally the company leitmotiv. Jack Tramiel, who took over Atari, and the affiliate managers would indeed often say: 'Technology is increasing, prices are decreasing.' And it is true that an Atari 1040 with a laser printer was worth a lot less than even a lower-range Apple Macintosh. What Atari lacked, though, was the meaning and latitude it would have taken to become more than just the name of the manufacturer of the 1040, Mega and Transputer. Nobody, in fact, knew what Atari's project, vision and source of inspiration were, nor what objective and subjective values it was trying to instil into the microcomputer industry by means of its products.

A successful launch requires that the new brand be treated as a real brand, right from the very start – not as a mere product name presented in advertising. Launching a new brand means acting before the product name becomes a brand symbol, with a much broader and deeper meaning than previously. Modern management must show results a lot sooner. From the very beginning, the new brand must be considered in full, ie endowing it with both functional and non-functional values. Creating a brand means acting straightaway as if it is a well-established brand, rich in meaning. This entails a few fundamental principles.

Defining the brand's platform

Unlike the product launch, the brand launch is, from the very start, a long-term project. Such launch will modify the existing order, values and market shares of the category. It aims at establishing a new order and different values and at impacting on the market for a long period of time. This can only be achieved if people are convinced of the brand's absolute necessity and are ready to give it all they have. In order to keep staff, management, bankers, clients, opinion leaders and salespeople mobilised for the long term, the company must be driven by a real brand project and a true vision. The latter will indeed serve to justify, internally and externally, why the brand is being launched and what its essential purpose is.

Creating a brand implies first drafting the brand's programme, which underlies the brand identity and positioning. Presenting the brand in a programmatic format (Table 7.1) is fruitful. It indicates where the brand stems from, where it draws its energy, what big project lies behind the brand. This is useful as a step in the brand thinking process itself, before the brand identity prism and brand positioning are defined.

Many brands no longer know why they exist, so they would be quite unable to answer questions such as those in Table 7.1 defining the brand programme. Such questions reflect a philosophy at the opposite of niche tactics. Only those who are driven by a grand project within can actually set out on the long journey of brand making.

Of course, this brand project will have to be transformed into 'strategic image traits'. In the car industry, we realise that Peugeot cannot be defined by simply a few of its features, such as dynamism, reliability and aesthetics. These image traits do help differentiate Peugeot from Volkswagen, which is rather positioned in terms of reliability and comfort. However, each brand reflects its own fundamental automobile project and its own philosophy. As a result, Volkswagen speaks of

Table 7.1 Underlying the brand is its programme

1. Why must this brand exist?
   What would consumers be missing if the brand did not exist?
2. Standpoint.
   From where does the brand speak?
3. Vision.
   What is the brand's vision of the product category?
4. What are our values?
5. Mission.
   What specific mission does the brand want to carry out in its market?
6. Know-how.
   What is the brand's specific know-how?
7. Territory.
   Where can the brand legitimately carry out its mission, in which product category?
8. Typical products or actions.
   Which products and actions best embody, best exemplify the brand's values and vision?
9. Style and language.
   What are the brand's stylistic idiosyncrasies?
10. Reflection.
    Whom are we addressing? What image do we want to render of the clients themselves?

cars, Peugeot of automobiles. Finally, without any industrial, marketing or commercial expertise, or any financial means, a project is just a wish.

The preliminary definition of brand identity is not the same for company-named brands as for brands that have their own name. Many companies nowadays act as brands. Alcatel is both company and brand, as are Siemens, Toshiba, Du Pont, Philips and IBM. On the other hand, Audi is one of Volkswagen's brands, as Persil is one of Henkel's and Dash one of Procter & Gamble's. Companies become aware that their name is actually a brand when they notice that the purchaser and user are just as important as the financial analyst in the markets in which they operate.

On an operational level, creating a brand with no direct reference to the firm offers a greater degree of freedom: everything is possible, which does not automatically mean that everything is relevant or easy. What it does mean is that we can create the brand's identity entirely from scratch.

In the case of company-named brands, the brand becomes the major spokesperson for the company. There must therefore be a relationship between brand identity and corporate identity. Brand identity has less freedom than in the previous case. The company-named brand is indeed the company's external showpiece: it is the messenger telling the company story to a larger audience. It is therefore vital for the company to identify with this brand as well as fully support this new spokesperson (which is different from the institutional spokesperson, the CEO). That is why we observe that company-named brands have the same culture as the companies from which they emanate (see Figure 7.1).

Now the brand is here to sell to customers, while the corporation itself has other stakeholders and markets (see page 29). This is why, although they share the same name, and thus strongly interact, it is important to differentiate for instance Nestlé as a corporate brand and Nestlé as a commercial brand. To help differentiate these two sources, the company itself has created two different visual symbols for each of its two facets. The same holds true also for Danone, which has created a specific symbol for Danone as corporation (a small child looking at a star in the sky), different from the geometric form of the Danone brand logo. Even if they did share the same graphic identity (as do Shell, BP and Total), the distinction remains to be made. The corporation is not the brand but is nourished by the brand (and vice versa).

Nestlé as a brand could never assume a fun and exuberant or greedy and permissive identity. This is because it bears the same

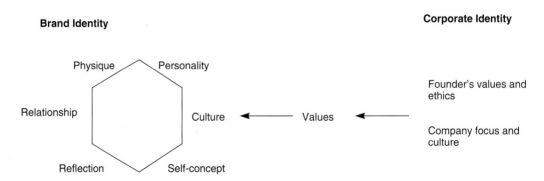

Figure 7.1 Transfer of company identity to brand identity when company and brand names coincide

name as the company, whose identity is none of these. Even though the public does not know this company, the Nestlé brand is nevertheless strongly influenced by the overall Nestlé corporate identity. Final acceptance of a new brand's identity is a company prerogative. And if the latter cannot identify with the new brand, the brand identity will be modified in order to be in tune with that of the company. This does not mean that the two perfectly coincide, but that there is a bridge between them.

Such a bridge is usually easier to build by means of the cultural facet (see Figure 7.1). There is a theoretical reason for this: a company coins its identity by focusing on one or two key values (Schwebig, 1985). These are the values which feed the brand, give it the company's outlook on the world and the impetus to transform the product category. This 'source-value' gives meaning to the brand. Underlying Peugeot's rigour and quality, there has always been the corporate determination to offer more than a strictly functional product: a car which drivers could truly enjoy.

Over time, this relationship between brand and company is switched around. The company's outward image is reflected inside and becomes far more effective in mobilising the workforce than all of the other here-today-gone-tomorrow 'company projects'. In order to take advantage of this positive feedback, many companies have traded in their old name for one of their leading brand names. Tokyo Tsuhin Kogyo, for instance, has thus become Sony Inc; Tokyo Denki Kagaku adopted the name of its famous brand TDK. Likewise, BSN became Danone throughout the world.

The identity of strong brands reminds us that identity is not just a matter of functional attributes. That is why choosing a new brand's symbolic references is just as important as choosing its product references. Apple is steeped in the Californian high-tech and 'counter-culture' imagery. Toshiba promoted its products, but never wove them into any particular symbolic reference. The brand has

no aspiration and no vision of its own either for the product category or for the microcomputer industry as a whole. Mitsubishi sells cars, but is not a brand in the full sense: we cannot perceive its values, its source of inspiration, its project, where it is heading and where it is taking us. It is just a name on a car, to which is attached the reassurance provided by the size of the industrial super-group, Mitsubishi. For non-Japanese people, Mitsubishi means little beyond Japan and a giant conglomerate. Imported Korean cars have only their price and quality to rely on. They are not yet real full brands, with both tangible and intangible values.

The process of brand positioning

By what practical process can a brand platform be defined that will maximise the chances of a successful brand launch? This concerns local brands but also global ones with the big challenge of finding a strong global identity, and eventually a global positioning (if not, one that can be tailored to different markets). There are five phases to this process: understanding, exploring, testing, strategic evaluation and selection, and implementing or activating the brand:

1. *The understanding phase* is about identifying all potential added values for the brand, based on its identity, roots, heritage and prototypes, as well as its current image. This is a self-centred approach: a brand's truth lies within itself. However, in order to detect which area of potential is most likely to be profitable for the business, an analysis of customers and competition is required. Markets are also analysed for this reason, as well as developments among consumers looking for 'insights' – consumers' aspirations or dissatisfactions on whom the brand can build. Lastly, the aim of analysing the competition is to identify opportunities,

gaps, exploitables and areas of interest. The tool for this is perceptual mapping, for in marketing the fight is over perceptions. Perceptual maps do produce a remarkably synthetic model of the mind of the consumer – the psychological battlefield.

2. *The exploration phase* is about suggesting scenarios for the brand. Finding the brand platform is not something that can be done in one fell swoop: it takes an iterative approach, using repeated eliminations and adjustments. For example, what would the possible scenarios be for a brand such as Havana Club? This is the only rum produced in Cuba, an island famous for the quality of its sugar cane (and thus its rum), and seeks to promote this quality on a worldwide scale. Going back to our four questions– against whom? why? for when? for whom? – we can identify four major scenarios, each of which uses its own approach to express the full richness of the imagery evoked by Cuba and its capital Havana, which have remained authentic and intact over time (see Table 7.2). Note that these four scenarios do not each rely on the same product. As is the case with many brands, preferences can differ from one country to another. For example, in the case of rum, some countries consume only white rum, while others consume only dark rum. Evidently not all of these countries could be penetrated using the same product. This has a strong impact on positioning, as the competition faced by a white alcohol will not be the same as that facing a dark rum. In one case, Havana Club will try to take market share away from gin and vodka, while in the other it will be up against whiskies, malts and brandies. Within the white alcohols sector, the question concerning the competition needs to be asked again: are we targeting the leader or not?

It all depends on the subjective category and the targeted competitors: to define oneself as rum is already to have specified the nature of the competition. In the UK, however, there is no rum market – despite the fact that Bacardi sells very well there. But to drink Bacardi, do you necessarily have to be aware that it is a rum? It is – thanks to Cuba – perhaps the very epitome of the party cocktail drink.

The angle of attack will differ depending on whether the target is Bacardi (the world leader), mixers and quality rums, or dark spirits in general (whiskies, brandies and so on).

3. *The test phase* is the time when scenarios are either refined or eliminated. It requires consumer studies to evaluate the credibility and emotive resonance of each scenario. What are being tested at this stage are ideas and formulations, but certainly not whole campaigns.

4. *The strategic evaluation* takes the form of a comparison of scenarios based on criteria, followed by the economic evaluation of potential sales and profits. The latter is conducted in 'bottom-up' fashion, through the summation of sales and contribution of forecasts from each country in question and so on.

Let us look again at some of the 10 criteria for evaluating positioning (see page 101). The second of these raises the question of the strength of the 'consumer insight' on which it is based. Is there a genuine business opportunity here? The fifth is a reminder that all positioning has to target a weakness in the competition – and indeed, a long-term weakness. Positioning itself is a durable decision. So you might ask the question, how do you find your competitor's long-term weakness? Paradoxically, through its very strength (Neyrinck, 2000). For example, what is the long-term weakness of the world leader, Bacardi? It is the very fact

Table 7.2 Comparing positioning scenarios: typical positioning scenarios for a new Cuban rum brand

| | White mixer | | Dark straight | |
	A	B	C	D
	Better-tasting mixer than the leader	Experience Cubania	The 'absolute' rum	An original spirit
Against whom?	The leader	All mixers	Premium rums	Whiskies, cognac
Why?	'Taste'	'The Cuban drink'	'The best rum'	'Be different'
When?	Cocktail/mixed	Night/mixed	Home/bars/straight	Home/after dinner
To whom?	25/40 Spain, UK, Canada, Germany Bacardi drinkers	16/30 Urban/B in Europe and Canada, non-rum drinkers	25/40 Urban/heavy rum drinkers in Canada, Spain, Italy, UK	30/45 Urban heavy spirit drinkers in Europe Canada, Asia
Product priority	White	White/3 yrs	Anejo (dark)	7 yrs (dark)
Pricing	–10 % vs leader	Par with leader	Premium	Par with whiskies
Communication	Mass media	2-step marketing	2-step marketing	2-step marketing

that it is the world leader. To sell in such quantities, you have to sell at low prices, and thus produce everything locally. Bacardi may have been born in Cuba; but its rum no longer comes from Cuba, for a variety of commercial and economic reasons.

To evaluate a positioning, one must always take the trade into account. For example, in the world of shampoo, would a positioning of the 'for men' type constitute good positioning? The answer would seem to be 'yes' when judged by certain strategic evaluation criteria. It achieves differentiation and it represents a 'customer insight' (a genuine purchasing motive). But adopting the philosophy of the retailer leads us to a different conclusion. Retailers such as Wal-Mart, Carrefour and Asda tend to have a special men's section for hygiene and cosmetics products. This would immediately attract those arguing for this positioning. But it tends to be women who buy for men, and these women tend to choose for their men a shampoo from their own section. Thus, in terms of sales potential, it makes more sense to leave the product in the normal shampoo section. If it were put in the men's section, sales would fall by 50 per cent. Furthermore, let us suppose that the brand was in the men's section, at which point the 'for men' positioning stops being a source of differentiation, since that section contains nothing but products and brands for men only!

5. The fifth phase is that of *implementation and activation* once the platform has been chosen and drawn up. This new term clearly expresses the fact that today, a brand's values must be made palpable and tangible; and the brand must therefore transform them into acts.

This is all about defining the brand's marketing strategy, functional objectives and campaign plan. Will it be mainly mass-media advertising, or mainly proximity marketing? How will the brand be activated? Here again, choices will be determined by the competitive environment. Consider the example of Dolmio – the European leader in Italian sauces – whose marketing strategy cannot be the same for both the UK and Ireland. In the UK, Dolmio controls a mere 20 per cent of the market, while in the latter it is the comfortable leader with 50 per cent. Furthermore, far more proximity marketing can be carried out in a country with a small population than in a very large country. Activation is the phase during which strategy becomes behaviour and tangible actions, thus transcending mere advertising and promotion. (See Figure 7.2.)

Determining the flagship product

In launching a new brand, companies have to be extremely careful in choosing which product or service to present in their first campaign and how to speak about it, even more so if the overall brand is particularly ambitious. This 'star product' should be the one that best represents the brand's intentions, ie the one that best conveys the brand's potential to bring about change in the market. Likewise, in terms of name, only those products that best support the overall project should prominently bear the brand name. On the less typical products, the brand name should intervene far less, serving only to endorse the product.

Not all products of a brand equally represent it. Only those which truly epitomise the brand's identity should be used as support in a launch campaign. Ideally, this identity must be visible. The major car manufacturers are well aware of this. Car design must be the outward expression of the brand's long-term design. The choice of the brand's best exemplar may conflict with short-term business objectives. The product that would sell the best might not be representative of the brand identity to be fostered. In this situation the long term should determine the short term, since it is evident that without business there is no brand.

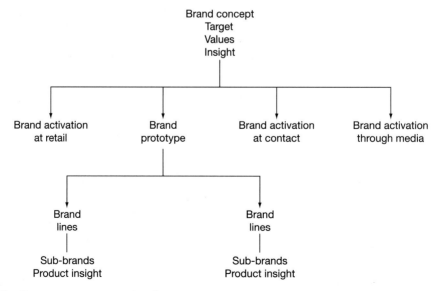

Figure 7.2 From strategy to activation

Brand campaign or product campaign?

Volkswagen has never produced communications about anything other than its products. Since the beginning, its ads have consistently reflected a deliberate choice of graphic style – that of purity: hence, the motif of a car on a white background. So, even if the brand treats the rational arguments aloofly, humorously, impertinently or paradoxically, the car remains the 'hero' of the ad. Sony occasionally launches so-called 'brand campaigns', which aim to emphasise the brand's slogan. Whenever a brand is created, there are two alternative strategies: to communicate the brand's meaning either directly, or by focusing on a particular product. Which path is followed depends on the company's ability to select one product which will fully convey the brand's meaning. It is no wonder that Volkswagen took the second option. The Beetle plainly demonstrated the genius of an original artist, an outsider, and obviously represented a different car culture.

In launching its brand in Europe, Whirlpool, the white goods world leader, decided to forbid any product ad for three years. It wanted to create a thrill around its name that no product campaign would have created, through a very imaginative and symbolic campaign.

The reason banks prefer brand campaigns is quite logical. As service companies, they have nothing tangible to show the potential customer. They can only symbolise their values and their identity. They also encapsulate the essence of their identity in slogans, in this way hoping to make up for their lack of visible products.

Brand language and territory of communication

Today's vocabulary is no longer just verbal, it may even be said to be predominantly visual. In this multimedia era, in which only a few split-seconds' attention are spent on advertisements in magazines, pictures are far more important than words.

A territory of communication does not appear from nowhere, nor can it be arbitrarily assigned to the brand. Brand language allows brands to freely express their ideology. Not knowing which language to speak, we merely repeat the same groups of words or pictures over and over again, so that the whole brand message eventually becomes clogged. There is such a great urge to create unity, resemblance and a common spirit among the different campaigns that in the end they all seem merely to repeat one another. Each specific campaign message thus gets obliterated by an excessive concern to find the missing code!

The code is always rather artificial whereas language is natural: it conveys the personality, culture and values of the sender, helping the latter either to announce products and services or to charm customers.

Brand language finally serves as a means of decentralising decisions. Thanks to the use of a common glossary of terms, different subsidiaries worldwide can adapt the theme of their messages to local market and product requirements and yet preserve the brand's overall unity and indivisible nature. Brand identity must reconcile freedom with coherence, a task which expression guides (also called brand charters) are meant to facilitate. These should not merely address issues such as the position of the brand name on the page and so on. They must also specify the following:

▮ dominant features of style;

▮ the audio-visual characteristics such as a gesture, a close-up of a customer's face, a jingle;

▮ the graphic layout or narrative structure codes, and the brand's colour codes;

▮ the principles determining if and how the brand – and its signature, if it has one – can be used in some circumstances.

Such cases must indeed be anticipated and defined in the expression guide.

Choosing a name for a strong brand

Manufacturers make products; consumers buy brands. Pharmaceutical laboratories produce chemical compounds, but doctors prescribe brands. In an economic system where demand and prescription focus on brands, brand names naturally take on a pre-eminent role. For if the brand concept encompasses all of the brand's distinctive signs (name, logo, symbol, colours, endorsing characteristics and even its slogan), it is the brand name that is talked about, asked for or prescribed. It is therefore natural that we should devote particular attention to this facet of the brand creation process: choosing a name for the brand.

What is the best name to choose to build a strong brand? Is there anywhere a particular type of name that can thus guarantee brand success? Looking at some so-called strong brands will help us answer these usual questions: Coca-Cola, IBM, Marlboro, Perrier, Dim, Kodak, Schweppes ... What do these brand names have in common? Coca-Cola referred to the product's ingredients when it was first created; the original meaning of IBM (International Business Machines) has disappeared; Schweppes is hard to pronounce; Marlboro is a place; Kodak, an onomatopoeia. The conclusion of this quick overview is reassuring: to make a strong brand, any name can be used (or almost any), provided that there is a consistent effort over time to give meaning to this name, ie to give the brand a meaning of its own.

Does this mean that there is no need to give much thought to the brand name, apart from the mere problem of ensuring that the brand can be registered? Not at all, because following some basic selection rules and trying to choose the right name will save you time, perhaps several years, when it comes to making the baby brand a big brand. The question of time is crucial: the brand has to conquer a territory of its own. From the very start, therefore, it must anticipate all of its potential changes. The brand name must be chosen with a view to the brand's future and destiny, not in relation to the specific market and product situation at the time of its birth. As companies generally function the other way around, it seems more than appropriate to provide some immediate information on the usual pitfalls to avoid when choosing a brand name, and also to give a reminder of certain principles.

Brand name or product name?

Choosing a name depends on the destiny that is assigned to the brand. One must therefore distinguish the type of research related to creating a full-fledged brand name – destined to expand internationally, to cover a large product line, to expand to other categories, and to last – from the opposite related to creating a product name with a more limited scope in space and time. Emphasis, process time and financial investments will certainly be different in both cases.

The danger of descriptive names

Ninety per cent of the time, manufacturers want the brand name to describe the product which the brand is going to endorse. They like the name to describe what the product does (an aspirin that would be called Headache) or is (a biscuit brand that would be called Biscuito; a direct banking service called Bank Direct). This preference for denotative names shows that companies do not understand what brands are all about and what their purpose really is. Remember: brands do not describe products – brands distinguish products.

Choosing a descriptive name also amounts to missing out on all the potential of global communication. The product's characteristics and qualities will be presented to the target audience thanks to the advertisements, the sales people, direct marketing, articles in specialised periodicals and the comparative studies done by consumer associations. It would thus be a waste to have the brand name merely repeat the same message that all these communication means will convey in a much more efficient and complete way. The name, on the contrary, must serve to add extra meaning, to convey the spirit of the brand. For products do not live forever: their life cycle is indeed limited. The meaning of the brand name should not get mixed up with the product characteristics that a brand presents when it is first created. The founders of Apple were well aware of this: within a few weeks the market would know that Apple made micro-computers. It was therefore unnecessary to fall into the trap of names such as Micro-Computers International or Computer Research Systems. In calling themselves Apple, on the contrary, they could straightaway convey the brand's durable uniqueness (and not just the characteristics of the temporary Apple-1): this uniqueness has to do more with the other facets of brand identity than with its physique (ie its culture, its relationship, its personality, etc).

The brand is not the product. The brand name therefore should not describe what the product does but reveal or suggest a difference.

Taking the copy phenomenon into account

Any strong brand has its copy or even its counterfeit. There is no way out of this. First of all, manufacturing patents end up being public one day. So what is left to preserve the firm's competitive advantage and provide legitimate recompense for investing in research and development and innovating? Well, the brand name. The pharmaceutical industry is the perfect example: today, as soon as patents become public, all laboratories can produce the given compound at no R&D cost and generic products start flooding the market. A brand name that simply describes the product and the product's function will be unable to differentiate the brand from copies and generic products entering the market. Choosing a descriptive name boils down to making the brand a generic product in the long run. That is exactly how the first antibiotics got trapped: they were given names indicating that they were made from penicillin – Vibramycine, Terramycine, etc.

Today, however, the pharmaceutical industry has become aware that the name is in itself a patent which protects the brand from copies. This name must therefore be different from that of the generic product: in becoming distinctive and unique, it also becomes inimitable. The Glaxo-Roche laboratory, for instance, discovered an anti-ulcer agent which it called 'ranitidine'. Yet the brand name is 'Zantac'. Their competitor, Smith, Kline and French, also identified an anti-ulcer agent called 'cimetidine', but sold it under the Tagamet brand name. This naming policy is a good hedge against copies and counterfeits. Doctors are under the impression that Vibramycine and Terramycine are the same thing. Tagamet, though, seems unique, as does Zantac. The inevitable generic products that will eventually take advantage of the cimetidine or ranitidine patents will not initate the Tagamet or Zantac names.

An original name can protect the brand since it reinforces the latter's defence against all imitations, whether they be fraudulent or not. The perfume name Kerius, for example, was considered as a counterfeit of Kouros: in litigation, legal experts do not judge counterfeit in terms of nominal or perfect similarity but in terms of overall resemblance. Thus Kerius became Xerius, while another cosmetics company had to pull out the products it had just launched under the name, Mieva because of Nivea. Descriptive names fail to act as patents. A brand called Biscuito would be very little protected: only the 'o' could be protected so as to prevent someone from naming a product 'Biscuita'! Even Coca-Cola was unable to prevent the Pepsi-Cola name! Quickburger, Love Burger and Burger King have similar names, whereas McDonald's name is inimitable.

Distributors' own brands have greatly taken advantage of descriptive brands' scarce protection. Planning to win over some of the leading brands' customers, distributors have chosen names for their own brands that are very similar to those of the strong brands to which they refer: this way, consumers are likely to easily mistake one for the other. Ricoré by Nestlé has thus been copied by Incoré, L'Oréal's Studio Line by Microline, etc. Because the packages look alike (Incoré is in a yellow can like Ricoré's, with a picture of a cup and table setting also like Ricoré's ...), consumers get all the more confused as they only rely on visual signs to find their way through the store aisles. As a matter of fact, recent research has shown that confusion rates are often above 40 per cent (Kapferer, 1995 (see also page 140)).

The way in which the pharmaceutical industry has been handling the copy problem is extremely promising in terms of the long-term survival of all brands. By creating at the same time a product name (that of a specific compound) and a brand name, they have avoided the Walkman, Xerox or Scotch syndrome. These proper nouns now tend to become common names, merely used to designate the product. In order to overcome such risk of 'generism', companies must create an adjective-brand (the Walkman pocket music-player), not a noun-brand (a walkman). When creating a brand name, it might therefore also be necessary to coin a new name for the product itself (in this case, the pocket music-player).

Taking time into account

Many names end up preventing the brand from developing naturally over time because they are too restrictive:

▌ 'Europ Assistance' hinders the geographical extension of this brand and has also facilitated the creation of Mondial Assistance.

▌ Calor etymologically (meaning 'heat' in Latin) refers to heating appliance technology (irons, hair-dryers), and thus excludes refrigerators, The Radiola brand never managed to impose itself in the field of household appliances: its brand name was much too reminiscent of one specific sector.

▌ As time goes by, Sport 2000, the sporting goods distributor, seems less and less modern and futuristic.

▌ The non-fat yoghurt name, Silhouette, was too restrictive in terms of consumer benefit: slimness for the sake of slimness does not necessarily prevail anymore. This is why Yoplait decided to change the name to Yoplait fat-free, after having invested over 20 million dollars since 1975 in advertising the first brand name.

Thinking internationally

Any brand must be given the potential to become international in case it should want to become so one day. Yet many brands still discover quite late that, if such is their desire, they are limited by their name: Suze, the bitter French aperitif wine, almost literally means sweet in German. Nike cannot be registered in certain Arab countries. The Computer Research Services brand name causes problems in France, as does Toyota's MR2. In the United States, the almighty CGE name cannot be protected against the famous GE (General Electric) brand name. Prior to internationalising a brand, one must ensure that the name is easy to pronounce, that it has no adverse connotations and that it can be registered without problems. These new requirements explain why there is so much interest in the 1,300 words which all seven major languages of the European Union have in common. It also explains the current tendency to choose abstract names which, having no previous meaning, can thus create their own.

Overcoming thresholds in brand awareness

Brand equity is partly measured by brand awareness: how many people around the world know the brand, if only by its name? This is nothing unusual: the brand is a sign. Brand awareness measures the number of people who know what the brand stands for and are aware of what promises this sign has given, namely in terms of know-how (which products, which services). A brand with no awareness is just something stuck on a product, meaningless and speechless. The purpose of investing in advertising is to reveal the meaning of the brand and convey it to the largest number of people: they should thus feel tempted to try the product being presented by the brand. Three types of awareness are usually distinguished:

▌ 'top of mind' awareness measures whether the brand is the first to come to the mind of people who are interviewed on the brands of a given product category;

▌ 'unaided' awareness measures the brand's impact, ie to what extent it is sponta- neously associated with a given product category;

▌ 'aided' awareness consists in asking the target audience if they have already heard of certain brands or if they have at least heard their names.

As we can see, the level of difficulty increases from one type of awareness to the next, from the cheapest – 'aided' awareness – to the most expensive – 'top of mind' awareness. From this hierarchy, it is often inferred that 'top of mind' awareness should be every brand's goal. It is a mistake. Each type of awareness has a

different purpose and specific implications. Depending on the market, it might or might not be appropriate to invest in order to reach a high rate of 'top of mind' awareness.

The purpose of aided awareness is to reassure – the brand has already been heard of. The brand is not totally unknown so that salespeople can allude to it when selling something to a hesitating client. Unaided awareness refers to the few brands which immediately come to mind: this will benefit them if the buyer, unwilling to spend too much time choosing among them, rather relies out of convenience on immediate memory. In industrial marketing, this awareness rate indicates a shortlist of names, which will be quickly scanned in a first phase of the decision process and among which some might later be more thoroughly analysed. 'Top of mind' awareness benefits the brand any time buyers have to make a quick decision (as when ordering a drink in a café, for instance) or want to decide without too much effort (because they are not very involved in the task), as is the case with many household products (Kapferer and Laurent, 1995).

As a result of these differences, it is clear that the pursuit of a particular type of awareness really depends on the way in which buyers of a product make their decisions and on their level of involvement. The financial investment which is needed by a brand eager to gain a strong unaided awareness is not always justified: the market share of a household appliance brand does not simply double if its unaided awareness doubles. However, if it has a satisfactory level of aided awareness, a white goods brand should invest to increase the number of its points of sale. Indeed, with regard to durable products, which are only purchased infrequently, clients do not always know beforehand either what is available on the market or what criteria they should use to decide. They usually decide on the spot, after lengthy comparisons with the other products on sale in the store. As long as the brand brings back a vague memory, customers are bound to evaluate its products. Thus, in Europe, Hoover has a low unaided awareness rate, but a very high aided one. Before deleting the Philips brand name, Whirlpool aimed at reaching two-thirds of Philips' aided awareness rate (see also p 362).

As for products that require less involvement by the purchaser, the unaided awareness rate has more impact on choice since customers neither perceive any great risk nor want to spend any great amount of time in choosing. Yet experience has shown that under certain market conditions, gaining any unaided awareness at all is almost impossible. The brand's aided awareness rate increases but not its unaided awareness? Why is that?

Unaided awareness is not a cold, merely cognitive measure: it has an emotional dimension. This is shown by the correlation that exists between awareness and preferences or global evaluations (see Table 7.3). Awareness, therefore, does not come simply from high pressure advertising. It comes from making people feel attracted and interested. It will thus be more difficult for an unfriendly brand to stand out because of the well-known mechanisms of selective exposure, attention and memory.

Unaided awareness is always acquired at the expense of another brand. If one brand's awareness increases, another's necessarily decreases. This is demonstrated by a fact that is commonly observed in most markets: people who are interviewed usually quote an average of three or four brands. Given such a limited number, accepting a new brand in such a selective club necessarily means that in turn some other brand will no longer be quoted. This results in the following: when three brands on the market are strongly rated in unaided awareness, scarcely any other brand has a chance of even getting quoted (Laurent, Kapferer and Roussel 1995). Access to such markets is said to be 'blocked'. The relationship between aided and unaided awareness is graphically represented by the curve in Figure 7.3(a).

In new markets, where no brands have strong unaided awareness, this selective

Table 7.3 How liking stimulates unaided awareness

Brands	Variation of unaided awareness	Variation of global image in the same period
Nissan	+6	+0.4
Toyota	+5	+0.5
Citroën	+4	+0.1
Renault	+3	+0.2
Mercedes	+2	=
Audi	+2	+0.2
VW	+1	+0.2
Peugeot	+1	+0.1
Mazda	+1	+0.2
Opel	=	+0.1
BMW	−1	=
Ford	−1	+0.2
Alfa	−2	−0.3
Fiat	−2	−0.2
Volvo	−3	−0.2

Source: Europanel, PSA

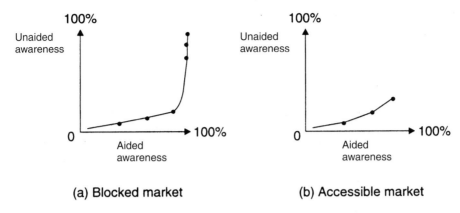

(a) Blocked market   (b) Accessible market

Figure 7.3   Dynamics of brand awareness

memory phenomenon does not exist. Unaided awareness can be pursued by investing in advertising and thus gaining a share of voice. In a competitive environment, it *must* be pursued: not only to escape the blocking mechanism described above, but also to benefit from the first mover's, or pioneer, advantage (Carpenter and Nakamoto, 1990; Nedungadi and Hutchinson, 1985).

In young markets, at the beginning of the category's life cycle, the brand which first enters the market and is aggressively marketed has what is called the 'first mover's advantage': most brands which start creating a market still dominate it several decades later, even in markets in which competitive advantage does not consist of technological know-how, learning curves or gains in productivity. The psychological explanation of this is that when a market first opens, buyers neither have a set of preferences nor any stabilised decision criteria. Thus, the first brand to get known in a new market becomes its prototype and main reference. In other words, this brand is the one to initially define the ideal brand, ie the cluster of attributes that will generate customer satisfaction. This brand is the one that defines the values. That is why later entrants have a handicap. Since they generally adopt a 'me-too' strategy and want to look like the first mover, they lose

some of their distinctiveness and become less conspicuous.

Making creative advertising work for the brand

In the world of mature countries, advertising is a challenge: it is costly, and its results are not always measurable. They are, however, measurable at the time of the brand's launch, at which time it quickly becomes apparent whether the public's demand and attitudes – as well as those of the trade – have changed.

The cost factor raises questions as to the appropriateness of advertising. There are sectors where launches are unthinkable without advertising: the FMCG sector, for example. But even in this case, it all depends on the precise category. The UK's current number one wine, Jacob's Creek (an Australian brand) was launched in the country in 1984, and its first large advertising campaign was in 2000. The brand has since stopped advertising, and now sponsors the *Friends* television programme. The brand's success was built on an excellent, multiple-award-winning product, trade support, public relations, plenty of in-store promotions, and encouraging consumers to try it at the point of sale, to say nothing of on-site promotions.

Top-of-the-range brands also work on winning the long-term support of opinion leaders, capitalising on word of mouth. In the world of the Internet, ebay – the only start-up company to have been profitable from the start, making it the Internet's real success story – operates only through online referral and public relations.

When advertising is needed to give a boost to sales and business, the familiar old maxim springs to mind, 'Half of my advertising budget is wasted – but I don't know which half.' Actually, we believe that this half can easily be identified. Wasted advertising is advertising that:

▌ is not sufficiently creative, and so will not be seen;

▌ misses its target, so will not be seen by the right people;

▌ will be seen in places with no stores, where there is no distribution system in place.

These three points are the true causes of the waste; and the first of them is the most important. The question it raises is not so much the quality of the advertising agency as that of the client/advertiser. An advertiser can make a major contribution to the creativity of its agency – and thus to the quality of the campaign – in two ways: through the quality of its brief, and by the ability to take creative risks.

With the creative process in advertising, everything starts and ends with the creative brief – and agency creative directors will have a better understanding of what is expected of them if they can empathise with the brand and understand in what direction they are required to take the target audience. The problem is that traditional marketing tools are perhaps no longer conducive to good briefs. It is significant that, in Unilever's Brand Key (its brand charter), nowhere is the word 'positioning' mentioned (that it, is does not say, 'the brand is the ... which offers the most ...

for such and such a reason'). No one even talks about the promise any more. Indeed, these concepts – derived from product marketing and based on product difference – have shown themselves to be unsuited to many markets, as well as to the competitive environment in mature markets. Implicitly, subtly, they promote the search for a significant difference or key compelling advantage in the product itself. This is all very well for Sensodyne, l'Oréal's new Revitalift cream or the Pentium 4, but how well does it work with Nescafé, Calvin Klein or Benetton, to say nothing of the monolith that is Marlboro?

Nescafé's big 'Open Up' campaign promotes friendliness and an open attitude to others. What promise does this make? Calvin Klein's Obsession, Eternity and Truth promise nothing either: they merely offer. Consider also the advertising from Benetton (United Colours of Benetton), which likewise promised nothing in particular, but constructed a challenging, inclusive brand which became a youth icon.

Today, therefore, we still have to ask the basic question, 'What does our brand want to be the brand of? What is it proposing?', rather than: 'What is it promising?' Likewise, we should now be asking, 'What is the reason to believe this brand proposition?' and not, 'Why is this promise true?' We therefore recommend that regardless of whether or not the word 'positioning' is used, the creative brief be limited to two pages. One of these should show the brand's identity prism (see page 107), to ensure that the creative directors obtain a good feel for the brand's body and soul, character and values. The other should be the creative brief proper, with its key items, which are:

1.   Why do we communicate this time?

2.   What is expected from this campaign?

3.   Target of this campaign.

4.   Consumer insight.

5. Brand proposition.

6. Reason to believe.

7. Executional guidelines (brand ownables, executional brand codes, media and so on).

To achieve a leap of creative genius, a great creative idea, the brand proposition must be incisive, not bland. What can a creative person do with a brand proposition coming from a typical McKinsey-style brand consultancy output, such as 'Brand X is the ultimate (whisky for instance)'. There is a real problem with the tools and consulting companies that excel in analytics but produce no ideas. Because of the reduction in the demand for strategic consulting, most of the big consulting companies have reoriented their staff. They want now to accompany the client all through the executional process. However, analytical people, recruited for data processing skills, produce thick and exhaustive reports and a mass of matrices, but a dearth of actionable ideas.

The mistake is to think one can rely on the agency to transform as if by a miracle the bland proposition into a great creative concept. It just does not happen this way.

The second condition for a creative leap is to realise that the advertising target must be radicalised. It cannot be a simple description of those who will buy, but should provide their reflection. If advertising is to break out of the clutter, it must not present plain people. Think of the Budweiser advertising saga 'Wazzup': by choosing quite radical characters in the commercials, the brand showed strong signs of modernity, of reinvention and of reinvolvement of the public. This was a challenge for this mainstream popular brand, which all Americans have known almost since they were born.

Building brand foundations through opinion leaders

Unless one wants to position the brand in a niche at the very high end, high market shares and sales will come from a mass market positioning. However, paradoxically in order to influence the mass of the market, the people less involved with the brand, the 'switchers', a brand must be carried by a smaller group of opinion leaders. Consumer behaviour relies too much on an individual approach to consumer choice, using the paradigm of a person deciding in a social vacuum. But everyone belongs to a network, a group, a tribe. Building a brand means getting closer to these groups, which are mediators of influence.

Proximity to opinion leaders

In all groups there are influencers, also called opinion leaders. The concept of opinion leadership is not new, but its significance has been hidden by an over-reliance on advertising. In fact, to build a brand one of the first questions to ask is, what group(s) will carry the brand? Here we do not speak of the market segment, but of the group(s) who will influence the market segment. A brand alone cannot convince. It needs relayers, committed relayers. Modern taste makers belong to tribes: microethnic, cultural and geographical groups. These groups need proper identification and a programme of continuous direct relationship. They must experience the brand, its values, and eventually interact with it. The brand must understand them, and present itself as being on their sides, sharing the same values.

Who are these influencers? Who are the opinion leaders? The two concepts need to be distinguished. Recent research (Valette Florence, 2004) suggests that opinion leaders combine three necessary traits. They are perceived as experts, are endowed with charisma and have a desire to be different from others, and have a high social visibility. Not all experts are opinion leaders: they are influencers, as are salespeople or prescriptors.

Influencers can be professionals. Canson would not have succeeded without the close ties that it is permanently weaving with the teacher community. Pedigree (pet food) relies on professionals too. L'Oreal relies on hairdressers, La Roche Posay on dermatologists.

They can be hobbyists. T-fal, positioned as tools for the successful cuisine, develops ties with cookery schools and with all the professionals engaged in developing a high level of skill in cuisine.

They can be the persons most involved in the category: all consumers are not equal. Some are more involved, more interested in all that concerns, not the product itself, but the need. They read more, use Internet much more, participate in chats and forums. For instance, mothers with more children play an influencing role.

Opinion leaders are to be found in specific community groups. We stress the word 'groups' because one should now speak of trend-setting tribes. As a result, the goal is to interact not with a sum of individuals, but with pre-organised groups, be they formal or informal. These groups can be met at specific places. Groups are organised, so it is easier to organise events with them. Salomon is obsessed with increasing the level of interaction with surfer groups all around the world, for they are trendsetters. Absolut Vodka succeeded because it came to be available at all the parties of the New York gay community. Bombay Sapphire gin did the same in Los Angeles.

To reach these groups, direct contact is needed and virtual intimacy on the net is necessary. One does not create strong ties at a distance. The goal is show that the brand is becoming part of their world, by means of participating in occasions that show the brand and group share the same values, in some way or another. Eventually the brand should be creating these occasions.

Creating a hard core of supporters

As soon as the brand is launched the reflex must be of creating a hard core of supporters, involved in the brand. Clarins, a very small cosmetic company when it started in 1954, facing giants such as Estée Lauder and l'Oréal, was extremely innovative in that respect, but it went unnoticed up to the point when market research showed to its competitors that the small brand was getting bigger, and that it experienced a high rate of loyal and even fanatical clients: with each product there was an invitation to write to the company and to Mr Courtin, its founder. One-to-one and CRM were already there, far before these became 'musts' for management.

There are many frameworks that have shown how consumers can be segmented on a dimension of closeness of the relationship to the brand. Typical segments range from hell to paradise, with a mix of behavioural and emotional dimensions:

1. Those consumers who dislike the brand, even hate it. It is really not part of their world.

2. Those who are not consumers because they consider the brand is underperforming on a sought attribute.

3. Those who simply are not consumers, without a specific reason (simply the brand has nothing salient to their eyes to induce trial).

4. Those who would like to buy but cannot (no availability, no accessibility, price problem).

5. Those who buy from time to time, switching between brands.

6. Those who buy more often.

7. Those buyers who are involved, engaged with the brand.

As soon as the brand is launched everything must be done to create and identify consumers in segments 6 and 7, the heavy buyers and the involved consumers.

Asking for identification is a sure way to build the precious database that will enable the organisation to give VIP treatment to these forerunners: specific tips, a specific code number on the Web site, specific invitations, specific offers, PR events and so on.

There is another way of creating a hard core of supporters. It can be summed up in one key phrase formulated 50 years ago by Paul Ricard: *faites-vous un ami par jour* (make a friend every day). Of course, this is easy to say if you happen to be – as Ricard was – the man who created what is now the world's third-largest spirits group. But the phrase deserves closer examination:. He did not say 'make a customer every day', but 'a friend'. Service, free gifts, responsiveness, personalised relationships, attentiveness and the sharing of enthusiasm at small and large gatherings alike are the rungs on this upward ladder.

Creating word of mouth

Status is not granted by oneself: it is given by opinion leaders, experts, and the press. Virgin, although it is one the very few brands known throughout the world, hardly spends a dime on advertising. However, everybody has heard of Virgin, or will hear about it. Paradoxically Richard Branson, the founder of the Virgin galaxy, is not an extrovert. However, he knew that by seeking publicity he could avoid spending a lot money on advertising – money he did not have in any case.

Branson has become a man of public relations: he knows how to create events that will become widely broadcast and diffuse the buzz.

Word of mouth should not however be seen as an alternative to advertising. Advertising is surely not dead. Brands have two feet: shared emotions and renewed products.

Advertising remains a fantastic tool to shape these common, shared imageries, or to create instant knowledge of an innovation.

How can one create the buzz, this modern, fashionable word for word of mouth, or positive rumours (Kapferer, 1991, 2004)?

The first approach is to make plenty of time for the press and media. Naturally, it is a good idea to recruit a specialist agent, but journalists will be flattered to be welcomed by managers themselves. This is where the work of making friends should begin: it is crucially important to know how to assist a journalist (for whom, as we all know, time is in short supply). We should also remember that everyone deserves attention, from the big-name television reporter to the freelancer from the small trade journal. The high-powered editor of the future is sure to be lurking among the dozens of freelancers you meet.

The second approach – which should become a discipline – is to do nothing without considering the press fallout. As the adage goes, every dollar you spend on public relations requires another to promote the fact. A buzz has to be activated and energised: it does not always start on its own.

The third approach is always to look for the difference and disruption in everything (Dru, 2002). It is said that in the world of PR, it has all been done before. This means that your job is to surprise, because surprise is what gets people talking. The search for suitable occasions must therefore always incorporate the three key aspects, which are:

▌ the target audience's areas of interest;

▌ the brand's identity;

▌ disruption.

Taking distributors into account

In the field of consumer goods that do not require much consumer involvement, it is no longer the consumer who is solely responsible for the success or failure of new brands, but the distributors. In deciding whether or not to give room to a new brand, they are the ones who can cause it to fail. They are also the ones who can cause the premature decline of a new brand if they judge its turnover to be too slow. Because of this, many projects based on excellent concepts and good products have not survived. New brands now have to fight distributors' own-brands which are pushed forward because of their higher margins, one reason why new brands are no longer easily admitted by distributors. The problem is that when the weighted distribution percentage increases too slowly, investments in advertising have little or no impact. If these are spread out over time or delayed, the new product on the market will not rotate quickly enough and thus will eventually get taken off the shelves after just a few months. Because distributors have such power, it is absolutely necessary to take their reaction into account when predicting a brand's chances of succeeding. A good example of this is Sironimo.

This new brand of fruit-flavoured beverage concentrate was an innovation offering real added value. The popular drink was introduced to the 6–11 age group in very different packaging: bottles that were fun, collectable and easy to handle, and were designed and shaped especially for children, unlike the large cylindrical cans of Teisseire (the local market leader) or those of distributors' own-brands. All six flavours in the line were bottled in bowling-pin-shaped containers, each one representing a different kind of animal. In tests, consumers unanimously acclaimed this innovation both in France and abroad, eg in the UK. A very creative, attractive and well targeted advertising campaign soon made Sironimo the leading brand in terms of unaided awareness among 6–11-year-olds. Unfortunately, though, Sironimo was not sold by enough distributors. The brand was based on a concept (a collection of six bowling pins) which required many shelf facings: this could only be achieved by reducing the leader Teisseire's facings or those of the distributors' own-brands, which were a major source of profit for the distributor. Without these crucial facings, the launch of the Sironimo product line concept could not be pulled off. Moreover, of the six flavours, some rotated faster than others and so were more likely to be out of stock if the sales reps did not pay attention quickly enough. All these factors were a serious handicap to the launch of Sironimo. In the end, the brand owner decided to sell the brand to the leader of this drinks market instead.

8

The challenge of growth in mature markets

Brand management is a challenge in mature markets. How to build the business where consumers have their needs amply fulfilled, face considerable choice, become price-sensitive and find allies in multiple retailers who want a larger share of the added value created by brands?

Drawing from multiple cases and models, we look at the main strategies that can be followed to find growth in no-growth markets.

The first, short-term strategy is to build on existing clients. Customer relationship management (CRM), database management and relationship marketing have not emerged so forcefully in the panoply of modern brand management without a compelling reason. It is necessary to get still closer to the consumer, one's own consumers, who may be faced with too much choice. Seducing new customers seems too costly (Reichheld, 1996).

The second one is to carry out more research. What needs, or lacks of satisfaction or untapped uses can be better met? For instance, packaging and design innovations, although not spectacular, are able to provide incremental sources of share, especially if they

are differentiated according to the distribution channel.

However, for the long term, the two main options are to explore foreign markets and to innovate. We turn to these strategies now.

Growth through existing customers

The first source of growth is to be found among the existing customers of the brand. There are growth opportunities to be searched, evaluated and exploited. This is too often overlooked by managers who wish to move quickly to some hot brand extension.

Building volume per capita

Brand management over time is the permanent pursuit of growth. One way of achieving this is to move from a pattern of low-volume use to a pattern of potentially higher-volume use. For example, Bailey's Irish Cream – a worldwide spirits brand created in 1974 – suffered from a serious restriction to its growth. Its consumption was highly seasonalised, and sales mostly took the form of Christmas and New Year presents. It was consumed mainly by little old ladies, partaking on their own as a sort of sugary treat. It was taken neat in small measures, on account of its sweet taste. If it was to grow in volume, things had to change. The brand's future also depended on its ability to compete outside its category (narrowly defined as Irish cream liqueur). A major campaign was thus launched around the concept of Bailey's on ice. The creative idea was to communicate how the sensuousness of Bailey's allowed you to connect to your friends and family. The intention was to encourage groups of people to drink Bailey's on the rocks (which in fact increases the desire for another glass). A creative media campaign backed this new positioning, exploring how to link the brand to the key sensual moments in the media. For example, Bailey's sponsored *Sex and the City*.

But most important were the on-premise implications of the campaign. Drinking Bailey's on ice required a normal-sized glass, not a liqueur glass as before. The marketers had to persuade the trade to take the campaign seriously. They designed a new Bailey's glass for bar chains, 6,000 ice consumer kits, 4,000 large-measure POS kits, and 16,000 optics to deliver a suitable measure of Bailey for drinking over ice. As a result on-trade sales grew from a low 46,000 cases in December/January 1989 to 107,000 in December/January 1996. It had become more hype, young and trendy to drink Bailey's on ice.

In the United States Jack Daniel's – suffering from its stereotypically 'macho' image – attempted to increase its per capita volume. To do this, the brand needed to create an association with parties (a consumption situation which has a galvanising effect on volume). The brand created a micromarketing plan specifically for this purpose, 'The Jack Daniel's occasion'. The exemplar for this was the barbecue people enjoy around the back of their car after arriving at a sports event a few hours early. The brand developed specific

paraphernalia and specific advertising designed to promote use in this context, which was placed in sports magazines.

Coca-Cola is a best practice exemplar in terms of increasing consumption per capita. Its goal is to bring consumers around the world closer to the consumption rate of American consumers, who drink 118 litres per person per year. Its first key strategic lever is not to use a cost-plus price fixing method, but to target the price of the most popular drink in each country: the price of tea in China, for instance. Because this put a strain on the profitability of local bottlers, the aim is to achieve a quick hike in sales. Profitability is guaranteed to the Coca-Cola Company itself, because it receives the difference between the cost of production of the cola syrup and its resale price (five times as high) to the bottler.

The second key lever is to gain local monopolies. 'Local' in this context means as close as possible to a thirsty person's impulse to drink. Ideally the product should be at an arm's reach, via automatic machines or small refrigerators, everywhere: in hotels, universities, hospitals, and also in bars and cafeterias, for on-premise consumption.

The third lever is to adapt pricing to the consumption situations, so that an identical litre of Coke is sold at very different prices according to when and where it is bought.

Last but not least, specific marketing plans are devoted to specific situations such as lunch and dinner, breakfast and evenings. In many countries consumers drink tapwater, bottled water or mineral water. They do this by habit and also for health reasons: consuming too many sugary drinks leads to obesity and other health problems, which are being faced by many Americans at present. Coca-Cola's plan is to modify local customs, starting with children and young people whose habits are yet to be formed. Hence the global alliance with McDonald's, a key social change agent and a chain of which young people are heavy users. Similarly, Coke has another alliance with Bacardi, the world's leading spirit drink. It is significant that advertisements for Bacardi Carta Blanca show a 'Cuba Libre' cocktail, which is made up of rum and Coke.

Building volume by addressing the barriers to consumption

Branding is too obsessed by image, and not obsessed enough by usage. Even though Coca-Cola is held up as the paragon of good brand management, if we are honest we have to acknowledge that it took almost a century for its managers to address perhaps the most important reason for its non-consumption: it is perceived as an unhealthy drink containing too much sugar.

Certainly the Coca-Cola Company has realised the growth of fitness and health as purchase motivations, in a country where baby boomers were ageing. It launched Tab in 1963, just after Diet Royal Crown Cola and just before Diet Pepsi. However, Diet Coke was launched as late as 1983. It soon became the leader in its category, and what the company calls 'the world's second soft drink'. Later would come caffeine-free Coke, caffeine-free Diet Coke Cherry Coke, Vanilla Coke, Coke and Lemon. Each of these products was an answer to a consumer problem. Some

consumers wanted to drink as much Coke as possible but were prevented from doing so by Coke itself. Some could not eat any more sugar, while others could not take caffeine.

Thus, there were huge opportunities for increased consumption per capita among Coke's own clients. They were probably heard, but never listened to. Identifying the barriers of consumption and relieving them was a service not only to clients but also to profitability: aspartame (the sweetening ingredient in Diet Coke) is less costly than sugar.

In the Coke example, the reasons for consumer's limited consumption were known, but the company was deaf. It confused the brand with the product. By claiming 'Coke is it', it had made Coke symbolise one product and only one, period.

In the task of growing volume through higher consumption per capita, identification of what blocks consumption is not always obvious. Research is needed. One way to do it is to segment the clientele according to the strategic matrix shown in Figure 8.1.

This matrix segments customers according to two dimensions, both related to behaviour. The first is the household's share of requirements (among 100 occasions to purchase, how many times is the specific brand bought?), and the second is the household's

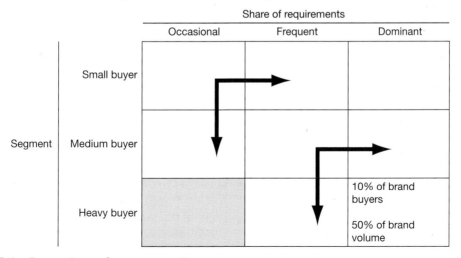

Figure 8.1 Increasing volume per capita

level of consumption (is it a small, medium or heavy buyer?).

This creates eight cells (not nine because one of them is theoretically possible but empirically empty), and each household can be allocated to one of these cells. Of course this matrix can be used for any type of purchase, or purchaser, including companies in B to B markets. Each cell represents a percentage of the total number of households, and a percentage of the total volume sold of the category and of the brand. These figures are important in themselves. The key segment is the bottom right of the matrix, which represents high-consumption households that allocate the highest part of their requirements to the brand. For instance, in Europe households in this cell consume 70 per cent by volume of Coke Light, but only 48 per cent by volume of Coke. These two figures highlight how a single innovative product can release the barriers that prevent people from consuming more.

The brand manager's task is to move as many people as possible progressively in the direction of this bottom-right cell. This can be done, starting from other cells and going vertically or horizontally. But it is first necessary to understand the very specific circumstances and motivations of consumers in each cell. To increase a specific type of behaviour requires behavioural segmentation, then an in-depth understanding of those in each of these behavioural segments. Who are they? Why don't they consume more? Is it a taste problem, a satiety problem, a price problem, a format problem, a packaging problem, an insufficient variety of line extensions, a distribution problem? It is very rarely an image problem, because those being considered here are already clients. In modern markets we know from panel data that even for loyal customers, the brand's share of requirements is never 100 per cent. It is sometimes no more than 40 per cent. However, managers lack information on why these consumers choose other brands 60 per cent of the time.

The result is a new marketing mix, often involving specific product improvement, higher experiential benefits, range extensions (formats, taste and so on), designed to target each behavioral segment.

Growth through new uses and situations

Like it or not, every product is consumed within a particular situation. This is one of the four aspects of the positioning diamond (see page 100). Customers are looking for solutions to problems related to highly specific situations. For example, different things are expected of a car depending on whether it is intended primarily for town use, town use plus other short trips, or fairly long trips. The growth of a brand is thus often a matter of tackling new situations of use, knowing that these situations may well include the same customers, as it is possible for one person to consume the same product in several different situations. For many companies, the situation of use is now the one real criterion for segmentation, rather than the characteristics of the users themselves. A product is always consumed in a particular situation – and it is this situation that defines the brand's competitive set. The situation is the brand's true battleground. Each situation is associated not only with a different subset of competitors, but also with expectations, needs, volumes, and growth and profitability rates.

It is understandable that brands should seek to grow by breaking into high-growth-rate consumption situations in which their attributes give them a high degree of relevance. Such a movement often requires the launch of a new product or line extension.

This is why Mars launched the mini-Mars bar, a new product designed for consumers of the brand aged over 35 who were reducing their consumption of chocolate bars. This new product also changes Mars' positioning: in terms of its physical size, it is a 'sweet'. The

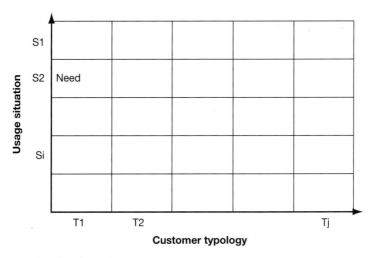

Figure 8.2   Segmenting by situation

situation into which it now fits is that of 'indulgence', rather than a meal substitute or re-energiser.

In the United States, Captain Morgan is a rum brand with a masculine personality: it is the rum of 'fun and adventure'. To achieve growth, the market was segmented according to the situations of use. Seeking to gain a foothold in the so-called 'partying' segment – a large group of friends indulging in noisy partying, dancing and drinking – the company launched Captain Morgan Spice. It then targeted the so-called 'lively socialising' segment – a smaller group of friends getting together for a cocktail – but the first attempt was a failure. Captain Morgan Coconut Rum suffered too much from the Captain Morgan umbrella name and its highly characteristic values. In the latter use situation, the key is to address a more feminine, elegant, romantic set of values, rather than some sort of macho ritual. This is why the second test product to be launched was Parrot Bay, a product merely endorsed by Captain Morgan.

Growth through trading up

A classic growth strategy is trading up. Customers may wish to receive an upgraded

service or product from the brand. Gift packs and 'special series' capitalise on collectors' motivations. Larger formats have a built-in attractiveness too.

Extending the range can also be a way to increase profitability. Thus if it costs 3 euros to produce a litre of three-star cognac (that is, cognac aged for 3 years), 4.5 euros for a VSOP (4 to 5 years), 15 euros for an XO (30–35 years) and 21 euros for a litre of *Extra Vieux*, the customer trade-up is very profitable, as consumer prices are around the 15 euro, 30 euro, 60 euro and 150 euro mark respectively, according to the type of cognac.

Line extensions: necessity and limits

Today, most new product launches are range or line extensions. Shelves are replete with line extensions. As the examples we have given have demonstrated, extending the range is a necessary step in the evolution of a brand through time. Just as living species only survive if they adapt through evolution to their environment and seek to extend their ecological realm, the brand, which historically is designated by a single product (like

Coca-Cola or McCain French fries) breaks up into sub-species. The extension of the line or range (we will address the difference between the two concepts later) typically takes on the following shapes:

▮ Multiplication of formats and sizes (typical in cars but also in soft drinks).

▮ Multiplication of the variety of tastes and flavours.

▮ Multiplication of the type of ingredients (for example Coca-Cola with or without sugar, with or without caffeine, types of motors in the Ford Escort).

▮ Multiplication of generic forms for medicine.

▮ Multiplication of physical forms such as Ariel in powder, liquid or micro formula.

▮ Multiplication of product add-ons under the same name, corresponding to a same consumer need in what is called line extension. Thus, Basic Homme by Vichy comprises a line of toiletries including shaving foam, soothing and energising balm, deodorant, and shower gel.

▮ Multiplication of versions having a specific application. For example, the Johnson company transformed its successful spray polish, Pliz, which was a mono-product brand for a long time, into a range called Pliz 'Classic', which offered products specialised for the type of surface. In doing so it also seized the opportunity to reduce its brand portfolio. Favor, a weak brand, became Pliz with beeswax especially for wood. Shampoo brands multiply endlessly, with varieties suited to different types of hair and scalp condition.

Line or range extension must be distinguished from brand extension, which is a real diversification towards different product categories and different clients. It is a highly sensitive and strategic choice that will be addressed in a separate chapter. Why does Yamaha brand both motorcycles and pianos? Line and range extensions represent 85 per cent of new product launches in consumer goods. It is the most common form of innovation in these markets.

Range extension naturally follows the logic of marketing and of even finer segmentation to better adapt the offer to the specific needs of consumers, needs that never stop evolving. At its beginning, we may recall, each brand was a unique product, in both meanings of the word: it is different and there is only one form of it. This was, for example, the case with the famous Ford: everyone could have it in the colour of their choice, as long as it was black. It was the same with the Coca-Cola and the Orangina bottle. With time, the brand becomes less narrow-minded, and acknowledging differentiated expectations, decides to respond to them. As the American advertising for Burger King, the competitor of McDonald's in the United States, says, 'Have it your way' (whatever way you like it, with or without sauce, onions, etc). Again, taking the example of Coca-Cola, while retaining its identity (the dark colour, cola taste, and other physical and symbolic attributes of the brand), the company was able to extend the power of attraction of its brand by allowing people who up until then were reluctant to try the product to indulge in Coke. The multiplication of versions (with or without sugar, with or without caffeine) increased the number of potential consumers. We therefore see that range extension can reinforce the brand by widening its market and its customer base. A variety of formats has the same effect. In the world of soft drinks, the launch of a new format may be considered the same as launching a new soft drink. Indeed, each new format allows the brand to enter a new usage mode.

In so doing, the brand proves itself to be full of energy and sensitivity. It recognises the different expectations of the public and responds to them. It follows the evolution of consumers and changes with them. Club Med was thus able to widen its offer beyond the simple Robinson Crusoe lodge to keep or attract families, then people in their forties seeking more comfort, and finally older people, children of the baby boom. The range extension is a token of the brand's attentive and caring character. Extending the brand range thus makes the brand interesting and friendly and maintains through these successive mini-launchings a strong visibility. From this point of view, instead of trying to force New Coke on Americans and make them give up the original flavour, the Coca-Cola Company would have done better to have launched the New Coke as an extension alongside the classic Coke!

Range extension is a way of revitalising many failing brands, by making sure they move closely to meet the expectations of today's customers. What saved Campari was the launching onto the market of a 'flanker' product: Campari Soda. Martini would have fallen by the wayside if it had not been for the launching of Martini Bianco, more in touch with the new modes of alcohol consumption. Smirnoff made a step towards customers who were not used to the strong taste of vodka by launching Smirnoff Mule and Smirnoff Ice in small individual bottles.

These motives may be worthy of praise, but the current proliferation of range extensions to be observed in all consumer goods markets results from frantic competition and from the new psychology of organisations.

In these markets there is a strong relationship between market share and the number of facings, ie the share of shelf space taken up. This is not surprising: the customer involvement in these products is average if not low and the number of impulse buyers (when the choice of brand is done on-site) never stops growing. It is, therefore, in the brand manager's interest to take up the most shelf space possible because it will attract even more attention from the customer, especially if a shelf is not extendible and competitors get

pushed out. In many markets, demand is no longer growing and DOBs also occupy a share of the shelf, so the brand manager tries to position his product as 'captain of the category' by presenting a unique offer and so dominating the shelf reserved for national brands.

Distributors have an ambivalent attitude towards range extensions. On the one hand they oppose what is now considered hyper-segmentation, the proliferation of range extension. But as each brand tends to offer the same extensions, this creates bottle-necks because of the obsession each brand has to gain access to maximum distribution. This fight for ever-reducing shelf space strengthens the power of distributors and puts them in a position to ask for increasing amounts of money as a listing fee (Chinardet, 1994).

The problem is that the turnover of extensions, because of their novelty and their price premium, is often lower than that of the original product. When the distributor realises this (if he ever does), he withdraws the extension and awaits the offer of other brands, along with any kind of listing fee that might come with it.

Criticised by, but at the same time popular with distributors, range extensions are appreciated by product and brand managers. First of all, the amount of time needed for development is shorter than that needed for the launching of a new brand. The costs are less than those for the launching of a new brand (they are estimated to be one-fifth), and sales forecasts are more reliable. In the short term at least, it seems an almost automatic way of gaining market share and thus creating observable results that can be attributed to the actions of the manager in a relatively short timespan. This counts for quick promotion within the company, or on another brand in another country. Few managers are willing to take the risk of launching a new brand, but would rather extend the range.

The proliferation of product extensions produces insidious negative effects that are not immediately measurable or measured. First of all, because of small production runs and the increased complexity of production, logistics and management, extensions are more expensive to produce, the cost of which puts up the higher wholesale and retail price. According to Quelch and Kenny (1994), compared to an index of 100 for the cost of production of a mono-product, the corresponding production cost index of differentiated products in a range is, for example, 145 in the car industry, 135 for hosiery and 132 in the food industry. Moreover, in companies which do not take into account direct costs (eg raw materials, advertising), many costs are considered as common to the entire range and are allocated to different products within it according to sales. The best-sellers therefore attract more of the costs than range extensions, which makes the profitability of the latter rather illusory.

Second, non-controlled extension weakens the range logic. The first to find problems with this are the salespeople: the salesforce of Ariel or Dash, used to promoting the brand against Skip, had to undertake within a few months a complete cultural revolution. They had to promote Ariel in powder, in liquid and in micro formula formats all together and without ever explaining that one was superior to the other, or what advantages one format has in comparison to the others. The more extensions multiply, the more the specific positioning of each extension becomes subtle. This is accentuated by the fact that extensions are added without withdrawing the existing versions. Organisations always have a good reason for not cancelling this or that version. The thought of losing the odd customer here and there rules the notion out. This thinking overlooks the fact that product withdrawals should also be managed to gently propel customers towards newer, better versions.

The range logic is also lost on the shelf: indeed, the distributor is reluctant to take on the whole range. He will shop around and take only part of a range, which undermines the consistency of the range on the shelf.

Finally, brand loyalty might be undermined by a proliferation of extensions. The hypersegmentation of shampoos according to new hair needs, leads the customer to take into account more needs in his/her choosing process. The brand is but a feature in an ever longer list of criteria. This result was verified empirically by Rubinson (1992).

In reaction to the proliferation of extensions, Procter & Gamble eliminated within 18 months 15 to 25 per cent of the product extensions that were not achieving a sufficient turnover. In the sector for cleaning products, the growth of new multi-usage products (all-in-one) is on the same principle of simplification. Economies of scale apply all the more since the product is designed for the worldwide market. The extreme strategy of counter-segmentation is applied by hard-discounters: there is absolutely no choice and products are generally only available in a single version with no variety. Thus, there will only be one type of diaper, whatever the weight or the gender of the baby, in contrast to Phases (boy or girl) by Pampers. On the other hand, because of this it will be 40 per cent cheaper than, say, Pampers.

Quelch and Kennedy (1994) recommend four immediate actions for better management of range extensions:

▌ Improve the cost accounting system to be able to catch the additional costs incurred by a new variety all along the value chain. This enables the real profitability of each one to be assessed.

▌ Allocate resources more to high-margin products than to extensions that only appeal to occasional buyers.

▌ Make sure that each salesperson can sum up in a few words the role of each product within the range.

▌ Implement a new philosophy where product withdrawals are not only accepted but encouraged. Some companies only launch an extension after having cancelled another with a low turnover. This withdrawal does not have to be brutal, but can be done gradually so that clients turn to other products within the range.

Growth through innovation

When Moulinex was asked why its results were bad, executives answered that the company had only offered 10 per cent innovation when the average in the industry was 26 per cent.

Innovation, source of growth and competitiveness, does not come easy. Here too, there are no miracles. The firms that innovate most, such as Procter & Gamble, L'Oréal and Gillette, devote on average 3.2 per cent of their sales to research and development. Is there a lesson here for the food companies competing against DOBs and price leaders? The giants in the food industry spend much less in comparison on R&D: Unilever devotes 1.8 per cent of its sales to R&D, Nestlé 1.2 per cent, Kraft General Foods 0.8 per cent and Cadbury-Schweppes 0.4 per cent (Ramsay, 1992).

As a consequence, own-label products account for 62 per cent of the 4,600 new product launches in the British food and drink market. In the chilled sector, own-label product launches represent 79 per cent of the 2,188 introductions! Retailers' brands do act as real brands.

Innovation does not have to mean a technological breakthrough. Gillette is an extreme case: the Sensor required 10 years in research and led to 22 patents, the Sensor Excel 5 years and 29 patents, Sensor Plus Pour Elle 5 years and 25 patents. Many innovations can be linked to the service brought by the brand, in its packaging for example.

The one common explanation for Oasis' leadership over competition in the fruit drink market is in their advertising strategy. The truth is nothing of the kind. Oasis was the first to give up glass bottles. The competitor, which had on the contrary recently invested in a new bottling plant, was wrong-footed and waited several months before carrying out the necessary reappraisal. It was too late: distribution channels had already made their choice and no longer wanted glass bottles that were heavy and breakable. The head start that Evian took over Contrex and Vittel lies mostly in the micro-services which it was able to provide the customer with first. This service, although not spectacular or linked to advertising, allowed a gain of 0.5 per cent in market share, which, given the volumes involved, is gigantic. Evian was thus the first to withdraw the metal capsule which sealed the bottle, which the consumer ripped off more often than not. That year, its sales jumped by 12 per cent when the market only grew by 7 per cent. The brand was also the first to introduce the handle which made the six-bottle pack carryable, the compactable bottle and so on.

On low-involvement products, benefits linked to the service are much appreciated by the consumer, the distributors amplifying the move if competitors do not react quickly – distributors prefer novelty.

In order to make milk a less ordinary product and to curb the surge of price leaders, the milk brand Candia multiplied its innovations, giving each its own specific name to accentuate the differentiation and allow for strong advertising support: Viva (milk with vitamins), Grand Milk (enriched milk), Grand Life Growing (for children), Future Mother (ie for pregnant women). These 'daughter brands' of Candia stemmed the advance of hard-discount products and enabled distributors to work with high-margin and high-turnover products. These were not major technological innovations, but were add-ons of vitamins, minerals and so on to respond to the expectations of demanding customers. In doing so, Candia made the whole category advance forward. Actually, nowadays Viva is rarely bought for its vitamins but for the brand and for what it stands for (a dynamic lifestyle, full of life, of youth). This product, which at first was advanced or premium, becomes the basis of milk, the reference. Candia was thus instrumental in enhancing the reference level for milk. The premium becomes a standard.

Innovation: a durable success factor

Innovation is the brand's oxygen, as well as the key to its growth and future-proofing. It is about time this fact was fully appreciated. Curiously, however, most books on brands hardly mention innovation, as though the brand was first and foremost a communication issue.

Remember that the brand has its beginnings in innovation. The brand is the name of an innovation that has succeeded and conquered the market. After all, at the birth of any brand, in the absence of recognition and image, one thing alone is capable of convincing retailers and opinion leaders: the innovative nature of the concept or product. Not only did this not exist before, but in addition, the concept or product appears to satisfy a real, strong expectation which had gone unheeded until then: it becomes obvious on first sight of the product or concept. This is the fact underpinning the origins of Nestlé, Kodak, l'Oréal, Nike, Sony, Amazon, Dell, Calvin Klein, Ralph Lauren, Armani, and in fact all brands. It is an error to suppose that innovation is required only at the beginning of the brand's life.

Although the brand is initially carried by a new product or service – an intangible concept carried by a tangible item – there is no reason why it should restrict itself to this product. Every product has its limits, and eventually becomes outdated or irrelevant in terms of meeting needs. It is thus the brand's duty to boost its value by renewing its range. This is also a way of increasing turnover.

Indeed, in the mass consumption markets, the brands that grow are those that invest in new or recent products with the greatest elasticity to advertising expenditure – a sign that they have touched on a latent (yet strong and widely felt) need. In fact, in modern groups of companies, advertising investment is allocated as a function of sales elasticity.

What are the virtues of innovation? What makes it an essential key factor of success, with such an ability to turn international companies and their worldwide brands into strong competitors?

Creating desire in saturated markets

With a few exceptions (telephony, the Internet, the need for clean water, safety, entertainment and so on), volumes in most markets are stable, or even on the decline. People who eat two yoghurts a day will not be induced to increase their consumption to four or six. People will only wash their hair a certain number of times a day. There is a limit to the number of cars any country can tolerate. The future therefore lies with 'value innovations', to use a phrase coined by Chang and Mauborne (2000). These are innovations that increase the value of the market and thus augment collective richness: their added value is strong for consumers or industrial clients. In this case, the question of price would seem to be of secondary importance.

Traditionally, market growth is achieved by lowering prices and the associated extension of distribution channels, which move towards the mass market or even – like Dell – direct marketing. Reduced prices introduced by Japanese, Korean and now Chinese brands have allowed anyone to have a television or coffee maker at home. Large retailers have democratised this progress, making low-margin products compatible with the economic equation of high throughput. But where do you go from there?

The average coffee-maker price is 30 euros. Would they become more desirable if sold at 28 euros? What about 25, or 20? In many categories, the motor of growth is no longer price, but desire – and desire is created through the innovation of value.

The crisis in the Japanese economy would be much worse if it were not for the remarkable rate at which Japanese companies innovate, and the civic responsibility of Japanese consumers, who consume and renew their products as a matter of duty – thus providing collective support for the economy.

A source of competitive advantage

In Europe and the United States, what innovation has revived the coffee-maker market? Nespresso – an original concept offering access to the best-quality coffee at home at a price of around 400 euros, thanks to a partnership between Nestlé and Krups. And what innovation has done the same for vacuum cleaners? Dyson, the 300-euros bagless vacuum cleaner, which has enabled the company to take 30 per cent of the UK market – which was previously assumed impregnable, as it was controlled by the majors (Hoover, Electrolux, Philips).

Which firm is currently Europe's number two automobile manufacturer, just behind Volkswagen? The answer is not Ford, GM, Renault-Nissan or even Fiat. It is PSA, the group that jointly controls the Peugeot and Citroën brands. How is this possible? Between 1987 and 1997, the company's annual sales rose from 1,952,474 to 2,077,965 vehicles, representing a growth of 6.4 per cent in 10 years. Sales figures soared between 1998 and 2002, rising from 2,247,121 to 3,262,146 vehicles – a growth of 38 per cent in four years. The new CEO, J M Folz, had identified lack of innovation as the key factor behind the group's stagnation (Folz, 2003). Between 2000 and 2004, PSA launched 25 new models and body shapes spread across its two brands, driven by restated brand values and a renewed understanding of today's markets and customers.

Only innovation can slacken pressure on costs: it generates desire and a temporary monopoly. However, modern competition is all about non-durable but constantly repeated advantages, and sometimes allows new segments to be opened in which the innovating firm becomes the market standard. This fact is important for mass retailers.

What mass retailers want

Mass retailers are on the lookout for innovations that create value rather than just move market share from one brand to another. They expect the creation of new categories or segments that will dynamise sales and margins.

A requirement for long-term survival

A brand will only survive in the long term if it can demonstrate its relevance with regard to the latent or expressed changing needs of a market which is in a state of constant evolution. It is through these new products and their associated advertising that this relevance is repeatedly demonstrated. Even brands whose success and business model are built on a single, durable product have been forced to change in order to survive and grow. Even Nivea, with its traditional little blue box, has had to take the path of innovation in a market where dreams are fed by the hope offered by each new development. Even Lacoste, despite its association with the legendary 12 x 12 René Lacoste shirt – a sign of sporting elegance and distinction since 1933 – now holds two shows a year to present its new collections in its three segments of sports, sportswear and 'dress-down' Friday wear. The same is true of Bic, whose worldwide success had until recently been based on a business model founded on two principles (one single brand, and single-product factories). Surely everyone is familiar with the Bic crystal ballpoint pen, disposable razor and cigarette lighter? Yet this model has had to be modified: the world has changed. Competition has come in the form of even cheaper ballpoint pens from China, but also from the Japanese Mitsubishi group, with ballpoint pens that are priced at above the 1-euro mark but are attractive, innovative and practical: they create value. Bic has now found itself forced to become creative too, and even to make modifications to its business model to outsource a portion of its new products – an approach which hitherto had been unthinkable.

The virtuous cycle of innovation

What managerial conclusions can be drawn from the above points? As Figure 8.3 shows, the brand can be managed in two ways.

Brand management is thus a balance between preservation, renewal, extension and growth of the prototype on the one hand, and on the other the creation of new products and services to capture new circumstances of use and new customers, and to open new segments. The first part maintains, feeds and consolidates the brand base, while the second opens bridgeheads into the future, carrying what will tomorrow become the brand's new prototype.

The effect of innovation on sales

Innovation does not merely work for itself: it benefits the brand in terms of both image and sales. It is what is known as the spillover effect, that is, the effect that advertising for one product has on the sales of another product in the brand. This effect, which is well known to companies, has been confirmed by

marketing research (Balachander and Ghose, 2003). Examining the sales of Dannon in the United States, the authors observed that advertising for a new Dannon product also had an effect on the sales of the prototype flagship product – the existing product most commonly identified with Dannon (which they wrongly name the 'parent brand' – strictly speaking, this term should refer only to Dannon itself, and not its products). Most importantly, this effect is three times greater than the effect that the prototype's own advertising has on its own sales (a 14.4 per cent rise in the probability of choosing the flagship product following advertising for the new product, compared with a mere 5.7 per cent following its own advertising).

There are several possible explanations for this phenomenon. The first – advanced by the authors themselves – is derived by reasoning. Since the prototype/flagship is strongly associated with the brand in consumers' memories, the stimulation of the brand name through the promotion of a new product produces a feedback effect which activates a path leading to the cornerstone product, the prototype. We believe there is another explanation. Every new product draws in new consumers distinct from those already consuming the established products. In so doing, they re-evaluate their overall perception of the brand, and are thus more tempted to explore its other hitherto ignored or undervalued products, and the brand's

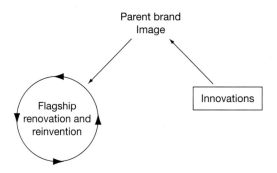

Figure 8.3 Two ways of managing the brand

flagship best-seller in particular. Innovation reframes the brand's image and feeds it with the new tangible and intangible attributes brought by this innovation. This is typically the case in the automobile sector, where the Peugeot 206 was named Europe's best-selling car of 2002. It has brought consumers to the brand who until then would never have thought of buying a Peugeot, but are now even considering buying higher-end models such as the Peugeot 307, 407 or 607. Innovation is the force that removes barriers to a brand's image – and the feedback effect modifies this image in a lasting way.

Disrupting markets through value innovation

It is well known that markets grow by the reduction of unit prices: this is how the computer became a household necessity, mobile phone sales skyrocketed, and so on. In mature markets, the goal is no longer to increase the market in volume, but to increase it in value. There are obvious limits to usage for most products: nobody wants to shampoo their hair four times a day. The main question is really how to make the consumer willing to pay more. This added value will then be shared between the distributor and the producer.

The goal of all brands is to look for value innovations, an unprecedented bundle of attributes that shifts the preference function of consumers (Chan and Mauborgne, 2000). 'Value innovation' consists in sacrificing some attributes (by suppressing them) in order to raise valued attributes to an unprecedented level. The best example is the Accor Formule 1 hotel chain created in 1985. This became the fastest-growing hotel chain in Europe. How did Accor, Europe's leading hotel group, achieve this?

The first point was in the identification of an 'oilfield', a source of growth nobody had thought of before, or that previously could

not have been served profitably. Many people never go to an hotel, because they cannot afford it. This is true of students, young couples, families, workers – a huge potential market. When they travel they tend to stay with friends or family. This matches their price expectations (it is free for them) but creates a number of disutilities (lack of privacy, obligation to eat and spend time with their hosts, lack of freedom and so on). An analysis of the value curve of this very competition (staying at friends or parents) reveals what bundle of attributes will move consumer preferences. The solution is still to be very accessible pricewise but to offer all the guarantees of a clean, safe, quiet, practical hotel.

How to do that profitably? How to base the brand on a valid economic equation? Only by sacrificing an attribute. The disruptive nature of the Formule 1 innovation was in suppressing some of the features that all previous players in the hotel market had held to be essential, such as ensuite bathrooms. In Formule 1 there were no baths or toilets in the individual rooms, but collective ones at the end of each hall, auto-washed and disinfected after each usage.

Formule 1 succeeded in tapping a hidden need, and also adopted a successful development strategy. This strategy consisted in quickly reaching the critical size (250 units) to be able to cover the country (that is, initially, France). Customer approval was transformed into loyal behaviour (which was only possible if they found a Formule 1 hotel wherever they went), and it was also possible for the brand to access television advertising, hence reaching the status of top-of-mind brand leader for the whole hotel category.

This brand did not meet the same success in all countries. In the UK for instance, land costs and the difficulty of find good hotel locations prevented the fast development of the chain, and hence access to the critical size, essential in the brand and business-building model.

The breakthrough brought about by Virgin Atlantic did not reside in its price or in the logo, but in the ability to create a different in-flight experience through a number of innovations that have now been widely copied. In addition Virgin offered business-class travellers a full service before and after the flight itself, adding new benefits to the Virgin experience. They could be picked up at their offices by chauffeurs in Volvo cars and driven to the airport. In addition they were offered access to a shower room after landing, to get ready for their business day. This not only attracted new clients but stimulated a higher frequency rate among all clients.

Another case illustrates the concept of value innovation: ballpoint pens. What made the success of Bic, which launched the ballpoint pen on a commercial scale in 1950? Mastering quality at a low price. The prototype is the Cristal model, the all-time best seller. It encapsulated the values of the brand: reliability, an excellent quality/price ratio and durability. Competition certainly came from lower-priced pens, with a lower quality, sold by discount chains or as distributors' brands. However the real challenge for Bic came from Pilot and Sanford, which introduced a lot of value innovations (ink gel, ink points, ink balls, more colours, better grip, new more sensual materials) at around five times the price of a Bic. When they encountered these products, which delivered experiential added values, closing the gap with classical ink pens, and provided a permanent thrill by frequently introducing new collections – as did Swatch, Gap and Zara in different fields – consumers were seduced. To survive, Bic had to change part of its business model, introducing variety to match what now emerged as very fragmented needs, thanks to an outsourcing policy, which had until then been forbidden within the Bic Group. Innovations now represent 25 per cent of each year's sales.

Increasing experiential benefits

Anyone who has visited a Nike Town cannot forget this experience. The same holds true for the House of Ralph Lauren, for Ikea and for Virgin Megastores. These places embody all the brand values in 3D, and in addition they deliver a memorable sensual experience. In developed countries, people have met their needs, and are now looking for exciting experiences. This creates a new source of growth: increasing experiential benefits.

The concept of experiential marketing has not emerged by chance over the past few years (Schmitt, 1999; Hirschmann and Holbrook, 1982; Firat and Dholakia, 1998). Consumers in developed countries and mature markets try to build thrills into their existence. This is why, for instance, they love to patronise thematic restaurants and amusement parks, and want to discover New World wines. Through these consumptions, their minds and senses are stimulated. They live differently through the product.

Swatch has based its success on the delivery of repeated experiential benefits to each of its clients, through collections, design and a general sense of fun. Garnier, one of the mass-market global brands of the l'Oréal Group, has defined itself as a full experiential brand: this is apparent in everything from the touch and colour of the packagings to the Internet site and the importance of street marketing in its brand building (with the creation of Garnier-owned buses, travelling around the country in Germany as well as in Shanghai). This also means that everything needs to change faster, to maintain the thrill: product lines, advertising, promotions, the contents of Internet sites and so on.

In this respect, service acquires more and more importance, even for product brands. This can take the form of making the brand 'mediactive', a mode which favours communications among members of a virtual community through consumer magazines, forums and chatlines, FAQs and other communication devices. It can also be achieved simply through levels of service, such as the call centres created by Pamper's and by Nestlé Infant Food to answer specific questions about babies.

Managing fragmented markets

Customisation is also a response to the slackening of desire among those who have become blasé. In Maslow chain, individualisation comes high in the ladder. Everything that creates an ability to tie the brand and its products to the singularity of each client is to be looked for, within an economically favourable equation, of course. One quarter of the revenues of Harley-Davidson comes from accessories. They enhance the experience of both bike riders and non-riders, and meet these needs for individualisation.

Customisation has its limits in terms of cost and profitability. Segmentation can circumvent them. It is very interesting to analyse the Ralph Lauren range, which takes seriously the issue of market fragmentation (Table 8.1). Actually there are no fewer than 10 ranges within the Ralph Lauren empire, from the very expensive Purple Collection (with jackets price ranging from US $2,000 dollars) to the more inexpensive Polo Jeans and RLX. Each label provides a full range of products and line extensions. This policy has a number of advantages:

▌ It creates a built-in coherence that distributors might not match without guidance.

▌ It allows the distributor to allocate specific labels to specific stores and locations.

▌ It matches the inclination of consumers to feel different in the morning, afternoon and evening, while continuing to wear Ralph Lauren clothes.

▌ It increases the perception of rarity, of exclusivity, a feat for a brand that in fact is more and more diffused.

The car industry has also discovered the virtues of range fragmentation. It is not certain that consumers would want a fully personalised car. The number of alternatives available would make the choice a chore. However, they do expect to be able to choose between prepackaged variations on the same model. This is why modern car-makers increase the level of involvement of consumers with their cars by planning in advance the line extensions that target specific highly conspicuous targets, or valued lifestyles. The sales of a new model are in fact made by the addition of segmented offers.

Mercedes decided to address the fragmentation of needs. It sold 700,000 cars in 1995, and has now reaches 1,250,000 a year. Meanwhile the number of models has made a leap, reaching 23 in 2005.

Nike's success can be explained the same way (Bedbury, 2002). It offers an increasingly broad array of niche products (a sign of mass customisation), thereby creating relationships

Table 8.1 Addressing market fragmentation

Ralph Lauren's situation brands, 'portraying core lifestyle themes'

Ralph Lauren Collection (Purple Label, etc)				
Ralph Lauren				
Polo Ralph Lauren	Polo Sport	Rlx	Polo Golf	Polo Jeans
	Ralph Lauren	Polo Sport	Ralph Lauren	Ralph Lauren
Ralph Lauren	Ralph Lauren Collection	Ralph Lauren Sport		
Ralph, Ralph Lauren				
Lauren, Ralph Lauren				
Chaps, Ralph Lauren				
Ralph Lauren, Children's Wear				
Ralph Lauren, Home				

with subsets of the market, with fragments. Being more involved with a product tailored to them, customers are ready to pay more. Nike now produces a number of collections even for a single sport. Also to maintain the thrill, product life cycles have been shortened from one year to three months.

As a whole, all these examples demonstrate the need for greater innovation in all aspects of the marketing mix, from product, channel and store to communication to match the fragmentation of demand.

Growth through cross-selling between brands

Is the brand perspective sometimes detrimental to growth? This provocative question has been raised by Accor Hotels, the number one European hotelier. Even though it had built a portfolio of strong brands, it wondered if, for growth purposes, it was not time to adopt a consumer orientation. With its complete portfolio of zero to four-star brands (Formule 1, Motel 6, Etap, Ibis, Novotel, Mercure, Sofitel and Suit'hotel), it realised that single-chain loyalty cards were causing its clients to defect to the competition.

This is because a businessperson travelling during the week does so at the company's expense, and his or her family cannot afford to stay in the same hotel at weekends. Although they were all Accor hotels, a loyalty card for Novotel (the three-star brand) conferred no benefits at Etap (one-star) or Formule 1 hotels. Seeing things from the client's point of view led to the planning not of product brands, but of a horizontal brand – Accor Hotels itself – as a loyalty vehicle. This allowed the client to be kept within the whole portfolio of the group's brands.

Seeing that Nivea enjoyed high levels of loyalty because of its umbrella branding architecture(all is Nivea), l'Oréal Paris decided to become a truly horizontal brand with a greater importance than that of its daughter

brands (such as Elsève, Plénitude and Elnett). The aim of this mother brand was to increase cross-loyalty between the daughter brands.

Analysing its client database, Unilever calculated that 78 per cent of the most valuable consumers (MVCs) of Skip were also MVCs for Unilever products in general. This was also true of 76 per cent of MVCs for Sun, 69 per cent for Dove, 66 per cent for Lipton Ice Tea, and 63 per cent for Signal. Ultimately, this posed the question of a horizontal Unilever brand – a tricky issue in an organisation founded on a variety of unrelated product brands, in a 'house of brands' architecture.

However, in the short term there was an opportunity to be exploited: for example, to tell Skip's MVCs about the group's other products. Hence the creation of group CRM, not only for this reason, but also as a way of shouldering fixed costs collectively.

The key questions with regard to CRM are those concerning the single-brand or multi-brand approach. Consumer magazines such as *Danoe* and *Living Magazine* (Unilever), and their Procter & Gamble equivalents, illustrate the multi-brand approach and customise each mailshot to a great extent, deciding what coupons and new products will be offered to which customers. These magazines place a strong emphasis on cross-selling. This does not stop each brand from conducting its own relationship-based programme, for example, by organising conferences on issues relevant to customers, either face-to-face or through forums on the brand's Web site. Other channels also exist to enable such contact: for example, call centres providing real consumer services.

Growth through internationalisation

If domestic markets are mature, brands should look for better markets. This is why all brands look eastward, towards the Eastern European countries and Russia, and towards India and China. The two-digit growth markets of tomorrow are there. We address these issues in our chapter on globalisation. Brazil and Argentina should also qualify as growth markets once the Argentinian financial crisis is over. Finally, brands meeting sophisticated needs can find in North America the wanted source of growth.

For instance, Evian water has since 1991 faced an unprecedented challenge in its home country: the emergence of low-cost bottled water, sold at a third of Evian's price. These waters are not 'mineral water', with a guaranteed proportion of mineral ingredients in them, but 'spring water'. (Another category is 'purified water', such as Coke's now famous Dasani, Dannon water and Nestle Aquarel. These brands are mostly sold in North America and in emerging countries, and hardly at all in Europe.) While Evian is still the leader in value share, the volume-share leader is a low-cost brand, Cristaline.

It is easy to see how difficult it is to have to suddenly justify a major price gap. In 1972, four brands represented 80 per cent of the 2-billion-litre bottled water market, and Evian was the leader with 653 million litres. Since then 17 major competitors have entered the market, and in 2003 the four main brands represented only 40 per cent of what had grown to be a 7-billion-litre market. Evian's annual sales volume is now 793 million litres. The brand succeeded in growing its sales in value through three strategic actions:

▪ Permanent innovations in the format, packaging and handling of the packs. All these apparently tiny improvements gain significance when one has to shop for water.

▪ Systematic repositionings of the brand, from generic health and nature to equilibrium and now to the concept of eternal youth, while remaining within the brand's identity.

▪ Extending the brand. As early as 1962, Evian was a pioneer in brand extension. In response to hospital requests it introduced

a spray to vaporise water on the faces of patients and babies. In 2001 Evian Affinity, another brand of facial spray, was launched in alliance with Johnson and Johnson. Two years after its launch it had become the number five brand by sales in the sector of mass market facial cosmetics. It now plans to launch in other countries such as Japan and Korea. This extension is consistent with the repositioning of Evian less as a water than as a source of health and beauty.

To make the business of Evian far more profitable, a simple calculus shows that a litre of water can be sold at a double price in developed countries such as the UK, Germany, the United States, Canada and Japan: there is a growing demand for healthy bottled drinks that is in reaction to the overconsumption of soft drinks, and the obesity syndrome attached to it. The real *un-cola* is not Sprite or Seven Up: it is Evian. Despite transportation costs, selling Evian in the United States delivers a high margin. The main problem is to access consumers and to justify the price premium in a market where Nestlé and Coca-Cola Corporation have established cheaper brands of purified water. This is why an alliance was needed with Coca-Cola to distribute Evian in North America in every outlet and vending machine.

Today, export represents 50 per cent of Evian sales. In each country the brand's role is to create the market for mineral water (not simply purified water), in order to build the business and become its referent, the brand with a fashionable, premium positioning. (See Table 8.2.)

As is shown in the table, this positioning was well perceived but failed to really convince the public that Evian was the higher quality water. As a result the initial positioning as a luxury water had to be replaced, in order to really make the brand become the referent of the category that was being created. Hence the new global advertising campaign, 'Another day, another chance to feel healthy'.

Table 8.2   How domestic and international images differ: the Evian case

Country	France	Germany	UK
Percentage seeing Evian as:			
Healthy	46	42	49
High quality	46	22	28
Traditional	23	8	13
Fashionable	12	19	19
For high-class consumers	3	15	11

9

Sustaining a brand long term

Many apparently modern and up-to-date brands have actually been with us for a long time: Coca-Cola was born on 29 May 1887, American Express in 1850, the Michelin bibendum appeared in 1898, Whirlpool in 1911, Camel in 1913, Danone in 1919, Alka-Seltzer in 1931, Marlboro in 1937 and Calvin Klein in 1968, to name a few. These are the brands that have survived – others have disappeared from the market even if their names do ring a bell.

The perennial appeal of some brands reminds us that, although products are mortal and governed by a more or less long life cycle which can be delayed but not avoided, brands can escape the effects of time.

Many great and well-known brands have disappeared, others are struggling. Why do some brands last throughout time and seem forever young, whereas others do not?

Time is but a proxy variable, a convenient indicator of the changes that affect society as well as markets, subjecting the brand to the risk of obsolescence on a double front – technological and cultural. With time, technological advances become more widely available and new cheaper entrants arrive that destabilize the balance of added value of established brands, forcing them into a never-ending cycle of constant improvement. For instance, the sudden growth of Daewoo in the car market is due to the fact that this conglomerate had access to GM assembly lines which were already 'obsolete' although they were just a few years old and were sold by GM at a low price. With the passing of time, consumers either become more sophisticated and expect customised offers, or become blasé and prefer a simplified and cheaper offer. Time also marks the cultural evolution of values, mores and consumer habits. As time goes by, current clients grow older and a new generation emerges which has to be won over from scratch all over again. Finally, time also wears down the signs, the words, the symbols and the advertising campaigns of brands.

Changes in the retail sector have far-reaching consequences. Take, for example, the rise of hard-discount in Europe, originating in Germany – where it has already become the leading form of retail, and is now getting close to a 20 per cent market share in Europe. In response to this, to pre-empt the risk that clients will desert them, hypermarkets have created low-price product ranges and – in order to avoid harming their store brand – have widened the price gap with the big brands. Stronger and stronger brands are needed to support this price differential, which has grown suddenly. In Japan, too, the retail sector is changing: in the wines and spirits market, bars have seen their market share fall from 32 per cent to 30 per cent, small independent stores have slipped from 14 per cent to 10 per cent and liquor stores are down from 34 per cent to 28 per cent. They have all lost share to the supermarkets, which have grown from 20 per cent to 32 per cent. Unlike the three first-named outlets, which offered little choice but could provide recommendations, supermarkets present a wide range – but in self-service style, with no recommendations. This change has come as a blow to all wines that formerly relied on a push strategy via in-store recommendation: it gives an advantage to Australian and US wines, which rely entirely on the brand's high profile.

Brands associated with a particular distribution channel are thus subject to the vagaries of the channel with which they are so closely linked. In terms of hygiene and beauty, the chemist's store channel is constantly losing ground to the hypermarkets and supermarkets. Indeed, the supermarket and hypermarket brands are improving their performance: Pond's, Olay, Bioré, l'Oréal Paris, Nivea, and so on. This makes the channel more and more attractive, and increases the pressure on other distribution channels. There are two possible responses to this, the first of which is to strengthen brands in the threatened channel and thus increase their attractiveness. This is the approach taken by the likes of Eucerin (Nivea), La Roche Posay and Vichy. The other approach is that of the twin channel, taking advantage of the reputation acquired in the chemist's store to sell the product in the supermarket. This is the Neutrogena option, tempting from the point of view of sales growth, but potentially threat-ening to brand equity. After all, sales may increase, but what will happen to the brand's reputation?

Is there a common feature of the seemingly everlasting nature of some brands? For convenience, one could say that an understanding of the brand logic, addressed in a previous chapter, offers the best bulwark against a brand slipping into decline and disappearing. A general definition also sums it up: 'to defend an added value that is constantly undermined by competition'. The following sentence epitomising the problem is attributed to Antoine Riboud (former CEO of Danone worldwide): 'I do not believe in the overpowering might of brands, but I believe in work.' A brand is not a once-and-for-all construction, but the aim of a constant effort to reconstruct the added value. The current product has to be continuously adapted to meet changing demand while at the same time the new concepts of the future have to be invented that will sustain the growth of the brand.

An analysis of the numerous brands that have survived the crises and lasted down the years may point to the key success factors of this virtuous spiral and is the purpose of the present chapter.

Is there a brand life cycle?

Curiously, the concept of brand life cycle is absent from most books on branding, as a review of their indexes shows. Does that mean that, unlike products, brands do not have a life cycle? In practice however the question whether brands have a life cycle is pervasive in a number of legal disputes. For instance, in 2002 LVMH, the world leading group for luxury brands and goods, sued the famous consulting group Morgan Stanley for having expressed the opinion that the Louis Vuitton brand (born in 1854) was now a 'mature brand', a judgement that carried implicit and explicit consequences for financial analysts and their clients, stock investors. Maturity is a typical phase of the product life cycle, the third after launch and growth, and just before decline. To describe a brand as in its maturity does indeed imply it is not far from decline, and so could hurt its reputation and the LVMH stock valuation.

The product life cycle does exist. Historical evidence proves it. All products (by which we mean the bundle of physical attributes) have an end. The problem is that the concept of product life cycle was mostly developed in hindsight. It is easy to reconstruct now the product life cycle of nylon, of transistors, of mainframe computers, of minicomputers, of word processing machines and so on. These products were replaced by more efficient solutions. Microsoft killed Wang: word processing software was a better solution than dedicated hardware. Looking at aggregate sales figures of the whole nylon industry, one finds the typical pattern: a birth and launch phase, a growth phase, a maturity phase and a decline. Maturity is signalled by a plateau, a levelling of sales.

As an after-the-fact concept, the product life cycle model is always correct. But as Popper showed us in the philosophy of science, concepts and theories that cannot be falsified are not thereby right. In practice, managers are never at their ease as to where they stand in the product life cycle. Should they interpret any stabilisation of sales as an evidence that the maturity phase has been reached, and make appropriate marketing decisions. Instead, they might argue that the decline was only due to weakened marketing, and that more work to identify and correct the causes of this stabilisation would make sales grow again. The routes to product growth recovery are multiple:

▍ through line extensions to capture the short-term new tendencies of the market and increase brand visibility;

▍ through distribution extensions to make the brand more available wherever customers are;

▍ through a reduction in the price differential from cheaper potential substitutes;

▍ through permanent 'facelifts' or innovations to deliver more value to customers and recreate perceived differentiation;

▍ through repositioning, and renewed advertising or communication in order to adapt the value proposition to the present competitive conditions.

A brand is not a product. Certainly it is based on a product or service: Nike started as a pair of sneakers, Lacoste as a shirt, l'Oréal as an hair dye. But as these examples imply, brands start from one product then continue to grow from multiple products. Louis Vuitton started as a luggage maker for the aristocracy: since then, it has become a full luxury brand covering many product categories. Recently the creative designer Mark Jacobs was hired to create the first Louis Vuitton clothing line. There should be perfumes soon. The brand surfs on new products and their intrinsic growth. As such, has this process an end? Must brands managed in this way reach a levelling-off stage?

One thing is sure. Brands that are not managed in this way, but remain attached to a single product, or even a single version of a product, are subject to the product life cycle. We all know of brands that in fact designate a very specific product: Marmite (that peculiarly English savoury spread), Xerox (photocopiers), Polaroid (instant cameras), Wonderbra and so on.

Certainly, brands such as Ariel or Skip are not growing any more in the heavy-duty low-suds detergent market. Their market share hovers around 11 to 12 per cent in Europe. They do try to create disruptions through regular innovations, but these are soon imitated, so this has become a yard-by-yard 'trench war'. Their growth will come from two sources. The first is geographical: the Russian market and all the former communist countries remain to be conquered, as does Asia (although this will be done by Tide, the equivalent of Ariel in the United States). The second is brand extensions. Why should Ariel be satisfied by just being the co-leader of the detergent market? Shouldn't it redefine its scope, its mission, as fabric care as a whole?

Of course, it can be said that once all countries of the world have been conquered and all possible extensions made, then a levelling-off in aggregated sales will unmistakably take place. This long-term prediction is as certain as J M Keynes's famous comment: in the long run we are all dead. But for practical purposes, in the short and middle term, sources of growth can always be found: it only requires more work.

In any case the emerging overriding rule of accounting for brand value (see page 444) has given a clear answer to the question of the practical existence of a brand life cycle. Brand values should not be amortised for the single simple reason that no sure forecast can be made about their span of life. To amortise over 5, 10 or 40 years one needs such forecasts. The accounting standards and norms that are coming to be accepted worldwide dispel the notion of a brand life cycle as an operating concept (rather than a historical explanation).

The fragile equilibrium of added value

Fundamentally linked to product differentiation, brands bring added values to the market. These can have a tangible basis (ie provides a superior 'augmented' product) and an intangible or immaterial basis. It is the latter that makes us go to McDonald's even if the Big Mac is no better than a Lotto's hamburger (its competitor in Korea), or that makes us buy a pair of Levi's even though the item is fairly uncomfortable. It is the added-value that justifies the difference in price to the customer. Either you want a yoghurt or you want a Danone! There is a natural equilibrium between material and intangible

added value on the one hand and price on the other.

The approach of the cheese-manufacturing company Bongrain is a typical example. The company has created more than 10 new brands of cheese, in each case systematically taking a generic category and adding a tangible quality edge to it. For example, the cheese 'Caprice des Dieux' provides a never-failing melt-in-your-mouth experience, which other camemberts cannot offer as their quality fluctuates too much. Moreover, the company adds on big value in terms of image, through name, packaging and advertising, as a basis for its unique proposition and to maximise its attractiveness. These two elements justify a high price premium, which when multiplied by the sales volume sustains a long-term profit rate partly reinvested in the manufacturing plant and research and development for quality innovations and partly in brand advertising. Figure 9.1(a) sums up this approach which is typical of manufacturers' brands in FMCG categories.

According to sound branding logic, the role of advertising is to accelerate the diffusion of a product that already sells well without it. For cheese, the difference in quality be organoleptic, dietetic, practical or aesthetic. The image stems from what is visible, ie the name of the brand, the visible aspects of the product, the pricing level and the advertising (see Figure 9.2). At Bongrain, the brand should be able to sell without advertising, a sign that the added value is perceptible on the shelf. At the same time, the advertising communicates that which is not visible – the intangible value added. That is why an image is made from both tangible and intangible values (see Figure 9.1(a)).

The problem is that the competition does not remain inactive. The basic level of the whole generic category improves at least as far as quality is concerned. This erodes the perceived quality difference of the brand (Figure 9.1(b)), but it also erodes its image, for instance, because of the progress made in terms of presentation by the private labels (sometimes bordering on slavish imitation). Unfortunately, since the price differential remains the same (when it is not increased by the willingness of distributors to increase the gap with their own brand) the equilibrium of added value is upset, resulting in a drop in demand. The company then responds by greatly reducing advertising spend, and so the image differential. The price premium of the brand remains but no longer corresponds to the added value. This is what happens to Bongrain and forces it to stop advertising support for some of its many product brands and to reinvent its branding model, introducing umbrella brands.

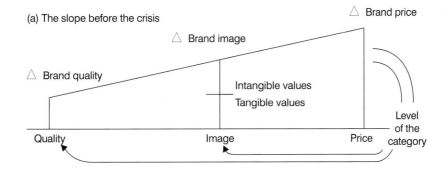

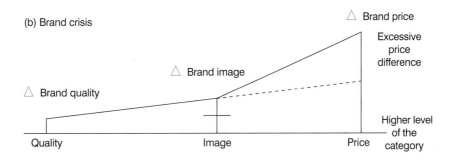

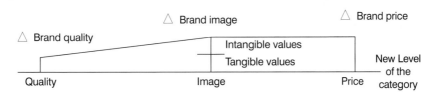

Figure 9.1   Brand and added value

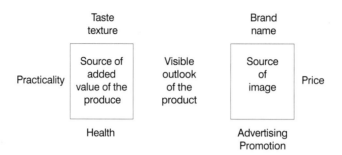

Figure 9.2   Sources of added value of a food brand

Which strategies can stop that spiral? First of all, one should consider returning to one's original vocation. The manufacturer's brand should excel in manufacturing. This means completely rethinking production, manufacturing plant and value analysis. All sources of cost which do not translate into value for the customer, all the squandering of resources which increases the brand premium, should be tracked down. Benchmarking and re-engineering may also find propitious grounds for consideration. Productivity gains may also stem from eliminating any marginal products in extended lines which have been mismanaged, thus cutting out the costs incurred by too many promotions (in terms of logistics, complexity and management costs).

The example of Procter & Gamble is quite revealing. In 1992 and 1993 Procter & Gamble launched its first gigantic productivity programme:

▌ First of all, it withdrew some weak brands (Citrus Hill fruit juices, Clarion cosmetics) and merged others (Puritan oil merged with Crisco, White Cloud toilet paper merged with its stronger cousin, the Charmin brand). Moreover, 7 of the 17 varieties of the famous Luvs diapers disappeared, and Camay did the same, letting go of one-third of its products in the line.

▌ Second, the firm adopted a policy called EDLP (Every Day Low Price), thus preferring a constant low price all year round to a multitude of promotional operations which only induced costs and made managing more complex.

▌ Third, Procter undertook staff reductions and closed some of its plants (30 plants were closed over three years).

All of these economies, which amounted to several hundred million dollars, were used to reduce retail prices spectacularly: 33 per cent on Camay soap, 26 per cent on Luvs diapers, 16 per cent on Pampers, and so on. In doing so, the brands came back into the core of the market, from which they had gradually been pushed out by an increasing price difference. Kellogg's also cut its prices in May 1996. However, it would be a mistake to believe that all the savings in productivity were passed on to distribution. One does not build a long-term brand loyalty by lowering prices; this is achieved by creating and injecting added value into the brand. The main part of the productivity gains should be reinvested in research, in the launching of new products or in renewing existing products by boosting their attractiveness through advertising. In 1992 to 1995, Procter increased its financial effort in favour of new products by 30 per cent. At Bongrain also, boosting the brand meant reinvesting a major part of the productivity gains back into the brands. Granting these savings to distributors who in turn would pass them directly onto consumers would have been a mistake, since distribution is often engaged on a path that leads it to the point of selling at a loss and to absolute discounting. Selling at a lower price does not resolve the quest for the means to increase added value.

Recreating a perceived difference

A brand is the name that progress takes to gain access to the market. The progress marked by the inclusion of enzymes in detergents is called Ariel or Skip or Tide. The progress in convenience coffee is called Nescafé. But progress does not stop. The latest level of quality or performance is quickly integrated by the market and becomes a standard. Before long it can be found in DOBs. Continuous, but from now on selective, innovation is the brand's fate. This also applies to products with a strong intangible added value: the cologne brand Eau Jeune (literally Young Water) can only survive if it launches new versions capable on each occasion of moving with the times. This applies just as much to stylish brands and to fashion designers as to luxury brands that have to renew constantly not their art but their products. Luxury must move with the times lest it become embalmed.

The exceptional longevity and leadership of Nescafé on the market can only thus be explained. Created in 1945, the brand has never stopped innovating, either by little imperceptible touches which when put together have produced an instant coffee whose taste is ever improving, or by major technological breakthroughs which helped recapture some of the 900 aromas that build a 'coffee taste'. The product has never stopped developing either in taste or in convenience (glass packaging replaced iron in 1962), or in its ecological considerations (the introduction of refills), or by its look. To signal the technical breakthrough and the progress made by lyophilisation, Nescafé took on the aspect of small grains under the name 'Special Filter'. In

1981, more aromas were recaptured, which was signalled by the creation of a real product range (Alta Rica, Cap Colombie), and new advertising focusing on South America. Later, a new manufacturing process called 'full aroma' was able to capture even better the aroma of freshly roasted coffee. Innovation and advertising are the two pillars of the long-lasting success of this brand. This incremental process never ends.

The leadership of Gillette follows the same pattern. Thirty-seven per cent of the sales of this multinational are accounted for by products that have been launched in the five previous years. In launching new products when the previous ones are barely established, Gillette keeps ahead of the pack, justifying a comfortable price premium and putting DOBs on short allowance (18 per cent volume on the disposables segment alone). Figure 9.3 demonstrates this well: there is a strict linear relationship between the innovation rate in a product category and the penetration of DOBs. When brands get lazy, cheaper copies can take a share of the market. It is significant that each year in the Lego catalogue out of 250 product references, 80 are new. In many sectors, the minute the innovation rate of a company goes down, it starts losing ground.

With their massive presence in distribution and daily presence on the table or in commercials, brands have become familiar, friendly and close, a source of empathy, even of loyalty and attachment. To maintain the strength of brands, it is vital to nourish the two pillars which make the relationship with the brand: one cognitive, the other emotional. Innovation serves precisely this purpose. It enables the brand to differentiate itself objectively and to draw once again the market's attention.

With time, it is noticeable that perceived differences erode faster than the emotional relationship. The liking persists even though we can see that the brand no longer has a monopoly over performance. A study conducted by the American agency, Young &

Rubicam, is a reminder of this psychological fact. The survey, called Brand Asset Monitor and conducted on 2000 brands worldwide, situates them against two facets of their relationship: cognitive and emotional (bearing in mind the fact that during the growth of the brand, the first facet precedes the second). The customer learns through communication and distribution the existence of a brand before grasping its difference, which then leads to its pertinence. In the meantime, the seeds of familiarity and esteem have been sewn, reminding us that prompted brand awareness precedes spontaneous awareness and that the latter is correlated with the emotional evaluation. The brands that come to mind spontaneously, as they belong to this group, also happen to be our favourite brands (see also p 159).

As shown by Figure 9.4, the decline of a brand, however, begins with a slide in the level of perceived difference between it and the competition and, in particular, with the opinion leaders of the product category. The esteem and the emotional ties are still alive and well, but the consumer realises that the quality gap has been bridged between the brand and its competition. He still likes it but may now become disloyal!

The benefit of this study is to underscore that the drop in differentiation signals the beginning of the decline, however strong the liking score may be. Unfortunately, many leaders are no longer considered as the qualitative reference of their branch. We like Lotus, Kleenex, brands that we have known since childhood, but we no longer think that they are the sign of superior product quality. They will have to refocus on the product to regain their leadership. The Coke vs Pepsi duel in the United States is a good example of this. One often reduces the struggle between the two giants to a battle of advertising budget size. Actually, Coca-Cola's philosophy lies in the so-called 3A principle: Availability, Affordability and Awareness. Coca-Cola must be within reach everywhere, cheap and on one's mind. Another phrase sums up Coca-Cola's ambitions: 'To be the best, cheapest soft drink in the world' (Pendergrast, 1993). What is exactly the strategy deployed by Pepsi-Cola? As it could not compete in the communication, sponsoring, animation and promotion race it focused on product and price. Pepsi-Cola has always tried to improve its taste

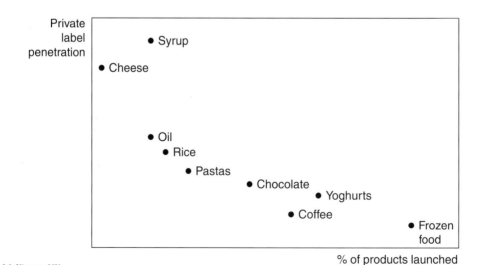

Source: McKinsey, UK

Figure 9.3   Innovation: the key to competitiveness

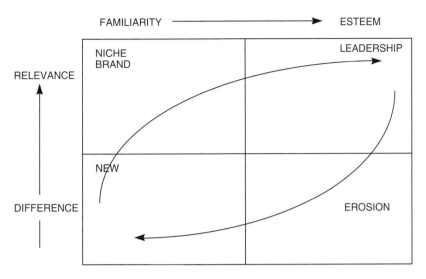

Figure 9.4 Paths of brand growth and decline

to fit as best it could the evolution in the taste of the American public. This is what founded the very aggressive advertising campaigns from 1975 onwards, such as the 'Take the Pepsi challenge', where surprised customers found they preferred the taste of Pepsi in a blind test. Moreover, Pepsi has always sought to be a couple of cents cheaper than Coca-Cola. The strategy proved effective: we know it forced Coca-Cola to change its formula in 1985 so as not to take the risk of being surpassed in taste. This was the famous episode concerning New Coke.

How do you preserve the superior image of a brand, this capital of perceived difference?

▨ One way is to renew the product regularly, to upgrade it to the current level of expectation. This is why Volkswagen introduced the Golf, then Golf 2, 3, 4 and 5. Detergent manufacturers make minor adjustments every two years or so, and make major changes in their formula every five years. This is how Ariel and Skip maintain their qualitative leadership, making them both the two most expensive brands and the leaders on the market. Moreover, for want of financial means, DOBs cannot keep up in the R&D

race, a race which can become an obsession.

▨ A second way is to integrate new and emerging needs while holding onto the same positioning. In doing so, any car brand, even if it is not specifically positioned on safety as is Volvo, must from now on show that it is equally concerned with security and even the environment.

▨ A third way is to constantly confirm one's superiority by extending the line. A brand of shampoo treating hair loss should rapidly propose line extensions covering the different needs of people suffering from this problem – creams, lotions and so on. These extensions demonstrate the concern of the brand to address as best it can the different aspects of the problem on which it focuses and to affirm its leadership by becoming the reference linked to the need.

▨ The fourth way lies in adapting to one's own customers who themselves change and become more experienced. Line extensions should propose new products adapted to their more sophisticated needs, to prevent them from trying the competition.

Jacob's Creek is a good example of this. Over 20 years, from 1984 to 2004, the UK became a wine-drinking country. Consumption per capita was raised from a low 7 litres per person per year to more than 21 litres. This was the result, as ever, of three converging forces:

▌ Multiple grocers realised that this new category was very attractive. They wished to made it a 'destination category'.

▌ Consumers travelling in Europe or Australia tried wine and wished to pursue the experience back home.

▌ New players understood the UK consumer better than existing competition did, and the New World wine makers understood them best of all. Jacob's Creek introduced its first two varieties in 1986 (a dry red and a dry white): it is now the UK's number one bottled wine brand (see page 58).

New drinkers are fast learners. Thanks to the magic of wine, they want to flex their newly acquired wine appreciation muscles and explore the category. Soon they wanted to discard their former simplistic brands in search of new experiences. This consumer maturity was soon perceived as a potential threat by Jacob's Creek, which it met by introducing gradual line extensions. A permanently renewed top range of special limited series was designed to keep up with opinion leaders' expectations (Parker's wine guide, wine buffs, restaurants), and a number of sub-brands based on more complex grape varietals were designed to keep customers and at the same time demonstrate the competence of the brand, as a true leader should. Jacob's Creek extended its line upwards: prices now (2004) range from a basic £4.59 to £6.99 for sparkling wine and even £8.99 for a rare reserve Shiraz.

In the banking sector, credit cards are constantly launching extensions to satisfy a customer base which, over time, is becoming more affluent and expects increasingly high-performance service and insurance products. After Visa came Visa Premier, followed by Visa Infinite. With their very low cost but high perceived value, innovations generate revenue for the entire chain, starting with the broker and continuing to the bank which promotes the product to certain segments of its clientèle, thus increasing the profitability of each customer. In addition, it produces a feeling of exclusivity among carriers of the most expensive cards, a feeling which is destroyed by the spread of so-called 'standard' cards. This is the typical American Express strategy.

Investing in communication

In 2002, the Danone group undertook a significant move. It decided to increase significantly (by over 20 per cent) the media budget of its strongest brands. Since then, their share of voice and market leadership have increased. Similarly the whole l'Oréal success story is based on two pillars: research and advertising.

Communication is the brand's weapon. It alone can unveil what is invisible, reveal the basic differences hidden by the packaging which often looks the same among competitors, especially when this similarity is precisely the impression sought by DOBs to create confusion. It alone can sustain the attachment to the brand, by promoting intangible values, even if this loyalty is eroded by many in-store promotions. Advertising is a result of the rise of self-service distribution and reductions in the numbers of salespeople. It is the necessary consequence of investments in R&D that have to pay off ever faster and therefore need an ever bigger public. That this has to be repeated over and over is the proof that there is a confusion in people's minds about the legitimacy of advertising, even within marketing teams, and is why we will use numbers to back our statements.

Share of DOBs

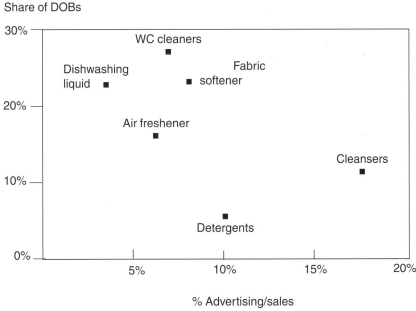

Source: McKinsey, UK

Figure 9.5   Penetration of distributors' brands and advertising intensity

As Figure 9.5 demonstrates, there is a linear relationship between the penetration of DOBs and the extent of advertising expenditure in a market, measured in percentage of sales spent on advertising. Advertising is a barrier to entry. However, upon examining the product categories, it becomes clear that the categories with a high investment in advertising are also those that invest in innovations and renovations, which are perfect opportunities for re-establishing the saliency of the brand in the public consciousness. It is the conjunction of these two factors (innovation and advertising) that produces added value.

The role of advertising in defending and sustaining the brand capital is shown by Table 9.1. With the exception of jam, where there is much consumption by children and the idealised reference to home-made jam favours small brands, advertising is quite efficient. Once more, we may notice that the categories that invest heavily in advertising are also those that regularly innovate and strongly differentiate their products.

No one is free from price comparisons

Even if innovation and advertising do increase added value, loyalty at all costs does not exist. Customers can be both sensitive to the brand but disloyal to it, estimating that the price of the brand goes beyond the price span that they are willing to pay for the product category, and beyond the brand premium that seems reasonable to them given the added satisfaction which is expected. Distributors also have the same attitude.

During years of economic growth, the biggest brands were tempted to regularly increase their prices to maximise the overall profit accruing from a strong price premium and a large batch of loyal clients. For financial directors concerned about showing ever-increasing profits, what does a price increase of a few pence or cents per unit represent? For the market, however, it now has the utmost importance. In April 1993, one of the most famous brands, Marlboro, noting a slump in

Table 9.1 Advertising weight and own-label penetration

	Advertising sales ratio %	Own-label market share %
Cereals	10	15
Detergents	8	11
Coffee	8	13
Jam	7	47
Butter	5	6
Soft drinks	5	20
Tea	5	26
Yoghurts	2	39
Cider	2	36
Fish	0.7	26
Wine	0.5	61

Source: McKinsey, UK

sales, was the first to put into reverse this inclination by unilaterally lowering its prices in the United States. Wall Street reacted badly, thinking the bell was tolling for brands: on that day the stocks of all consumer goods companies dropped significantly. More than a year later, in August 1994, Marlboro's market share reached unprecedented heights (29.1 per cent), seven points more than in March of 1993 just before the famous 'Marlboro Friday'. In France 10 years ago, Philip Morris decided to bring down the price of Chesterfields from 11.60F to 10F at at time when competitors were preparing to pass on to customers the 15 per cent tax increase imposed by the government. Within two months the sales of Chesterfields jumped by 300 per cent. The market share of the brand went from less than 1 per cent to 12.2 per cent in two years. It became, in a year, the favourite cigarette for young people (71 per cent of buyers were under 25).

One may recall that Procter & Gamble significantly reduced the price of its brands in the United States in accordance with its brand-boosting programme, thanks to the allocation of part of the savings accruing from an impressive programme to increase indus-trial productivity, marketing and sales. These price reductions were part of the EDLP (Every Day Low Price) policy which put an end to the myriad of micro-promotions.

These price reductions show that the brand has to stay within the core of the market if it wants to continue. This was discovered by European car manufacturers after first the Japanese and now the Korean invasion: they forced all car OEM (original equipment manufacturers) suppliers to reduce their prices by 20 per cent. Portable computer manufacturers also know that they must both innovate and reduce their prices. Indeed, the price premium that pays for the superior added value is a differential concept. It says nothing of the standard, the reference level of the brand with which it is to compare. But nowadays in many markets this standard is falling in absolute value. If hard-discounters spread through Europe as they have in Germany, they can impose in certain sectors their own levels of price and quality as the standard that the branded products have to reckon with when setting their price levels. If brands leave their price premiums unchanged, they will not be able to hold their ground.

The preceding argument is *a fortiori* valid if the price premium is higher than the perceived added value of the brand. The brand then gets into a niche at a high-end segment of the market and watches its volume drop. As is shown in Figure 9.6, the latent savings unexploited by industrialists could represent up to 30 per cent of costs. It is true that part of the benefits linked to the product are sometimes not valued by customers or that the upgrade in production costs is not worth it in the customers' eyes. There is more to be gained by suppressing these costs and finding a new price competitiveness again. Besides, trade-off analyses demonstrate that the logic of 'bigger and better' can be counter-productive if it entails an increase in price. Beyond a certain performance threshold, utility slumps. There are also acceptable price thresholds: the rule for home computers is to always give the client more as long as the retail price does not go beyond the $2000 barrier.

The analysis carried out by OC&C has, however, two limits. First, it neglects, as do most economic analyses, the perceived value of the reputation and image of the brand: a brand does not only bring a product benefit. Second, it is not obvious that price leaders set the standard price that will be the reference for customers when they compare prices. It all depends on the level of involvement of the customer and of the perceived difference! For years, low-priced colas existed but attracted no consumers. Only recently have the Sainsbury's and Virgin colas been able to challenge Coca-Cola. Creating a large shelf space for price-leader detergents will not in itself create a significant sales volume: the quality reference is set by Skip and Ariel. Customers know they are not getting the same quality when, for want of buying power, they fall back onto secondary brands and *a fortiori* on unknown brands. At the other end, the Viva milk created by Candia, far from being perceived as a premium product, has become the milk that all milks should be like, the standard for milk, both modern and advanced. There are indeed other price-leader milks, but they are considered ordinary and lacking in character.

Any price decrease, if it does occur, should not therefore be conducted in comparison

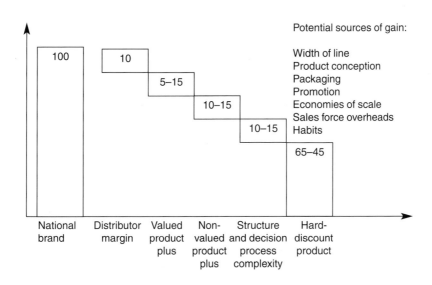

Figure 9.6 Sources of price difference between brands and hard-discount products

with the cheapest product of the category but with the products in the same segment aiming at the same need. The so-called 'trammel-hook analysis' (Degon, 1994) demonstrates empirically that the brands which are successful are most of the time those that have the lowest price within their own segment. To return to the Chesterfield case in France, the brand was withdrawn as early as 1988 from the declining segment of upmarket Virginia cigarettes (Marlboro, Stuyvesant, Rothmans) to be positioned in the segment just under it, that of 'popular Virginia cigarettes' (Lucky Strike, Gauloises Blondes). By pricing its pack at 1.5 euro, it became the cheapest alternative within this segment and quickly became the leader. Since then, the brand has had to increase its price due to budgetary constraints from the government, but has kept this price positioning.

As a conclusion, a decrease in price has never in itself solved the problem of making sure a brand lasts. It does not increase added-value but reduces costs. Moreover, a decrease in price on the part of the leader has important consequences in the long term: it will jeopardise the profitability of the whole sector for 20 years to come. The leader should instead aim either to retrieve the standard of quality that the customer knows he is leaving behind if he chooses a cheaper product, or to enlarge the market. But to do this the company must invest: lowering prices too much will make financing this effort impossible.

Image is an art at retail

Where marketing is concerned, he who is in contact with the end-user often has a decisive edge. This is a major handicap for manufacturers who are not in control of their distribution network. It may be an illusion to consider that you can bypass supermarkets to sell significant food brands, but this is not the case for many other outlets. Selective distribution is such an example. The evolution of

European Union law on selective distribution networks has substituted qualitative criteria for the old quantitative criteria linked to minimum volume quotas.

In the case of Levi's, the brand is quite selective in its distribution. While not permitting the sale of its products to supermarkets, Levi's expects its retailers to respect five criteria:

- the first one has to do with the offer range: the latter must comprise quality clothing and only brands that are recognised by the customer where jeans are concerned (therefore no price-leader or anonymous jeans);

- the environment must be as high quality as the offer;

- product ranges that could alter the image of Levi's must not be found close by;

- the service must be in tune with the brand and the staff must be adequate and competent in the field of clothing;

- last of all, the shop must be part of a fixed construction (not a market stall) with adequate space reserved for jeans and capable of attracting youths aged 15 to 25.

Through this mastery of the channel, Levi's is, in fact, controlling its image and preserving its brand capital. A brand cannot be narrowed down to its advertising and to its products, it involves the customer in the purchasing act and even thereafter. This is also the strength of Benetton, Ikea, Häagen Dazs and Louis Vuitton. Coca-Cola itself does indeed have to contend with competitors in supermarkets and even with copies from distributors. But the reputation of a soft drink is enhanced by its distribution in cafés, hotels, restaurants and night-clubs. Moreover, the Coca-Cola company offers a wide range of non-colas that make it an exclusive distributor at the sales outlet. Hence, where there is Coca-Cola there usually is neither Pepsi Cola nor any product from Cadbury Schweppes.

Creating entry barriers

This last example draws attention to the importance of entry barriers in sound brand management: offering a full portfolio of brands helps the Coca-Cola Company extend its dominance, outlet by outlet. The bar owners and restaurant operating companies are satisfied: they can offer their clients a full range of famous soft drink brands, and in addition they often receive bonuses from Coca-Cola for providing full exclusivity to the whole Coca-Cola portfolio. (This was the source of lawsuits in Europe by the other soft drink companies.)

By focusing exclusively on the consumer's psychology, brand analysis has overlooked the crucial role of the management of the offer itself, which can make it impossible for competitors to enter on the market. This is one of the key questions in the analysis of the financial value of a brand, of the present value of its future profits. The impenetrability of the market is the best warranty for the latter, and the example of Black & Decker is quite revealing.

Why are there hardly any DOBs in the drilling machine market? Because Black & Decker makes it economically impossible for them to enter the market. DOBs sprout up when one or more of the following conditions are fulfilled:

- there is a high volume in the market;

- there is little product innovation;

- brands are expensive;

- customers perceive little risk;

- customers make their choice essentially according to the visible characteristics of the product;

- technology is accessible at low cost.

Much to the contrary, the market for drills is small, and moreover is cut up into many segments. Black & Decker drives the market and makes it develop at a fast technological pace. In addition, Black & Decker has globalised its production: each plant produces one single product for the worldwide market. The production cost level thus becomes unbeatable, and as Black & Decker is not over keen to increase its retail price, it does not leave much room for copycats to manoeuvre. Lastly, the customer feels safe when buying such a well-known and ubiquitous brand.

What are the main sources of entry barriers?

- The cost of the factors of production is the most important, which leads to a long-lasting competitive advantage. This is the strategy of Dell, and also of Decathlon, the world's fifth largest sports goods retailer and eleventh largest producer. Decathlon may become for some sports the European number one manufacturer far ahead of any others because of the economies of scale accruing from its products developed at a European level.

- Mastering technology and quality is a key success factor for Procter & Gamble, Gillette, L'Oréal and 3M. Turning down any offer to yield an iota of their know-how to DOBs, these companies keep for themselves their main added-value leverage. This is what enables them to constantly innovate and to remain the reference of the market in terms of quality. Kellogg's even goes to the extent of indicating on its boxes that it does not supply DOBs.

- Domination through image and communication is Coca-Cola's mainstay, although it does not hinder a K-Mart or a Sainsbury brand cola from borrowing as much as possible the distinctive signs of Coke and selling at a lower price. In hard times, sensitivity to price is exacerbated. But as a worldwide brand, Coca-Cola had access to the sponsoring of the Olympic Games in Atlanta and was able to pass on the benefits to bottlers worldwide. This is also the weapon of Nike, Reebok and Adidas. Domination as a result of their fame and image is not solely a result of the titanic size of these companies' budgets. Focusing all their communications on the name itself and applying a brand extension logic beyond the initial segment, many brands are thus able to dominate in brand awareness.

▌ Quickly using up all the aspects of a promising concept through range extension is a method that hinders the entry of competitors. In the United States, and in Europe, the Snapple brand is surfing on the wave of so-called 'New Age' drinks and offers a wide variety of tea-based soft drinks. Dim, as we have seen, was quick to offer under one hosiery brand name a wide range of products covering different needs and satisfying distributors' and customers' expectations. In the agricultural market, it is possible to count the different kinds of Decis (the leader in insecticides) according to the type of plant, thus reinforcing the worldwide leader status of this brand.

▌ Putting a name on a product in itself yields a uniqueness of offer and an added value that competitors will lack. All the giants of the chemical industry produce elastane, a fibre that makes stockings and foundation garments soft and shiny. On the other hand, only Du Pont de Nemours has Lycra, a fibre whose name in itself is used as a sales ploy by Du Pont and by all lingerie brands. Actually, Lycra is the trade mark used by Du Pont to sell elastane. It is not the name in itself which adds value to the fibre: it is 10 years of worldwide communication about the glamour linked to the Lycra name which gave the brand its exclusive attractiveness. The same strategy applies to Gore-Tex and Coolmax.

▌ Controlling the relationship with opinion leaders is one of the key success factors for a brand looking to the future. Canson, a

school-supplies brand which is part of the Arjomari-Wiggins group, provides an illustration. What is more natural than a sheet of tracing paper or drawing paper for a schoolchild? However, despite the share of supermarket shelf space given to DOBs' drawing and tracing paper, only that of Canson sells. For more than 20 years the brand has developed a close teachers relationship with organising for instance drawing competitions between classes on a national level. The long-lasting presence of Canson on a child's shopping list for school supplies is due to the excellence of what is now called relationship marketing. The main asset of Canson is its loyal teachers within the public education system.

▌ Controlling distribution is also a major handicap for new entrants. McDonald's will soon have 1,000 restaurants in France, and Quick, the second largest burger chain, will have 350. This sheer number closes the hamburger market off to competition. Mass-distribution brands also freely use this barrier to entry: by imposing their own brand on the shelf, they thus exclude manufacturer's brands. The ice-cream maker Häagen Dazs does indeed control the market of upmarket ice creams through the provision of a high-quality ice cream and through a well-managed word-of-mouth campaign from opinion leaders, but most of all through its own exclusive refrigerator present in all supermarkets and hypermarkets.

▌ The last barrier to entry is based on legality. The brand must defend its exclusive image against counterfeit products, models or signs. It should not hesitate to defend the exclusive character of its distinctive signs against imitations and distributors' copycat brands. The latter, under the pretence that these are signs of the category, actually try to make their brands benefit from the value of signs developed by the leading brand. The imitations of Coca-Cola try to get as close as possible to the red that Coca-Cola has with time associated with its quality. Beyond the deliberate sought-after confusion, which leads the customer, if he or she is not careful, to mistake the copy for the original, the similarity between the signs induces a perception of equivalence (Kapferer, 1995). Just as Dior, Chanel and Cartier invest heavily in law suits against counterfeiter networks, the brands must sue imitators or, at least, state to them that they will tolerate no imitations or copying. From this point of view, the brands which from the start chose non-descriptive signs withstand the test of time and imitation better. The Orangina label is blue: it is not a generic colour and protects this orange-flavoured soft drink brand well.

Defending against brand counterfeiting

As soon as a brand starts to enjoy success, it is imitated: copies appear and multiply. The competitive advantages offered by innovation are short-term only, and this is why today's brand is built on the continual flow of innovation. Ideas, concepts and products can all be the subject of imitation. For example, shortly after the launch of a peach-flavoured low-alcohol drink named Carlton, targeting the top end of the range, lower-cost competitors such as Claridge began to appear. Competition is even more intense where it applies to intellectual property: this includes patents and designs, but also trade dress, and even trademarks (the name or pictorial image of the brand). This imitation stems from producers and retailers whose imitation of the leader is the first step towards building a store brand (see page 128).

It also comes from counterfeiting. Top-of-the-range brands such as Nike and Adidas, as well as various luxury brands, are directly targeted in this way. The markets and bazaars of foreign countries are filled with fake Cartier watches and Ralph Lauren polo shirts. No sooner has a Dior or Chanel fashion show finished than Asian factories begin to reproduce their designs, introducing them into parallel distribution channels even before the brand itself has sent out stock. More dangerous still is the practice of counterfeiting medicines or automobile spare parts, which can often deceive customers and potentially put lives at risk. Lastly, we have already discussed protection against brand imitations conducted by the brand's own retailers (see page 129).

Intellectual property must be defended and extended (for example, Harley-Davidson has patented the characteristic sound of its engines, as has Porsche). It is not our intention here to cover in a few lines a subject as important and strategic as trademark laws, particularly since, with the advent of globalisation, it is becoming obvious that not all countries have the same sensibilities when it comes to counterfeiting. In China, South-East Asia, Morocco and Italy, a considerable number of micro-companies make a living in this way. It is always more or less directly linked to money laundering, and sometimes receives covert government protection. Such divergent attitudes allow brands that could not legally exist in the West (or any country that upholds intellectual property laws) to become established. Everyone in Singapore, Hong Kong and Shanghai is familiar with the Crocodile store chain, an obvious imitation of the world-famous Lacoste brand, whose symbol since 1933 has been its famous crocodile. The Asian store chain has exploited lax local brand laws to position itself in Lacoste's slipstream: it even goes so far as to boast in its slogan, 'Enter the legend'.

The basic precautions to be taken in order to avoid losing protection rights for one's brand are well known. For example, never use the trademark as a noun, but as an adjective: in other words, we should say a Budweiser beer, not just a Budweiser. Let us also add that if a brand colour is to be protected, it too requires protection within the company. Brand product lines are frequently segmented, which leads to the use of different colours to identify each segment. As a result, it becomes harder to maintain that a brand is characterised by any one single colour.

How should the brand respond to counterfeiting and imitation? First, we should identify the difference between the two types of attack. Counterfeiting is the identical, trait-for-trait imitation of the brand and its identifying components: it is unlawful in the most direct sense, and there is no need to provide evidence of customer confusion. It simply needs to be identified, and legal action taken. However, longer-term work is necessary in a number of countries where it is more than simply tolerated, and indeed often accepted:

- Joint action aimed at the Ministries of Foreign Affairs and Justice. This works at the level of inter-state relationships.

- Collective information programmes to improve local laws directed at, for example, world trade organisation.

- Advertising for the original brand in the country in question. The extent of the phenomenon of counterfeiting in China, where there are no laws over brands, is well known. Chinese culture traditionally praises those who share, and condemns those who do not. Faithful reproduction of the master's work is a virtue in traditional Chinese education and teaching. Lastly, in the communist economy that dominated the Chinese way of thinking for 50 years, the notion of property itself did not exist, and it was common for all Chinese factories to go under the same name. We should add that counterfeits are the only financially accessible option for local consumers. Lastly, in these countries, after years of deprivation in terms of consumption, people are keen to show their neighbours they have finally 'made it'. Western brands are familiar to all, but

very few actually have first-hand experience of them: they are unaware that what they are buying is a fake. Research has confirmed this point (Lai and Zaichkowsky, 1999): local consumers who choose a counterfeit or an imitation do so because they lack knowledge of the original.

- Counterfeit-related advertising in tourists' countries of origin. Western consumers are well aware which products are the originals: imitations and counterfeits are a game for them. Our own qualitative research of the phenomenon reveals five underlying motives for them to buy a counterfeit:
  - The sense of having obtained a bargain. After all, everyone knows that luxury goods and Nike products are made in third-world factories. Such consumers deny there is any difference in quality between the original and the copy: they are therefore getting a bargain. This makes them very discriminating buyers: they will only buy copies of Vuitton bags that are 'identical' to the original, and they admire the quality of the copy. It is this quality, combined with the price, that makes it 'a real saving' and enables them to wear or carry the copy on a daily basis, even while with friends, who will not spot the difference. A buyer of a fake Bulgari watch – which is of very good quality compared with the genuine article he himself wears – will not hesitate to give it to one of his sons as a fifteenth-birthday present.

    Revealingly enough, the buyers themselves often own the original product. This is what qualifies them as experts and lends status to the copy chosen for the quality of its resemblance. They know what they are talking about.
  - The desire to put a little sparkle into everyday life. Fake Ralph Lauren polo shirts may be only approximate copies, but they are good enough for tasks such as housework, gardening or cleaning the car.

– An original present. Instead of going to Thailand and bringing back cheap knick-knacks as gifts which will immediately be hidden away in a drawer, a tourist buys friends what is these days a typical item from that country: a good imitation, a counterfeit scarcely distinguishable from the original. It will always surprise the recipient and lead to conversations about how well made (or not) the counterfeit is; furthermore, it is bound to be used.

– Some consumers willingly buy counterfeits because they cannot or will not pay the price differential for an original. They consider it ridiculous and pointless to pay 60 euros for a Ralph Lauren polo shirt, because they are not sufficiently involved.

– Lastly, some buyers of counterfeits are motivated by 'moral' considerations. They believe that the price of the original is scandalously high because, considering that it was made in a South-East Asian factory, the cost price of the product is actually infinitesimally small. They consider their actions as just retribution: given that the brand itself has committed theft by selling at a price way above its cost price, it is legitimate to steal it in return.

Preventive action with Western consumers in their country of origin takes the form of education. It needs to be pointed out that counterfeiting is linked to Mafia-style networks and the laundering of drug money. There is also a legal side: a consumer bringing back a counterfeit product is an accomplice, and is thus committing a crime punishable by law.

From brand equity to customer equity

The financial value of a brand is a function of the amount of its future expected return and of the degree of risk on these returns. A brand can only be strong if it has a strong supply of loyal customers. This established fact led to a revolution in the practice of marketing, under way since the beginning of the 1980s: the major concern is loyalty and its related factor, client satisfaction. Leaving behind an approach which implicitly concentrated on conquering clients away from the competition, firms now do all they can to keep their own clients. This is to be expected at a time when, as a result of the abundance of offers, buyers tend to jump from one brand to the next, from one manufacturer to the next. Rather than zero defaults, the aim is zero defections.

A lifetime client at British Airways brings on average £48,000 to the company in revenues. Thus under no circumstance should one customer be lost. It is the same for Carrefour where a loyal client brings £3,550 in annual sales. Besides, loyal clients are more profitable. According to a study from the Bain company, a household spends 330 euros/ francs per month in the supermarket to which it goes most often, 85 in the second most frequent and 22 for the one where it only goes occasionally. And not only do loyal clients spend more, but their expenditure grows with time, they become less sensitive to price and they are the source of positive word-of-mouth reports concerning their favoured supermarket or brand. Moreover, they are five times less costly to contact than non-clients. That is why, also according to Bain, by lowering the defection rate of clients by 5 per cent, benefits go up 25 to 85 per cent. The example of Canal Plus is significant: this pay-TV channel benefits from an unprecedented loyalty rate: 97 per cent of its 6 million clients are loyal to it. Bearing in mind that a yearly subscription costs 310 euros, if the loyalty drops by as little as 1 per cent, it would mean 11 million euros less in annual revenues!

All strong brands are currently establishing loyalty programmes. Nevertheless, a cautionary remark is necessary: no programme of this kind will make up for a service that is not adapted or sufficient. The actions required to keep loyal customers have two aims: the first is defensive, to give the customer no reason for leaving the brand or the company; the other is offensive, to create a personalised relationship with the client, the basis of a more intimate and therefore more involving bond, what Americans call 'Customer bonding' (Cross and Smith, 1994).

The essential part of the defensive side is the identification of the causes of disloyalty and dissatisfied clients. Thus, dissatisfaction linked to the food provided induces, because of disloyalty, a loss in revenue amounting to £5 million pounds at British Airways. The dissatisfaction linked to bad seating costs close to £20 million! Paradoxically enough, the company seeks to get as many voiced dissatisfactions as possible. Indeed, the worst thing is a silent dissatisfied client who, saying nothing to the company representatives, spreads negative rumours among his relatives, colleagues and friends. And there are statistics to prove that a dissatisfied client who is well treated becomes a real proselyte, and even more loyal into the bargain. When asked if they will fly with British Airways again, the rate is 64 per cent 'yes' among those that have never contacted the complaints office. It is, however, 84 per cent among those who have. The treatment of complaints with diligence, care and respect becomes a key lever in customer loyalty.

Seeking client satisfaction implies adding a touch of management spirit where spirit of conquest reigns exclusively. This is why L'Oréal Coiffure is nowadays a company with a conquering as well as an innovative and entrepreneurial spirit. It launches new products one after the other. Hairdressers like the L'Oréal products and L'Oréal knows their product needs well. Unfortunately, this led the firm to somewhat overlook the management spirit: some deliveries were wrong, stockouts occurred, discounts were unevenly granted, etc. The firm responded well to sophisticated needs but somewhat forgot some of the more down-to-earth needs. The hairdresser who put in an order on Tuesday for a tube of light golden brown colouring for a client coming on Friday could not be sure it would be there on time. He could not always count on the company. That is why even when its product launchings were successful, and even if customers were attracted, the sales of L'Oréal Coiffure stagnated for a while. When focusing on client satisfaction, the product alone is not sufficient if the basic service is deficient.

When going over to the offensive, a brand must become a landmark of personal attention. More emphatically, Rapp and Collins (1994) talk of becoming a 'loving company', interested not in the client but in the person. This marks the end of anonymous marketing: attention has to be customised if it is to be efficient. But it has to be acknowledged that even if the terminology of market studies distinguishes between big, medium and small customers, up until recently few companies had developed programmes designed specifically for big customers, who as a rule are also the most loyal. But the loyal client wants to be recognised. He or she therefore has to be identified, a direct bond has to be established and he or she should be the focus of special attention. This is why what is commonly called relationship marketing (McKenna, 1991; Marconi, 1994) uses databases, customers' clubs and collective events, which unite the best customers of the brand. Moreover, realising that a brand that does not have direct contact with customers becomes further and further out of reach – literally as well as figuratively – many brands have stepped out of mere television advertising and off the shelves to establish a direct relationship with customers. Nestlé offers to its customers a dietician, reachable by phone. Six days a week, Nintendo helps out 10,000 children who are stuck in a video game. As long ago as 1992, IBM France created an assistance hotline working around the clock seven days a week all-year-round.

Treating clients as friends instead of accounts is the basis to a long-lasting relationship.

In their efforts to increase brand loyalty, brand companies have realised that they have to care about their customer equity or market share. In other words, these companies should focus not only on augmenting brand preference as a mental attitude, but also on increasing brand usage, especially among the best customer prospects: the heavy buyers. Recent findings, for example, recognise that mass market brand profits come not from the mass market, but from the top third of category buyers. Furthermore, a brand's greatest potential for additional profit rests on its ability to increase share in this high-profit, heavy-buyer category (Hallberg, 1995).

Unfortunately, advertising misses the mark with these prime prospects. Instead, it reaches mostly non-buyers or small-quantity buyers. On the other hand, promotions *do* touch the high-profit segment. That is, frequent buyers are more likely to encounter price promotions, coupons, rebates, etc. However, promotions over-sensitise consumers to price and tend to decrease brand loyalty in the high-potential, high-profit segment.

As a consequence, most mega-brands are now experimenting with database marketing on a grand scale. The database marketing concept is twofold:

▨ All marketing actions should target the prime segment more effectively. The goal is to increase this segment's rate of brand use.

▨ Effective targeting requires companies to identify each of these customers or households, almost nominally. As a consequence, a by-product of all promotional activities should be a database, ultimately comprising 100 per cent of the high-profit customers.

At this time Procter & Gamble's database in the USA holds more than 48 million names. Danone's database in France holds 2 million names. Nestlé is building its own in each major country, as is Unilever. And this ignores all the broker-created databases for rental to smaller companies.

The function of these selective databases is to deliver customised offers to specific targets, to bring the store shelf to the home (thus decreasing impulse buying and distributors' power), and to promote a 'private image' among loyal and heavy-user customers. Generally, these customers are more involved in the brand, so they deserve recognition and special treatment. They also merit specific information to nourish brand image and equity. These activities constitute the nurturing of a 'private image', as opposed to a broader, general public image.

The recent concern about managing customer equity is illustrated in Figure 9.7. Many consumers hold very favourable attitudes *vis-à-vis* particular brands. Nevertheless, their loyalty is insufficient to inhibit switching within a repertoire of brands. These customers are potential loyals only if a tailor-made programme is devised to increase the rate of purchase of a particular brand. On the other hand, some repeat buyers are actually pseudo-loyals: they do not hold strong attitudes regarding the brand. Perhaps, for instance, they buy the brand because of its price or availability. To increase their brand preference, these buyers require a reinforcement of their choice and an increased perception of the brand's superiority. Finally, active and committed loyals should be induced to try more and more new products, whether line or brand extensions. Figure 9.8 illustrates Sony's situation, where committed loyals comprise 19 per cent of Sony's entire customer franchise. The potential loyals represent 4 per cent, and the pseudo-loyals 35 per cent. Each group deserves a specific marketing proposition.

The customer demand for dialogue

Although most brands claim to put customers' needs first, this does not extend to creating a

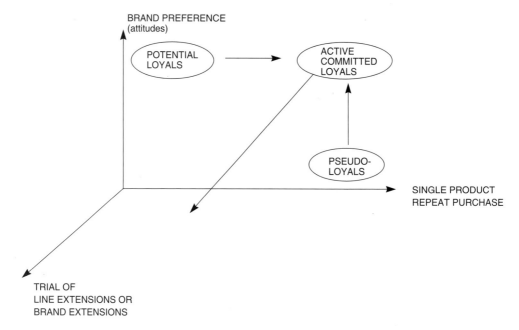

Figure 9.7   The three facets of brand loyalty

dialogue with them. Advertising does not count as dialogue. Neither does a relationship with a seller with clear marketing intentions, and neither do satisfaction questionnaires: they may be very useful in obtaining feedback on perceived quality, but a series of questions does not constitute a dialogue. Do consumer magazines provide a dialogue? Once again, no. And the same is true of direct marketing mailshots from sellers inviting consumers to see or try out a new product, and the like.

Why do we say 'customer demand'? Because customers want to be valued, listened to and heard, and not merely as an averaged-out statistic in a market segment, but for themselves as individuals. Furthermore, the new Internet firms, with their ability to amass 'intelligent' information (which learns from the most recent call, person by person) and use this information in future contacts, have made them accustomed to a responsive reaction and a listening ear.

A relationship with a brand automatically creates a need of this kind. Take banks and insurance companies, for example. Once the customer has initially been won over, the brand–client rapport will last for years. There are bound to be problems along the way, but if these are managed well, the result may be lasting loyalty. The problem is that they are often not managed well, and negative word of mouth can be the only means of retribution available to customers who feel ignored, or treated with contempt. Indeed, the retailer is not only the brand's best ally when things are going well; it can also become its worst enemy when problems arise. It is the enemy of the brand because it is perceived as the enemy of the customer. We believe that at such a time, the customer should have direct access to the brand itself, its ultimate recourse.

Saturn – the recent automobile brand created in the United States by GM as a response to Japanese brands – was a pioneer in customer relations. Following the example it set, every new buyer – whether large or small – should be given the name and telephone number of a brand employee who can if

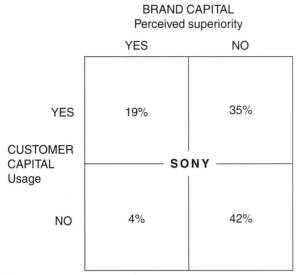

Source: Sofres, Megabrand System

Figure 9.8   Brand capital and customer capital: matching preferences and purchase behaviour

necessary be contacted by the customer in the event of unresolved problems. This is the real one-to-one relationship, and is what customers expect above all else when problems occur. The brand cannot delegate crisis management to third parties.

Without becoming the enemy of its own selective network, the brand must assume a benevolent 'the buck stops here' attitude, eager to find a solution for the customer. After all, the customer has bought a brand, not a retailer. Furthermore, what is the point in conducting customer intimacy operations and public relations exercises if, the minute a real need presents itself, the brand suddenly becomes distant and fails to return the customer's calls? The 'boomerang' effect is the only possible outcome here.

Over and above these crisis situations, which create the immediate need for genuine dialogue and invoke the first duty of any brand (the guarantee), remember that the need for dialogue is very closely linked to customer segmentation. Needless to say, not all customers have the same expectations.

Do all customers want:

- to be listened to?
- to be recognised?
- to be gratified?
- to be involved?
- to be informed?

Some of these are true of all customers, but not all of them. We must therefore separate the approach described above – which is a universal truth demonstrating the brand's acknowledgement that every customer, big or small, is worthy of attention – from other approaches that target particular segments. For example, in the automobile sector (a prime example of an area that generates involvement), the following groups can be identified:

- Automobile fans who want to know everything about the brand's past, present and future. They want to be involved in live or media-covered events (such as live Internet coverage from the cockpit of a rally car, or on CD-ROM). Brand fans also want to form themselves into a community, under the aegis of the brand. The brand should be media aware and encourage the building of relationships between its 'fan' customers.

▎ Loyal customers who are not automobile fans respond well to being acknowledged as loyal, and are thus gratified when they receive the attention they deserve from the brand: highly personalised, and thus incorporating the one-to-one element.

▎ New customers can be segmented by lifestyle or by their stage in the family life cycle, and be informed of news that is relevant to their own lifestyles – presenting another opportunity to listen to the customer. For example, women with children will be interested in anything related to children's active (or even passive) safety.

▎ All (non-segmented) customers must have the ability to make themselves heard and to obtain information – for example, via a call centre – and to obtain a personalised response within a set time period.

The customer is then entered into a database and is targeted by segmented relational actions.

The concept of the relationship demonstrates the way in which all product-based companies are moving towards the concept of service, and the notion of 'clientèle' is being redefined as community.

More ethical customer relations are needed. All too often, the relationship has been dictated by legal departments seeking to avoid abuse by placing detailed restrictions on customers' rights – but by substituting the anonymous for the personal, such a legalistic approach kills customer relations.

Is relational marketing profitable?

Customer relations are certainly a good idea, but are they profitable? Here again, we must reconcile the brand (the creation of value) with the economic equation. Convincing statistics abound with regard to the profitability of loyal customers. However, studies also show that most customers who become disloyal to a brand were previously very satisfied with the brand: their requirements have simply changed. Another way of looking at these figures is to conclude that the customers' attachment – their desire to stay with the brand – cannot have been especially high to start with. This is where relational marketing comes in.

Attachment to a brand is evidence of a customer's desire to stay in a lasting relationship with the brand. This attachment is characterised by loyalty, which is a behavioural measure of repeat purchasing. Loyalty may be a consequence of attachment, but it can also be generated by means of bonuses and so-called 'loyalty cards'. Attachment to a brand is a one-dimensional concept of varying strength. Its opposite state is detachment, indifference and non-involvement.

Attachment is a different thing altogether from satisfaction. This is why attachments can be mainly rational (a desire to continue the relationship with the brand because it meets the buyer's implicit requirements, albeit without generating any real emotional involvement). Conversely, some customers remain very attached despite considerable dissatisfaction with the product or service (the Harley-Davidson/Jaguar syndrome).

Research has identified six sources of attachment. As we shall see, each of these points to specific levers for managerial action:

▎ Attachment based on the hedonistic satisfaction conferred by the use of the products and by the quality of the interaction with the brand's representatives (network, call centre and so on).

▎ Attachment based on the quality of the relationship established by the brand: appreciation of the individual and his or her uniqueness, personal recognition, ethical behaviour.

- Attachment based on shared values which affect the consumer; a shared vision.

- Attachment based on the increased self-image generated by the brand through its image, advertising, rallies, behaviour and so on.

- Attachment based on the pleasure of a lasting relationship. The brand has often played a part in the development of individuals, their family and their children. In a sense, it has become a part of the life of individuals and their 'clan'.

- Attachment based on the brand's association with people to whom the customer is emotively linked. Managers have little power to influence this particular factor, but it is real nonetheless ('Proust's madeleine syndrome') (Heilbrunn, 2003).

Many different types of behaviour result from attachment. A relational brand must respond to them in order to feed attachment:

- a desire for rituals and participation therein, like a community;

- a desire for information;

- a desire for participation in the life of the brand and company;

- a desire for shared creation and involvement in the process of creating new products;

- a desire to be heard;

- a desire for community;

- a desire for intimacy;

- a desire for customer involvement with the brand: evangelising, prescribing and acting as an ambassador for the brand;

- automatic repeat purchasing (loyalty in the strictest sense of the word).

Customer relations increases the effectiveness of brand promotion. An offer is never perceived as 'touting for business' when it arrives at the right moment! Only a relationship with – and deep understanding of – customers, informed by an awareness of their recent requests, can transform what is usually perceived as commercial harassment into an impression of genuine service. There is thus no real contradiction between increasing client profitability and nurturing a relationship. A fan will be delighted to be able to download historic advertising for the brand. A young mother will be pleased to receive child-related ideas, services or products from the many brands aimed at parents and children. It all boils down to the timeliness of the offer.

How can this synergy be achieved if there is no information; no ongoing relationship with the customer; no means of listening to that customer's needs and being able to store and update the information thus received through a variety of media (e-mail, text messaging, telephone, fax, post)? As we can see, well-targeted, relevant business offers that come at just the right time create satisfaction because of the service they provide and the understanding they demonstrate of the client's needs. They are thus one of the key ways of creating attachment.

Having said this, we should not deny the power of the service in creating loyalty and repeat purchases. For example, Courtepaille – the European high-quality fast-food restaurant chain – has no loyalty programme. Certainly, the customer will find very few other restaurants with such friendly service and hearty fare at prices of under 10 euros. But margins are so tight that the benefit of a loyalty card is still uncertain: happy customers will come back anyway.

Such examples are rare: in mature countries, bad brands scarcely exist any more. The competition is divided between very good brands and merely good brands. An in-house engineer will say that his or her product is the best: the customer and retailer will not see things in this way. However, the brand will have played a successful part in influencing preferences if it has been able to draw alongside the customer and promote a relationship based on service, communication and community – a source of affective involvement.

Segmenting loyalty programmes

Does this mean that the concept of loyalty is outdated? The conceptual explanation above clearly shows that loyalty behaviour (automatic repeat purchasing) continues to be relevant because it concerns information of critical importance to the company: it is based on observation. Even so, there may be many reasons behind a lack of loyalty (as we have seen above), which should be linked to the level of satisfaction.

The modern nature of competition is such that the issue is no longer 'or', but rather 'and'. It is therefore essential to avoid neglecting strategies for increasing loyalty (repeat purchases) that operate at the strictly behavioural level. They have an immediate effect: they raise the brand's share of requirements and create an exit barrier – as has been shown by airlines and store-card promotional offer coupons. In the sphere of commodity sales, given the competition from low-cost sources, loyalty cards are – along with service – an essential component of the economic equation. In petrol stations, for example, nearly 40 per cent of petrol by volume is sold to customers with loyalty cards.

However, the real aim is to shift clients from behaviour towards attitudes. In traditional marketing – symbolised by the AIDA (attention, interest, desire, action) model – purchase follows desire, and thus attitudes. Given the number of competitors, and the degree to which products resemble one other, the priority is now to stand out from the herd. Creating a well-known, high-profile brand with emotive impact is one way of doing this. Another way is to introduce a surprising,

tempting innovation. A third way is to provide direct purchasing and repeat purchasing incentives. However, this last approach has meaning only if it creates long-term value: that is, if behaviour initially motivated by the lure of an incentive is subsequently transferred to the brand and its products or services. Repeat purchasing is the customer's way of giving the brand a unique chance to prove itself.

In terms of loyalty management, Accor, the European hotel sector leader, offers an interesting and rare example. A hotel chain's profitability is based on the occupancy rate in its hotels, and particularly in cases where prices are tight, such as the budget hotel sector. Accor has a strong presence here, with a brand portfolio which covers all segments: zero-star (Motel 6, Formule 1), one-star (Etap hotels), two-star (Ibis), three-star (Novotel and Mercure) and four-star (Sofitel), not forgetting the new luxury Suit'Hotels segment. However, despite its customers' sensitivity to price, Accor charges for its loyalty cards. It has created an entire range of cards, each addressing a different client segment and governed by its own precise terms of use, acting as a replacement for single-brand cards. An additional service is being offered to customers by allowing them to move freely between the various brands of the group as dictated by their own wishes, budget and situation. This is the competitive advantage of having a portfolio of brands.

The premier card is Accor Hotels Favourite Guest, an individual card sold at the high price of 270 euros/year. It offers significant advantages to customers, and is therefore aimed at 'heavy stayers' who spend more than 20 nights a year in a hotel. It offers guaranteed reservation up to three days prior to the stay date, as well as immediate reductions and loyalty points – and can be used at Ibis, Mercure, Novotel and Sofitel hotels.

The second card is targeted at lighter users who spend an average of 13 nights a year in hotels, and costs 45 euros a year. To make it more attractive in terms of points earned, it is a combined payment and loyalty card thanks to a partnership with Amex.

This left the loyalty of 'small users' to be secured. An ordinary free card would be of no benefit here, since a quick calculation shows that it would take a customer who spends three nights a year in a hotel 15 years to earn enough points for a free night. One option might have been to take part in a Smiles-type frequent buyer programme – that is, a card allowing the user to accumulate points at a large number of sales outlets of all kinds (department stores, hypermarkets, super-markets, specialist stores such as Delheze and Kaufhof and so on). But how much benefit does such a programme actually bring to the individual brand? None. Naturally, the aim of loyalty is to increase the brand's share of requirements, but also to feed its own values. The Total petrol company positions itself on its service, and so the main thrust of its loyalty programme is to provide access to additional quality service (such as Total Assistance breakdown cover); points are a secondary consideration.

It is for this reason that, with its so-called 'small-user' clients in mind, Accor joined forces with a number of partners, each of which shared the same client philosophy and operated in the same line of business (journeys and travelling) to create the Accor Compliments Mouvango card. This improved the services offered to customers and allows points to be accumulated more quickly than would have been possible if they had visited hotels even five or six nights a year. This partnership has its own brand – Mouvango, the sign displayed by partners to show that the card is accepted. It includes restaurants, Total service stations, Carlson-Wagons Lits, travel agencies and so on. Total's version is called the Club Total Mouvango card, and so on. As we can see, the brand remains pre-eminent among all partners in this scenario, for it is here that the customer contact and relationship exists:

Mouvango is an exclusive additional service to sweeten this relationship.

From the product to attentions: from the client to the VIP

Segmentation leads rapidly to the realisation that not all customers carry the same sales potential. It is also true that not all customers have the same interest in an involvement with the brand and becoming its ambas-sadors. A brand cannot survive without loyal followers and ambassadors, especially if it has premium positioning in its segment: there are women who will spurn all washing powders other than the top-dollar Tide or Ariel brands. This is even more true in high-involvement markets such as automobiles and cosmetics.

Such markets have traditionally been driven by a product-oriented approach: this is why l'Oréal, the world leader, relies totally on research. The goal of its 1,000 PhD-holding researchers is to invent new products which will inspire dreams of beauty and youth among women of all ages and all countries. The l'Oréal Group's flagship brand, l'Oréal Paris, only discovered relational marketing fairly recently, in 2002 – the date when it launched its first advertising campaign aimed at building a relational database as a way of offering services to women. The same is true of the luxury brand Lancôme, which took its first steps in this direction in South America at a time when a brutal economic recession had had a colossal impact on purchasing power. It was essential to retain existing customers and thus enable the business to survive. Clearly, it was not enough merely to expound the virtues of the products themselves: this was necessary, but insufficient under such circum-stances. This is why Lancôme's local teams reacted by innovating – not with new products, but with the attention it paid its customers. This example is even more pertinent in that it involved retailers, and thus also created a trade relationship tool which generated business.

Lancôme instructed its authorised retailers to distribute a small smart card – the Lancôme beauty card – and to use equipment that would store the client's last few transactions when the card was presented. This was a revolutionary approach, since the retailers believed that a client record was their own property. In order to 'earn' the card, the client had to make an initial purchase of US $100. All subsequent purchases – regardless of the store, as long as it was a participant in the scheme and had an electronic recorder – would earn points. These points could be exchanged for Lancôme products, lingerie, jewellery and famous-name bags. Cards were also given to journalists and top fashion models. Once a database had been created, it became possible to create campaigns targeting VIPs, who are generally also big spenders, making repeated visits to their local sales point.

The company's first act was to produce and mail to these clients a woman's beauty magazine, paid for by advertising (from airline, jewellery, lingerie and similar companies). 'Sneak preview' announcements were also made of new products, and specific samples were provided, along with access to a dedicated, interactive MyLancôme.Vip Web site. The VIP card was accepted in selected restaurants and shops. Lastly, selective invitations to public relations events and fashion shows, offering meetings with leading figures, were issued regularly.

The database also becomes a tool for building a relationship between the brand and the sales outlets, for coordinating the promotion of new products, or performing a 'diary' function (reminding store clients of key dates – such as birthdays – appearing in the database, and prompting post-purchase calls). The aim of this is not only to make customers visit sales outlets, but also to enable them to be recognised as special and unique – receiving personalised attention to increase the pleasure of their visit. A VIP wants to be recognised as such.

Sustaining proximity with influencers

Today, mass targets have disappeared. Statistics should not create an illusion. What might appear to be mass targets are in fact made up of an aggregation of smaller ones, of micro targets. Even if mass advertising campaigns are still used, what is needed for a brand is a shared image, a collective bonding tool within societies. To develop the brand over time entails improving the brand's relationship with each of the strategic micro targets. These strategic targets are made of more involved customers, or those who are currently non-customers but have the potential to become involved. Once involved they can act as influencers. They can re-energise a brand image that is weakened by the deleterious effects of time.

This is critical for sustaining the equity of mature brands, facing new entrants. Such brands run the risk of losing contact with the trend-setting groups in a society. The risk is that they will be perceived as yesterday's brand. Recreating contact with trend-setting 'tribes' or micro-groups is of paramount importance even for brands that are not involved with fashion in any direct sense. Otherwise they run the risk of becoming just another supermarket brand.

Ricard provides a good example of best practice in its long-term engagement in recreating lost ties with critical groups. It is a historical leader in the aniseed-based alcoholic drinks sector, which comprises the fifth largest spirits sector in the world. It has introduced relational programmes aimed at three groups: women, those of high socio-economic status (SES), and young people. Ricard faces competition both from spirits such as whisky, vodka, gin, rum and tequila, and thus from world-famous brands such as Johnny Walker, J&B, Absolut, Bacardi and Cacique, and from fashionable modern brands of beer. Finally, it is 40 per cent more expensive than the distributors' brands and other low-cost brands of aniseed drinks. Part of its resistance to these massive attacks has been to remain close to its core clients and to invest in reconquering proximity with the trend-setting groups, those most attracted and seduced by international competition.

Women may like the taste of Ricard but they did not like its image. They perceived it as a male, popular brand, not a sign of good manners. As a response, Ricard runs very specific adverts in trendy women's magazines, and sponsors events involving women. The brand sponsors literary events where new female writers are promoted. It is a major organiser of St Catherine's Day, a promotional event for national design schools. It continues to try out specific relational operations such as a cooperation with Mod's Hair, a youth-oriented hairdressing franchise. Typically, this involves the hairdresser's customers being offered a Ricard to drink while waiting in the salon in the summer. The new format RTD – ready to drink – is very useful for this purpose.

High-SES people of all sexes and ages are addressed through Espace Ricard, an art gallery, open to the latest forms of painting, thus creating a proximity with the most advanced artists and art lovers. In addition, advanced designers are regularly asked to redesign the basic 'tools' that accompany a drink of Ricard, a carafe and an ashtray. The world-famous designers Garouste and Bonetti did the latest versions.

To gain proximity to young people interested in music and sport, Ricard has developed three long-term actions supported by a specific budget allowance. One is creation of the Paul Ricard car racing circuit, compatible with F1 international racing standards, and now the most modern and safe circuit in France. It hosted most of the major international car races, until a law was introduced preventing sports sponsorship by alcoholic drink brands. It was then sold but the name has been retained.

The second innovation is the Ricard Live Music Tour, providing the largest free music events in Europe, featuring famous rock stars. It has attracted more than 1 million people each year, and its name has become synonymous with quality music and concerts. The company has gained unique know-how in organising open concerts in the middle of major cities and synchronising sales events around them to maximise synergy. Each concert attracts a great deal of free publicity.

The third youth-oriented initiative is the organisation of 1,000 integration parties (for students just going up to university) and graduation parties each year. The targets for these are the top business and engineering schools, since their students will be the elite of tomorrow.

Of course, it is not possible to remain a popular brand without also maintaining a proximity to core consumers, existing heavy buyers and the engaged segment (see the segmentation scheme on page 170). Locally, at the micro level, pétanque contests are still sponsored by the brand in Provence (the birthplace of the brand) and elsewhere. In summer, a squadron of Ricard 'fire girls' runs onto major beaches and offers sunbathers free drinks. For image management purposes, each brand needs to decide which of its many PR activities should receive publicity.

Nine lessons can be learnt from this example:

▌ Because change is permanent, and new competition is always coming in and can be very seductive, the brand's profile is always threatened over time. It must be nurtured and proximity eventually reconquered.

▌ No brand can stay apart from trend-setting tribes in its sector.

▌ Proximity and strong ties can only be built at points of direct contact.

▌ Strong ties need to be continuous: this is not a 'coup' policy, but a continuous decision.

▌ This activity must be supported by a strong investment.

▍ It must be done by courageous people. Trend-setting groups are not waiting to be approached by a currently unfashionable brand, and sometimes they will look down on its promoters.

▍ Again, targeting is key.

▍ Again, creativity and disruption are of paramount importance, to surprise and create a buzz.

▍ Finally, this is the occasion for creating selective publicity, deciding which of these ties should be most squarely in the spotlight.

The necessity of dual management

Regularly, the same question arises: should the brand aim at its existing customers or at its future buyers? Should it try to maximise its present customers' satisfaction or should it think of the new generation?

For sure, the global mantra of management today is to focus on existing customers. They are the most profitable source of cash flow. This is why all companies and brands invest in building up large customer databases, CRM software, and undertake in-depth surveys on customer satisfaction with the product or service. This leads to necessary improvements, and in theory it increases customer loyalty. We write 'in theory', for all automobile surveys show that 60 per cent of the consumers who did not buy the same brand on their next purchase were very satisfied with their former brand. Why then did they change? Because consumption is situational. New situations create new expectations: this is called 'value migration'. New generations too develop a new set of values and expectations.

Existing customers are essential for short and medium-term growth and profitability, but listening too much to existing customers is the main reason companies do not innovate

enough. Professor Christensen has shown that the main reason companies disappear is that disruptive innovations transform the market and rapidly make their products or services obsolete. What prevents these companies, which are often adjudged to be excellent, from innovating? Arguably they are too well managed (Christensen, 1997). Well-managed companies select the innovations that please their clients and that provide good profitability forecasts with a high degree of certainty. Disruptive innovations are just the contrary: they are not well perceived by current customers, and nothing can be said with certainty about their profitability. But disrupting the market is how the minicomputer made mainframe companies obsolete, then the PC did the same for the minicomputer and so on.

Collins and Porras (1994) have reminded us of the power of the 'and'. Most of us keep on asking questions about alternatives: should the brand do this or do that? It is a mistake. We must do both. Brands must think of their present clients as the immediate source of growth, but they must also look to the future generation.

At present Smirnoff has 60 per cent of the UK vodka market. For most managers, this would be a good reason to be satisfied. Instead, the management of Smirnoff innovated to react to new entrants such as Absolut and Finlandia. Most importantly, it invented a vodka for the new generation, who were not interested in drinking vodka as their parents did, but could be persuaded to drink it outside pubs, not from a glass but straight from the bottle, like a beer. This is called dual management: already thinking of the emerging trends, new behaviours and customers, those who will be dominant tomorrow. As we analyse below (page 228), Salomon also had to follow a dual approach. Choosing one instead of the other would have been suicidal. All brands should do the same if they intend to remain as successful brands in the immediate future.

Nivea provides a good example of the so-called dual strategy. The lifespan and growth of this world-leading skincare brand can be explained through two key factors: the modernisation of the prototype product, Nivea cream, in its round blue box, and systematic brand extension via daughter brands (which Nivea calls 'sub-brands').

The little round box is the prototype of Nivea, and carries the brand's values (see page 122). In every country it is introduced first, and made available at all sales points, explaining its penetration into all social environments. Next come the extensions (see page 233), in a pre-established order, to build the brand: first care products, followed by hygiene, then hair products, and lastly make-up. The daughter brands expand these categories, with their specialisation based on age (Nivea Baby), purpose (Nivea Sun), gender (Nivea for Men), and so on.

However, if it is to maintain itself, the brand must work tirelessly to recapture its relevance, and this is why it must innovate. Each advertisement for a Nivea daughter-brand now places the emphasis on innovation. But even the prototype has needed an update: this has been the role of Nivea Soft, with its white box, as modern generations look for a cream which is less greasy and penetrates the skin more quickly. Nivea Soft is bringing the brand's foundation up to date.

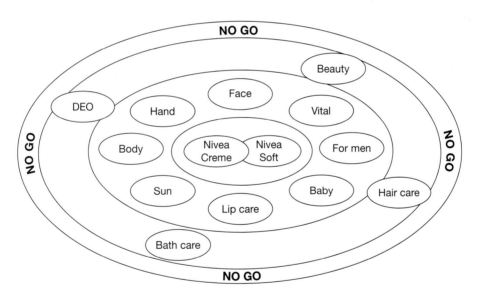

Figure 9.9 The Nivea extensions galaxy

10

Adapting to the market: identity and change

The only way a brand can grow is through movement. You cannot expect growth and lack of change. The brand is continually looking to create new markets, new segments in which it can become the reference and above all the market leader. It was said, for example, of the Twingo that Renault had invented 'the car that hadn't existed' (Midler, 1995). According to this plan the brand's image is, like its environment, in perpetual evolution. To fail to evolve is to appear to be shackled by the present, to have a dated and immobile image.

Mercedes could have repeated its famous sedans indefinitely, while always improving them, since they were the global image of what a luxury car should look like, to the point at which the Japanese Lexus copied their contours exactly. Meanwhile customers had changed. Those at the edge of leading opinion, who influence the opinion of 90 per cent of the rest, had changed their lifestyle and their points of reference. They were no longer wedded to sedans, but were looking for niche designs of car to suit them. The brand's hopes went into the Class A, the 'little Mercedes': a break with what had been the

brand's contract with its customers. It represented a disruption, but not an incoherence or a contradiction. Mercedes could not afford to confine itself to a conception of a car that was becoming a minority taste. Its mission of offering the most reliable cars in the world needed to adapt itself to the requirements of the world.

Only radical change is visible. Otherwise, according to the psychological principle of 'perceptual assimilation', what we see is based on our preconceptions. Accordingly, brands should not hesitate to push their boundaries far from their original prototype. The frontiers of the brand's territory are made always to be pushed back, in the directions of products, geography and meaning. If, in order to manage the brand in the medium term (three to five years) there is a need for tools that fix its limits (such as the prism of identity), it is necessary to review them regularly, to adapt to changing circumstances, and indeed to prompt change. Equilibrium for a brand in a world in perpetual movement does not consist of staying static, but of introducing movement, of fighting a continual battle.

The luxury US brands surprise us, because they have an air of incoherence. Calvin Klein went from the provocation of Obsession to the idealism of Eternity. Ralph Lauren jumped from the Boston WASP image of Polo to the Safari ambience of 'Out of Africa'. In reality one product does not follow on neatly from the previous one, in the sense of a repetitive coherence that continues the same concepts to infinity, leading the brand inevitably down a path of decline. These products are signs of a brand in movement. Calvin Klein is not either Obsession or Eternity. It is both, a brand both more complex and more open than others had imagined. Renault comprises both the Megane and the Espace. The future belongs to brands that are able to handle this type of 'and', and to abandon the dichotomous choice of the 'or'.

This is also the message that Collins and Porras conveyed in their *Built to Last* (1994). Chanel surprised us in launching Coco and associating it with Vanessa Paradis. There was an incoherence, a break with the image it had conveyed through its previous figurehead, Carole Bouquet. But this kind of radical move does more to ensure the long-term survival of the brand in an era when it is faced with competition from American and Italian designers who know how to seduce the young.

The paradox is that at the same time, the brand only develops on the basis of a certain permanence, or perhaps a duration. The key concept of the brand's identity carries within itself the necessary continuity of 'identification': the meanings and expressions of the brand. We should not forget that the brand is a point of reference: it indicates a proposition, certain values. That is its first function. To create and build up a point of reference, the brand needs to have a clear sense of itself, a direction. A certain amount of continuity is also essential to the construction and development over time of the brand.

The parallel pursuit of these two requirements (identity and change) leads us to view the brand from two angles: the timeless angle of its basic meaning and identity, and the offensive, disruptive angle of its new developments. This is the theme of this chapter.

The necessity of change

It is known that a brand only grows over a long period by remaining consistent. The concept of identity implies that some facets of the brand remain identical through time: continuity is essential to the brand's formation and longevity.

Nevertheless, a brand which does not change with the times fossilises and loses its relevance. Time is merely the indicator of changes in lifestyles, consumer expectations, technology and competitive position. The question of management of the time factor therefore becomes: how do we adapt to these new conditions while keeping our identity? What should we change and what should we leave untouched? Since a brand only exists by means of its products (or services) and its communication strategy, managing the time factor will necessarily involve these two vectors of evolution and continuity. On the communication side, we have the rare example of Marlboro, who initiated the image of the lone cowboy in 1964. Few brands have, in fact, been steeped in such a myth rooted in a specific time and space. Jack Daniel's is another example. Coca-Cola, Volkswagen, Nestlé, Philips and Adidas have updated their advertising and products to adapt to social changes. Brands must therefore learn to change their style and products in order to keep up with the times. It is by staying up to date that a brand survives the test of time.

Technological progress and research ensure a permanent flow of innovations which the brand should incorporate to safeguard against obsolescence or downgrading. Whenever the product does not change, the brand becomes mortal: Volkswagen almost disappeared with the end of the Beetle. Linking a brand's destiny to one single product is a major risk for any company whose product is at the end of its life cycle. Without an ongoing renewal of its products and services, and without non-stop attention to its task, the brand falls by the wayside. Innovation and new products give the brand the opportunity to demonstrate its mission and direction, and to construct a coherent and specific image. This concerns just as much IBM or Dell in the crowded computer market, as it does Coca-Cola. Certainly, the basic Coca-Cola formula has remained unchanged throughout the world, but its format and ingredients have evolved in response to changes in lifestyle – eg family packs for the weekly shopping in super-markets, aluminium cans for more conven-ience when taking home and taking out, derivatives without caffeine or sugar, etc. Recognition of the purchaser's basic needs should be a brand's primary occupation, and requires constant vigilance.

Values, customs and behaviour patterns are constantly changing with time. What seemed revolutionary in 1995 is insignificant in 2005. A brand that anchors its survival on one particular feature is threatened with extinction. Findus is the brand that gave credence to frozen foods by legitimising a new social behaviour. At the time, the advent of frozen foods helped shatter the traditional concept of the role of women – that their place was in the kitchen. The Findus repu-tation and its public voice on TV gave authority to the changes which women had long been seeking. Times certainly have changed – the housewife has been replaced by the working wife. The basis of Findus's original argument is now as outdated as Women's Lib.

Generally speaking, such effigies can bog down the brand, wrapping it in a symbolism which is prone to change as society evolves. This is why Exxon ceased for a while to communicate through its tiger, deemed too agressive, although it has since been revived. Bibendum does not run this risk – it is an original symbol with no prior connotations. Only Michelin gives it meaning, and vice versa.

Brands created around a living personality also need to face up to changes in meaning. The personality has his or her own life and acquires a dimension and symbolism which may not always coincide with the brand's strategic interests. Pepsi-Cola discovered that with Michael Jackson. Lancôme abandoned Isabella Rossellini, judging her 'too old', and switched to more universal top models.

Brand identity versus brand diversity

What is the main characteristic of modern markets? This is a tough question and there is probably no single answer. For us, in any case, the most important thing is that needs are satisfied. This has two considerable consequences.

First, economic growth will rest on sustained consumption only if consumption itself can be stimulated. This means that brands will have to stimulate desire. This has great implications for brand management. Brands should now deliver experiences, and one of the first is to surprise their consumers.

Another key factor of modern markets is the wish to consume better. Globalisation is now a reality for consumers. They are aware that first-world companies have their products made in China or Brazil, that underdeveloped countries will only be able to develop if trade is more equitable, that some companies are more ecology-conscious than others. These considerations have no impact on consumers when their main problem is to fulfil their basic needs. Maslow reminded us that higher-level needs become important when lower-level ones are satisfied. This means that modern consumers do not want bigger brands, but better brands. Sustainable devel-opment is here to stay. It is no fad. Perhaps many companies now mention sustainable development in their corporate annual reports purely because their competitors do so, or because they feel forced to do it. Meanwhile their competitors have realised that sustainable development and fair trade are sources of competitive edge. Today intelligence is moral intelligence.

The fact is that classic brand concepts fail to address this new situation. Certainly the key concept of brand management is identity: we have been stressing it since 1990, when the first edition of this book was published. 'Identity' means that the brand should respect its key values and defining attributes. However, there is a point where too much repetition of the same creates boredom. Too much predictability is a drawback in modern markets.

This is why the role of modern brands is to stimulate the consumer to have new experiences. The role of the brand in providing reassurance and generating trust is not dead, far from it: but it needs to be used to encourage the consumer to take more risks, explore new behaviours, try new unexpected products. In order to do so, disruptive innovations become very important. To grow through time while keeping its identity, the brand should continue differently.

To this end there is a need for new research tools. Why are all companies now listening to forecasting consultants, trend spotters? Because they need to think now about what consumers are not thinking about today, but will think about tomorrow. Classical marketing research analyses sources of satisfaction and dissatisfaction with the product or service or brand. The outcomes can be used to prompt immediate and continuous improvements. But can disruption come from this type of marketing research? Satisfaction is always linked to customers' existing values and goals. Research is needed also to spot how these values and goals will change, leading to new insights.

Brand management needs a set of boundaries. This is called brand identity, which covers how the brand defines itself, its values, its mission, its know-how, its personality and so on. A clear sense of identity is necessary, for the brand meaning to be reinforced by repetition. On the other hand-market fragmentation, competitive dynamism and the need for surprises call not for reinforcement but for diversification. As ever, brand management will act as a pendulum, going from an excess of sameness to an excess of diversity. There is nothing wrong with this. The same holds true of the local/global dilemma, or the ethics versus business dilemma.

Another consequence is the need to know the identity of the brand. More precisely, what is its kernel, the attributes that are necessary for the brand to remain itself, and what are the traits that can show some flexibility? If all the attributes of the brand belong to its kernel, that is to say, they are all necessary to its

Table 10.1   From risk to desire: the dilemma of modern branding

Brand = capital	Brand = impulse
Capitalise	Surprise
Repeat	Diversify
Sameness	Variety
Identity	Change

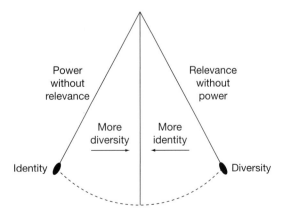

Figure 10.1   The identity versus diversity dilemma

identity, its ability to change will be hampered. How can a brand surprise customers, evolve, adapt to new uses, situations and markets, if it is too rigidly defined? Peripheral attributes can change, or be present in some products but not in others. Eventually, innovations introduce new peripheral attributes, which may become incorporated into the kernel at some point in time. This is how brands evolve through time, how innovations have an impact on their identity. Peripheral traits act as the key long-term change agents within brands (Abric, 1994; Mischel, 2000). The tools to identify the traits held by consumers as kernel traits of a brand are known (see page 272) but their use is not sufficiently widespread.

The brands that ultimately last are those that are able to surprise their customers, and the customers of tomorrow in particular. This sums up the challenge facing modern brand management in a nutshell. Far from seeking to capitalise on its past – and thus to repeat itself – the brand should surprise, and promote change. This is what should be termed the 'exploratory function', which plays an epistemic role for the brand

(Heilbrunn, 2003). But how can you know what will surprise the customers of tomorrow?

Market studies provide a good understanding of today's customers; or at least, of the expectations they express. So much needs to be done to improve customer satisfaction. How long ago did readers receive a satisfaction questionnaire from their bank? Their car dealers? Their telephone company?

To surprise customers, you need to take a long-term view – hence the growing use of trends in brand management. Trends are hypotheses relating to change that occurs within small groups in our societies, but could potentially create a tidal wave among the general public. These trends are established on the basis of combined information regarding the demographic, technological, social and cultural future of our societies.

We thus need to define three levels of vision: long, medium and short term. Car concepts in the automobile sector, for example, are governed by long-term considerations. Decisions regarding models that are already part of the seven-year production plan are considered as medium term.

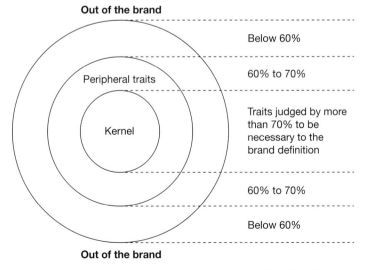

Figure 10.2   How brands incorporate change: kernel and peripheral traits

Consistency is not mere repetition

Brand messages and slogans are bound to evolve. Evian was, initially, the water of babies, then of the Alps, then the water of balance, later the water of balanced strength, and now a source of youth. These changes in positioning occurred over a long time period: they demonstrate the evolution of the consumer's attitude towards water, the maturation of the market and the evolution of competitive position. The functions and representations of water are not fixed: they depend on external factors linked to urbanisation, industrialisation, rediscovering nature, discovering pollution, new representations of the body, health and food hygiene. Positioning is the act of relating one brand facet to a set of consumer expectations, needs and desires. As these needs change through time, the brand is obliged to follow suit. However, Evian's identity remained consistent throughout these re-positionings.

But within a brand's lifetime these changes in positioning should not happen too often, about every four or five years. However, the brand's means of expression can move faster to integrate with the evolution of fashion: new speech modes, new signs of modernity and new looks. It is essential that the brand is perceived as up to date although such necessary adjustments and changes make the brand run the risk of a loss of identity.

To retain their identity while changing, brands often stick to their communication codes, that is their fixed visual and audio symbols. This is undeniably a factor that contributes to a brand and what it represents being recognised. Even when not named, Coke commercials can be picked out: their music and their style are unique. But the style itself is subject to obsolescence. Continuing with it could prove fatal to the brand.

Unfortunately, it has to be acknowledged that brands have a hard time parting with their communication codes, even when they feel it is necessary. This is to be expected: they are afraid of losing their identity. But this reluctance is largely due to the fact that brand management concepts are essentially static. Time is not taken into account when it is a key parameter in markets. In that sense, the concept of 'communication territory' is a vision that clings to the ground: it has to do with all the visible signals that the brand uses to communicate its definition and what it represents. However, an identity that defines itself only through signs is subject to an alteration of their meaning. The brand is indeed recognised, but no longer in control of its meaning.

The three layers of a brand: kernel, codes and promises

The evolution of a brand needs a direction. Considering the brand as a vision about its product category, it is important to know in which direction it is looking. The brand being a genetic memory to help us manage the future, we must know what drives it, what is its prime reason for existing.

All these concepts (source of inspiration, statement, codes and communication themes) work together in a three-tier pyramid that is useful in managing the balance of change and identity.

▌ At the top of the pyramid is the kernel of the brand, the source of its identity. It must be known because it imparts coherence and consistency;

▌ The base of the pyramid are the themes: it is the tier of communication concepts and the product's positioning, of the promises linked to the latter;

▌ The middle level relates to the stylistic code, how the brand talks and which images it uses. It is through his or her style that an author (the brand) writes the theme and describes him- or herself as a brand. It is the style that leaves a mark.

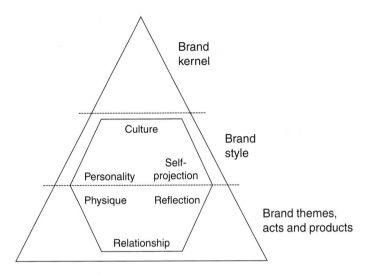

Figure 10.3   Identity and pyramid models

Of course, there is a close relationship between the facets of the identity prism of a brand and the three tiers of its pyramid. An examination of advertising themes reveals that they refer to the physical nature of products or to customer attitudes or finally to the relationship between the two (particularly in service brands). They are the outward facets of identity, those that are visible and that lead to something tangible. The style, as with one's handwriting, reveals the brand's interior facets, its personality, its culture, the self concept it offers. Finally, the genetic code, the roots of a brand, inspires its whole structure and nurtures its culture. It is the driving mechanism. There is, therefore, a strong relationship between stylistic codes and identity. In Volkswagen's case, its sense of humour is the consequence of solidarity because it demonstrates the rejection of car idolisation, the cult which leads to a hierarchical ranking of drivers and therefore to their animosity towards each other.

This idea of levels or tiers within the brand provides a tool which allows freedom for the brand in the sense that the brand no longer has to define itself by repeating the same themes. The choice of the theme has to inte-grate the needs of the times. It is founded on the reality of products and services. It corresponds to a concern or a desire of a particular market segment. Alongside these criteria, one must respect the brand's identity.

Brand communication can thus vary in its facets. Over time it seems first to start with the physique, goes through the reflected image and ends with the cultural facet. Benetton first launched its colourful sweaters, then modernised to appear more dyamic, before identifying with a set of universal values (friendship, racial tolerance, the world village). This evolution is normal: the brand goes from tangibles to intangibles. It starts as the name of a new product, an innovation and later acquires other meanings and autonomy. Benetton is now a cultural brand and addresses a range of moral issues. Nike moved from product communications to behavioural values (just do it!).

The pyramid model leads to a differentiated management of change. The brand's themes (its positionings) must evolve if they no longer motivate: it is obvious that Evian had to move from balance to youth. All themes tend to wear off and competitors do not stand still. The stylistic code, the expression of the personality and culture of the brand, has to be more stable: it enables the brand to gently pass without disruption from one theme to another. Finally, the genetic code is fixed. Changing it means building another brand, a homonym of the first, but different. This is how, even if the positioning of Evian has changed with time, from being the water of babies, to that of the Alps and that of the strength of balance, there is a strong sense that the basic identity has been preserved. Evian never was a water against something, but a water for something, natural and loving, a source of life. It is not for nothing that its label has always been pink: this colour is linked to the brand's kernel, its essential identity, those traits that are necessary to the brand. Without them, it would be another brand.

Finally, the idea of different tiers within the brand gives particular flexibility to those brands which embrace many products. In managing these products one must respect their individual position in their own markets. They may carry different promises for each product, provided they appear to emanate from a common source of inspiration. In this respect, brands work as a superstructure.

Taking into account the importance of this genetic code, how do we recognise it? All brands do not always have this identity basis. Some of them have only communication codes, or a style. When one says that Cacharel is romantic, one talks about a common style and source of coherence between Anaïs-Anaïs, Eden and Gloria. Its products carry within them a very precise and hidden driving principle.

Consumers, clients and even managers are rarely aware of the brand's pivotal guiding force. They readily talk of its visible facets and of its codes, but without penetrating the brand's programme. Nor is the brand's creator aware of it, but carries it subconsciously. He transmits it through his actions and his choices. Thus when Mr Robert Ricci died in the summer of 1988, his successor commis-sioned an analysis of the identity of the Nina Ricci house alongside its worldwide best-selling perfume L'Air du Temps. The death of a creator signals the birth of a brand: respect for it demands understanding. An analysis of identity lies more in the history of the brand than in opinion surveys. The most typical products of the brand are closely examined throughout time: from what unconscious programme do they seem to emanate? Why does Nina Ricci haute couture sparkle with its dazzling evening dresses? Why did Mr Robert Ricci find in the photographer David Hamilton's 'fuzzy' style a sort of revelation, to the point of signing a long-term and exclusive contract with him? What is the link between the dresses, L'Air du Temps and Hamilton? Once the highest point of the Ricci pyramid is known, the problem of the necessary replacement of David Hamilton's style becomes less acute. We know what he was expressing. Other means of expression will achieve this without using fake Hamiltons. Long-established brands seeking such an overhaul should undergo an inner search before projecting themselves into the future.

Respecting the brand contract

Each brand should be seen as a contract. It binds, promises and engages each side: the company and its clients. The brand expects loyalty from consumers but it must in turn be loyal to them. With time, it is normal that the brand should seek to widen its client base by offering other products and services. In doing so, it communicates more and more on its margins and less and less on its core, on the basic contract.

The source of the current problems of Club Med, which feels it has lost its identity, may also find their source in the forsaking of the founding principles of the brand. However, it was not without reason that the product range was differentiated to fit a particular market segmentation which, as customers were growing older, expected more comfort in the rooms and sometimes wanted to withdraw from the group and not sit down at mealtimes at the famous eight-people tables. What aged in Club Med's offer is the value system portrayed in its advertising, and which a part of the population no longer identifies with, in particular its opinion leaders. The concept of 'happiness' in groups is a cliché and no longer corresponds to the intense need for meaning expressed by our society. What made the inspired strength of Club Méditerranée was forgotten when the brand was restructured to make it international and renamed Club Med. Indeed, the Mediterranean Sea is not, as one would think, just a reference to the original location of the vacation villages or to some water sports. It is, on a symbolic level, a source of life. The intense need for Club Méditerranée lies in its brand kernel: to replenish, to find one's self again. This drive, remarkably transposed in its time by the famous advertising campaign coined by the FCA agency (love, live, play, talk…), has disappeared and does not seem to inspire the current brand any more, as Club Med has become a vacation club like all others, only more expensive than most, and no longer promotes a particular vision.

The pressures that lead a brand astray from the initial contract by little nudges are numerous and create the risk of identity loss. The management of the Paloma Picasso perfume brand is a good example of this. Through the roots of the brand and the creator whose name it bears, this brand symbolises a violent Latin character, the South, a haughty, self-asserting pride. Its codes of red and black are Latin codes, signs of a strong character, but such an identity creates territorial boundaries for the brand. It is strong in South America, in the Sunbelt in the United States (Florida, Texas, California), and in Europe in all the countries where Spain exerts an attraction (Germany, Great Britain, France). On the other hand, it has not been able to penetrate the Asian market (where the preference is for pastels, tenderness, softness), or in Oceania, Australia and Scandinavian countries. Hence the question that arose at the launching of the third perfume: should one respect the brand contract – what it has stood for up until now, the basis of its success – or put on the market a softer version?

Revitalising brands also implies the rediscovery of one's roots. With time, we tend to forget the founding principles accumulating compromise after compromise. The Novotel management called the programme which redefined the orientation of the brand 'return to the future'. The aim was not to reconstruct the Novotels from the good old days but to take up again the historic mission of the brand, updated to meet the needs of its clients in the year 2000. In the car industry, it is also symptomatic that the success of the C5 and C2 signalled the reawakening of Citroën after many years in the wilderness. It reactivated the kernel, the genetic programme of Citroën and brought it up to date.

Managing two levels of branding

Managing both change and identity is helped by a double level of brand architecture. This is how Calvin Klein, Chanel and Volkswagen are organised. How does one consistently manage such brands? They are called source brands in the sense that they include products that have their own individual identity and brand name. In this sense we talk of mother brands and daughter brands, or first-name brands. Thus, there is Renault but there are also the personalities of Clio, Twingo, Megane and Val Satis, each with its own identity. As we will see in Chapter 12, the Renault brand is not content just with endorsing, it adds its own values and creates a coherent environment. It is no longer an umbrella brand because there are two levels to the brand (the family name and the first name), whereas an umbrella brand includes products without first names (such as a Philips TV, a Philips razor, a Philips coffee machine …). The problem that surfaces is that of the balance which has to be struck between coherence and freedom, family resemblance and individuality. This concerns, beyond the examples just cited, all industrial groups that maintain the strong identities of corporate brands, and that do not want to be considered as merely a holding company. The key lies in a systematic approach to the source brand, analysing what each daughter brand brings to or borrows from the whole.

One should always start with understanding the whole (the mother brand or house brand) and how this impacts on its products.

In 1986 Garnier brand management undertook an exercise aimed at understanding the brand's roots, its genetic code. The initial and founding product of the brand (before it was bought out by L'Oréal as soon as it got too threatening) was the herbal shampoo created by Mr Garnier himself. One could already find in it certain key attributes of the brand: naturalness, beauty through care (thus a certain medical benefit), no narrow USP (unique selling proposition) but a large promise and a distribution through pharmacies. Later, after the war, Moelle Garnier was to be the second successful shampoo: it nurtured the hair and still offered beauty and shine through care. Mr Garnier innovated by distributing it not only in pharmacies but in hair salons and finally in what at the time stood for mass distribution. L'Oréal then bought Garnier along with another brand, Roja, creating Roja-Garnier, an idea which completely diluted the brand-capital and led it to sink into oblivion from 1976 to 1986.

In 1986, the coherent relaunching of Laboratoires Garnier was decided. A European study was conducted to apprehend what was left in consumers' memories as buried, semi-buried or conscious traces of the old Garnier brand. This analysis revealed that there still existed a rich and lively basis and that beyond the differences in advertising for each of the product lines of the brand, there still stood

out a Laboratoires Garnier brand that was coherent, structured, deliberate and sustained by a real aim. The constituent features of the brand were close to the roots of the Garnier mother house, a taste for a wide range of benefits could still be found (beauty through care, not mere dermatology) aimed at active women (but not hyperactive). The brand would not be limited to shampoos, but would extend to 11 product lines. To manage the products and the daughter brands to come, it was paramount to define a philosophy of production. After all, if the brand defined itself at that time as a laboratory, it should hold firm all the underlying principles and apply them to the creation of the products themselves.

The research process resulted from the key principle of brand management: the truth of a brand lies within itself. Taking the 11 products considered the most typical of the Garnier brand and which represented best the brand manufacturer, one searched for what the scientific principle was, the common stream defining the know-how of the brand. Everything was thus brought together to establish the charter of the brand. In this way, it came to be much more than just an umbrella brand endorsing other brands, but a real source-brand, carried by its own set of values, entrusted with a mission and having scientific principles, a philosophy which precisely reflected the woman who uses it. The charter was communicated by audio-visual means in a deliberate fashion to the subsidiaries (by area and country), to the networks and to the reporters, thus putting an end to all the remaining connotations associated with Roja-Garnier. Being more than an endorsing brand, it had now established the basis for a real corporate culture which could be decentralised. This would have to be found in all the lines, current and to come, even a line like Graphic, whose aim was to open the brand to a younger clientele, girls and boys concerned about their looks. Bearing this in mind, it is significant that Graphic was the first line of Laboratoires Garnier to be launched in Great Britain. Conscious that it was doing much more than just launching Graphic but that it was actually launching the source-brand Laboratoires Garnier, the communication emphasised the philosophy of the brand and portrayed Graphic as being inspired by it. It is a known fact that the first steps in creating a brand model its long-term image: its first product acts as a prototype of the brand meaning.

In 2000, for globalisation purposes, Laboratoires Garnier became Garnier, and undertook another revitalisation of its attributes around the same brand kernel (see page 221). The degree of adaptation of the brand identity to changing market conditions needs to be assessed regularly.

Checking the value of one's identity

Over time, brands should regularly ask themselves whether their values are still relevant. Are they still even 'values'? Put another way, are they still valued by today's customers, or have they become commonplaces which are simply taken for granted, an attribute of the category itself, rather than the brand? Some brands have become icons and institutions because, at a certain stage in their life, they espoused values of growing importance in society to such an extent that they virtually became spokespeople for those values. These are emblem brands, and are well known: Levi's, the icon of youth rebellion; Benetton, the icon of the cultural melting pot; Moulinex, whose slogan boasts of 'liberating women'; Gap, praised as anti-fashion, and so on.

It is a rude awakening for these brands once their mission is no longer the issue of the day: women have been liberated, young people now aspire to Armani jeans, Benetton has been overtaken by Zara and Gap by Abercrombie & Fitch. Since values constitute the source of the brand's shared energy, it is

vitally important to recognise when these values and their ability to differentiate the brand are weakening.

Long-term survival relies on rediscovering the brand's values; not betraying it, but instead reinventing it. The question to ask is, what will become the value of today? Moulinex was associated with the liberation of women. This domestic appliance brand, recognised and distributed in more than 100 countries, claimed to give women time to do something other than housework: it was a woman's friend, urging her to enjoy herself rather than stay at home. This message now sounds a dated one to modern young women – and therefore it *is* dated. The question is, what is important today? Is it still the liberation of women, in the sense of 'women's lib' and the dominant woman? Surely what every couple is now talking about is gender equality – the true shared responsibility of men and women for everyday chores? This is the direction in which the cultural facet of the Moulinex identity prism should develop.

A second way of surviving over time is to realise that even if one value remains the same, the meaning of the words themselves change; their significance is not what it was 20 years ago; the consumer insight has changed. For example, dynamism is a key value of Peugeot – the 'lion' automobile brand. In 1983, the previously dormant brand was relaunched in explosive fashion by the little 205, and in particular the version that defined its era, the 205 GTi. Although it was not the best-selling 205, it stamped its personality on the 205 brand as a whole. The 205 GTi gave thousands of young people in Europe access to an intense experience at the wheel of a car. As with the Golf GTi, the GTi suffix is associated with the 1980s.

In 2004, the question is how to express automotive dynamism nowadays. The key is no longer raw engine power, but other attributes such as more space, better design and so forth.

Reinventing the brand: Salomon

The problem with brand management over time is how to deal with change. Customers change; society values change; and competitors change too. Few examples illustrate the challenges of change as well as the case of Salomon, the world winter sports leader with 30 per cent of its sales in Japan, 30 per cent in Europe and 30 per cent in North America.

In 1995, in an executive committee long-term planning meeting, a hypothesis emerged that established a scenario for the future, in which it was probable that the young teenagers who were giving up skiing to take up snowboarding would never go back to skiing and the other traditional winter sports that had established the reputation of not only Salomon but also Rossignol, Kneissl, Dynamic and others. On the basis of this prediction, it was decided to present a full range of snowboards at the forthcoming professional winter sports world exhibition. However, the stand remained bereft of visitors throughout the exhibition: visitors (who were all retailers) walked past without even stopping. For a company ruled by technical innovation, (for example, Salomon's safety bindings are world leaders), it was a major shock. Meanwhile, Salomon's overall sales shrank from 442 million euros in 1993/4 to 437 million in 1994/5, 396 million in 1995/6, and then 365 million in 1996/7 – a lower figure than in 1992/3. It should be said that between 1994/5 and 1995/6, world snowboard sales doubled while ski sales fell by 16 per cent.

The diagnosis was a shock, too. Salomon was perceived as an anti-model by new generations of anti-conformist, rebellious 'snow surfers' worldwide, who were opposed to the values prevalent in alpine skiing and in the sporting system in general. After all, a brand is always more than just a name. It is a point of view about a category, a vision, a set of values. As a pillar of the Olympic ideal and the Winter Games, and the first choice of the world's top ski teams, Salomon was becoming the symbol of a world from which the snowboarding community wanted to distance itself, standing as it did in total opposition to its values. Indeed, what are the typical values of traditional winter sports in which all participants ski along wide avenues of well-packed snow? What are the Olympic values if not individuality, competition, beating competitors, shaving off hundredths of a second, order and hierarchy? By contrast, snowboarding – which is after all a direct descendant of surfing – is about getting together in groups, going off-piste and enjoying unique snow sensations centred on the values of fun, groups, friendships, anarchy, freedom, pleasure and a disdain of competition.

Breaking with traditional values, snowboarders form tribes with very well-defined dress codes, in sharp contrast to the traditional clothing of the piste skier. Surfboarders generally shun the reds, whites and blues of traditional ski suits in favour of fluorescent colours straight out of the Timothy Leary psychedelic movement. Furthermore, snowboarding is a combination of sport and music: participants always wear their personal stereos on the slopes. This makes it more than just a sport: it is a sect.

Salomon's very future was at stake. The diagnosis was that there was no question of creating a new, dedicated snowboarding brand: to do so would ultimately be to sign a death warrant for Salomon and entomb it within the practices of yesterday. Surgery was required on the brand itself in order to bring about a profound change in its identity. Winter sports are not a segment or an activity, but instead represent a fundamental shift in western society. Therefore, no winter sports brand can afford not to play a part. A brand identity overhaul was thus set in motion.

The second part of the diagnosis was that Salomon should continue to maintain a presence in the ski and snowboard markets. The former market was the source of its current revenue; the latter would generate the revenue of the future. This left the brand with no choice: a dual marketing approach was needed. However, there is no room for schizophrenia within a brand. There is room for only one value system to be attached to any given name. When it comes to values, a brand cannot serve two masters. The answer was thus to reduce the values gap between skiing and snowboarding, bringing the former increasingly closer to the values of surfing: fun, sensations and pleasure.

This is where concept and product innovation came in. Salomon invented parabolic skis, freeride skis, X-screams skis and improved mini-ski technology. All of these new products offered new sensations and delivered the snowboarding feel without the snowboard. By means of these innovations, Salomon achieved an effective reduction of the distance between skiing and snowboarding or snowblading. Salomon thus dragged skiing out of its traditional mould – a case of the category leader changing along with the category as the key to its survival.

But the hardest work was yet to be done. How was the firm to make up its lost ground in the opinion-leading teenage target market to which it remained the anti-model and very epitome of tradition? Of course, it could already count on the democratisation of the snowboard and snowblade. Assuming that this process continued, reaching increasing numbers of less radical people, the assets of the Salomon brand could offer them reassurance. However, the world of sport is dominated by fashions and by opinion leaders, who saw brands such as Quiksilver as the real stars.

Three radical decisions were taken to bring the brand closer to its reticent (or even hostile) targets: listening to customers, the creation of Salomon Stations, and a strategic extension into rollerskating.

Listening to customers became Salomon's main method of conducting market research. Young people were sent out to spend time

alongside – and learn to understand – surfers and young teenagers on the US West Coast, since they are opinion leaders. Using this ethnographic method of participatory observation, they could feed back continuous information on forthcoming trends, expectations, key words and so on.

Another step was the creation of Salomon Stations, friendly places right at the heart of winter sports towns, offering a listening environment at the bottom of the pistes. The exercise was not about selling products, so as to avoid competing with local retailers, but rather about stimulating dialogue in a relaxed setting, thus furthering the values and practice of the sport. However, considering the significant set-up costs and times, another approach was needed: this took the form of brand stretching into the rollerskate and inline skate market.

This strategic extension was triggered by a simple observation: young people only spend one month a year playing winter sports. If Salomon is to become their brand, they must be approached during the preceding 11 months – and snowboarders are one and the same group as the die-hard rollerskaters found in town and city streets the world over. Furthermore, with regard to the actual rollerskates, Salomon's technical expertise could offer a significant advance over the performance of existing rollerskates in two key areas: comfort and safety. As a world leader in mountain shoes and safety bindings, Salomon alone had the means to take a significant forward step through innovation. This led to the 1999 launch of a new range of rollerskates whose performance characteristics were widely acknowledged.

The third strategic decision was based on an observation: in snowboarding, 'software' is just as important as hardware. It was not enough merely to be a manufacturer of products, however technically excellent. What was needed was the introduction of design, colour and hyper-modern codes capable of attracting young people brought up in the culture of tag graffiti and comic books. Most importantly, a plan was needed for marketing the 'software', extremely modern clothing ranges which would reflect the changes within the brand. Hence the purchase of the Bonfire textile brand, which enjoyed a high profile among surfers – and, more importantly, enlisting the help of Adidas in 1997 to assist in these changes. After all, who better than Adidas to master the balance between aspirational hi-tech and textiles and sportswear, worn by the young and not-so-young alike, immersing them in the crucible of worship of sport (and thus of the body)? Furthermore, there is great profitability in textiles, which are sports deriva-tives. Until then a family company which had been founded by Georges Salomon, Salomon discovered in Adidas the financial resources and expertise to assist in the transformation of its identity and business model.

The same strategy continues today: in a nautical twist, Salomon is now entering the surfing market. This is the result of a redefin-ition of its identity and business: it has moved from a product-based definition (mountain shoes and safety bindings for skis) to an identity based on the activity itself (winter sports) and on values (sensations and pleasure). It has developed from a cyclical business threatened by the vagaries of the climate ('Will it snow this year?') to a permanent business with its grassroots in the tarmac roads of New York and Oslo. Tomorrow, they will also be in the waves of Australia, California and the South of France. This product extension also satisfies the goal of profitability: it will enable the follow-up launch of a complementary textile range. After all, a textile range in this sector needs legitimacy, of the sort that is conferred by the equipment. The extension into surfing has no other aim than to provide this legitimacy.

Lastly, on the communication front, Salomon developed a relational marketing system and created communities. It initiated the Salomon X-Adventure ski trek in Europe, the United States and Japan, created 'free-ride'

stages and offered a host of 'challenges' for inline skaters and snowbladers. It also put an end to superficial sponsoring. Now the cham-pions, and opinion leaders for young teenagers, are more than just a brand vehicle – they are co-creators with Salomon.

What can we learn from this? A brand can only survive change if it is constantly re-earning its relevance among target groups of which it may have had little understanding. Paradoxically – as has been shown by Christensen (1997) – in their quest for 'good' management, companies often become slav-ishly devoted to understanding their existing client base. In the process of satisfying their own customers better and better, brands become these customers' hostages and neglect the weak signals of social or technological change. Considering that this change generally takes the form of a break with existing habits and products, it is rejected by the brand's existing customer base. The brand then works harder and harder to please a clientèle that does not represent the future, thus becoming an anti-model for innovators and tomorrow's customers.

The necessary process of winning customers over again takes time and requires a systematic, coordinated, focused approach which involves all areas of the company. It implies an internal revolution – at the management, organisation and identity levels.

It starts with a redefinition of identity. What parts of the old identity do you keep? What do you change to help in coping with changes in society and the rise of all the new sports that were still unknown 10 years ago?

Salomon's slogan – which defines its business and field of competence – is now 'freedom action sports', which applies equally to the mountains, the town – and in future, the sea too. This shows the path followed by the brand over time:

- In 1950, its identity was based on a product – the 'binding' safety fastening, an essential component.

- In 1980, the brand's entire identity, skills and value system could be summed up as skiing.

- In 1990, its identity became focused on mountains, with the introduction of hiking boots and the like.

- In 2000, the brand expanded its target and field of competence to a particular area, a conceptualised sport: freedom action sports. It became a specialist multi-sport brand, serving this concept and its under-pinning values. What are these values? Freedom means unrestricted sensations and 'my style'; action means energy, gravity and the environment as a play-ground; and sports suggests gliding, adventure, riding and so on.

To equip itself against competitors and changes among consumers, distribution channels and competition, the brand continues to capitalise on its historic skills: its unique know-how in working with profes-sionals to design pure, simple, unique, inno-vative products.

It has had to acquire new skills in order to communicate with – and indeed, enter into a genuine relationship with – a new generation of young sports enthusiasts worldwide.

Salomon has thus widened its target to young people and teenagers, tomorrow's trend leaders. Activating this identity implies a long-term commitment and substantial human and financial resources dedicated to:

1.   Product innovation (brand extensions play a strategic role here). For this purpose, Salomon sets aside 7 per cent of its turnover for research and registers 80 patents per year. The company has also reduced its product-to-market timescales to one year for composite products and two years for mechanical products

(bindings). In addition, opinion leaders are involved at an early upstream stage in the creative process, and surfers can contact the brand via the Internet to influence research into new products.

Furthermore, Salomon's product range marketing is no longer segmented simply into the old three categories of age, sex and skiing ability: a fourth category has now been added (the type of sensation sought after).

2.   The brand's role as an engine for moving 'old-fashioned' but still majority activities (such as skiing) towards something more modern via new sensation-based products, and in so doing narrowing the gap that exists within both the brand and winter sports as a whole. In addition, snowboarding has become an Olympic event, and Salomon has been able to forge a link with Edgar Grospiron, an emblematic figure in winter sports.

3.   Offering a complete range of experiences via challenges, competitions, ski treks and so on, and also via sportswear ranges.

4.   Communication that has at last become more interactive, guerilla-styled and street-focused.

5.   Proximity to the customer; perhaps even a direct relationship in locations devoted to the brand, during events and the like.

The commercial and financial results reflected the radical effort which had gone into adapting to this change: sales rose from 390 million euros in 1997 to 435 million euros in 1998, and 500 million in 1999. The company reversed its 1997 deficit to move back into profit in 1998. Bought out for 1.2 billion dollars by Adidas – 40 times its profit in a sector where the average multiple was just 20 – the Salomon group was keeping its promises.

11

Growth through brand extensions

Brand extension is on the increase. When they wish to enter markets from which they have been absent, more and more companies do so using the name of one of their existing brands, rather than using a new brand name created for that purpose. Yet brand extension is not a recent phenomenon (Gamble, 1967). It is inherent in the luxury goods sector: the luxury brands originating in haute couture have extended to accessories, fancy leather goods, jewellery, watch-making, even tableware and cosmetics.

In the same way, the first distributors' brands (Migros in Switzerland, St Michael in Great Britain) covered several differentiated categories of products. Industrial brands themselves were extended beyond their initial product type to cover a range of diversified activities under the same name: Siemens, Philips and Mitsubishi have been using brand extension for a long time. Indeed, brand extension is even used systematically by Japanese conglomerates: Mitsubishi includes shipyards, nuclear plants, cars, high-fidelity systems, banks and even food under the three-diamond brand (the visual symbol of Mitsubishi).

Brand extension has become common practice. What was reserved for luxury goods is becoming a general managerial procedure: Mars is no longer only the famous bar but an ice cream, a chocolate drink and a slab of chocolate; Virgin covers everything from airlines to soft drinks; McCain covers French fries, pizzas, buns and iced tea; Evian now endorses cosmetics. For all those executives brought up on sacrosanct Procterian dogma according to which a brand must correspond to one, and only one, product, the present situation leads to thorough rethinking; even Mars, for so long the typical example of a product brand, has become an umbrella brand covering very different segments and products. Such development is the direct consequence of the recognition that brands are the real capital of a company and a source of competitive advantage.

Brand extensions are one of the hottest topics in brand management. They have spawned a rich and intense body of research. Some experts keep claiming that brand extension should be avoided (Trout and Ries, 1981, 2000). However, today, most companies, even those that were culturally the least prone to engage in brand extensions, have extended their brands. In fact, as we shall demonstrate, brand extension is a necessary strategic move at some point in the life of a brand. It is an essential way to sustain the brand's growth, once other approaches have been explored. Let us remember that growth should be built:

▪ First, by increasing the volume of purchase per capita of present customers of the present product (see Chapter 8).

▪ Then by new product development and line extension to increase the brand's relevance and address the needs of more specific targets or situations. Line extensions are, in fact, proliferating in modern supermarkets.

▪ By the globalization of business in countries offering high growth opportunities (see Chapter 16).

▪ By innovating to modify the competitive situation, create new competitive advantages or open new markets, thus benefiting from the pioneer advantage. At this time the question of naming the innovation becomes acute. Should one extend the brand portfolio by adding a new brand (as when the Coca-Cola Company added Tab to its portfolio) or call it instead by the name of an already existing brand (Diet Coke, for instance)?

When an innovation is not in the core market of the brand, it means that the brand will extend out of this core, a process also called brand stretching. This is why brand extension is such an important topic: it is about the redefinition of the brand meaning. It is not

possible to grow the business indefinitely without changing some facets of the brand. Hence the question, is the essence of the brand intact? Does the extension preserve the kernel? Also, what does the extension bring to the brand equity, to the brand image, beyond growing the business? These are indeed strategic questions.

Beyond branding itself, extensions are often diversifications, entries into unknown markets, with a different product from previously (see Table 11.1). As such they are a strategic move.

What is new about brand extensions?

Why has brand extension become such an important topic? In fact, most companies have discovered the virtues of brand extensions only recently. Certainly some luxury brands have thrived through extensions, and so have Japanese brands, and indeed Nestlé, but in North America and Europe most marketers have been trained in a 'Procterian' vision of marketing. At Procter & Gamble, since its foundation, a brand has been a single product with a benefit. As a consequence, the rule has been that new products should form a new brand. P&G's Ariel (known as Tide in the United States) is a specific low-suds detergent. Other detergents have other brand names such as Dash and Vizir. This practice is thoroughly product-based.

The brand extension perspective introduces two radical modifications. First, it maintains that a brand is a single and long-lasting promise, but this promise can or should be

Table 11.1 Relating extensions to strategy

| Markets | Products | |
	Present	New
Present	Intensive growth	Market development
New	Market extensions	Diversification

expressed and embodied in different products, and eventually in different categories. 'Palmolive' represents softness, and from this perspective it makes sense to have Palmolive hand soap, dishwashing liquid, shaving cream, shampoo and so on.

Second, it asks us eventually to redefine the historical brand benefit by nesting it in a higher order value. Brand extension exemplifies the move from tangible to intangible values, from a single product-based benefit to a larger benefit, thus making the brand able to cover a wider range of products. Is Gillette simply the best shaving product, or 'The best a man can get'? as it says in its advertising baseline? This latter brand definition easily backs up the Gillette Sensor, or Mach 3, aimed at continually increasing the quality of a man's shave. It allows also the brand to grow by leveraging its reputation and trust to introduce a line of male toiletries, a profitable, growing market.

Brand extensions are an emotional topic because they are the first occasion on which the identity of a brand is redefined, when all the unwritten assumptions that may have been held for decades about the brand within the company are questioned. In addition, unlike mere line extensions, brand extensions are associated with diversification, so there is a sizeable impact on the company as a whole. Research on brand extension has been so obsessed by the brand itself that this has tended to foster a tunnel vision in marketing circles. The only focus of that research was to determine consumers' attitudes to various possible extensions for a specific brand (Aaker and Keller, 1990) This is why so many companies have gone through a phase where they extended their brands in all directions, just because the consumers said they could do it. This phase has ended; this early research neglected the company. It is a form of tunnel vision to focus on the brand only and exclusively. Diversification is a strategic concept, which has implications for the whole company. Will it be able to learn all the new

competences required to meet competition in the new market? At what price? With what delays? At what cost? Is it worth it? Is it sustainable? The brand and business perspective promoted by this book calls for a reinsertion of brand extension issues into the context of corporate strategy.

Finally, it is an involving topic because it is generally tied to a new product launch, which as for all new products commands time, energy, allocation of resources, and creates a situation of risk. This risk is increased by the fact that unlike line extensions, brand extensions lead the brand into new and unknown markets, which may be dominated by entrenched competitors. There is not only a straightforward financial risk should the extension fail, there is also potential damage to the image of the brand, in the distribution channels, among the trade, and among end users. A good example is the problems encountered by Mercedes when it launched its new Class A, a radical downward extension, after it decided to go where the market was and compete against Volkswagen. The car could not pass the 'elan test', thus destroying the sacrosanct image of Mercedes as one of the most secure cars in the world. The whole conception of a Mercedes car had to be redefined. One does not move easily from a high historical competence in manufacturing large sedan cars with rear wheel drive to making small compact cars with front wheel drive. Also for the first time, one could buy a new Mercedes for around 20,000 euros.

This example illustrates the fact that brand extension decisions should not be looked at only through consumer research. As a rule, when expensive brands stretch downward, their existing clients are frustrated. They feel less exclusive, therefore their attitude to the extension is negative (Kirmani, Sood and Bridges, 1999). However consumers are in that respect quite conservative. They do not have a full picture of the Mercedes situation, and finally they do not have a long-term view. Very few people knew, for instance, that the average age of purchasers of the Class C, at that time the entry-level Mercedes, was 51. Also, very few people knew that unless the company was able to produce more than a million cars rapidly, its production costs would be too high to sustain modern competition even in the premium segments. Higher production costs provide no value to consumers.

Managing brand extensions is about identifying the growth opportunities. It aims also at maximising the chances of success of the new product launch, while increasing the value of the parent brand. This entails managing the whole product range: to maintain its equity. Mercedes reinvested to innovate in the high-end segment of its market through the new Class S and now a spectacular top-end model. On this occasion a naming problem arose: it was not called 'Class Y' but received a name, a brand: Maytag.

Since the first edition of this book in 1991, the brand extension field has changed. Companies have all gained experience in extending their brand. Some have made timid but successful extensions (Mars ice cream), others have experimented with at least 10 extensions, which may have all failed, as did Becel extensions, Unilever's anti-cholesterol margarine (Kapferer, 2001: p 222). All acknowledge the necessity to reintroduce more focus, and more corporate parameters into the process. The decision to extend the brand is a strategic one, and relying on consumer's attitudes to possible extensions is now held to be seriously insufficient. Decision grids have to encompass other dimensions. In brief, because a brand could create an extension, it does not follow that it should do it. To a far greater extent than it has been said or written, it is necessary to assess the competitive status of the extension and of the company behind it. The question what the extension really brings to the business and to the brand itself has also become more acute.

On an academic level, recent research is now revealing the limits of early research on brand extension. Some of the models and rules presented in pioneer studies should be questioned if not forgotten.

Brand or line extensions?

When should one speak of line or of brand extension? We developed the case for line extensions in Chapter 8. This is a necessary step in growing the brand through:

▌ An extension of the line to enrich the basic promise through diversity (like providing new tastes, new flavours for a jam brand or a crush brand such as Minute Maid).

▌ A finer segmentation of a need (like the many variants of each shampoo brand according to the type of hair, age of customer, or kind of scalp problem).

▌ Providing complementary products. As mentioned in the discussion on line brand architecture (page 298), a brand might provide all the products involved in solving a specific consumer problem. A brand fighting hair loss would not limit itself to its first product, a shampoo for instance, but also provide a gel, a hair dye and so on.

What is noticeable is that through these line extensions, the brand aims at intensive growth. It deepens its problem-solving ability more or less to the same customers, for the same need and consumption situation. This is not viewed as a diversification (which involves different clients and different products).

At the other extreme no one would quarrel with describing as brand extensions, rather than line extensions, Virgin Airlines, Hewlett-Packard's entry into the digital photo business, the Mercedes Class A, the Porsche Cayenne (its entry into the 4 x 4 market), Yamaha bikes (from a company originally known for its musical instruments), the Caterpillar fashion line, Salomon new surfboards (for the Hawaiian and Australian beaches), Ralph Lauren domestic paint, Evian cosmetics, Merlin Gerin moving from switchgears to electrical distribution products, or GE extending from electricity to capital investment. Typically in such brand extensions, the brand moves to another remote category, in which it is open to question whether it has the ability to deliver the same benefit, and therefore to stay the same. The buyers may be different, or the same: the first to buy the Porsche Cayenne were existing Porsche owners who now have two Porsche cars. In fact most of the early research on brand extension has focused on remote extensions, far from the prototypical product. Some of these brand extensions are more than simply brand extensions: they are real diversifications. The company wants to develop itself in new categories that may become dominant in its future sales. Certainly this is not the case for Caterpillar, but it could be the case for HP, stuck between Dell and IBM in its core activity. Few people recall that Findus, the name for frozen food, comes from 'Fruit Industry', the core original business of that Scandinavian company.

Where does line extension end, and where does brand extension start? Perrier is a case in point. To grow its sales the brand has launched three new products in three years:

- In 2001 it launched its first 'Pet' bottle, nicknamed 'rocket' because of its specific shape. It was the first time since the brand creation (in 1847) that a non-glass bottle had been created. It was aimed at mobile consumers and out-of-home consumption situations (such as stadiums and offices).

- In 2002 Perrier Fluo was created: it is an aromatised water in a plastic fluorescent-coloured small bottle. It is aimed at the young and competes in the soft drink market.

- In 2003, Eau de Perrier was launched to try to achieve better penetration in the table

water market. The famous Perrier bubbles, which are the essence of the brand, prevent the brand from appealing to those who like to drink less bubbly water with meals. This extension had finer bubbles (like San Pellegrino) and a finer and more elegant bottle.

How should these extensions have been described? At Nestlé Water, the owner of Perrier, they are called line extensions for the sake of simplicity. However, despite the fact that all these new products are basically water, the soft drink entry qualifies as brand extension more than the others. It aims at a market dominated by other competitors, which is subject to other success factors, and is aimed at different consumers.

The ability of any product given the Perrier name to meet the demands of the soft drink market is surely a long-odds bet. Here promotion and place are essentials. Also, the brand evokes less fun than any other soft drink brand. This is why the decision was taken to have Perrier only endorse the product, the big name on the bottle being 'Fluo'. This refers both to the very odd colours of the bottle and to the fact that it is fluorescent in the darkness, a typical situation in discotheques and late-night bars. However the main question will be the ability of Nestlé Water to cater to these new circuits of distribution and consumption.

For Aaker and Keller (1990), brand extension refers to the use of the name of a brand on a different product category. This was the case when Bic went worldwide from ballpoint pens to disposable lighters, disposable razors, and even stockings and hosiery in central Europe. One should then speak of line extensions when the brand launches new products in the same category. Therefore Diet Coke should be called a line extension. Interestingly, at the Coca-Cola Company, Diet Coke is called the second 'brand' of the company, which says it has two worldwide leading brands: Coke and Diet

Coke (called Coke Light in Europe). These differences in perception are not an academic problem. They hint at the fact that, although the product may be the same, the market, the 'category' may be different. Since the emergence of 'category management' we know that category does not mean product (Nielsen, 1992). Therefore, Perrier Fluo would be considered as a line extension by those who focus on the physical resemblance with the core product of the parent brand: basically it is the same water. For us, it qualifies as a real brand extension, for it aims at a different category of need, and of usage situation, and of users, and of competition. The same would hold true *a fortiori* for Evian spray, which vaporises water onto the face. The product, created in 1968, holds the same water as any Evian bottle, but the need and usage are very different.

As for all concepts, the best tactic is also to realise that they are relative, and that they cannot obey simple yes/no cut-off points. One should acknowledge that there are both highly continuous extensions, which apparently capitalise on the real or perceived know-how of the brand (as with HP's entry in the digital market), and highly discontinuous extensions, which do not capitalise on this know-how but on a mission, a set of values driving all the behaviours of the brand whatever the market it decides to compete in. We analyse the Virgin case below.

This scale of discontinuity has a lot of implications. It is a measure of the risk taken by the corporation itself. The current brand literature focuses heavily on the intangible facets of brands, probably because they are treated as intangible assets in accounting terms. But this is a semantic confusion: a performance-based brand is also an intangible asset. Overlooking the performance source of brands leads us to underestimate the weight of corporate abilities. Some companies just do not have the know-how or resources necessitated by the extension of the brand into specific categories. Certainly they can use

licensing as a way of circumventing the problem: for example Evian Affinity (a cosmetic line) is managed by Johnson & Johnson. The other possibility is to outsource. It is a classic way of moving more quickly and benefiting from low import prices. However this often means reducing the perceived difference between brands, if most of them outsource to common OEM suppliers.

Another implication concerns the branding strategy itself. Should one give a brand name of its own to the extension, thus moving to a double-level branding architecture (that is, an endorsing or source brand architecture)? It is noticeable that Perrier is very discreet about Fluo, as all endorsing brands tend to be. Experimental literature shows that giving the product a different name prevents dilution of the parent brand image, especially in the case of downward extensions (where the product goes from a premium price to a mainstream price) (Kirmani, Sood and Bridges, 1999). One should therefore distinguish 'direct extensions' (without a specific name) and 'indirect extensions' (with a specific brand name in addition to the parent brand) (Farquhar *et al*, 1992).

The limits of the classical conception of a brand

Most brand limitations are self-imposed. This is why brand extension took so long to emerge as a normal practice of brand management. This is also why some authors still hold it in disrepute. These prejudices are based on a classic conception of brands, which reigned over marketers and all business schools for almost a century. However, it cannot resist the conditions of modern markets.

The classic conception of branding rests on the following equation:

$$(1 \text{ brand} = 1 \text{ product} = 1 \text{ promise})$$

For instance, in the Procter & Gamble tradition, every new product receives a specific name, which is totally independent from the other brands. Ariel corresponds to a certain promise, Dash to another, Vizir to a third. Mr Proper is a household detergent, and nothing else. Let us compare this policy with that of Colgate-Palmolive: Palmolive is a toothpaste, a soap, a shaving cream and a dishwashing liquid; Ajax is a scrubbing powder, a household detergent and a window cleaning liquid.

The classic conception of branding leads to an increasing number of brands. If a brand corresponds to a single physical product, to a single promise, it cannot be used for other products. Under this conception it is a rigid designator, the name of a product, a proper noun, just as Aristotle is the name of the famous Greek philosopher (Cabat, 1989). It names a specific reality, as a commercial name is linked to a specific company.

Under this conception of the brand, few extensions are possible. The brand is in fact the name of a recipe. All that can be done is range extension, that is a variation around the central recipe either by:

▪ ameliorating the quality of its performances. The brand then gets a series number: for example Dash 1, then Dash 2 and Dash 3;

▪ increasing the number of sizes in order to adapt to the changing practices of the consumer (packet, tub, mini-tub);

▪ increasing the number of varieties (Woolite for wool and Woolite for synthetics).

The classic conception of branding is actually limiting. It does not differentiate the history of the brand from the reality of the brand. Of course, a brand originally begins with a new single product which is better than the competition, thanks to the know-how of a firm.

With time, and through communication, packaging, advertising, etc, the brand becomes rich with features, images and representations which give it its style. The brand thus has personality along with know-how. After designating an origin (the manufacturer's brand), or a place of sale (the commercial name), the brand conveys after some time the signs of non-material elements, which take root in physical production (the products) and iconic production (advertising images, logos, symbols of visual identity). The relationship between the brand and the product is therefore reversed: the brand is no longer the name of a product, but the product itself carries the brand in a sense that it reveals the exterior signs of an interior imprint. The brand has transformed the product, endowing it with both objective and subjective features.

In this reversed perspective, there is no other limit to brand extension than that of the ability of the brand to leave its mark on a new category of product, ie to segment it according to its own attributes. Bic, ignoring the dissimilarity of products, left its mark by creating sub-segments of simple, cheap and efficient goods wherever these attributes are valued. Bic failed where these were not valued – in the perfume segment.

The classic conception of branding is nominal: the brand is the name of an object. If one looks beyond this object, and wonders what project it conveys and what vocation it embodies, one can grasp the full meaning of the brand, its etymological meaning (the brandon), the exterior sign of an internal transformation, on behalf of a key value (the brand essence).

Thus, the classic conception of the brand takes the history of the brand for its long-term reality. But, although the brand originates from a product, it is not the product. The brand is the meaning of the product.

Products cannot speak for themselves. The consumer is perplexed in front of a tin of brandless frozen lasagna. How can he or she foresee the satisfaction that will be derived from this tin? The brand reveals the intention of the maker: what values did he try to into this tin? What did he want to introduce in this product: the love of tradition, an example of work well done, a respect for modern tastes, the will to find a compromise between fat and light food?

Extensions cannot be made in all directions. The direction is defined by the brand itself. A brand works as a genetic programme. It carries the code of the future products which will bear its name.

What does this new conception of branding change for brand extension? According to the classic conception, brand extension barely goes beyond very similar products. They key concept is product or usage similarity. This does not explain how perfumes by jewellers – Van Cleef, Bulgari, Boucheron, etc – are successes. It reduces brand identity to one single facet, the physical. This logic would exclude the idea of a Swatch car.

The larger conception of branding leads to extensions out of the initial category. The brand is different from the original product. It is a way of dealing with products, of transforming them, of giving them a common set of added values, both tangible and intangible: this way, a Swatch car is possible. An alliance with a company which has the technical know-how (Mercedes for example) suffices. This alliance, eventually made explicit through co-distribution, will give reassurance as to the car's quality and free consumers' desires.

The case of Lacoste helps to compare the operational consequences of each of the two conceptions of branding. Lacoste gained its reputation in 1933 through its tennis shirt made out of knitwear (called the 12 × 12), so a logical extension of Lacoste could be made not only toward other knitwear products, but also to polo-shirts, T-shirts, sportswear and textiles in general. Under this conception, shoes and leather items are excluded (apart from tennis shoes), since they do not use the same know-how as textiles and knitwear. Under Lacoste's broader brand conception, the crocodile signals a typical attitude: with

Lacoste, one is casual when smartly dressed, and smart even when dressed casually. Lacoste is beyond fashion: it is a classic. From this perspective, Lacoste can brand shoes or leather goods as long as they preserve the brand's originality; it must not brand products that have already been seen. The other condition is to brand only products which embody the values of the brand: flexibility, casualness, extreme finish, durability, distance from fashion, unisex use, etc. What enables Lacoste to brand a product is not the physical fit, but whether the product belongs to the Lacoste culture.

The new perspective opens new sources of growth for brands. Instead of looking at themselves as product brands, they become concept brands, defined by a set of values and not by a single instance (Rijkenberg, 2001). Indeed, brand logic is additive. The brand is the sum of its attributes: it is revealed by the products that it covers. The case of McCain is typical. The brand generally penetrates new countries through its frozen fries (it is actually the main supplier to McDonald's). They later introduce a frozen pizza ('deep pan', typical of the American way of life and of eating). They then launch buns to aim at the snack market. McCain also launched an iced tea to penetrate this high-growth market. Brand identity is actually uncovered by the sum of all these products. McCain's identity in Europe is that of 'American fun and generous food'. Generosity is both a relationship trait and a physical trait: all portions should be bigger when signed by McCain. Hence the surname 'deep pan pizza' or the higher cap of its iced tea (surnamed Colorado to refer to a mythical view of America). Future products may come from anywhere as long as they embody this enlarged identity of the brand, and fall within the territory of legitimacy the brand has created step by step, through each of its product launches.

History should not determine the future. In order to remain up to date, the brand must also be able to evolve; this is achieved through extension towards products which lead it in new directions and modify its meaning. Nestlé, known for dry foods (its prototypical products are instant milk and chocolate), did not enter the ultra-fresh market of yoghurts just to increase its turnover. The move was also intended to nurture its image thanks to this more modern segment, capable of updating its traditional and classic image traits.

Why are brand extensions necessary?

Brand extensions are necessary. They are a direct consequence of competition in mature markets and of the fragmentation of media. The only justification for brand extension is growth and profitability.

Brand extension is not new: it is the core of the business model of luxury brands (see page 69). It can increase the power of the brand and its profitability. Typical margins in the ready-to-wear premium market are 53 per cent, but the average is 71 per cent for bags and 80 per cent for watches. This is why fashion brands extend so quickly to these categories. As to perfumes, sold under licence by l'Oréal, Procter & Gamble or Unilever, they provide royalties, and a considerable boost in international visibility to the extended brand. This is why extensions are strategic in the fashion and luxury sector. No name can survive without them. The first thing a capital investment fund does after having bought a name is to extend the brand. What would Armani, Ralph Lauren or Calvin Klein be without their licences and extensions?

Often, perfumes become the most visible part of the fashion brand, because of the high advertising budgets involved. In addition the perfume increases the brand awareness and dream value, a prerequisite before other extensions. In fact, without a perfume, can a designer brand succeed and be profitable? Success in modern competition means the ability to access a critical size and visibility. Although not always successful, launching a perfume under one's name is a classic, if not the only, way to build the brand and business. Interestingly, this is the argument used by an as yet little-known designer brand that sued P&G for damages when the latter decided to stop its plans of launching a perfume under its brand name. Without this expected boost, would the brand meet its growth and profitability objectives?

As long as growth and profitability can be achieved through the present customers and products, or through minor variations in these products and their benefits (also called line extensions) there is no need to extend. Globalisation in search for the new areas of consumption in the world is also a natural route, but this does not solve the problem of growth in domestic markets, which are often saturated. Brand extensions allow brands to compete in less saturated markets, with a perspective of growth and profitability, as long as the brand's assets are assets in these markets. That is to say, the brand image must be able to act as a driver of purchase in the other market.

Brand extension relies on the ability to create a competitive advantage by leveraging the reputation attached to the brand name in a growth category, different from the brand's present categories. This bold move, which often surprises the competition in the category of extension, makes five crucial assumptions:

▎ The brand has strong equities (strong assets): it is strongly associated with a number of customer benefits (tangible or intangible) and it inspires a high level of trust.

▎ These assets are 'transferable' to the new and attractive destination category, that of the extension. Its buyers will still believe and acknowledge that the new products (that is, the extension) are endowed with the benefits associated with the brand.

■ These benefits and brand values are very relevant to that new category (extension). In fact, they should segment it in a previously unforeseen way, and leave the competition unable to react rapidly.

■ The products and services (extension) named by the parent brand will deliver a real perceived advantage over the competition, both consumers and the trade.

■ The brand and company behind it will be able to sustain competition in this new category over the long run. This refers to the question of resources needed to acquire leadership in the market in order to remain in it profitably.

As a consequence the most important part in the brand extension process is the selection of the destination category. This requires the company to assess various strategic parameters: the intrinsic attractiveness of the new category, the company's ability to acquire leadership in this category, and its ability to segment it profitably. These factors are to be found in the brand image, but also in the company's more general abilities and resources.

A second set of reasons that has pushed corporations to extend their brands is more defensive, or tied to efficiency and productivity factors:

■ Facing higher media costs, companies have felt the limits of their former brand architecture and wish to create more encompassing brands, so called mega-brands, in which a larger product portfolio can be nested. Most companies that started with a product brand architecture have realised the impossibility of sustaining growing advertising allowances behind each product or brand. They have transferred some of these formerly independent products or lines to a single mega-brand, which acts either as an endorser (Kraft or Nestlé) or like a source brand (l'Oréal Paris),

as a quasi-branded house. This is why brand transfers have become so frequent. The goal is to capitalise on a single name and to nurture it by a constant flow of innovations.

■ The fight against distributors' brands that themselves are mega-brands and are practising extension (as is, for example, President's Choice) has called for the reorganisation of products and innovations under a small number of banner brands.

■ In 1995 Nestlé decided to extend its name into the yogurt market. Until then the group had been present in this market through a regional brand, which was Chambourcy in Europe. However, the competition with Danone was leading to rising marketing and advertising investment. As a result it was decided to leverage the Nestlé name, thus enabling the products to benefit from all the trust and equity attached to this name, and from the advertising investment in other product categories where the group was already competing under its house brand. All products were transferred from Chambourcy to Nestlé (see page 366). In the meantime this extension provided the opportunity to nurture the brand image, by adding important facets that had been lacking up to then. Born in the larder, in the realm of dry goods, Nestlé as a brand was not associated with modern chilled and fresh products. These represent the future of modern food. It was necessary to reassociate the brand with these values, in order to avoid losing some relevance and equity.

■ Some brands are in declining product categories. To avoid disappearing with their product they must move to another category. Why did Porsche enter the 4 x 4 market in 2003? As we shall see later (page 383), there is a danger in resting always on the same product, even if it is continually face-lifted, revamped and renewed. All over the world, data show that the share of the coupé in the overall car market is decreasing. If Porsche stayed in that niche without reacting to this trend, it would be competing in a shrinking market. In addition, the 911, Porsche's keynote product, was coming to look at odds with the trend in values among elite and niche car buyers worldwide. Some of their newer values are captured by the 4 x 4 category. It remained to Porsche to build a 4 x 4 which would be a 'real' Porsche at an acceptable price. The only way of producing one at a realistic cost was to capitalise on the platform of the Volkswagen 4 x 4.

Another example is that consumption of brown tobacco is strongly declining, a sure threat for Gauloises, the prototype of dark cigarettes. After decades of uncompromising battle against blond tobacco, the company had to make a hard choice. Should it let its banner brand die? It decided to extend it into the blond category, creating Gauloises Blondes, which now represent the largest part of its sales.

Finally, in the UK, the reference brand for toilet paper was Andrex. This brand had a 39 per cent value share in 1987. By 1994 this had dropped to 28 per cent, as a result of the market becoming a commodity market, and also of the rise of hard-discounters (selling at no more than half the price of Andrex). Thankfully, Andrex had already started on an intensive extension policy, and it now offers kitchen paper, paper tissues and a range of related products.

- In the business-to-business market, the logic of continually increasing customer value leads in itself to brand extension. Take a service provider, say a company providing cleaning services for hospitals. How can it increase its sales to its core clients? Rooms cannot be cleaned two times or three times a day. There is no other avenue than to propose extended services, for instance supplying flowers for hospital rooms, lobbies and offices. This is another competence, an extension.

British Gas faced the same problem after the deregulation. How could it defend its business against all the new gas providers? It realised that its strength was its customer proximity: its engineers actually visited millions of households. It was time to leverage that competence and competitive advantage, and provide an extended set of home services including insurance and financial services to the customer base. This naturally entailed a change in name to facilitate consumer acceptance.

- Labeyrie is a brand that originated in the 'foie gras' sector. This is a very cyclical market, where most sales are made in three months of the year. To be able to advertise and gain a competitive advantage, Labeyrie decided to enlarge its scope and extend to other luxury foods such as smoked salmon and caviar. The resulting increase in its sales volume made television advertising a realistic investment.

- Many companies make a brand extension because they do not have the resources to sustain two brands nationally and internationally. This is why in Spain Don Simon sells wine, gazpacho and orange juice under the same name. This small company invests all its resources in productivity and quality. It fights head on against Tropicana in the juice sector, and has now extended its market throughout Europe. We shall see later that although they are governed by necessity, such decisions may prove later to be a real blessing.

- Some sectors are under growing advertising constraints: cigarettes, spirits, beers and wine are all limited by law in their types of advertisement and sponsorship. They have to create brand extensions to circumvent these limitations. Such extensions actually act as surrogate brands. The most known and successful is Marlboro Classics, an offshoot of the cigarette brand, which has become a real outerwear fashion brand worldwide. It has a very specific design, and exclusive stores and concessions. This is a typical case of a successful licensing approach.

The Camel Trophy did not survive the introduction of laws forbidding any association of cigarette brands with sports sponsorship. Pharmaceutical laboratories are another typical case where extension makes it possible to increase competitiveness even though the core product is tightly constrained. In all countries, pharmaceutical laboratories have to make a choice: whether to produce freely available over-the-counter (OTC) products, or products that are only available on a doctor's prescription. OTC products are allowed to be advertised, but they are generally not prescribed and they tend to be expensive. Part of the cost of prescription drugs is usually reimbursed through the national security system or by health insurers, so they can cost less to the end-users. However, manufacturers are generally not allowed to advertise prescription drugs to consumers (although there are some exceptions: specific types of direct-to-consumer advertising are often permitted for asthma products, for instance). In France, the market leader for paracetamol is called Doliprane. This is a prescription drug, so consumers can be reimbursed for its cost, but in addition it can be bought freely without a prescription. As a prescription drug, however, Doliprane is not allowed to advertise. To circumvent the regulations it launched two extensions, Doli'rhume and Doli'tabs ('rhume' means catching a cold in French). These two variants could be advertised, because they are only sold in the OTC market. The heavy advertising campaigns not only boosted the sales of the two new products, but had a positive spillover effect on the core product.

What should one think about Caterpillar line of shoes and clothes aimed at the youth market? Was it necessary for the tractor brand to extend itself in this way? Of course not. What then was the rationale? When asked that question, the CEO answered that it was intended to increase the share value by giving more visibility to the brand name, beyond the trade circles in which it had previously been known. Many small investors now buy shares, and familiar corporate names act as symbols of value to the lay investor. In addition, Caterpillar clothes and shoes were able to express the exact values for which the Caterpillar was known: tough work, reliability, security and so on.

Similarly, why did Michelin extend its brand from tyres to guidebooks, over a century ago? The first Red Guide was produced to tell readers where to find a garage in the event of a breakdown. Soon it came to be aimed at inducing car owners to travel more, with tips about hotels and good restaurants. It was a great example of relational marketing before the word was ever invented.

Recently, Michelin, working with a partner, The Licensing Company, has created a dedicated company, Michelin Life Style Limited, based in London. It is marketing snow chains for cars, a product with obvious marketing synergy with tyres. There are plans to extend the brand into sport equipments such as ski shoes and running shoes, areas in which the use of rubber can increase comfort and security. These are the two key benefits of Michelin tyres.

In a slightly different way, My First Sony and My First Bosch are tactical extensions, designed to create early familiarity with the brand among soon-to-be clients.

Building the brand through systematic extensions

In 2003, the three giants Procter & Gamble, Henkel and l'Oréal bid against each other to acquire Nivea, putting in very high offers – a sign of their extraordinary confidence in the growth potential of the company and its brand. What an astonishing outcome for a German company founded in 1912 in Hamburg on a single product: a little round, blue metallic box containing skin moisturising cream, which was treated almost like a medicine.

However, the company and its brand were split up after the war, and like other German brands (such as Persil), its assets were given to other companies across the world as war damages. This is why the brand had to be rebuilt with great patience, with the assets being bought back whenever and wherever possible, such as in the United States in 1974. In 2003 Nivea was the world's leading skincare brand, with a turnover of 2.5 billion euros and an average growth of 15 per cent per year. The brand's growth has been achieved entirely through progressive, carefully planned extensions repeated in country after country. As we shall see, each extension constructs a specific facet of the brand while penetrating new markets or new needs, all the while remaining faithful to the brand's heritage and key values.

Extensions very soon came to form a part of Nivea's business model An analysis of its brand launches in all countries – from the United States to Russia and China – reveals a fixed, well-planned pattern of development. The brand is launched in each country using its cornerstone (founding, prototype) product, portraying itself as a healthcare brand. Next follows Nivea Visage, a sub-brand which is key to its long-term business development. Nivea Visage is the perfect symbol of care: we entrust our faces to it.

After that follow the daughter brands judged to be most relevant for each different country, deepening this role and mission: Nivea Hand, Nivea Body, Nivea Sun, Nivea Lip Care, and three brands that are segmented by customer type: Nivea for Men, Nivea Vital (for the older market) and Nivea Baby (formerly known as Babyvea). The next to arrive are hygiene products, via the Nivea Deo and Nivea Bath Care daughter brands. Finally, these are followed by Nivea Hair Care and Nivea Beauty.

Thus, the order of entry in each new country is always carefully planned: care products first, followed by hygiene, then hair products and lastly make-up. Similarly, women's care products come before men's: Nivea Visage is always launched before Nivea for Men. Nivea's philosophy is that each country organisation is free to choose to launch a daughter brand, depending on the available potential in that market. However, Nivea Visage is of key importance. For example, although the care products market in Brazil is small in comparison to hygiene products, the brand construction order is still maintained. After all, Nivea is not Dove. The latter (Unilever) brand is based on hygiene (with as its core product a soap containing 25 per cent moisturising cream), but is now successfully expanding into the entire hygiene and beauty market worldwide.

The brand architecture is an umbrella, in the sense that each daughter brand is named descriptively, and thus represents a statement of the brand's values as they pertain to that category. However, note that the logos of each daughter brand are not uniform. This tiny difference makes the brand open, living and non-monolithic. Furthermore, each logo reflects a personality and values specific to the daughter brand. In this respect, the Nivea brand is also a sort of branded house (source brand) with two clear brand levels, even though the mother level is dominant in this case.

Indeed, each daughter brand has its own personality, and this is a deliberate decision. Furthermore, the aim of each extension is to provide not only a deepening of the core competence (loving care for the skin) and greater penetration of the category, but also specific components of the overall image. For example, Nivea Sun is where the family and protection aspect is communicated, and so advertising for Nivea Sun shows mothers and children, and fathers and children, together.

Likewise, the final extension – the one farthest from the core of the brand – is Nivea Beauty. By now we have come a long way from long-lasting products, simplicity and harmony. In this category, the key words are accelerated range renewal (four per year), the game, fun, seduction and so on. However, in highly developed, sophisticated countries this extension is necessary. It brings young girls to Nivea who would not otherwise have come, and who will subsequently try out other products from the range. It also adds a necessary touch to the brand image: more modernity and 'fashion'.

We can therefore see that under this system, daughter brands are not extensions in the iterative sense, as they would be for a hypothetical brand X asking itself what else it could do. In reality, they are the means through which the brand's 'big plan' takes shape. Extension presupposes the existence of a long-term vision. Before sinking the pillars for a bridge across a river, one must first have picked a clear destination point on the other side. These extensions are not extensions in the traditional sense, but rather components of a pre-planned whole which accumulates its meaning, coherency and scale through them.

As with any new product launch, the key question is that of perceived distinctiveness from the existing competition. Of course, the brand brings its own intangibles and image equities, but they are not enough on their own: a physical basis for differentiation is needed. This is, therefore, where innovation comes in:

▌ Nivea Visage launched Patch in Europe (the fruit of an alliance with the Japanese firm Kiaoré.

▌ Nivea for Men provides more care during shaving.

▌ Nivea Vital is developing the concept of mature skin.

Lastly, as with any system, there are certain no-go areas – such as, for example, anticellulite products. This is not because no market exists: it does exist, and it is a thriving one. Rather, it is because none of the existing products work well. To enter this area with another product that did not really deliver its promise would therefore be to break the link of consumer confidence in Nivea –and more than any other brand in its sector, Nivea wants to be the brand of confidence.

There are many examples of companies that have built their meaning around successive extensions. For example, the Canadian company McCain has three divisions, frozen fries, pizzas and soft drinks. In high-potential countries, it enters by means of frozen fries, then after three years launches its pizzas, and lastly soft drinks (for example, Colorado iced tea). McCain is thus no longer a fries, pizza or soft drinks brand, but instead symbolises North American cooking (rich, plentiful, playful, modern, relaxed) in the eyes of non-American consumers. This process of scope enlargement takes time, and presupposes that the brand is able to carry it off, as we shall see below.

Extending the brand to internationalise it

As world leader in cosmetics and beauty, l'Oréal has to create barriers to entry against a major source of threat: pharmaceutical laboratories. These have the potential to innovate in cosmetics, thus endangering l'Oréal's market share. This threat was exemplified by Johnson & Johnson launching a new active ingredient Retinol in a number of its brands (such as Neutrogena and Roc).

L'Oréal bought a niche brand called La Roche Posay (LRP), named after a town known for its dermatological water and spa. The town hosts more than 10,000 patients per year, including about 3,000 children as young as five months. LRP's business model was based on medical expert prescription. When working with dermatologists, it takes two or three years before any new product can safely be introduced to the shelves of pharmacies. But the brand faced growth problems:

▌ It was imprisoned in its therapeutic niche, and limited to patients rather than the general public.

▌ It was remote from the public. A user might be satisfied by the performance of, say, Antelios XL (an LRP product prescribed by dermatologists), but without another prescription, he or she would not buy a different LRP product.

▌ As a consequence the brand was below the minimum critical size. LRP sold 560,000 units in 1998, while it needed to sell at least 1 million units.

L'Oréal's strategy is to build its growth on truly global brands, and this requires a minimum sales level of 150 millions euros per brand. LRP was intended to be the eleventh global brand of the l'Oréal Group, but as it was, it was not easily exportable. To thrive against modern competition it is necessary to move quickly in global markets with promising growth potential. L'Oréal's target markets were Europe, Brazil and Argentina in 2000, Scandinavia and Asia in 2001, and India 2002. It needed the brand to have a presence in four market segments: hygiene, facial care products, solar protection and make-up. These last two categories were intended to release the first two sources of limitation in the brand's growth, and make it truly attractive to pharmacists all around the world.

In some markets pharmacists' shops were not appropriate outlets. The strategy here was to create another form of outlet, such as a concession in a department store (the solution in Canada), with a qualified pharmacist in attendance.

Because LRP did not have existing products in the solar protection and make-up cate-gories, strategic extensions were planned for these. This was done by means of a brand transfer. LRP took over the products sold under another l'Oréal brand, Phas, which had been positioned on non-allergenic products (see page 368 for the brand switch description).

Identifying potential extensions

It goes without saying that before making any brand extension it is imperative to know the brand well. What are its attributes? What is its personality? What identity does it convey to its buyers and users? What are its latent associations or traits? The answers to these questions are based on both quantitative studies (to discover the popularity and the image of the brand) and qualitative interviews of the target public. A simple listing of the image characteristics does not give a full picture of the brand. Defining the prism of identity requires qualitative investigation.

Armed with this information, the second step of the investigation procedure involves the extrapolation of the brand's distinctive features in order to assess their consequences. If Dove is personified by gentleness, then what other products need to be gentle? If Christofle is a brand for knives, forks and spoons, could it, by metonymy, be extended to glasses, plates or other tableware in general? Since Rossignol is active in one area of sport (skiing), could it not also extend into tennis rackets and golf clubs?

Luxury product brands often find the reason and the inspiration for their extensions from within their own history. Thus René Lalique, founder of Lalique, made jewels, scarves and shawls. The extension of Baccarat into small items of furniture, jewellery, perfumes and lamps is also symbolic of the reconquest of unexploited areas.

Whatever the source, a long list emerges from this process of introspection and investigation into brand identity and extrapolations based on it. It is then subject to internal feasibility filters. Brand extension is a strategic choice that is also accompanied by other changes: in production, know-how, distribution channels, communication, corporate culture. These have to be financed either internally or by forming alliances. Thus, Boucheron sold 22 per cent of its shares, not those of its core business (high-fashion jewellery), but those of the company that managed the so-called 'first circle' extensions (jewellery, watches, spectacle frames, pens and perfumes) in order to increase its resources.

This shortlist is then tested with the target public. Opinion surveys are often used to achieve this. For every extension proposition consumers evaluate the product on a scale of interest to them such as 'very interesting, so-so, not interesting'. This leads to a popularity rating of the possible extensions.

This method is advantageous in that it is simple and that the grading is done by numbers. Its one drawback is that it is conservative. When a series of questions about a multitude of products are thrown at them, interviewees tend to comment only on the basis of the most striking features of the brand. Therefore, this technique is biased and conservative. Thus, when Bic was only making ball-point pens, this strategy would have ended up by exhausting all the possibilities in stationery and completely rejecting the idea that Bic should sell razors.

Davidson (1987) distinguishes a number of concentric zones around an inner core: the outer core, the extension zones, and finally the no-go areas (see Figure 11.1). Close-ended questions in surveys provide information on the immediate vicinity of the brand (the outer

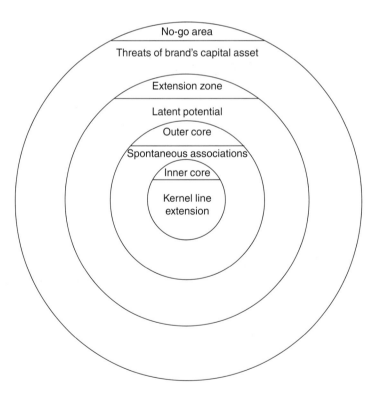

Figure 11.1 Perimeters of brand extension

core). In-depth qualitative phrases explore the remote extension zones.

Once again, it is necessary to proceed with a qualitative investigation to bring out the latent potential of a brand and to see how it can or cannot adopt each of these extensions. Through this same investigation we can also tell whether the resulting refusals were due to a conservative attitude linked to the actual situation, a lack of imagination on the part of the interviewee, or due to incompatibility with the brand.

The qualitative phase is a constructive one. Bearing in mind that a brand has to bring some added value to the product category, one would also like to know under what conditions the envisaged product would be legitimate for the brand. What attributes – objective and subjective – would be necessary for it to be able to bear the brand name? How is the product superior to the present market offer?

Thus, it is not enough to say that Lacoste could make jackets. One also has to describe what the characteristics of a Lacoste jacket would be and those of a 'non-Lacoste' jacket. The Lacoste identity prism encompasses the following characteristics: knit, finish, durability, discretion, harmony, social aptness, conformity and adaptability. The reputation of the original Lacoste product is that of a second skin: it induces a distancing effect which constitutes the central value of the brand. It nurtures an image of supple transition between the personal and social – personal ease and social ease. The aerated knit is analogous to the skin and its pores. This identity prism defines the territories which are not Lacoste and which should be avoided for fear of losing the very meaning of the brand:

- since it conforms to a sporting ideal, Lacoste is transversal and cuts across all barriers of age and sex, thus it should not put its name to products which are exclusively feminine (in fact, the Lacoste aerobic line was a big failure), or hyper-masculine (eg hunting);

- Lacoste does not sell either garish colours or short-lived 'in' products;

- being a 'second skin', Lacoste does not make either heavy knitwear or shiny leather clothes.

One understands why there are no Lacoste leather jackets. They are very masculine, virile and fashionable, and they do not last. Only the suede jacket is capable of possessing Lacoste characteristics.

The qualitative stage also permits an understanding of the functions of the brand for its users. Is the brand a sign for itself or for others? Where would consumers like to see the brand signed? This information is essential for branding. On the pocket of a Lacoste blazer should the signature be Lacoste, the crocodile or Lacoste Club?

Fundamentally, the testing phase should not only find out whether the success factors of the extension category are coherent with the brand, but also whether the product is superior to its competitors when deprived of its brand. In spite of the many explications about image failure, many extensions fail simply because they are inferior to existing products and are more expensive. Above all, an extension is an innovation and its added-value should be considered. Finally, these projection techniques allow the tricky question of the boomerang effects on the brand capital to be dealt with.

The economics of brand extension

By capitalising on the brand awareness, the esteem and the qualities attached to an existing brand, the practice of brand extension can help to increase the chances of success of a new product and lower its launch costs. These two alleged consequences have been verified.

As shown in Figure 11.2, only 30 per cent of new brands survive longer than four years, whereas the rate is over 50 per cent for brand extensions.

How does extension increase chances of survival? First, distributors themselves will allocate more space to an already well-known brand than to a newcomer. But brand extension also has an impact on the consumer (see Figure 11.3):

▨ in the trial rate, inducing a higher rate (123 vs 100);

▨ in the conversion rate (17 per cent vs 13 per cent);

▨ in the loyalty rate (index of 161 vs 100 for new brands).

Thus, for an equal facing and an equal unweighted distribution/weighted distribution ratio, consumers have a higher probability of trial, conversion and loyalty when the product bears an existing brand name, as this second OC&C analysis shows.

As far back as 1969, Claycamp and Liddy had measured the impact of a 'family name' (extension) on the trial rate of the new product. Their forecasting model, known as Ayer's model, rested on a database of 60 launches in 32 categories, half of these being in the food sector. The basic structure of the model is presented in Figure 11.4.

The estimate of the parameters of the model (through double regression) resulted in a very positive weight for the 'brand extension' variable. A previously known name directly and strongly induces the consumer to try the product. Moreover, Liddy and Claycamp noted that this variable was not correlated to advertising recall or even to weighted distribution. This last point is surprising: perhaps American distributors do not act as barriers to entry as much as their European colleagues.

What conclusions can be drawn from these studies? It would be wrong to think now that all new products must be launched under a known brand. This would mean forgetting the usefulness of multi-brand portfolios in the maximisation of market coverage. Moreover, as will be discussed later, some brand extensions can hinder the success of a new product,

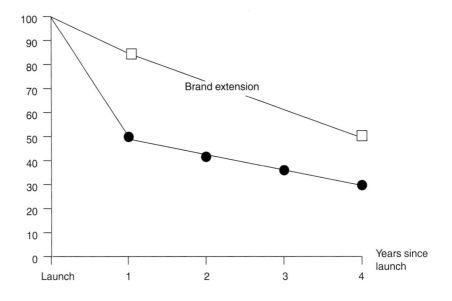

Figure 11.2   Rate of success of new brands vs brand extensions (OC&C)

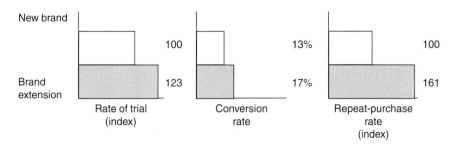

Figure 11.3   The impact of brand extension on the consumer adoption process (OC&C)

or be detrimental to the brand capital itself. Thus Hermès refused to lease its name, in exchange for royalties, to the Wagons-Lits Group, which wanted to launch a top-of-range service of individual or package holidays. The service risks of hotels in exotic and far away countries were too high for Hermès to be willing to associate its name with that venture.

These figures also reveal that the consumers' view of the product is generally far less conservative than that of management itself. Quite often the latter is too blinkered by the origin of the brand and considers the manufacturing history of the brand as its definition. For management, Mars could not mean anything else but the chocolate bar. And yet the Mars ice-cream bar has been a success and the Mars biscuit launched in 2003 was also a hit. This proves that consumers distinguish rather well the brand from the

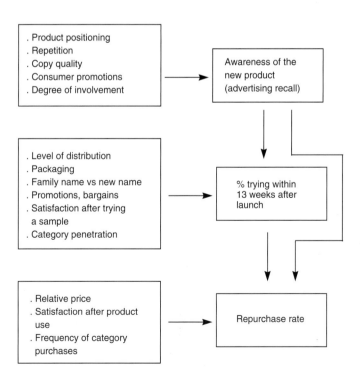

Figure 11.4   Ayer model: how a family name impacts the sales of a new product

product, or at least that they do not associate them irreversibly.

The second economic argument put forward to justify brand extension has to do with cost: launching a new brand would cost more than launching a new product under a well-known brand. Indeed, for consumer goods one estimate is that, as a result of lower expenses in 'push' and in 'pull', in promotion (to consumers and above all to distributors) as well as in media advertising, the savings due to the choice of brand extension amount to 21 per cent. Since the trial ratio is higher, the strategy of brand extension proves economical as far as cost per trial is concerned (see Table 11.2).

However, another study from Nielsen based on 115 launches gives apparently contradictory results: the new products launched under new names get market shares twice as high as those of the products launched under known brands (except for health and beauty products, for which the results are identical: 2.7 per cent vs 2.6 per cent) (see Figure 11.5). The reason for this difference can be seen in the second column. The extension strategy would not in fact be less efficient: the lower market shares are due to the fact that management uses smaller communication budgets in cases of brand extension, which lowers the share of advertising presence.

For an equal percentage of advertising presence, brand extension results in equivalent or even greater market shares in the field of health and beauty where, the risk perceived by the consumers being higher, there is a preference for known brands.

What can be deduced from these two studies? Are they contradictory? The first one concludes that extension is more efficient even with a lower budget. The contradiction could be solved by considering the fact that many managers, confident in the productivity of brand extension, reduce the advertising budget dedicated to the extension launch (thus the results of the first column of Figure 11.5). For equal budgets, the extension strategy has a slight advantage which is not significant in the cleaning products and food sectors but significant in the health and beauty sector (0.46 vs 0.39). In addition, the fact that OC&C analyses efficiency in terms of trial rate (very tightly linked to the familiarity of the brand name) whereas Nielsen's is based on market share over 24 months, which reflects the marketing mix and product quality as a whole, may have some bearing. Finally, this low launch budget of the extension may be linked to a desire to keep the bulk of advertising on the core product of the brand to preserve its sales (a mistake since it underestimates the reciprocal spillover effects of advertising a new product on the sales of the core product (Balachander and Ghose, 2003).

A hidden factor in each of these two studies is the moment of entry on the market. A risky, new market cannot be approached in the same way as the same market at a more mature stage. Sullivan's (1991) analysis of 96 launches

Table 11.2 Brand extension impact on launching costs

	New brand	Brand extension	%
Launching budget:			
– pull	100	78	–22
– push	30	24	–20
Total	130	102	–21
Trial rate	100	123	+23
Cost/trial	1.3	0.83	–36

Source: OC&C

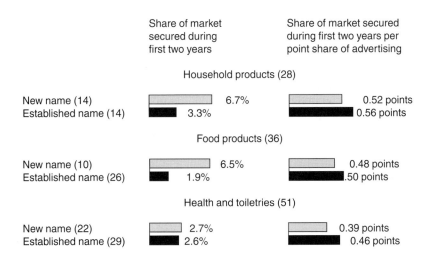

	Share of market secured during first two years	Share of market secured during first two years per point share of advertising

Household products (28)

New name (14) — 6.7% — 0.52 points
Established name (14) — 3.3% — 0.56 points

Food products (36)

New name (10) — 6.5% — 0.48 points
Established name (26) — 1.9% — .50 points

Health and toiletries (51)

New name (22) — 2.7% — 0.39 points
Established name (29) — 2.6% — 0.46 points

Figure 11.5 Comparative sales performance during first two years (Nielsen)

in eleven categories of products gives interesting descriptive results (see Table 11.3).

First, this analysis noted that companies preferred to penetrate new markets with new brands. Of the 48 launches studied that had taken place on emerging markets, only 13 were brand extensions. However, in mature markets, 40 out of the 48 launches analysed were brand extensions. Sullivan also noted that the brands which used their own names in order to penetrate a young market were rather weak brands. For example, in the United States, Royal Crown Cola was the first brand to penetrate the diet cola segment under its own name. It was followed by Pepsi-Cola with Diet Pepsi. Coca-Cola had preferred to launch Tab and not to put its brand capital at risk. It introduced Diet Coke last. The survey shows that the brands which have become leaders in these markets were almost always new brands (Diet Coke is an exception).

Why do strong brands hesitate to penetrate young markets? Of course, they would benefit from the fact that there is no competition yet. But creating a market entails more risks for the creator (Schnaars, 1995) and a negative effect on the brand and its capital. In a young, badly defined market, a brand must be flexible in order to find the best positioning. Brand extension does not permit such flexibility. The attributes of the brand must be respected. Furthermore, launching a brand which is specific to a new market enables the brand to become the reference on that market, by benefiting from what is called the pioneer advantage (Carpenter and Nakamoto, 1991). Finally, many new markets are created in reaction to old ones. For example, the snow surfing market is a counter-culture against

Table 11.3 Success rate of two alternative branding policies

	Market development	
	Growth	Maturity
Launches of new brands	57%	43%
Launches of brand extensions	46%	68%

Source: Sullivan (1991)

alpine skiing and its competition-oriented values; its proponents have their own brands and have refused the surfboards of Rossignol, the established brand.

Apart from the case of weak brands trying to dominate a new market, it can be attractive to be the only known and reassuring reference on a market where neither the offer nor distribution is structured, and where the consumer perceives a high risk. The consumer will appreciate the presence of a famous brand, even if it is far from its original market. Only its fame and serious reputation count. That is why Tefal penetrated the fledgling market of domestic appliances under its own name.

Finally, the analysis of success rates of the two launch strategies, depending on the degree of maturity of the markets, reveals a slight advantage for the new brand strategy in the market creation phase. But with time, the brand extension strategy seems more successful (see Table 11.3).

What research tells us about brand extensions

Since 1990, extension has attracted the attention of all marketing researchers and academics. This barren ground was seducing, and in addition the stakes were high. This research, mostly experimental and quantitative, has focused on identifying the determinants of consumers' attitudes to an extension. Would they find the concept attractive or not? It has also looked for the conditions where the brand equity could be diluted by an extension, which is generally true when an extension fails to bear the 'brand contract'. What is the impact on the parent brand image or on the sales of its core product?

This research has thus focused on only a small part of the brand extension process, which involves eight key steps:

1. Assessment of the brand equities (its image, or emotional assets, its key competencies among various segments of the population).

2. Assessment of the intrinsic attractiveness of likely extension categories.

3. Assessment of the transferability of the brand assets in the chosen extension category.

4. Assessment of the relevance of these assets: are these assets real benefits in this category?

5. Assessment of the ability of the company to deliver the expected benefits subsumed by the brand name.

6. Assessment of the perceived superiority of the extension to existing competition.

7. Assessment of the ability of the company to sustain competition in the extension category and to acquire leadership through time.

8. Assessment of the feedback effects on the parent brand and on the sales of the core product. What does the extension bring to the brand (new clients, new image traits, new sales?)

Academic research mostly addresses issues 1, 3 and 8. It aims at answering such questions as: When is band equity transferable? What causes positive consumer reactions to extension proposals? When can brand equity be damaged by an unsatisfying extension? Its dominant paradigm is experimental research, using consumer evaluations (I like it, I do not like it) as the variable to be explained. Only recently have researchers analysed back data, and the historical sequence of market entries, to focus on sales and segment leadership and try to understand the determinants of success and failure. (See Figure 11.6.)

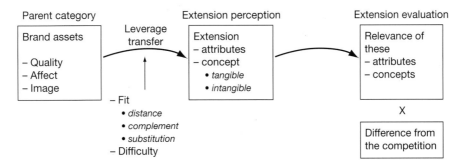

Figure 11.6   The brand extension model

Early experimental studies on brand extension

The first study was presented in 1987 during a symposium on brand extension at the University of Minnesota. The attitude towards a fictitious brand of calculators (Tarco) was manipulated through the presentation of the results of tests evaluating six Tarco calculators. These tests concluded, according to the experimental group, that none of the six calculators were of poor quality, or one out of six, two out of six … up to six out of six. Naturally, the general attitude towards Tarco was much influenced by this manipulation. Then a list of new products to be launched by Tarco was presented: these ranged from a new calculator

and 'close' extensions (microcomputers, digital watches, cash registers, etc) to 'further' extensions (bicycles, pens, office chairs). The interviewees in each group were asked to state their feelings about each of these new Tarco products before having even seen them. The correlation between the attitude towards Tarco and the attitude towards these extension products of Tarco was measured. As shown in Table 11.4, the correlation is stronger when the extension is close. In short, the transfer of attitude increases with the perceived similarity between the category of brand origin and the category of the product extension.

Naturally, the bases of 'perceived similarity' vary with the individuals. As another study has shown, experts and non-experts use

Table 11.4   Is reputation transferable? Correlation between the attitude towards a parent brand and the attitude towards each of its extensions, ranked in order of decreasing similarity

Extension		Correlation
Close	Another calculator	0.85
	PC computer	0.76
	Cash register	0.75
	Digital watch	0.63
	Video recorder	0.62
	Radio	0.58
	Colour TV	0.51
	Office chair	−0.11
	Bike	−0.11
Remote	Ball pen	−0.17

Source: Consumer Behaviour Seminar (1987)

different indexes to evaluate the degree of similarity between two products. For example, the two following types of extension were shown to two groups of individuals, non-experts and experts:

▪ one was a superficial extension, using superficial similarity and relatedness (from tennis shoes to tennis rackets);

▪ the other was a 'deeper' extension, using the same know-how (that of carbon fibre, enabling a brand of golf clubs to introduce tennis rackets).

When asked about their perception of similarity between the starting category and the final category (tennis rackets), non-experts found the superficial extension very similar, but the experts not as much. On the other hand, an explanation of the process and material used convinced the experts more easily of the fact that tennis rackets and golf clubs are close products, while for non-experts they remain quite dissimilar. Thus, identical composition is not a factor of perceived similarity for non-experts: they base their opinions on more superficial signs. They are sensitive to extensions based on relationships of complementarity or substitutability between products, which this creates a sense of 'fit':

▪ Uncle Ben's sauce is complementary to Uncle Ben's rice;

▪ Nesquik cereals are substitutes for Nesquik milk chocolate.

Experts are not satisfied with these peripheral cues. They need a stronger rationale, such as that of Look's extension. This brand, famous for its ski bindings, was extended to the upper-range mountain-bike market, for it could apply here its mastery of the automatic grip pedals and of new composite materials.

In the first study, the fact that Tarco was a fictitious brand was intentional. This way, the brand had no capital – no particular trust and emotion were associated to the brand. This explains the importance of the criterion of similarity of products to facilitate the transfer of attitudes. In a normal situation, if the brand is a strong one, the relevance of its key values in the product class it wishes to enter is what determines the attractiveness of the extension even if the categories of products are very different (Broniarczyk and Alba, 1994). The success of Bic in pens, razors and lighters illustrates this fact.

The first sign of awareness of a mechanism independent from the product and stemming from the brand itself appeared in 1991, among Park and his colleagues. Two lists of products were given to the persons interviewed: functional products and expressive products:

Functional products	Expressive products
TV	
compact disc	perfume
cassette-player	shoe
radio	wallet
video tape	shirt
VCR	bag
walkman	pen
car radio	ring
video camera	watch
record-player	belt
headphones	crystal
	tie

Two questions were asked:

1. the traditional question about the degree of similarity between the products of each column;

2. a question about whether the products of each column 'fit' together.

The researchers asked these two questions in two ways:

▪ blindly, as above;

▪ using a brand, here Sony for the first list and Gucci for the second.

What were the results?

▌ For the symbolic products, the fact that the brand was mentioned or not did not modify the judgements of low perceived similarity between the products. However, the presence of the Gucci brand name created a considerable fit between products which did not seem to fit much without the brand (3.68), but suddenly fitted together (4.74) under the brand.

▌ For functional products, the presence or not of the brand did not modify the judgements of perceived similarity and of 'fit'.

In short, the authors hinted at two processes by which consumers build an opinion on an extension:

▌ If the brand is mainly functional, the extension is evaluated from the bottom up, according to inherent links between the category of the original product and that of the extended product. The consumers' evaluations rest on the degree of perceived similarity between product categories.

▌ If the brand is symbolic, the concept of the brand creates a link between products which otherwise would not have one. In this case, the judgements on extension are independent of the physical characteristics of the products. Each extension is evaluated according to its belonging to the brand concept and to its coherence with the value system of this brand. This is a top-down process.

Some extensions bear the risk of dilution of the brand. Like an elastic band that has been pulled too much, the brand can become weak. Many factors explain the weakening of a brand by excessive extension. Evaluating this risk is no mean task: what would be the impact on Tuborg if a sparkling mineral water were introduced under this brand (such an extension does exist in Greece)?

A study demonstrated the existence of this risk. It focused on a well-known health and beauty brand, Neutrogena. Two extensions were presented to the consumers, one very unusual for Neutrogena, the other very typical of Neutrogena. The experiment consisted of informing the consumers that both extensions did very poorly in the two dimensions that make Neutrogena famous, softness and quality. What would be the impact of such a statement on the image of Neutrogena itself (Loken and Roedder, 1993)? Would the image of softness and quality of typical Neutrogena products be affected, too? The study considered product A1, the brand prototype associated with Neutrogena by 83 per cent of consumers; product A2, associated by 61 per cent; product A3, by 55 per cent; product A4, by 39 per cent; and product A5, by 5 per cent. Here are the conclusions:

▌ Although of poor quality, the remote extension did not stain the image of the brand, nor the image of its other products. This phenomenon is well known to researchers on stereotypes: the exception does not harm the rule. The extension is atypical, therefore without influence on the heart of the brand.

▌ The situation is different for the more typical extension of Neutrogena. Its poor quality had a negative influence on both the image of the brand in its key attributes, and that of products typically and spontaneously associated to the brand. (A1, A2 and A3 had a statistically significant poorer softness image after exposure to the extension.) There has, indeed, been a negative impact on the brand and on its most significant products, but only in the case where the extension is typical of the brand. The danger concerns line extensions much more than brand extensions.

How attitudes about extensions are formed

Much research has been carried out into brand extension. As with any field of research, the pioneer articles are followed up by endless variations on the theme, exploring contextual aspects such as other products, countries, and interviewee types along with in-depth analyses (Leif Heim Egil, 2002), summaries, and then – much later – re-analyses and meta-analyses. Meanwhile, the results of the initial research have done the rounds, and have assumed the status of intangible truth. Only later do their limitations become apparent. This is why in 2004, for this new edition, it is possible to sort through the results of these summary analyses and critiques.

For example, Bottomley and Holden (2001) re-analysed data from all research that faithfully adhered to the basic Aaker–Keller paradigm (1990) to explain attitudes with regard to an extension. In this pioneering study, consumers were asked to evaluate ideas for extensions (a good idea/not a good idea; good/bad). The aim was to gain an understanding of the determining factors behind these evaluations from among a series of suggested values, such as the parent brand's reputation for quality, the perceived fit between the extension and the category of origin, and the perceived difficulty of constructing the extension, along with a number of other variables, without considering the interactions between variables. The perceived fit is the main variable to emerge from this pioneering research. It measures the psychological – and thus subjective – gap between the extension and the brand's typical product (its prototype). Traditionally, the fit is measured in three dimensions: the degree of perceived synergy between the extension and the prototype, the degree of perceived substitutability, and the perceived transferability of know-how.

Bottomley and Holden's re-analyses of the initial study and seven repeat studies produced conclusions somewhat different from those that were circulated following the initial research:

■ Consumers' evaluations of an extension are in the first place influenced by the perceived quality of the parent brand and the perceived degree of fit. Clearly, extensions are not a way of saving weak brands: they must have a reputation for quality before being it is possible to attempt brand stretching. With regard to the dimensions of fit, 'synergy' and 'transferability of know-how' are more important than 'substitutability'.

■ These evaluations are also influenced by the interactions between the brand's perceived quality, the degree of synergy and the transferability of know-how, as well as by the interaction of the brand's perceived quality with the perceived difficulty of manufacturing the extension. (In short, the importance of the brand's perceived quality grows along with the perceived difficulty in carrying out this extension.)

■ Last, there is a small direct influence produced by the perceived difficulty of manufacturing the extension: when this rises, the evaluation rises. Consumers do not like brands that are happy to put their names to excessively trivial products. However, this result is not confirmed in all cases. It is true that the success of brand licences among children casts doubt on the extent to which they are influenced by this variable: the Harry Potter name has appeared on some of the most banal products (exercise books, erasers, pencils, pens, clothing and so on). However, perhaps the effect does apply to parents, helplessly watching the tidal wave of demand for licensed products bear down on them. It may also apply to technical brands, which would explain their reluctance to move down-range by manufacturing oversimplified products.

The Aaker–Keller paradigm has provided an initial step in brand understanding. However, as can easily be seen, it has its roots in a traditional, cognitive view of the brand defined by its competence, objective attributes and know-how. To evaluate an extension, consumers are thus supposed to analyse the proximity of the extension product to the product that in their eyes most accurately represents the brand (its prototype). This is a bottom-up approach: the consumer's starting point is the similarities between products as a means of evaluating the brand extension. This applies well to so-called 'functional' brands.

But how much proximity is there between fries and pizza? Or between fries and buns, or fries and iced tea? There is little in a physical sense, and yet these products constitute the McCain range. In fact, the common factor behind the unity of this brand and the fit between its products is not the products themselves, but the brand concept, American food. In the future, McCain could start to sell brownies or ice cream. We may thus suppose that there is another way of evaluating fit other than just the three dimensions examined above: the evaluation of the fit with the intangible concept of the brand itself. In this case, consumers would use a top-down approach. Starting with the concept, they would ask themselves whether the product extension conforms to the concept.

Furthermore, extension serves to move a brand from being product-based ('McCain makes excellent frozen fries') to being concept-based ('McCain makes delicious American food products'). Becoming a concept brand enables preparation for future expansion via other new product introductions, thus increasing the brand's market power, turnover, profile and visibility: it becomes a mega-brand.

In acquiring an intangible dimension on which its identity is founded, the brand thus gains access to expansion. For as long as it stays a product brand, it remains confined to a product segment: if what you sell is Bic biros, how much further can you go than, say, erasers, marker pens and pencils? But when perceived as 'the brand of cool, simple, practical and plastic products', Bic can put its name to ballpoint pens and disposable razors and become a world leader in both these markets, as well as in the disposable lighter market.

The research can thus be summarised as in Figure 11.7.

The limits of early research on extension

Who knows Genichi Kawakami? He was the CEO of Yamaha for 52 years, and died in

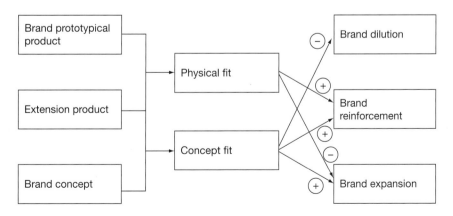

Figure 11.7   The consequences of product and concept fit and misfit
Source: Mischel, 2000, Vuibert

2002. When he succeeded his father as CEO in 1950, Yamaha was an harmonium and piano company. In 1954 the company made a radical diversification into motorbikes. In parallel, it also created synthethisers and acoustic and electric guitars. Then it extended its activity to skis, tennis rackets and carbon-based golf clubs. Later it was to enter the hi-fi market, positioned as a premium product, followed by extensions in the video market and now multimedia. At the heart of all these strategic moves lay the belief that product innovations are the only way to enter markets and to remain profitably in these markets. They were also underwritten by a genuine vision of this CEO, that of the leisure society. Of course, it never came to the mind of Genichi Kawakami to call any of these innovations by any name other than Yamaha.

The problem is that, according to early brand extension research (Aaker and Keller, 1990), these extensions should have all failed.

The prime factor for consumer acceptance of an extension, stemming out from this research, is 'the fit', the feeling of perceived similarity between the core product and the extension. This result has been amply confirmed by subsequent research (Leif Heim Egil, 2002; Bottomley and Holden, 2001). What fit or resemblance is there between a piano and a motorbike? None. However, Yamaha is the world's leading brand for musical instruments and the world number two manufacturer of motorbikes. What fit is there between a ballpoint pen and a lighter, or a lighter and a disposable razor? None. However, Bic is the world leading brand in these three markets. It successfully managed its very dissimilar extensions under the same name. According to its CEO, having the same name was precisely one of the factors of their success. Certainly, consultants told him not to launch the lighter in 1973 under the same name as the ballpoint pen (launched in 1950) or the disposable razor, launched in 1975. But

the management had another vision. These three products now make 53 per cent of their sales in North and Central America.

Why are the findings of this early research so far from this reality? In fact, this kind of pioneering work (Aaker and Keller, 1990) rested entirely on laboratory research. In this special context, consumers were presented with ideas about extensions and had to make an immediate evaluation. In the real world, the extensions were launched as all-new products, with information about the intrinsic value of the extension and trust relayed by publicity and word of mouth. In the laboratory research setting, the interviewees had none of these, and this is why they relied on perceived fit, a measure of 'global sameness', or similarity between the extension and the brand. In brief, the conclusions of that research present the consumer as very conservative. Recently, Klink and Smith (2001) confirmed that the results were determined by the method. The interviewees have too limited information, are exposed only once to the concept (in contrast to the multiple exposures of a real advertising launch campaign), and typically are not the risk-taking innovators who try new products first. Klink and Smith demonstrated that the effect of fit diminishes when consumer innovativeness increases, and that multiple exposures increase the perceived fit between an extension and the brand.

Now that after 10 years or so we have achieved a meta-analysis of all the articles or studies focusing on the overt discrepancies between generally held beliefs stemming from research and the reality of brand and business, it is time to look at research with a different eye, that of external validity. It now appears that laboratory research by its very nature produces conservative statements about brand extension. In the real world consumers are more informed and can better evaluate the extensions.

The new perspective of typicality

Above, we have spoken of typical and atypical extensions. This raises the question of how to judge whether the product resulting from an extension is at the heart, at the limit or outside the territory of a brand. This question is one more application of a more general question at the heart of research on cognitive psychology: according to what criteria is an object considered part of a category?

Indeed, the psychological study of classification by categories aims at identifying the processes by which we form categories, and assigns certain objects to one category rather than to another. The brand is, in that sense, a category.

For decades, the dominating, or 'classical', theory answered this question in the following way: a product or an object belongs to a category if it has the necessary and sufficient features of this category. This leads one to question 'the' definition of the concept (or the category), ie about the nature of these features determining the belonging or non-belonging. This model works well for certain categories (for example the category of 'even numbers'), but it seems less reliable for others. Specialist or niche car makers such as BMW or Saab have definite image and physical traits, which can qualify a new car as belonging or not to the brand. This is not the case for the generalist brands such as Ford, Opel, Vauxhall and Nissan. The same holds true for Braun vs Philips.

Indeed, in this classic model, all examples of the category are equivalent since they all have these necessary and sufficient traits: two is an even number as much as 18 or 40! All BMWs are BMW.

Experience proves that the situation is different for many categories: for example, some birds are more 'birdlike' than others, and even a butterfly is more 'birdlike' than an ostrich. Belonging to a category does not seem to be a clear-cut binary function (yes/no) but a probabilistic one. The frontier between the 'bird' and 'insect' categories is unclear. This does not nullify these two categories: indeed, we all have in mind the prototype of a bird and that of an insect, and these two prototypes cannot be mistaken one for the other! However, the frontiers of each category are not that separate.

Thus the new tendency of research on categorisation, led by Rosch (1978) and Lakoff (1987), admits that categories can also be groups with unclear boundaries which are not defined by a series of necessary and sufficient features: what common features would link bridge, hopscotch, a doll and Monopoly? All are prototypes of games, but games in a different way for each one of them. This is important as these objects are more linked by a 'family resemblance' than by the possession of specific features common to all. Family resemblance means that if A resembles B, B resembles C in a different way, and C resembles A in an even more different way. The same goes for mega-brands such as Whirlpool or Philips, which are characterised by typical products more than by typical image traits (see Table 11.5).

Although the theory of categorisation has evolved and its authors have reintroduced the possibility of features that define the meaning of natural categories – called 'most typical' features – various consequences can be drawn from this new approach.

Basically, an extension is considered acceptable if it 'fits' the idea that consumers have of the parent brand. This feeling is based either on a high perceived similarity to the most typical product – or products – of the brand (also called pivot products), or on the coherence between the extension and the brand contract (also called its concept or identity).

When the extension is distant from the mother brand, which attributes of the latter are transferred to the extension product, and which are not? As the notion of distance is linked to a comparison with the prototypical product – or products – of the brand, the objective characteristics of the brand are the ones which will be transferred the least to

Table 11.5   How brands differ: their prototypes are not the same

	Philips	Whirlpool
Television	9.10	5.06
Magnetoscope	8.65	4.97
Hi-fi	8.45	4.61
Electric razor	7.82	4.01
Walkman	7.73	3.44
Video-disc	7.68	3.34
Compact disc	7.64	3.49
Vacuum cleaner	7.57	5.85
Video cassette	7.45	3.65
Refrigerator	7.40	8.69(1)
Hair-remover (woman)	7.21	4.19
Coffee machine	6.97	5.06
Food-processor	6.94	6.05
Freezer	6.86	8.57(3)
Washing machine	6.83	8.69(1)
Dish washer	6.81	6.37(4)
Microwave oven	6.81	5.87
Iron	6.73	4.77
Hair dryer	6.67	7.83(7)
Cooker	6.60	8.12(6)
Tumble dryer	6.47	7.83
Electric oven	6.38	8.16(5)

Base: How typical of each brand is each product?
        (Answers range from 0 to 10)

Source: Kapferer and Laurent (1996)

remote extensions. On the contrary, the intangible, more symbolic characteristics ignore distance and have an influence on all extensions. The doctoral thesis of Gali (1993) under supervision of the author, demonstrates this, as seen in Table 11.6. Consumers were asked to evaluate the Miele brand according to various image dimensions, then to evaluate according to the same dimensions the most typical product of Miele (the washing-machine) and two extensions, one slightly atypical (a television) and one very atypical (a microcomputer).

Table 11.6 reveals several facts:

▌ First, the very atypical extension receives very little of the Miele functional values, as shown by the comparison of correlations in columns 1 and 3. Its role could be the

opposite: to introduce into Miele values which the brand lacks. The more typical extension (column 2) receives more values from the brand.

▌ Generally speaking, objective qualities are not transferred as well as symbolic qualities. Thus, typical physical features of Miele – quality, innovation, reliability – are weakly transferred to the image of the two extensions. On the contrary, the extensions receive the following features: for the young, to show off, for innovators. For that reason, in a different context, luxury brands have little difficulty in practising extension even into dissimilar categories. Their primarily symbolic qualities ignore the distance between concrete objects.

Table 11.6   Which brand attributes are transferable to close or remote extensions? The case of Miele

Image attributes	Correlation between brand image and its prototypical product image	Correlation between brand image and a close extension image (TV)	Correlation between brand image and a remote extension image (PC)
Expensive	0.89	0.70	0.40
High quality	0.75	0.45	0.30
Innovativeness	0.71	0.24	0.17
Reliable	0.70	0.55	0.55
Design	0.61	0.45	0.41
Trustworthy	0.60	0.38	0.31
Ease of use	0.36	0.31	0.25
For modern people	0.87	0.78	0.63
To show off	0.84	0.65	0.71
For young households	0.89	0.73	0.68
For experts	0.90	0.70	0.45

Source: Gali/Kapferer (1993)

How extensions impact the brand: a typology

Brand extension is a leap out of the category of origin to grow the business. Here again it is necessary to see the difference between close extensions, also called continuous extensions, and discontinuous or remote extensions. A brand of spark plugs for automobiles can undertake a close extension into other automobile accessories (batteries, windscreen wipers, etc), as is the case for Bosch and Valéo. A brand that masters optics can extend into photocopying: this is the case for Canon, Minolta, Ricoh, Kodak and Agfa. A sports brand can cover other sports goods (Adidas, Salomon). Discontinuous extensions eliminate technological synergies and physical links between products: they are real diversifications. For example Yamaha sells both motorbikes and classical pianos. The Carrefour distributor's brand covers the entire field of mass consumption goods and even quality goods.

Thus, there are extensions which are far from the original territory of the brand, and extensions which are close. This leads to brands with a narrow spectrum of products – specialised brands – and brands with a wide spectrum (such as Philips or General Electric). Is it better to be a specialist or a generalist? Both strategies are valid. A brand is arbitrary, in theory it can go wherever it wants to. Nothing can stop Bic from deciding to brand windsurfing equipment. If the corporate strategy puts forward synergies of brand awareness and savings on advertising, it will adopt a wide spectrum strategy. As a general rule, it can be stated that beyond the growth of sales and profits, brand extensions influence the brand and its capital in six different ways:

1. Some extensions exploit the brand capital: the new product sells thanks to its name. This is what happens when the product receiving the brand is no different from the existing competitors on the market: the brand has not entirely played its transformation role, but it enables the product to benefit from its image. By using this practice too frequently – through a loose licensing policy for example – the brand capital

wears out as the brand becomes associated with these now commonplace products, and with their unjustified price premium. Industrial brands often fill up the gaps in their lines by buying the missing items from their competitors. This is typical of the copiers' market.

2. Other extensions destroy the brand capital, for instance when the extension is downwards. Porsche has cancelled its 924 range, cars which only justified their considerable price difference against their competitors (the Golf GTi) by the prestigious name. None of the objective or subjective values of Porsche could be found in the 924 model: neither masculinity, nor technology. This model seemed to announce the end of the Porsche myth. Since at that time the brand no longer took part in Formula 1 racing and was losing in the Le Man 24-hour endurance race, the only communication element of the brand was advertising, of which a large part was dedicated to the 924. To return to its source, the brand ceased to manufacture the 924 and reinvested in the 911.

3. Some extensions have a neutral effect on the brand capital. The product is not out of place but is in tune with what is expected from the brand. Significantly, in the field of home appliances, some brands are thought to offer many more types of products than are actually produced, but if they decided to actually penetrate these markets, their image would not suffer. This shows that consumers have a perception of the brand which is different from that of those who manufacture it. They attribute to the brand areas of competence which are larger than and not limited to just the existing products.

4. Some extensions influence the meaning of the brand: when Rossignol added branded tennis rackets, the status of the brand changed. It is now less specialised and is characterised by a wider range of interests. Yet the two sports covered by Rossignol were not chosen randomly: the brand is still offering the equipment which extends the individual's body to help gain access to pleasure and performance. Nestlé increased its modernity by competing upfront under its own name with Danone on the ultra-fresh market (ie yoghurt).

5. Some extensions are regenerating. They revive the brand and its core, and re-express its base values in a new, stronger manner. Thus, the classic green blazer is a regenerating product for Lacoste. It represents a rare symbiosis between the features building the Lacoste brand: conformity, discretion, sociability but also a certain distance on fashion. As for the green colour, it is more casual than the blue blazer (too uniform for Lacoste) and refers to the green grass of the original tennis courts at Wimbledon. The green blazer brings Lacoste up to date and at the same time expresses its roots. The 'Marlboro Classics' line allows the brand to recommunicate its history, its roots and founding values.

6. Finally, some extensions, although not desired by the brand, are necessary to defend the brand capital: their purpose is, above all, to prevent the use of the brand name by another company in another category of products. Thus, Cartier may not want to develop along those lines, but they have to in order to prevent another company from registering the brand name Cartier on an international scale in the textiles category.

Avoiding the risk of dilution

In our many brand extension consulting missions, the recurring question concerns the risk of diluting the image capital. Could the business extension harm the brand's assets: its reputation, and the traits that comprise its value in the eyes of the market? For example, what will be the long-term effect on Danone's image if it starts selling Danone water too? What will be the long-term effect on Mercedes' image when it produces its A-Class range? What will be the long-term effect of Chanel's decision to start selling glasses at Afflelou, a discount franchise chain of opticians? What will be the long-term effect on the image of a brand that has sold only to professionals, but now starts selling to the general public too? What will be the long-term effect of an extension towards lower prices? What will be the long-term effect of selling not only pens but also cigarette lighters and razors under the Bic brand?

As these typical questions show, the problem lies in estimating the long-term effects. No study can predict the future. Second, the answer will depend to a large extent on the ability to perform the extension successfully and well. After all, an extension is more than just a brand extension: more importantly, it is a departure from the brand's tried and tested sphere of competence. Some learning will be necessary, and this may take time. For example, the little A-Class car revealed that Mercedes had not sufficiently mastered the engines and stability issues for this chassis type, thus reneging on the brand's traditional basic contract and its three essential attributes: reliability, safety and standing.

Extensions also entail taking risks other than just image-related ones. A brand extension generally brings about changes in target markets, distributors (and perhaps even buyers, from a mass retail perspective), prices, manufacturing and logistics. These changes may be a source of annoyance to the brand's historical distribution channel, opinion leaders or existing customers. There is thus a genuine business risk – and this may affect sales of the current flagship product which constitutes the main sales platform.

An example of brand dilution: Vichy

Vichy is an example of a brand whose changes over its history have led to a loss of identity and value. It started out as a cosmetics brand that promoted itself as the dermatologists' brand. However, in an attempt to increase sales, it dropped this label and began developing products with a strong cosmetics base. Freed of its dermatology tag, the brand was able to advertise on television and develop products which, in accordance with women's wishes, had a much more cosmetics-based slant – as well as bigger margins. The brand was able to launch more new products every year, as the whole clinical tests process was no longer necessary. In just a few years, it became just another run-of-the-mill pharmacy product.

Vichy's sales increased very rapidly, as did its margins. However, at the same time its image was being eroded. This policy, although a winner in the short term, had caused a loss of identity in the eyes of consumers who could no longer perceive the brand's distinctiveness or added value. It was no longer what chemists wanted either, at a time when the pharmacies channel as a whole was attempting to re-establish its legitimacy against new distribution channels also seeking the right to sell so-called 'para-pharmacy' products.

It was back to the drawing board for Vichy's business model and brand mission. Vichy, the dedicated chemist's brand, needed to bolster its distribution channel. The brand was repositioned around the theme of health, and thus the brand slogan became *La santé passe aussi par la peau* ('Health is vital. Start with your skin'). Most importantly, all items and products that did not fit this philosophy were axed.

Such losses of identity are common: large groups often seek to make a profit out of their acquisitions and force small brands with a strong identity to move quickly into other distribution channels and categories.

Neutrogena, for example, is facing this threat: it is expanding its presence in the worldwide food channel, but at the risk of losing the key values that make the brand truly distinctive.

Is the consumer book-keeping or subtyping?

Academic research furnishes important information on the risk of image dilution. Unfortunately, however, it focuses exclusively on the misfit with the brand image: it does not consider risks arising from the fact that an extension is usually also accompanied by strategic changes in distribution and targets.

The foremost paradigm in research on dilution is a failure to honour the basic contract. What happens when the expectations created by the brand's name are dashed by the brand extension? Apart from this failure in itself, is there not a risk to the brand's image, or even to the sales of existing products? Basic research (Loken and Roedder John, 1993) has shown that any failure to honour the basic contract has a negative impact on the brand and its image for each image aspect that is ignored. A brand is constructed out of the sum of all of the impressions accumulated in consumers' memories. The only exception to this is if customers find themselves asking the question, is the unsatisfactory extension typical or atypical of the brand? If the extension is perceived as being atypical, the brand's image is safe. However, extensions that are fairly typical of the brand are the ones that dilute its image the most if they disappoint with regard to the brand contract. The problem is that there is no guarantee consumers will ask themselves whether the extension is typical or not. In the aforementioned study, researchers put the question to half the sampled group. The question did not spontaneously occur to the other half. It would therefore seem that consumers adopt a 'book-keeping' approach in which the brand is responsible for everything it does, whether good or bad.

A second, more recent piece of research considered the question of the effect of breaking the brand contract during an extension on sales of the current flagship product (Roedder John, Loken, Joiner, 1998). Disappointment with the performance of a Johnson & Johnson brand extension did indeed impair the brand image with regard to the attribute that constituted its differentiating value: gentleness. However the sales of the prototype, or flagship product, was not affected. This suggests an 'experience effect'. Consumers who have already used the product are confident about qualities. They might view a brand extension negatively but this will not alter this confidence about the flagship product. However, J&J's flagship product (baby shampoo) *was* affected when the disappointment stemmed from a line extension (a simple modification to the basic product). Such very closely linked extensions are the ones that cause the most collateral damage to sales of the flagship product.

The risk of downward stretch

It is a well-known fact that price is an indication of quality, and can on its own create the image of a product with a high standing. In their extensions, some top-of-the-range prestige brands have been prompted to sell cheaper products in the search for a client base that is more numerous but less willing to pay a high price. This is the approach taken by brands such as Mercedes with its A-Class and Cartier with its Must de Cartier range. What effects do such acts have on the brand's existing clients?

Given that an expensive brand derives its value in part from the fact that it indicates the buyer has the financial means to afford expensive products (consumers' reflected image), it is hardly surprising that there is a negative reaction: their status has to be spread more thinly, and thus reduced. This has been confirmed by a study on 'The ownership effect in consumer response to brand stretches

(Kirmani, Sood and Bridges, 1999). People who do not buy the prestige brand (BMW in this study) are pleased by its more accessible price extension; existing buyers are much less impressed. Current buyers, however, appreciate price-increasing 'upward-stretch' extensions far more than non-buyers do. With brands that are not of high standing (for example, Accura cars), there is no effect of this kind. This study also confirms that the act of using a sub-brand protects the top-of-the-range brand from image dilution in the event of a price-lowering 'downward-stretch' extension. This is what Cartier did with Must de Cartier, selling pens, cigarette lighters and leather goods in large retail stores to reach a wider clientele and increase its recognition, which until then had been restricted to a well-off elite.

Another interesting piece of research (Buchanan, Simmons and Bickart, 1999) analysed the risk of devaluation if a prestige brand adopts a less selective channel when entering a non-prestige market. For example, the luxury hairdresser J Dessange granted a licence to l'Oréal to use its name on a shampoo to be sold in supermarkets. The findings of this study were that it all depends on merchandising, and – in this case – on three factors. What is the brand's relative visibility, price gap and distance from one or more lesser known or lower prestige brands? If its relative visibility, distance from the competition and price gap tally with the consumer's impression of the brand's standing, the risk is reduced. If they do not, the consumer mentally lowers the brand's standing. For example, it is crucially important for a brand of standing to have a clearly separated display which is distinct from competitors. If it does not, and the display is mixed, the consumer interprets this as a signal from the (supposedly expert) retailer that the brand of lower standing placed alongside the brand of high standing is just as good.

What can we draw from this research on the risk of dilution? First, we can conclude that customers of prestige brands are happy where

they are: they form a conservative lobby. In so doing, they demonstrate a lack of awareness of the economic conundrum faced by the brand or company. As Jürgen Schremp, the CEO of Daimler-Benz, observed in 1998, Mercedes could either stay where it was and – like Rolls-Royce – go bankrupt; or it could change, and sell over a million cars. Conscious of the risk of losing the attachment of its existing customers, the brand has to take precautions:

- Even in its lower cost extensions, the brand contract must be honoured – and the first consideration is quality.

- The brand should manage its downward extension while at the same time continuing to nourish the legend that ensures its high standing. After the A-Class, Mercedes relaunched the S-Class – voted by experts as the best car in the world – and announced Maytag, an even more luxurious model.

- The brand can use a sub-brand for its downward stretch.

- It can also split its distribution into segments. Chanel boutiques concentrate on products with a minimum price of 1,000 euros, while Chanel sunglasses and cosmetics are intended for wider channels.

- Current buyers benefit from a greater level of attention and distinctive signs of recognition, following the model established by credit cards. There is a basic card for everyone, but also far more exclusive Gold and Platinum cards which provide a way of re-establishing the differentiation from other cardholders.

The brand is extended to grow through changing its scope of influence. It is not possible to grow while at the same time keeping everything intact and unchanged.

With regard to non-prestige brands, the risk of dilution can often be exaggerated internally.

For example, all spirit brands have asked themselves what the impact would be if they were to enter the ready-to-drink (RTD) pre-mix/alcopop market. Would this not have an effect on their image among the buyers of their basic products – Smirnoff, Ricard, Johnny Walker, Bacardi and so on? In fact, company studies reveal that this is far from the case. Buyers of established but somewhat elderly brands are delighted to see that the brands are consumed even by today's young people, albeit in a very different way, a fact that is flattering to their parents. This is not to suggest that such extensions are entirely without risk, but the risks are business-related. The first of these is that the new product launch will fail. The second is that older buyers with a high volume potential will be replaced by younger buyers who – at least initially – will consume less. The trick will be to encourage them to migrate at a later date from an RTD-type product to the far more profitable 'real' product. Even if Bacardi Breezer is a genuine worldwide success – like Smirnoff Mule or Ice before it – and even if the products are high-margin on account of their low actual alcohol content (5 per cent), it is still a fact that Bacardi-Martini is a spirits group that expects the high profits commensurate with the spirits sector, not the lower profits of the RTD sector. The challenge is therefore to migrate current RTD customers in future to the proper Smirnoff and Bacardi products. We should add that the real risk would have been to do nothing and watch as young people deserted the brand as a result of its failure to adapt its products, consumption methods, sales and consumption locations and prices to new consumers. Extension is a necessity.

The traditional problem faced by professional brands is their desire also to address a less professional audience. Modern management techniques advocate talking to the customer's customer. By communicating with the general public to publicise the merits of aluminium verandahs, Technal – at that time a subsidiary of Alcan – increased demand from its actual clients (craftspeople and businesses that make aluminium verandahs for their customers). Somfy, the worldwide manufacturer of tubular motors for household automation products, did something similar: it produced advertising for automated blinds, even though its actual customers were the blind manufacturers themselves. Will such a strategy tread on professionals' toes? Such questions overlook the main issue: these extensions are strategic because they seek to maintain the domination of the channel, ensuring that the company does not become a mere OEM, parts manufacturer and subcontractor. Not to take such an extension risk is to take a much more serious medium-term risk instead. This is certainly one way for a leader to increase its recognition, and thus its brand's status. More importantly, it is the way to increase the size of the market, by directly influencing downstream demand from its own clients – who have a natural inclination to go on selling whatever sold well last year, and not to promote innovations. However, only innovations can make the market grow: this is why they must be 'pushed' by the distribution channel. If they are not, demand has to be 'pulled' instead.

Business-to-business brands start out as specialists, and grow via integration. The delicate phase comes when they stop being single-product specialists and expand their range to include another speciality. For example, could a company that has made its reputation in high-voltage switching gear also manufacture medium-voltage or low-voltage switching gear? More importantly, could it also distribute electricity distribution hardware (plugs, cables, conduits and so on) without losing its status? After all, switching gear is a key component of any industrial installation: safety comes first, especially in high-voltage equipment. The same cannot be said for electrical distribution hardware. But it also seems obvious that while we continue to look at the problem from the sole angle of brand extension, we are viewing things the wrong way around. The real question is one of leadership. Clients and distributors want more integration, because it makes their business life simpler. Furthermore, in emerging countries, the pursuit of critical size is vitally important. Can this be achieved with a single line of products? No.

However, it is important to maintain the image capital, which can be achieved in two interlinked ways. The first is by entering the new market (electrical distribution) with a differentiated range based on the attributes for success in this market, with an additional 'plus' as insurance (even if this is not a determining expectation for this new market), in the interests of brand identity and commercial success. The second is the pursuit of innovation and communication in the switchgear market to reinforce the brand's leadership in this sector.

By way of conclusion on the risk of dilution, let us remember that all extensions are a form of change whose aim is to ensure growth and profitability. It is impossible to expect both growth and a lack of change at the same time. Of course, the basic values and attributes of the brand's kernel of identity (see page 223) must be preserved. However, the extension is certain to add new attributes, which start out as being peripheral but may one day become part of the kernel themselves.

What does brand coherence really mean?

The risk of dilution is often mentioned when a brand innovates in an unexpected way which does not fulfil the brand contract to the letter. However, is a lack of coherence the same thing as incoherence?

In 1990, the Fleury Michon charcuterie (cooked pork meats) company conducted a strategic analysis: the share of distributors' brands in the category would continue to rise, as differentiation would be increasingly difficult and the price of imports too low. It

decided on a strategic diversification into shrink-wrapped ready-cooked meals for the quality 'ready to eat' market. The aim was to provide a product that was better than frozen food technology could make. Of course, analysts advised against the use of the Fleury Michon brand: carrying too much of an association with traditional charcuterie, its attributes were contrary to expectations in the new category. The company – a dynamic, pragmatic, family-run SME – chose instead to invest its financial resources in an ultra-modern production and logistics tool which broke down the barrier to entry and transformed the brand into the category leader in the space of just a few months, rather than invest in creating a second brand. This counter-intuitive extension, dictated by scarce resources, turned out to be the best possible decision.

Today, the 'ready meals' division has modernised the brand's image, while the charcuterie division has provided a gastronomic dimension to the ready meals business. A synergy therefore existed around the concept of modern haute cuisine, balance and nutrition. In the meantime Fleury Michon has made changes to its charcuterie line, concentrating on high-end pre-wrapped products. It should be added that if the company had followed the advice to set up two brands, it is possible that no one would now be talking about Fleury Michon: charcuterie would not have been enough on its own to change the firm's image, and ready meals do not constitute a sufficient volume to permit investment in television advertising. The individual brand would have remained weak.

The same thing happened in the case of the Spanish Don Simon company, which sells fruit juice, sangria and table wines under this brand name. The decision was initially taken because of a lack of funds; now, the aim is to capitalise on one single brand and inter-category synergies.

We should therefore be wary of simplistic advice maintaining that the brand is always something highly specialised and should stick to doing just one thing (Trout and Ries, 1990): this creates a strategic situation which is often untenable. Of course, consumers expect specialist brands, but they also expect general-purpose brands, which allow them to confront their own contradictions as consumers, wanting everything and wanting the opposite. For example, Danone is home to very health-oriented products (Actimel, Activa/Bio, Taillefine/Vitalinea) as well as pure pleasure products such as Danette, with its high sugar and fat content. A brand rule that enforced strict coherence would forbid such a practice. However, the consumer is happy to see Danone as a serious, high-quality, thoroughly comprehensive brand whose extensions put a health gloss on sweet treats and lend a pleasurable dimension to diet products. Without this, Danone would be a brand like either Weight Watchers or Cadbury's.

We thus have to draw a clear line between the incoherent and contradictory on the one hand, and the merely non-uniform on the other (see Figure 11.8). Even when selling Danette, Danone talks in terms of calcium.

Balancing identity and change

Brand extension capitalises on the brand's 'assets'. It hopes that there will be a transfer of these 'assets' between the parent category and the extension category, given the perceived subjective proximity between the two categories. It is therefore a question of capitalising on identity: the intended result is an identity-based brand.

However, the success of an extension depends on its ability to deliver value to the client. In what way are these assets relevant? What makes them superior to the competition? This presents the problem of the extension's ability to exploit a genuine opportunity or real consumer insight in its market.

There is therefore always a balance to be struck between these two (equally legitimate) requirements. Since a name is a promise, the brand cannot make different promises with different products; but at the same time, unsuitability for the target market is the number one reason that new products fail: each market has its own 'drivers' and customer preference levers.

One way of avoiding this dilemma is to extend only into categories where market drivers (preference factors) correspond with the brand's equities. This is the approach used by Schneider Electric in electrical equipment and control panels. The company also analyses extension opportunities for its daughter brands, Merlin Gerin and Telemecanique, by auditing potential extension categories. What

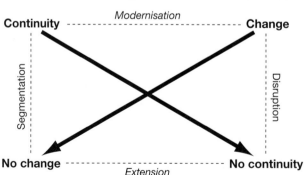

Figure 11.8 The issue of brand coherence

are the key factors in their success? In what way are they also the key factors of the brands themselves?

However, an extension category may also be chosen for its contribution towards building the future brand. Nivea, for example, owns a raft of daughter brands, each positioned on extensions that have a highly specific role in building the Nivea brand over time (see page 245). The hygiene and beauty market – as the name suggests – consists of hygiene and care on one side, and make-up on the other. Why would a brand such as Nivea, positioned on skincare and having successfully offered all possible skincare permutations worldwide, use Nivea Beauty to enter the world of seduction, play and appearance against such well-established giants as Maybelline, Max Factor and Bourjois?

As always, the answer has to be growth, image and profitability. After all, the make-up market is a rich seam of double-figure growth. Furthermore, it attracts new young customers. This fashion aspect lends the brand image a very modern appearance. And lastly, it is a profitable category.

However, Nivea still had to acquire legitimacy in this unexpected area. The first advertising campaign of Nivea Beauty was a failure; during extension, brands are often (naturally enough, perhaps) more preoccupied with their brand identity than with the customers in the target market. Nivea relied on bad insights. The sub-brand's positioning was 'All the colours of care' – but to a young target audience in the mass retail channel, this is not a relevant promise. At a chemist's it would have been a different story, hence the existence of La Roche Posay and Roc cosmetics. The brand re-positioned its beauty line on the market expectations and the long-term weaknesses of the competition. The new promise was, 'The most beautiful me'.

As we can see, this promise is no longer a straightforward translation of the essence of the brand (loving care for the skin), but neither is it inconsistent with the brand's equities. Nivea Beauty's promise is that it preserves a woman's natural beauty. This capitalises on Nivea's fundamental intangible values: respect, humanity, love, naturalness, simplicity. The promise derives from a consumer insight as a reaction against the totalitarian line taken by many make-up, cosmetics and beauty products brands, urging women to look like top models and stars. This time around, the relaunch was a success. In terms of extension, the challenge lies in the balance between market appropriateness and faithfulness to the brand's identity: it is created through successive adjustments.

The McCain example provides another illustration of the difficulty inherent in brand extension. Remember that McCain is a Canadian company, operating worldwide, with three branches: frozen fries (it supplies McDonald's throughout the world), frozen pizzas, and soft drinks. In 1998, noting the rising popularity of tea-based drinks in the soft drinks market, it decided to launch an ice tea, Colorado by McCain. The firm justified its choice of an endorsing brand architecture by the over-prominence of the 'raw' product's image (in light of the previous launch of McCain fries and pizzas in the relevant countries). Consumers were therefore intended to ask for the Colorado tea drink, with its intangible youthful Tex-Mex connotations, thus fitting it into the overall American brand identity.

The marketing team was not limiting itself to image. Mindful of the competitive nature of the market, it also created a highly differentiated product embodying an essential McCain identity trait: generosity. As a result, the can of tea contained 33 cl instead of the competitors' usual 25 cl. This decision was based on sound logic: it differentiated the extension in terms of the brand's equities, both intangible and tangible. Sadly, this was also one of the causes of the extension's failure. In reality, this differentiation, embodying the brand's spirit of generosity (and thus larger portions, as befits the stereotypical American), proved to be a problem. The can, being taller than other standard cans in the category:

▌ was unsatisfactory to retailers, who like to keep storage issues as simple as possible;

▌ was rarely drunk in full by customers, who thought it contained too much;

▌ appeared more expensive in terms of its retail price, even though the per litre price was the same.

Paradoxically, then, this differentiation generated long-term dissatisfaction – a fundamental error in the cut-throat environment of this double-figure growth market.

The most serious problem faced by this extension was probably the fact that it was up against Lipton, the world's number one in tea products, aggressively pushing its two megabrands (Lipton Ice Tea and Liptonic), with their associated promotional expenditure, to capture this market. Not even Nestea could compete, despite a strategic alliance with the Coca-Cola Company which ensured the distribution of its drink in all Coca-Cola vending machines. In the hypermarket – and thus the home consumption market – Nestea was powerless against Lipton.

At this point we should take another look at why strategic analysis is a higher priority than marketing analysis for the extension.

Assessing what should not change: the brand kernel

All extensions are real products or services, and real decisions have to be made concerning their attributes and characteristics. Typically the first extensions are very conservative. Then bolstered by success, extensions gain their degrees of freedom (from the prototype). This is the time when the issue of what should be left intact, unchanged, and what can change is asked.

Extension and respect for physical identity

One of the first questions raised in extensions is how far the brand can go from its physical basis. This especially true for brands whose identity rests heavily on their physical facets. Dove positioning for instance is based on its moisturising power, and the claim of 25 per cent moisturising cream content. This claim is maintained across extensions. All Orangina's extensions respect the ratio of 10 per cent real juice and 2 per cent real pulp in the bottle or can.

Typically, first extensions are very close to the original: Mars introduced a Mars ice-cream bar, for Mars looks like a bar. Only later would it dare to move to other formats and shapes. However, growth can only be found by gaining more degrees of freedom: self-imitation cannot suffice. In addition, extension is an extension of the same benefit elsewhere: it accentuates the move of the brand from pure product to concept, from pure tangible values to intangible values as well. Taillefine/Vitalinea is a leading yogurt brand based on good taste with 0 per cent fat. It made a successful extension in the biscuit market, but with a promise of 'less fat'. Finally it was extended to purified water, a product with no taste but with slimness benefits.

At some point in time, it is then possible and even necessary to forget the tangible root. Smirnoff is a vodka. However, Smirnoff Ice, the world's number one ready-mixed drink, is based on not vodka but malt whisky. Skyye Blue also is not vodka but whisky-based. Of course, this is not a guaranteed way to success. In the United States everyone knows that Captain Morgan is a brand of rum. To grow the business it too introduced Captain Morgan Gold, a ready-mixed drink. Instead of rum, it too used whisky as a basis. This ingredient switch created a number of strategic advantages:

▌ lower taxes;

▌ access to greater distribution than is possible for rum, for instance through beer distributors;

access to television advertising (not permitted for spirits in the United States).

The new product however failed. Consumers did not like the taste enough, a classic in food and drink new product failure.

In brand management, identity plays a key role – and this is doubly true in extensions management. If consumers reject the very idea of an extension, it is either because they cannot see what benefits it offers that the competition does not (the number one reason for the failure of extensions), or because they cannot see the logic of the extension under this brand. In other words, the extension is in conflict with their concept of the brand's essence and kernel of identity – that is to say, the handful of attributes without which the brand ceases to be the brand. So how can we gain an understanding of identity as perceived by consumers?

To return to basic theory for a moment, the brand – like any concept – is defined by essential and less essential traits. The former are identifying traits, and are thus crucial. The latter are variable: they may be prominent in some brand products and less prominent in others. In his work on the perception of stereotypes, Salomon Asch showed that some traits had a consid-

erable impact on overall perception, while others could be absent (or even contradictory) without affecting overall perception. Abric (1994) extended this theory to include social perceptions, and Mischel extended it to brands (2000). According to the theory, the brand changes over time by incorporating traits into its kernel which had until then been peripheral, featuring only in some of its products. These traits form the heart of the brand's vitality, the source of its ability to adapt to its ambient environment (see Figure 10.2, page 221).

So how do we find out which traits, from the consumers' point of view, are crucial to identity (the kernel), and which are peripheral? If the replies we obtain are to be valid, it is clear that we cannot put the question to consumers in a direct way.

An image study does not satisfy this objective, as it measures brand associations: for example, what tangible or intangible attributes are associated with the McCain brand? The first column of Table 11.7 shows the results. But which of the traits most strongly associated with McCain are actually identifying traits?

To find out, we have to ask an indirect question. The only way to find out if something is necessary is to take it away. This is

Table 11.7 Identifying and peripheral traits for a brand: the McCain example

Brand image (perceived typicalness, graded 1–7)		Brand kernel (percentage of 'no' votes for an extension that is not ...)
American	6.70	92
Fries	6.31	61
Pizzas	5.96	59
Handy	5.81	71
Modern	5.80	80
Young	5.79	62
Plentiful	5.35	74
Fun	5.27	62
Original	5.20	60
Friendly	5.16	58
Family-oriented	5.07	55
Dynamic	5.01	61

Source: based on Mischel, 2000, Vuibert

why we must ask interviewees whether the brand could make new products that are not fries and pizzas, are not American, are not in generous sizes, and so on. Wherever a consensus forms that a brand could not do this (more than 90 per cent 'no' votes), it is the sign of a trait belonging to the brand's kernel. The second column of Table 11.7 shows kernel traits and peripheral traits.

Two observations should be made about this example. First, the image order is not the same as the identity order. Fries are the second largest association, but not a kernel trait of the brand (nearly 40 per cent of interviewees would accept McCain innovations that were not fries). Second, none of the products associated with image is in the kernel. The essence of the brand lies elsewhere, in its tangible and intangible traits (American, modern, plentiful and available). The other traits are peripheral, and thus variable.

This method provides an understanding of what constitutes the kernel at a given moment, as perceived by customers or non-customers. It is a point of view that is heavily influenced by the past and by the brand's history. Management can bypass this if long-term considerations so dictate. The kernel measured here will identify the areas of possible resistance.

Preparing the brand for remote extensions

Not all brands lend themselves to extension. Some brands are defined only through their prototypical product or know-how. This is the case with cosmetic brands such as Clarins, Roc and Vichy. Their field of extension has to be limited within appropriate boundaries which combine both science and beauty.

Other brands are almost like sects and have quasi-religious principles: St Michael, the brand owned by Marks & Spencer, covers everything from food to clothes, from toys to para-pharmaceutical products and furnishing.

Through its signature it imparts legitimacy to all that is in conformity with the Marks & Spencer ideology. Like a patron saint (etymologically, patron means pattern, ie model to be followed), the brand transforms and elevates all the products that it sanctifies.

If the brand is to remain intact in the eyes of the consumer and not be fragmented into disconnected units, the prerequisites of a remote extension must be taken into consideration. For the extension of one brand into various remote categories to look coherent, one has to draw upon the deeper meaning of the brand. This supposes that the brand either has such meaning or has the potential to acquire it. The Swiss brand, Caran d'Ache, built its reputation through up-market pencils and writing tools. Its extension into scarves, wallets and leather items failed. The brand was missing the necessary deep meaning.

Figure 11.9 demonstrates the demands arising out of brand extension. Every degree of product dissimilarity changes the meaning and the status of the brand. Close extensions (B) are compatible with product or know-how brands: Heinz can market not only ketchup, but also mustard sauce. Extension one degree further (C) corresponds to brand benefits: Palmolive softens all that it embraces and Bic simplifies everything from pens to razors to lighters, making them disposable and cheap. A further extension (D), in order to be coherent with the initial product (A), assumes a brand defined by its personality. In the beginning, Sony was a brand exclusively for hi-fi systems. But in a few years it has acquired fame in the field of television sets and videos and has therefore modified its image and its significance, but its core values still remain technology, precision and innovation with a specific elegant and refined personality. The last extension (E) assumes a brand that is defined by deep values. Virgin is a good example.

Thus, the only way for a brand to give a single meaning to a collection of extensions is to regard them from a higher viewpoint. To

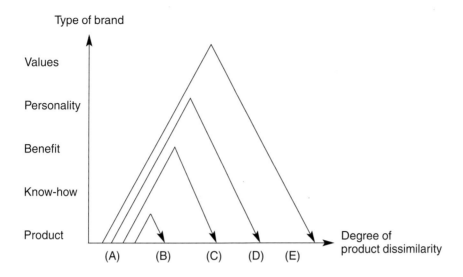

Figure 11.9   Type of brand and ability to extend

make distant extensions fit, the brand has to distance itself physically and serve more as a source of inspiration and a value system that can embed itself in different products. This is the case with Nestlé, a brand with a very large spectrum of offers. The distance helps to maintain the angle between the brand and its capacity to lend itself to different products. The steeper the angle, the greater force it exerts on the products (from A to E). The flatter this angle, the less is the force available to the brand to unify the products. Like an over-stretched rubber band, the brand becomes weak, loses its grip and finally breaks.

More concretely, brands having only a physical facet (a product, a recipe) and no intangible identity do not lend themselves to remote extensions. They become diluted and are no more than numbers (see X in Figure 11.10). This is the case with Mitsubishi. It no longer operates as a unifying brand but is only a corporate name and a factory trademark. It carries no signification other than the generic characteristics of Japanese technology and the image of industrial power that is associated with the group. Mitsubishi cars do not seem to

embody any particular ideal and neither do Mitsubishi televisions or tools. This is also the case with Philips to a certain extent.

Originally, Philips signified a certain know-how associated with products such as televisions, videos and hi-fi systems. But the brand did not carry with it any other meaning. Therefore, its extension into small household appliances and white goods was too far-fetched given the elasticity of the brand capital. Consumer surveys are proof of this fact: 80 per cent of people interviewed stated that Philips was a specialist of brown products, that these products belonged to its domain and that it was competent in this area. Only 60 per cent of the respondents thought the same for the household appliances and 40 per cent for white goods. Thus, Philips lost half its credibility as far as washing-machines and refrigerators were concerned. On these products the name was scarcely more than a simple guarantee, like that of a retailer or a quality seal. The need to economise having led to the policy of a single brand, its limitations were seen in the fact that different signatures were used for different products. But the brand signature

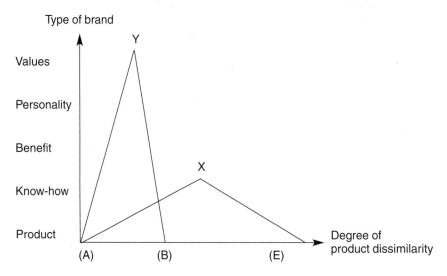

Figure 11.10   Under- and over-exploitation of a brand capital

should not exist in different forms. The brand is, after all, unique. The multiplication of slogans reflected the tensions imposed on the brand which was looking in vain for a unifying factor. The subsequent (and foreseen) phase was a concentration on only the core business of the brand and the sale of the white goods unit to Whirlpool.

At the other end of the spectrum are the underexploited brands. These (see Y in Figure 11.10) cover a very narrow product field but have an inner meaning which makes them legitimate over a large range of products. The initial objectives of the multiple retailer, Carrefour, were limited to the food sector, but soon found larger and larger areas in which to express themselves: textiles, bags, banking services. The social objective of Marks & Spencer, which is also the key to its identity, permits it to operate in a very large field of extensions. These brands do not promise a function, but a selection principle for their goods. In Marks & Spencer or Carrefour stores there are only St Michael or mostly Carrefour products. One might lose out on the freedom of choice, but that is normal because these brands are almost a cult in themselves.

The brand Dole was a typical example of under-exploitation. This brand underestimated its growth potential for a long time. Management considered the brand as a product and confined it to pineapple juice. But for consumers, Dole signified much more. Beyond its attributes (good taste, freshness and naturalness), lay a deeper core: sunshine. Dole was actually the sunshine brand and in this capacity could cover not only other fruit juices, but other products, eg ice creams. Very well known for a long time as a shoe brand, Salvatore Ferragamo has now successfully diversified into ladies' handbags, cardigans and ties.

As shown in Figure 11.9 (see page 275), the further a brand wants to move from its origins, the more it needs to have acquired a relevant tangible meaning. The senior citizens' brand, Damart, did not progress in one step from being an anti-cold mono-product (thermolactyl underclothes) to light ready-to-wear clothing for the summer and even swimming costumes. After 20 years of intensive television communication focused exclusively on thermolactyl, to the point that it was practically considered to be a product brand, the offer of ready-to-wear clothing was totally unacceptable under this brand. Furthermore, leaving aside all considerations about the brand, even in product terms the Damart ready-to-wear line did not offer anything more than the catalogues of the large direct-mail companies. The extension procedure consisted of two parallel actions, which reinforced each other:

▫ The evolution of the brand concept and its disconnection from the strict physical, material plane was achieved by giving it more tangible meaning so as to allow it to legitimise and nourish, equally, the ready-to-wear line offer and the traditional offer of winter underwear. As a result the brand changed its signature also: moving from the product slogan 'Cold? Me? Never!' to the brand slogan 'Living Fully'. This corresponded perfectly to the lifestyle needs of senior citizens. The latter slogan is based on the need for warmth in winter and the accent on active lifestyle in summer.

▫ Gradual extensions were made, starting from underclothes. Damart was a manufacturer's brand and had to propose a product that offered more. They first extended the thermolactyl to corsets, sports undergarments, panty-hose and socks. Then they developed a line of snug-fitting products that were both well adapted and comfortable. Finally, even in the ready-to-wear line they sought to develop clothes where a special element could be introduced.

Being well aware of the gradual nature of the process, Salomon did not want to repeat the failure of Rossignol in the field of snowboards and snow-surfing. This culture, which arose in opposition to the traditional skiing environment, refuses to support existing well-known brands. It looks for and worships its own cult brands. So, before entering the snowboard market with an innovation, the company decided to spend some time getting accepted by the youth, penetrating their world through another of their sports where a real value-added product could be offered: roller skates and inline skates (see page 228).

Research does, indeed, demonstrate that the order in which intermediate extensions are made affects consumer reaction to the final extension. Thus, in an experiment, consumers were presented with a sequence of five extensions for a number of brands. These extensions were chosen to represent five degrees of perceived distance or fit with the brand. In one case, consumers viewed an ordered sequence of extensions (from the closest to the farthest); in the second case they saw an unordered sequence of extensions (Dawar and Anderson, 1992). Two results emerged from this laboratory experiment.

As expected, there is a decrease in perceived coherence due to the distance between the extension and the brand's present product. However, the decrease in perceived coherence due to the distance is less steep when consumers saw the remote extension after a series of prior extensions presented in order of increasing distance. Each one may have acted as a stepping stone and prompted a category (brand) extension mechanism known as 'chaining' (Lakoff, 1987). The same result held true for the purchase likelihood for extensions.

Interestingly, it took less time to evaluate the farthest extension's coherence with the brand when that extension was seen at the end of the ordered sequence (4 seconds vs 4.34). Actually, the ordered sequence had itself modified the meaning of the brand, making it clear that it was not a product brand but a larger brand with a wider territory.

Again, a real-world illustration of this process is that of McCain. This brand entered the market with its frozen fries. After two years, it moved to large American pizzas, then to buns and recently to the fast-growing iced tea market. The meaning of McCain is now clear: American food, simple products, generous portions, fun to eat and innovative in their category. This brand territory will determine McCain's future extensions.

A second experiment demonstrated another basic rule of brand extension: only the coherence between extensions can create a brand territory. Two extensions may be equally remote from the core of the brand but not in the same direction. When a remote extension is presented to consumers after an intermediate extension in the same direction, this sequence increases the perceived coherence of that remote extension and its purchase likelihood (compared to the case where the intermediate extension is not in the same direction) (Dawar and Anderson, 1992).

Keys to successful brand extensions

What advice can one give to increase the probability of success of brand extensions? Based on both research and consulting, there do exist key steps and questions in the extension process which require particular attention.

Think of the big plan first

Extensions used to be managed too much on an ad hoc basis. Every new idea was screened and evaluated, then eventually implemented. Now this era has ended. Brand management entails a long-term vision for the brand itself. There should be a clear statement of where the management wants to lead the brand. The brand wants to be a leader of what? How should we define its leadership – by product? by category? by need? by target? One thing is sure: the ambition must be to construct some kind of leadership.

This long-term vision can be compared to a stairway. It shows the direction of the stairway and the steps to get to the desired position. Each proposal is then evaluated in relationship to this objective. A brand cannot just

stretch in all directions, but strategy should guide it. There is for instance a big difference in stating that Tide (Ariel) wants to lead the low-suds detergent market, and that it wants to be the brand for those who take trouble over the care of their textiles.

The limits of consumer research for managing extensions

The role of consumer research is to assess the level of risk. It indicates what difficulty may arise when using the same name on an extension. But research is not management. Brand management needs to integrate all dimensions of the decision. This is the fundamental rationale of this new edition of this book. Decisions about extensions will take into account production, financial, strategic and competitive factors, beyond the immediate reaction of consumers. Management is risk taking, a source of competitive advantage. Let us recall that consumers' reactions to brand extensions are reflections of the past. They rest on prior learnt associations. They are also short-term oriented. Management of brand extensions is based on a long-term vision. Prior to any extension, one question must be asked: what do we want the brand to look like in the future? Each extension is a step up the stairway to this goal. Consumers have no idea of the stairway.

Are our assets here really assets there?

Many extensions fail because someone has overestimated the value of the brand assets in the extension category. Are they really assets there? Do they really have a motivating value? Do they deliver an unprecedented array of benefits? Too often someone overestimates this point, making the assumption that the brand assets are relevant. For instance, most perfume brands are tempted to launch cosmetic lines, but very few have succeeded. The drivers in the latter market are focused on confidence and hope in research, and this is not what a perfume brand can provide. It has no credentials.

A second key question concerns competition. Does the proposed extension really beat its competition? Too much of extension research is concept testing: it asserts the attractiveness of the concept. However, in stores customers compare offerings, and assess their relative attractiveness. Certainly an extension may be welcomed in research exercises, but that does not mean it will win out in the purchasing decision. Customers may be reluctant to change their existing purchasing patterns for the new brand and product. At the moment of truth, is curiosity enough? There has to be a strong incentive (perceived difference) or a pioneer effect (acting first).

It is noticeable that Nestea, Nestlé's entry in the iced tea soft drink market, has not been successful in Europe, despite its strategic alliance with Coca-Cola, which distributes the product and offers it in all the vending machines it controls. However, there is one country where Nestea is leader: Spain. There and only there, Nestea was launched before Lipton's Ice Tea, and so benefited from the pioneer advantage.

Think of the full marketing mix of the extension

An extension is not simply a new product or service, it entails a full new marketing mix. It requires in fact that the organisation think more about the consumer than the brand. When Nike launched its Nike Women extension, its management was so infatuated with the brand itself that it forgot consumers. This is why it was a failure: the products (shoes and clothes) had the same design as their male counterparts, and only the sizes were adapted to women. Nike Women was not really a line for women at all. Soon it was discovered that to succeed in this extension, it was first necessary to create relevant products. Female designers were hired to rethink the product offerings.

In Europe, Perrier has always been hampered by its most differentiating attribute, its strong bubbles. This is why Nestlé (which owns the brand) has restored it to growth via two innovations/extensions. The first, called Perrier Fluo, targets young people who perceive Perrier as being the brand of their parents. It offers a sophisticated taste (for example, peppermint) and finer bubbles, making it easier to drink than the original Perrier. Perrier Fluo also has lower production costs, because the packaging is plastic (rather than glass), and the water used is not taken from the Vergèze spring, the brand's historic source. The second extension, called Eau de Perrier, targets adult mealtime drinking. To this end, a finer, more elegant bubble was created, and the sparkle of the product was adjusted to make it lighter.

As we can see, extension often takes the form of the adaptation – indeed, sometimes the radical modification – of the product or entire marketing mix. The main and only real reason for extension is growth. Often, the brand needs to go beyond a mere range extension to achieve a significant leap. Thus, in the United States, Smirnoff – currently the world's number two spirits producer – decided to enter the store multiples channel in addition to its traditional channel (liquor stores). To do this, it launched a new ready-to-drink (RTD) product, Smirnoff Ice, with a low alcohol content, backed by an advertising investment of US $70 million. It has sold more than 30 million cases and produced 'a positive spillover effect on Smirnoff's image'. The extension also led to the acquisition of competence in this new distribution channel.

When Ricard launched its own RTD in order to penetrate the night clubs, discotheques and night bars it had failed to enter with its core (and till that point, only) product, did it think enough of the new consumption situation associated with these places? After midnight, this simple RTD competes with all kinds of cocktails. It should therefore have been aromatised to better answer the needs of that situation. This extension is consumed in a specific place, at a specific time, and this had implications for the product itself. The same holds true for distribution. Extensions are often ways to get out of the classic distribution channels and become closer to the public's need.

Extension should meet trade expectations too

In its desire to maintain its dominant share of market in the UK, Smirnoff has shown the way by following a dual strategy. One part is aimed at adults, its present target market, with the introduction of Smirnoff Blue, Smirnoff Lemon and Smirnoff Black for instance, to compete with Absolut and Finlandia. The other is aimed at the youth market through Smirnoff Mule and later Smirnoff Ice, two ready-mixed drinks which gained high success and were soon imitated. The success of Smirnoff Mule demonstrates that all good innovations must provide value to the distributor *and* to the consumer.

The strategic goal was to establish these new products among young people for on-premise consumption. On Friday or Saturday nights, many pubs are literally full up and people gather outside them. Smirnoff Mule brings bartenders a faster way to serve clients than a draught beer, with a better margin: they just have to hand the bottle over to customers, without the need for a glass. Meanwhile, the bottle with its highly visible branding acts as a badge, an identifier for customers, unlike a glass of beer which generally does not carry a brand name. This is a very important motivation for 18/24-year-olds who are insecure about their image. In addition, advertising reinforced the modern status of the new drink. More than £4.5 million was spent on Smirnoff Ice to launch it among young males (Mule having been mostly chosen by females).

The question of resources

The main source of failure of extensions is a lack of resources for the launch. Companies should remember that if an extension is aimed at a different market, its launch should be treated as a new product launch. Unfortunately many companies extend their brand, thinking that it is a way to save money compared with launching a new brand, and that a simple mention at the end of the regular 30-second television ad will suffice. It might do for a simple line extension, a variant, but not for a brand extension.

Companies also hesitate to divert investment from core products to finance an extension. They feel that by doing so they will put their core product at risk from competition. As a consequence, they decide at the last moment not to support the extension with the required budget. This reasoning underestimates the reciprocal spillover effect. Communicating the benefits of a new product has an effect on the sales of the core product (see page 178). This is one of the virtues of mega-brands covering multiple products: they get re-energised through communication about their new products.

Can we implement it?

Concepts are one thing, but success requires a perfect implementation. Too often people try to explain extension failures by suggesting there are deep psychological reasons that it could not have worked. In fact the truth is much more prosaic. For example, most food extensions fail because the product does not taste good; and if an extension forces the company to master new many competences at the same time, it may fail to master some of them, creating disillusion in the channel, if not anger. This is why so many companies prefer alliances.

Advertising the extension

The problem of identity versus diversity is most visible in advertising the extension. The brand should set simple, precise rules for managing this balance. For example, Nivea operates a very strict code in this respect. This is what creates the brand's typical 'Niveaness' in all its advertising worldwide, despite its 14 sub-brands. The essence of this brand is 'loving care for the skin', thus making it a proximity brand, which in practical terms translates into remarkable continuity and 'Niveaness' over time:

▮ There is no over-promise.

▮ Nivea speaks to each woman through people she can relate to: unpretentious blonde models who are pure, healthy and vital, but not excessively made up (in other words, no stars or top models, unlike l'Oréal Paris).

▮ Nivea believes that beauty is a pleasure, while l'Oréal Paris sees it as a battle. in all advertising the colour code remains blue, with a cool, calm, relaxed atmosphere.

However, the sub-brands have certain distinguishing characteristics in what they communicate. Each is there to lend something to the brand: its own individual personality, as well as certain customer segments and peripheral attributes. This is embodied in advertising that is remarkably unified, but not uniform. The brand flourishes by stating its diversity. Lastly, it is significant that each sub-brand has its own brand design: the standard Nivea logo may remain intact, but diversity rules.

From a budgetary point of view, companies are discovering one by one that a successful extension gives consumers a chance to discover or rediscover the brand. It must therefore be allocated all the resources it requires for its launch. Although it would be wrong to cease all investment on the central flagship product if launching a dissimilar, distant extension, such investment can – indeed, must – be stopped when the extension is closer. The reciprocal spillover effect explains this logic.

Extending the brand extensions

After a successful line or brand extension is created, one major question that soon arises concerns its geographical extension. In what countries should it be developed? In answering it is important to remember that extensions are often created in response to a specific market problem. For instance Orangina Red (with red oranges and guarana energising ingredients) was created to challenge Coke's appeal among the major soft drink gulpers, the teens. Coke's appeal is based on thrill and mystery: it is a black drink with a secret formula that can be mixed with forbidden (to teens) alcohols. Orangina Red was created to be the more thrilling and adventurous extension of Orangina. However, this logic only applies in countries where Orangina is in fact competing across flavours. In the United States for instance, it held a niche position within the 'new age' segment of orange-flavoured drinks. Orangina Red would make no sense there, while Orangina Light would.

Nivea's sub-brands are not present equally in all countries. The fashionable Nivea Beauty is not sold in the United States, for instance, although in this case it is because the sub-brand roll-out strategy (see page 245) has not reached this point.

Another reason for differences between countries is based on the potential of the country and the status of the parent brand within it. For instance, should Evian launch Evian Affinity in Japan or Korea? This extension is in line with the latest Evian positioning based on health, aesthetics and eternal youth, and Evian water is certainly known in Korea and Japan, but it commands a very low market share.

What name for brand extensions?

Why is Chanel's entry in the cosmetics market called Precision, and why does Biotherm call its entry in the male market Biotherm Homme? Obviously the question of the name cannot be separated from that of the chosen brand architecture (see Chapter 12). If it is decided to follow an umbrella brand architecture there should be no specific names. Architectures based on source brands and endorsing brands allow for another name.

The naming decision must satisfy two demands. First, it should help the extension succeed. By a name one can underline specific traits or benefits of the extension, or counterbalance possible negative thoughts. Second, it should not dilute the parent brand equity.

Fashion and perfume brands are not that legitimate in the highly scientific cosmetic market, where women are looking for innovative ingredients, not just dreams or fashion. Chanel's choice of Precision helped bypass the negative prejudice against this type of extension for perfume and couturier brands.

Many years ago, when there was still a lot of male prejudice against cosmetics, Vichy decided to name its male line Basic Homme de Vichy. Men were just not ready to buy Vichy for Men. In fact, at that time Vichy had not repositioned itself on effectiveness and health, but was a mid-range cosmetics line. Now its message is that health is tied up with skin condition. This message, this vision, has no sex, and is extendable directly to men. In addition the market has changed, and men are more open to buying cosmetic products. Basic Homme de Vichy was renamed Vichy Homme.

The name should also not dilute the parent brand equity. Too often, just because the parent brand is old, or seen as such in public surveys, the extension receives a new brand name, and the parent brand is hidden, in a typical endorsing architecture. This creates a self-fulfilling prophecy: hidden, the parent brand gets older and older in the public perception. The role of new products and brand extension is always to take from the brand equity but also to give to brand equity: imbalanced exchanges should be avoided.

As a rule, and as was discussed with reference to the multicircular picture (see page 248), the more remote an extension from the brand core values, the more it should have an endorsing architecture and as a result a brand name of its own. The closer it is to the core, the more it should adopt an umbrella architecture, and receive a generic or descriptive name. For instance a prepaid card for mobile phones could be called Mobicard or BT Nomad Card, but surely not Nomad ... by BT.

Checking what the extension brings to the brand

An extension uses brand capital. This is not surprising, since it was created to do so: the brand is a business development tool. It is therefore logical that we should seek to exploit this capital by putting it to productive use in new growth categories. However, we must also ensure a win–win outcome. After all, what does a brand extension really deliver? Sales alone are not enough. The benefits to be derived by the brand from this extension must be clearly specified:

Each extension from Kinder confectionery is aimed at a particular target, age segment or situation of use. Each also gives the brand widened relevance and less of a narrow image. This must be specified clearly in advance, and then measured afterwards.

Of course, we must be all the more careful to avoid any risk of dilution, as can happen when the values associated with the extension category contradict those of the brand, or when it is known that implementing the extension will be risky. After all, the implementation is the part customers see.

Is the market really attractive?

The first thing to evaluate in a brand extension is not the extension, it is the market attractiveness of the category. The key question in evaluating a brand extension is the intrinsic value of the category. Later, we examine this from the point of view of the business and the brand. This presupposes that we are considering not only the present but also the future of the category. An extension is not an overnight affair, it marks the beginning of a desire to invest in a new market. The extension itself is no more than a bridgehead. A realistic analysis of existing strengths, threats and opportunities is therefore required. Clearly, this corresponds to the traditional SWOT model.

Opportunities derive from the relationship between the factors for success in the category and the organisation's key competences, both tangible and intangible. They also derive from the brand's ability to segment the category according to its own values, or in other words to create genuinely relevant differentiation. Strategic analysis also analyses the future of competition and the organisation's relative strengths. Will its entry into the market trigger a competitive reaction, and if so, how big? To answer this question, it is necessary to evaluate the importance of the category to competitors.

To repeat, the fact that a brand *can* be extended does not mean it *should* be extended. One must take into account future competition and the costs of remaining a significant player in the category (the rate of innovation, rate of launches, marketing and sales investment and so on). Extension is not an inside feat: it must deliver a sustainable advantage. For instance, many food companies have thought of launching a frozen pizza, but what would they do next to capture shelf space from Buitoni or McCain, or to defend their own shelf share? In the middle term, who is the best position to innovate most often? Table 11.8 presents a multi-criteria strategic analysis evaluation.

The question of resources

As mentioned above, the main source of failure of extensions is the lack of resources for the launch.

Should we implement it alone? Partnerships and licences

It is difficult for a company to master the many new competences needed for an extension at the same time, which is why so many companies prefer alliances:

▌ Nestlé won the battle in Europe against Kellogg's once it decided to find a technical partnership with the American General Mills.

▌ Weight Watchers' expansion in the pre-cooked meals category was made possible through a co-branding agreement with Fleury Michon, a leader in this field.

▌ Evian asked Coca-Cola to distribute it in the United States, where its core brand urgently needed to be made more available. It also asked Johnson & Johnson to develop and market Evian Affinity (its cosmetics line) worldwide.

One of the criteria in the strategic matrix for evaluating extensions concerns the company's ability to produce this extension. Of course, we are not suggesting that extensions should be restricted to categories that the company is itself capable of producing. Mars had no expertise in ice cream, nor did it have any knowledge of the buyers in this category, and hence it subcontracted production of Mars ice cream, its first major extension outside the chocolate bar market. All Cacharel extensions are based on licences: Playtex for hypermarket lingerie until 2004, l'Oréal for perfumes, household items by Arnolfo di Cambio and so on. In total, of a turnover of 35 million euros last year, royalties (extensions) accounted for 7.6 million euros.

Table 11.8 Extension strategic evaluation grid

	Extension 1	Extension 2	Extension 3
Is it a growing market?			
Are its success factors close to our strengths?			
Are the brand assets transferable?			
Are the brand assets still assets in this market?			
Will it impact positively the brand equity?			
How entrenched are competitors?			
How fast can they copy?			
Does the product have a clear differentiation?			
Is it a motivating difference?			
Can the company produce it?			
Can it produce at a normal cost?			
Will distribution accept it?			
Is it consistent with brand or company identity?			
Does it capitalise on the brand or company's present customers?			
Is it consistent with the brand or company's positioning?			
Does it capitalise on the company's expertise in:			
– production?			
– advertising?			
– logistics?			
– sales forces?			
– retail location?			
– pricing/promotion?			
Does is meet the company's profitability objectives?			
Can the company sustain competition			
(does it have the financial resources needed to compete)?			

Licences can enable extensions to move quickly into categories in which the brand has no experience of production, logistics or distribution. Some famous brands have never produced or even distributed their own products, but have instead operated on the basis of production and distribution licences throughout their existence, along with regional sub-licences, while retaining control over design, creation, strategic marketing and communication.

A few classic implementation errors

After the event all successes or failures of extensions can easily be explained. The problem is that decisions are made at a time of uncertainty. Brand extension is much like a new product launch, and as is well known most product launches fail. However launching new products is a necessity to sustain a competitive advantage.

All managers know that the most difficult question in the brand extension process is, how far can one stretch the brand? Let us be clear: going far is not an end in itself. However, growth markets are where they are. In fact, paradoxically, it is the brand extensions that reveal the limits. Before they are tried, research is always somewhat ambiguous. When it failed in the perfume business Bic learnt its limits, but also its strengths.

Bic, an innovating company, had always succeeded by disruptive innovations. Who before Bic would have dared fight against

Gillette by creating the segment of disposable razors for a cool shave? Bic management thought that among the young generation there would be at least 10 per cent of unconventional types who would appreciate a real natural quality essence, made less expensive thanks to low-cost minimalist packaging with a twist of humour. Unfortunately, although the product sold well in Italy, it did not reach the profitability objectives set by Bic worldwide. Success or failure is only ever relative to a set of assigned objectives. From this experience Bic management learnt that perfume purchases are driven by intangible values, and most important, that it should not ask its brand to deliver sensuous, intangible benefits.

The same holds true for Unilever's best-selling margarine Becel. After having failed to extend the brand as widely as had been hoped (Kapferer, 2001), it learnt when, in what situations, what kind of consumers really did need a low-cholesterol spread. Its other attempts had appeared to be relevant, but it had not dug deep enough into purchase motivations in these extension categories. A Becel-based chocolate is rationally attractive, and makes sense, but in reality it was not purchased. Chocolate purchases are dominated by the indulgence motive: even people who worry about their health forget their problem once in a while in order to taste a real treat.

Brand extension is a strategic procedure that deals with both the future and the capital of the brand. It is a delicate act which explains the need for a safe methodology and studies of potential. There are certain pitfalls along the road of extension and we will study them presently.

A restricted vision of the brand

Many companies have a very restricted vision of their brands. They take them to be nothing more than descriptive names. Thus, the brand extension programme is limited to a few variations of the main product. It is this conception of their brand that prevented Orangina from

benefiting from the rising popularity of grapefruit at the outset. Clinging to a notion that Orangina meant orange and only orange, the brand shut itself off from this growing demand. Young consumers were far less conservative. To them Orangina represents a cool soft drink, and they do not restrict it to only one flavour. Palmolive does not contain any extracts of olive either in its soaps, shaving foam or dishwashing liquid. In fact the brand obliterates the semantic associations of the words that support it: when one thinks of Palmolive, one never thinks of olives.

Does this mean that the presence of the word 'olive' has been completely neutralised? The reality is that the meaning of the word has been suppressed but it still remains deep within the brand as latent potential. Palmolive carries in its name a vision linked to the olive which entrenches itself in the objective and subjective qualities of the products that are signed with the name. There is no need for these products to have olive extracts; it is the signification of the olive and not its physical presence that forms the extension programme for the brand.

Opportunism and identity incoherence

Aware of the boom in the sector of 'light' foods, many companies jumped at the opportunity to profit from it. But, it was a wrong move for quite a few, which is why there is no 'Heineken Light'.

Extension is rife in the luxury goods market where opportunities for licensing abound. One can thus find china and cutlery in a Nina Ricci boutique. It is not the right brand for such extensions. What is right for Hermès isn't necessarily so for Nina Ricci because Nina Ricci's identity is based on the image of the woman whose virginal symbol is the hymen, and china belongs to the social universe of the lady of the house, the lady with status. It is compatible with brands such as Hermès or Dior, which are based on a social status, or a brand such as Yves Saint Laurent, which is based on seduction. It is not coherent with the identity and the universe of Nina Ricci.

The trap of mundane products

Choosing a category of very simple and mundane products prevents a brand from segmenting the category and leaving its own traces. The brand can only add its name as an imaginary halo but cannot change the product in any distinctive manner. In the short term this can lead to an additional flurry of sales due to consumers attracted by a well-known brand name and its promise of excellent quality. In the medium term this can weaken the brand. Attaching the brand to a product whose added value as a result of the inclusion of the brand name is not immediately obvious renders the brand extension artificial and only a commercial act. A true brand is one whose image is embedded in the product's characteristics.

A category of mundane products does not permit the establishment of qualitative differences so a big brand cannot exploit all its potential and knowledge. For example, Thomson did not benefit from the image of Thomson Industry (radars, weapons and electronics) when it tried to sell household appliances.

The case of luxury goods: Licences and accessories

Are Chanel T-shirts and Cardin cigarettes examples of this syndrome too? Big signatures expand into mundane categories such as handkerchiefs, socks, cigarettes, etc, through licensing agreements. The only difference between a handkerchief and a Cardin handkerchief is the brand name. The Cardin version supports the brand through the motif and the consumer wears it as a sign of his allegiance just as people wear religious symbols or their candidate's logo during elections. That is why the watch is adopted by any and every

brand. In showing the time; it serves as a medium to display the brand also.

The brand, as we have said, is additive – it is the sum total of its own attributes. The long-term danger for Chanel is that their T-shirts might come to be considered as an attribute of Chanel. Made in China, generic but sold at a high price, they may evoke the excess of luxury brands. And one has to accept that the T-shirt is an uninspired garment that is worn by people who do not exactly have the Chanel look. A very wide distribution of the garment can be detrimental to the guarantee of refinement which is one of the pivotal features of the brand's identity.

When a brand proliferates, not in all directions but into uninspiring products such as cigarettes, handkerchiefs, ties and various other accessories, the brand's capital asset is drained. Cardin is the prototype of this phenomenon. When the name is splashed on all kinds of products, it becomes insignificant just like the word 'de luxe' which is today used for everything from cars to cheap beers. Or was it perhaps part of Cardin's plans to exhaust the brand by spreading out in all 'cardinal' directions?

Complementarity is not guarantee

The graveyard of brand extension is littered with extensions that were considered risk-free. Panzani pasta failed in their efforts to sell Panzani tomato sauce. Yet one can understand the temptation to market the sauce, an indispensable accompaniment to a good pasta dish. Campbell, the soup brand, considered it quite natural to launch a spaghetti sauce. This seemed obvious for a brand whose leading products included tomato sauce. But, it was a failure and was relaunched under the name Prego. Similarly, Becel margarine was never able to launch Becel oil.

Therefore, it is not the products themselves which determine the possibilities of extension, but the fit with the brand's core identity. Barilla succeeded where Panzani could not, and it was not because Panzani's management was incompetent. The pure Italianness of Barilla legitimised its extension. Similarly, Lacoste sold tennis rackets but not the strings. These always wear out very quickly and disappoint the player. No brand proclaiming durability would want to attach their name to such a product.

Underestimating the risks for the brand

Certain extensions include some risks which cannot be excluded. The worst-case scenario can always happen. This is the reason why, in spite of all temptations, Fisher-Price did not enter into the child-care products market. This would have been consistent with the brand, but accidents are very common with these products and the resultant publicity could have had unwanted repercussions on the other activities of the brand.

The group Wagons-Lits decided to enter the market for luxury travel that was targeted towards the elite. Approached for the use of their name, Hermès eventually refused. The unforeseen risks of the service sector – especially the travel world – would have exposed the brand to risks that it did not want to undertake. They are well able to control events in their shops in the Faubourg St-Honoré, but would be helpless when it comes to problems with hotels in Tibet.

Not anticipating negative evocations

On a psychological level, brand extension assumes three hypotheses: first, that the positive associations linked with the brand will be transferred to the new product; second, that negative associations will not be transferred; third, that a positive trait of the brand will not become negative when associated with the new product. The purpose of market research is to verify these hypotheses. The role of communication is to ensure that the second and the third hypotheses continue to hold true.

Thus, the concept of Colgate or Signal chewing gum will spontaneously evoke the sensation of a pharmaceutical taste. This attribute may be positive when associated with toothpastes, but becomes negative when linked with chewing gums. Moreover, it would be a mistake to focus communications around dental hygiene as that would only serve to reinforce the negative associations stemming from the imagined taste. Communications should, on the contrary, stress the pleasure of the taste of chewing gum and the taste of mint. Communication therefore helps to block the risks of the transfer of the negative aspects of the brand. This is why Diet Coke stresses its taste.

The temptation to under-invest

Advertising costs cannot be supported for too many brands and so the brand portfolio has to be trimmed. Furthermore, since the brand is already known, its seems normal to under-invest on communication for an extension as compared to the launch costs for a new brand. An analysis was carried out by Nielsen under the supervision of Peckham (1981) illustrating the dangers of such an attitude in the consumer goods market (see page 253).

Nielsen studied 115 new product launches in three segments: body care, food and hygiene. Results showed that within two years new products launched under their own name achieved twice the market share of products launched under an already existing name (6.7 per cent versus 3.3 per cent for body care, 6.5 per cent versus 1.9 per cent for food). Is brand extension a mistake?

Deeper analysis revealed the true reason for this difference in performance. Products launched under their own name had launch budgets twice as big as those for brand extensions. To eliminate this bias they recalculated market share obtained on a proportional basis. The results were then equal for both.

When advertising hides the new product

Well-known brands should treat with extreme prudence the forecast sales figures emerging from consumer reactions and test market simulations (like Bases or Assessor). In these studies consumers are well aware that they are dealing with new products, but in national launches of extensions many of the target clientele might not even know that it is a new product. The advertisement is well seen, but not the product. This risk is augmented when the brand uses a symbol or a person who has become so familiar that the public no longer awaits (and therefore, does not hear) any informative message. They believe that every appearance of the brand is a friendly reinforcement and not an announcement for a new product. In fact, people often attribute to well-known brands products that are not actually made by them. This is exactly what happened to Andrex when they decided to challenge Kleenex in the paper handkerchief market in the UK. The attack tactic was the development of a family-size format in combination with the inherited values of the Andrex name (Yentis and Bond, 1995). Based on test market simulations, sales were predicted at 11.6 million units. In reality, they were only 10 million units in the first year. The reason for this was that even before the launch, Andrex handkerchiefs had 6 per cent spontaneous awareness and 60 per cent assisted awareness. These users were therefore not even conscious of a new launch (unlike the consumers used for the simulation and the test marketing). Thus, the commercial had to be reshot a second time to highlight the real novelty of the product both for Andrex and for the market. This problem is aggravated when one can only use the press as the medium of communication for a launch.

An extension-based business model: Virgin

Most brands conjure up an image of a product or service: shoes for Nike, yoghurt for Danone, ballpoint pens for Bic, a holiday village for Club Med, and so on. This is not surprising: before they became brands, they started out as a simple product or service, driven by marketing and sales. Virgin is an exception: who associates that brand with only one product or service? Indeed, Virgin now comprises 200 companies and 25,000 people working for the brand worldwide. It has a turnover in excess of 7 billion euros, and has become one of the world's top 50 brands. Even in countries in which it does not operate, it is still a famous brand.

It all started in 1969, when Richard Branson decided to launch a direct record-selling operation, enabling many groups without distribution by the 'majors' to gain access to the general public. The brand's DNA is already apparent in this founding act: Branson seeks out opportunities in markets choked by 'false' competition. He asks himself how he can operate differently from the leaders – who have usually frozen the market to their advantage. The Virgin name was chosen because it was friendly and modern, and could be applied to sectors other than just music. This last consideration alone presaged the business model that would follow.

Virgin's originality lies in the fact that it is held together by one entirely intangible 'glue', its brand. This is why the brand architecture is umbrella branding. Every year, Virgin launches itself into new businesses and pulls out of others. In under 20 years, Richard Branson has extended the brand to the following sectors (and subsequently pulled out of some of them):

▌ First business: mail order (1969).

▌ Records: Virgin Records (label created in 1973 and sold to EMI in 1992).

- Radio: Virgin Radio.

- Video games: Virgin Games (1983).

- Distribution: Virgin Vision (1983), Virgin Megastores (1988) and Virgin Bride (1996) for brides-to-be.

- Cosmetics: Virgin Vie.

- Drinks: Virgin Cola, Virgin Vodka (1994).

- Computers: PCs manufactured by ICL Fujitsu (1996), Internet terminals manufactured by Internet Appliance Network (2000).

- Air transport: Virgin Atlantic Airways (1984), Virgin Cargo (1984), Virgin Express (1996).

- Rail transport: Virgin Railways (1997).

- Tourism: Virgin Holidays (1895), tour operator, Virgin Sun.

- Hotels and pensions: Virgin Hotels, Virgin Pensions (for senior citizens).

- Financial services: Virgin Direct Financial Services (by telephone, 1995), Virgin Bank.

- Internet: Virgin Net (1996).

- Utilities: Virgin Power House (2000): water, gas and electricity.

In a sense, Virgin is like the Japanese *keiretsus*, horizontally structured conglomerates consisting of independent companies that share one name and one set of values. How can a brand spread itself in so many directions without specific competencies and with minimal investment? Of course, the more widely the brand spreads itself into apparently dissimilar extensions, the greater the need for an intangible link (see Figure 11.11) – and this link consists of the Virgin brand's values. Its extensions actually form a family of independent companies that share the values of the Virgin brand.

To finance his expansion, Branson usually seeks support from appropriate partners in order to minimise his own investment, even if this means not being the majority shareholder. The partner thus provides the sector know-how, the money, and its own energy as an entrepreneur. For example, Virgin Megastores in the UK are 75 per cent owned by the W H Smith group. Similarly, Virgin Vodka was manufactured and distributed by William Grant in a 50/50 partnership with Branson.

Virgin allows start-ups to begin with a world brand as their 'birth gift', significantly reducing their necessary advertising expenditure – particularly as Branson is well aware

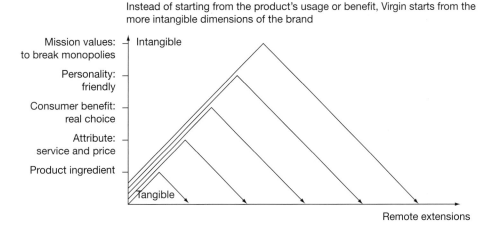

Figure 11.11 The Virgin extension model

of the financial benefits of repeated public relations exercises such as his balloon trip around the world, or riding down Fifth Avenue in a Patton tank to celebrate the launch of Virgin Cola. Branson also resells his businesses, but only after having added what makes them valuable in the eyes of the public – his brand. For example, the French Megastores were sold to Lagardère, and Virgin Atlantic Airways went to Singapore Airlines. Of course, the Virgin brand remains the property of Virgin Enterprises, a company of which he is the sole owner.

Virgin's extensions are remarkable in that they are truly based on a strategic analysis of the sector. But in addition, like any healthy extension, they deliver far more than just a name to customers: they represent true innovation which remains consistent with the brand's values. As its name so prophetically suggests, Virgin aims to take a brand new, 'virgin' approach to markets and operate in a different way from the 'majors'. Virgin has a rebellious, extraverted personality. Its ambition is to 'unblock' markets and liberate consumers from meaningless choices between dominant market leaders. Its commercial proposition is innovation, quality and fun. The result is a product range totally different from those of its competitors, targeting a younger audience and better value for money, all under the 'gis of an aspirational brand.

After all, in order to succeed, innovation is required at every stage, even if it means being copied: Virgin Atlantic Airways was the first company to offer a Volvo-chauffeured collection service for its business class clients from their offices, and a bathroom at the arrival airport. On board, Virgin innovated with the first personal video screens, followed by relaxing massages and the like. Another example is Virgin Cola, which innovated by offering an excellent taste, produced by the Canadian firm Cotts (bought out by Virgin in 1998), at a price nominally 10–15 per cent lower than that of Coke, with widespread distribution.

However, the system has its limits: extensions do not always work (a fact that applies to Virgin just as it does to any other firm, of course). The further you get from the British zone of influence, the weaker and less emotive the Virgin brand becomes. This makes the high visibility associated with the Megastores music and entertainment brand a prime tool for generating recognition and empathy among young people from all countries.

Paradoxically, Virgin's failures do not seem to have damaged its business model. In situations where many brands would have packed up and gone home, Virgin simply continues to expand elsewhere. After all, should we criticise David if he loses to the Goliaths every now and then? At least he tried. But can this brand and business model last forever? Not if the extensions fail too frequently. An analysis of the failures readily shows when an extension has been inappropriate:

- When it adds nothing other than just competition. This was what happened with Virgin Clothing, abandoned in 2000. London already buzzes with creators, rebels and anti-conformists. In a fragmented market with extremely wide price variations, what could Virgin add?

  The same is true of Virgin Cola. In Europe, Pepsi already plays the role of the fly in Coca-Cola's ointment. Furthermore, the multiples' purchasing centres chose not to stock the brand, thus starving it of access to the public. A question mark also hangs over Virgin Express: despite the fact that Virgin Atlantic Airways and its battle against British Airways assumed emblematic status, the act of starting yet another low-cost airline to compete with Ryanair failed to connect with the brand's mission. There are no dominant leaders in this sector, and customers do not feel trapped.

- When the scale of investment required pushes the fulfilment of the promise back into the long-term future. This is what has happened to Virgin Rail. In the UK, the brand's entry into commuter railways has not made any real difference to commuters' daily life: it has not been able to deliver a better experience. True, the dilapidated state of the rolling stock and infrastructure, handed over to the firm 'as is' under privatisation, ensured there could be no miracle: a network cannot be changed that quickly. Similarly, profitability issues concerning the MGM cinemas taken over by Virgin in 1995 prevented any real price reductions – one of the terms of the brand contract.

Without Richard Branson himself, could the Virgin group succeed? Given its founder's aura, and his ability to attract the attention of the media and to concentrate energy and investors around him, it must be concluded that Virgin is Branson himself. This is the brand's strength, but also its weakness. As with luxury brands, we should remember that a brand only truly begins with the loss of its founder.

12

Brand architecture: managing brand and product relationships

Why did l'Oréal stop calling its professional line 'Tecniart by l'Oréal' and use instead 'l'Oréal Tecniart'? Why do Japanese companies market their products under one brand name, which happens to be the same as that of the corporation? Why do such retailers as Dominick's, Carrefour or Sainsbury use their store name as a brand name for their own-label products whereas Kroger's used to carry completely different store labels (before moving recently to one single name)?

All these issues refer to brand–product relationship. All companies have to deal with this once they stop producing only one product.

The difficulty of the decision is linked to the dual function of brands. The World Organization for Industrial Property defines a brand in legal terms as a name or symbol serving to guarantee the product origin and to distinguish the products or the services of one company from those of another. Thus, globally, a brand has two functions:

▌ to distinguish different products from each other;

▌ to certify a product's origin.

But as the company starts growing over a period of time, the simultaneous realisation of these two objectives becomes difficult. Philips puts its own name on its televisions (what is usually called corporate branding): but what then are televisions called which are also made by Philips, but are of a lower standard and price than the former? To differentiate between them, they named the latter Radiola and, in doing so, they concealed any clues to the origin of the product. On the other hand, Holiday Inn preferred, initially, to emphasise the origin of their hotels of a higher grade by calling them Holiday Inn Crowne Plaza.

As one would suspect, the multiplication of products in a company first calls for some thought to be given to how the system of names and symbols (emblems, colour etc) given to products will be organised. This system should clarify the overall offer and structure it in such a way that it is easily understood by prospective buyers. It should be logical and follow rules that can be understood and applied by the various divisions of the company. The system should also help sales and product promotions in the short term and the establishment of brand-capital in the medium term. Lastly, it should be able to anticipate the future and possible evolutions in product-lines and ranges in order to last and be applicable to all new products.

There are six structural models of the brand–product relationship. We will discuss their advantages and disadvantages presently. These models can be applied to the corporation itself and its corporate brand, and to the many brands it promotes, thus creating more variants as shown in Figure 12.1. Second, armed with concepts and models, we will study why many companies have chosen one or the other or a mixed model. Third, we will identify the principal failures and dysfunctions appearing in brand–product relationships and in the development of brands. In the following chapter we will also tackle the problem of the number of brands to keep for a certain market or a certain company.

Branding strategies

An analysis of company strategies reveals six models in the management of brand–product (or service) relationships. Each model denotes a certain role for the brand, its status as well as its relationship (nominal and/or visual) with the products which the brand encompasses:

- the product brand;
- the line brand;
- the range brand;
- the umbrella brand;
- the source brand;
- the endorsing brand.

To each of these six forms of brand–product relationship we can ask another question: should the brand name be that of the corporation or distinct from it?

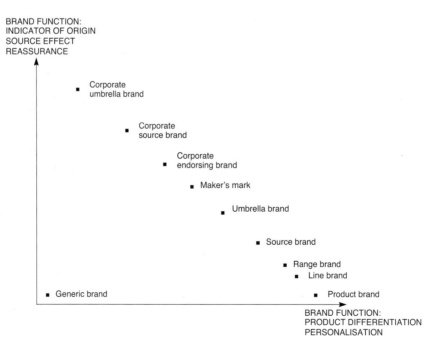

Figure 12.1   Positioning alternative branding strategies

This creates nine typical architectures, which can be positioned on a two-dimensional graph (see Figure 12.1), related to the two essential functions of a brand: either to certify the authenticity of the source (source effect) or to personalise, to differentiate the product.

Branding strategy and brand valuation

Branding strategy should not be seen as a formal design problem but rather a matter of deciding on the value flows to be created between the different parts and products of a company. The central issue is therefore the valuation of the offering, through the agency of the company itself.

The business angels and investment funds have got it right. For example, in the cosmetics sector, there is more to be gained from the resale of a 'branded house' than a basket of mixed brands, however well known, grouped together within a 'house of brands'. For example, Garnier has become a 'branded house', a house with a house spirit and house values that in return influence the positioning of the brands under Garnier. In fact, Garnier is itself a brand with a specific identity. SCAD, on the other hand, is a 'house of brands' that groups together brands as diverse as Dop, Vivelle, Dessange and J L David. SCAD is merely a commercial and marketing organisational structure.

In the cosmetics sector, a 'house of brands' is valued at six times the profits, while a 'branded house' enjoys an overvaluation that brings the P/E (Price-Earnings) ratio to 7 or 8. Similarly, as soon as a company is quoted on a stock exchange, all internal separatist tendencies – such as sub-brand logos protected jealously from the corporate brand – must cease. What had previously been of little consequence becomes unacceptable. All value flows must converge on the stock brand, since the market valuation of the company presupposes that the company capitalises on all sources of value created by its subsidiaries and sub-brands. Everyone and everything in the company contributes to this, including branding strategy.

Industrial companies are only just beginning to appreciate the importance of brands in terms of their profitability.

The product brand strategy

It is widely known that a brand is at the same time a symbol, a word, an object and a concept: a symbol, since it has numerous facets and it incorporates figurative symbols such as logos, emblems, colours, forms, packaging and design; a word, because it is the brand name which serves as support for oral or written information on the product; an object, because the brand distinguishes each of the products from the other products or services; and finally, a concept in the sense that the brand, like any other symbol, imparts its own significance – in other words, its meaning.

The product brand strategy involves the assignment of a particular name to one, and only one, product (or product line) as well as one exclusive positioning. The result of such a strategy is that each new product receives its own brand name that belongs only to it. Companies then have a brand portfolio that corresponds to their product portfolio as illustrated in Figure 12.2.

This brand strategy can be found in the hotel industry where the Accor Group has developed multiple brands for precise and exclusive positions: eg Sofitel, Novotel, Suit' Hotel, Ibis, Formule 1 and Motel 6. The company Procter & Gamble has made this strategy the symbol of its brand management philosophy. The company is represented in the European detergent market by the brands Ariel, Vizir, Dash and in the soaps market by Camay, Zest, etc. Each of these products has a precise, well-defined positioning and occupies a particular segment of the market: Camay is a seductive soap, Zest a soap for energy. Ariel

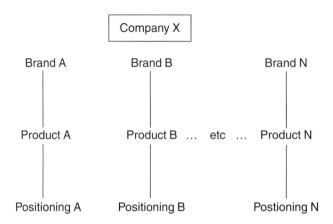

Figure 12.2   The product–brand strategy

positions itself as the best detergent in the market and Dash as the best value for money in the intermediate price range. Both have developed a product line including powder, liquid and tablets.

Innovative companies in the food sector create new speciality products which are then distinguished through individual names and therefore these companies have a large brand product portfolio. The cheese company Bongrain markets more than 10 brands, such as St Moret, Caprice des Dieux and Chaumes. The mineral water market is composed of only product brands: one asks for Vittel, Evian or Contrex, knowing very well that there will be no ambiguity and one will get the product asked for. Here, the brand, the name of a product, becomes a strict indication of identity.

In an extreme case, the product is so specific that there is no equivalent, and the product is not only a product, but an entire product category of which it is the sole representative. This phenomenon has been described by some through the neologism 'branduct' (Swiners, 1979), an abbreviation of brand product. These products are so unique, so specific that they have no other name than their brand name. We see this in 'Post-it', Bailey's Irish Cream, Malibu liqueur, Mars, Bounty, Nuts, etc.

How is the strict relationship between one name, one product and one positioning maintained over a period of time? First, the only way to achieve brand extension is by renewing the product. To keep the product at its height and original positioning, the Ariel formula has often been improved since it was launched in 1969. Ariel receives the best technological and chemical inputs from Procter & Gamble (like its competitor, Skip, from Lever) (Kapferer and Thoenig, 1989). Often, to emphasise an important improvement to the product, the company adds a number after the brand name (Dash 1, Dash 2, Dash 3). To keep up with changing consumer habits, the brand name is applied to various formats (for example, in packaging: packets, drums, in powder or liquid form).

What, then, are the advantages of the product brand strategy for companies? For firms focusing on one market, it is an offensive strategy designed to occupy the whole market. By indulging in the practice of multiple brand entries in the same market (Procter & Gamble has four detergent brands), the company occupies many segments with different needs and expectations and therefore has a greater consolidated share of the market: it becomes category leader. However, this remains unconspicuous, for the corporate name is kept discreet if not hidden.

Some companies do wish to remain at the back and focus the lights exclusively on their brands. The cases of Procter & Gamble, Unilever, Masterfoods and Bestfoods are well known, that of ITW is less so. ITW stands for Illinois Toolwork. It is a billion-US-dollar corporation, very acquisitive: it owns more than 500 companies throughout the world. Its brands aim at the construction professional: they are called Paslode, Duo-Fast for wood products, Spit and Buidex for steel and concrete. The goal is to provide very specialised tools to specialised workers: a policy of niche brands, addressing segmented needs, craftspeople and channels is a direct consequence of this goal. People working with wood want to be reinforced and differentiated from people working with other materials. ITW does not wish to hurt this desire, and AS resisted all temptations to grow the ITW brand itself, for instance as an endorser. ITW's success rests precisely on the exact contrary.

When the segments are closely related, choosing one name per product helps customers to perceive better the differences between the various brands. This may also be necessary when the products resemble each other externally. Thus, one sees that although all detergents are composed of the same basic ingredients, the proportion of these may vary according to the factor that is being optimised: stain removal properties, care for synthetic materials, colourfast control or suitability for hand washing. The association of a specific name for a type of need underlines the physical difference between the products.

The product brand strategy is one that is adapted to the needs of innovative companies who want to pre-empt a positioning. In fact, the first brand to appear in a new segment, if it proves to be effective, has the advantage of the first player in the market. It becomes the nominal reference for the thus innovative product and maybe even the absolute reference. The brand name patents the innovation. This is particularly important in markets where the success is likely to induce

copying. In the pharmaceutical world where copies are a certainty, every new product is registered under two names: one for the product, the formula, and another for the brand. Even if they have the same formula, future copies appear different because the originality of the brand name (Zantac, Tagamet) provides an aura of exclusivity and of legal protection. On the other hand, where the law cannot provide protection, forgeries and copies attempt to exploit the potential of the brand name by imitating it as closely as possible. That is why large mass retailers often use product brands or, to be more precise, counter–product brands. Thus, Fortini copies Martini, Whip copies Skip, etc. Scared of having their other brands cast out of favour manufacturers have, until now, hesitated to legally challenge the distributors for forgery or illegal imitation. (See also page 201.)

Product brand policies allow firms to take risks in new markets. At a time when the future of the liquid detergent was still uncertain, Procter & Gamble preferred to launch a product brand: Vizir. Launching it under the name Ariel liquid would have threatened Ariel's brand image asset and launching it under the name Dash would have incurred the risk of associating a potentially powerful concept with a weak brand and thereby overshadowing it. Coca-Cola did just the same when it first launched Tab to test the diet market.

Product brand policy implies that the name of the company behind it remains unknown to the public and is therefore different from the brand names. This practice allows the firm considerable freedom to move whenever and wherever it wishes, especially into new markets. Procter & Gamble moved from the creation of the soap, Ivory, in 1882, to the culinary aid, Crisco, in 1911, Chipso in 1926 and the machine detergent, Dreft, in 1933, Tide in 1946, Joy, the dishwashing agent in 1950 and then Dash in 1955, the toothpaste, Crest, in 1955, the peanut-butter, Jif, in 1956, Pampers in 1961, the coffee, Folgers, in 1963, the antiseptic mouthwash, Scope, as well as household paper rolls, Bounce, in 1965, Pringle chips in 1968, sanitary napkins, Rely, in 1974, Always (Whisper) and Sunny Delight later on.

Since each brand is independent of the others, the failure of one of them has no risk of negative spillover on the others, or on the company name (in cases where the company name remains relatively unknown to the public and different from that of any of the brands).

Finally, the distribution parameter also favours this strategy heavily: the shelf space accorded by a retailer to a company depends on the number of (strong) brands that it has. When a brand covers many products, the retailer stocks certain products and not others. In the case of product brands, there is only one product per brand, or one product line per brand.

The drawbacks arising from product brands are essentially economic. Thus multi-brand strategy is not for the faint-hearted.

In fact, a new product launch is often a new brand launch. Considering today's media costs, this involves considerable investments in advertising and promotions. Furthermore, retailers, unwilling to take risks with new products whose future is uncertain, stock them only when reassured by heavy listing fees.

Multiplication of product brands in a market due to the increasingly narrow segmentation weighs heavily on the chances of a rapid return on investment. The volumes required to justify such investment (in R&D, equipment, and sales and marketing expenses) make the product brand strategy an ideal one for growing markets where a small market share could nevertheless mean high volumes. When the market is saturated, this possibility disappears. On the other hand, in a stable market it is sometimes more advantageous to nurture an existing brand with the innovation in question rather than attempt to give it product brand status by launching it under its own name.

The role of fire curtains between product brands is certainly important in times of crises, but in other times it prevents the brand from benefiting from the positive spillover effect created by other products under the same name. The success of brand A will not help other products because their names, B, C, D, etc are different and do not bear any relation to A. As we can see, in this strategy, the firm gives the brand a completely distinct and exclusive function and almost no hints about its origin. New products do not benefit from the renown of one of the already existing brands nor from the economies that one could derive from it. On the other hand, this advantage has no role among distributors who are well aware of the company name behind the brand and its reputation for success or failure.

The case of 'branducts' is even more marked. Since they represent an entire category of products on their own, they have to invest twice as much in advertising. While a brand of whisky only has to associate itself with the whisky category for the customer to recall the brand when he wants to buy a whisky, other products such as Sheridan, Malibu or Bailey's cannot fall back on the cushion of a product category. They therefore need a permanent spontaneous awareness: either one thinks of Bailey's or one does not (in which case the probability of a sale is zero). Furthermore, isolated due to the lack of a category shelf, branducts suffer from a lack of prominence and visibility on the shelves. This makes their fame their only strong point. In times of recession, they are the first to undergo budget reductions.

The line brand strategy

Deglaude Laboratories launched a product brand, Foltene: a single product associated with a single benefit, the regrowth of hair. A strong TV advertising campaign made the market explode and Foltene became the leader with a single product and a 55 per cent market share. They should have remained thus, but consumer logic prevailed. Bald people were not looking for a single product. They wanted an all-encompassing service, a total care routine. They wrote asking that shampooing be combined with the Foltene treatment. In 1982 Deglaude launched a mild shampoo (which was later subdivided according to hair type) followed by a daily-use lotion. All this was by way of response to customer demands.

Christian Dior launched Capture, an anti-ageing liposome complex for the skin. Following its success, a first spin-off was soon launched: 'Capture, eye shaper', followed by lip shapers and then other products for the body. The Capture line was born.

Thus, to take up Botton and Cegarra's definition (1990), the line responds to the concern of offering one coherent response under a single name by proposing many complementary products. This goes from variations of the offer, as in the case of Capture or with the fragrances of an aftershave, to the inclusion of various products within one specific effect, as in the case of Foltene. This is also the case with Studio Line hair products from L'Oréal, which offers structuring gel, lacquer, a spray, etc. Calgon (a Benckiser brand) markets a dishwasher powder together with a rinsing agent and lime-scale inhibitor. That these products are completely different for the producer makes no difference to the consumer, who perceives them as related.

It should be clear that the line involves the exploitation of a successful concept by extending it but by staying very close to the initial product (eg Capture liposomes or the Foltene principle). In other cases, the line is launched as a complete ensemble, with many complementary products linked by a single central concept (for Studio it was allowing youngsters to do their own hair and give themselves a 'look'). The eventual extension of the line will involve only the marginal costs linked to retailers' discounts and to the packaging. It does not need advertising. It

should be compared to the marginal number of consumers that could be won. As one can see, the line brand strategy offers multiple advantages:

- it reinforces the selling power of the brand and creates a strong brand image;

- it facilitates distribution for each line extension;

- it reduces launch costs.

The disadvantages of the line strategy lie in the tendency to forget that a line has limits. One should only include product innovations that are very closely linked to the existing ones. On the other hand, the inclusion of a powerful innovation could slow its development. Thus, even though Capture was the result of seven years' research in collaboration with the Pasteur Institute, received three patents and brought with it a revolutionary anti-ageing principle, Dior decided to attach it to a currently existing anti-ageing line. This did not prevent the success of Capture, but unnecessarily delayed it initially.

The range brand strategy

Campbell's Soup, Knorr, Bird's Eye and Igloo all propose more than 100 frozen food products. But not all range brands are this extensive. The Tylenol range now covers a number of different products. Range brands bestow a single brand name and promote through a single promise a range of products belonging to the same area of competence. In range brand architecture, products guard their common name (fish à la provençale, mushroom pizza, pancakes with ham and cheese in the case of Bird's Eye). In the Clarins cosmetic range, products are named 'purifying plant mask', extracts of 'fresh cells', multi-tensor toning solution, day or night soothing cream, etc.

Range brand structure is found in the food sector (Green Giant, Campbell, Heinz,

Whiskas and so on), equipment (Moulinex, Seb, Rowenta, Samsonite) or in industry (Steelcase, Facom). These brands combine all their products through a unique principle, a brand concept, as is shown in Figure 12.3. The advantages and disadvantages of the structure are as follows:

▌ It avoids the random spread of external communications by focusing on a single name – the brand name – and thereby creating brand capital for itself which can even be shared by other products. Furthermore, in such a structure the brand communicates in a generic manner by developing its unique brand concept. Thus, the range brand of pet food, Fido, covers many products but in its advertisement it only has a taster dog who marks his approval on a product with a paw print. This commercial transfers the brand focalisation and its pre-eminence to the animal. Another approach consists of communicating the brand concept by concentrating only on certain of the most representative products through which the brand can best express its meaning and convey consumer benefit. This can then be shared by other products of the range which are not directly mentioned.

▌ The brand can easily distribute new products that are consistent with its mission and fall within the same category.

Furthermore, the cost of such new launches is very low.

Among the problems that are most frequently encountered is one of brand opacity as it expands. The brand name Findus covers scores of savoury frozen products. It is a good brand – high quality, modern, a specialist in frozen products and a generalist as well because it makes all kinds of dishes. For years, product names were the names of the recipes. But these names are banal. Any brand can claim that it has the same recipe. To enrich the brand and to express its personality on one hand, and on the other hand to help the consumer choose from the mass of products that are on offer, an intermediate level of categorisation must be created between the brand name and each actual product name. This is the role of specific lines such as:

▌ 'Lean cuisine' that regrouped 18 dishes all recognisable by their white packaging;

▌ 'Traditional' covering nine dishes with maroon outers;

▌ 'Seafoods' comprising nine kinds of dishes and assorted products (previously simply called hake cutlets, whiting fillets, etc) in blue packaging.

Such names for a line throw light on the products and also help to structure the range in the same way as retailers organise their

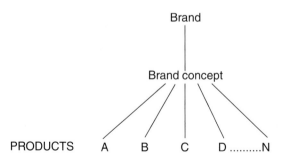

Figure 12.3   Range brand formation

shelves. The criteria for segmentation and for the creation of families of products depend on the brand. Thus, should we make the distinctions according to the content (poultry, beef, pork etc, as in a butcher's shop) or according to consumer benefits (light, traditional, exotic, family orientated ...)?

The line structures the offer, by putting together products which are undoubtedly heterogeneous, but all of which have the same function. Thus, in the Clarins cosmetic range brand, the offer is also made more clear and structured by way of lines. To assist the consumer in deciphering the scientific terms used on the products, the brand proposes lines as one would a prescription. For example:

▐ the 'soothing line' for sensitive skins includes a mild day cream and a mild night cream as well as a restructuring fluid in capsules;

▐ the 'slimming and firmness' line regroups an exfoliating scrub, a slimming bath, a 'bio-superactivated' reducing cream and an 'anti-water' oil.

The Clarins offer ceases to be a long list of creams, serums, lotions, balms and gels and now forms structured and coherent groups as seen in Figure 12.4.

Umbrella brand strategy

Canon markets cameras, photocopying machines and office equipment all under its own name. Yamaha sells motorbikes, but also pianos and guitars. Mitsubishi regroups banks, cars and domestic appliances. Palmolive is a brand name for household products (dishwashing liquid) and hygiene products (soaps and shampoos for the entire family, but also shaving cream for men). These are all umbrella brands: the same brand supports several products in different markets. Each of them has its own advertising and develops its own communications (sometimes even has its own advertising agency). Yet, each product is called by its own generic name. Thus, we speak of Canon cameras, Canon fax machines, Canon printers. Figure 12.5 illustrates this structure. (Chapter 11 is

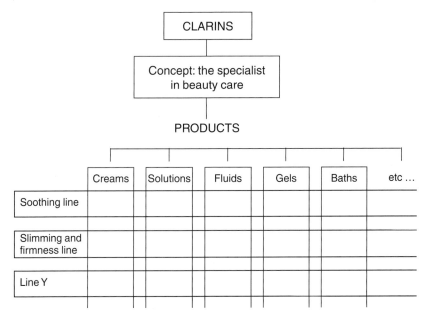

Figure 12.4   Range brand structured in lines

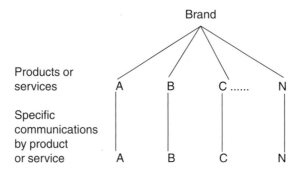

Figure 12.5   Umbrella brand strategy

devoted to the crucial question of brand extension beyond its original domain of activity. Is Philips right in using the same name to cover hi-fi, television, bulbs, computers, electric shavers and small electric appliances?)

The main advantage of the umbrella strategy is the capitalisation on one single name and the economies of scale on an international level. Not even one of their undertakings, products or communications fails to contribute to Philips' reputation. Even the occasional setback can add to public awareness of the brand. As a result, this allows one to capitalise on the brand which is already well known and on the reputation to enter markets where the company is not present. The awareness gives rise to nearly instantaneous goodwill on the part of the distributors and the public concerned.

Firms enjoying such awareness find the umbrella brand useful to penetrate sectors where little marketing investment is required. In smaller sectors, they can even succeed without any specific communications. It also permits considerable savings when they enter new strategic markets.

The importance of this last point should not be underestimated, especially in the present era of over-communication. Today, in many markets the quest for brand awareness is nearly out of reach given the advertising expenditures of the players already in the market. This is what led Jack Tramiel, former boss of Commodore microcomputers, to buy Atari in 1984 – a very well-known brand, albeit primarily for its video games at the time. This was done so as to be able to penetrate once again the market for home and office computers. Tramiel chose to buy a brand with an established reputation, even if it was associated with other products, rather than create another brand. The same reason explains why one revives ancient brands (like Commodore, Sunsilk, Talbot) to serve as supports for new products that may or may not be close to the original product that people have certainly forgotten, even though they still remember the name. It is better to take advantage from a glimmer in the public mind rather than start from scratch. Research on memorisation and the impact of advertising campaigns shows that their main determinant is brand awareness: it boosts advertising recall.

An umbrella brand strategy allows the core brand to be nurtured by association with products with which it was not previously associated. McCain's meaning changed as the brand became the signature for not only frozen fries, but also pizzas, buns and iced tea. The same holds true for Virgin.

Finally, the umbrella brand imposes very few constraints, unless it is managed as a real 'branded house' that is to say with a very clean set of values and a delineated territory.

Each product is often a company division or a business unit, with worldwide scope and a lot of autonomy. It has its own communications to increase its market share and to emphasise the specific qualities of its own brand: Toshiba hi-fi and low-fi targets the younger generation while the laptop division aims its outstanding, practical, portable computers at modern executives, and its television sets at families. However, in each of these markets the general brand competes against a multitude of specialist brands, forcing it to demonstrate the relevance of its products in each of the segments where it wants to acquire a dominant position. Brand awareness does not automatically signify a legitimate product – even less so an excellent one – in the eyes of the purchaser. Only companies able to launch superior new products can use the umbrella brand strategy. In each new market, the product will have to succeed on its own merits, despite its brand name. This is typical of Japanese companies.

The problems encountered in umbrella brand administration stem from the failure to appreciate its demands. It sometimes happens that in wishing to save money by diversifying under an umbrella brand, the firm forgets that the purpose of the brand is, above all, to gain money. Awareness is not sufficient in this respect. Every division must use its financial and human resources to communicate and convince that its products and services are as good as those of specialist brands and even superior, something that is not usually evident. The core of the brand is always stronger than its extensions.

The umbrella brand must not cast a shadow. Bic's image undermined the attractiveness of its perfumes. Furthermore, an accident occurring with one of the products can affect other products under the same umbrella (Sullivan, 1988).

An over-stretched rubber band weakens. Similarly, the result of putting a large number of heterogeneous products and services under the same brand is called the 'rubber effect' by Americans (Ries and Trout, 1987). The more a brand covers different categories, the more it stretches and weakens, losing its force like a rubber band. It then becomes a simple endorsement on the products, a mere indicator of their origin, thereby a small guarantee of quality. Distributors do favour umbrella brands for that reason: the large umbrella distributor's brand indicates that all its products are acceptable because they have been selected by this distributor. Strong brands with a precise meaning can also embrace heterogeneous products, because they impose their meaning on the products. Sony, for example, is a refined technological innovator and ground-breaker. The brand can cover many categories since the factors contained in the Sony image are attractive and relevant to these product categories even if they are unrelated. Palmolive seems to add softness to everything that it touches: this factor is important every time a product is in contact with the skin, from dishwashing liquid to facial soap. The brand can also cast its net over hygiene as well as beauty, and be relevant for both men and women.

Horizontal extension of the brand is less of a handicap than vertical extension by which brands try to cover all levels of quality and status. The automobile market is a segmented one – lower range, mid-range, upper mid-range and high range, not to mention luxury and sports cars. But it would be wrong to think that the brand programme can have the same impact on all segments. The creative strength of Mercedes is prominent in the high range but loses its edge when faced with the constraints of producing cheaper cars such as Class A.

The freedom allowed by the umbrella brand sometimes leads to a patchwork brand. It is one thing to allow each divisional manager to take care of his own product communication and another to accept too many variations in brand positioning from one division to another or from one product to the next. The manager may be free to make detailed promises in line with their particular market; however, even though each product has its individual identity, the codes of expression should be homogeneous for them all. Customers do not have just an isolated view of the brand, they come across all the products, each with its own particular message. To them, the brand should appear as an indivisible whole even though it is organised in commercial and industrial divisions. This is why companies adopting the umbrella brand strategy try at least to enforce the use of a brand identity charter, a minimal and formal tool for communications. Later they tend to become almost a source brand or a ' branded house', imposing more than a same dress to all its products: a common spirit, vision and identity. Virgin and Nivea are typical cases of this stronger umbrella approach.

Thus Nivea's growth has been achieved by stepwise extensions, well planned and repeated in each new country where the brand is sold. Despite these many extensions, which all have their specific personality, Nivea remains an umbrella brand:

▌ Each sub-brand has a descriptive name (Nivea Sun, Nivea Vital, Nivea for Men).

▌ There are remarkable executional continuities in all the advertisements. This is called the 'Niveaness' (intimate tone, blond models, not too flashy but very natural types, and so on). The message is always the same throughout the full range (loving skin care).

▌ The key colour is always blue.

Source brand strategy

This is identical to the umbrella brand strategy except for one key point – the products have their own brand name. They are no longer called by one generic name such as eau de toilette or eau de parfum, but each has own name, eg Jazz, Poison, Opium, Nina, Loulou, etc. This two-tier brand structure, known as double-branding, is shown in Figure 12.6.

Since this strategy is often confused with the endorsing brand strategy, it is important to specify the differences at the beginning. When Nestlé puts its name on the chocolate Crunch and Galak, on the bars Yes, Nuts and Kit Kat and on Nescafé, Nesquik, etc, the corporate brand is endorsing the quality of

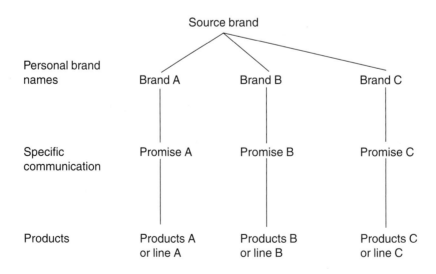

Figure 12.6 Source brand or parent brand strategy

the merchandise and acts as a maker's mark. The Nestlé name dispels the incertitude that certain products can create. Nestlé takes a back seat position. The product itself is the driver of the consumers' choice; it is the hero to the extent that few customers of Crunch attribute it to Nestlé. On the contrary, when we see the Yves Saint Laurent name on a perfume such as Jazz, this name is more than a simple endorsement. Here, it is the brand name which holds sway and which accords Jazz the seal of approval and the distinction which it would not otherwise enjoy. Yves Saint Laurent is the driver of purchase, not Jazz. Jazz is another key to the door of the Yves Saint Laurent cultural universe. The problem with many brands is that they have converted from source brands to endorsing brands. Within the source brand concept, the family spirit dominates even if the offspring all have their own individual names. With the endorsing brand, however, the products are autonomous and have only the endorsing brand in common. Today, where do Nestlé, Kellogg's or Kraft stand? What about Du Pont or Bayer, Glaxo or Merck?

The benefit from the source brand strategy lies in its ability to provide a two-tiered sense of difference and depth. It is difficult to personalise an offer or a proposition to a client without any personalised vocabulary. The parent brand offers its significance and identity, modified and enriched by the daughter brand in order to attract a specific customer segment. Ranges having 'Christian names' allow a brand which needs to maintain its own brand image to win over newer consumer categories and new territory.

The limits of the source brand lie in the necessity to respect the core, the spirit and the identity of the parent brand. This defines the strict boundaries not to be infringed as far as brand extension and also product communication are concerned. Only the names that are related to the parent brand's field of activity should be associated with it. All product aids should share the same spirit. If greater freedom is sought, then the endorsing brand strategy is more suitable.

Garnier for example wanted to become a source brand and abandon its previous endorsing brand strategy. This is a delicate process for it means moving from patchwork to unity.

Creating a source brand: from patchwork to unity

Companies need to improve their efficiency on a regular basis. One way of doing this is to put an end to the natural dispersion of brands and identities, and reorganise supply under proper parent brands that fulfil more than an endorsing function. These parent brands would be a source of strong, differentiated and unique values shared by all products and sub-brands, which also have their own particular personality based on their target group, product territory and specific function. What the present work refers to as a 'source brand' partly corresponds to what some people have called a 'branded house' (as opposed to a 'patchwork' or 'house of brands') (see page 319). It should be remembered that, unlike the umbrella brand, the source brand is a strategy with two layers of branding.

So how does a company convert a 'patchwork' into a real 'house'? The first thing it has to do is define the identity of the brand for the future. The real identity of a brand lies within the brand itself, while its future lies in its ability to adapt to the markets. It is therefore by analysing the roots and origins of the brand, its early products and performance that it is possible to isolate its core, its key values, the source of its influence and legitimacy. But this analysis must then be considered carefully within the context of the development of tomorrow's markets and consumers.

Garnier provides a good illustration of this process. Until 2002, this internationally renowned brand was known as Laboratoires Garnier. Its task was to become the other international brand of the mass-market network, alongside l'Oréal Paris, which was positioned as a more glamorous, more expensive product within the same shelf ranges. It was a question of finding values that were positive, aspirational, internally and externally motivating, and had popular appeal since the brand had been allotted a more accessible market position.

Historically speaking, the origins of Laboratoires Garnier date from 1904, when M. Garnier first invented a herbal hair tonic. This original product already had some of the key attributes of the brand – naturalness and beauty care. Some time later, after the Second World War, a hugely successful shampoo called Moëlle Garnier not only revitalised the 'genes' of the brand but also boosted business. Relaunched in 1986, the brand was extended by its sub-brands – Synergie (cosmetics), Ambre Solaire (sun care), Graphic (hair care), Ultra Doux (skin care) and Lumia (hair colour).

The brand achieved international renown and established a strong position on several European markets. However, its sub-brands declined in popularity and remained regional. All except one, that is, which had already been extremely successful outside Europe and appealed to the younger generation in countries throughout the world – Fructis, the first strengthening shampoo with active fruit concentrates. Fructis was a direct descendant of the Garnier line but with a more modern image. The real reinvention came with Fructis Style, a range of revolutionary styling products containing fruit wax and characterized by a complete range of strong, tactile sensations – the colours, consistency and aroma of fruit. With Fructis, a new generation of sensual products was born.

But to conquer the world market the brand needed a new identity that, while respecting its origins, would nevertheless make it an aspirational brand for modern young people worldwide. Fructis and especially Fructis Style would be the new prototype for the brand,

while their casual and ironic tone would provide the basis for its reinvention.

What were the consequences for Garnier? In order to be attractive and accessible to young people in countries throughout the world, the brand had to change its name from Laboratoires Garnier and simply become known as Garnier. It was no longer a scientific or a French brand, it was accessible and international. Furthermore its brand contract, its values, were now written in English.

How does Garnier define its aims? 'Garnier believes in beauty through nature. Scientifically developed and enriched with selected natural ingredients, our products help you look healthy and feel good everyday.' This contract is outlined in six core values:

- Natural high tech (which distinguishes it from Yves Rocher, which is not high tech, and l'Oréal Paris which does not focus on the natural element).

- Healthy beauty: Garnier is a healthy brand, which does not use top models, but unknown models who look and feel good (like the girl next door).

- Total experience: Garnier is not selling just a product but a complete experience that appeals to all five senses.

- Universal: it is multi-ethnic, multi-racial, multi-generation.

- Accessible, as evidenced by price and distribution.

- Positive irreverence: this is a distinctive personality trait, found in all Garnier advertisements.

How was this new identity projected across all Garnier's daughter brands?

- The first stage was one of identification. Apart from modifying the name, a new logo was created in green, orange and red, the colours of fruit but also traffic lights.

▨ The next stage involved bringing the sub-brands portfolio into line with the source brand. Since Garnier is a source brand, the sub-brands must reflect its core values. So the Neutralia sub-brand (shower gel) was abandoned because its clinical purity no longer corresponded to the Garnier 'house' image, while the Ultra Doux brand was extended to replace Neutralia. Similarly, the Synergie sub-brand (cosmetics) became Skin Natural which was much more in line with Garnier's values.

▨ The third stage consisted of developing business by organising an attack on growth markets, that is, deciding which sub-brands would target which countries and which segments. What would be the consequences in terms of range and adaptation to multiple niching (universality value)?

▨ The fourth stage involved defining how the advertising was to be handled. What distinguishes a Garnier advertisement? They all begin with a light-hearted statement of the problem, followed by the presentation of the solution, and involve a wide range of different people, all looking and feeling good and reflecting the cultural and racial diversity of the country in question. The advertisement always refers viewers to the website GarnierBeautyBar.com.

▨ In the fifth stage, the promotional principles were established – an accessible brand that offers a full experience – and Garnier developed massive sampling and street marketing initiatives involving direct contact with consumers in all countries.

It is significant that the Web site is called GarnierBeautyBar.com. Visually, it is presented like a real 'house' where you can visit each room and discover and/or personally experiment with one of the Garnier sub-brands. The 'branded house' has constructed a 'virtual house' in which all the brands in the family are brought together with a view to offering an intense product experience. Garnier's (male and female) customers enter via the Garnier Hall from where they can go to the Beauty Lounge, Style Room, Tonic Area or Game Zone and try out their future looks, carry out personalised diagnostic tests or simply experiment and develop their customer loyalty.

From this it can be seen that the source brand is a structure that restructures all its parts. Many groups use this type of brand architecture to give greater impact to their diverse product ranges by making them converge on a common image. For example, all Danone products and brands now focus on health, the core value of the source brand, in the knowledge that there are seven types of health, and therefore seven different ways of presenting it. Danone has also changed its status from an 'endorsing brand' to a 'source brand'.

Endorsing brand strategy

Everyone recognises famous car brands such as Pontiac, Buick and Chevrolet in the United States or Opel in Europe. Next to their logos and to the signs of the dealers of these brands we always see the two letters: GM. It is obviously General Motors, the endorsing brand. Again, what is the link between the cleaner Pledge, Wizard Air Freshener and Toilet Duck? They are all Johnson products. The endorsing brand gives its approval to a wide diversity of products grouped under product brands, line brands or range brands. Johnson is the guarantor of their high quality and security. This having been said, each product is then free to manifest its originality: that is what gives rise to the different names seen in the range.

Figure 12.7 symbolises endorsing brand strategy. As one can see, the endorsing brand is placed lower down because it acts as a base guarantor. Furthermore what the consumers buy is Pontiac or Opel: they drive choice. General Motors and Johnson are supports and assume a secondary position.

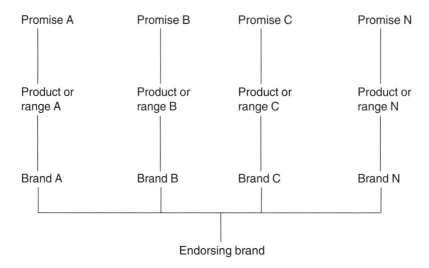

Figure 12.7 Endorsing brand strategy

The brand endorsement can be indicated in a graphic manner by placing the emblem of the endorser next to the brand name or (when signed above, it acts as maker's mark) by simply signing the endorser's name.

The advantage of the endorsing brand is the greater freedom of movement that it allows. Unlike the source brand, the endorsing brand profits less from its products. Each particular product name evokes a forceful image and has a power of recall for the consumer. There is little image transfer to the endorser.

The endorsing brand strategy is one of the least expensive ways of giving substance to a company name and allowing it to achieve a minimal brand status. Thus, we can see the initials ICI (Imperial Chemical Industries) on Valentine or Dulux paint pots, the name Bayer on packets of garden products and Monsanto on Round Up. The high quality of these brands is guaranteed by the names of these major organisations. On the other hand, through their presence in everyday life these companies become more familiar and close to the people, as in the case of ICI in Europe. Since the scientific and technical guarantees are assured by the endorsing brand, product

brands can devote more time to expressing other facets of their personality.

Therefore, as one can see, there is a division of roles at each stage of the branding hierarchy. The endorsing brand becomes responsible for the guarantee that is essential for all brands and, today, these guarantees not only cover areas such as quality and scientific expertise, but also civic responsibility, ethics and environmental concerns. The other brand functions are assumed by the specifically named brands: distinction, personalisation and even pleasure (Kapferer and Laurent, 1992).

Mixed approaches

The six branding strategies presented here are models, typical cases of branding. In reality, companies adopt mixed configurations where the same brand can be, according to the product, range, umbrella, parent or endorsing brand. For example, L'Oréal is a range brand of lipsticks. It is a source brand for Studio, Elsève or Plénitude. The hybrid character of the usage of the brand L'Oréal and the strategies adopted reflect its willingness to adapt to the decision-making processes of consumers in different sub-markets (hair care products, perfumes or cosmetics) or according to the distribution channels (ie self-service or specialist stores). In certain cases, L'Oréal guarantees reliability and technical capacity. In others, it wants to achieve recognition (ie in cosmetics) and therefore needs to place itself to the forefront. And finally, in still other cases, L'Oréal has to be invisible – either to avoid being associated with a low-price segment or to avoid hurting one of its prestige products. Nevertheless, many hybrid situations result out of the series of small decisions that are taken as and when a new product is launched. Due to the lack of an overall plan for a brand's relationship with its products, a number of non-coherent branding decisions often exist side by side.

3M provides an interesting example of the accumulation of separate branding policies, with as many as five denominational stages (quintuple branding). This is shown in Figure 12.8. 3M is a company focused on high-tech research into industrial and domestic applications of adhesives. This covers a vast area

which includes glues, obviously, but also films, cassettes, medical plasters, transparencies and overhead projector products, etc. The 3M name is synonymous with seriousness, power and heavy R&D. But this also leaves an image of coldness. Thus, to humanise the contact with the general buyer, the umbrella brand Scotch was created. Video cassettes, glue sticks and sellotape are all branded Scotch directly. But for the scouring pads, on the other hand, a line brand called Scotch-Brite was created. To counter the challenge of a rival product from Spontex (who simply call them scouring pads) Scotch replaced the generic name by a particular name, the 'Raccoon' (just like the Volkswagen Beetle). This differentiated its product and explained its advantages in a unique manner and gave it a closer and more friendly image.

The 'Raccoon' itself has been expanded into many versions – green, blue, red – depending on its shape and use. For its general consumer products, such as sponges and glues, 3M was used as an endorsing brand with a signature in small print. Curiously enough, 3M is scarcely

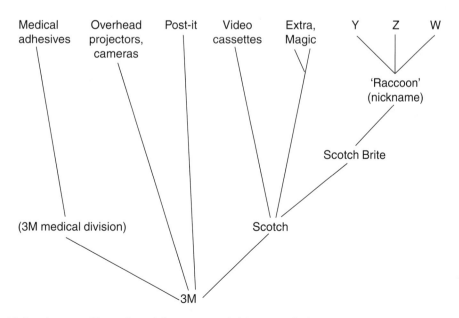

Figure 12.8   A case of brand proliferation and dilution of identity

in evidence on Scotch cassettes. Is this to distinguish better from the video cassettes marked clearly and exclusively 3M and targeted at professional use? In fact, while 3M provides a guarantee of good performance and an endorsing brand for general consumer products, it serves as an umbrella brand for professional products: all the power and significance of the 3M name is reflected in products such as cameras, overhead projectors and dental cement (coming from the 3M health division). Post-it, the famous 'adhesive notes that serve as a memory tool or a message carrier', is also signed 3M. In order to patent this invention in a better way and to define it in a better manner than the long description used above, that it be given a proper name was to be expected.

Thus, depending on the level of professional end-use that a product has, or the need for an up-to-date image of excellence and performance, it is either signed 3M in a prominent manner or even perhaps exclusively. If not, 3M is present through the brand Scotch. Perhaps this is why the sellotape, Scotch Magic, used the name 3M only as a recall tool. On the other hand, aerosol glue for communication professionals bears the Scotch name in small print and 3M in large letters. There are also differentiated product advertisements for the 'Raccoon', general-use sellotape, Scotch cassettes and Post-it. Beyond the endorsing brand, there are no common codes of expression which appear independent in form and intent.

Choosing the appropriate branding strategy

Which is the best branding strategy? Procter & Gamble are firm supporters of product brands; are they right and L'Oréal, their more flexible competitor, wrong?

Each type of brand strategy has its own advantages and disadvantages, as has been described. However, a simple list of the pros and cons does not provide a procedure for making a choice in a given company in a given market. The choice of brand policy is not a stylistic exercise, but more a strategic decision aimed at promoting individual products and ranges as well as capitalising the brand in the long term. It should be considered in the light of three factors: the product or service, consumer behaviour, and the firm's competitive position. Brand policy is a reflection of the strategy chosen by a particular company in a specific context.

What parameters should be taken into account when choosing a branding strategy? The first is *corporate strategy*, of which branding strategy is in fact the symbol. For example, in 2003, Schneider Electric, one of the leaders in the field of electrical distribution and industrial control, decided to revitalise its Merlin Gerin and Telemecanique brands, which were well known to research departments and electrical integrators and installers throughout the world. In so doing, Schneider ended an initiative launched some 10 years previously with a different aim in mind, namely to replace individual brands with a single, group brand. The company's new director, who had come from Steelcase, outlined the strategic positioning of Schneider Electric against GE, ABB and Siemens. Compared with these general electrical and electronic giants, Schneider Electric is not a small general electrical company but rather likes to see itself as a multi-specialist company. In fact, because it sells intermediate products, its customers are looking for a specialist company. On the other hand, when compared with its many single-specialist competitors, Schneider Electric is more of a general electrical company. So if it wants to position itself as a multi-specialist company, the specialities must be offered by specialist brands, united by a group brand, a single entity, which facilitates customer relations. This is why it was decided not to follow the single-brand path, but to bring the range of 50

product brands together under three integrated international brands – Merlin Gerin,
Telemecanique and the US company Square
D, in 130 countries. There is therefore a
Schneider Electric front office and a Schneider
Electric sales force organised by type of
customer, and these customers are able to
purchase products under different product
brands.

Another consequence is that distributors
will once again become the official distributors of Merlin Gerin or Telemecanique
without there being any obligation, as in the
past, to automatically reference both brands.

Similarly, Groupe SEB, world leader in small
household appliances, decided to form itself
into a multi-brand group, with four international brands – Moulinex, Tefal, Krups and
Rowenta. Why not follow the tempting
single-brand path, like Philips? Precisely
because of Philips. The strategy lies in the art
of being different. The single brand is an
advantage if you are already a single brand
like Philips, one of the few international
brands whose reputation is based on the fact
that it is distributed throughout the world –
even, via its light bulbs, in the depths of the
Amazon basin. It is basically too late to try to
emulate Philips. In today's fragmented
markets, with their aggressive distribution
networks and consumer segments, it is far
better to exploit the targeted reputation (in
terms of product and values) of the brands
that people have bought precisely because
they were brands.

The second parameter is the *business model*.
In this respect it is interesting to compare
companies within the same sector, since their
brand policy is often a reflection of their
business model, the driving force of their
competitive edge and their profitability. This
can be illustrated by comparing three giants of
the European cheese industry – Bel, Bongrain
and Lactalis. Bel develops range brands
around a central innovative product, thereby
giving rise to an entire range of products with
The Laughing Cow, Kiri or Mini Babybel

signature. Bongrain develops product brands
– Chaumes, Vieux Pané, Caprices des Dieux,
Haut Ségur – while Lactalis uses a single brand
(Président) as an umbrella for all its cheeses
and butter, and even milk in Russia and Spain.
So why the different brand policies?

In fact, the business models of these
companies are not the same, hence the
different brand strategies. Bel likes to see itself
as the inventor of modernity, anti-tradition-
alism, accessibility and everyday values. It
does not deal in those speciality cheeses
bought as a weekend treat. As the inventor of
modernity, it must therefore create brands,
with their own particular shapes and characteristics, that can subsequently be offered in a
variety of forms to capitalise on the
investment in promotion. Bongrain decided
to develop processed AOC (*appellations
d'origine contrôlées*) cheeses to make them
more accessible in terms of taste, price,
preservability and usage. Vieux Pané is a
processed version of the AOC cheese category
called "Pont l'Evêque" but, as such, does not
have the right to use the name of the appel-
lation. Bongrain therefore has to give each of
the specialities it creates a new name – hence
the product-brand policy. The disadvantage of
this is that it has to promote each new brand,
meanwhile supporting through advertising
many small volume brands.

The business model of Lactalis is to segment
generic categories in order to bring them up to
date and into line with everyday life and the
modern lifestyle. This model gives rise to an
umbrella-brand policy – under a single brand
(Président), there are descriptive names for
each of the varieties, each of the various
forms, with low-fat butter remaining a quality
butter, Emmental a real Emmental, and Brie a
real Brie.

The third parameter for choosing a brand
architecture is *cultural*. The United States has
developed the culture of the product brand – a
brand that produces a single product. Ivory,
the founder brand of Procter & Gamble, is and
continues to remain a soap, which explains

the company's reluctance to extend the brand and even the ideological opposition of such authors as Trout and Ries who have berated it in their work for the past 20 years. But the US domestic market favoured this product-brand policy. On the other hand, it also explains why Europe and Japan have been the main exponents of the umbrella-brand policy. Nivea and Nestlé are just two of the many European examples. In Japan, apart from the size of the domestic market, the concept of the company has also counted for a lot in the sense that, the more products and sectors a company covers, the greater its reputation. It would simply not occur to the director of a Japanese company not to use the corporate name to promote all kinds of brand extensions. Yamaha is a typical example, putting its name to such widely diverse products as motorcycles and pianos.

The fourth parameter is the *pace of innovation*. How do you develop product brands in a sector that updates its offer on an annual basis? In this instance, a single-brand policy covering the entire range is preferable, as in the case of Nokia, Sony-Ericsson, Alcatel, Samsung and even Whirlpool and GE.

A fifth parameter is the a*dded-value lever* on which a product is based. This point is illustrated in Figure 12.1, giving the relative positioning of these different strategies. When the added value in a particular market is linked to reassurance, reputation and scale, a single-brand umbrella strategy is recommended (in the world of industry, this is often the corporate brand), although a source-branding strategy with two levels – a real 'branded house' like Garnier or l'Oréal Paris – can work equally well. However, the more segmented the market, with top-quality, personalised products, the more one has to favour either a portfolio of l'Oréal product brands or an endorsing brand strategy that sanctions the sub-brands (the logic of Danone or Nestlé in dairy products).

Next there is the problem of *resources*. In the absence of sufficient funding, a company should concentrate its efforts on a single brand, especially if it is international. The need to achieve a visibility threshold comes before all other considerations. However, in case of co-branding, it is impossible to do so: this is why Philips and Douwe Egberts (a leading coffee company) created a separate name (Senseo) to designate their joint innovation in coffee machines.

Finally the brand vision impacts the choice of architecture. In the cosmetic market there are thousands of products and many scientific terms, and innovations are essential. This is what leads to an opacity in the market. Brands serve as milestones and a question that is frequently asked is which naming strategy should be used? There is no single answer to such a general question: it depends a lot on the brand's conception of itself.

Lancôme prefers a mono-product policy with only a small range derived from the leading product (Progress for the face, eyeliner, anti-wrinkle cream, etc). Thus, recently the brand chose to launch mono-products for body care, each with its own brand instead of a line under one name. There was Cadence for the body (moisturiser), Exfoliance (scrub) and Sculptural (slimmer). Lancôme is not an endorsing brand. It wants to be a source brand and therefore the creator of a precise vision, that of French elegance. The brand wants to serve as a vehicle to express:

▮ the product's technological level and its performance;

▮ luxury as perceived in a French manner, that is to say natural sophistication; Lancôme makes laboratories appear charming.

Lancôme expresses itself through its products and the services that surround them (the dialogue and the advice of salespeople). They want a brand policy that is coherent and easily understandable on two levels: the consumer and the seller. But, consumers actually respond badly to brand policy in this sector: they do not usually memorise brand names and may simply ask for the 'moisturising cream from Lancôme' when they enter the shop. The sales assistant then explains that there are two: Hydrix and Transhydrix. The two names help the assistant explain the existence of multiple products. Through these different product names, the customer understands the different products and the assistant can subsequently promote each one by stressing their individual functions, use and specific characteristics. Thus, at Lancôme, they try to give each product a different name to reflect a function (Nutrix nurtures the skin, Hydrix moisturises it and Forte-Vital makes it firmer) or the main ingredient if it is something new or revolutionary (eg Niosome contains niosomes, Oligo-Majors has oligo elements). This naming policy makes the sales pitch clearer because it explains the differences between the products and other closely positioned products and therefore avoids the confusion that could have occurred had they been in the same line and under a single common name.

This would appear to close the argument clearly between product brands and line brands in favour of the former as far as cosmetics are concerned. But, at Clarins, as a general rule, there are no mono-products and their 70 products are all grouped into lines. Since Clarins is not Lancôme, it does not have the same image, the same identity or the same conception of itself. It projects itself as a Beauty Institute and the profession of beautician is very important to them. This concept implies the use of many products belonging to the same line, just as in a prescription. A mono-product cannot do everything and from this arises the preference for product lines that act in synergy. Clarins wants to create stable lines that can last for years and are in conformity with its identity, personality and brand culture. Finally, it prefers objective product promises rather than a plethora of slogans for mono-products

that all play on one factor, presently 'victory over ageing'. From this arises the names for their products, which are always in the beauty sector. The names are always descriptive of the product's actions and do not play upon dreams and fantasies as did Christian Dior when he launched 'Capture'. At Clarins, names are constituted of two or three words, for example, 'Multi-Repair Restructuring Lotion'.

In the past, the creation of any new product was usually also accompanied by the creation of a new name. In christening the new product, the product manager gave it life. Without a name, the product had no real existence. Once branded, it had a life. In 1981, at 3M, 244 new brands were created and registered. In 1991, only four new brands were created. The same thing happened at Nestlé: in 1991, the company created 101 new products but only five new brands. The age of brand multiplication is over. What has led to this change in practice?

The realisation that brands are the true capital of the company has led to this revolution. By capitalising on fewer brands, companies had to sustain their equity by nurturing them through constant innovations and line or range extensions. Therefore, the question 'what name do we choose?' becomes 'which new product should we put under which already existing brand?'

Companies with decentralised management are particularly susceptible to brand proliferation. Thus, 3M, in spite of its high rank in the Fortune 500 companies and its 60,000 products, remained relatively unknown. One part of the explanation for this was the excessive number of trademarks with which it was burdened: over 1,500. In order to solve this problem, 3M decided to take the cat by the tail and created a branding committee at the highest level (Corporate Branding Policy Committee) whose mission was to establish a precise doctrine regarding brand policy. Its approval was necessary before the creation of any new brand. To make 3M become a real corporate brand, it was decided that from then on 3M would be used to sign or guarantee all products (except the cosmetic line). The second decision was the banning of the use of more than two names on one product (as was the case with Scotch Magic) in order to abolish brand pile-ups, as is shown in Figure 12.8. In order to facilitate the integration of the new brand policy that capitalised on a few mega-brands (also called primary or power brands), 3M distribute to all its subsidiaries a guide explaining the policy to be followed in case of branding when faced with a new product. The creation of this guide led to a drastic fall in the requests for new brand creation: be it parent brands (like Scotch) or daughter brand (like Magic).

The decision tree shown in Figure 12.9 puts each innovation through four questions which serve as filters to limit the creation of a new brand to certain very specific circum-stances (like Post-it). The first filter question asks if the innovation satisfies one of the following four criteria: Is it a top priority innovation? Does it create a new kind of price/quality relationship? Does it create a new product category that did not exist until then? Is it the outcome of an acquisition? The second filter question asks whether the brand could not be used to nurture an already existing parent brand in 3M's primary brands portfolio. The third filter question seeks to discover whether the new product can provide the occasion for the creation of a new parent brand. The last filter question evaluates the capacity of the new product to justify the creation of a new secondary brand (daughter brand). From the decision tree emerge six exhaustive branding possibilities that are based on measurable market parameters. They go from the extremely simple (slides for overhead projectors from 3M) to multiple level branding (Scotch Magic, the sellotape from 3M). As expected, the creation of a new brand (primary or secondary) became the exception rather than the rule. A number of restrictive conditions had to be fulfilled first: mainly, that the innovation creates new primary demand and that none of the existing primary brands are suited.

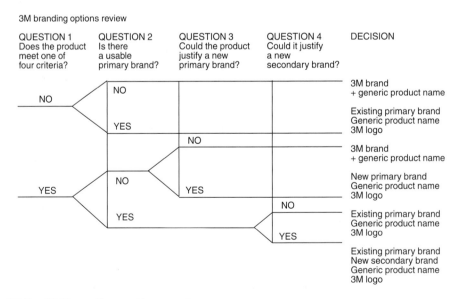

Figure 12.9　3M branding options review

Retailer branding strategies

Nothing illustrates the strategic dimension of brand architectures better than a comparison between similar companies in competition in the same sector. This is the case with the retail sector. Faced with the same potential clientele, they opt for different branding policies that reflect their individual identities and strategic preferences. Given that in the retail sector brand policies have their own jargon, we will clarify them first before linking them to the concepts and terms presented in this chapter.

The retailer's brand is not a recent phenomenon. Sainsbury started it as far back as 1869. The first retailer to officially register its brand in France was the Coop in 1929. These were umbrella brands, exclusive to the retailer and comprising a number of products within the same category (groceries or household-ware or cosmetics). The main function of these brands was to serve as a defence tool for the retailers against suppliers that would not supply to them.

In 1976, with Carrefour, the establishment of a new type of retailer brand known as the banner brand was seen. This brand was named 'freedom products' at Carrefour.

Grouping many products under it, the 'banner brand' was an umbrella brand. It appeared in no-nonsense packaging without artwork or embellishment and in a single colour (white, orange, etc). It bore no signature, only a guarantee in the visual form of its emblem or initials.

As its name suggests, the banner brand represented an offensive strategy, against manufacturers' brands. This was an occasion for an in-depth renewal of the communication strategies of those hypermarket chains that could thus promote their vision and competitiveness through support from specific products. Carrefour was thus able to present itself as the consumer's champion, hence the choice of the term 'freedom' to name its new product line. Its positioning was simple: 'as good as national brands and cheaper' (20 per cent cheaper). Thus, these banner brands gave the retailers a new visibility and also, for some, the beginning of an identity. They were moving away from the price–choice–quality–service type of communication and were starting to affirm their culture, motivation and focus.

Besides the competitive interest between distributors, banner products were also interesting in the sense that they won over public opinion in their favour, an indispensable factor in the competition that was inevitable between distributors and manufacturers in the future. In fact, while the image of the large retail stores had greatly suffered due to the elimination of smaller neighbourhood grocery stores, Carrefour's 'freedom' banner products advertised, in all kinds of media, that manufacturers' brands were only an instrument of slavery for the customer and that it was time to liberate the consumer from their clutches. And silence meant consent: manufacturers, unused to collective actions, did not react and thereby lost a battle because of their inaction.

Increasing competition led to the appearance of many generic or unbranded products on supermarket shelves. Though admittedly of lower quality than national brands, they were 30 to 40 per cent cheaper. These products came without any frills, usually in simple white packaging and with nothing but a simple description of the product (eg sugar, oil, etc). This led to a confusion in the consumer's mind as to the difference between low-priced generic products and banner brands. The confusion threatened to have the reverse effect and drag the image of the retailer down. Carrefour therefore stopped selling its 'freedom' line and launched instead a policy of corporate branding. This policy consisted of putting the store's own name on the products. It was not new – Sainsbury's, Migros in Switzerland and Jewel in the USA had been doing it for a long time.

The retailer name can be used in many ways:

■ On its own on the products concerned. In such a case it is an umbrella brand and covers a number of different products. Thus, there exist not only Carrefour corn flakes, but also frozen fish, yoghurt, fruit beverages, sports bags, car fluids, etc.

■ Alone, on the products, it serves as a line brand if these different products are united by some common benefit, some concept. This is the case with Monoprix Fitness or Monoprix Bio Line. Under the retailer brand name we have the family name of the products that fulfil certain criteria (health products or biologically-based products).

■ As a signature with another name. In such a case it is an endorsing brand. Carrefour signs its name in fine print on the lower right-hand corner of F. Delacour champagne. In the same manner, the name Printemps appears on ready-to-wear brands such as Essentials and the name is marked both on the tags as well as the products.

The third kind of retailer's brand is called 'own-brand' or private label and it has a name different from that of the retailer. Private labels can be used as:

■ a product brand: as is the case with many beers, biscuits and other food products (Sainsbury's Crunch);

■ a line brand: Micro Line hair gel at Auchan hypermarkets is a copy of L'Oréal's Studio Line;

■ a range brand: Tex for fabric at Carrefour, or Kenmore, the home appliance brand of Sears Roebuck;

■ an umbrella brand such as St Michael, President's Choice, World Classics.

Compared to older, pioneer own-brands, the latter are different in that they are often

product or line brands and they are meant to attract the clientele of a targeted manufacturer's brand. It is this that led to the name 'counter-brand' or 'copycat brand'. For instance, Asda Puffin was a copycat of the Penguin biscuit.

The basic advantage of copycat brands is the possibility of their multiplying indefinitely. Faced with a market that is being segmented more and more, the retailer can put a copycat brand in each segment, which was not possible under a common single label. This policy allows for a great flexibility to enter into niches. Compared to other retailers who put their name on products and then reject the manufacturers' brands by simply delisting them, own-brands achieve the same results but more discreetly. The consumer here has the impression of having a much larger and varied choice and reacts less to the disappearance of the big brands.

To maximise their sales, the counter-brand strategy consists of choosing a brand name, packaging, an outer design and colours that are as close as possible to those of the target brand. This creates a confusion in the consumer's mind. (See also pages 128 and 129.) Realising that a flux of clientele had been created by the manufacturer's brand due to heavy investment in research and development, quality, performance and marketing, the distributor creates a copy and packs it in the same manner as the original. The simplest way of reducing costs and risk is to imitate closely the marketing strategy employed by the manufacturer's brand. There is a fine line between a counter-brand and a trademark infringement and several retailers have already crossed it. But the law can do little about it: most manufacturers are reluctant to sue retailers on the grounds of unfair competition for fear of seeing their products thrown off the retailer's shelves. (See page 139.) Recently, however, the manufacturers of the Penguin biscuit won such a case against the Asda copy, Puffin.

As we can see, in spite of a difference in terminology, it is possible to establish a link between the manufacturers' branding strategies examined in this chapter and the concepts involved in retailer branding (see Table 12.1). They are, however, separate on two counts: manufacturers are unable to copy each other as much as the copycat brands, not only because counterfeiting is illegal but also because manufacturers do not hesitate to sue each other. Second, except in rare cases where the retailer has also vertically integrated the production process, the name of the actual producer of the private label is always hidden and cannot be verified. This also poses the problem in giving a quality certification to a retailer's brand, because manufacturers may be changed from time to time.

Besides the major functions expected of a brand, the choice of branding strategy by a retailer depends on many parameters:

▌ The value of the store name weighs upon the choice. If it uses the store name, the retailer brand assumes the name is a potential guarantor and benefits from close proximity and familiarity;

▌ The strategy also depends on the product's degree of involvement. All products do not bear the same importance for the consumer: some are more important than others and some may even be totally secondary. The sources of this importance may vary:

– 'necessary' products are bought out of necessity: we expect functional utility of them and that is all. These range from paper handkerchiefs (less involving) to vacuum cleaners (more involving);
– 'pleasure' products have a pleasure function and can vary from caramel custard to a hi-fi system;
– ego-expressive products have a social function and through them the buyer reveals his/her personality: this concerns cigarettes, soft drinks, beers and also ready-to-wear clothing.

Naturally, the products can have more than one source of involvement and it is difficult to apply one retailer brand to ego-expressive products: when these products are displayed, one does not want to create a bad impression, unless the store is one of great renown and distinction (eg Hediard, Fauchon, Harrod's, etc). The fact that Carrefour puts its name in really small letters even if it is offering champagne speaks more of the desires of the enterprise than consumer choice. When the source of involvement is strictly functional, a single umbrella brand can cover many different categories. In such a case, the brand signifies an excellent price–quality relationship, and can embrace a range of prices.

Table 12.1   Relative functions of retailers' and manufacturers' named brands

Brand's main purpose	Brand owner	
	Manufacturer	Retailer
To capture the clientele of a targeted brand		Counter-brand Copy-cat brand
To personalise the product	Product brand	Private label
To incorporate the product among others	Line brand Range brand	Private label
To identify the source of product	Umbrella brand Source brand Endorsing brand	(Banner brand) Retailer named brand
To indicate the manufacturer	Corporate branding	

The motivation of the distributor is also a determining factor. Brand management for the retailer is not, as is often wrongly believed, an exercise in graphics and creativity, and is not restricted to finding a name and good packaging. It is a new profession which implies a consumer orientation and the application of both human and financial resources to analyse the market and the consumer's demands, to research and development, to the establishment and follow-up of clients, to permanent quality control checks, and, more and more important, to the capacity for new product development.

These three parameters explain why many retailers do not want to have their name on the products, while others practise it to a certain extent and yet more follow it with a passion. The choice reflects an evaluation of the constraints and the identity of the retailer. Right from the start, Casino, like the Swiss Migros, saw itself as an alternative solution to the classic channels of distribution. The retailer must follow his own vision. He has a mission. That is why the retailer name acts as an umbrella brand everywhere. The only exceptions are so-called products of status needing a strong product brand. In such a case, the retailer's name manifests itself only as that of an endorsing brand.

Carrefour wants to be the quality multiple retailer in the world. After its 'freedom products' came the 'concerted products', comparative surveys and other manifestations of its consumer orientation. The retailer obviously puts its name to many of the products, but not all of them. Doing so would give an impression of uniformity and the loss of the freedom of choice. Also, Carrefour uses its name primarily in the grocery section which is at the core of its historical competence. Carrefour also puts its name to innovative products and thereby nurtures its image through these exclusive products. At the same time, textile products have their own umbrella brand, Tex.

Intersport is, above all, a retailer. Here, there is hardly any philosophy, project or vision. The chain does not really have an identity. But, it does have a concept of positioning: choice. That is why they have own-brands: Etirel for clothes, Techno Pro for tennis, McKinley for winter sports, Nakamura for bikes, etc.

Empirical research has demonstrated that the effectiveness of a branding policy interacts with other variables such as the type of packaging (differentiated or copycat), the reputation of the store name and the objective quality of the distributor's product (compared to that of the market leader). Thus, the Lewi and Kapferer (1996) field experiment showed that (see page 133):

If the private label quality matches that of the leading brand (with blind tests as evidence) and if the store name has a strong image, in order to maximise market share the best strategy is to use the store name and a highly differentiated packaging. In brief, the distributor's brand should behave as a real brand. This option is superior to that of using look-alike packaging and trademark infringement.

The reverse is true, however, if the retailer does not wish to use its own store name as a brand name. Then, although inferior to the former cases, the best strategy is that of copycat branding.

New trends in branding strategies

Companies do evolve in their branding strategies. An analysis of their international behaviour reveals significant trends.

Why the rise of branded houses?

An interesting classification of branding architectures is that of 'branded house' versus 'house of brands'. As it names indicates, the 'house of brands' refers to a company which operates through well-known brands but itself remains discreet if not hidden: this is the case of the ITW (Illinois Tool Works) operating with such brands as Paslode or Spit, and well known in professional circles. Procter & Gamble and Georgia Pacific also operate that way.

The branded house is the inverse case: the company itself is the one and single brand, acting as a banner and a federating force. For Aaker and Joachimstahler (2000), the models of such architecture are GE (GE Capital, GE Medical and so on) and Virgin. In fact, it is over-restrictive to assimilate the branded house to this type of case. The branded house is a strategy by which the corporation is the source of reputation and the federating force. This can be achieved by two branding architectures: the *corporate umbrella brand* (Sony, Philips, GE and Virgin are examples), and the *corporate source brand*, where there exist sub-brands or branded subsidiaries, but the leader is the parent company. This is typically the policy followed by HSBC, which puts its name or logotype before that of all subsidiaries, as long as these subsidiaries keep their name.

Two brand architectures correspond to the so-called 'house of brands': naturally what is called the *product brand* approach, and also the *endorsing brand* approach. When 3M puts its name at the bottom of all its products, is it really driving customers' perception of value? No. Although present, visibly it

remains discreet: this is the sign of a 'house of brands'. The brands of the portfolio act very independently.

Paradoxically some corporate umbrellas are also very close to being quasi houses of brands. This may look as a contradiction with what has just been said. In fact, the whole issue is that of power and organisation. Take Toshiba for instance. This conglomerate is organised in business units: computers, hi-fi, television, cookware (in Japan) and so on. Not only are the business unit directors totally independent, the country managers are also very independent. Their role is to sell the products coming from Japan. As a consequence, there is no desire at all to coordinate the communications between business units, and for a given business unit between countries. The result is that although their wear the same name, Toshiba hi-fi products do not have the same image than Toshiba computers, Toshiba television sets and so on. The Toshiba corporation up until now never thought of itself as a brand that needed to be managed globally as such. It is only recently that a VP was named with that objective, with worldwide responsibilities and authority. His or her first task will be to establish the Toshiba brand platform and to enforce it throughout all communications of any product in the world. Philips is itself now acting under the 'one Philips' internal motto.

Why do so many organisations move towards this branded house architecture? to

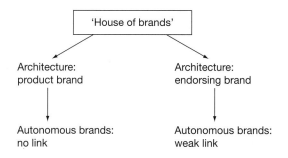

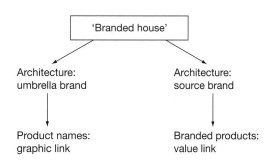

Figure 12.10   Strategic alternative

recreate identity where there is diversity, fragmentation, if not a patchwork. In modern
developed markets, unlike the emerging
ones, it is no longer sufficient to be known.
One must also consistently evoke a set of
values and stimulate emotional resonance.
This supposes some discipline and less
autonomy. Sales-oriented organisations, such
as those of Korean and Japanese companies,
assign high sales objectives to their country
managers. In exchange they have a lot of
freedom. This is why their communication is
generally managed at the local level. Creating
a branded house will meet resistance because
one source of autonomy, and not least, advertising freedom, will be affected. However, a
branded house does not automatically mean
a global campaign: the spirit of the brand
may emerge through different and even
localised communications.

Loyalty and the rise of transverse brands

There is another reason for changing brand
strategy – when the emphasis shifts from
product logic to customer logic, from a desire
to conquer new markets to developing
customer loyalty. Accor Hotels, the European
leader in the hotel industry, is a good example
of a company that was able to react and
modify certain fundamental principles of its
brand policy. Accor owes its success to the
creative brilliance of its two founders who
invented the product brand in the hotel sector.
Novotel, their first hotel chain, was based on
the concept of total standardisation –
whichever hotel they stayed in, businessmen
and women felt at home, down to the very
layout and decoration of the rooms. Then they
covered the different market segments with
other product brands: Formule 1, Etap Hotels,
Ibis, Mercure, Novotel, Sofitel and Suit'Hotel
in Europe, and Motel 6 in the United States.

According to the original logic, Accor – the
name of the holding company – was limited
to that single function and was therefore

invisible. Then, in view of the requirements of
stock exchange valuation, it was decided to
make the corporate brand more visible. It
began to appear in small print on the hotel
brochures, before being incorporated as the
trade name – Accor Hotels – in the actual logo
of each product brand.

The growth of the group's market share
recently led to another reassessment: the
decision to move from individual loyalty
programmes for each brand to a corporate
loyalty programme (Accor Hotels Favourite
Guest).

It was this same need to develop loyalty
that led l'Oréal Paris to break with its historic
brand strategy in 1995. The decision was
made in response to Nivea, whose simple
strategy maximised brand loyalty within an
increasingly broad portfolio of sub-brands
that were in direct competition with the
brands in the l'Oréal group. L'Oréal realised
the limitations of a flagship-brand strategy in
which l'Oréal Paris merely endorsed a large
number of independent sub-brands – Elsève,
Elnet, Plénitude and so on. Apart from the fact
that the publicity budget was fragmented,
there was no effective capitalisation. The
group therefore switched from a 'house of
brands' logic (with l'Oréal Paris as the
endorsing brand) to a 'branded house' logic, a
source brand with a basic unity and a very
distinctive form. This is when the so-called
'dream team' appeared on the international
scene – a collection of internationally
renowned top models and stars, each
promoting a sub-brand from the l'Oréal Paris
house, using the same creative platform and
publicity signature ('because I am worth it').
At the same time, the l'Oréal Paris brand name
became larger, more visible, and more
prominent for such sub-brands as Elsève, on
the packaging and in-store merchandising.
Finally, the denominative logic was applied to
brand extension categories that were not yet
sufficiently attributed to the brand (due to its
historic associations with hair products).
Plénitude, the brand then in competition

with Nivea, was abandoned in favour of Dermo Expertise, Pure Zone and Solar Expertise, whose more descriptive names immediately suggest competence in the area concerned.

By doing this, l'Oréal Paris was also aiming to develop real customer loyalty across the different sections of the brand and thereby make up the time lost to Nivea in this respect. In 2002, in an extension of this customer loyalty objective, l'Oréal Paris launched its first advertising campaign with a view to creating a relational data base.

Industry discovers the importance of branding

When branding policy is considered, the industrial sector does not immediately spring to mind. Paradoxically, since promotion in this sector is not done through costly publicity but through catalogues, the sales force and trade exhibitions, companies do not hesitate to register trademarks. Air Liquide, for example, has registered a total of 880 trademarks (effectively, brand names).

As well as representing a considerable cost, these trademarks also create confusion and opacity further down the line, at sales team and at catalogue level. The problem is that they are specialist names which it is hoped will be passed on by word of mouth and recommendation: 'I want some X.' But this is quite clearly impossible as there are far too many, which is why the industrial sector is beginning to incorporate the concept of the endorsing or source brand, and even the mega-brand, which creates an umbrella for a series of specialist products.

Internationalising the architecture of the brand

Should companies globalise their branding architectures? Should they just duplicate

them when entering new countries and continents? It is a fact that most branding architectures have been created slowly, through time in the domestic market. They benefited from low media costs, and a lower competition. This is why we so often find 'product brand' architectures. They resulted from the acquisition of a company by its main competitor: to avoid loosing market share, the acquirer decided to keep the brands apart. Can the same portfolio architecture be applied when entering Russia or the United States?

In Russia, as in many former communist countries, there is a unique opportunity to rapidly take a dominant position by investing fast and heavily as long as western competitors are not there, and media costs remain low. This is what Frito Lay did. This means capitalising on one brand, used as source brand or endorsement, and rapidly pushing new products into new segments.

In the United States, the challenge is the media and distribution costs. The consequence is the obligation to nest products under an umbrella brand which remains to be created. As a result we see what can be called a 'vertical crunch' of brand architectures. There are in fact two types of ''vertical crunch'. The first is a bottom-up crunch, when a mere descriptor becomes a driver (the way consumers name what they buy). For instance in Europe, the whole shampoo line of l'Oréal Paris is sold under the brand Elsève: its many products have names such as Color Vive and Energance. In the United States, Elsève has not been launched. Instead of three levels, there are only two levels (l'Oréal Paris and a wide range made of names like Vita Vive, Nutri Vive, Hydra Vive, Curl Vive, Color Vive and Body Vive).

The other is a top-down crunch, when a mere endorsing brand becomes the driver. For instance in Europe the famous biscuit speciality Pim's is called Pim's by Lu. In the United States, it is Lu Pim's.

Companies also exploit local equities to carry international brands. For instance, all

Unilever's global ice cream concepts (Magnum, Solero and so on) are endorsed by a local house brand, acting as reassurance by its long-established proximity and familiarity in the country.

Group and corporate brands

Since 1990, there has been a basic tendency for corporate brands to be as visible as possible on the products themselves. For example, Pharmaceutical Laboratories now regard themselves as a brand in their own right and take much greater care to ensure that their brand name is clearly visible on the packaging of brands of medication. In the professional electrical equipment sector, the name Schneider Electric appears on the packaging of products from the Merlin Gerin, Telemecanique and – in the United States – Square D brands. The back of all Nestlé products bears the Nestlé corporate brand name and the customer service phone number. It is the same for Danone, which has taken great care to create a logo for its Danone corporate brand, as distinct from the Danone commercial brand used for chilled products, and water and biscuits in Asia.

This tendency is part of a basic trend – the demand for responsibility and transparency. The company presents itself as the ultimate endorsement and no longer hides behind its brands. This also has the effect of increasing its visibility, and therefore its attractiveness to students, executives and the employment market in general. In Asia, television ads for Procter & Gamble and Unilever brands bear in the last seconds the signature of the companies themselves. This is not the case in the United States or in Europe, although – influenced by this Asian experience – Unilever is looking for some kind of higher public visibility to boost its corporate brand profile. In Asia, however, these two companies do not enjoy any reputation and this must therefore be established.

Finally, once a company is quoted on a stock exchange, it must try to influence the share price since, over and above the financial results published on a regular basis, market predictions are influenced by the company's name and reputation. So anything that makes people dream a little adds to its goodwill.

Companies regularly change their name and take the name of their flagship commercial brand. For example, the company formerly known as BSN changed its name to Danone Corp (it nearly became Evian Corp), while the Volkswagen group and l'Oréal group have both taken their name from their flagship brands. Mars, on the other hand, changed its name and became known as Masterfoods, as other companies are called Bestfoods (Unilever) or General Foods. So what are the reasons for these two diametrically opposed attitudes?

Capitalising on a flagship brand by applying its name to the group makes it possible to take advantage of the halo effect, even if this involves two clearly distinct sources, since the image of the one influences the perception of the other. For example, the press regularly refers to Volkswagen as Europe's number one brand when it was not the brand but the multi-brand group that earned the title through the cumulative sales of each of its brands. In fact, at the beginning of 2003, Europe's number one group was PSA Peugeot Citroën.

The l'Oréal group does not advertise a great deal. However, its brands use heavy advertising, along with research and development, as one of their main weapons. By sharing the name of its glamour ('l'Oréal Paris') brand, the l'Oréal group benefits from the impact of an international image that inspires confidence in shareholders and defines what they do.

It was for entirely opposite reasons that Mars took the less transparent name of Masterfoods. Apparently, it was difficult to sell brands of pet food such as Pedigree and Whiskas under the Mars corporate or group name, particularly since Mars conjures up the image of a single product, a legendary chocolate bar, which has growth limits in an extremely segmented market. There was also a risk of a negative halo effect on financial predictions. LVMH, the initials of Louis Vuitton Moet Hennessy, uses both strategies. On the one hand, the experts are familiar with the significance of the acronym, which refers to internationally renowned luxury brands. On the other, by retaining the acronym, the group demonstrates its intention to remain discreet by placing the emphasis at brand level rather than corporate level, and leaving the brands to develop through their own creativity, publicity and the quality of their distribution. From this, it can be seen that the position of the corporate brand in relation to its subsidiaries is in fact a reflection of the group's internal organisation.

This essential part of group strategy is developed below.

Group and subsidiary relationships

In the industrial sector where external growth is the norm, the question of the status of corporate brands that have been acquired crops up again. Should they be left independent? Should they disappear? Should they be endorsed with a simple visual symbol of the parent company? Or joined to the name of the parent company? If they behave as mere holding companies such firms should not be surprised by their low public recognition. For instance, although it was founded in 1969 and was one of the largest chemical companies in the world, Akzo remained largely unknown. No wonder: all the companies acquired had kept their own company names and brand names (Warner Lambert, Stauffer, Montedison, Diamond Salt, etc). Akzo thus acquired a poor image in terms of technology because of its lack of visibility. It had become the biggest unknown company in the world.

General Electric has defined four brand policies and specifies the conditions for their application. These policies range from:

▌ The so-called monolithic approach where GE behaves like an umbrella brand and replaces the corporate brand which has been bought (either immediately or after a transitional period of double branding). The brands GE Silicons, GE Motors and GE Aircraft Engines have all emerged from this process.

▌ The endorsement approach where GE signs its name beside the name of the product or the company that has been acquired.

▌ The financial approach where GE behaves like a holding company and is only discreetly mentioned (X, member of the GE group).

▌ The autonomous approach where the acquired company or product makes no reference to GE.

To decide upon a policy, GE uses six selection criteria:

1. Does GE control the company?

2. Does GE have long-term commitments in this company?

3. Does the product category have an image value? Dynamic or not?

4. Is there a strong demand for GE quality in this industry?

5. Is the corporate brand which has been bought strong?

6. What could be the resultant impact on GE?

Group style and branding strategy

At regular intervals, the major industrial groups ask themselves whether their branding strategy is as effective as it could be. There are three formal types of strategy that can be implemented within industrial groups. Although the terms 'subsidiaries', 'holding companies' and 'companies' tend to be used in this context, structurally speaking they represent the typical figures of branding strategy – source brand (A), endorsing brand (B) and umbrella brand (C). But beyond these terms, the impact on level-one subsidiaries (sub-brands) is self-evidently not the same. Above all, each branding architecture has organisational repercussions, with each playing a different role for the group in relation to its subsidiaries and sub-subsidiaries:

▌ The strategy in which the group is a source brand can be likened to the role of an orchestra conductor or band leader.

▌ The strategy in which the group is an umbrella brand makes it a unifier.

▌ The strategy in which the group is an endorsing brand makes it a coordinator.

It is obviously not up to the branding decisions to determine the management style of a particular group – that would be a reversal of roles – but it should explain management choices and the criteria on which these choices are based.

Internationalising the group/ subsidiary architecture

The world is complex. Groups must face the fact that their different branches have a very different competitive status in different countries. In addition, in some regions high equity brands/companies were purchased as a means to penetrate the channels of distribution. This creates a question as to the longevity of these brands.

Architecture has a connotation of something nice, square and fixed. In fluctuating and fragmented modern markets, one should be careful not to harness operations under too many constraints that would prove to be counterproductive. This is why it may not be ideal to have the same branding architecture across all products/services and regions of the world.

Let us analyse the Lafarge case. This worldwide company is known for its core business: concrete and cement. Less known is the fact that Lafarge has many other branches: roofing systems, plaster, granular products and paints. If internally the goal of creating a feeling of belongingness to the group is justified, the same does not necessarily hold true as far as branding is concerned.

As for all brands, two criteria need to be taken into account. First, is the activity core or not? If it is not, it could be sold in the future. For instance, in the plaster business, if BPB (British Plaster Board) takes over Knauf, then Lafarge would become stuck in the number three position in this market. There is no reason to stay in a business where one is number three: resources might more profitably be invested in other businesses. Second, are there strong local brands in the portfolio and are they key drivers to customer loyalty?

As a consequence Lafarge has not chosen a uniform, monolithic umbrella brand architecture. It is definitely umbrella on the core activity: after acquiring the Korean Ala Cement company, this local leading company soon became Lafarge Ala Cement, or in India Lafarge Tata Cement. For non-core activities, Lafarge acts as an endorsing brand when there exist strong local names in key mature markets. This is the case for Redland in the UK, Braas in Germany and Klaukol.

Should Redland have become Lafarge Roofing UK or Lafarge Redland? Here a distinction must be made between the legal name of the company and the commercial brand. Marketing research has shown how much these names conjured emotional attachment among local professionals: the company became dual named, and the local brand became endorsed by the branch (Lafarge Roofing). However, in Malaysia from the start it created Lafarge Roofing Malaysia.

This shows that the question of the name of societies, branches and brands needs to be well understood as implying different criteria. Not all societies are brands, or divisions that are organisational classifications subject to change. Brands are made to convey values to one or many targets.

Corporate brands and product brands

For years, companies have hidden behind their brands. Through prudence and fear of being affected in case of brand failure, company names have been separate from those of the brands. Thus Procter & Gamble remain unknown to the public while their brands are the stars (Ariel, Pampers). In fact, it is this that allowed the company to keep its turnover stable when the rumour of it being linked to a sect raged through the United States. The brands, autonomous from the company itself, suffered no setback. Nevertheless, such instances are rare and the tendency is more towards transparency due to communication obligations. Also, the public wants to know, in larger numbers than before, who are the actors behind the brands. Journalists want to disclose who is the 'brand behind the brand'. This also explains why so many companies have taken on the names of their most famous brands (eg Alcatel-Alsthom, Danone). They get more visibility and acknowledgement. This helps the stock exchange investor also, in cases where he is not an expert or very well-informed, to understand better what he is buying. It may also create a beneficial confusion for the brand itself. After it bought Audi, Seat and Skoda, Volkswagen Group is now co-leader in Europe on a cumulative basis. However, many people mistakenly speak of Volkswagen as a brand being the number one in Europe.

The trend towards greater visibility of corporate names also has other causes. Distribution is one of them. Distributors, multiple retailers and hypermarket chains are not very interested in brands. Their fundamental relationship is with corporations, not with brands. It is a business to business relationship. The name of the powerful corporation is therefore a potent reminder of that relationship.

Only corporate names can endow brands with stature, an extra-dimension calling for respect. Would Audi have succeeded in its remarkable recovery had it not been known that Audi belonged to the Volkswagen Group? The same holds true for Seat and Skoda. Nissan's status will change because it is now part of the Renault group. As long as car makes are only brands and not part of a larger and more dynamic corporation, they arouse perceived risk among consumers and do not guarantee a long-term presence.

Many companies sell in industrial and commercial markets at the same time. Here, there is the problem of having to choose between the use of product brands or the use of the corporate reputation to support the products. This depends on the quality of the company's endorsement and the degree of visibility that it wants to acquire. In practice, the respective weight to be attributed to the product brand and the corporate brand depends on a case-by-case analysis of the returns brought by each of them on the many targets concerned. Table 12.2 presents the outline of such an analysis.

At ICI three kinds of brand policy were used (see Figure 12.11):

▉ The first policy is the classic umbrella brand where the products keep their generic names and are signed with the corporate name. Most often this concerns raw materials and undifferentiated products where the company guarantees a certain quality and the differentiation is essentially commercial (ie special conditions offered to the client on a case-by-case basis). An example would be ICI polyurethanes.

▉ The second policy is that of the endorsing brand. The company puts its name beside the product brand and this confers a status of high technology and reliability to the

Table 12.2 Shared roles of the corporate and product brand

Targets	Product brand	Corporate brand
Customers	+++++	+
Trade associations	++++	+
Employees	+++	++
Suppliers	+++	+++
Press	+++	+++
Issues groups	++	++++
Local community	++	++++
Academia	++	++++
Regulatory authorities	+	++++
Government commission	+	++++
Financial markets	+	+++++
Stockholders	+	+++++

product. Thus, Dulux paints are accompanied by the ICI logo.

- The third policy makes exclusive use of the product brand. Tactel is one of the most widely sold fibres but it never mentions ICI. The product is sold to the textile industry and to the fashion world, and it is feared that the mention of the ICI name may alter the positive images linked to Tactel. Similarly the insecticide, Karate, which is sold throughout the world, also does not make any mention of ICI. Does this have

anything to do with not wanting to step on ecological toes and avoid the possibility of blame regarding the harmful effects of pesticides on ground water? This situation is not only changing through time, but it also changes according to the company. Decis, the world leader in pesticides, makes a reference to Roussel Uclaf (Agrevo division) on its packaging. Similarly, to benefit from its innovations, Du Pont de Nemours mentions clearly 'Lycra by Du Pont' on all its communications for Lycra, the fabric that has revolutionised women's lingerie.

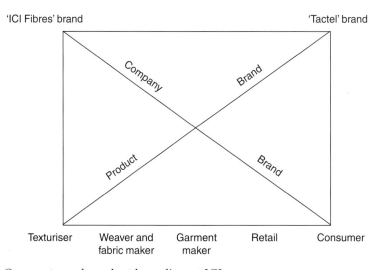

Figure 12.11 Corporate and product branding at ICI

Product innovations generally provide an ideal occasion to ask fundamental questions about the branding policy. How to name these innovations? Let us suppose that the Lafarge Roofing Division decides to launch a radical innovation in roof maintenance and rebuilding, associated with a guarantee for 10 years or more: an 'all in one approach', service oriented instead of technology oriented. How should it be called? Would a name like Lafarge Roofing Total Solution be better than a new specific international name for that innovation?

It is surely an occasion to demonstrate the ability of the group to deliver more than cement, its core symbolic product and star (which in this sense means, offering high growth and high profitability). However, roofing is a high involvement decision, with both a high perceived risk and dimensions of emotion. It may be hard for the corporation ego to recognise it, but would a Lafarge name be able to evoke the sufficient emotion needed in all real brands within a realistic timespan? Wouldn't it be better to use it as a guarantee, and let a specific good commercial name foster the benefits, tangible and intangible, of this total solution, against the small local companies with which it will be competing?

13

Multi-brand portfolios

Although the main function of a brand extension is growth, there are limits to what a single brand can achieve. However, the other way in which a company can grow is by creating new brands to meet the demand that existing brands cannot satisfy. But it takes courage to launch and position new brands in a bid to dominate the market.

It takes courage because, at a time when extensions are the order of the day, it is difficult to admit that even a mega-brand has its limits. Companies prefer to attribute failure to production problems so that they can try – and fail – again. Thus Mattel is facing the challenge of the 'tweens' (see Lindstrom, 2003) who are no longer really children but not quite teenagers or adolescents. There is a saying in the business that today's kids are getting older younger.

In concrete terms, this means that the company's business model for the 1970s, 1980s and 1990s is defunct. In the past, Mattel treated children in the 4–10 age group in exactly the same way, as a homogenous group. This had a major advantage in terms of cost (economies of scale) – they were all sold the same Barbie doll, which represented 40 per cent of the company's sales.

Mattel's first response to the tweens challenge was to segment the target group and create a special Barbie for 8–10-year-olds, the Barbie Generation Girl with the single Barbie signature. Then, to counter the success of MGA's Bratz dolls for 8–12-year-olds, Mattel relaunched My Scene Barbie, still with the Barbie signature but smaller. However, the company had to make up its mind to take the plunge and create a genuine new brand rather than a brand extension, and in 2003, the multinational launched Flavas to succeed Barbie. After all, there comes a time in every little girl's life when she no longer wishes to play with Barbie.

Levi's had already taken the plunge by launching Dockers after initially trying a simple brand extension – Levi's Tailored Classic. But the same brand cannot be simultaneously rebellious and classic. In the car sector, brands seem to represent progress up the social ladder. Thus, Honda created the Accura in the United States, just as Toyota created the Lexus and Nissan Infinity, since customers worldwide seem to equate changing the brand of their car with proof of financial success. This is why Renault really needs to buy Volvo or Jaguar to add some top-of-the-range brands to its portfolio.

This same rationale applies to the distribution networks. For example, Hanes – the largest apparel brand in the world – is sold in the big department stores but could not be sold in supermarkets, so Eggs was created for this network.

Basically, therefore, the purpose of multi-brand portfolios is to better meet the demands of segmented markets, and any reassessment of the portfolio raises the question of the segments to be retained. So when Procter & Gamble decided to dispose of a number of brands in Europe, in 1999, it was because they did not fit into the group's European segmentation – premium, smart buyer and low-price.

Inherited complex portfolios

The question of how many brands should be kept in each market has become a primary concern of all senior marketing managers. The fact is that, due to historical reasons, most firms have to manage a large portfolio of brands. The natural tendency during the growth of firms has been to add new brands each time they wanted to penetrate new market segments or new distribution channels. This was done so as not to create conflicts with former segments and channels which could have endangered their old brands. The vogue of company mergers and acquisitions brought additional brands that managers were reluctant to dispose of or merge with other brands. The size of brand portfolios, therefore, just grew and grew, with increased complexity and waste.

Times have changed though, and now the trend is to reduce the size of portfolios as quickly as possible. There are several reasons for this reverse in trends:

▊ Although it is easy to maintain several brands simultaneously in industrial markets where different brands are sometimes used for the same product to ease relations with distributors, in the retail market it is nearly impossible. The direct consequence is that only a few brands in a portfolio will be promoted, to gain a significant market share. The others will be abandoned.

▊ The concentration of the distribution trade has reduced the number of retailers and has even almost suppressed certain retail channels and small businesses. Brands that were previously uniquely handled by specific distribution channels and sold only in certain stores may now be found in a single wholesaler or purchasing group. This tends to lead to the reduction in their numbers. The trade has also pursued a policy of creating distributors' own brands. This, coupled with the fact that supermarket shelf space is limited, leads to the reduction of space allocated to the other brands, another factor causing a reduction in the number of references or brands themselves.

▊ Industrial production has also become concentrated. International competition has put the emphasis on high productivity and low costs and has led to the regrouping of production units and research and development activities. There is less justification for large brand portfolios when the products, however varied, come from the same factories, and even the same production line.

▊ Consumers, however, still have the last say and despite the fact that the objective of a brand is to clarify the market, their most frequent complaint is that they are confused by the growing number of brands. A company is fooling the consumer if it sells two identical products under two different brand names. Manufacturers respond by rationalising their brands.

▊ The last point, but not the least, concerns brand internationalisation. In many areas today, national barriers no longer make sense. In Europe, for example, class, lifestyle and consumer needs are no longer exclusive to a single country. The luxury goods industry has long been targeting the world market, as indeed have most industrial companies. Not all brands are suited to the international arena, however. The investment required to establish a significant global presence means that firms can only maintain a small number of brands, or indeed just a single one for a mono-brand strategy such as that of Philips, Siemens, Alcatel, Mitsubishi or ABB.

How many brands, therefore, should be retained in a portfolio? It is obvious at this stage that there does not exist any magic formula or number. The question of the number of brands to retain is closely linked to the strategic role and status of the brands. In keeping only a single brand, we are assuming that an umbrella brand policy is possible and indeed pertinent in the market being considered. For decades, the Philips brand included both brown and white products, yet they parted with the latter markets, selling them to the American company Whirlpool. The decision regarding the number of brands to be retained should therefore be closely linked to an analysis of the brand's function in its respective market. Every market can be segmented, by product, customer expectation or type of clientele. This does not mean, though, that a market divided into six segments, for example, should necessarily call for six brands. This depends on their function (do we need endorsing, umbrella, range or product brands?). It also depends upon the long-term corporate objectives, the degree of competition and the resources of the company. The appropriate number of brands results from a multi-stage, multi-criteria decision process whereby various scenarios are presented and evaluated. A good example of this approach is Michelin.

From single to multiple brands: Michelin

Companies' attitudes to brands are changing – should they adopt a single-brand policy or penetrate markets from several different angles (multiple entries)? Some have decided to concentrate on a small number of international brands, which does not prevent them from promoting strong, local brands in their countries of origin – as l'Oréal did with Dop. Some have concentrated on a single brand (Philips), while others have changed from a single-brand policy to a real portfolio – as in the case of Michelin, the world's leading tyre manufacturer. This last case is extremely interesting.

Initially, Michelin found it difficult to accept the need for a brand portfolio. The company's success was based on the fact that it focused on research in the interests of quality, under a single name – the name of the family that had created a set of values and the means to achieve a valid long-term policy. Culturally speaking, everything at Michelin revolved around the Michelin name. Of course other brands existed, but they were often found in the basket of factories bought locally to penetrate the market – there are 80 Michelin factories worldwide. These factories did not receive any form of innovation or marketing support – they were purely tactical brands.

The problem with this is that the market is segmented. In the US automobile market, for example, there are certainly customers who want the best quality in the world, but there are also customers who want a major brand that offers good value for money, and those who only have US $100 to buy a set of tyres. There are also the 4 x 4 and pick-up drivers who are conscious of changing fashions and want customised tyres. For these drivers, the Michelin brand is too staid. A single brand cannot meet such a diverse demand, whereas a group can. This is why BF Goodrich is positioned as a sports brand in a flourishing market that pays little attention to price, namely the 4 x 4 market.

In the United States, Uniroyal targets the cost-conscious customer and is referenced by General Motors. This market segment is serviced by the Kleber brand in Europe where, following a series of mergers and the restructuring of groups, Uniroyal is still managed by Continental, Michelin's German competitor. In China, the role is fulfilled by the local brand Warrior, which has the largest market share. Distributor requirements also have to be taken into account since distributors are now demanding a quality tyre with their own brand name. Michelin has two policies in this respect. The first is to supply a tyre with the distributor's brand name, according to the latter's specifications. Thus, Michelin manufactures tyres for the Liberator brand, sold exclusively by Wal-Mart in the United States, and for Norauto in Europe. The second is to supply the distributor with a brand that belongs to Michelin. Thus Warrior, positioned as a middle-range brand in China, is used as the name for low-cost tyres in the United States and Europe. The same applies to the Japanese brand Riken, the Hungarian brand Taurus and the Czech brand Kormoran.

Michelin's global strategy aims to encourage customers to move from mass-produced products to middle- and then top-of-the-range products, with the different brands making it easier to emphasise perceived difference. Second, it involves adapting to the market. For example, the Chinese market was for a long time small and elitist because of the high proportion of top-of-the-range vehicles. Michelin's major share in this market was aided by the ill will created by accidents in Formula 1 racing that were linked to quality defects in the tyres produced by the Japanese group Bridgestone-Firestone. As the Chinese car market becomes increasingly democratic, there is a need to offer new buyers quality tyres, since those produced locally are dangerous at the speeds that can now be reached on the new Chinese motorways. The Michelin group must

therefore provide a response to the middle range and the economical segments (if not it will be marginalised), but without endangering the reputation of Michelin as the world's number one brand for quality. The acquisition of the leading local brand Warrior has enabled it to complete its brand portfolio in this segment. In Japan and Korea, there is also a segment of clients demanding products 'made in the United States'. This demand has been satisfied by the acquisition of the US company BF Goodrich.

The last aspect of Michelin's global strategy, required to complete the picture, is that, because tyres are relatively inexpensive to transport, the tyre market is truly global (unlike the car market: see page 397). Today, the group's Chinese factories manufacture tyres for distributors' brands (private labels) in the United States, and will soon be producing Uniroyal and BF Goodrich tyres for Michelin North America. One day, they will also be making Michelin tyres. Furthermore, the globalisation of production makes it possible to circumvent customs barriers. For example, Japanese car manufacturers cannot export cars to the United States unless they include a minimum percentage of parts made in the United States, which is why these manufacturers fit their cars with Michelin tyres made in US factories. This has enabled Michelin to penetrate the reputedly nationalistic and closed Japanese market through this, as yet, fairly low-key distribution.

This example illustrates the flexibility and adaptation made possible by a brand portfolio – from local brands through middle-range brands to lifestyle and top-of-the-range brands, not forgetting the connection with the distribution networks via distributors' brands. All this adds up to global segmentation and the logic of globalised product platforms. Even so, as has been seen for the Michelin group, the branches are totally independent and the positioning of the brands is completely different in aviation, agriculture, the truck division and the car industry.

The benefits of multiple entries

At the beginning of this chapter, we looked at the practical reasons why the number of brands had to be reduced, sometimes even to a single brand. They all correspond to a strategy of domination and competitive advantage via low cost. While recognising the market segmentation, it has been decided not to take it into account at brand level, but only in terms of products.

The multi-brand approach, on the contrary, is the logical consequence of a differentiation strategy and as such cannot coexist with a low-cost policy, in view of reduced economies of scale, technical specialisation, specific sales networks and necessary advertising investments. Nevertheless, with the exception of exclusive luxury brands, pressure remains. In order to take advantage of productivity gains, there is a tendency to fragment the production chain in the cause of differentiation at the last possible moment, thus exploiting the benefits of the learning curve. This is the case in the domestic appliances industry, making industrial regrouping a necessity, as well as in the food processing or automobile industries. The policy of having general car brands makes the most of all possible production and corporate communication synergism, and breeds the loyalty of the customer who progresses from one model to another within the same make.

With all the advantages of a mono-brand policy, what makes it necessary to have several brands on the market at the same time?

To start with, market growth. No single brand can develop a market on its own. Even if it forms the sole presence at the outset, once the brand has created the market, its development requires a multiplication of players, each investing to promote their respective differences. The collective presence of a number of contributors helps to promote a market. Beyond their differences, their combined advertising accentuates the common advantages of the product category.

A multiple presence is necessary to support the market as a whole. It would not be in Philips' interest to see its competitors in the electric razor market disappear. This would only decrease the number of messages praising the merits of electric razors, which could only benefit Gillette and Wilkinson Sword. Philips should acquire a brand and maintain it as an active brand in the market. In the pharmaceutical industry, a laboratory discovering a new formula could certainly profit from 'co-marketing' it with other laboratories in order to accelerate its impact. An example of this is found in the case of aspartame.

Multiple brands allow for best market coverage. No single brand can cover a market on its own. As a market matures there is a need for differentiation and it becomes necessary to offer a wider range; the market is becoming segmented. A brand cannot be targeted at several different qualities at the same time without running the risk of losing its identity. In any case, consumers and retailers themselves will object to further brand ascendancy. This dual process is illustrated by the case of Rossignol. The company Rossignol follows a dual brand policy:

▌ a mono-brand multi-product policy: the hallmark Rossignol covers its skis, ski suits and ski boots (those coming from its acquisition of the Le Trappeur Brand, since then debaptised);

▌ a multi-brand mono-product policy, with the Dynastar brand on skis, Kerma brand on sticks and Lange brand on boots.

With 20 per cent of the world ski market, Rossignol is the leading manufacturer. Its share in the upmarket ski sector is thought to be even greater, of the order of 40 per cent or more. This is an area where the company should not offend people's susceptibilities by expecting them to dress from head to toe in Rossignol products. If the world leader wants to grow even bigger, it should be the one increasing the choice, rather than its competitors. In this market, the distribution is still handled by a large number of small independent retailers, who fear the control of a single supplier. This is why each company brand has its own sales force. In the United States the Rossignol company presence is assured by two separate companies, Dynastar Inc. and Rossignol Inc. In the industrial sector, Facom and Legrand, two dominant leaders, successfully increased their hold on their market by creating apparently separate and autonomous brands. This enabled them to find new distributors, who were only too happy to have at their disposal a near exclusive brand, different from those of other retailers in that zone.

Multiple brands offer a tactical flexibility which also enables one to limit a competitor's field of extension. In this way Delsey, the leading European luggage manufacturer, cornered Samsonite. They created a new brand, Visa, positioned to undercut Samsonite prices, while at the same time Delsey restrained them from moving into the top-of-the-range market.

A multi-brand policy can stop any new competitors entering a market. A strong entry barrier to a market can be created by offering a complete range to retailers, with a brand name for each sector of the market. This is why in on-premises in the European market, soft drink companies create barriers to entry by providing the full range of products needed (Coke, Fanta, Sprite and so on).

A multi-brand policy is necessary to protect the main brand image. This partly explains why the Disney Corporation uses a number of brands in film production, for example Buena Vista and Touchstone. This enables them to produce films of every type without endangering the revered Disney name. Similarly, when the success of an innovation is not certain, it would be foolish to risk associating it with a successful brand. This is why Procter & Gamble launched their first liquid detergent under the brand name Vizir and not

under the name of the leading market brand, Ariel. The inverse policy was adopted by the Cadbury Schweppes group when it decided to launch its new fizzy drinks not under the brand Wipps but as Dry de Schweppes. This was not only because Schweppes' name helped the sales but because it was thought that the new brand Wipps would reinforce the slightly old and stuck-up image of Schweppes, and would have, in the long term, threatened the value of the brand. In order to avoid having to lower the prices of its leading products, 3M created the sub-brand Tartan which only covers the products where 3M is the dominant leader. This minimises the risk of unwanted cannibalisation. Where 3M is not dominant but a challenger, retailers might be tempted to move directly to the lowest priced alternative from 3M.

Linking the portfolio to segmentation

The brand portfolio is indicative of a company's desire to better meet the demands of the market, not only through differentiated products but also through different brands and therefore different identities. The organisation of the brand portfolio reflects the type of market segmentation chosen by the company. Ferrero (Kinder) bases its market segmentation on age groups and user status, l'Oréal bases it on distribution channels, Legrand on types of consumer motivators, Procter & Gamble and Volkswagen on price brackets, SEB on consumer populations and value systems, Evian on the benefits sought from the water, Guinness on occasions, and so on.

The following sections illustrate how portfolio brands and segmentation are linked.

Socio-demographic segmentation

Although certain people regard socio-demographic segmentation as an outmoded concept, it is still a useful tool when it comes to understanding consumer behaviour and preferences, and as such, can be used to establish a brand portfolio. Ferrero (Kinder) is Europe's leading confectionery company. Unlike the Mars bar, Kinder has developed a portfolio that adheres rigorously to segmentation by age, with the development of needs and situations corresponding to each age group – from Kinder eggs for the very young to snacks for adolescents. All magazine editors produce different titles based on age and gender. Their magazines target extremely narrow age groups and reflect progress at school or rather the child's cognitive development according to Piaget. Lego also has a brand portfolio based on different age groups, from the very young to pre-adolescence.

Benefit segmentation

A key criterion for segmentation is the main benefit looked for by consumers. Companies can organise their brand portfolio by positioning each brand on one single motivation/benefit, as long as of course it is a profitable business. This is the basis of Danone Waters brand portfolio in Europe. Recent marketing research revealed the following motivations to purchase: status, good life (13 per cent); health (57 per cent); and price (30 per cent). The macro motivation for health needs to be sub-segmented: for 16 per cent it refers to an aesthetic vision of health, for 15 per cent it means vitality and for 26 per cent this refers to specific problems. As a result, Danone Waters reorganised its brand portfolio of non-carbonated waters as follows:

▪ Evian targets 29 per cent of the consumers (those seeking status and aesthetic health).

▪ Volvic is positioned on vitality (15 per cent of the market), against Nestlé's Vittel.

▪ New brands were created on physiological needs: Taillefine against Contrex (Nestlé),

both on remaining slim, and Talians, another new brand.

▪ A host of source waters to fulfil distribution expectations of a low-cost brand.

In this portfolio, Evian's role is to be the referent of the market, and to valorise water as much as possible (in addition, this is consistent with the fact that Evian's supply is not unlimited: it takes time for the Alps to create this water). As a consequence, some brand extensions are forbidden, such as the growing area of aromatised waters. The second brand of the group, Volvic, priced 10 per cent below Evian, has the ability to stimulate the market through such extensions. Taillefine (known as Vitalinea in other countries) is actually an extension in the field of water of a dairy brand positioned on 0 per cent fat. To compete in the weight-conscious segment, against Contrex (segment leader, from Nestlé), instead of launching from scratch a new brand, it was decided to extend this global franchise to water.

Attitude segmentation

Unlike most automobile manufacturers, which organise their portfolio along a vertical price line, PSA has chosen to develop two parallel generalist brands, Peugeot and Citroën. In 2003 PSA was the second largest European car manufacturer. What is the basis then of the segmentation? Peugeot has in its roots, its identity, a number of core values (reliability/quality but also dynamism and aesthetics) which address primarily the consumers who like to drive, to master their car, deriving pleasure out of it. Citroën, although its cars share 60 per cent of their hidden parts with the Peugeot models, delivers a totally different driving and living experience. Once a brand with character, ingenuity, innovativeness, it went bankrupt twice before being bought by Peugeot. Reinventing Citroën, PSA has made it a car brand for people expecting their car to foresee the evolution of life styles (Folz, 2003).

There are strong gains in having two parallel brands, beyond sharing the same platform for manufacturing. Aiming at the same price segment, when one model of a brand starts declining in its life cycle, the other brand launches its own model. As a result, the rate of innovation of the group within each price segment is exceptionally high compared with competitors, a key success factor in modern markets. Also, with only two brands, one avoids the problems of Volkswagen with its four brands largely overlapping, a factor that negatively affects the profitability of the global portfolio. Salespeople trade consumers down by suggesting they consider Skoda or Seat cars, entry brands, which are essentially the same as Volkswagen cars. In addition, these two entry brands now face growth problems: where should Skoda and Seat go? To capitalise on their recently built brand loyalty, they wish to trade their own consumers up with higher-priced models, but run the risk of increased cannibalisation, and of a still larger lack of differentiation from Volkswagen's lower lines.

Channel segmentation

This is a growing mode of segmentation and organisation of brands. The rationale is that channels are fighting against each other. An allocation of different brands to each channel avoids conflicts, price harmonisation problems, and maximises the adaptation of the brand to the motives of channel patrons. In addition, taking the small appliance business for instance, being sold exclusively at Wal-Mart prevents brands from having a presence in the selective distribution channels, which still represent more than 55 per cent of the market in the United States. This is why a portfolio is very helpful in allocating brands to channels.

The paradigm of this approach is l'Oréal: all its brands have to be sold in one and one only channel:

- There are brands for selective premium distribution and department stores: Lancôme, Helena Rubinstein, Biotherm, Kiehl's and Sue Emura.

- There are brands for mass channels: L'Oréal Paris, Garnier and Maybelline.

- There are brands for pharmacies: La Roche Posay and Vichy.

- There is a brand for direct sales by mail order: CCB (Club des Créateurs de Beauté) although this name is really a handicap for the globalisation of the brand.

- There are brands for the professional hairdresser channel: L'Oréal Paris Professionnel, Redken, Matrix, Kerastase and Inné.

The first segmentation criterion is the channel. When this channel is not already present, it is reconstructed thanks to the presence of two or more brands in the channel so that costs can be shared. For instance, if pharmacies in Canada do not sell cosmetics, a specific counter can be developed in department stores, with a pharmacist to assist consumers, selling both La Roche Posay and Vichy.

Of course there is another segmentation criterion: price. In each channel, there is a premium brand and a mainstream brand. Finally each brand epitomises one universal model of beauty. In the mass channels, everywhere in the world, l'Oréal Paris symbolises Paris, and Maybelline the American style of beauty.

L'Oréal's profitability rests largely on this systematic channel-based brand portfolio organisation. It gives this group the ability to price the same product very differently from one channel to another, capitalising on the fact that consumers' price sensitivity is not at all the same across channels and purchase situations. For instance, a hair fixing gel sold to consumers at a hairdressing salon for 9 euros under the brand Tecniart (l'Oréal Paris

Professional) is bought by the hairdresser for half this price, that is to say for more or less the price at which a consumer would find the product under Fructis (Garnier) or Studio Line (l'Oréal Paris) in mass distribution. Kerastase shampoos are sold at 8 euros to the consumer in a hair salon, but the same product is sold at 2.5 euros under the Elsève brand at a multiple retailer.

The same holds true for an industrial group like Saint Gobain. This group has created a portfolio of stores aiming at building and construction:

- from Platform du Bâtiment, a cash and carry for small general contractors;

- to the mass multiple retailer Point P aimed at craftspeople;

- to Lapeyre aimed at the DIY expert, able to buy a window and install it without professional help;

- and K par K (literally, case by case), a chain of mini-stores selling tailor-made new windows, fully installed.

Of course, the last option is the most expensive (1,000 euros for a replacement window, with everything included), but in most of the cases, the windows that need replacing are standard in size and design. It is therefore a standard window that is bought (not a customised one), essentially the same product as could be found at Lapeyre for instance at a fraction of the price, but without any service. The same reasoning applies to the other brands in the portfolio.

Occasion segmentation

An increasing number of companies have become aware of the importance of occasion segmentation (see also page 170). All products are in fact purchased or consumed on a particular occasion. The real issue is therefore to influence the occasions affecting consumption rather than the consumers themselves. In fact, the same person can consume a product in different ways during the course of the same day if he or she has encountered several clearly differentiated occasions. Each occasion gives rise to clearly differentiated expectations, and therefore to a specific type of competition for the brand since, on each occasion, the brand does not encounter the same set of circumstances.

In the case of Guinness, the occasion not only forms the basis of the brand portfolio but also structures the organisation of sales and marketing. Today, there are occasion managers, just as there used to be brand managers. Thus Guinness is positioned on the so-called 'affiliation' occasion typical of the pub environment, while Carlsberg corresponds to the 'release' occasion in nightclubs and Budweiser targets the 'relaxing at home' occasion.

When dealing with occasion segmentation, the first thing a company should do before developing several new brands is to consider whether line extensions could enable a particular brand to expand by gaining a foothold in situations or places that have so far been inaccessible. However, there are limits to this extension, which is where the brand portfolio comes in.

Price segmentation

This is a most classic organisation of the portfolio. The whole Group Volkswagen brand portfolio is based on it, with entries ranging from the low-end Skoda or Seat to Volkswagen itself, Audi and luxury brands like Rolls-Royce. Accor, Europe's leading hotel group, has achieved its success by launching a set of product brands, all positioned at a specific price. The Chanel-Bourjois company has two entries, the luxury brand Chanel, and Bourjois for the mass market.

In the construction market, Velux is one of the most global brands: it stands for roof windows in 40 countries all around the world. It has just introduced Roof Light as a low-cost alternative, targeting the price-sensitive market segment. The price gap with Velux is 30 per cent, less expensive than Velux's main competitors (Roto and Fakro), which are sold with a 20 per cent price gap. It is also sold as a private label of large multiple retailers in the DIY market.

In fact, very few brands have successfully managed to cover substantially different price ranges. It is true that generalist car manufacturers like Renault build a wide range of cars, from the Twingo to the Val Satis. But they cannot really enter the top-of-the-range market, even when they add a flattering extension to their brand name such as Avontime. This was also one of the aims of their association with Volvo, a brand more easily associated with top of the range cars. Toyota took the approach of creating a separate brand, Lexus. A brand portfolio makes it possible to cover the different price sectors without affecting the reputation of each brand. The Sanford group, having taken over Parker, Waterman and Paper Mate, can specialise its brands in terms of price and style. By reputation, Parker represents the top of the range in each product segment, from the ball point pen to the ink pen. Waterman represents the middle of the range. The Whirlpool group allocates to each of its brands a price bracket. The average price of the Whirlpool brand itself must be that of the middle of the market. The average price of the Laden brand corresponds

to the lower quartile of the market price range and that of Bauknecht the higher quartile (see Figure 13.1).

A multi-brand portfolio only makes sense if, in the long term, each brand has its own territory. This is not always the case – companies hang on to brands whose images are not different enough to justify the economies of the multi-brand policy.

Linking brand portfolio to prescription segmentation

In the business-to-business sector, the type of key influencer targeted constitutes a strategic criterion for segmentation. The market can in fact be segmented according to the decision-making process. Along the value distribution chain several participants play a key role, and brands have different ideas of what they consider to be a key role.

For example, in the aluminium systems market for the residential and service sectors, the leading European company HBS (Hydro Building Systems) has three brands – Wicona from Germany, Domal from Italy and Technal from France – all represented to varying degrees in Europe, depending on the level of maturity and development of the markets. In reality, each brand targets a different operator-prescriber:

▪ Wicona targets architects, research departments and engineering companies.

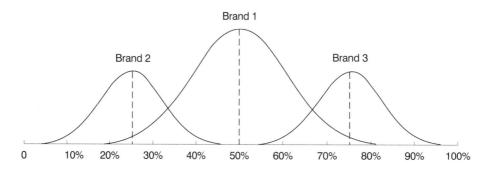

Figure 13.1 Segmenting the brand portfolio by price spectrum

- Domal targets installation companies, general companies that win tenders associated with building sites. It supplies flexible and inexpensive extruded aluminium systems manufactured in its small plants.

- Technal aims directly at the end-users via television and a network of well-known registered installers who also co-finance the advertising.

Legrand, Europe's leading electrical appliance company, uses the same type of organisation. Legrand's expansionist policy is based on external growth. In the electrical equipment sector, standards vary significantly from country to county in order to prevent access to national markets. There is also a great deal of intense lobbying by operators who want to perpetuate a situation that creates a network of local markets. The only way to penetrate these markets is to buy the leading local company, which is why Legrand acquired the Italian company Bticino. It then specialised the brands, allocating Bticino to the prescribers, engineering bureaux and research departments, while Legrand became the installers' brand, offering them a broad and totally integrated range of products in which ease of installation is the cardinal virtue.

Another example of this type of brand portfolio organisation is provided by the UK company Arjo Wiggins, a leading manufacturer of top-quality paper for companies and professionals. Since 2002, this company has reorganised its basket of brands to create mega-brands, whose size is critical, bringing together what were previously small product brands under the umbrella of each one. The new organisation is structured as follows:

- AW Curious Collection targets creators and designers in advertising and design agencies, since they are the key influencers for projects and creations in which innovation and creativity count for a great deal.

For example, the Curious Collection ranges include aluminium and steel paper.

- AW Impressions targets the printers who are the key prescribers for a great many of the jobs they are asked to do by companies – for instance, letterheads.

- Conqueror targets the general public, the end-users who want a quality paper to reflect their company or their personal image.

Global portfolio strategy

For the last few years big groups have been carrying out a policy of stuffing their portfolios with additional brands, either through acquisition or partnerships, at the same time as extending the product range of some of their brands. Nestlé has become the world's number one food processing company thanks to its acquisition of Carnation and Stouffer in the USA, Rowntree in the UK, Buitoni-Perugina in Italy and Perrier in France. Philip Morris is another busy company; its foodstuffs division is made up from Kraft (cheeses), General Foods (coffee, corn-flakes, confectionery, chocolate) and Jacobs-Suchard (coffee, chocolate).

In the mineral water market, outside Evian and Badoit, the Danone group, which already owns Volvic, has bought La Salvetat, a sparkling mineral water spring. Kraft General Foods owns three strategically important chocolate brands: Milka, Suchard and Côte d'Or.

This trend towards company size growth is partly motivated by the gains that can result from joining forces in research and development, logistics, manufacturing, distribution and sales. Another reason is due to the levels of financial and human resources that are now necessary to compete on the world market. A third reason is the desire to buy a dominant position and be able to restrict the market to a duopoly or an oligopoly. A final reason is to be able to resist the pressure exerted by the concentration of distributors.

It is worth remembering that besides this quantitative aspect, the idea of a portfolio implies a global vision of the competition in a market or category. A portfolio also forces the relationships between one brand and the others in the portfolio to be considered, the idea being that a brand's value can be enhanced by belonging to a larger portfolio. There are several decision grids, the most famous being the Boston Consulting Group's. Hence at Pernod-Ricard one speaks of growth products (Clan Campbell, for example), contributors (Ricard, Pastis 51, Orangina) and the famous cash cows. To these can be added the concept of a 'strategic brand': Pacific, a non-alcoholic aniseed drink, may not be financially interesting but is vital for the long-term prospects as it accustoms future customers to the aniseed taste. Unisabi (Mars) control half the cat food market thanks to a portfolio that is made up from the following brands: Ronron, Kit-e-Kat, Whiskas and Sheba. These can be classified into strategic, value and tactical brands. Whiskas is strategically aimed at being the invincible brand in the market, with the biggest range, large profits, central consumer benefit (best nutrition) and the most expensive advertising campaign. Sheba is a value brand: its market share in money is three times as much as its market share in volume. Sheba, a high-quality product, is targeted at the most dedicated owners. Ronron is a buffer brand, low in price and hardly given any advertising support; it is there to counter-attack the distributor own brands. Strategic, niche and tactical brands can also be distinguished in the Heineken Breweries.

The case of industrial brand portfolios

In the industrial world, multi-brand strategies either have very few constraints, or there is a multitude that is very often underestimated.

The first case is illustrated by the chemical industry in the agricultural market. As each herbicide brand is associated with one unique active principle, a single company often stocks 500 trademarks or even more!

When a brand is strategic and the portfolio corresponds to the segmentation of the final market, the brand must mean more than a mere difference in name or logo on the product. In this way BASF sells paint to coach builders worldwide under two brands, Glasurit and RM. They are, in fact, the same product. In the car world there is a difficulty with the idea of two different qualities – no one would buy the inferior one. The two brands are thus supplementary and not complementary.

Glasurit is aimed at the technically minded coach builder. As its international slogan points out, Glasurit is the 'Preferred Technology Partner'. As its slogan indicates, RM is the thoughtful coach builder partner, 'The key to your success'. It is aimed at the other segment of coach builder who expect service to increase their activity. They see themselves rather as company directors than as painters.

To maximise their chances of success, BASF gave each brand the necessary means to defend itself. Dictating who did what would only weaken both brands and give the advantage to their competitor Akzo. Instead BASF decided to:

- create two separate management teams (as opposed to a common marketing department, which was for a long time the case), based in two different countries;

- have two separate sales forces in charge of the distribution, so as to minimise cannibalisation from the inside;

- avoid all references to the parent company BASF, in order to increase the perceived difference between the two brands;

- develop services in line with the positioning of each brand;

▌ have different advertising campaigns on a worldwide scale.

This is how BASF maximised its cover of the market. It adapted itself to the two distinct segments of the car re-finish market and to the psychology of the constructors. Mercedes, for instance, would not like the idea that its paint supplier also supplied Lada!

The constraints associated with multi-brands are often underestimated in the industrial world, where a brand is considered just a name or a reference in a catalogue. When a brand corresponds to a strategic segmentation this underestimation can undermine or even break the strategy. In the industrial electrical equipment market, the manufacturers have to decide whom to favour, the installing company, the wholesaler/distributor or the end-user. It is impossible to favour all three at the same time. Merlin-Gerin, who concentrated on the distributors, were losing touch with the fitters. For the latter, the Sarel company was created. This increased the proportion of the market that could be reached, provided that all links with Merlin-Gerin were hidden. In practice, in the various countries they operated in, because of the different turnovers of Merlin-Gerin and Sarel the constraints of their multi-brand strategy were soon forgotten for the sake of saving costs.

▌ Sarel could sometimes be found in the same office block as Merlin-Gerin's local headquarters.

▌ The published organisation charts did nothing to hide the Sarel–Merlin-Gerin link. Sound management on the organisational front could instead dictate that, despite its small size, Sarel be directly linked with Schneider's, their common parent company, and not Merlin-Gerin's local manager.

▌ On occasions, in order to save money, both Sarel and Merlin-Gerin shared the same trade exhibition stands.

The organisation of brands in the business-to-business sector poses specific problems that need to be addressed as such. For example, industrial groups whose growth typically involves the acquisition of companies soon begin wonder whether or not to keep the brand name of the newly acquired company, and how much independence it should have in relation to the purchasing group.

Furthermore, the engineering culture might make the product central to the group or company identity, while the brand is little more than an appendage and is often the name of a reference. This explains the increasing number of references, registered throughout the world, that preoccupy companies' legal departments and give rise to regular complaints about the excessive number of brands. However, although there may be a brand name in legal terms, there is every reason to believe that these names are not in fact real brands with real market power.

It is therefore a question of reducing the number of brand names in the portfolio, and reorganising them around a few valid mega-brands that serve as an umbrella, a central point of reference. From this it can be seen that the task of rationalising the brand portfolio is in fact indicative of the need to reorganise the business. How do you manage multi-product mega-brands within a structure of business units, knowing that the mega-brand may well cover several business units? Do you need to create a brand committee, from across the business units, that meets on a regular basis with a view to making decisions about problems of coherence in the development of the brand – coherence in terms of products and services, price positioning on the various markets, advertising and catalogues? At this stage, large-scale industry begins to consider how other more 'lowly' sectors – the mass-consumer market and FMCG market – have resolved this type of problem.

The role of the sales force in designing the portfolio

In business-to-business contexts, it is essential to include sales in any consideration of brands since it is ultimately the sales force, the technical and commercial engineers, and the front office who represent the brand. It is therefore important to distinguish four types of brand:

1. The *integrating brand* is usually the corporate brand when it is used to sell a global service to a single client. To this end, it brings together the skills and synergies of the different business units. The front office and sales force represent the name of the group. Typical examples of this are Vinci, Schneider Electric in its promotion of global services, and Suez Industrial Solutions.

    The integrating brand (usually the group) also ensures the transversality of the product brands at the level of the catalogue, invoicing and shared vision (for example, when the brand/group issues a communication on 'security').

2. The *integrated brand* is usually the name of an acquired company, internationally renowned for a particular application, a particular need or a particular area of expertise. However, the front office and sales force operates under the name of the group

3. The *endorsed brand* only uses the name of the group as an endorsement (as with, a company that is a member of XXXX) and has its own name and front office. This is typically the case when the brand uses a business model that is different from the group's area of expertise.

4. The *independent brand* is presented as completely independent, with no links to the group, which in theory implies separate offices in the different countries concerned. It therefore has its own name

and front office and there is no visible relationship with the group. This type of brand makes it possible to overcome the problem of expanding market coverage when a brand is already dominant. Thus, when a brand in the group already covers more than 30 per cent of a particular market, it is logical to launch an independent brand for all those who do not want to work with the first. Furthermore, the independent brand is often used to advocate a policy that contradicts the official policy of the group, in order to increase market coverage without placing the group in a precarious position. The US group Rockwool is a typical example of this type of portfolio organisation.

Linking the brand portfolio to the corporate strategy

So how many brands does a company put on the market? Does it adopt the single-brand or the brand-portfolio model? These are the type of questions asked by modern company and group managers. And this is how group policies evolve, based on the lessons learnt from the development of their market shares and from the diagnosis of the causes of a possible upper limit on profits.

As has already been seen, Michelin is a typical example of a group whose global market share reached an upper limit in spite of the widely acclaimed excellence, not to say superiority, of Michelin tyres, including Formula 1 versions. After years of using a virtually single-brand model, the Michelin group decided to change its policy. Michelin certainly remained the flagship, but it was no longer the only brand to be the focus of innovative ideas and new advertising. In the private car market, Michelin realised the advantages of double segmentation – the first linked to price, the second to the fashion for status tyres. There are customers throughout the world who want value for money but, while recognising the superiority of the Michelin brand, are not committed enough to want to buy Michelin tyres. But should they simply be left, as in the past, to turn to the competition in the form of Bridgestone? The demands of this segment of smart buyers needed to be met, and this was done via Kleber in Europe – an old brand in the portfolio that has been revitalised through innovation, such as the non-puncturing tyre – and Uniroyal in the United States.

But there is also a segment of drivers, usually drivers of pick-ups and 4 x 4s in the United States and Europe, for whom tyres are a kind of status symbol. They want their tyres to be flashy and ostentatious and are not attracted by Michelin because, in their eyes, a brand that focuses on safety, performance and long-term development is too staid, not fashionable enough, not different enough. It is to these drivers that the group dedicated its US brand Goodrich, with a policy of offering a regularly updated range of large, custom-made tyres. However, while Kleber is cheaper than Michelin, Goodrich is positioned in the same price bracket.

SEB, world leader in small household appliances, decided to concentrate on four major brands (Moulinex, Tefal, Rowenta, Krups) to compete with Philips on the international market, while for the moment retaining certain local and regional brands such as Calor, SEB and Arno. However, there was a strong temptation to emulate Philips and its single-brand policy on the domestic market. But this would have been a mistake since there is no point in imitating a market leader on a smaller – and therefore less visible and less successful – scale.

The growth of Legrand, the market leader in small electrical appliances for the residential and service sector, was achieved through the acquisition of specialist brands. Then Legrand picked up 80 per cent of its catalogue and 'Legrandised' it, making it simple, ergonomic, user-friendly for installers and electricians, and above all compatible with the rest of the catalogue (based on the Lego model). Legrand became the reference catalogue for the sector – a business model that is repeated worldwide. So what does Legrand do with the brands it buys? It keeps them to create a protective barrier, using them in a preventative capacity to ensure its domination of the market. The electrical installation market is no different from other markets and Legrand, like other market leaders, creates the desire to be different among certain customers, making sure they do not want to have the same brand as their colleagues and competitors. So, rather than leaving them to turn to its competitors, Legrand keeps their custom by offering – albeit much reduced – specialist brands. As already stated, these brands also create a protective barrier for Legrand so that a newcomer trying to penetrate the market could not replace Legrand in the eyes of wholesalers. It would be offered the place of a small specialist brand.

There are also parameters linked to the distribution strategy that explain why the Volvo truck division that bought Renault Trucks has maintained the Renault brand name. But this can only be understood by taking account of the general strategy of manufacturers in response to the liberalisation of the European car and truck market. Agents are now no longer obliged to deal exclusively with a single brand so, if they want to prevent another manufacturer from filling the breach, it is better to offer two fairly well differentiated brands, but which belong to the same group. And this is exactly what Volvo did. To prevent the risk of any drift towards the lower-priced models (as is happening in the Volkswagen group), the price of Renault Trucks was re-evaluated, which helped to greatly increase the profitability of the division.

The l'Oréal group continues to buy new brands and thereby extend its portfolio. In fact, it is moving out of Europe, is currently targeting the United States and has plans for Asia where it is still a modest player.

To accompany this expansionist strategy, the group buys strong local brands either because they are the leaders in their market segment or because they anticipate the trends of the future. This is why it bought the US mainstream brand of makeup, Maybelline, as well as Softsheen Carson, which specialises in hair care for African-Americans. It has also bought the US brands Redken, a very fashionable hair care brand for professionals, and Kiehl's, a 'long-term development' and 'niche' brand of cosmetics. In Japan, it has bought the Sue Uemura brand. One interesting fact that will be examined in the chapter on globalisation is that l'Oréal subsequently globalised these local brands.

Key rules to manage a multi-brand portfolio

There are a few principles to be followed to optimise the results of multi-brand entries in a competitive market. Although simple to express, they pose implementation problems to organisations built and organised on other principles than brand logic.

Portfolios need coordination

Brand portfolios do not manage themselves, they need some form of coordination and even a coordinator above brand level. Experience has shown that companies are 'porous', with ideas passing between departments, across corridors and even between buildings. This gives rise to an – albeit involuntary – tendency to duplicate brands within the same portfolio. The allocation of innovations also gives rise to difficulties, with each brand wanting the innovation before the others. This is why companies have either a brand coordinator or a brand committee responsible for addressing these problems.

Allocate innovations according to each brand's positioning

It is a well-known fact that innovations are the life-blood of a brand, since they renew its relevance and differentiation. This is why it is essential to have clear and precise platforms (a charter of identity) for each brand – a tool for clarifying the main lines of development and innovation of the brand. This makes it possible to allocate innovation according to brand values and not under pressure from the sales force, which wants each brand to enjoy the same advantages. In fact, it should be quite the opposite – it is through innovation that the brand reveals its identity. It is therefore important to distinguish between exclusive innovations (such as coupés for Peugeot) and innovations that will be introduced over a period of time (phased innovations), and also to establish the order in which these innovations will be allocated to the brands.

Apart from brand values, positioning and market share also influence the allocation of innovations. For example, there is no point in allocating a specialised innovation (targeting a small number of households) to a mass-market brand. It is far better to reserve an exclusive innovation for a top-of-the-range brand which, by definition, targets a more limited clientele. This is how Elcobrandt manages the allocation of innovations between its mass-market brand Brandt and its top-of-the-range brand Thomson.

However, the rule for allocating innovations as a function of brand identity comes up against another type of logic, the logic of cost reduction. For example, the logic of platforms where an increasing number of parts are shared between different brand models totally contradicts the principle of allocating innovations according to brand value. Nothing could be more a function of identity than Citroën's hydro-pneumatic suspension, which reflects the identity and very essence of the brand – overcoming technical constraints to increase passenger comfort. This suspension – the historic attribute dating from the famous DS models – is only found at the very top of the Citroën range. But if it had to be invented today, what industrial group governed by the logic of production platforms would agree to create and develop such an innovation for a single brand, let alone a single model?

Conversely, to increase the relevance of the Peugeot 607, it could be necessary to adopt the rear-wheel drive option typical of the German top-of-the-range models that set the international standards. The 607 is constructed on the top-of-the-range Citroën platform which, as everyone knows, is a front-wheel drive. Given the design issues and costs of a production line for a rear-wheel drive, it is easy to understand why an industrial group might hesitate to commit itself to this option for the only top-of-the-range model of a single brand. The future lies in partnerships with other manufacturers.

Do not 'rob Peter to pay Paul'

Since the aim is to create a portfolio of strong brands, you must avoid making this mistake. Although it is standard practice to position brands clearly in relation to one another in order to maximise their appropriateness for the segments targeted, a brand should not be prevented from becoming strong. Thus innovation is an integral part of the key values of PSA's two general brands Peugeot and Citroën. Limiting this value (innovativeness) to one brand would destroy the other. There is simply no future for non-innovative brands in the car market.

A brand portfolio is not an accumulation of independent brands but the reflection of a global strategy of market domination

This makes the procedures and intervention of the US Federal Authorities and the European Commission rather paradoxical since, for these bodies, the fact of maintaining a sufficient level of competition is essential to accept or refuse a proposed merger or an acquisition. But there is no point in hiding the naked truth. Corporate mergers and brand acquisitions are largely determined by a single objective – market domination – over and above the synergies and cost reductions achieved by pooling resources. Why did Coca-Cola want to buy Orangina and pay US $1 billion for this predominately local brand? Quite simply because it would have enabled the group to force Pepsi-Cola out of the market. Since it did not have a fizzy orange drink in its portfolio to offset Coca-Cola's Fanta, Pepsico had in fact signed a strategic distribution agreement with Orangina.

A portfolio is therefore a global approach on the chessboard of competition, with a precise role allocated to each brand. Brand managers should therefore receive a set of instructions so that they understand their role and do not deviate from the global plan by carrying out a series of independent initiatives over a period of time.

A portfolio is not a simple collection of brands that just happen to be there as a result of the vagaries of history, but a well-structured and coherent group in which each brand has a place and clearly defined role:

- For example, this may be a financial role, in which the brand contributes to the financing of another brand. This is typically the case of local brands which are leaders in their own market. These brands are and must remain important contributors to enable the portfolio under construction to develop as a whole.

- The role of a brand may also be to defend the brand leader. For example, Colgate Palmolive, thinking that a price war was about to be declared on its leading fabric softener Soupline, was prepared to lower the price of its 'flanker' brand Doulinge to avoid lowering the price of its brand leader.

Legrand successfully covered the market and rendered its general brand impervious to attacks from competitors by a precise allocation of roles between the Legrand general brand and the specialist brands it had bought and maintained (Arnoult, Planet Watthom and so on). These brands formed an outer barrier at wholesaler level in the event of foreign competitors trying to enter the market. If the wholesalers were disloyal to Legrand and referenced a newcomer, at least they only affected the escort ships and not the flagship.

▌ A brand can also fulfil the role of group banner brand, especially if the brand has the same name as the group.

▌ It is worthy of note that this rationale is equally valid for daughter brands and their role in the construction, reinforcement and defence of the parent brand. It has already been seen that, apart from their specific positioning relating to a particular need or clientele, the 14 daughter brands of Nivea all had a specific role to play and made their contribution to the Nivea 'house' in terms of a specialised area of competence as well as an input of innovation, sensuality and fashion. There is no doubt that they are all very much Nivea brands but nonetheless each adds a personal touch, which is why, in spite of a very strong 'Nivea-ness' and very precise guidelines on how the brand should be presented, it does not come across as monolithic.

▌ The consequence of the portfolio logic is that it is dangerous to acquire a brand leader without the brands that go with it. If Schneider had succeeded in merging with Legrand, it would have been crucial to preserve the network of more modest, more specialised brands maintained precisely because they created an effective barrier that protected the star brand, Legrand. All too often, company rescuers, especially if they are investment funds, do not have this long-term vision. They resell the small brands without taking account of their collective role.

Within all large companies, there is an inevitable tendency to replicate

This must be combated since it destroys the competitiveness and imagination of the brands concerned. It is partly because there is always an underlying competition based on prices, since the basic function of groups is to reduce costs by pooling as many resources as possible. The main danger of groups is that, in the interests of making economies (which is quite natural), they tend to erode the identity of their brand in their portfolio by giving the common areas too much prominence when they should be concealing them, or by publicising too much information on the fact that the different brand models come from the same platform. It is crucial to ensure that all the visible parts of these brands are different. Now 'visible' does not only refer to design: companies that buy trucks look at the engine and some key hidden technical parts of the truck, especially for long-haul models.

Focus on a very specific and carefully targeted external competitor

This is one way of preventing the brands in a portfolio from replicating each other, apart from permanent surveillance by the brand committee or brand coordinator. This reminds managers that the best way to cover the market is via the logic of multi-brand portfolios and not by 'narrowing the focus'. Choosing a target competitor for each brand increases the chances of achieving this objective.

A classic risk of brand portfolios is their complexity

This is true since exaggerated fragmentation does not allow each brand to achieve its critical size. This is what business-to-business companies look out for since, for them, a brand – even registered – is merely a name and not a long-term publicity and promotional medium. This is why their legal departments are gradually collapsing under the cost of registering and monitoring trademarks (brand names), and it is what led Air Liquide to reassess its entire portfolio of more than 700 'brands' in 2003. Distributors are also susceptible to the same risk when they rethink their portfolio of distributors' brands (private labels). Décathlon managed to avoid this pitfall; when it changed from the single Décathlon brand to the so-called 'passion brands' portfolio, as many as 13 brands were envisaged before some were merged and the company decided on 7.

The Volkswagen group is currently subject to this risk. Although Seat and Skoda should, in theory, have been separated geographically, the four brands Seat, Skoda, Volkswagen and Audi are still found in several countries, each with its own network of agents. Sustaining an independent commercial network requires a large product range and the ability to create customer loyalty. This means that Seat and Skoda have to move upmarket, but where do they stop and how are they to be differentiated from the very similar newcomers from Volkswagen and Audi? Price is one solution, but the publicity based on the fact that these four brands come from the same factories and even the same platforms has created the ideal conditions for internal cannibalisation. The agents selling Seat and Skoda use it as a sales argument.

Design and portfolio management

Design plays a crucial role in the battle for differentiation. It is design that structures customer expectations, design that evokes brand values, creates visible differences and develops new favourites on mature markets. This is why it has to observe several key principles:

- The principle of radicalisation. Design cannot be vague – since the strategy is to attack the market with a small number of brands, they must be clearly defined, with a specific design, all the more so since organisations have a natural tendency to soften the hard edges, which leads to a resemblance on the shelves that has a dramatic effect on perceived differentiation. Radical design must also compensate for the increasing lack of differentiation due to the industrial logic of platforms. There is no place on today's mature markets for half-hearted designs. If there is a brand identity, it must be clearly visible.

- The principle of externalisation. If the company is responsible for defining the story to be told by each brand, that is, creating its identity, it is important to seek outside help for the design itself by appointing a designer for each brand who is totally committed to that brand. Thomson did the opposite and entrusted the design of its four brands, Thomson, Saba, Telefunken and Brandt, to the same designer, Philippe Starck, who was a brand in his own right. This is why, within an organisation, design must be positioned at brand level, not corporate level, even if this requires robust coordination to avoid replication between brands, a tendency that is all too frequent. But this risk is avoided if the company appoints an external designer, for each brand, who is inspired by its strategic platform.

- The principle of business. The function of design is to promote and develop business, not art. Design should not become self-absorbed. For example, the aim of designing a coffee pot is not to enable consumers to invite their friends round to admire their coffee pot, but to offer them a good cup of coffee. In short, the purpose of design is to enable the brand not just to look good but to function efficiently.

▌ The principle of courage. The key question in design is whether a design can be properly tested. Certainly, the ergonomics and functionality of a product must always be tested at user-status level. But apart from that, what is the relevance of a few individuals' (interviewees') opinions of a design when it is, by definition, the opinion leaders (the press) who decide whether or not a product is in good taste when it is launched in a few months' or years' time? Design is a risk. In the car sector, for example, how can you predict which design will be perceived as avant-garde in another four years, in the event that the brand could be said to be a trend setter? Renault took the risk with its audacious (some will say over-audacious) design. But four years ahead of its time, it is difficult to forecast perceptions with any degree of accuracy.

Does the brand portfolio match the organisation?

A brand is only successful if the factors governing its production work together in a coordinated and motivated manner. The success of a group logic and a brand portfolio cannot be assessed without analysing the conditions of its development and, above all, the type of organisation. Since this is not widely publicised, or may even be deliberately played down, it tends to be overlooked as a key factor in the success of a brand portfolio policy.

The main risk of a brand portfolio is the gradual de-energising of the brands, reduced to the state of increasingly undifferentiated 'outer casings' that are little more than publicity devices. This is exacerbated by the fact that the economic press only talks in terms of groups and therefore publicises the fact that brands that were once different are now produced by the same group. Its readers, often opinion leaders, are within their rights

to ask certain questions, behind the bodywork, what remains of the brand identity? Do Jaguars still have a Jaguar engine or do they have a Ford engine? Will the specificity of Saab disappear with its integration within the GM group?

The essence of a brand is differentiation. Anything that detracts from this is a threat – within the context of a favourable economic equation, of course.

To a certain extent, over-centralisation is responsible for the loss of differentiation. At Fiat, the different brands are managed within the same department, with Alfa Romeo alongside Lancia and Fiat, a type of organisation that leads one to wonder whether the company still believes in its brands. Conversely, PSA – Europe's second largest car manufacturer, almost on a par with Volkswagen – may use the same factories but Peugeot and Citroën remain separate organisations with their own product plan, marketing, design, publicity, sponsorship and, of course, distribution network (Folz, 2003). Volkswagen has abolished the VAG (Volkswagen Audi) network and given each brand its own distribution network. It has to be said that the sales force in the VAG network had a strong tendency to push the Volkswagen models rather than the very similar Audi models, which were 10 per cent more expensive.

Part of Seagram's problems can be explained by the over-centralised organization of its international brands. The development of international campaigns at all price levels is a classic tendency among all centralised organisations. It is significant that the first thing the buyer of Seagram did was to decentralise the organisation of the brand portfolio. Thus the management of Martel, the flagship of cognac worldwide, was relocated in Cognac where famous brandy is produced, while Chivas was returned to London.

LVMH, world leader in the luxury market with such famous brands as Christian Dior,

Christian Lacroix, Vuitton, Moet, Hennessy and Tag Heuer, has an interesting business model. The group manages 45 international luxury brands. When asked about the upper limit on the number of brands in such a portfolio, the group's CEO, B Arnault, replied that there wasn't one. In fact, success in the luxury sector depends on there being three types of people able to work together – in design, management and marketing – but this is impossible to achieve at a centralised level. At LVMH, however, each brand is a 'house', a mini-company, and this makes it possible to create the optimum conditions under which extremely talented people from these three areas of competence are able to work together. As heads of their 'brand-company', they are more motivated and their remuneration is directly proportional to their financial results and the international reputation of the brand.

Although it not as widely known, l'Oréal functions in the same way. It is significant that within the l'Oréal group, reference is made to the Garnier 'house', the Lancôme 'house' and so on. These 'houses' are autonomous operational units that manage their business with an international approach.

In the field of distributor brands, changing from the single brand – usually a store brand – to private labels also affects the organisation. The recent transformation of Decathlon (the world's fifth largest retailer of sports clothing and equipment), from the Decathlon brand to the so-called 'passion brands' portfolio, had far-reaching repercussions for the organisation – is it in fact possible to develop 'passion brands' within a centralising structure? The first people who have to be inspired by this passion are those within the organisation, the managers and the teams, then the co-designers, the fans and the opinion leaders. There is a need to recreate a formal autonomy.

Auditing the portfolio strategically

Companies regularly reassess the relevance of their brand portfolio. Numerous matrices have been devised to help them do this – all derived from matrices used for the evaluation of the activity portfolios created by consultants such as the Boston Consulting Group, McKinsey and Mercier. These matrices incorporated profitability, the competitive situation and the potential for growth. But can matrices for the analysis of an activity portfolio be simply converted into matrices for the evaluation of a brand portfolio?

There are two possible levels of analysis. The first is the intra-brand level which evaluates the portfolio of brand products (sub-brands or daughter brands) according to the criteria mentioned above – are they in declining or non-cash generating segments, what are the growth vectors for the future? The second level asks the same questions at multi-brand level, on the global chessboard of actual and predictable competition. The lines and columns of the matrix are growth and profitability. The markets are then shown as circles whose size reflects the actual size of the market. Brands are represented as portions of these circles (markets) where the portions reflect their market share.

The most classic way of structuring a portfolio is to divide the brands into groups according to attractiveness and function. This makes it possible to identify:

▮ Global brands, which should theoretically be the largest source of growth in the brand contribution, and as such should receive the lion's share of investment in advertising and promotion.

▮ Local or regional growth brands, which have the potential to one day become global brands.

▮ Local or regional brands that can be qualified as 'fortress' brands and which are often the historic market leaders, 'entrenched', and therefore very profitable. There is therefore a strategic interest in maintaining these 'fortress' brands since they in fact finance the development of global brands in their own country. They are often brands in mainstream segments.

▌ Local or regional 'cash-cow' brands, which have a low growth rate but a strong contribution margin.

Another form of audit consists of regularly evaluating the ability of the current portfolio to ensure the profitable coverage of future markets. Is the current portfolio the right response to market developments and competitive logic?

Thus, in the insurance sector, everyone is familiar with the growth of new distribution methods, like the telephone and the Internet. An insurance company cannot afford not to be represented in this way. However, since the conditions offered are so very different from those offered by the network of general agents and brokers, they need to be represented by a specialist brand. This is how UK insurer Aviva structured its brand portfolio. Eurofil was created to cover the growing segment of low-cost car insurance without creating conflict with Aviva's other insurance distribution networks.

The segmentation of a market by user status (linking volumes, expectations and competitors to the use made of the product) also makes it possible to identify unexploited pockets of growth in the current portfolio. The first question to be asked is whether a range extension would offer an opportunity to gain a foothold in these areas. In this respect, all Nivea's sub-brands reflect this determination to exploit all the potential sources of growth on the beauty-care market by capitalising on the single Nivea brand.

When this cannot be done, a company must have the courage to launch a new brand. For instance, in 2003, after trying everything

under the global Barbie brand, Mattel decided to launch the new Flavas brand (see page 329).

Auditing the portfolio can also reveal that it does not constitute enough of a barrier to prevent competitors entering the market, or even an incitement for them to leave. For example, it is impossible to find Orangina on the French TGV (high-speed train) network or in many airports and stations, even though it is the second largest soft-drinks brand in the country. The logic of the operators of the café-hotel-restaurant network is to choose a soft-drinks distributor offering a complete portfolio – from cola to lime and fruit juice. So clients of the Coca-Cola Company receive Fanta (a fizzy orange drink) and Minute Maid (fresh orange juice) but not Orangina. This therefore creates a local monopoly and prevents free choice among end consumers.

A local and global portfolio – Nestlé

How do the multinationals organise their brand portfolio to improve the efficiency of their brands simultaneously? Nestlé is an interesting example of this.

The Nestlé portfolio of 8,500 brands is organised by geographical status and role. Together they create a 'hierarchy of brands' in which each product is associated with at least two brands, at different levels in the hierarchy (not to mention brands of ingredients). The geographical criterion allows three groups of brands to be distinguished – international, regional and local brands.

These brands fulfil different functions and roles, depending on the customers, and represent the principal families of brand architecture. There are 'family brands' (or source brands), range brands, product brands and endorsing brands. Eighty per cent of the Nestlé Group's activity is brought together under six strategic corporate brands – Nestlé, Nescafé, Nestea, Maggi, Buitoni and Purina. Seventy strategic international brands, designating either ranges or products, come under – or even outside – the umbrella of these six corporate brands. They include Nesquik (an extensive range of chocolate milk products), but also product brands such as Kit Kat, Lion, Friskies and the mineral waters Perrier, San Pellegrino, Vittel and Nestlé Pure Life.

A third category of brands groups together 83 brands known as 'strategic regional brands', which are regional rather than international, such as mineral waters like Aquarel and Contrex, the Nuts bar, and Herta cold meats. Finally, there is a fourth category of local brands sold only in their country of origin.

Thus the Nestlé brand refers to several levels and roles:

▌ It is a corporate brand and as such acts as an endorsement for all the products and brands in the group. This endorsement function means that the corporate brand usually appears on the side of the packaging or on the labelling on the back.

▌ The Nestlé brand is also one of the six strategic corporate brands, with the status of a family brand or source brand. It covers categories as diverse as baby products, products for children, chocolates, ice cream, chocolate bars and fresh dairy products.

▌ The Nestlé brand is sometimes simply a product or range brand, as for example Nestlé chocolate or Nestlé condensed milk. These are the basic products, the symbolic products that lie – both literally and figuratively – at the heart of the Nestlé galaxy.

To help identify the different extensions of Nestlé the commercial brand, according to category, the categories have a different symbol. This means that, beyond the unity, there is recognition of the fact that what customers expect from a yoghurt is not the same as what they expect from baby food. Similarly, there is also a logo and symbol for Nestlé the company, that is, the corporate brand.

It is worth pointing out that 20 per cent of Nestlé's turnover is not produced under the six famous 'strategic corporate brands'. This is the case with mineral waters, for example. Perrier, which is classified as a recreational drink for adults, is indeed managed within the Nestlé Water division. But this division does not have a brand – its identification is a matter of internal organisation. For clients the world over, Perrier is simply Perrier.

14

Handling name changes and brand transfers

One of the most spectacular aspects of brand management, but also one of the most risky, is the changing of brand names. Some cases immediately spring to mind: Philips–Whirlpool, Raider–Twix, Andersen–Accenture, Pal–Pedigree, Datsun–Nissan. The industrial world is now used to external growth by company acquisitions and to the creation of large groups such as Novartis, Zeneca, Alcatel and Schneider by the fusion of identities which were previously separate and independent.

This growth in brand transfers is normal: it is the consequence of capitalisation, the key to modern brand management. The reorganisation of multi-brand portfolios and the reduction in the number of brands has meant that the products under brands due to disappear will have to be transferred to one of the remaining brands. The same applies for companies themselves. This approach is risky: the abandonment of a brand means that the market is going to lose one of its benchmarks, one of its choices or even one of the loyal customers' favourite choices. The risk of losing part of your market share is high. This is why the transfer of a brand is a strategic

decision that is not to be taken lightly. To this day, empirical studies on the question are either scarce (Riezebos and Sneller, 1993), or private and confidential (Greig and Poynter, 1994). It is possible though, thanks to the accumulated experience of ten or so cases, to define the conditions for successful name changes on a local level or multinational plane.

Brand transfers are more than a name change

Brand transfers are too often thought of simply as name changes, though admittedly this is the most risky facet of the change. In the customers' minds a well-known name is linked with mental associations, empathy and personal preferences. However, a brand is made up of many components, which cannot be reduced to just one, the name. In fact, when you examine the numerous examples that have occured both in Europe and the United States, the situation is far from simple. Many of them involve other changes in the marketing mix.

Some brand changes are also product changes. What disturbed Treets fans, apart from the loss of a product they loved, was that M&Ms included two different products: peanuts covered in chocolate and a sweet similar to Smarties. It was therefore a transition from a simple and familiar situation to a totally confusing one where all references had changed, as, indeed, had the product itself. When Shell changed the name of its oil from Puissance to Helix it also modified the characteristics of the product. However, the fact that these characteristics are 'hidden', hardly perceptible by the customers, meant that this was not a risky move for Shell. The change of the oil formula could be used as an alibi for the introduction of the new name.

As regards name changes, the risks associated vary immensely depending on whether we are dealing with product brands, umbrella brands, endorsing brands or source brands. Examples of the first two cases are Raider/Twix and Philips/Whirlpool respectively. The change only affects the one and only nominal indicator of the product or products. Conversely, Puissance has become Helix but still remains under the mother brand Shell. Changing a name when the product is defined by a hierarchy of brand names is far less problematic (see Table 14.1).

With self-service, visual identity has become crucial as an aid to customers to quickly pick out their brand. Distributors' own-brands capitalise on this: their imitations, which aim at confusing the customer, rely less and less on similar names (for example Sablito against Pépito) and more and more on near identical copies of colour codes of the national brands that are targeted on the shelves (Kapferer and Thoenig, 1992). In this way, in the UK, a fierce conflict arose between Coca-Cola and the retailer Sainsbury, whose colas totally imitated the Coca-Cola colours: red for classic cola, white for sugar-free cola and gold for sugar- and caffeine-free cola. Conversely, some brand changes are accompanied by profound modifications of the colour codes. Thus, the brown Shell Puissance 5 oilcan became the yellow Shell Helix Standard oilcan. The long and gradual change from Pal to Pedigree was accompanied by the adoption worldwide of a

Table 14.1 The different types of brand transfers

What brand attribute was changed?	Treets M&Ms	Andersen Consulting Accenture	Shell Puissance/ Helix	Philips Whirlpool	Chambourcy Nestlé
Name:					
Umbrella name		X		X	X
Product name			X		
Product-brand	X				
Visual identity:					
Colour	X	X	X		
Packaging					
Logotype	X	X		X	X
Visual symbol	X	X	X	X	
Audio identity				X	
Brand character					
Physical product	X		(X)		
Consumer benefit or brand positioning	X	X		X	(X)

new colour, bright yellow, striking and eye-catching, to reinforce the impact on the shelves. Since colour is the first thing that consumers notice in a self-service situation, how risky such modifications can be is all the more evident.

The shape of packaging is the second most important visual recognition factor. This is why, despite the savings that could have been achieved by adopting a unique European oil can, Shell immediately refused to abandon its easily recognisable and very practical 'spout' can. Part of Shell oil's added value comes from this can. Finally, brand transitions can be accompanied by changes to the logo or trade mark as well as to visual symbols. As regards this last point, the impact of the disappearance of visual brand symbols shouldn't be underestimated. Replacing Nesquik's gentle giant Groquick by a rabbit in some countries for reasons of international coordination is playing with the relationship children have with Nesquik. The same applies to people associated with a brand. The disappearance of emblematic figures can have drastic consequences for a brand.

Finally, with written and musical slogans now under copyright, it has to be realised how important they are, as they are what people will remember. When Raider was changed to Twix, Mars hesitated but decided not to keep the same brand music. Music is one of the vehicles of a brand's personality. A slogan is also, in the long run, an integral part of a brand and can now be put under copyright. The famous slogan 'Melts in your mouth not in your hand' was lost when Treets became M&Ms.

Reasons for brand transfers

What are the aims behind the numerous brand changes that we are witnessing? The reasons are numerous:

▌ Many brands are bought with the intention of transferring their activities to the buyer's own brand. In this way, as there is only room on the market for two national brands, the third brand sometimes decides to buy the second one.

▌ Firms decide to transfer brands when they decide to stop some of their activities. So when General Electric wanted to withdraw from the small domestic appliances market, Black & Decker took over with the agreement that they could only use the GE name for a limited period. No brand would want part of its image to be controlled by another company. It was the same for Philips and Whirlpool: the takeover of the former's 'white goods' activities by the latter included the agreement that the Philips name could only be used for a limited period. Looking to concentrate only on its 'brown' products and small domestic appliances, Philips only conceded its name to Whirlpool temporarily. Whirlpool bought the white activities for the European market share it immediately gave them, as well as the chance to be the world's number one domestic appliances manufacturer.

▌ The search for the critical size also provides an explanation for brand transfers. The Mars group abandoned its European brands Treets and Bonitos to merge them into the global brand M&Ms. To compete against McDonald's, the European Quick bought Free Time and changed its trade name.

▌ The creation of worldwide companies leads to the same results. Ciba-Geigy and Sandoz merged under the new name Novartis. Alcatel was born out of the joint venture between CGE and ITT. In a few years all the company brands of both companies and even a few product brands (such as their telephones) were given the Alcatel name.

▌ Brand transition is a common tactic used when trying to access a foreign market. It is basically the same ploy as the 'Trojan Horse'. The local industries in a country are often highly protected using all kinds of domestic regulations to prevent foreign product invasions. The electrical equipment market is a typical example. Desperate to grow internationally, Merlin-Gerin bought the famous Yorkshire Switchgear company as a way to penetrate the British market. The transfer was carried out progressively. Yorkshire Switchgear received the endorsement of Merlin-Gerin, then the names were switched round before finally being replaced uniquely with Merlin-Gerin UK, now Schneider.

▌ The fact that international markets are now more homogeneous than ever before is also an explication for the number of brand transfers. Companies that favour global brands are replacing all their local brands with global ones. This is why Raider in continental Europe became Twix, Pal changed to Pedigree, and why the paint brand Valentine will be transferred to Dulux, the worldwide brand of ICI. In order to make sure European motorists can spot their products in all European countries, Shell gave their lubricant a unique name, Helix, and where possible used the same colour codes.

▌ With time, the name attached to a brand can become a burden to the brand's development, for example when wanting to access new activities, international markets or simply when wanting to rejuvenate a brand. Corporate names that attract bad will have to change: Philip Morris became Altria Group, Vikendi became Veolic. BSN became Danone in order to instantly gain international recognition, which would have been lengthy if not impossible with an acronym.

▌ Brand transfers can also be the result of lost court cases. For example, Yves Saint Laurent had to abandon the name of its brand of perfume Champagne in several countries, turning it into Yvresse. The

sportswear brand Best Montana lost its case against the luxury brand Montana and had to become Best Mountain.

The challenge of brand transfers

Brand transfers are everywhere. This is hardly surprising since this is the age of mergers and acquisitions, which always give rise to the rationalisation of ranges, products and brand portfolios. Companies have to choose between brands that have hitherto been competitive with parallel ranges. On mature, low-growth markets, the need to make economies, create synergies and increase efficiency has the same result. Finally, globalisation brings its share of brand transfers to the advantage of the global brand. For all the above reasons, reducing the number of brands is the order of the day.

This explains the wealth of publicity announcing – if you know how to read between the lines – an imminent brand transfer. For example, the Swedish company Electrolux, the world's leading manufacturer of household appliances, is preparing the worldwide transfer of its local brands – the historic leaders of their market, acquired country by country. From now on it will act as the endorsement for these local brands – Zanussi Electrolux in the UK, Arthur Martin Electrolux in France, Rex Electrolux in Italy, and so on – and will appear as such in the promotional publicity. It has to be said that, in 2003, only 15 per cent of sales were made under the brand name of this international group. The aim is to increase this figure to between 60 and 70 per cent by 2007, so that 55 per cent of consumers will include Electrolux among the 'three brands they have in mind when entering an electrical appliance store' – what is known as an 'evoked set' or 'consideration set'. In 2001, this could be said of only 21 per cent of consumers.

Berated by financial analysts the world over for not having enough global brands with a turnover of more than US $1 billion, the Unilever Group made the decision to reduce drastically the number of these brands in a process known as the 'path to growth'. The group's Elida-Fabergé division played a pioneering role – by reducing the number of brands from 13 to 8, growth increased from less than 2 per cent to 11 per cent.

But this objective of reducing the size of brand portfolios also creates challenging problems in certain product categories. This happens when the brands to be merged are well established and do not have the same positioning on the market. For example, the famous detergents category is not particularly profitable compared with other categories since distribution costs are extremely high and the market is fragmented. Many of the smaller brands no longer justify the promotional support. Throughout Europe, Lever has organised its portfolio in three price-related segments – the premium segment with Skip (in competition with Procter & Gamble's Ariel), the smart buyer segment with Omo for example, and the economy (or low-price) segment with Persil (except in the UK where, for historical reasons, Persil replaced Skip). The question therefore arises, given the market shares and Lever's declared intention of concentrating its business around strong brands, how to unite the brand in the smart buyer segment with the brand in the economy segment. The difficulty becomes all the more apparent since in many countries, these are well-established brands that, over time, have forged a very specific bond with a section of the public. The issue should involve the distributors who, throughout Europe, are wondering about the future of the low-price segment, positioned just above their distributors' brands. Should this segment in fact be allowed to survive?

Another illustration of the risks associated with brand transfers is provided by the example of Phas and La Roche Posay, two brands of cosmetics in the l'Oréal Group that were merged in 2000. Each represented approximately 15 per cent of the market share in a sector that was losing momentum, namely pharmacy. This should make it possible to begin internationalising the brands under a single banner, with critical mass. Named after a thermal spring used to treat skin disorders, La Roche Posay is associated with a guarantee of proven effectiveness in the treatment of skin conditions. Its business model was based on recommendation by dermatologists. Conversely, Phas was a brand of cosmetics – with no dermatological endorsement – for skins that were extremely sensitive to ordinary make-up. Its strength was hypoallergenic tolerance rather than effectiveness. It is easy to understand why this – albeit necessary – transfer ran the risk of diluting the brand capital for La Roche Posay. The brand was going to have to put its signature to products formerly under the Phas label and which had no guarantee of effectiveness.

When the risks are too great, it is better to avoid them and choose another strategy.

When one should not switch

The internationalisation of companies raises the question of the globalisation of brand portfolios. This involves changing the name of the products or services of a well-known and very popular local brand to that of a less well-known and less familiar international brand. However, before considering how a company goes about making such changes in order to effect a brand transfer, the following caveat should be borne in mind. There are occasions when this transfer should not be made, if it presents too great a risk for the business and the brand capital. Thus, when BP bought the German Aral service stations in 2003, it decided not to change the brand name as it had done in California when it bought Arco. In the same year, Shell bought the other major German service-station group, DEA, but decided to bring it under the Shell banner. So who was right – BP or Shell?

In fact, they were both right. Aral is a very strong local brand, almost a national symbol, rather like the Continental tyres fitted on all Mercedes manufactured in Europe. So why would BP run the risk of severing this extremely rare bond that generates customer loyalty, in a sector already threatened by 'commoditisation'? Conversely, although DEA has a good customer service record, it does not inspire the same emotional attachment and its transfer would therefore be less risky. Customer service relations are created by the people who work for the company. So, if these people remain in situ, the continuity of satisfaction is maintained and customer loyalty guaranteed.

There are other instances when a brand transfer should not be made to the advantage of a new, global brand and when it is better to retain the local name, for example when the meaning of the name to be internationalised proves problematic in the other country. Procter & Gamble's German competitor Henkel could not extend its product brand 'Somat' – designed to make glassware shine – in the UK since the word 'matt' is the opposite of shiny.

There is no shortage of examples where, to an outsider, the local brand seemed little more than a legacy from the past but was regarded locally as an icon. This happened in the case of many leading Eastern European brands, which the multinationals decided had to be replaced by the global – European or US – brand. But they had not taken account of the consumers who are often extremely emotionally attached to the local brands that are part of their everyday life and past memories. The Danone Group had to reverse such a decision in the Czech Republic. After abandoning the Opavia brand in favour of the global Danone brand, it had to reintroduce Opavia – famous for its biscuits and the country's favourite food brand – because it was a national symbol.

In this respect, the Bel group was well advised not to pursue a potential brand transfer which involved replacing the German brand Adler, famous for its processed cheese portions, with the international mega-brand, The Laughing Cow, whose prototype is also processed cheese portions. However, the symbol of the Adler brand, familiar to all Germans, has long been the imperial eagle. It is hard to imagine the juxtaposition of two more paradoxical animal logos.

L'Oréal is pragmatic when it comes to brand transfers. In line with its expressed intention of developing mainly via its 17 global brands, the group bought Maybelline, a brand of make-up sold on the US mass market. In the space of a few years, it launched the brand in 80 countries but to do so had to effect a transfer with the local brand in the principal countries concerned. The problem was that the local brand was often a strong brand that was popular with both distributors and customers – Jade in Germany, Colorama in Brazil, Missiland in Argentina, Gemey in France – while Maybelline means nothing in these countries. The group has carried out a deliberate policy of double branding for five years, introducing an increasing number of US concepts and innovations but, even so, there is still no question of setting an exact date for phasing out the local brand. Yet, as far as the financial analysts and major multinational distribution groups are concerned, l'Oréal has achieved the desired effect – by increasing the sales of co-branded products in each country, the group can say that Maybelline is the leading international brand of make-up in the mass-market sector.

When brand transfer fails

Companies that are over-confident in themselves often underestimate the emotional attachment created by local brands, long since written off by the advocates of globalisation. In so doing, they do not realise to what extent brand transfers can destroy value and, above all, the value of the market share.

This is illustrated by the example of Fairy in Germany. In 2000, the buzzword at Procter & Gamble was 'globalisation' at all costs. In Europe, the group introduced global segmentation and all the brands that did not fit within the framework were eliminated (Kapferer, 2001, p 52). Furthermore, local brand names were to be replaced by the global brand name corresponding to each segment.

In Germany, Procter & Gamble had been successfully marketing a washing-up liquid under the name Fairy for years, with the brand reaching 12 per cent of the market share in terms of value. In the middle of 2000, the Fairy brand became known as Dawn, the name of Procter & Gamble's international brand. Nothing had changed except the name, which is a good measure of the power of the brand. However, in spite of colossal investments to inform people that Fairy was now called Dawn, the market share plummeted and, in the last quarter of 2001, stood at just 4.7 per cent, whereas it was still at 11.9 per cent on the day before the name changed. It was estimated that, in 2001, Procter & Gamble sustained a loss in turnover in Germany of US $8 million (Schroiff and Arnold, 2003). The group made the same mistake in Austria when it tried to replace Bold with Dash. In view of the destruction of value caused by these two costly mistakes, it was decided to return to the previous brand names.

What was the reasoning behind these two brand transfers? Because Fairy used the same consumer benefit as Dawn, the ability to cut through grease, Procter & Gamble thought that the brand transfer would be easy. However, this transfer was not even attempted in the UK, possibly because Fairy was positioned according to a different consumer benefit from Dawn. But the brand can also be much more than a name – it can be the sign of a certain product guarantee. Local brands inspire customer loyalty through their origins, their being a part of everyday life, their proximity, their confidence (Schuiling and Kapferer, 2003) (see also page 408). There is a real emotional dimension in the attachment to certain brands, as has been shown by Fournier (2001).

So what lessons can be learnt from this example? A transfer must first of all take account of consumer opinion. A transfer must offer some form of benefit and create value for consumers. This is the key to successful transfers. Second, in the process of convergence implemented within the multinationals, the principle source of productivity is the product platform. But people tend to focus on the visible part of the product, the actual change of name, whereas this is not in fact the real issue – far from it. In globalisation,

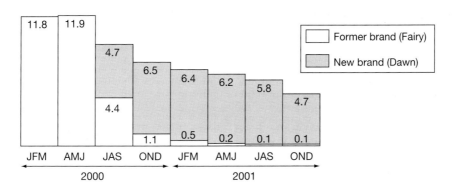

Figure 14.1 When rebranding fails: from Fairy to Dawn (P&G)

the homogenisation of names should be the last problem to be solved. There are also a great many fringe benefits to be gained by unifying and reducing the number of different packages, non-standardised parts and product platforms. Furthermore, productivity is vastly improved by the convergence of brand platforms, which makes it possible to use a single agency and employ the best designers. It is not important if a product has to have a different name in different regions. To quote just three examples, a leading line of male toiletries is known as Axe in Europe and Lynx in the UK, a brand of washing powder as Skip in Europe and Persil in the UK, while the Opel brand in Europe is Vauxhall in the UK.

Analysing best practices

There is not much academic research on brand transfers. It is however possible to draw on some brand and business models to clarify the conditions of a successful transfer. We selected them because they illustrate very different market situations and brand role, from mere impulse to highly risky purchase decisions, from products to services.

From Raider to Twix

In the autumn of 1991, continental Europeans were informed by a massive advertising campaign that the chocolate bar Raider was to be henceforth called Twix, Twix being the name used everywhere else in the world from New York to Tokyo and London. The difference from the Mars group's previous brand transfer (from Treets to M&Ms) where everything had changed, including the product, was that this time, great care was taken not to disturb the customers. Nothing was changed apart from the name. It was a success.

Why was the brand change necessary? Philippe Villemus, the marketing director of Mars, explained (for more details see Villemus, 1996) that Mars was a worldwide group with six brands each worth more than a billion (US) dollars, and that it wanted only to have mega-brands which satisfy the five following conditions:

- is able to meet an important, durable and global need;

- represents the highest level of quality;

- is omnipresent all over the world, and within every one's reach both physically and financially;

- creates a high level of public confidence; and

- is the leader in their segment (when this is not the case the brand is simply removed, like Treets and Bonitos).

For legal reasons it can happen that a trade mark cannot be registered in a particular country or region. This was the case with the Twix name in continental Europe. As soon as the legal aspect had been dealt with by the acquisition of legal rights in certain countries, the group did not hesitate to rename Raider and to give Europe the global name.

What were the objectives behind this change of brand? In the first instance, it was to gain more market share and increase sales, otherwise, according to Villemus, there would have been no point to the operation. It is important to remember that a brand transition is not an exercise in style, but a unique opportunity to increase the share of the market. It is a competitive move. A second objective was to have a global brand. A third objective was to reduce production, packaging and advertising costs. A fourth objective was to make its management easier. Finally, it was desirable to have one brand name so as to make the preparations easier for the intended brand extensions towards new sectors such as ice creams.

Raider had a strong brand equity in Europe so the transition was no small matter. It was the second most popular chocolate bar after

Mars and it had an annual volume growth rate of 12 per cent. This was thanks to its specific concept and its slogan, which included a physical description of the product as well as its benefits for the customer. In France, for example, spontaneous recognition was 43 per cent, assisted recognition was 96 per cent and that of the slogan was 88 per cent. Eighty-five per cent of all adolescents had tried Raider and 44 per cent bought it on a regular basis. Knowing this, Twix was marketed as the ideal snack for adolescents and young people between the ages of 15 and 25.

Even though the customers thought that the transition was rapid, in truth it took over a year. From October 1990 to October 1991, the Raider's wrapping carried the words 'known globally as Twix' and for six months after the transition, 'Raider's new name'.

The communication objectives given to the campaign by the marketing director were:

▐ to communicate clearly and simply that only the name was changing;

▐ to transfer all Raider's values to Twix;

▐ to quickly obtain a high brand awareness within the target group of young people (30 per cent unaided, 80 per cent assisted);

▐ to make the change popular using the alibi that the new name was in tune with the rest of the world, and that Twix was a global brand for young people all over the world.

The key elements of the success of the operation were due to the flawless implementation of the strategy:

▐ it was very rapid: 15 days to change everything in one country (the whole transfer in Europe took three months);

▐ Mars made a big event of it, which maximised its visibility and the awareness created;

▐ promotional activities at sales outlets contributed to the impact and trial of Twix;

▐ finally, great care was taken to ensure good coordination with field activities. It was decided that, even if it meant buying back stock, on the day of the transfer no stocks of Raider should be left in any shops.

Looking more closely at the different means of communication that were used, we see that the packaging was the first medium. It was used for one year before the transfer to warn customers of, and to familiarise them with, the new name. It was used for six months after that to explain the transfer. In order to meet the communication objectives the advertising campaign was characterised by:

▐ a strong emphasis on the pack-shot to maximise the recognition;

▐ the interruption of all communication of the Raider brand six months before transfer day to hasten the drop in its awareness;

▐ a high-impact European commercial starring David Bowie;

▐ a strong concentration of means: in three weeks as much as the total advertisement budget for two years was spent on television advertisements alone (it is now easy to understand why it was absolutely vital that all Raider packets were removed from all sales outlets).

In shops, Twix was given prominence and was put on visible display. Twix was the focal point of all the sales force, and all other brands were sidelined in terms of priority. Supermarkets had, of course, been informed well in advance. The bar code was kept the same so that supermarkets did not take Twix to be listed as a new brand and hence claim a listing fee.

Six months after the operation, Twix's market share was the same as Raider's had been. But from then on there was only one brand name, one factory and far less complexity. Due to its young and international status, Twix's image was more modern than Raider's.

Looking back, all the decisions taken seem logical. All successful operations give the impression of being easy. But the decisions were not taken without debate. For example, some people recommended improving the recipe and announcing 'even better'. In the end it was decided, after reflection on the opposite approach of Treets/M&Ms, to change the product as little as possible. It might also have been a good idea not to change the Raider music in the change-over film to Twix. Was the modification necessary? It is said to have disturbed some customers, which goes to show just how much the brand's music is an integral part of its identity and personality.

From Philips to Whirlpool

On 1 January 1989, Philips and Whirlpool joined together to create the world's biggest household appliances group, Whirlpool International, owned 53 per cent by Whirlpool and 47 per cent by Philips. This partnership was formed with the intention of attaining a significant global size which would enable and ensure the development of a long-lasting manufacturing firm. Besides, Philips wanted to concentrate on its core activity. Finally, both companies were highly complementary, in their plant layout and industrial capacity, in innovation and in their geographic market coverage. Philips was the most important domestic appliances brand in Europe. Whirlpool, for its part, was the number one in the United States, Mexico and Brazil. With 11.1 per cent of all the goods manufactured, Philips Whirlpool overtook Electrolux (9.6 per cent) to become the world leader in the household appliances market. In 1990 the Philips Whirlpool brand was launched in Europe by a spectacular advertising campaign (50 million US dollars). In 1991, Whirlpool bought the remaining 47 per cent held by Philips. In January 1993, the Philips Whirlpool brand became Whirlpool in all communications, but the dual brand was kept on its products. In the last countries to make the switch, Philips was removed from all products in 1996. Via this brand transfer Whirlpool became the world number one domestic appliance brand. The importance of what was at stake and the risks involved during the brand transition become evident when one looks at the significance customers put on a brand when buying durable goods which are perceived as high-risk investments. According to a study carried out by Landor, in Europe Philips was the second-most powerful brand over all sectors. In France, another study showed that when customers were asked to mention names of brands from any sector off the top of their head, Philips was placed fifth after Renault, Peugeot, Adidas and Citroën (Kapferer, 1996). Nevertheless, it is worth noting that Philips' market share and its public brand recognition differed from country to country. This is why it was quickly apparent that it would be impossible to carry out the change in different European countries simultaneously. In the same way, the guarantee role of brands in the domestic appliances market rules out a sudden, quick transfer as was the case with Raider/Twix.

In January 1990, the assisted brand awareness of Whirlpool in Europe was non-existent. This was why a stage-by-stage progressive approach was decided upon. This included a Philips Whirlpool stage before Philips was abandoned. The case is different, therefore, from that of Black & Decker's takeover of General Electric's domestic appliances activities in the United States where both names already had a good reputation.

Another reason favoured the stage-by-stage approach. In order to ensure global coherence, Philips' products left in stores would have had to have been bought back, as Twix had been for the transfer to Raider. But this of course would have been impossible for both practical and financial reasons.

So what was Whirlpool's transfer strategy and why did they choose it? In the first instance early research had shown that customers perceived favourably the Philips Whirlpool partnership. Both companies had very different images. Whirlpool had potential, it evoked change, fluidity, movement and dynamism. It had the ideal qualities required to give the brand transfer a positive image. The fusion of both companies gave the Philips Whirlpool brand an ideal image, the dynamism of one was tempered by the solidarity of the other. Research showed that the Philips Whirlpool couple was perceived as 'sure and dynamic, solid and robust, classic and stylish, reliable and innovating'. In Europe, the arrival of Whirlpool was seen by consumers as bringing new impetus to Philips, a touch of high tech to a reliable classic brand, imagination to a brand characterised by experience.

The first thing that needed to be done was to decide upon the nature of the dual brand and its visual form. To start with, should it be called Whirlpool Philips or Philips Whirlpool? Tests revealed that the first option did not inspire confidence and that it evoked a confused perception. People associated it with jacuzzis and all 'water equipment'. On the other hand, Philips Whirlpool evoked a healthy equitable partnership or even a slight predominance of Philips. Only a minority thought that it referred to a Philips product range like that of the Philips Tracer razors. The second question regarded the graphic trade mark. Should both names be written on the same line or one on top of the other? The first choice was adopted because it inspired an image of partnership and looked better. Figure 14.2 shows the synergy brought by Philip's association with Whirlpool. It represents

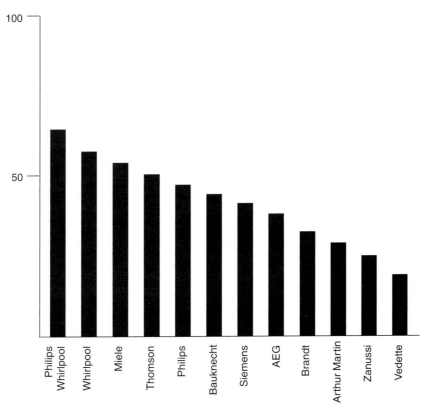

Figure 14.2   Perceived innovation of Whirlpool before its introduction in Europe (1990)

brand images, in terms of innovation, in France before the launching of the transfer campaign.

With regard to the communication, what target should it be aimed at? Obviously the priority was the distributors. Only 20 per cent of domestic appliance customers visit a shop with a specific brand in mind, and only 10 per cent, ie half of them, actually buy that brand. This shows the importance of sales outlet staff in the sale of these products. Whirlpool started in 1990 a considerable communication effort aimed at retailers – this is a little known facet of brand transfers. This, of course, was addressed to the big European or national retail bosses, but it was also used by Whirlpool's sales force with customers, shop owners and sales staff whose opinions were so influential on consumers. Moreover, Whirlpool's image was that of an innovating leader, so merely confining oneself to innovations in products and services would have been limited. Whirlpool brought about a revolution in producer–distributor relations, a new approach that distributors weren't accustomed to, which not only touched on services but market information and more besides. As regards the consumers, the plan was to reassure them as quickly as possible by the rapid acquisition of brand awareness and a strong image of quality and innovation.

These communication objectives had several important operational consequences. On the one hand, wanting to associate with Whirlpool an image of quality and innovation implied that the brand transfer on the products themselves had to take place progressively, in line with the launch of new products and the rejuvenation of Philips' old ranges. If this had not been the case the project would have suffered from the Talbot-Chrysler syndrome, where the only thing that was changed on the vehicles was the name on the bonnet. The Whirlpool brand on its own was not to be found on an old product. Launching a new brand implies taking great care over the early impressions the brand would create among the European audiences. Giving Whirlpool a quality image involved prohibiting all promotional advertising of any sort in the media during the first years of establishing the brand in Europe. Finally, as it is impossible to pursue an image objective and an awareness objective at the same time, it was obvious that to the classic advertising a media action had to be added so as to quickly reach the required level of brand awareness before the final brand transfer, ie two-thirds of the assisted awareness of Philips. It is certainly true that, in the case of durable goods, the involvement of consumers is low when they are not actually engaged in the buying process – which is most of the time. When the consumer is not considering a purchase, the means of persuasion that should be adopted are very specific. When consumers' attention disperses, a multiple contact approach should be privileged, even if received incidentally. This calls for a high number of (gross rating point) GRP. Consumer resistance can become weak; in this case contact should be received in an agreeable ambience to benefit the effect of the affective transfer to the brand. Finally, when the consumer is not ready to make a cognitive effort one must repeat the consumer benefits of the brand rather than point out the difference between specific products.

This is why, in some countries, Whirlpool invested large amounts of money sponsoring prime-time TV programmes. This choice was no coincidence; they represent viewers' favourite moments on the most popular channels, and are often associated with a relaxed family atmosphere. Thanks to this strategy, the brand awareness made considerable progress, as shown in Figure 14.3. In all the countries where only traditional commercials were used, the awareness reached was less significant.

Figure 14.3 also points out the structural relationship between assisted and spontaneous awareness, as described earlier (see page 161). On first analysis, it might be thought that for durable goods only assisted brand

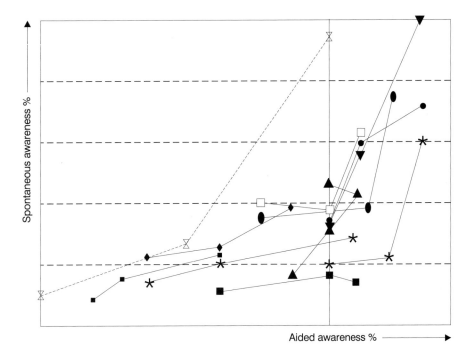

Figure 14.3   Growth of Whirlpool brand awareness in 11 European countries

awareness counts (recognition being reassuring) but this cannot be the case for a brand aiming to be seen as the quality reference and the leader of the sector. Yet, it is known that a high level of assisted brand awareness must be reached before there is any hope of increasing spontaneous awareness. This is even more the case when the market is 'closed', ie when there are already three brands with high levels of spontaneous awareness. This is why Whirlpool wanted to reach the critical zone of 70 per cent assisted awareness as quickly as possible. Thus, it would be possible to gain the status of market leader associated with spontaneous awareness. Then it would also be possible to safely remove the Philips brand from the products in the shops.

It was indeed important to separate the treatment of the Philips brand in the media and in sales outlets. In the media, it was necessary to stop mentioning the brand as quickly as possible, otherwise the brand would only have been reinforced when the

objective was to see a decline in its spontaneous awareness. This is why, during the short period when the dual brand existed, Philips Whirlpool adverts finished with the dual brand but the signature tune only mentioned Whirlpool. This was to ensure that only this brand was associated with the innovations.

As early as January 1993, it was decided to remove Philips from all TV adverts. This put an end to any reinforcement of Philips' awareness. What is more, it sent the message to retailers that Whirlpool, the market leader, no longer needed the Philips guarantee and that the transfer programme was ahead of schedule.

On a European level, how was the multiplicity of countries to be dealt with? Taking into account the differences in the market shares and the brand equity that Philips had from country to country, all monolithic approaches were ruled out. Some countries wanted to pass to the single brand, Whirlpool, quickly. Others would have liked more time:

where Philips' reputation was excellent, it could not be removed overnight if the objective was not only to maintain market share but also use the transfer to increase it. The order in which each country was to have the Whirlpool brand transfer was decided using a multi-criteria analysis, which took into account, for each country:

▌ Philips' market share;

▌ the presumed reaction of the distributors (based on an ad hoc survey);

▌ the strength of the brand in the eyes of consumers (brand recognition, evoked set, preference);

▌ the influence of retailers on the customers' decisions;

▌ the feeling that the management in the country was ready for the abandonment of the Philips brand.

Recent research on the transfer from the local brand Libertel to Vodafone seems to indicate that a dual branding phase does not in fact transfer values from the former to the latter. In fact brand values must be built, they are not simply transferred by this tactic of dual naming for a while. Attaching two names is creating a third one. In the Philips–Whirlpool case, the dual naming gave saliency (brand awareness) to Whirlpool, but did not transfer the values of Philips onto Whirlpool. Its first objective was to maintain the consumer or customer loyalty and the trade franchise, which would have deserted if the name Philips had not been maintained as an endorser of the totally unknown American newcomer.

From Chambourcy to Nestlé

In 1985, Nestlé bought out Unilever's European activities in the chilled foods sector. Nestlé had been synonymous with milk worldwide, but knew little about refrigerated dairy products.

Ten years after, in 1995, it was decided to transfer all of Chambourcy's products to the Nestlé brand. It was true that Chambourcy seemed to be threatened in several segments in the 'ultra fresh' dairy market and there was no way that on its own it was going to reduce the market share margin that separated it from Danone (17.6 per cent vs 33.6 per cent). As for the segments of products where the brand was either leader or in second place, it was the daughter brands of the products that carried the image and the preferences of the customers: La Laitière, Viennois, Yoco, Kremly, Sveltesse, Marronsuiss. The consumers of these products did not take any notice of the mother brand, Chambourcy. The advertising war was very uneven: in France, for instance, Chambourcy spent around 10 million euros in 1994 compared with Yoplait's 15 million and Danone's 40 million. Danone's strength enabled it to invest heavily in its strategic products: 4 million euros on Danette, 4 million on Velouté and 5 million on Bio. The conquest of market share had therefore to be accompanied by an increase in the advertising budget, something which was difficult to justify for the Chambourcy brand. The fact was that all adverts on Nestlé's chocolate products had a positive knock-on effect on all Nestlé products in general, apart from the 'ultra fresh' segment under the Chambourcy label. The effects of brand awareness synergy could not be counted upon. Besides, without having to spend as much as Danone on advertising, a transfer to the Nestlé brand name would instantly benefit all the 'ultra fresh' range. Nestlé, according to a Landor study, is the most powerful foodstuffs brand in the world after Coca-Cola.

In any case, it also seemed necessary that a brand as valuable as Nestlé should finally put its name to 'ultra fresh' products. There is, in fact, an evolution of food products over time, starting with dry products, then dry groceries, then frozen goods and then finally fresh products. It is the case that the future of the agricultural processing industry lies with fresh goods, that is goods that have not had to endure the physical shock of being transformed into powder, put into cans or frozen. It would not be prudent for the Nestlé brand to be absent from this evolution. Not doing so would have branded Nestlé a manufacturer of dry foodstuff, products for the cupboard, therefore 'not fresh' and far removed from modern healthy produce. Quantitative research carried out on clients and non-clients to test the acceptability of the Chambourcy–Nestlé transfer in several market segments (fitness and health, desserts, children's products and traditional specialities) revealed that the Nestlé brand was already starting to suffer from such an image.

Indeed, it was desirable to know what the public would think of the brand change. Wasn't there a risk in updating the 'powerful multinational' facet with the removal of Chambourcy in favour of Nestlé? The credibility and legitimacy of Nestlé's penetration into each of the 'ultra fresh' segments, either as a signature on daughter brands or as a direct product brand, also had to be evaluated. In fact, some of the Chambourcy products were likely to be ill at ease under the Nestlé umbrella, others would benefit from it, while others would inject it with new life.

The 1996 brand transfer posed several strategic questions:

▌ How to convince the customers that the arrival of Nestlé, normally associated with dry produce and far removed from Chambourcy territory (natural, gourmet), in the 'ultra fresh' market was legitimate?

▌ Should the change be given a high profile with extensive communication at the time of the transfer, or, on the contrary, should the consumers and the distributors be disturbed as little as possible?

▌ Should a global 'ultra fresh' brand communication be adopted or should it concentrate on individual products according to each item's market segment?

▌ What should be retained of Chambourcy: the signature tune associated with desire and pleasure? The joyful 'Oh Yes!' slogan? Should Chambourcy become a daughter brand like Danone had done with Ch. Gervais?

▌ Should there be a transitional period where both brands exist side by side on the products or should there be a quick break changing from Chambourcy to Nestlé in one go, as in the Raider–Twix case?

The answers that were adopted resulted from the analysis of the information in Table 14.2. It was well understood what Nestlé would gain as a brand in this name switch (new peripheral attributes such as freshness, lightness, sensuousness, pleasure). However, it did not create much value to the consumer. Nestlé did not really beat Chambourcy on the key success factors of the category.

Knowing that in the short term at least the products would not evolve, it was not possible to make an event of this name change: no big bang campaign was planned. There would be campaigns for each product, and each new advertisement would stress some change in the formula to increase sensuousness and pleasure (Nestlé's main deficit). Similarly, the desire not to disrupt Chambourcy fans demanded that some of the Chambourcy communication codes be maintained:

▌ The Nestlé brand did adopt the former Chambourcy logotype, a very recognisable sign on each product.

▌ The new advertising tag line would not be very different from the former in content.

▌ Finally, Chambourcy itself did not fully disappear: it was just retrograded from family name to product name on three prototypical products.

Table 14.2   Assessing the image gaps between the new and the former brands

Brand	Chambourcy	Nestlé	Advantage/deficit
Category success factors			
Most important attributes			
The real taste	71 %	74%	+3%
Appetising	88%	89%	+1%
Natural	75%	75%	=
Sensuous, pleasure	89%	84%	−5%
Important attributes			
Fresh milk	62%	54%	−8%
Freshness	92%	85%	−7%
Light	69%	60%	−9%
Non-important attributes			
Chocolate	44%	93%	+49%
For babies	41%	89%	+48%
Reminds me of when I was little	38%	74%	+36%

Source: Charbonnier and Lombard, 1998

From Phas to La Roche Posay

Brand transfer is a sure way to make a brand reach the critical size needed to become a global player. Instead of trying to launch two half-brands in many countries, the goal is to create a single full brand with globalised resources. As previously discussed LRP had to become the eleventh global brand of the l'Oréal Group. But to do so it needed to extend its product range beyond the prescription products that had made it famous as a therapeutic brand but prevented its growth into impulse products for individuals who were not, and perhaps never had been, users of the prescription products. The product sectors for these impulse products were solar protection and make-up.

In the brand portfolio of the l'Oréal Group, Phas was the brand for which the viability of its economic equation was most in question. It was a competitor of Clinique (Estée Lauder) and Roc (Johnson & Johnson). A brand portfolio audit revealed that the group had two middle-sized brands, LRP and Phas. Today, middle-sized brands cannot compete in global markets. Second, Phas was being sold on a double promise, of security and beauty.

However, the problem, as with most dual promises, was that each of these promises was held by a competitor: security by dermatologists' brands (such as LRP) and beauty by Clinique, for instance. The Phas model was unstable and had growth threats.

It was decided to merge Phas into LRP, but since LRP's historical equity was based on proven effectiveness in treating dermatological problems, Phas was an anti-allergenic brand selling 4 millions units of make-up, this brand transfer was a challenging one. How could former Phas consumers be moved across to LRP? And what could be done to avoid diluting LRP's brand capital and reputation?

▌ The first phase of the merger had to be internal. It is too often forgotten that brands are managed by people, represented by people. They needed to understand the merge, and the new emerging brand. Obviously LRP before and after would not be the same. No extension leaves the brand untouched: in fact the merger is done in order to modify one brand on some peripheral values while keeping the core values intact. LRP sales forces and its whole staff had to learn about make-up, while reciprocally the former Phas people had to learn about science.

▌ The second phase was a double branding on the packages.

▌ The third phase was the launch of post-merger new products, epitomising the complementarity of the values of both brands. For instance, Phas Novalip had been sold as a lipstick that was comfortable and moisturising for dry lips. The core question for all LRP products is, how would a consumer speak to a dermatologist about her problem? The new lipstick brand was launched as the first lipstick to treat sore lips or dry lips. It also needed to be usable by people with more serious dermatological problems. As this example shows, changing names often means changing the contract: the former Phas products had to be reinvented by LRP. On the other hand LRP was to become more comprehensible, more accessible to the consumer, more human.

Transferring a service brand

Services need to be analysed separately. On the one hand, unlike product brands, service brands have nothing to show: they are intangible. Their name is the proof of their existence. Brand awareness and saliency is of vital importance. On the other hand, their nature can make brand transfers easier, because they are often tied to a place (the specific geographical location of service delivery, of 'servuction'). In addition, the driver of loyalty is the direct relation with the salesperson, agent or staff. This is not too say that the brand is of no importance: when BP and Shell took over two German networks of petrol distribution, much care was taken in handling the situation. Not recognising the name and visual identity of the gas station they have historically, if not ritually, used acts as a deterrent for many German consumers.

However, global brands are created by replacing local leaders by global names. This is how Axa built its global worldwide brand recognition, acquiring local leaders and instantaneously moving them to Axa, as a way of immediately indicating internally what the strategy was, namely to become the local arm of the first worldwide insurance brand. In the service business, hesitations and dual brandings may create some internal doubts about the future strategy, and lead people to defend their former identity instead of thinking of the new future. As a result, the internal phase comes first and foremost in service brand transfers. A lot of discussion groups must be created, for the sake of communication and release of tensions, whereby all parts of the company that has been taken over can express how they see the future and concretely build the pathways to become the quality arm of the new global brand. Two recent cases are interesting in that respect, Accenture and Orange.

The Accenture case

On 7 August 2000 the International Arbitrage Court, in the case between Andersen Consulting (AC) and Arthur Andersen and Andersen Worldwide, ruled that among others things, AC would not be allowed to use its existing name after 1 January 2001. It had less than 145 days to transfer its intellectual, technological and reputational capital to a new brand.

The first step in this process consisted of an internal wide-scale and in-depth interrogation on what was expected from the new brand:

▌ What new values should it foster?

▌ It should attract what types of new consultants?

▌ How could it contribute to the development of business?

▌ How could it reinforce differentiation?

▌ What changes could be suggested?

The process of name choice was also internally managed by means of a 'brandstorming' process. All employees were asked to participate. On 1 September 2000 various names were proposed by Landor, a globally known design agency. On 21 September, 2,677 proposals were made internally, for such names as Future Creation Group, Global Already, Deep Thought, Mind Rocket and Global Curves. On 5 October, 68 names were screened for legal registrability, international semantic connotations, availability of the domain name and so on. On 12 October, 29 finalists were submitted to a vote at the firm's Miami Congress, and 10 of these were discussed by a brand steering committee on 23 October. Finally, on 25 October, Accenture was selected. This name had been proposed by the Norwegian senior manager, to convey putting the accent on the future. To help fulfil the mission (reinventing the business to win in the new economic context), the key words linked to this brand would be agile, visionary, well connected and passionate.

As a rule, communicating a new brand aims at creating an immediate boost of unaided awareness and suggesting the new values of the brand. To regain its status within the very closed club of the big five accountancy/consulting firms, a blitz communication strategy was chosen in this case. US $175 million was budgeted to reach these two objectives worldwide, and the goal was to reach 30 per cent awareness in three months.

Here again, the emphasis of service brands is on employees. For the sake of an efficient brand alignment, 50 work groups were created to manage the name change in 137 countries. This involved creating a new Internet site, internal communication kits, communication with 20,000 managers in client companies, communication with thousands of potential candidates, and of course communication for introducing the name on stock exchanges. As the global campaign put it, the company was renamed, redefined, reborn.

Moving to Orange

On 30 May 2000 the UK's third largest mobile phone operator, Orange, was acquired by FT, the incumbent national French operator. As with all former monopolies, FT needed a commercial brand to carry its offer and eventually extend it to other services internationally. British Gas had created a precedent with the creation of a commercial brand to offer services to households, including its traditional utilities but also insurance and financial services. The goal of FT was to make Orange the second largest operator in Europe, after Vodafone. In 2005, the objective was to be present in 50 countries.

In each country, the strategy was to rename the local operating company as Orange, exploiting this opportunity to capture the high-consumption-rate young consumers segment. Up to then the former monopoly telecomms organisations had not looked very attractive to them. The success of Orange in UK had been based on a disruptive approach to the mobile phone business, epitomised by the simplicity of its name. In fact, its six brand values were dynamism, modernity, simplicity, transparency, proximity and responsibility. These values contrasted strongly with those of the UK's former monopoly telecomms company, BT. Orange in the UK had been a challenger brand, proposing a true relationship with consumers, an innovation after decades of monopoly offerings.

In the countries in which Orange would now operate, the challenge became to make a local former monopoly, often still the market leader, acquire the brand and adopt its values. The goal of the brand transfer was first and foremost to get across the 'Orange attitude'. The difficulty was to align the company itself, the employees and the newly acquired brand values in each country. The process was divided into three steps: 'Let's build Orange' (defining the brand's values, and understanding them), 'Let's live Orange' (understanding how to put these values into action), and 'Let's launch Orange' (the communication launch itself).

The second phase involved an in-depth immersion of each employee in the new values, both individually and within his/her functional team. Scores of focus groups, internal meetings, and global sessions would slowly build up that understanding over a period of one year.

The director of human resources would naturally be part of the process of 'Let's live Orange'. For instance, an evaluation grid was created, to help measure how each participant stood in achieving the brand values. In addition, to foster group adhesion, this form was to be completed by all the members of the individual's team, as a measure of how others saw each person's performance. Two other regular features, 'all in store' and 'all on line' were intended to help employees understand in practice the challenges of selling the Orange way.

The 'Let's launch Orange' phase was designed to provide the opportunity to make a strong impression, accentuating the idea that a radical new offer was now present in the marketplace. The media were key in conveying this impression and helping to immediately capture new consumers. Employees were also involved, and each one was sent a cassette and CD-ROM outlining the full launch process. Finally, all existing clients were to be contacted individually to tell them about the name change and what it would mean for them.

Which brand to retain after a merger

Reductions in brand portfolio sizes are the main source of brand transfers. As soon as a brand has been diagnosed as weak it naturally

follows that its flagship products will be transferred over to strong brands in the portfolio. When a company gives up part of its activities to another company, it is the brand of the latter which inherits the products of the former. This we have seen in the Black & Decker–General Electric and Philips–Whirlpool cases. But it can happen that the decision of which brand to keep after a merger is not as simple. For example, which of the following names currently used in different countries will Johnson keep as its European brand name: Pledge, Pliz or Pronto?

These decisions are not necessarily rational. More Pal was sold in continental Europe than Pedigree in the UK, yet the decision was taken to use the British brand name hitherto unknown on the continent.

One can also assume that Pedigree has an international feel understood by all dog owners, and that this name is closely tied to the creative concept which presents the product as the one preferred by pedigree dog owners. The Merloni group was wise, too, when it chose its European portfolio brand, opting for Indesit rather than Ariston. Indesit had an image of lowest-price products but was well known in Europe. Ariston was the group's historical brand and had a good image but was hardly known in Europe.

A good illustration of a methodological approach worth following in such situations is that of the Accor group's takeover of Pullman International Hotels. Looking to reach a critical size, the group found itself with two international prestige hotel chains, Sofitel and Pullman. Capitalisation meant that one of the two trade names had to go, but which one? In order to make that choice both names were compared using 12 criteria judged to be important for the decision. They were:

- The degree of spontaneous awareness of each brand among top executives.

- Clients' preference for one or the other brand. Clients from each chain were asked if they preferred that the new chain be called Sofitel or Pullman.

- The level of customer satisfaction with the service of each chain. This was calculated using the following style of question, 'overall Pullman (Sofitel) is a hotel chain that meets my needs'.

- Customer tolerance of the other name in case of a change. When questioned about their hotel preferences in the case of the disappearance of their usual chain, the Pullman clientele preferred the Hilton first and Sofitel second, and the Sofitel clientele preferred Novotel.

- Customer preference based on the level of service associated with each chain. This was tested with the following question, 'would you like the new chain amalgamated from the previous two to have the Pullman or the Sofitel level of service?'

- The difference between the name and the reality of the product.

- The perceived positioning of each chain compared with a luxury chain.

- The perceived clientele satisfaction and pleasure.

- Staff attachment to their chain.

- The financial consequences of choosing one or the other name and the necessity of constructing a homogeneous network at the level required by the positioning.

- Contractual constraints resulting from the trade names, where renegotiating difficulties are foreseeable.

- The risks that the change would inflict on the hotels which were particularly sensitive to a change in their name.

The analysis led to the abandonment of the Pullman name. Its hotels were, depending on their location and level of service, transferred either to Sofitel or to Mercure or sold off.

When choosing a new brand name for a product whose old brand name is about to disappear, it is important to incorporate the conditions under which the brand is distributed. In other words, the store and merchandising must be taken into account. This is what led l'Oréal to abandon its l'Oréal Progress for Men brand and place its products under the umbrella of l'Oréal Elsève for Men.

The supermarket chains Carrefour and Wal-Mart created special sections for grooming products exclusively for men. But the segregation of these products had a negative effect on the number of people buying them and the turnover. The products were immediately relocated in the standard – and much busier – hair-care products section where most of the customers are women buying products for their husbands, friends and children. It appeared to be easier to market these products under the Elsève brand, the leading European hair-care product, rather than in a separate men's section under Progress for Men.

Managing resistance to change

It is a fact that brand changes arouse hostility, which can be a real danger in terms of the effect on market share. The source of the opposition can be found with consumers, with distributors and also internally. From the clients' point of view a brand change is not a superficial act, but it affects the very identity of the product. There is therefore a perceived risk of altering the implied contract. This is especially the case in emerging countries. A change of design is interpreted as a sign of a counterfeit product. It is also the case in the service industry. When there is a lack of any tangible element the brand becomes the heart of all contractual relations. Besides, we have already seen that a brand can only be successfully extended to cover a new category of products if it is seen to be legitimate (Chapter 8). This was Black & Decker's principal challenge when it took over General Electric's domestic electrical appliance activities.

A successful brand transfer also has to deal with distributors. In the industrial world with long distribution channels, retailers tend to choose a few complementary brands that they stick with. Having promoted these brands, they have inevitably linked their reputation with them and their customer loyalty derives from them. To change a brand is therefore like questioning 10 or 15 years of good and loyal service. A retailer loyal to a brand expects something in return from the company. A simple presentation of the strategic reasons why a company should replace brand X by brand Y is not enough, even if the products remain identical. There must be some compensation. The situation is completely different when dealing with supermarkets who care far less about brands apart from their own. Here their analysis is much more down to earth: is this an opportunity to receive a listing allowance for the new brand or a contribution to the temporary hassle incurred by the transfer? Also, distributors will not hesitate to criticise any operations aimed at placing a weak brand under the umbrella of a strong one in order to improve its shelf prominence.

Finally, one must not forget the internal and human elements of resistance. Generally speaking, all brand changes have to pass through managers who will inevitably be attached to their own brand. When L'Oréal decided to give Ambre Solaire a modern technological dimension by placing it under the umbrella brand Garnier, the division came up against numerous pockets of resistance in Europe. In the UK, where Ambre Solaire had a good name and Garnier was unknown, the partisans against the change pushed forward the fact that the future signature brand Garnier had little recognition. The opposite was true in France: the Garnier management argued on the basis that Ambre Solaire suffered from a bad reputation, and that the change might devalue their brand. In the end

the operation did take place and Ambre Solaire sales increased from 4 to 20 million euros.

The precautions taken by the British group ICI when it made an apparently insignificant brand change, transferring the leading paint brand in the French market Valentine to 'ICI Dulux Valentine', illustrate the need to take into account these three stumbling blocks. The precautions aimed solely at the personnel showed just how much they were involved. The personnel at Valentine were attached to their brand so much that they saw themselves as its trustees and looked after it as if it were their own. This is why they took any brand modification to heart, and the dividing line between evolution and dispossession was very fine. The importance of internal communication during this brand change was therefore absolutely crucial if feelings of loss of identity were to be avoided and all thoughts of disappearance kept at bay.

As a result, one of the first things to be done was the setting up of a selective information policy. Only the people who worked closely on the project were informed of progress. The project itself was given a code name rather than a title which would have given the game away. Afterwards, when the deadline date was imminent, the personnel were told. The operation was presented as a step forward and not as the end of the Valentine company once bought by the ICI giant.

The sales force was gathered for a big presentation on the evolution of the European market, on ICI and on its Dulux brand. Particular attention was given to the worldwide importance of Dulux, to its long history (founded in 1930), to its sympathetic and relaxed communication strategy (projection of advertisements), to its content and to its corporate values. The change was presented not as a big event but rather a natural evolution which would bring real and important benefits to the customer.

This gathering was held six months before the brand change. A notable consequence of this date was that all internal rumours were avoided, at least on a large scale.

Some of the distributors were informed very early on of the name change. It is worth remembering that they were part of the cause of the decision to change, because they also favoured a European extension and therefore wanted a European brand. They could not therefore oppose the principle of a brand change. All that was needed was to show them that everything would be done to assure a smooth transition.

Some retailers were informed a whole year before the name change directly by Valentine managers, when internally only the people responsible for the project knew about it. On the other hand, shopkeepers were forewarned by Valentine sales representatives only three months beforehand. Finally, department or shelf managers were informed by mail, just before the change, that on 23 March 1992, ICI Valentine was to become ICI Dulux Valentine. The letter was accompanied by a free luxurious badge of the Valentine mascot, a panther. And when the Valentine sales force next came by they distributed an ICI Dulux Valentine watch (blue background, 12 yellow stars for the 12 hours of the clock and a black panther in the middle) which was such a great success that some people still wear it.

In fact, if this brand transfer was carried out without any hitches, it is because it was presented as an adaptation to meet the constraints of the retailers, and therefore more for their benefit than a revolutionary brand change. What is more the new packaging was intended to make the distributors' life easier and the product clearer and more comprehensible for the consumer, and it permitted a more homogeneous organisation of the shelves.

It had already been established that it was more practical, from the clients' point of view, to organise shelves according to purpose (paint for floors, for ceilings, for wood, for steel, etc), rather than according to brands. Thanks to the new packaging, customers could easily find all the information they needed, paint for the kitchen, for the bedroom, etc.

What is more, Valentine made sure that the brand change would not upset the shelf layouts and that no extra work was needed by the distributors. They also decided that at no point should there be the two different brand names on the same shelf. This is why 180 people carried out the necessary relabelling when the transfer took place in each of the 620 shops concerned. What is more, a freephone number was made available to the retailers should any kind of problem occur.

Tests to measure consumer reactions were also carried out before the brand change. Tachytoscope tests (successive presentations of the old and new packaging) revealed that both versions of the packaging were equally well associated to the brand.

Another benefit for the customer was the opportunity to quickly reorganise the whole range of paint products into sectors according to the main kinds of uses. In normal circumstances this would have taken three years. This makes the customers' choice much easier when they do not know what kind of paint to use in the room or on the surface that they are repainting.

Factors of successful brand transfers

Although the cases looked at and their particular situations vary a lot, it is still possible to draw an overall lesson from the principal experiences in this domain. For fast-moving consumer goods a good summary is by Philippe Villemus, former marketing director of Mars, who remarks:

> Above all, this kind of operation requires a combined effort from all the company departments: production, logistics, sales force, marketing and general management. All will be concerned and any false note will be a source of problems.

Secondly, it is vital that this event be considered an opportunity and not a constraint. The transfer must be an occasion for reappraisal, when the strengths and weakness of the brand can be rethought, and an occasion to gain new market shares by profiting from the extra attention that the new brand will have for a while. In this respect the transfer has to be seen positively by the personnel, the distributors and the consumers, so the benefits that the new brand will bring for each of them must be specified.

A brand transfer cannot be improvised, it must be well prepared. The retailers, prescribers, opinion leaders and the personnel must all be warned well in advance.

The time factor is crucial: one must wait until all the customers are aware of the change, and if the operation has to be carried out quickly, one must have, at one's disposal, the communications means necessary to be able to let them know.

You cannot force a brand change on retailers. Not only should they be informed but everything possible should be done to facilitate their work. That means no double stock. The same product codes should be maintained. This approach not only reduces demands for listing allowances, it makes the rotation of the new brand easier. In the case where a new code is introduced, the chances are that the optical check-outs will not be able to read them because the new reference has not been registered at a central level nor in the shop's computer system.

Even when the transfer is to take place in transitional phases, like a double brand phase before the actual inversion, one should still opt for the quickest time frame. It is true that the average purchase frequency should be taken into account; the frequency of paint purchases compared to that of ultra-fresh produce leads to very different minimal transitional periods. To linger too long only results in being bogged down and losing one's way. This was the case of the Pal to Pedigree transition which took several years. Retrospectively, the process would have benefited if it had been shorter, or even, as in the Raider/Twix case, instantaneous and accompanied by a strong advertising campaign.

Nothing is more shocking to the customer than the strategy of 'fait accompli', imposed without warning, information or explanations. The loyalty to the brand is dented by this sudden disaffection and lack of consideration. Lessons have been drawn from the Treets/M&Ms mishap.

(Villemus, 1996)

A typical 'fait accompli' is the sudden change from Coke to New Coke on 8 May 1985. That event was called the marketing blunder of the century. In fact the brand change nearly created a revolution in the United States that forced the return of the classic Coca-Cola to the shelves and the disappearance of New Coke. After having advertised during more than a century that Coke was the real thing, it was odd to force consumers to change without any warning. Consumers need to be respected: they want to understand how a change will create value for them. A brand transfer is always an act of violence, unlike mere extensions which preserve the consumers' freedom of choice. A brand is much more than a name, it is an emotional link (Fournier, 2000). One does not lose a friend without harm and pain, even resentment.

Today, most brand transfers are explained to clients or consumers. They are forewarned and reassured. They learn how the new brand intends to provide more value to them. Also, in order to not lose consumers at the point of purchase, the former brand recognition signs are maintained for a while. Finally, a tag line can be added on the packages, after the shift, reminding that 'this the new name of ...'.

Last, but not least, to achieve successful brand transfers it is important to know what the customer identifies with the brand and where its equity lies. The Shell Helix case is revealing in this respect. Having decided to replace all its local lubricant brands with one European brand, Shell left the coordination of the transition to its subsidiaries. France was a particular problem in view of the share of the automobile oils market enjoyed by the self-service supermarkets (more than 50 per cent). The strategy that was adopted consisted of the launch in September 1992 of a top-of-the-range oil called Shell Helix Ultra. It was added to the local Puissance range of products, keeping its characteristic can with a practical spout, but in a different colour, grey. Shell Helix Ultra was launched in the automobile press and sold only in Shell service stations. The print advertising campaign slogan, aiming at making Helix the market reference, was: 'One day all oils will be like Helix.' In the meantime the name Helix Plus was added in small letters to Puissance 7 and Helix Standard to Puissance 5. In October 1993, in order to follow the European transition, all the 'Puissance' brands were replaced by Helix. A small mention of Puissance under Helix survived for a few months. The Puissance 7 blue can became the Shell Helix Plus blue can, but the Puissance 5 brown can became the Shell Helix Standard yellow can. The advertisement campaign put the old Puissance 7 can and the new Helix Plus can side by side under the slogan: 'It may have changed its name but the spout remains.' The problem was that the advertisement agency focused on the name change while the clientele paid more attention to the colour of the can. Yet nowhere in the advertising campaign did the yellow can appear. The customers looking for their brown can could not find it: instead they could only find a yellow can the name of which they had never heard of. In reality, despite the brand awareness scores of the name Puissance, the strength of the brand was in fact associated not with its name but with its colour! The customers should have been informed of a transition from brown to yellow rather than soley a name change from Puissance to Helix.

In durable goods sectors and in service sectors, in fact in all sectors with high perceived risk, it is important to stress the role of internal communications. Brands are not abstractions, they are literally carried by people who identify with them. To changing the brand is to change their identification. They need to adhere. This is of paramount importance for corporate brand changes.

Changing the corporate brand

On 1 January 1991, CGE became Alcatel 'to have a brand with a higher profile'. It had up till then been handicapped by the confusion that was occurring due to its similarity with General Electric. In 2000 CGEA became Connex because its name, unpronounceable in international markets hindered expansion and the effectiveness of all communication. To the precautions to take when changing a brand name a few more can be added when dealing with company names. These are based on the fact that there is always a strong internal public and a multitude of external micro-publics.

The first problem that should be avoided is that of rumours, which will always portray a different picture of the change than the reality. The internal public is quick to interpret any change in terms of a crisis, serious problems or shareholder pressure, especially when new majority shareholders have arrived. A big effort is therefore needed to explain the situation. As regards the external public, they generally under-evaluate internal problems. The name change does not bring them any specific advantages so there is no reason for them to pay too much attention. But if they did understand they might go along with the decision, so the name change must be made relevant to them. Finally, each micro-public demands a specific action. In this way, with regard to the transfer to Connex, the first problem that had to be resolved was that of the stock market traders. The company was quoted in about 10 markets around the world, so they had to be certain that right from day one all financiers would be looking for the letter A and not C in the finance sections of their newspapers.

In July 1999 a small energy company, Total, took over the large Elf company, thus creating the fourth largest energy company in the world, and the only one that was not Anglo-Saxon in origin. Naturally, the success of such corporate mergers goes far beyond the topic of the present chapter. Reducing it to a name change would be looking through a tunnel. However, names do play a role in such mergers. In this case the names were not changed immediately to increase the chances of success of the whole operation.

According to the general management of TotalFinaElf, the merger was a success because of the following factors :

▎ It was well prepared by the company taking over. For instance, they had already analysed all the personnel of the target company. Just one month after the takeover, a new organisation chart was issued, so all the employees in the former Elf company learned quickly where they would now stand.

▎ The company taking over had the courage of respecting a 50:50 equilibrium in all assignments, teams and staffs and did not act as a victor.

▎ Hundred of committees were created to discuss all types of topics, so that yesterday's enemies became less hostile, learnt to know each other and eventually became friends.

▎ After the takeover the group took as name TotalFinaElf and kept it for three years. This name was chosen for internal purposes. It indicated that no one was defeated.

Keeping the name of the companies that had been taken over was a sign of respect. Externally it was a sign of power.

▎ Only in 2003 was the group name changed to Total, after an intense probe of the internal climate. However, the Total logo did change at this occasion. The new Total is not the same as the former Total: the new logo conveyed the new values of this leading European fuel company. A merger is an unique opportunity to create a leap forward. Why come back to a former name, and not start with a clean slate as Novartis (formerly Ciba Sandoz) or Aventis (formerly Hoechst Rhone Poulenc) have done? These laboratories have brands as assets, their medical and pharmaceutical product brands. The assets of an energy company are found in its petrol reserves. They depend heavily on the reputation the company has built up under its name in all oil-producing countries over 50 years of activity. Total was a key asset: it meant trust all around the world. In addition, the international financial community expect the Total financial management team to continue in place, and the continuity was intended as a way of reassuring them.

15

Ageing, decline and revitalisation

Because brands are assets, companies try to make them produce earnings as long as possible. They do not believe in the brand life cycle (see also page 186). This is why even though their sales may have come to a minimum, or even after a number of years of inactivity, it is frequent to witness efforts to relaunch this activity. Investment funds and business angels are fond of sleeping beauties, brands whose name still evokes resonance in our memory. There are good reasons for that. As assets, these brands are still endowed with brand awareness, attributes, beliefs: it is less costly to start from these premises than to restart from scratch. This is why, for instance, in 2003 Unilever relaunched Sunsilk shampoo for the third time in Europe.

Second, as old brands they capture a value enhancing emotion, nostalgia. Part of the past of many consumers in our ageing societies, they evoke the ebb of life and good times past. Some of these consumers may want to recapture these emotions, as a symbolic way to stop the passage of time (Brown, Kozinets and Sherry, 2003).

It is necessary to differentiate clearly between a number of close and related concepts: an old product relaunch, a reinvention, an old product facelift and a brand revitalisation:

- An old product relaunch consists in taking a product from the past and selling it as it was. In 2001, Wal-Mart listed a new and unknown brand, Lorina. This brand comes from a small company selling lemonade. For all distributors, lemonade is a commodity: the cheapest is the better. One litre of standard lemonade is sold at around a quarter-euro. Lorina sells it for 4 euros. It has recreated the exact lemonade people used to drink in the 1950s, with a typical glass bottle, a very specific cap and a recipe from that time. Who are the buyers? People of 50 and older.

- An old product reinvention is the new VW Beetle. No one, except collectors, would be prepared now to drive an old Beetle: it is too insecure, uncomfortable, by modern standards. This is why Volkswagen decided to reskin it a little while keeping its unique design, and to completely revise of all its functionalities to match a modern consumer's bottom-line expectations. Who are the buyers? Old consumers and those younger people who are willing to adhere to the brand community.

▊ Brand revitalisation in the narrow sense consists of recreating a consistent flow of sales, putting the brand back to life, on a growth slope again. When the brand is made up of many products, we shall see that this typically entails two actions in parallel: keeping the old typical product globally as it is (to keep its franchise) and reinventing it for new and younger consumers (that is to say asking the question, what would this product be today, if we had to invent it from scratch for the needs of modern consumers?).

▊ Brand facelifts (Bontemps and Lehu, 2002) are part of the revitalisation process. They refer to an upgrading of the performance and/or design of the brand to keep up with the competition.

A lot of people are interested in brand revitalisation:

▊ Young investors or venture capitalists who buy an ailing brand at low price, often an old brand, with the objective of reselling it in a few years at a profit, after revitalising it.

▊ Small businesses that will never have enough money to create their own brand, but are willing to buy the name of a formerly active brand for a reasonable price. For instance, 10 years after having stopped selling the European yogurt brand Chambourcy, Nestlé thought it could sell it. A small company bought it, but the fact that the name was still known did not guarantee the success of the revitalisation, and it soon went out of business. A brand alone without a viable economic equation is of no use. Nestlé had, of course, put a number of restrictions on the use of the brand, since it did not want to find it competing against itself). In addition, the sales of a brand are the result not only of the attractiveness of

that brand to consumers, but also of the muscles of the corporation operating it. Modern mass retailers also tend to value much more the capacity of a company to sustain competition, and to deliver products efficiently to their storage facilities, than its possession of a known but old brand.

▊ Large companies are also interested in revitalising old brands, but only if these brands are not perceived as old, that is to say as brands with no relevance for today, associated exclusively with older consumers. This is how Ford bought Jaguar and had to invest as much money again into put it back to use as a marque for quality cars.

▊ Global companies might buy a leading local brand in order to ease and finance the local development of their international stars. The local brand is a door opener with local distribution. However, it is often found that these so-called local leaders present the clear symptoms of ageing (no innovation, too few younger clients, little challenge of the past practices, no systematic upgrading of packages, designs and communication).

The decay of brand equity

Although they may have ceased their commercial activity, brands do not immediately lose their assets. Learnt through time, their brand image is not erased from consumers' long-term memories. Indeed, after many years a brand can still evoke a number of positive or negative associations. What is lost however is the key brand asset: brand salience, the capacity of the brand to be evoked spontaneously in consumers' minds as soon as the need to buy the product type appears. This is why belonging to the consumer 'evoked set' (or consideration set) is a key measure of brand equity, signifying both brand presence and its perceived unique relevance for that need.

Table 15.1 illustrates how brand equity decays over time. Brand X is a FMCG food brand in a very popular category (with almost 100 per cent penetration). Until recently, this brand was the number two in its market. Then it was bought by market number three, which immediately sold all Brand X's factories so that the acquisition of the brand paid off immediately. Most important, it discontinued its activity and as a result became the market number two in volume and number one in value. Eight years after the end of any kind of commercial activity, the brand equity had not disappeared. Top-of-mind awareness had dropped from 13 per cent to 5 per cent and aided awareness from 86 per cent to 55 per cent. Interestingly, there are still 13 per cent of consumers who declare that they have bought it at least once over the preceding 12 months. This latter figure casts doubts on the validity of such indicators of brand equity in this FMCG category: it seems to be a mere reflection of spontaneous awareness.

How much would this brand be worth if its owner decided to sell it? Not far from zero. The owner would never take the risk of selling it so that it could be revived in its own market. Out of this market, it is just a name with faded remote credentials: there will be no buyer. Could the owner itself revitalise that brand? Probably in specific segments or niches. As far as the mainstream market is concerned, a return to the shelves would be impossible. They are now overcrowded, first by private labels, and second by the few remaining producers' brands, which have become mega-brands. Typically, a shift of channel would be possible. For instance, a drink brand might be sold via on-premise distribution (for consumption in canteens and business restaurants), if this were a channel where it could add value without meeting fierce competition. Channel and use changes are a classic form of revitalisation for this very reason.

This example illustrates a fact too often overlooked: the value of a brand does not lie in its assets, but in the ability of a company to make a profitable business with these assets. After eight years of inactivity the whole commercial environment will have changed. Nature abhors a vacuum, and business does too. As so as the brand disappears from the stores, the shelves are filled with other products from other brands, including the distributors' own brand. In order to sell the original again, they would need to be displaced. It costs a lot to induce the modern distribution to reallocate space for a comeback, with very little guarantee of success. A brand is not enough to stage a comeback, one needs an innovation.

It is clear why it is essential to prevent decline, and how a brand loses value after a period of inactivity. But what are the factors of decline?

The factors of decline

Following the analysis of the factors of a brand's longevity in Chapter 9, one could

Table 15.1 How brand equity decays over time

Years after the end of the brand's commercial activity							
	1	2	3	4	5	6	7	8
Top of mind (saliency)	13	12	7	7	6	3	1	5
Total unaided awareness	26	28	20	29	15	14	11	16
Aided awareness	86	83	76	73	68	50	55	55
Bought last 12 months	27	29	17	19	12	15	10	13

FMCG food brand; sample size 450/year; all figures are percentages.

simply say that in contrast, brands decline when they are not respected. In fact, their decline always comes from mismanagement. When a producer ceases to be interested in its brands (thus creating a lack of innovation, advertising or productivity), it can expect the consumer also to lose interest. And if the brand loses dynamism, energy, and shows fewer and fewer signs of vitality, how can one possibly hope that it will arouse passion and proselytism? Apart from these rules, which are so basic that it is astonishing that they can be forgotten, there are some factors that accelerate decline. These will now be studied.

When quality is forgotten

The first and surest road to decline is through the degradation of the quality of the products. The brand ceases to be a sign of quality. Economic factors oblige companies to cut corners with regard to quality, albeit in minor steps, and unfortunately, far too frequently. For instance, when L'Oréal bought out Lanvin, its leading perfume Arpège was a mere shadow of its former self. The fragrance had originally been made up of natural oils but by then included a fair amount of artificial ingredients. The bottle had even lost its round shape. Consumers around the world were conscious that they were no longer respected since Arpège had been so badly mistreated. L'Oréal's first step was to give back to this perfume the case, the bottle and the ingredients of the quality that it deserved. This task, which was not spectacular but was expensive, was absolutely necessary. It enabled contact to be re-established with the consumers who had been forsaken, and the rebuilding of acceptable foundations for the brand.

Beware of non-significant differences

The change in the level of quality of a product is rarely abrupt, but results from the insidious logic of statistical tests. Each change is tested against the product's previous version: if consumers have a lower opinion of the changed product but statistical analysis reveals that the difference is not significant, the company will not hesitate to carry out the change to provide a source of financial savings. The problem entirely rests with the expression 'significant difference'. All the decisions are based on the so-called 'alpha risk threshold' (generally 5 per cent). As long as the difference observed in the sample, just due to chance, affects less than 5 per cent of the cases, it is declared non-significant. In sciences, the aim of this high-risk threshold is to avoid taking for real a phenomenon which would not exist in reality. The problem is that in marketing, it is the 'beta risk' that should be taken into account, the aim of which is to avoid considering as false a hypothesis that is in reality true. For, through modifying a product even by the smallest amount which each time has been declared 'non-significant', a considerable risk is taken. Consumers are not fooled. They avoid the product, then abandon it, even sometimes spreading by word of mouth a very negative opinion. From then on, any modification of the product must be approached with caution if it is rated below the standard product, even if the difference is said to be non-significant.

Missing the trend

The third factor of decline is the refusal to follow immediately a durable change. Thus Taylor Made, for a long time the world reference for golf clubs, did not believe the gigantic head launched by the Callaway brand under the suggestive name of 'Big Bertha' would catch on. By clinging to a different conception that was more demanding for the average player, ie for the majority of the market, Taylor Made suddenly lost its leadership. In the same way, Banga orange juice continued to believe in glass bottles when the market, following the market leader Oasis, turned towards plastic.

In 2001, according to Zandl, a specialised US marketing research company, the jeans was still number one in the youth clothing preference. However, young people now quote 112 different brands as being their 'preferred brand for jeans'. The market has become fragmented, a challenge for Levi's, whose image and sales are very much associated with a mono-product, the 501.

Fragmentation led tribes, small groups to prefer new types of jeans, more adapted to new usages, and new brands. A lot of new competitors filled niches. Pepe and Diesel addressed the urban rebel, 'For us by us' and underground streetwear. Gap also became a major player. Levi's had expressed disbelief in streetwear and neglected the rappers and gliders, who are in fact the opinion leaders of the new youth. Tight 501s are totally unadapted to skateboarding and rollerskating. Skaters wish to wear an XXXXL rolled up their knees, and rappers like multi-pocket trousers. On the other end of the spectrum, girls desired Tommy Hilfiger and Polo jeans, not to speak of Armani and Versace jeans. It was clearly the end of the mass market. Levi's had not foreseen it, and worse, it had not reacted when the trends were there.

The mono-product syndrome

Still at the level of product policy, the brands associated with a single product are more vulnerable. They risk being carried away by the decline of that product. This again is part of what happened to Levi's, with its too-long association with the mythical 501. Wonderbra is another clear instance of a brand that fell into the mono-product trap.

Who has never heard about Wonderbra? Very few, either women or men. Although the product is in fact comparatively old (it was invented in Canada in 1953 by Canadelle Corp), its real launch in Europe was quite recent (1994). Sara Lee had bought the company and gave Playtex the responsibility of launching the Wonderbra in Europe. The fantastic advertising campaign ('Hello boys') and accompanying publicity made this innovation famous. The brand helped women who felt they had small breasts look more sexy and gain self-assurance as a result. It created a new segment. In 1995, 5 million units were sold in Europe, and 86 per cent of its consumers were less than 35 years old. Now where is Wonderbra? Still trying to find pathways for growth, if not prevent decline. Despite an aided awareness level of 70 per cent, its goodwill has come close to bad will in some countries, in the trade channels.

After the peak sales of 1995, sales started to decline. Competitors with known brands entered this segment too.

The problem was that Wonderbra became associated not with a brand but with a product, and its brand name became a generic name: people spoke of 'the wonderbra'. This highly technical product (it had 42 parts, and needed a specific manufacturing technology) was much adored inside the company. Everyone was very proud of it. Where to go next? If innovation is the key to market penetration, a brand has to become more than a name of a product. But Wonderbra did not innovate sufficiently, and consumers did not repurchase its products. Today, 61 per cent of Wonderbra consumers possess only one Wonderbra. They wear it for special occasions, and rarely on weekdays. Wonderbra might instead have capitalised on its sexy positioning but offered new products based on different reasons for purchase. The very same benefit could have be expressed using different materials or shapes. Instead it remained too narrow, preventing the consumer from move freely within the brand.

Another difficulty was the global management of the brand. New models were designed essentially for the UK, its leading European market, because of an excess of centralisation at Playtex (Sara Lee). The management did not recognise that the tastes and wishes of Italian, French and Spanish women were not those of Englishwomen. As a result European sales became one-country sales.

Distribution factors

The relationship with a distribution channel can be a factor of decline if the brand does not live up to the new expectations of it. Because companies such as L'Oréal developed particular brands for supermarket distribution, such as Plénitude for cosmetics, Vichy's status in the field of pharmaceuticals is under threat. Consumers who go to a chemist shop to buy such products expect from them a higher level of quality as befits the laboratory guarantee. But over time, Vichy had become a generalist brand more focused on lifestyle than scientific quality. It found itself, in 1995, carrying products which no longer corresponded with the products which consumers wanted to buy in a chemist shop. Vichy's survival was contingent upon a qualitative upgrade of all its products and its repositioning on the benefit of better health through the skin.

Other brands have collapsed because they have allowed themselves to become trapped in a declining distribution network. The recent rise of large liquor stores in Japan, at the expense of small convenience outlets, has caused the immediate decline of all the brands lacking a sufficient level of public awareness. In small outlets, they did not need it: the store owner pushed the brand, sold it to his clients. In modern distribution the brand has to sell itself, it needs market pull.

Weak communication creates a distance

Finally, communication can accelerate the decline of brands. Beyond the obvious fact that ceasing to advertise means ceasing to exist in the market and ceasing to be a key actor, the sensible management of communication consists of modernising the signs, but keeping the essence.

If the daughter brands are too much in the spotlight, the mother brand can be adversely affected and give the impression that it is in decline. This happened with Dim, a Sara Lee hosiery brand. Although the brand was by far the main advertiser in its hosiery market, and even in the textile market in general, it seemed to be declining, less active. Such an imbalance between the actual share of voice and the feeling of loss of energy felt by the market worried the management of the Sara Lee group. In fact, the diagnosis was clear: the promotional tactics of the daughter brands had been carried so far that they had fragmented Dim's image. Indeed, it was appropriate – as we have seen in Chapter 7 – to clarify Dim's wide range by attributing names to different products which did not propose the same customer benefits, hence the appearance of Sublim, Diam's and other lines. On the other hand, this measure produced a dispersion of the Dim image, even the disappearance of Dim to the benefit of the daughter brands. The first symptom of this condition was the packaging. There was no longer any homogeneity between the different packagings, and the mother brand appeared in a minor endorsing role in variable places. Moreover, in the context of the organisational change, further divisions had been introduced (tights, lingerie, men's items). Unfortunately, there was no longer anybody in charge of coherence between the divisions and of the defence of the Dim mother brand's capital. Finally, since the Dim logotype only appeared clearly on bottom-end products and was concealed on advanced products, this increased the perception that its quality had declined. At the same time, the market was moving towards opaque tights, a more durable and more top-end product, which could easily make Dim the symbol, not of today's woman, but rather of a poor quality.

In order to correct these dangerous impressions, Dim undertook to increase the added value of all its products, including the basic product, to upgrade all its packagings, to return the status of source-brand by replacing the first-name brands under a visible umbrella, and to clearly advertise 'Dim presents the new

Diam's' instead of 'This is the new Diam's by Dim'. (This example illustrates, in passing, a tendency which is fatal for a brand: its systematic distance from the best new products, thereby confining it to an offer which is static, obsolete or old-fashioned.) To complete the story, it should also be mentioned that, in parallel with the excessive exposure of the daughter brands, the Dim brand had been extended to leisure and indoor clothing. This created an added danger for the brand, that of dilution. By leaving its field of competence (everything which is worn close to the body) to enter the sector of regular clothes, its added value became less tangible. The existence of clothes with a Dim label without any tangible added value could only raise doubts about the brand's actual contribution, not only in this new market, but also in its basic markets: tights and lingerie. So, in the context of Dim's renewal plan, an end was put to this extension, which was causing the dilution of the brand's capital. The priority was to return Dim to the field in which it was recognised to have expertise. The history of ready-to-wear clothes contains too many examples of brands which have abandoned their initial concept to experiment with new extensions and so lose their identity. This has been the case with Newman, which can no longer be associated with a typical product, of Marlboro Classics which has moved away from its founding style, and so on.

When the brand becomes generic

The highest degree of dilution of the brand's added value occurs when the brand becomes generic. The brand is considered a descriptive word, part of everyday vocabulary with no distinctive properties. The classic examples are well-known: Scotch, Kleenex, Xerox, Nylon, Velux. What causes a brand to be reduced to the point of becoming generic? The abandonment of any communication on the brand's specific nature and purpose can

cause its decline. Thus, any dominant brand of a new product risks becoming a generic name. This can be prevented by taking certain precautions, for example:

▮ create a word to designate the product of the brand;

▮ never mention the brand's name alone, but together with the product's generic designation;

▮ never use the brand's name as a verb (in the United States, for instance, to xerox means to make a photocopy) or as a noun, but as an adjective;

▮ systematically protest whenever the brand's name is used as a common noun by third parties and the media; for instance, request that an erratum be published. Through not having reacted strongly enough, Du Pont de Nemours lost the ownership of Nylon and Teflon, which have since become generic terms;

▮ nurture the perceived difference between the brand and competitive products, either with tangible attributes or with intangible values. In any event introduce new products.

The ageing of brands

It is frequently said that a brand is ageing, shows signs of ageing or seems aged. This impression may be felt by customers, non-customers, suppliers, distributors or employees themselves, who acknowledge a difference between them and their competitors. Ballantines, Martini, Black & White, Club Med, Yves Saint Laurent and Guy Laroche have all been described as ageing.

The concept of ageing has in fact two different meanings:

▮ The general meaning suggests a slow but systematic decline over a long period of time. The brand is not destined to end rapidly but seems likely to be inevitably phased out with time. Yesterday strong and active, it appears today much more mundane, as if it no longer had anything to say or to propose to the market and lived exclusively on its loyal clients. One symptom of this is the widening gap between the spontaneous awareness and the assisted awareness. The brand still rings a bell, but it is not one of the brands which has an impact on the market. It does not launch new products as often as the category actors. It does not surprise. It repeats itself. There is only a small difference between repetition and boredom.

- The second meaning refers to the reflected image of the customer. Everything points to the typical customer being older. And even in the case of a company whose marketing is deliberately targeted at older customers, it is never advisable for the image of a brand to be too closely associated with an older clientele. Although it is aiming at the flourishing older customer market (that is, customers over 50), Damart must make sure not to be associated with the clientele who are 60 or 70. Without going to that extreme, the Yves Saint Laurent label appears to young people to represent a clientele older than that of Dior's and Chanel.

What is that produces these impressions of ageing? Most of the time these impressions are well founded: the brand no longer seems to belong to its time and has lost its inner energy.

Many brands allow themselves to be associated with the products of another age. With the acceleration of time, the notion of another era now refers to a close past. In all markets dominated by technology, obsolescence can occur very rapidly. Little can be done for brands linked to a dated technology, or those which seem not to have kept up to date with progress or with the Internet.

A brand can be 18 years old and threatened with ageing. The challenge for the eau de toilette Eau Jeune (ie Young Water), launched by L'Oréal for supermarket distribution, is to be still considered Eau Jeune by the next generation of 18- to 25-year-olds, but who are so different. If this brand had remained a single product, it would have disappeared. What symbolised youth in 1987 no longer symbolises it in 1997.

The point of view expressed by the brand on its market can also sometimes seem to be suddenly behind the new dominant values. As long as decisions regarding Playtex in Europe were taken in the United States, the brand never seemed to take into consideration the role of femininity in women's choices. Even though the products were of high quality, they were purely functional, that is based on the tangible problem of breast support. What was relevant in the United States was totally opposite to the way European women related to their bodies. In its tone and inflexibility, Playtex seemed to be addressing the mothers, not the daughters.

Although it was still the world's leading brand for shoes and ski bindings, Salomon recently realised that it was in great danger of ageing within a few years. In fact, Salomon, in the same way as Rossignol does, has represented the values of alpine skiing for half a century: effort, order, competition, gaining one hundredth of a second, beating all others by a microsecond. The new generations no longer subscribe to these values: a counter-culture, originating in the surf, is dominant on the slopes, bringing with it new sports and new values. What has been called the 'glide generation' has not learnt alpine skiing and probably never will. They instinctively practise snowboarding on the slopes in winter and roller-skating or roller-blading in the streets. They put as paramount values friendship and emotion: they eschew competition and the brands associated with yesteryear. They have elected their own gods: Burton, Airwalk, Quicksilver, Oxbow. All these brands are new and symbolise another vision of sport.

The lack of evolution in a brand's outward signs indicates its present lack of interest in attracting new customers.

Certain brands also come to a standstill because they remain associated with the same images. The fact that Yves Saint Laurent seems more dated than Dior or Chanel is connected with the omnipresence of the ageing creator himself and association with Catherine Deneuve. Lancôme was sensible enough to bring in younger and international stars.

As for the clientele, the loss of direct contact with young people is the surest symptom of ageing. This is what differentiates Johnny Walker from Jack Daniel's or Martini from Bacardi.

Without necessarily having to appeal to young people between the ages of 20 and 25, the brand should always be attractive to tomorrow's consumers. The buyers who are today in their forties will modify their functional expectations when they reach their fifties. But they will also like to show that they have not changed by staying with their usual brands. They will refuse to support the ghetto brands which signal their entry into old age. This is why Damart's future depends on its image among 45-year-old men and women even if its marketing is rather targeted at the 55-year-old senior consumer. Damart has to work on the evolution of its image, not of its target clientele. To do so, they must improve their image so as not to appear a last-frontier brand. This is why, besides the modernisation of their main product, underwear, they have left behind their old methods of distribution: some department stores now have a Damart lingerie department next to Playtex, Rosy or Warner. Damart also advertises products that cross the generation barrier, allowing them to dissociate their image from one based merely on age: thick and coloured tights are just as appropriate for a young girl in a short skirt riding a motorbike as they are for skiers and autumn hikers. Through these significant actions, they address their future customers and put an end to the stagnation of their clientele, for in 1990 Damart was attracting hardly any new buyers, but was selling more and more to loyal customers.

As has been noted, keeping in touch with young people implies a cultural revolution among management. The efforts to be made may seem huge to an older internal team who often do not appreciate the danger they are facing as their own reference points always seem secure. Finally, with consumers living longer, the effects of the clientele's ageing may pass unnoticed. The decline is slow and never spectacular. But unfortunately, as with a cancer, without an obvious sign of decline to react rapidly to, it may sometimes be too late.

To make the radical internal changes required to energise an organisation which has aged with its own reference points, there should be no hesitation in rejuvenating the entire management with younger people. The revitalisation of brands always starts with a major work of internal rejuvenation.

Rejuvenating a brand

How should one rejuvenate a brand? How can a declining or a past brand revive? How do you recreate a durable growth for a brand that has for long been declining? Although there exist a wide variety of situations, the goal is the same: to bring a brand back to life. This leads to the core question, what life? Whose life? As a rule, it will rarely be the same as formerly.

There is a big difference between respecting one's roots and cultivating the past. Revitalisations, revivals are based on an updating of the overall offer of the brand while staying true to part of its identity. Revival means aiming at a new growth market. The brand must find a new relevance and differentiation. The term 'revival' of a brand is not quite accurate since it always implies a change in the product, or in the market, or in the target market. It is a relaunch but not necessarily among the same people as before, or in the same distribution channels, for the same uses, or whatever. With time the consumers, the markets and competition will have changed.

Redefining the brand essence

Even forgotten brands have an internal meaning, a domain of legitimacy to be exploited. The first task in a brand revitalisation is to understand which values of this brand still have a high relevance, and which have lost meaning. Old brands have disseminated bits of associations in people's memories, even among non-customers or newer generations. These weak memories act as a 'humus'. It is important to analyse this humus. What is left about the brand essence? What are the potentialities emerging from it? What market opportunities could be met? It is useful to analyse this as shown in Figure 15.1.

As a rule, declining brands have few positive salient evocations, or these evocations are generic and lack differentiation. The real potential usually lies in the latent associations. It will be the role of marketing to choose the right set from among these buried positive associations. Then the brand will have to embody them in new products or services and channels aimed at the new target.

Revitalising through new situations

The revitalisation of a brand usually follows new paths that are very different from those that led to its initial success. If there has been a decline, it is because these paths did not lead to any new demand or pocket of growth.

Revitalisation involves establishing new parameters for the brand. Since its original consumers are no longer able to ensure its success, it has to attract a new clientele, develop new user occasions, new distribution channels and new consumer networks.

Brandy is a classic example. It is typically associated with the 'after-dinner' and 'connoisseurs enjoying a brandy together'

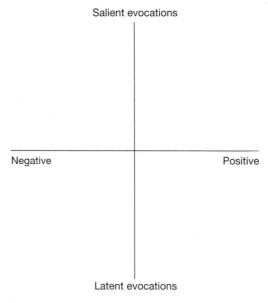

Figure 15.1   Analysing the potential of an old brand

type of occasion, an image and occasion that have been responsible for a massive decline in the volume of brandy sales worldwide. After years of decline in the face of competition from white spirits, which are much easier to drink and much trendier (Bacardi, Absolut, Seagram's Gin and so on), brandy sales have recently soared in the United States. But with one major difference – 50 per cent of the volume of brandy currently consumed in the United States is consumed by the black community, which represents 12 per cent of the population. It has become the favourite drink of African-American males, within the context of a lively social situation, where status value is essential. They ask for Martell or Hennessy, as well as Thackeray (gin) and Crystal Roederer (champagne).

To target a new consumer group, a company must be ready to call its traditional marketing into question and define an optimum marketing mix for its new target group. The process begins with new customers, their lifestyle and new occasions on which the product is consumed or purchased. Innovation is therefore central to the revitalisation of old brands.

Revitalising through distribution change

In fact, it seems that a classic revitalisation strategy is to use known brands in different distribution circuits. For instance, a super-market food brand could be moved to a channel that rests on 'push' marketing rather than 'pull' marketing. This is why one sees many formerly famous brands in canteens, or office restaurants for instance. It creates value in the eyes of the clients (more than an unknown brand or a private label) and these brands are cheaper than well-known leading brands. The obverse is also true. One company has specialised in purchasing old medical products, with 100 per cent aided awareness, but that are little prescribed these days. Some of them have become generic names. The

strategy consists in selling them on the shelves of supermarkets, where their name triggers immediate recognition and trust.

Revitalising through innovations

Barely 10 years ago, Mercedes was under threat. The brand had certainly gained international acclaim, but the signs were nevertheless worrying. In California, where new consumer trends are created, Mercedes was no longer an aspirational brand. It had been replaced by Lexus, the top-of-the-range brand from Toyota. And in Europe the average buyer of the smallest Mercedes of that period, the C-Class, was 51 years old.

Clearly Mercedes was becoming a brand for older people. The company's CEO made a harsh but accurate diagnosis: either the brand remained as it was and the company would go bankrupt (like Rolls-Royce) or it would have to evolve.

The first step was to re-establish the conditions that would create a favourable economic equation – the company would have to produce 1 million vehicles to lower production costs to an acceptable level. The second was to attract a younger clientele – they could not be left to the competition until they reached 51! To do this, the company had to break with the standard design of all Mercedes cars for the previous 60 years.

This is why the event that revitalised Mercedes was the launch of the A-Class. This little car, which was in direct competition with the Volkswagen Golf, was the brand's new 'prototype' in Europe. It departed from the traditional Mercedes image on two counts – it had front-wheel drive and a completely different design. However, it still had the interior space of the C-Class and the safety of the E-Class. In fact, it currently accounts for 30 per cent of Mercedes sales in Europe. Above all, it has attracted a younger clientele (with an average age of 37), more women and the style conscious.

In the United States, the new Mercedes prototype is the luxury 4 x 4 M-Class, which has re-established contact with the trendy set of California and elsewhere.

To target even younger consumers, the beautiful CLK Roadster was deliberately positioned at an attractive price. Its beauty, sensitivity and design are now part of the new Mercedes brand contract. Of course, any form of extension modifies the original brand, and Mercedes is no longer an exclusively luxury brand. The new Mercedes management is more segmented, more attuned to the needs of its consumers and their lifestyle. The brand regularly renews its status as the world's leading car manufacturer via its top of the range models, of which the S-Class is the symbol.

Back to the future

Often a brands decline is tied to forgetting the brand's mission. Little by little small adjustments have been added to the strategy, and cumulatively they have led the brand astray. This is how heavy discounters become less heavy discounters, luxury brands become less luxurious, feminine brands become less feminine and so on. 'Back to the core' is a classic revitalising strategy. It does not mean being obsessed with the past, but if the early vision and mission are still valid, trying to come back to it while acknowledging that the product itself may need to be updated.

Many groups act preventively by regularly checking the relevance of their identity and the fact that the operations are actually in line with this strategy. For instance, at Decathlon, as soon as operating margins get higher, the alarm bell rings. Decathlon's deep culture focuses on making people happy through sport and physical activities. This is achieved through a remarkable policy of providing own brands with the best performance/price ratio on the market. Higher margins seem to indicate that this ratio is becoming less exceptional than it should be.

This is also very typical of hotel management. Regularly at Accor Hotels, each brand (holds a seminar called 'Back to the future'. The goal is to assess if the strategy is being followed or if in fact it has subtly changed. If it is the case, what services should be deleted or added in order to once more fulfill the brand's mission?

Revitalising by contact with opinion leaders

Ageing brands have generally lost contact with the trend setters in their category, the tribes that prefigure change. Advertising and product innovation will be of no help without the active support of these trend-setting tribes. It is not easy to make friends again with people one has not called for years, during which time they have been seduced by the competition, including new entrants. In addition the ageing brand is held as an icon of the past, and may attract bad will, not goodwill.

The task of recreating proximity through direct contacts and shared emotional experiences will be difficult, but it is an essential part of any comeback. Salomon, which had lost contact with the surfers who were its future market, had to create an internal cultural revolution, changing its management and hiring young people who were likely to be able to recreate the lost connection.

Apple had lost contact with today's new trend setters, who are no longer advertising agencies, but the kids seduced by Napster and whose use of the Internet is now mostly to exchange music within their virtual tribe. Ballantines, formerly at Allied Domecq, realised recently that it too had lost all contact with youth. Managers more concerned with their own fate in the midst of mergers and acquisition in their sector concentrated on the brand's core clients, not the future clients. They forgot that sustaining brand equity means addressing current and future business alike. For instance, in 1995 brand equity monitoring showed that in some European countries, brand spontaneous awareness among 18–24-year-olds had dropped from 47 per cent to 13 per cent in seven years.

It is not possible to get out of this dramatic problem just by changing one's advertising. Sometimes creating a new product is needed, because in between, everything has changed: consumers, their habits, the competition, places of consumption and so on.

Regaining contact is a preliminary. A brand is not a product with a name, it is a relationship. After years of indifference, not to say neglect by Ballantines, the brand had to reconquer the lost relationship. It might still have been number one in some countries, but that was because of a core of frequent buyers, all ageing. Benchmarking the best practice of Pernod-Ricard, the brand decided to invest massively in Europe, and also in South America, to reconquer proximity by contact. Targeting is crucial: what key tribe? The management identified snowboarding as representing the core values of the new generation.

In cooperation with the International Snowboarding Federation, which was fighting against the International Ski Federation, it sponsored all alpine snowboard events, and created a night event in discos. However, to be effective today at regaining contact, sponsoring must go far beyond just stamping the event with the brand name everywhere. The brand must be at the centre, or a key ally of the event.

Step two entailed recognition that urban youth was the target. Ballantines decided to bring snowboarding to cities through the 'Ballantines Urban High' Tour. In the middle of capital cities from Berlin to Rio de Janeiro, or on their beaches, Ballantines had a huge ramp built, covered in artificial snow, to host three-day national contests to find the best freelance snowboarders. The contest was preceded by country-wide selection phases, thereby creating a mounting buzz through word of mouth. The event fuelled involvement. The first event of the series took place in October 1995 in Berlin, symbolically at the Brandenburg Gate (which used to be the only gate in the Berlin Wall where people from the former East Germany could come through to the free West). Because among young people everything goes together, during the contest there were an open air concert (with the group Prodigy), grunge fashion shows, and night-time promotions in all the city's discos around snowboarding themes. In addition for the cream of the cream, Ballantines created Ballantines orbit, a huge mobile tent, with restricted invitation to those perceived as style leaders to listen to live techno music. After Berlin the tour went on to Prague, Milan, Moscow, Rio de Janeiro – it still goes on.

The lessons that can be drawn from this case are that proximity today means bumping into the lives of the target group, not just being there. A multidimensional event was created, merging fashion, sport, music, dancing, entertainment and video games, showing a high level of investment, and a very good understanding of the target audience's desires. A special logo was created, Ballantines Urban High, which could eventually become a label for licensed products (a clothing line, T-shirts, music and so on), certainly a Web site, and why not a franchised store chain in the future?

The event was well prepared for through the selection phases and brand presence across the country,. The budget commitment was high: about 600,000 euros) for the Berlin event, which was attended by 100,000 young people (so it cost 5 euros per person for a contact that should create a long-lasting emotional memory and involvement with the brand).

Changing the business model

Once in a while daring entrepreneurs buy an old and ailing brand and decide to revitalise it. It also happens that big groups do so. What is often presented as a brand revitalisation is actually a change in the business model. In Chapter 1 we emphasised that a brand that cannot provide benefits has no real value. By benefits is meant financial benefits, economic value added (EVA) once the cost of capital had been paid (see also page 450). What makes an ailing brand more valuable is the new business model on which it will rely.

For decades l'Aigle, a former subsidiary of Hutchinson, was known for its rubber boots. Its name was also its symbol: it came directly from the American Eagle. It had become a cult brand among fishermen, hunters, nature lovers and country landowners. But Chinese imports and modern distribution created too many problems, the company went broke, and it was bought in an LBO. Now, in 2004, there are Aigle stores opening everywhere in the world. Has the brand changed? In name terms it has lost a letter, moving from l'Aigle to Aigle, gaining simplicity and internationality. Most important, it moved from a boots brand to a leisurewear brand, whose prototype (most symbolic product) has moved from the rubber boots to a parka, a solid product, as the main value of the brand commands. The vintage rubber boots are still there to nurture the myth, but business grew through the new prototype. There are a lot of benefits in this change of business model:

- Brands that rely too much on a mono-product are always in danger, as they cannot smooth out a drop in sales. Boots sell less when climate becomes dryer. Also, since the rubber boots were of excellent quality, they lasted a long time. Brand loyalty was high but the time between purchases was too long.

- Extending the line to leisurewear made it possible to free the brand from the grip of modern distribution and build its own selective distribution network. The extended line made it more than possible to fill each store.

- Leisure wear is fashion conscious: people buy new garments each year even if they already own similar ones. It is also a less price-sensitive sector.

This example is a reminder that too often the success of the revitalisation is attributed to 'the brand' as a short cut, because there is a lack of information on the company itself, the strategy, the back office. Certainly the brand reputation was an invaluable asset, but that asset was worth nothing as long as it was not supported by a valid business model.

Growing older but not ageing

One way of understanding revitalisation is to consider brands that have not 'aged'. How have they done it? Typically, the brands that have defied the passage of time have adopted a dual logic, as illustrated by Nivea and Lacoste. To follow their example and stay young, a brand must implement three types of initiatives towards the product. These can also be used as a model for relaunching a brand.

Facelifting, reinventing and innovating

The management of a brand involves maintaining the present (what the brand is now) while at the same time working for the future. It is the present that constitutes the source of income and therefore allows the development of the growth products of the future. As shown in Figure 15.2, in order to stay young, a brand must implement three types of initiatives at the same time:

- It must continually modernise the 'prototype' in the same way that Nivea introduced Nivea Soft to modernise its basic in the famous metallic blue jar. Nivea Soft is lighter and less greasy, and is marketed in a white jar. Lacoste regularly improves its famous 12 x 12 polo shirt in terms of the quality of the wool, the colours, the sleeves and so on.

- It must also reinvent the 'prototype', just as Lacoste produced a tight-fitting shirt with

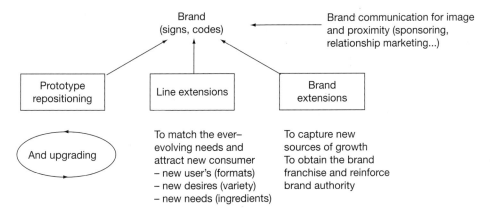

Figure 15.2 Sustaining brand equity long term

Lycra since this is how the woman of today likes to dress. It was an immediate hit. For example, imagine a brand of hair-care products whose basic product is a lotion. It would certainly have to modernise it in terms of the packaging, and update the formulation. But it should above all consider how today's customers would want to apply the product. It is quite possible that rubbing a lotion into the scalp is something that is no longer done, even though the product itself is extremely relevant. In this case, another method of application would certainly be the best form of innovation. You only have to think of Nivea, which invented the first spray-on sun lotion.

- Finally, it must innovate by actively seeking out the trends and behaviour that currently dominate the younger consumer segments, since these are the segments that will generate customer loyalty in the future. To return to the example of the hair-care brand, it simply cannot afford not to create new products – which are of course in line with its brand contract. Young people are mad about hair gels, styling products and hair colour. These markets certainly exist already, but the brand can create new segments within these markets that work in its favour.

Actively seeking out new types of behaviour means opening up to the idea of exploring new distribution channels, since new behaviour is often linked to new places and situations. These innovations also provide an opportunity to launch new and truly ground-breaking publicity campaigns, both in terms of their basic structure and especially their style. In this way, the brand sends out clear signals that it is reinventing itself. At the same time, these campaigns aim to launch the business of these innovations, just as they would for any new product.

Detecting the symptoms of ageing brands

Brands are built by the sum of all their behaviours creating value at contact points with customers. This is why brands should regularly monitor their behaviour. There are many sure symptoms of a brand dropping off, and they can be grouped into seven main types.

Insufficient preparation for the future

- Insufficient rate of new products in the yearly sales.

- Low rate of patent registration.

- Low rate of trademark registration (a sign of little need to name new products and services).

- Insufficient investment in R&D, in market sensing, in trend spotting.

- Insufficient knowledge about new uses and new emerging situations of use.

- Date of the last executive committee meeting to address these issues.

Insufficient dual management

- Insufficient knowledge about non-consumers, modern consumers, tomorrow's consumers.

- More and more sales to a reduced number of clients.

- Following the demands of existing clients, not foreseeing the changes in the market.

- Slow but regular increase of the average age of clients.

Insufficient capacity to capture growth pockets as they emerge

- Thinking the brand only through its historical product, without being ready to capture emerging new materials and demands.

- Excessive vision of what is called brand coherence, thus limiting the types of extensions to be made by the brand.

Insufficient relevance

- Weakening of the present positioning and values.

- Weakening of the way values are materialised.

- Date of the last customer satisfaction questionnaire.

- Date of the last interview with lost customers.

- Increase in proportion of customers declaring they are 'moderately satisfied'.

- Date of the last blind test.

- Lowering rate of repeat purchase.

- Decrease in spontaneous awareness (saliency).

- Decrease in number of spontaneous press quotes.

Insufficient vitality at contact

- Lack of regular updating of the quality of the logo and visual symbol of the brand.

- Date of last change or facelift for the packaging (design, ergonomics).

- Lack of regular facelifts for stores or concessions.

- Lack of organised merchandising, lack of plans to regularly rethink it.

- Lack of service (call centres, Web sites and so on).

- Lack of brand proximity marketing.

- Lack of advertising.

Insufficient self-stimulation

- Lack of curiosity.

- Lack of desire to surprise.

- Lack of PR events.

- Lack of contacts with new opinion leaders, with the press.

Insufficient staffing

- Lack of young managers.

- Sex imbalance among executives (100 per cent male or 100 per cent female).

16

Managing global brands

Geographic extension is the necessary fate of brands. On it depend the brand's growth, and its ability to innovate and to sustain its competitive edge in terms of economies of scale and productivity. As such, marketing directors are no longer questioning the principle of international expansion, but are preoccupied with the means by which this can be accomplished. They ask themselves: Where should we go? What balance do we maintain between a global brand which shuns linguistic and national frontiers, and one which makes provision for local requirements and context? Which brands are destined to have global significance and which should remain on a national footing? Finally, how do we rationalise the portfolio of national brands into a small number of global brands? Any such transition must be carefully managed, as we have seen in Chapter 15.

The debate between advocates of brand globalisation and those of a sound adaptation to local markets was set in an academic fashion in the 1980s through the articles of Levitt (1983), and Quelch and Hoff (1986). One had to choose sides almost ideologically. Twenty years later, we are able to learn from past experience which was more or less successful. If on a global scale we cannot deny the existence of certain factors that bring together countries and cultures, we must not forget that the speed of this coming together is sometimes slower than reckoned. Moreover, if at a certain level of generality or social and cultural trends consumers in many countries declare the same motivations and expectations, a closer look reveals slight differences that must be taken into account. This chapter urges us to a pragmatic approach. The empires built by Marlboro or Coca-Cola will not be replicated, as they benefited from particular historical and time factors. The international expansion of Coca-Cola was fostered in great part by two world wars and the presence of GIs in Europe and Asia. It took Marlboro 35 years to conquer the world and McDonald's 22 years! A contemplation of these models, however agreeable it may be, is quite useless for Danone, for example, whose brand image varies from one country to the next because the products through which it penetrated these countries cannot be the same: creamy desserts in Germany, plain yoghurts in France, fruit yoghurts in Great Britain. How do you then create a uniform image around the concept of health if in concrete terms the brand does not have the same products in each market or country? This is the reality for most brands today. They are not much helped by the models of brands that have created a new category (Coke, Amazon, IBM, Chanel). They need other models, more relevant to the situation most companies and brands are facing, when they operate in already existing categories.

The latest on globalisation

In 2003, the last session of the G8 summit coincided with an anniversary that went unnoticed. Twenty years earlier, in May–June 1983, an article entitled 'The globalization of markets', by Professor Theodore Levitt was published in the *Harvard Business Review*. The direct and simple nature of its argument was to make it one of the most quoted and influential articles in the field of business management. According to Professor Levitt, national differences and preferences would no longer carry any weight in the face of the progress and reduced costs associated with international products and brands. With everyone in the world travelling either physically or, in most cases, via satellite television, the desire to buy products and brands sold in other countries would also greatly increase.

In short, while recognising that the world was indeed round, companies had a vested interest in regarding it as flat, and treating it like a single market. This was the strategy adopted by Coca-Cola, McDonald's and Microsoft, and by the many companies that followed in their wake. The main obstacle to the globalisation of markets was decentralised organisation and its symbol – national marketing directors who, by their very nature, could not help but promote the opposite argument, the one that justified their position.

Twenty years later, how far has this prediction of globalised markets been fulfilled? Anyone who travels knows that the same brands are found in countries throughout the world, whether it is Philips, Michelin, Sony, Hugo Boss, Nike, HSBC or Axa. However, beneath the surface, what do companies really think of globalised brands? Is it still what they want? Is it still their ideal?

It should first of all be pointed out that Professor Levitt's prediction was based essentially on factors associated with production and on the unmistakable competitive advantages of economies of scale. In fact, most globalisation has taken place at production level, which is why it has been the target of some of the criticisms levelled by the anti-globalisation lobby. In her very interesting book *No Logo* (1999), Naomi Klein berates the companies that do not have factories and, as a result, wash their hands of anything that goes on in the archaic factories of their Asian subcontractors. Nike is a good example of this. By contrast, when Jean Mantelet, the creator of Moulinex, tried to keep employment in Upper Normandy at all costs, it ultimately cost him his company (but not the brand). The movement towards globalisation of the upstream (production) stage is therefore unavoidable. Successful companies have globalised their factories and supply chains to bring them closer to their markets and/or take advantage of lower costs. The car industry is a typical example.

It should, however, be recognised that this is a movement that has affected products more than services. While the circulation of the flow of money and information no longer encounters any barriers and is instantaneous, the movement towards the relocation of, for example, the processing of financial information, data files and bank databases is only just beginning. UK banks and insurance companies have taken the initiative by finding in Bangalore, the Indian equivalent of Silicon Valley, a well-qualified but much less expensive work force. Call centres serving

French customers are often based on the island of Mauritius.

There is one point on which the forecast of globalised markets can be challenged – the downstream stage of brands and products that are a long way from the predicted standardisation. Of course, you find Porsche and Jaguar worldwide, but these are exported brands, like Chanel. They are the standard bearers of a particular country or culture, and appeal to an international clientele. The car industry provides a good illustration of why the concept of the global product is in fact a myth. Paradoxically, the most global product that ever existed in the car sector was Ford's famous Model T – it was totally standardised, with 20 million cars manufactured and sold worldwide. Even though the domestic market was by far its principal market, the Model T was a truly universal product. In 1981, the launch of the famous Ford Escort in the United States and Europe appeared to be a sign of globalisation. In fact the US and European models only had one part in common – the radiator cap. Hardly a global product! More recently, the Ford Focus was launched in Europe (1990) and the United States (2000), and this time the models from these two world regions had 65 per cent of parts in common. But Ford does not think it can go much further – there are too many structural and long-term factors against it. So what are they exactly?

- The first is that energy is very cheap in the United States, which it will never be again in Europe. Low-energy innovations that have an enhanced value in Europe are regarded as irrelevant in the United States. This is why the engine type cannot be the same in both regions.

- The second is that vehicle standards and testing remain primarily national and in any event regional. Manufacturers therefore have to adapt their vehicles to suit the specifications and requirements of local test centres. Safety standards in the United States are less stringent than in Europe and Asia.

- The third factor concerns structural differences such as the type of roads, climate, humidity and the resulting use of vehicles. This therefore involves very different drivers of preference on either side of the Atlantic.

- The last factor is the customers themselves. Everyone knows that the Germans like a certain type of comfort, the British and French another. Today, manufacturers are flocking to China which alone will shortly represent 25 per cent of the growth of the world car market. They are opening factories and establishing joint ventures like PSA Peugeot Citroën, but not with the aim of slavishly duplicating European models. It is impossible to appeal to a market of 300 million Chinese who now have the financial resources to access the market without taking account of the customers themselves.

The time has in fact come to recognise the post-global brand – the brand that no longer tries to adhere unreservedly to the model of total globalisation, which is no longer perceived as ideal. Of course, globalisation at the upstream or production stage remains a priority in many sectors. Like the car sector, which has reduced costs by sharing production platforms, companies can still save more money by creating a smaller number of product platforms that are able, if the need arises, to produce differentiated models. The service sector could also benefit from upstream globalisation.

However, the further you go downstream and the closer you get to the customer, the more obvious it becomes that the global concept tends to be replaced by the regional or local concept in the case of a large country. There will therefore never be a car that is truly global, but a more American type for the

United States, and other types that are characteristically European and Chinese. This has already happened on other mass-consumption markets. For example, the strategy of the US company Procter & Gamble is based on regionalisation, with the US flagship brands Tide, Whisper and Clairol becoming Ariel, Allways and Wella in Europe. The company has a factory in Europe for all its detergents.

It is becoming more and more common for companies to develop products for specific geographical regions, in the way that Hennessy created Pure White for Europe. Dannon (USA) could not sell its drinkable, low-fat yoghurts in Europe since they neither correspond to local taste nor meet the current food standards requirements. It is however true that initiatives designed to open up regional markets, such as the EU, Mercosur and Alena, help to make the region, in the broader sense of the term, a relevant market segment. Furthermore, it is at regional level that the world's markets, and even its historical and cultural communities, are at their most permeable.

Finally, even when a brand appears to be global, when it is distributed and well known in countries throughout the world, closer examination reveals that the product is often far from standardised – it is more of a composite, hybrid or highly adapted product. For example, l'Oréal differentiates between the cosmetic products of its so-called global brands by basing them on the four types of climates in China, since they determine four skin types.

The idea of a global market and the standardisation that it implies, has usefully served to start a basic movement in all companies. But over-globalisation leads to loss of relevance, a lesson that companies have often learnt to their cost since 1983. This is why today's brands are post-global – they have assimilated the myth and distanced themselves from it without exactly renouncing it. Today, it is more appropriate to refer to selective globalisation.

Why are American brands ideologically more global, and the European ones less so? We hypothesise that the American globalised brands were exports of successful brands that had taken many years to find their optimal functioning and positioning in the United States. The idea that this equation of success would simply apply elsewhere seemed to be taken for granted, for the United States themselves constitute a non-homogeneous market. As an example, it is noticeable that Wal-Mart's first store outside the United States, in Mexico, was created 30 years after the creation of Wal-Mart (Bell, Lal and Salmon, 2003). Its worldwide competitor Carrefour opened its first foreign hypermarket in 1969, only six years after it created its first store. Unsurprisingly Wal-Mart applied the rules that made its success in the United States, but in some countries, more remote from the United States than Mexico, such as Brazil, the golden rule of everyday low price does not seem to work. The average Brazilian consumer is instead eager to capitalise on special bargains. Carrefour, being unsure about its optimal formula, was more open to the specificities of the new countries.

The same holds true for Nestlé, number one food company in the world. How can Nestlé be sure that the situation is the same everywhere when it comes from a small country like Switzerland? In fact Nestlé internationalised to four countries its first-ever product, powdered milk, four months after it was launched in Switzerland.

We tend to favour extreme solutions (to be or not to be global?), for they are rhetorically more provocative. Real life is in the middle, but it is more complicated. People have to collaborate in the organisation. Then the question becomes how to build a collaborative organisation (Hansen and Nohria, 2003).

What is new then? Realism in globalisation, the mark of the post-global brand.

Patterns of brand globalisation

Before we move forward, it is important to specify the meaning of global. For most managers a brand is global when it is sold everywhere in the world. Finding ads in all airports about Nokia, Dell, IBM or Alcatel seems to be a living sign of real globalisation. However, this may be a superficial vision.

We know from Chapter 1 that a brand is a system relating three facets, a concept, a name, and a product or service. It can be pictured as a triangle. As a consequence, when one speaks of globalisation, one should specify of what?

We saw that there are strong compelling economic reasons to globalise products or platforms. There are also good reasons to use the same name, for the sake of capitalising on one single name and exploiting the extra value of global perception. Finally, some concepts are reflections of the existence of global segments. Actually, the combination of these three poles creates eight possible alternative strategies as far as the continuum from globalisation to localisation is concerned (see Table 16.1).

When people refer to globalisation, it is generally in a loose sense, a feeling that the brand is known, visible and distributed everywhere. When we travel abroad some brands do seem global: we see them on billboards as soon as we land at an airport. It is this vision that creates negative attitudes about globali-

sation, the feeling of an inescapable loss of country differences. All commercial centres sell now the same stuff, the same brands, throughout the world. Human richness and diversity now seem dangerously eroded by the law of economies of scale. Of course, those who do not travel are pleased by the possibility of accessing the brands and products they see on television while watching the world.

What are these eight structural types obtained by combining the two possible answers on each part of the brand system?

▌ Type 1 is the fully global model. Here there are very few adaptations, except for details.

▌ Type 2 recognises the need for different positioning strategy: Mars is a meal substitute in UK (have a Mars a day), but an energiser in Europe. Cars follow the same approach. What is a small car for the German market is seen as a family car in Portugal.

▌ Type 3 acknowledges the need for important product adaptations. Different countries have different tastes for coffee. The skin and hair of Brazilians are not the same as those of Argentinians. In China, according to the l'Oréal Group, because of the differences in climate, sun, and humidity, there are four types of skin balance to be respected from north to south, east to west. Connex is a world

Table 16.1 From global to local: eight alternative patterns of globalisation

(Yes = global, No = localised)

Type	1	2	3	4	5	6	7	8
Name	Yes	Yes	Yes	Yes	No	No	No	No
Positioning	Yes	No	Yes	No	Yes	No	Yes	No
Product	Yes	Yes	No	No	Yes	Yes	No	No
Examples :	Coke	Mars	Nescafé	Persil	Ariel/	Volks-	Cycl-	Pure
	Chanel	Martell	Garnier		Tide	wagen	europe	local
	Amex		Connex			(Group)	(Group)	
	Sony							

ground transportation brand: it operates railways, buses and metro systems wherever municipalities want to create concessions for this public service. However, the same concept, 'security', means very different things in Stockholm, where Connex operates the metro, and in Rio de Janeiro. Thus, obedience to the same brand values cannot mean providing the same secure product everywhere. Local expectations are not as high in South America as they are in Scandinavia for instance, or the capacity to pay the price.

▍ Type 4 is the result of brands being split between companies. This is the case of Persil: this brand is operated by Unilever and by Henkel. The same holds true for Gervais, an ice cream brand at Nestlé, and a range brand of dairies at Danone.

▍ Type 5 results when the company cannot use the same name for legal reasons everywhere. For instance Vauxhall in the UK is Opel in Europe.

▍ Type 6 results when almost similar products are sold under two world brands with different price positionings. It is what is currently happening at the high end of the Volkswagen range, where the cars are very close even in design to the Audi entry models.

▍ Type 7 is the business model of Cycleurope, leader in the bicycle market. Cycleurope is a Swedish company, which has bought the market leading bike brands in other countries. These are typical local names, with high recognition and proximity. There are strong differences in the bike standards expected by the Dutch, Swedes, Germans, French and Italians: the size of the wheel, the gear, the height of the bike are different. Standardisation can only concern the frames.

▍ Type eight is the fully local model.

Looking more specifically at two of these variables, the brand name and the product platform (is it common or are there widely different products?), there are four strategies.

Danone for instance, like Unilever, is not obsessed with common names, but with the creation of products/concepts that reach an annual turnover worldwide of 1 billion euros. The CEO, Frank Riboud, states that 'our ambition is not to develop brands that are number one in the world, but brands that are number one locally with global world concepts/products'. For instance 'taillefine' (literally, slim waist), whose name changes according to the country (Light'fit in the United States, Silhouette in Canada, Corpus in Brazil, Ser in Argentina, Vitalinea in Spain, Vitasnella in Italy, Vitaline in Greece), is a concept of adult tasty food aimed at those maintaining a low-fat diet. It is stretched over the three divisions of Danone group, dairies, water and biscuits. As such one finds the products of this concept either as purified water, or as biscuits under Lu source brand, or as dairies under Danone source brand. But in Argentina the group has kept the endorsing local brand Serenissima, with its 65 per cent market share, to reinforce its competitiveness. This local brand, number one in Argentina, now endorses the global concepts.

Another global concept is Actimel, a specific yogurt designed to reinforce the body's natural defences. It is sold in 22 countries, with a sales turnover of half a billion euros, and a sales growth of 40 per cent in 2002. A final example of a world concept is the aromatised water sold as Danone Activ'Aro in the UK, Volvic Magic in France, and Bonafont Levite in Mexico. On the whole more than 60 per cent of the Danone group sales are made by concepts that are the market leader in most of the countries where they are sold.

Unilever has been criticised for having more than 1,400 brands, none of which reach the critical size (US $1 billion) to become a world mega-brand. It is now engaged in a fierce reduction of the number of brands. However, to take the ice-cream business, it is operated under the endorsement of the well-known names of the former local market leaders (Walls in the UK, Miko in France and so on), all presenting a common international logo. But their sales are made through power products that are sold globally and managed as real brands: Magnum, Solero and so on. In the margarine business, trust is very important. Local names have been maintained, but the whole company operates four typical product platforms for the whole European market.

The matrix in Table 16.2 reminds us that most companies started in quadrant A. They were international in sales before they thought they had an asset called a brand, and by default before they realised they had to globalise their business. Mostly operating in existing categories, and they do not consider Coke or McDonald's as a valid benchmark for them.

From A they can move either to B or C. B entails rationalising the products: it is the main source of profits and synergies. C means creating brand transfers to reduce the number of brands. The output is less strong and the risks higher. However, for all disruptive new products such as Actimel, the quadrant D strategy should be adopted.

Why globalise?

An economic necessity

Very few people dispute the need to internationalise business. World commerce has existed since caravans brought spices from all over Asia to Europe. The great naval explorers of the 15th and 16th centuries were also motivated by the prospect of opening new routes to merchandise. Colonisation had economic motives: access to raw materials, to gold, then wheat, then oil.

Production was the first business function to be delocalised. Finance is international. It is the time of marketing. Why then global brands? Why not simply international or multi-local brands?

In the competitive race, economies of scale provide a strategic lever in that they contribute to competitive pricing. A company designing a car with worldwide market potential in mind has a competitive advantage over the manufacturer who only sets his sights locally. Even though the latter may produce a car which better reflects the tastes of his own country, the difference in price from that of a Japanese or a Korean car designed from the start with a worldwide market in mind will naturally make even the most patriotic motorist hesitate. This is why Renault's Twingo, whose low price is a key element of positioning for the easy-to-live-with car, was designed from the start for a whole continent: the same product everywhere.

Table 16.2   Globalisation matrix

	Different brands	Same brand everywhere
Same products or concepts	Different brands, identical platforms (Unilever, Danone) **(B)**	Global brands, no adaption (Coca-Cola, Chanel, Sony) **(D)**
Different products or concepts	Sum of local tastes Franchises **(A)**	Nestlé (Nescafé) Yoplait President **(C)**

The local company – even if it is positioned in a niche – has no other way of overcoming the price handicap than to extend its outlets while innovating. Geographical extension is an essential condition in the race for survival.

If the brand is to remain competitive, its innovation must be offered immediately to all at the lowest possible price. The marginal cost of each progressive feature rises day by day. Hundreds of researchers are needed to even hope to innovate. Industrial investments and research costs must now be set against low unit margins. Using the awareness and public confidence which it has acquired, the brand provides the firm with access to outlets on an ever-widening scale. Without these, such investments could not be economically justified. The manufacturer's brand opens the way to progress and, at the same time, makes it available for all.

To summarise thus far, globalisation particularly affects products by allowing overall savings and leaps in the experience curve. But a global product does not necessarily signify a global name, in other words moving from a single product to a single brand needs further discussion on the subject of economy of signs and symbols.

The global name: a source of advantages

In certain market areas, the global brand is a necessity, whereas in many other cases it is a means of exploiting and taking advantage of new opportunities in communication.

The single brand is a necessity whenever the clients themselves are already operating worldwide. Firms using IBM or Dell in London would see no sense in having the same equipment in their Bogota or Kuala Lumpur offices under a different brand name. The same applies to most technological industries. Caterpillar, Sumitomo, Schlumberger, Siemens and Alcatel are of necessity world brands – quite apart from the fact that they are global enterprises.

It is also necessary to retain a single brand when the brand itself corresponds to the signature or *griffe* of its individual creator. Take the luxury trade – Pierre Cardin is Pierre Cardin wherever his products are found, just as Ralph Lauren is Ralph Lauren. Their creations are bought around the world because their signature bears witness to the values of their creator. Whether or not the creator lives on in body or in spirit does not change the rule: from a single source comes a single name.

These cases apart, the single brand permits the exploitation of new international opportunities:

▌ As tourism develops, for instance, it is a disadvantage that certain products have different names in different countries. If this were not the case, tourists could find their brands. Seeing the queues of comforted tourists from all countries in front of McDonald's instead of Quick is enough to convince anyone. This argument applies, however, more to some sectors than to others: to food more than lingerie and to car oil more than cooking oil. But the main advantage is linked to the synergy: the exposure of an American executive to DHL in Europe will benefit the renown and the reputation of DHL in the United States. Brands acquire additional credibility when they prove to have international appeal. This is why in 1989 Ariel brought out the first advertising commercial featuring testimony from housewives from different European countries.

▌ The more international media develop, the greater the opportunities they provide for the single brand. This has long been the case with traditional media; it now concerns satellite, cable and the Internet. Real opportunities for worldwide coverage are provided by such events as Grand Slam tennis tournaments, the Tour de France, the World Soccer Cup, the Olympic Games, Formula 1 motor racing, etc. Through its sponsorship of the Roland Garros tournament, the BNP Bank is known as far afield as California where they speak of the tournament as the 'BNP Tournament', just as there is a 'Volvo Grand Prix'. These programmes reach an international audience and therefore in practical terms exclude on-the-spot local brands, since the costs involved in appealing to only part of the audience would be prohibitive. Only global brands can be present in worldwide events such as the Olympic games or Formula 1 motor racing. Only the global brand can justify the cost of sponsoring such worldwide stars as Tiger Woods, or Michael Schumacher.

From single name to global brand

How far do we push the global idea? To what extent do we continue to make marketing decisions on a national level? Should we globalise positioning, creative concepts and even the ads themselves? The fact is that, though no one denies that a single name is often an advantage, there is some dispute over the brand strategy to be adopted, together with the form it should take. For some, the essence of marketing is to stick close to customers, while for others, the advantages offered by homogeneous marketing on a global scale offer no alternative.

Before dealing with the respective arguments, it is important to be precise about the terms used. Global marketing implies the wish to extend a single marketing mix to a particular region (eg Europe or Asia), or even to the world. It also denotes a situation in which a firm's competitive position in one country can be significantly affected by its position in other countries. The global approach sees the role of individual countries as only part of a wider competitive action.

The global approach considers countries and their roles in a widened competitive field. The aims of marketing in each country are no longer determined by the local subsidiary, but

are decided upon according to the global competitive system. Thus, whereas traditionally each subsidiary planned their activities based on their own resources and the domestic market, within a global strategy the following is the case:

- Certain countries have the task of developing a marketing mix for a new product, testing its capabilities in their home markets before its extension to other countries. This therefore constitutes a test, not of the best marketing mix on single national lines but of a global marketing mix prior to extension. As a consequence, nowadays it is insufficient to keep an eye on the competition in one country alone – every country should be included.

- Certain countries are assigned to develop know-how on a particular brand or a type of product brand so that they can act as a precursor and coordinator for others.

In contrast to the global approach, many multinational firms follow a 'multi-local' philosophy, preferring to follow specific trends in each country's market. Not only will the same brand differ from one market to the next both in positioning and in price level, but it is also supported by its own specific advertising campaign. Coca-Cola follows a global marketing policy, while Nestlé prefers multi-local marketing. Thus Maggi ready-snacks were launched:

- in Germany under the name 'Maggi, 5 Minuten Terrine' and positioned as a practical nutritious food for men and women and between 30 and 40;

- in France under its own name 'Bolino' (with Maggi in small print) and positioned as an instant snack for the young single person;

- in Switzerland under another name, 'Quick Lunch', and positioned as a quick meal approved by mothers.

In these three countries, the product achieved its sales objectives. Manichean comparisons should, therefore, not be made between global and multi-local policies in terms of either customer appreciation or sales. However, a company's ultimate aim is not simply to achieve maximum sales – marketing globalisation leads to profitability.

▮ In the first place, it cuts out duplicated tasks. For example, instead of bringing out different TV advertising for each country, the firm can use a single ad for the region in mind. Bearing in mind the high cost of producing these ads (up to US $1 million), the potential for savings is considerable. The McCann-Erickson agency was proud of the fact that they have saved Coca-Cola $90 million in production costs over 20 years, thanks to producing ads with world appeal. Even if production costs are, from now on, low compared to the investment in the media themselves, rendering the economy argument less forceful, it is still worthwhile for middle brands used to developing one campaign per country!

▮ By launching a product in several countries simultaneously, it eliminates the problems which arise when a new product appears at staggered intervals from one country to the next, depending on the local situation. This has the drawback of allowing competitors time to pre-empt certain ideas in one country which they have seen in another.

▮ Globalisation allows a firm to exploit good ideas wherever they come from. Since good ideas are rare, they must be made maximum use of. By getting representatives in several countries to put their minds to a particular question, there is a better chance of coming up with a strong idea that can be used on a global plane. This is how the global idea 'Put a tiger in your tank' came to be used around the world. The Timotei shampoo was developed in Finland and spread to other European countries to benefit from the emergence of a trend towards natural goods. The worldwide drink Malibu was created in South Africa.

▮ A global policy allows a firm to slip the stranglehold of the major retailer, whose commercial demands are closer to a systematic toll than to a payment for real services to the producer. A national brand may have few means of extricating itself; such is the intensity of distribution concentration that it is forced to use a small number of major retailers in order to reach the consumer. The global brand is fortunately less susceptible to local pressures.

▮ When a brand goes international, it can however benefit from the internationalisation of its main domestic retailers. Thus Wal-Mart acts as bridgehead to many North American brands, and Carrefour to many European brands.

The emergence of global segments

All sociocultural studies underscore the convergence of life styles. There are fewer differences between top executives in Japan and in Germany than between executives and employees within Germany. In addition identification models act on a worldwide basis: some Chinese women identify with American woman, others with the French, and a growing number now identify with Korea's style of beauty. The same may be true in Holland or in New York. This is why l'Oréal has developed a wide array of global brands: far from pushing towards uniformity, this group diffuses heterogeneity. This is why it takes much care in offering brands that symbolise not one single type of beauty but all of them, from Softsheen Carson for the black community worldwide, to Sue Uemura or Maybelline. The group takes much care in leaving each of its brand's headquarters in its home country to preserve its specificity.

However, they must globalise their concept and products and communications. Global segments should have each a global brand corresponding to their needs.

Pricing issues

Finally, the price factor will be a key component of the homogenisation of brand strategies in the future. Indeed everything points to reducing the price span within which the same brand can evolve from one country to another, from one area to another.

▮ The existence of a concentration of distributors on a regional or international level creates a major destabilising threat to brands that optimise locally their price policy. There is nothing to prevent the distributors from demanding the lowest price to be seen in Europe, which may be in Portugal for instance, or in a country that has lowered its prices as a means of competition.

▮ The emergence of parallel markets needs to be avoided as these would destabilise the normal distribution channels of a country and therefore the relationship between a brand and its distributors.

There is indeed a close relationship between price positioning and market positioning. A brand cannot be the most expensive on the market in one place and in the mainstream in another. The price level situates the brand in terms of perceived quality, performance and prestige. In the market for special vintages of champagne, for example, to be the most expensive, on a par with or cheaper than Dom Perignon, does not position its challenger Veuve Clicquot in the same way. Reducing the international price variance of a brand is a factor which encourages uniform positioning and, by extension, affects the whole brand policy. Unless a policy is explicitly chosen that allows optimum prices locally and strong

price differences from one country to another, identical products need to be sold under different brand names in each country. This is the strategy followed by Benckiser, which buys strong local brands. R&D are indeed by necessity European, using the principle of a 'lead country' for the development of new products and the definition of the marketing mix.

Fighting the grey market

A classical consequence of economic heterogeneity is the grey market. To reach public accessibility, brands must align their prices on the local economic level. However, when a gap exists among countries not too far apart in distance, a grey market grows, disturbing the sales and trade goodwill in the country invaded by parallel imports. Of course, in the case of luxury goods with selective distribution agreements, the first reaction is to install some form of trace, in order to identify those commercial agents that break these agreements, reselling outside their zone.

A second approach is to change the brand. Thus in Northern Europe Viakal, an anti-limescaling household product, became Antikal to stop the grey market of Italian Viakal products, which were sold there at a price 30 per cent lower. Without going to such extremes, Hennessy cognac decided to stop selling its VSOP product in Western Europe, and instead created a customised product called Fine de Cognac. Europe was in any case drinking less and less VSOP, but it had become a source of a grey market for Russia. In fact, throughout the world, global brands are developing more and more regional products for these commercial reasons.

A final approach of course is to create a price corridor across all countries of a region or continent. This cuts the risk of a grey market growing, but handicaps the sales where the brand is overpriced for the sake of respecting the international corridor. As an example, the net trade price of Absolut vodka in Europe is around 5.5 euros on average as evidenced in Table 16.3.

The benefits of a global image

A great deal has been written on the subject of global brands, but what exactly do we know about them? In fact very little, until recently when the subject was further clarified by the three studies outlined below. Two of these studies focus on the benefits of having – that is, being perceived as having – a global image. But how does perceived brand globalness (PBG) create value? There are a number of reasons for creating a global brand – economies of scale, synergies between countries, the speed with which innovations created worldwide can be brought onto the market, the existence of exploitable global segments and finally, as has already been suggested, the benefits of having an international image. Today, in the age of cultural integration, modernity is expressed via internationalism. The perception of globalness would therefore increase perceived value. It is symptomatic that, in countries throughout the world, young people's favourite brands are usually international, whereas the reverse is true for adults.

One of the studies (Alden, Steenkamp and Batra, 1999) set out to validate this hypothesis. In a quantitative study carried out in the United States and South Korea, the authors demonstrated that perceived globalness (the fact of being perceived to be selling products worldwide) exerted a strong influence over purchase decisions. But contrary to expectation, this influence was not because perceived globalness enabled consumers to participate in a global culture. In fact, perceived globalness primarily influenced the perceived quality, and second the perceived prestige, of the brand. These effects were however not quite as strong for ethnocentric consumers, that is, those who were more focused on national values. These results needed to be extended to other countries and include other criteria for consumer segmentation, since the cultural connections between South Korea and the United States are well known.

This was done by Holt, Quelch and Taylor (2003) when they studied how global perceptions drive value, using a sample of 1,800 respondents in 12 countries. According to the study, perceived globalness influences brand preferences via five levers:

▓ As an indicator of quality (higher quality due to perceived globalness). This effect is in fact the most important, and explained 34 per cent of the variance in preferences observed by the study.

▓ The second effect is the increased status conferred on the brand by its perceived globalness. This explained 12 per cent of the variance and coincides with the results of the previous study.

▓ The third lever is linked to the images and special characteristics attributed to individual countries. Global brands are often associated with a country of origin and therefore a stereotype of competence, such as clocks and watches (Switzerland), TGV high speed trains (France). This accounted for 10 per cent of the variance.

▓ Increased responsibility, fostered by perceived brand globalness. Because they are represented worldwide, global brands

Table 16.3 How Absolut copes with the grey market: corridor pricing

Country	Germany	France	Spain	Italy	UK	Greece	Portugal
Net price	5.21	5.81	5.16	5.35	5.97	5.66	5.77

Prices are estimates of net/net trade retail prices in Europe in euros have a higher profile and therefore have to be more environmentally and socially aware than other brands. Being big is equated with being more responsible. This effect only explained 8 per cent of the variance. However, it was extremely important for 22 per cent of respondents, and important for 41 per cent of this group.

▍ Finally, the American image, or the American dream, is associated with a number of global brands. This effect did not explain the variance in preferences between brands when consumers were taken as a whole. However, as soon as these international consumers were segmented, the American image was a dream for 39 per cent, which made it a factor of preference, while it was anathema for 29 per cent and therefore a negative factor and rejection.

To their credit, Holt, Quelch and Taylor segmented the consumers. In the seven segments that resulted – from 'pro-west' to 'anti-globalisation' – the hierarchy of the five levers was completely different. How people understand and value global brands is very segmented. Countries are also heterogeneous. China, for instance, is both pro and anti American values: it has consumers belonging to both groups. Muslim countries such as Indonesia, Turkey and Egypt are very influenced by the perception of globalness. However, one should recall that the interviewees were not lay people, but well off ones, probably with a westernised life style. People in India, Brazil and South Africa were not very much influenced by perceptions of globalness; is it because they have a strong local culture they are proud of? Finally, those least influenced by the perception of brand globalness are US consumers.

This should not be a surprise: the Americans do not consider that the choice of other countries is relevant. It is an ethnocentric country. Also, since many of the so-called global brands are American in origin,

their status is ambiguous. They are selling everywhere in the world but they seem to be deep local brands.

Schuiling and Kapferer (2004) have compared the distinctive properties of local and international food brands, separating, however, international brands in their home country from the same brands in other countries. In fact, their data show that the best brand profile is that of the international brands in their home country. No wonder: countries export their best in class brands. The data also show how global brands really differ from local ones. Working on a database of 507 brands in four countries, and 9,739 respondents, Schuiling and Kapferer have isolated the discriminant properties of each type of brand: local (that is, sold in one country, whatever its perception by the public) and international (sold in all countries, whatever the perception of the public). The authors first notice that on the whole local brands that have been present for a much longer time in the country are endowed with a higher brand awareness score than more recent international arrivals. Since brand awareness is correlated with image (see page 21), are the so-called differences of image only an outcome of this brand awareness gap? When the data are adjusted for awareness, there do remain differences in image, some negative, some positive, as evidenced by Table 16.4.

It is noticeable that, compared with local brands, global brands have a significant deficit on:

▍ health value (–3.29 per cent);

▍ reliability (–3.05 per cent);

▍ trust (–1.88 per cent);

▍ serviceability (–1.03 per cent).

On the other hand, they outperform local brands on the following levers:

Table 16.4   How global and local brands differ (in percentages, after adjusting for brand awareness level)

	Local brand	Global brand (B. Aw = 85%)	Global–local (B. Aw = 85%)
High quality	25.29	27.07	+1.78
Trust	22.11	20.23	−1.88
Reliable	22.11	19.06	−3.05
Fashionable	14.04	15.50	+1.46
Original	13.57	14.64	+1.07
Distinct	12.56	13.70	+1.14
Sympathetic	11.74	13.19	+1.45
Funny	9.76	12.90	+3.14
Pleasing	7.08	12.90	+5.82
Healthy	15.56	12.27	−3.29
Innovating	6.08	11.50	+5.42
A leader	8.07	9.33	+1.26
Unique	4.40	7.61	+3.21

(Base 9,739 respondents , 507 brands)

Source: Kapferer and Schuiling (2004)

- sympathetic (+ 5.82 per cent);
- innovativeness (+5.42 per cent);
- uniqueness (+3.21 per cent);
- fun, thrill (+3.14 per cent);
- high quality (+ 1.78 per cent);
- fashionable (+ 1.46 per cent);
- sympathetic (+ 1.45 per cent).

Conditions favouring global brands

Certain situations make global communication and brand policy easier. They are linked to the product, to the markets, to the force of brand identity and also to the organisation of companies.

Social and cultural changes provide a favourable platform for global brands. Under these circumstances, part of the market no longer identifies with long-established local values and seeks new models on which to build its identity. Turning its back on prevailing national values, it is open to outside influence from abroad. In drinking Coca-Cola, we are drinking the American myth – in other words the fresh, open, bubbling, young and dynamic all-American images. Youngsters form a target in search of identity and in need of their own reference points. In an effort to stand out from the rest, they draw their sources of identity from media-personified cultural models. Levi's are linked with a mythical image of breaking away down the long, lonely road – the rebel. Nike encourages them to strive to surpass themselves, turning its back on the national confines of race and culture. Women also constitute a clientele looking for new models; Estée Lauder could portray the free, independent and seductive woman, and use this image for its own globalisation. Brands corresponding to new eating habits also have to impose forcefully their view of the world in order to rally consumers in search of change. In this way, the brand is seen as a new flag-waver.

New, unexplored sectors have not, by definition, inherited a system of values.

Everything is there for the making, and it's up to the brand to do it. This is why there is nothing to prevent the global marketing of high-tech, computer, Internet, photographic, electronic and telecommunications or service brands. Dell can, and must, spread its brand everywhere, because brands themselves are the only point of reference in these markets. Only the themes of the campaigns will change to take into account the country's level of economic development, hence its preoccupation. Globalisation also applies to new services: Hertz, Avis and Europcar globalised their campaigns by portraying the stereotype of the hurried businessman – and in any event an Italian businessman wants to identify more with being a businessman than with being an Italian. The argument of novelty works also for McDonald's, Malibu or Corona!

The world has been standardised by the increasing and levelling power of technology – this is Levitt's point (1983). Its products no longer stem from local culture but belong to our times. They are the fruit of science and time. They therefore escape the local cultural contingencies that hinder global communication.

In general terms, globalisation is possible – and indeed desirable – in markets which revolve around mobility. This applies to multi-media, the hotel industry, car rental, airlines, and also the transfer of pictures and sounds. When the brand is perceived as being international, its authority and expertise are automatically accepted. Again, brands have a clear opportunity to organise and structure those market sectors which symbolise the disappearance of time and space constraints. It is their role to deploy their system of values, which can only be unique faced with mobile clients.

Globalisation is possible when the brand is totally built into a cultural stereotype. AEG, Bosch, Siemens, Mercedes and BMW rest secure in the 'Made in Germany' model, which opens up the global market, since the stereotype invoked is a collective symbol breaking national bounds. It conjures up a meaning of robust performance in any country. The Barilla name is another stereotype built on the classic Italian image of tomato sauce, pasta, a carefree way of life, songs and sun. Volvo, Ericson, ABB and Saab epitomise Sweden.

Finally, certain brands represent archetypes or 'universal truths', to paraphrase Zaltman (Wathieu, Zaltman and Liu, 2003). Snuggles fabric softener not only arouses the same notion in every country – that of gentleness (which is not in itself original) – but also the image of reliance, love and security as in one's childhood, as symbolised by the teddy bear. This is why, in order to express the notion of 'snuggling, caressing, cajoling', the brand name is translated as Cajoline in France, Kuchelweib in Germany, Yumos in Turkey, Mimosin in Spain and Cocolino in Italy. La Vache-Qui-Rit, which corresponds to the archetype of the generous mother, is likewise translated (Die Lächende Kuhe or The Laughing Cow). Marlboro embodies the archetype of the macho man – alone and untouched, authentic, yet modernised and popularised throughout the world in Western sagas of the conquest of America. Maybelline expresses American beauty. Lancôme expresses the French woman.

Several of the above factors explain why luxury brands and *griffes* have gained a worldwide appeal. In the first place, they bear a message – each creator is expressing his or her own personal values. They were not conceived as a result of any market study or consumer analysis from one country to the next. It is the creator's identity and his or her desire to express his or her own values that form the automatic basis of the brand's identity, in no matter what part of the world. Second, behind every luxury brand there is a guiding standard – sometimes even an archetype. Cacharel and Nina Ricci represent the dawning of femininity, a dawn tinted with shyness and modesty. Yves Saint Laurent stands for female independence, even rebellion. Finally, the 'Made in France' label and the myth of Paris imbue these brands with definitive cultural undertones. All these are reasons why such brands are able to impose their own vision of the world on national outlooks. Like any religion, brands that set out to convert must believe in their message and spread it unerringly among the multitudes.

On the whole, brands whose identity focuses on the product and its roots can more easily go global. Jack Daniel's whiskey builds the pivot of its brand identity from its distillery and its tradition, which leads to advertising which has been remarkably stable throughout time and similar in all countries. Even though it is working with different agencies, the articles and conditions are such that each one produces commercials or announcements that are typically Jack Daniel's.

Certain organisational factors also ease the shift to a global brand. One-man companies and brands that bear the name of their creator who is still alive are from the start more global. Countries have less ability to modulate locally the identity of Ralph Lauren since the head of the company is precisely Ralph Lauren. It is also true for Bic or Paloma Picasso.

American companies are more ready to globalise because marketing on their domestic market is in essence global, considering the social and cultural diversity of the American melting-pot. Organisational factors also point in the same direction. When expanding towards Europe, these companies created European headquarters from the beginning, based most often in Brussels or London. Individual countries therefore had to account for their results to these European centres. As seen from the US, there was very early on the need for a centre for 'European operations', for considering Europe as a single and homogeneous area.

Finally, a single centre for production in Europe or South America is also a strong factor for globalisation, at least for products. The fact that one factory centralises the production of detergents for Procter & Gamble in the whole of Europe leads to a standard product offer throughout and to the spread of technical innovations to all countries at the same time. In markets where the product advantage is key in the positioning of the brand, this centralisation of production and of R&D leaves little room for differentiation on a local basis.

Disruption versus optimising products

Apart from factors linked to the market or to the organisations themselves, the same company may have to follow two different policies according to the status of its products. One analysis that explains the differences in observed behaviour is linked to the type of marketing. Certain products are the optimisation of an existing offer. Others are complete breaks from what is on offer, innovations even to the extent of creating a new segment that did not exist before. This distinction has an impact on the chosen international policy. Optimisation marketing leads to more flexibility when there is a need to adapt to local conditions. Strong innovation, however, that which conveys new vision, tends to impose itself on all countries and hardly needs any adapting.

Generally speaking, a strong new concept is capable of breaking the rules and borders. For example, alcoholic beverages are generally promoted using local strategies. What is more cultural than alcohol? Moreover, it is drunk by adults and as we get older our tastes and preferences solidify (unlike with soft-drinks for teenagers). However, very new concepts in this field are able to have a worldwide impact: Corona, Absolut, Bailey's, Malibu. It is the same for cheese: La Vache-Qui-rit is a global concept.

The excess of globalisation

Arguments against globalisation are, in fact, arguments against a strict and rigid monolithic international marketing policy. In fact, there are plenty of examples of failure resulting from undue haste in adopting a global marketing policy without certain precautions. These examples have been analysed by corporations. They have learnt their lessons.

Globalisation has become associated with deafness or blindness. Naomi Klein (1999) has called the attention of global brands to the fact that some of them have become businesses without any production facilities. They outsource all their production. However, the absence of plants does not mean the brand can feel unconcerned by what takes place in the plants of its suppliers: working children, sweatshops and poor conditions of work all impact on the brand image. Today, big means responsible: ethics will be part of the evaluation by the financial markets (see Chapter 17). In the present chapter we address another issue, strictly managerial: the lack of adaptation to salient differences between markets.

Arguments against globalisation are in fact arguments against a strict and rigid monolithic international marketing policy. There are plenty of examples of failure resulting from undue haste in adopting a global marketing policy without certain precautions. Thus, in January 1984 Procter & Gamble launched in France the anti-dandruff shampoo Head and Shoulders relying on exactly the same marketing mix and positioning which had led to its success in the UK and the Netherlands. At the end of 1989, Head and Shoulders still had only 1 per cent of the French market. The problem was that they had not taken sufficient account of a feature particular to the French market and present nowhere else. Consumers either buy anti-dandruff shampoos in pharmacies, the pharmacy being a guarantee for efficiency and treatment, or they pick up the line extension of their usual brand in their hypermarket (Palmolive dandruff shampoo, etc) for everyday use. In between these two brand groups, there is scarcely room for a brand positioned on efficiency, sold in hypermarkets and much more expensive than usual brands. The adopted communication mix in no way bettered the situation of this shampoo:

▌ Procter & Gamble had decided not to translate the name, relying on the evidence that it had been well accepted in Holland as it stood. However, outside the UK, Holland is the EU country that speaks the best English, so there is a considerable inherent risk in extending a policy tested in Holland to a country such as France.

▌ For its launch, Procter & Gamble used their British film showing a face divided in two so that the results could be seen. The punchline was 'Dandruff talks behind your back'. In France, however, dandruff is seen as a social problem – one should not point the finger in blame, but should sympathise with the problem. The tone adopted in the British approach was perhaps in keeping with Dutch levels of sensitivity, but scarcely applicable to the French.

Head and Shoulders illustrates the harsh realities of different levels of sensitivity and competitive forces in the market place, both of which make a monolithic global policy a perilous strategy.

Such reverses do not, as such, amount to a rebuttal of global policy, since we have such universal successes as Dell, Sony, McDonald's and Volkswagen. The idea of global marketing has an inescapable draw, even though its implementation has been seen to vary considerably in speed according to the markets, the public and the companies themselves, and in spite of the fact that certain idiosyncratic brands are destined to remain on a local footing.

Barriers to globalisation

What are the strongest barriers to globalisation? What are the parameters that, according to managers themselves, make difficult, even impossible, brand globalisation? Table 16.5 is particularly revealing in this regard.

The first and only factor that justifies for most people interviewed (55.2 per cent) the non-application of a global strategy is legal differences. It is true, for example, that laws which deal with the definition of products, the right to sell, the authorisation and manner of advertising of alcohol and the use of children in advertising vary considerably. However, because of the Single European Act, Mercosur in South America or the GATT, these differences in legislation will have to be evened out, thus suppressing the major obstacle to globalisation. The second factor is linked to the local competitive situation (number and strength of competitors, levels of brand awareness, type and level of distribution, stage in the product life cycle). Taking the example of Orangina once more, it is not possible to approach the market where Orangina is a close second to Coca-Cola in the

same way as the English market, where it occupies a niche in the premium segment of carbonated orange soft drinks and competes with Fanta, Sunkist and Tango, the local dominant brand. This has a deep impact on market strategy and positioning, but the Orangina identity is nevertheless the same. Moreover, since they are known in advance, these very different market situations can be integrated when filming commercials. Some commercials destined for countries where Orangina is not known will need longer sequences on the product and on shaking the pulp. At the other end of the scale these sequences can be reduced in other countries. The significance of this factor concerning the local competitive situation explains in some measure global success of brands such as Mars, Gillette, McDonald's, Coke, Bailey's, Dell, eBay, Ryanair, Somfy and so on. They didn't really have any competitors in the market, and they were new products, creating new segments or revealing the start of a latent transnational demand. They were driven by

Table 16.5 What differences between countries would compel you to adapt the marketing mix of the brand?

Type of difference	Necessary adaptation (%)
Legal differences	55
Competition	47
Consumption habits	41
Distribution structure	39
Brand awareness	38
Brand distribution level	37
Media audience	37
Marketing programme success	34
Consumers' needs	33
Media availability	32
Brand images	30.5
Norms for products manufacturing	27.5
Brand history	25.2
Lifestyle differences	25
Cultural differences	25
Subsidiary sales	23
Consumers' buying power	22
Consumers' age differences	12

Source: Kapferer/Eurocom pan-European survey

the feeling that they had an excellent product and extended their programme to all countries. The third factor hindering globalisation is the differences in consumer habits: these are, as we have seen, fatal for products such as Ricard that are deeply rooted in a particular culture. Moreover, to become truly global, a brand must play down its ethnic component. As long as Bailey's was an 'Irish Cream' its potential was limited. An 'exotic' beverage coming from afar, its 'strangeness' relegated it to small sales volumes, to fans of Ireland who would sip it in the evening by the fireplace. But how many people know Ireland throughout the world? Who will still drink alcohol as a liqueur? The globalisation of Bailey's consisted of breaking away from the association with the liqueur set ('The Bailey's moment is whenever') and the promotion of Ireland as a tourist destination, and promoting instead 'Baileys on ice' (see page 168).

Table 16.6 presents the facets that are most easily globalised for pan-European brands.

As we can see, the percentage varies from 10 per cent to 93 per cent. Such a variance is linked to the fact that the phrase 'brand globalisation' refers both to identity and to action

Table 16.6 Which facets of the brand mix are most often globalised?

	%
Logotype, trade mark	93
Brand name	81
Product features	67
Packaging	53
After-sales service	48
Distribution channels	46
Sponsoring (arts)	32
Sponsoring (sports)	29
Advertising positioning	29
Advertising execution	25
Relative pricing	24
Direct marketing	18
Sales promotion	10

(the marketing mix). It is the fixed image of the brand (its fixed logo) that is the most globalised, a sign that image precedes sound. What counts is that the exclusive typography and the red colour of Coca-Cola can be found throughout the world, even if it isn't written 'Coca-Cola'. Unilever does not use its Motta brand of ice cream everywhere, but its local equivalents use the same colour and signal codes. The brand name comes in second. It is true that most companies have inherited some odd situations where what is called Dash in Italy is called Ariel in Europe and so on. When brands are local strengths it is not a good idea to risk standardising too fast. The operational facets of the marketing mix are naturally adapted to local markets, all the more so as we approach below-the-line activities or local financial optimisation regarding the price. In the era of television and multimedia, image wins over word. All the more so in Third World countries where illiteracy is common. Colour codes and graphics must be global: Coke is red, Heineken is green. However, even the strongest brands hesitate when the question arises of what to call them in the enormous Chinese market (see below).

Let us analyse in depth how these barriers impact the internationalisation of brands.

Coping with local diversity

How do global brands integrate the true diversity of the world, economic, legislative and cultural? How do they build a global brand in such heterogeneous conditions? Can the brand be in fact truly global?

Coping with economic heterogeneity

How should the global brand cope with the reality of widely differing levels of development of markets? This certainly concerns emerging countries, but also the very advanced countries when a new category is concerned.

The first approach is, of course, by adapting the product lines to the markets. One does not sell the same cars in China and in Europe. Car manufacturers use more entry-level models in China. Interestingly, since they want to build a global brand, which means a global perception and not only a global name, care must be taken in launching these models under the same brand values as any upper model of the range sold elsewhere in the world. This causes difficulties in creating a homogeneous concept.

For instance Wyborowa, probably the most exquisite vodka (made in Poland, the homeland of vodka), has to expand in two widely different markets: the most advanced and largest market for international brands (the United States), where there already exists a premium and super premium segment, with very sophisticated brands as Skyy, Belvedere, Grey Goose and Ketel One, well above the prices set by Finlandia and Absolut, not to speak of Smirnoff; and Europe, which is just discovering the category, and in comparison many consumers hardly know what vodka is and why they should drink it. Clearly, to succeed in the United States the brand needs to launch a super premium version, used as the prototype of the brand, but this is not needed in Europe. How then can a brand present a united concept with two different prototypes?

A second approach is by segmenting the product line. For instance Arc International, the leading group in the world for glass tableware, has recently rationalised its brand portfolio, concentrating on four brands, along a double market segmentation by channel of distribution and by price level. Luminarc is to be the unique mass market brand. The whole range has been subdivided into three subsets, casual, modern and formal, and each of these families has a positive name. In developed countries, many people would not consider buying products from the 'casual' family, but these same products are used as gifts in many developing countries.

The third approach is by a phased introduction of innovations. Thus, Danone as a group is totally positioned on 'good health'. However, this concept is a broad one, and cannot mean the same thing in India and in Scandinavia. As a matter of fact, Danone distinguishes three stages of development corresponding to three levels of market maturity: quality /security, health and nutrition, and active health. Markets at each of these stages will see the launch of products that correspond to their meaning of this large concept, 'health'.

Interestingly, although it is very much centralised, Absolut adapts its advertising to the level of maturity in relation to its category of each country. Thus the consumer benefit used in advertising varies according to a fixed ladder of market development and sophistication, from purity (Absolut Perfection ads) to closeness, topicality, taste variety (such as Absolut Lemon) during the growth phase, and creativity/originality in the maturity phase.

A fourth approach is to stick firmly to the brand values through different levels of operationalisation. The best example is Connex. This world brand of public ground transportation was launched in 2000. Its market comes from the growth in the privatisation of former public transport services. Connex has been promoted on a number of added values – regularity, safety, comfort – but because of wide differences in the level of economic development and cost constraints, it is impossible to operationalise each value the same way all over the world. Expectations of service regularity are not the same in Lagos (Nigeria) and Perth (Australia), for instance. Connex could have decided to restrict use of its name to circumstances that met the highest service delivery standards, but this would have created a very elitist and restricted brand, and would have been contrary to its global strategy: Connex's future growth potential is mostly found in countries that want to accelerate the level of satisfaction attached to public services by outsourcing them.

As a consequence, it was decided to stick to the brand values but to define locally how they are operationalised. In addition, since a brand represents a permanent search for added values, in each city or region where Connex operates, these operational standards must be upgraded year after year, and the result made public.

Coping with differences in legislation and norms

Best practice seminars and books are replete with examples of globalised brands such as Coca-Cola, Mars and Microsoft. Certainly they are interesting examples. However, they also have their limits, imposed not least by differences in taste, in legislation, in norms. Thus none of the yoghurts sold by Dannon USA could be described as yoghurts in the EU, because they contain too high a proportion of starch and stabilising agents, and their taste too is unlikely to meet with public acceptance in Europe. Why? Because Dannon USA, since its creation in 1942, has tried to build its business in the United States.

In the United States there was no custom of eating yogurt when Dannon began, unlike in Holland, Germany and France. Moreover, the fact that it is eaten with a spoon gave a childish personality to the category. As a result, the whole market started as a niche market, mostly aimed at women, promoting the health benefits, a little like Slimfast. Also, unlike in Europe, Dannon yoghurts actually compete in the snack market, and US consumers typically drink a cola (diet or otherwise) while consuming the product. As a consequence, the yoghurts needed to be sweeter and thicker.

Coping with category differences

Although products may have the same name, they do not mean the same thing from a country to another. Thus, the same apparent product needs to be positioned in accordance with the significance of the category in the different countries.

The example of yoghurt is relevant. At first glance it would seem possible to sell plain Danone yoghurt to everyone in Europe in the same way, whether it be flavoured Danone Kid or Danone Bio. However, despite appearances, yoghurt is a typical case of non-transversality because of the different circumstances in each of the markets when yoghurt was first introduced. In France, the market is still influenced by the fact that yoghurt was first introduced as a health product and therefore was sold exclusively in pharmacies (in much the same way as mineral water). Though this is no longer the case and most younger consumers would not be aware of it, this has a deep and unconscious impact on attitudes in the market. Thus, in France the product reference is a plain yoghurt, a symbol of good health, while fruit and flavourings were only added a long time afterwards. In Anglo-Saxon countries, on the other hand, where there weren't any pharmacies in the French sense, yoghurt was first introduced as a low-fat product containing fruit for enjoyment, and in this sense it was a product for adults. The motivation to purchase in the yoghurt market therefore comes from very different impulses in different countries because of the way the market was first created in those countries. Moreover, as a result of these differing motivations, the same product will be regarded in a different light in the various countries involved.

For example, in the UK, the origins of the yoghurt market mean that the product is regarded as being one for pleasure, for the enjoyable experience of eating. Flavoured yoghurt, ie yoghurt without the fruit, is therefore a lesser product, and also means it cannot be positioned in the market for children. Moreover, plain yoghurt without either flavouring or fruit – and therefore without pleasure in the eating – is thus a boring product only for those on a diet. In Spain and Portugal, on the other hand, where fruit is abundant, the fruit yoghurt does not have the position of product reference in the market. Indeed, there, where the standard of living is lower than in other European countries, flavoured yoghurt constitutes the main segment, and is eaten as much by children as it by adults: it is a family product and does not need a first name (such as Kid). Again, in Italy, the reference is blended yoghurt with a different texture, and flavoured yoghurt is positioned for very young children. Yet again, in France, flavoured yoghurt is regarded simply as a plain yoghurt with added flavouring, so the logic of the health benefit prevails, as testified by the slogan 'Petit à petit on devient moins petit' (literally 'Little by little we become less little'). To emphasise this promise and to differentiate it from competitors, Danone chose to give the first name 'Kid' to this type of yoghurt, thus identifying it with a child reaching a later stage of development.

In a similar way the reaction to Bio is different depending on the country. In France Bio is perceived as the rebirth of plain yoghurt, conveying health and pleasure. In the UK Bio was the first to introduce the health aspect of the product to the market. In Italy, on the other hand, cultural morality frowns upon the taking of pleasure in the taste of food and it is not considered possible to taste good and and be healthy at the same time. This is reflected in the related commercials – the internal body clock of the UK commercial instead of the nude woman chosen in France.

Thus by considering one of the few food markets that does not have a long history but is actually an industrial product, we can clearly see that the conditions under which the market was created in each country have determined the long-term perception of that product in each specific market. Only Yop crosses these borders. Positioned for teenagers like a soft drink around the concept of freedom, Yop has a European commercial that works well in all countries, provided of course the market understands the concept of a drinkable yoghurt.

Coping with differences of segment

The same product may belong to different segments in different countries. It then faces different competition and aims at different targets. In the car industry, the small car segment represents 38 per cent of cars on average in Europe, with extremes reaching 59 per cent in Portugal and 18 per cent in Austria or Germany. In Italy, the small household car is nevertheless the main car, in which the whole family fits. This determines a stream of structural expectations (five doors for example) very different from France where the segment corresponds to the second or even the third car. Another problem arises when Germany is considered: in this country the segment simply does not exist. Here it is the Golf that is considered the small car, when it is in the middle range segment everywhere else in Europe. It was, therefore, difficult to speak of the Peugeot 106, for instance, in the same way in all countries. In France, in order to compete with the Renault Clio and not to poach sales from the Peugeot 206, the amount of interior space was emphasised, despite the small size of the car (hence the slogan 'la surprise de taille' – 'the size surprise'). In Germany, the 106 was positioned like the Austin Mini, as a second car, small, feminine and urban, and after that as the most environmentally friendly because it was the smallest. In the countries of Southern Europe the interior space was again emphasised to make it a good first family car. In the UK the 106 was positioned as a feminine car which was small but which allowed escape through its comfortable and dynamic aspects – two qualities that make Peugeot a valued brand in this country.

Coping with differences in meaning

The danger with international communication is that there may seem to be a common understanding of words, where in fact there is not. Simple words as ' nature' and 'well-being' do not mean the same thing across countries. If they did, it still remains to be proven that the best way to communicate the concept is similar across countries. Often it is not.

According to the country, the same idea must be expressed through different symbols. This established fact has the paradoxical consequence that it is not by using the same brand name from one country to another that one stays closest to the initial brand concept. The concept behind Jif is better expressed by Viss in Germany and Cif in France. One can change a local name to a global name when the former has little intrinsic meaning and the name precisely encompasses the concept of the product. Otherwise, a fundamental element of the identity is shattered. The diversity of names draws the product closer to its consumers in each market. This is why Playtex applies a modular policy: the Playtex name is worldwide. On the other hand, the company adapts the names of individual products to the markets. Indeed, Playtex only launches new product concepts if they are international. The marketing strategy is homogeneous within large geographic areas (Europe for example): thus the 'Cross Your Heart' range has the same positioning, the same consumer benefit, the same advertising theme and the same execution in all countries. Cross Your Heart adapts to local markets in terms of fabric (cotton in Italy for instance) or of packaging (to take into account differences in distribution circuits). As for the name, it is 'Coeur Croisé' in France (a direct translation), but 'Crusado Magico' in Spain (a slight shift to a 'magic cross'). To stick to the common concept and convey it as best it can, Playtex does not hesitate to change the name of the products if necessary, to provide a more appropriate translation.

▌ Thus the line of bras without underwires is called 'WOW!' in the US ('WithOut a Wire'), but 'Armagiques' in France.

▌ The line of girdles that feature long-lasting comfort is called '18 hours', which can be translated in each country.

▌ A line of bras is called 'SuperLook', a name which in this case needs no translation. Wonderbra itself was launched untranslated.

Despite the legitimate willingness to globalise, we must not overlook real cultural differences and differences in perception. This is why Procter & Gamble has created different versions according to the country for the Mr Clean brand, while nevertheless remaining within the limits of a common strategy (shine). Indeed, the symbols of 'shine' change with the culture. In France, it is expressed by the idea of the mirror ('You can see yourself in it'), while in the USA, the emphasis is on reflection off water ('Is it water? No it's the shine!'). Throughout the world, Camay is the soap which implies 'seduction'. This is the line which Procter & Gamble have always taken. However, though customer habits and expectations are the same the world over where soap is concerned, cultural blocks call for different approaches when speaking to a woman about intimate moments.

▌ In France, the seductive power was portrayed by a woman beautifying herself in her bath for her husband. The success of this commercial tempted the Japanese to introduce it in their market where it caused fury when the advertisement was screened. In Japan it is considered an insult for a man to enter the bathroom while his wife is performing her ablutions.

▌ In Italy, they preferred to show a fawning wife and her macho man.

▌ The Austrians just use Paris as a backdrop to signify seduction.

▌ In Greece, they added a more sensual note, bringing in the proverbial vamp.

Flexibility at the creative stage not only satisfies local cultural requirements, but also allows Camay to establish its own status in different countries.

Building the brand in emerging countries

Today, all eyes are turned towards the East, where companies are keen to compete in countries that were once part of the Soviet bloc. Beyond lies Asia – the five 'tiger economies' and China. Pioneer managers sent into the field are faced with the task of achieving major sales objectives within a short space of time. There is a great temptation to use an internationalised version of the flagship brand as far as possible, for example the Kraft, Müeller or Campina dairy brands. In fact, everything encourages managers to do so:

▌ Their managerial freedom – in these distant countries they feel less restricted by the constraints of head office.

▌ The pressure of sales and objectives, combined with a lack of resources.

▌ The pitfalls of market research – since the brand is weak and not yet crystallised around a prototype, it seems able to be used anywhere.

▌ It is therefore tempting to actually use it anywhere, on all products, all the more so because this type of initiative proves effective at sales level. As a symbol of quality, in countries that are not used to quality, a brand is reassuring and boosts the sales of anything it endorses. Any new initiative works.

It is a well-known fact that the first thing multinationals do in these countries is to rationalise production. The skill of manufacturers lies in their ability to significantly increase the quality of production, which gives local consumers access to levels of quality worthy of the name. Is not the primary function of a brand to guarantee quality? The brand therefore serves to endorse production and symbolise the newly acquired quality and reliability. By adopting this logic, the international brand becomes a strong umbrella brand from the outset, a source of reputation and power. The way to creating a strong brand appears to be clearly mapped out.

It should be pointed out that most examples of globalisation cited in managerial literature written in English are in fact 'product globalisations' based on a model of geographical extension from the country of origin, as with McDonald's, Mars and Coca-Cola. In many cases, however, this model is not applicable since companies are not seeking to impose specific tastes on the inhabitants of other countries, but to recreate their brand (Kraft, Müeller or Président) at local level. For example, while it is reasonable to assume that most Russians would not want to eat Camembert, it is quite legitimate for Lactalis to try to globalise its flagship brand Président. But this can only be done via large-volume local products to get the business off to a good start, otherwise it is not worth investing in a sales force or advertising.

The first problem is that, by covering all segments in a new country, the brand may deviate from the strategy (positioning) that has been fixed for it, in Europe or the United States for example. What is not a problem for Thailand or China can be a serious issue in Russia. But the strategy is global and has to be reflected in each country. Creating an umbrella brand that covers all segments in a country from the outset may favour short-term sales but does not really prepare for the future.

The second problem is that establishing an umbrella brand quickly from the outset may fill the brand catalogues but does not really create a strong brand for the future. So what will happen exactly?

It will not take long before all the brand's western competitors will be in the country as well. The levels of quality between these competitors will therefore be comparable. So what will differentiate the brand from all the others? It will be a general brand, with no real identity, no prototype, no strong differentiation.

How long can you go on introducing new initiatives that keep working? This type of success can be short-lived if a competitor also decides to launch an innovation. Taking the easy option does not lay foundations for the future. It is essential not to lose sight of the long-term objective and to bear the middle and long term in mind when considering short-term initiatives, for example when promoting difference(s) to create preference over future competitors.

It is therefore essential to build firm foundations at the outset and extend the brand later. This means making choices and selections, despite the temptation not to do so. But this is the way global brands are constructed.

Naming problems

The ultimate symbol of successful globalisation is the ability to use the same name worldwide. However, a brand name often poses problems for globalisation. The main ones are outlined below:

▌ First of all, there is the problem of prior registration by a local company. For example, the name Eurostar had already been registered by a service company and had to be bought from that company, a solution that is not always possible. Less straightforward was the problem of the Crocodile brand, registered by a Chinese company and rapidly reinforced by a vast network of stores known as The Crocodile Shop, just as the global brand Lacoste accessed the Asian market. Lacoste's logo is a crocodile.

▌ Second, the name can be a problem in terms of its meaning in a specific language. There is no shortage of anecdotes about brand names that have sexual connotations in other countries.

▌ A less common problem is the translation of descriptive names. Traditionally, the Americans do not translate their descriptive brand names – Pampers are Pampers the world over, as is Head & Shoulders. But for an international brand of cheese such as La Vache Qui Rit (The Laughing Cow), the name is important because it conveys a message and permits the correct interpretation of the brand symbol (a cow's head). Without it, the cow could appear stupid, smiling or mad. In this case, there is a link between the brand name and brand symbol. The question therefore arises as to whether or not to translate this descriptive brand name for each country, and if so, whether to keep a reference to the brand name in French. If this is done, should this reference be above or below the local translation? Finally, should the answers to these questions be different for each region, since the answers depend on the added value desired?

In certain areas, there is a real problem of counterfeited goods and therefore a need to reassure consumers that the product is in fact the real thing. In some areas (such as Saudi Arabia, the Middle East and Germany), the added value comes from the reference to France, while in others, the 'made in France' label can be a negative factor due to changing economic circumstances, for example in the United States in 2003.

▌ Finally China poses a specific problem because of its very different regional dialects.

Naming in China

Naming in China often forces managers to face a choice: should they name semantically or phonetically?(Schmitt and Zhang, 2001). The dilemma is as follows: should one respect the sound of the name even if it has no local meaning and is therefore difficult to pronounce and to memorise, or should one respect the concept even if it means parting from the international sound of the brand name? Ideally of course, one would say both. The Chinese sound should resemble the international pronunciation, but the meaning should also be appropriate. Microsoft's semantic name would be Wei Jua, which means micro flexible and soft. In addition it is a pleasant sound to a Chinese ear. Coca-Cola and Carrefour found both a semantic and phonetic appropriate translation: Keu Ko Keu Leu means 'good to drink and makes happy', Tia-leu-Fu means something close to 'the house of happiness'. The leading worldwide brand of insecticide, Decis from Aventis, is pronounced Di-Cha-Seu which luckily means 'at them until death'.

Others are less lucky. Peugeot is said as 'Piao Je', but in Cantonese, it evokes a prostitute. Orangina starts with an O: in Chinese there are no nice words starting with an O.

There is a danger however in localising the name too much in China. Foreign brands are now valued much more than local brands. All signs which accentuate the perception of being a local brand may erode brand equity in the long term. The size of this market requires that all due precautions be taken.

Achieving the delicate local–global balance

Each company has to find its own balance between localisation (the adaptation of its products to local markets) and the deep-rooted *raison d'être* of globalisation, the pursuit of a competitive advantage through reduced costs. It is therefore possible to say that there is a contradiction between the need to create value – via the adaptation of products and symbols to suit a particular country, market segment and even ethnic groups, communities or individuals on a one-to-one basis – and the economic requirement of reducing costs. As with any dilemma, every company knows there is no single solution, just progressive adaptations and even policy reviews when they have placed too much emphasis on localisation or standardisation.

Cosmetic groups (such as Estée Lauder, Shiseido and l'Oréal) and car manufacturers are in the throes of this dilemma since they are both 'high-tech' and 'high-touch'. It is a well-known fact that globalisation was born of technology, and aids the diffusion of research via the ever-decreasing costs of that technology. However, because cosmetic brands target the beauty of individual women, they must be ultra-sensitive and therefore 'high-touch' and, as such, adapt as far as possible to specific physiological characteristics, as well as to the basic and cultural characteristics of women in countries throughout the world. There is no longer an overall concept of beauty, but an acceptance of the diversity of different types of beauty within the same country and between generations. The dilemma is equally acute for the car industry when a car is not simply positioned as a low-priced vehicle. A car has a special significance for individual consumers, and since each consumer is different, there is not only an expectation of diversity at brand level, but also in respect of models, line extensions and even the personalisation of the relationship with the brand.

Each to his own balance?

To take one category, cosmetics for example, it is significant that the brands positioned as 'mass market' have to develop their proximity much more than the so-called elitist brands. As such, they not only make greater use of direct-contact marketing but also tend to adapt products and publicity much more within the well-defined framework of the brand identity, on the one hand, and the brand's economic equation, on the other. Thus Garnier and Maybelline adapt much more than Lancôme, and in the case of Garnier, this adaptation is automatic and built in from the outset. For example, Garnier offers the most extensive range of cosmetics to meet the demands of all skin and hair types in Europe and the United States. Depending on the country, its subsidiaries select the products best suited to their requirements, since each country develops its own market. The same applies to the format of the packaging and labelling. The differentiation is situated at national level and not at the level of the region or zone, since the women of – albeit geographically close – countries such as Korea, Taiwan and Japan in fact have very different expectations. The Lancôme customer, on the other hand, is widely travelled and expects to be able to buy the same products in Tokyo or Paris – by being over-adapted, these products would lose their status. Naturally, Lancôme develops specific skin-whitening products to meet the very strong demand among Asian women in these countries.

So how do companies reconcile this fine-tuned adaptation and the economic equation? By making the economic equation the criterion for the acceptance of the adaptation. Thus for l'Oréal, innovation assumes the status of a religion, with over 500 patents registered each year. This innovation can come from one of three sources:

▌ one of four basic research laboratories – two in the United States, one in Europe and one in Japan;

▌ from brand marketing teams throughout the world;

▌ from any of the various national retail distribution subsidiaries.

Sometimes there is a strong local demand in a particular country. For example, in 1997, Brazil expressed a desire for a specific hair-care product since Brazilian hair – the result of the country's ethnic melting pot – is characteristically dry and unmanageable and needs a moisturising conditioner. Brazilian women are proud of their hair, which they regard, even more than their faces, as the symbol of their sensuality. They therefore want it to be long and flowing, to move with their body, what the Brazilians call *cacheado*, or curling and wavy. So the European laboratory developed a unique formula and then l'Oréal considered the economic equation. Could enough of this new product be sold in Brazil and, of course, elsewhere in the world? It was called Elsève Hydramax and soon became the most popular hair-care product in Brazil before being extended to other countries.

Maybelline provides another example. Although it is a US brand and its teams are based in New York, the Japanese laboratory discovered an innovative active ingredient that was able to meet the very specific demands of very trendy and 'hip' young Japanese women, typical of Tokyo's Shibuya district, for a particular type of lipstick. These are young women with small mouths, and in Japan mother-of-pearl is very popular. This molecule created the effect of water, giving the lipstick a 'wet look'. After careful economic analysis, the product was developed in Japan under the name Maybelline Watershine Diamonds. In the space of a year, it made Maybelline the best-selling mass-market make-up brand in Japan, and was subsequently extended to the United States and Europe where it enjoyed a similar meteoric success.

In both these cases, the local innovations were only accepted when they were considered 'globalisable' with the potential for global successes. This is a far cry from the 'think global, act local' business model. It is more a case if 'think local, act global'.

Competitive advantage through adaptation

Globalisation at all price has a cost: failure. On the other hand, some examples, not much publicised, show how market adaptation helps in developing a profitable business and slowly gaining market leadership.

Year after year, Nestlé has tried to compete against Kellogg's in the cereals market. This is normal: cereals are close to the core product of Nestlé, milk. They address the same target too (children), and the same benefit: growth.

As long as Nestlé copied Kellogg's it was unsuccessful. In addition, Nestlé had no know-how in cereals. It needed an alliance. General Mills in the United States was itself looking for a way to enter Europe, after Kellogg's, Quaker Oats, and the private labels of strong or even dominant multiple retailers. To compete against a leader one needs an innovation. Because of Nestlé's decentralised culture, local subsidiaries have some autonomy. The French subsidiary identified a need so far untapped by Kellogg's: children love chocolate. They wish to have chocolate for breakfast. Why didn't Kellogg identify this need? First, it was a local need, and centralised global companies are not fitted to adapt to local needs. Second, it did not fit with the ideology of cereals for growth and health. Finally, leaders tend to defend their acquired position instead of looking for new markets (Christensen, 1997). Also, as a chocolate brand, Nestlé had more insight into this market. The result was the launch of a local new product, thanks to the know-how of General Mills, marketed and distributed by Nestlé: Chocapic, the first cereals in chocolate. Soon this product became the market leader with a share of 11 per cent: all multiple retailers had to distribute it. This is how Nestlé fought back successfully. It innovated in a high-volume market, then Chocapic was rapidly extended to other European and world countries.

Everyone has heard about Malibu, a white rum and coconut light drink. What about Soho or Ditta, which recently passed Malibu in volume and value sales? Soho and Ditta are the two names of the same product, a mixer based on lychees. Why are there two names?

Because it is not possible to sell a lychee mixer drink the same way in Japan (where it is now the number one brand) and in Europe. In Japan, Ditta is aimed at young women who typically go to bars to chat together, a classic of Japanese social behaviour. The communication target was the bar staff who promoted imaginative new cocktails. In Europe, the brand called Soho is mostly sold off-premises, in multiple retailers, thanks to in-store wet trial campaigns. The target market is women as a basis for cocktails (with grapefruit for instance). Here again, leadership came from adaptation.

Adaptation: a necessity for growth through time

A final example is Barilla, a mainstream popular pasta brand that is number one in Italy. It decided to extend geographically in Europe, by means of a positioning very different from its own domestic positioning: it created the premium pasta market in Europe. Barilla was introduced almost as a luxury brand (see Table 16.7, page 429).This was implemented through cartons with a specific design and the launch of a collection of forms of pasta unknown in most countries. Naturally the price was 25 per cent higher than the local leader, which itself often had an Italian name but did not play on this image dimension, having lost all links with Italy a long time ago.

Barilla's goal is not to remain a niche player in all foreign countries, but to become the number two if not the number one. This necessitates addressing the local habits of average consumers, not elitist ones. As a consequence, the brand has to widen its range and lower its prices on new lines adapted to children and family consumption, even if this means producing products that are hardly typically Italian but represent a large part of local consumption (like noodles). This also entails packaging these lines in a far less premium style (no more cartons). Finally, the advertising itself should bring the brand closer to the markets: it has to stop being perceived as the brand of Italians. Positioning a brand on export markets as the one preferred by consumers in its domestic market contributes to reinforcing an alien image. Some consumers may like to imitate the choices of foreigners, but becoming a local leader means addressing the needs of this market, the first one being to be relevant for that market.

Being perceived as local: the new ideal of global brands?

A curious turnaround appears to be taking place. In multinationals the world over, CEOs are proudly producing figures proving that their brand is perceived as 'local'. In fact, brands that have been very successfully 'globalised' for some time are now perceived as local brands, a phenomenon that is just as true for Nivea and Kodak as it is for brands of medication (Aspro and Rennies), washing powder (Ariel and Omo) and even Shell, which the Swedes firmly believe to be their national brand. Is this desire to appear local a concession to fashion, a concession to the World Social Forums against capitalist globalisation, or does it reflect a deeper awareness?

It should first of all be pointed out that this trend does not affect all brands, only those that want to be accessible, popular brands reaching a wide public in countries throughout the world. By definition, 'high-tech' is not local – if it is, it is perceived as 'low-tech'. It is technology that unites the world, which is the essential factor of globalisation and the attendant standardisation, by creating the same desire for a particular piece or pieces of new equipment in consumers the world over. Thus, the big technological brands are clearly perceived as global, a perception that invests them with additional perceived quality and prestige. Similarly, 'high-touch' brands are also global – their customers are, in

part, buying a value based on the idea that, if they travelled to Paris, New York or Tokyo, they would find exactly the same product. This is why luxury goods and top-of-the-range cosmetics do not try to appear local – their added value stems from their global image and their foreign origins. Finally, this basic trend does not affect brands whose added value stems from their association with a particular country. For example, Coca-Cola and Levi's are universal symbols of the United States, while Lacoste symbolises French sporting elegance. Today, young consumers worldwide, who have grown up with mixed cultures, tend to favour brands with a strong national identity which allow them to experiment with their own particular identity.

However, the search for popular success on the world market forces companies to recognise that being close to consumers is a key factor of this success. L'Oréal was quick to realise this and, within its very diverse brand portfolio, the name of the typically French brand Laboratoires Garnier was changed to Garnier in 2001. The change of name was not accidental – it was designed to facilitate the brand's acceptance by countries on all five continents. In spite of a 'brand identity' platform that is the same in all countries, Garnier readily adapts its products and ingredients to suit local hair and skin types, as well as adapting its packaging to suit local practices (large formats in Portugal, tiny formats in Korea) and its advertising (using local models) to appeal to local consumers. This strategy is therefore the direct opposite of that used by the group's top-of-the-range brand Lancôme, which is extremely globalised in all aspects of its marketing mix. Thus, the higher up the range the brand, the less it has to adapt.

If brands are seeking to maximise their integration within a country, it is because companies have realised that the global brand was above all a consequence of the pursuit of economies of scale and the competitive advantage they provide. Consumers have never been known to ask for global brands. There is, therefore, a difference between being a global brand that is represented on all continents because it meets a universal need, and proclaiming a global brand from the rooftops. Furthermore, our recent research has shown that the key asset of local brands is confidence, and in these times of doubt, food scandals and capitalist crises (like Enron), the confidence factor is a distinct advantage.

This is why groups like Danone say they want to be 'a local global company', but in Danone's case the brand is actually – and legally – a local brand in several countries. (See page 425.)

Being relevant before being global?

The global brand results from a deliberate will to rationalise its management and less from a demand from the market. The typical consumer does not buy a global brand *per se*, but on the contrary, individualistic brands that correspond exactly to his/her specific needs. Even when it is global, the brand is bought in an individualistic fashion. The buyer of Mr Clean in France compares it to Ajax and to other local competing brands: he/she has no notion of the existence of Mr Clean in another country, with the same positioning and the same promise of shine. The buyer is sensitive to the latter and to the personality of the brand, just like the buyers of Mr Clean in these other countries. Thus, when in several countries, groups of buyers appear sensitive to the same advantages and expect the same features, there is an opportunity for a global brand. We should speak here of 'coincidence of globalism', referring to the fact that globalism expresses a corporate view, whereas at the consumer's level in each country, in spite of so-called similar needs, their choice remains individualistic and egocentric (Buzzell and Quelch, 1988). The brand must therefore often be a chameleon and seem 'just like back home'. This does not apply to international high-tech, service,

luxury or alcoholic beverage brands. But Kodak and Philips are considered French by a third of the French population, as Bic is thought to be an American brand in the USA.

Integration factors

How does a company speed up perceived integration and acquire the desired level of assimilation in a country? This is an issue that even involves high-tech companies if they do not want to be perceived as cold, distant and indifferent to public concerns, simply content to sell and therefore a symbol of the predatory multinationals. The first thing is to tune into local needs and then implement a local marketing campaign – on the streets, in sports stadia, as part of local life. Media advertising should be balanced by direct contact and involvement in a country's everyday life. It was not by chance that Garnier launched its new Fructis Style product on, among other things, more than 100 buses in each country – buses that would travel back and forth across towns and cities, in direct contact with the general public.

Last but not least, and bearing in mind that the brand and company are one and the same thing in the eyes of the general public, it is a distinct advantage to have factories and produce the product in the countries in question. This not only helps the brand to put down roots but also increases its status, since it provides employment. If the company also has a well-developed social policy, people will talk about it and it will gain respect and confidence. Far from behaving like a coloniser or a predator, the brand will be seen as seeking to share its success. The local publicity given to the social initiatives of Danone (the company) in Mexico greatly helped to speed up the brand's assimilation in this key country. As can be seen, in the age of the responsible and ethical brand, companies no longer hide behind their brands (quite the opposite, in fact) in their penetration of foreign markets.

Local brands make a comeback?

The criticism of local brands has therefore been exaggerated (Kapferer, 2001) and their strength underestimated. Because they tried to replace local brands with global brands too quickly, Procter & Gamble and Danone were forced to back-pedal and try to win back the customers they had lost. It should be remembered that pro-global propaganda was a one-way street and did not brook any form of opposition. However, it is worth considering how many leading brands are in fact not local. The leading brands on a number of markets – fruit juices, beer, cooking oil, butter, cheese – are all local brands. It could be argued that these are traditional products, but it is significant that in Korea and Japan, the number one hamburger is not McDonald's or Burger King, but Lotteria (an offshoot of the Lotte department stores). The same is true in Belgium where Quick is still the market leader, more than 10 years after the US giant penetrated the Belgian market. The paradox is explained by the 'first mover advantage'. In these countries, it was the local brands that established the hamburger restaurants and the market for which they became the referents. There is no difference in the structures of these competitors, but the key factor of the success of any restaurant is its position – when McDonald's arrived in Korea and Belgium, the best sites were already taken.

Today, many global brands affirm that they try not to appear global. This is certainly true in the case of Danone, which is in fact legally the local brand in four different countries. The Danone brand, the result of an innovation, was created in Spain in 1919 by Isaac Carasso, who named it after his son (Danon is the Catalan diminutive for Daniel). Danone was registered in France in 1929, while Dannon Milk Products, Inc. was created in New York in 1942 by Daniel Carasso, who had emigrated to the United States. The brand was subsequently extended to Mexico. In each of these four countries, Danone or Dannon is regarded as a local brand. Strangely enough, according to its directors, the German brand Nivea also aspires to be perceived as a local brand even though it is one of the most widely distributed brands in the world. The same applies to the Danish brand Velux, the number one roof window manufacturer, Bic, Garnier and others.

In 1998, the trend was for globalisation at all costs, and having bought the Czech company Opavia, the Danone group decided to replace this local brand with its own global brand. However, Danone had seriously underestimated the strength of the local brand and had to back-pedal. Opavia had more than 70 per cent of the market share in the Czech Republic. During the communist era, the only 'treat' available to the Czechs was biscuits, and Opavia had become their friend and ally. Last but not least, Opavia was also the name of a Czech town, which made it a patriotic brand. All these factors were difficult to appreciate when legislating from a distance. Each country has its own icon brands and globalisation simply cannot afford to ignore the consumer.

The international study referred to earlier (Schuiling and Kapferer, 2004; see page 408) identified the levers specific to local brands – confidence and proximity. These are key factors of success if the local brand also knows how to market its products effectively.

Developing local brands

Since many brands are and will continue to remain local, how can they be developed in the face of international competition? The strength of local brands has already been demonstrated (Schuiling and Kapferer, 2004) and their strong points compared with global brands. But confidence and proximity will not provide indefinite protection – they have to be maintained, and the strategies that maintain them are therefore particularly important. But it is equally important to address the weaknesses of local brands – a lack of innovation, fun and fashion, according to the new, younger generation of consumers. Local brands also suffer from a number of weaknesses and limitations at management level, and these are outlined below:

▌ The first is often inertia – too used to simply being there, because of their history rather than their ambition, local brands often lack energy because they lack ambition. The brand therefore needs to be revitalised from within, and its aims, mission statements and advantages clearly redefined.

▌ Local brands are often too widely dispersed. It is therefore crucial to refocus resources on certain markets or market segments in which they can hope to dominate or at least be joint market leaders. They also have to accept the need to part with some of their business in order to concentrate on the segments with the potential to dominate the market. Alternatively they can target niches, small but profitable markets, in a way that the multinationals are unable to do.

▌ Local brands often lack innovation – they rely too heavily on loyalty as a driver of preference and have therefore lost their relevance because their products are no longer modern enough or sufficiently well adapted to meet present-day demands. It cannot be said often enough that innovations are the life-blood of a brand. There are several types of innovation. Some demand huge investments in R&D and are beyond the scope of local brands, while others are more closely identified with the user values of the products and are therefore more accessible. A third type is related not so much to basic research (new active ingredients) as to the search for new concepts that are linked to a consumer insight.

▌ Local brands tend to have an established form of management. There is a need to bring in new managers who relate to and

therefore understand the new markets and segments, who can identify consumer insights and convert them into ideas.

▌ Local brands are too self-restricting. In an age that glorifies globalisation, there is little in the way of advice or articles to support local brands (Kapferer, 2001). They therefore run the risk of being too self-restricting, as in the case of the Norwegian company DBS, a local market leader in the bicycle sector. DBS did not think it would be able to sell modern mountain bikes under its own name, in the face of competition from Giant or the US company Cannondale. In fact, it was a huge success – consumers were delighted to be able to buy quality products throughout Norway (due to the extended distribution of the brand), under the national brand name. Of course, there are always people who will only buy international brands, but it is important to take account of the less obsessive majority.

▌ There is another form of geographical self-restriction. There is no reason why a local brand should not seek opportunities for growth in neighbouring countries, which are often familiar with the brand or have cultural similarities that favour its assimilation. Thus, it is quite natural for local Estonian brands to be sold in Lithuania and Latvia, or for Polish brands to be sold in Hungary and the Czech Republic. But the geographical area can extend further afield. One of the key factors of the success of small and medium-sized enterprises is their assimilation at international level very early on in their development (Simon, 2000). It is significant that in the case of Wal-Mart, the world's leading distributor, a development team travels the world in search of innovative products that will differentiate the store's ranges from those of its competitors and add an element of surprise for customers. This was how the micro-company Lorina, which had relaunched the 'orange crush' drinks popular in the past, was spotted at a trade exhibition for new products and then referenced in the United States a year after its creation. This referencing with a mega-distributor is often tied to an exclusivity agreement that guarantees a certain continuity for a brand's international development.

▌ Finally, local brands must not appear local. Except in the case of ethnic or traditional craft products linked to a particular region, modernity is expressed via cultural integration. Who knows whether or not Hollywood chewing gum is a local brand? Or Gemey, Dop, Tango or Wall's ice cream? The top three brands in the world's largest market in terms of volume (France) for Scotch whisky are all local brands. Certainly these whiskies come from Scotland, where whisky is produced to excess, but these brands were created by wines and spirits merchants – two low-price brands, based essentially on trade marketing (William Peel, Label 5), and a mainstream brand (Clan Campbell). It was these brands, less expensive than the big international brands, that enabled the French market to double in size in the space of 15 years.

A good example of management of local brands against increasing international competition is Amore Pacific, Korea's dynamic and leading cosmetics company, and strong market leader thanks to a wide brand portfolio. How did Amore Pacific strengthen its brand proactively?

▌ First, the brands are allocated by distribution route: one brand, one channel. This includes the very dominant direct sales channel (door to door or through customer-led parties), a channel imported brand cannot penetrate for it requires a know-how and resources it will not possess.

▌ Second, small brands have been merged into larger ones, to create mega-brands and reach a higher critical size, a condition of higher marketing investments

▌ Third, brands are permanently nurtured by innovations.

▌ Fourth, local brands do not look at all local. La Neige for instance aims at the youth market, with a French looking name and capitalises on its proximity to French customers. Hera (the name of a Greek goddess) is a direct competitor of Lancôme and Estée Lauder: as such it is strongly visible in all premium department stores as in the duty free zone of Korean Airports.

▌ Finally, Amore Pacific has extended its best brands to other countries. La Neige has been successfully launched in Hong Kong and Shanghai, as Hera. There is a growing demand in Asia for Asian brands that understand Asian women better than western imported ones.

The process of brand globalisation

While there is no shortage of examples of globalisation in books, articles and at conferences, most focus on product brands such as Coke, Marlboro, Starbucks, McDonald's, Amazon, eBay and Intel. However, these examples are centred around unpredictable and/or radical innovations which, after becoming leaders in the United States (a domestic market that is equal to 50 per cent of the world market), were able to be exported on the basis of their reputation. They do not correspond to the reality of most global groups and brands, which often have a small country of origin and have to become global from the start. This was true in the case of Nestlé (the world's leading food company), which originated in Switzerland, Unilever (the Netherlands), Absolut (Sweden), Grey Goose (the Netherlands), Finlandia (Finland) and Velux (Denmark). It is significant that, four months after the launch of the first product ever manufactured by Nestlé (baby cereal), it was already being sold in five different countries. Nestlé made diversity part of its strategy from the outset and still continues to do so today – Nescafé currently offers a range of no less than 32 different coffee-related products in Europe. This is a far cry from the single Coke-style product. Whereas US brands promote the 'American way of life', this does not apply to other brands and groups throughout the world. The object of this chapter and indeed the entire book is to try to re-establish a certain balance and to suggest alternative, and sometimes more relevant, models.

Key stages in the process of brand globalisation are:

▌ defining brand identity;

▌ choosing regions and countries;

▌ accessing the markets;

▌ choosing the brand architecture;

▌ choosing products adapted to the markets;

▌ constructing global campaigns.

Defining brand identity

Brand globalisation presupposes the definition of the brand to be globalised. That is, the brand must have an identity that will serve as a medium for its globalisation, in both tangible and intangible terms. The company must therefore start by defining and writing the parameters of the brand's identity. This is essential for coherence, all the more so since globalisation will greatly increase the brand's centrifugal tendencies, with everyone wanting to interpret it in their own particular way. To limit these tendencies, there must be a clear and concise platform with salient points and flesh.

It should be remembered that the modern brand is no longer a simple 'product plus' (a mere definition of a product with a plus value, like 'the best toothpaste for helping prevent tooth decay'). It is a source that has to be defined. To avoid problems of understanding and translation, globalisation very often involves the choice of all-purpose words that have the advantage of creating consensus the world over, such as 'high quality', 'client focused', 'dynamic' and 'competent'. But it is important to be wary of international consensus since it usually reflects a certain weakness in the brand definition and therefore the brand identity.

Brands are based on differentiation. They have to have character, salient and original points. But would Marlboro dare to launch its brand today using the symbol of a solitary, macho, craggy, outdoor figure?

Global brands and universal truths

As a rule each brand should be based on a consumer or customer insight. An insight is literally an insight into the consumer or customer, a short sentence encapsulating the state of mind or expectation or attitude the brand is responding to.

As a consequence, global brands tend to address universal truths, global insights. Taking the spirit market, what are the universal truths of alcohols? Here consumption is conspicuous: by drinking, men try to enhance their male status. By its symbolic character, and the values it promotes (keep walking, that is to say persevere) Johnny Walker represents the adult male achievement. It is about masculinity, about being a real male throughout the world. J&B is about social success. Chivas encourages joy and conspicuous consumption. Bacardi is an escape to paradise.

Give flesh to your identity

There are several ways of preventing the salient points of the brand identity becoming lost in the globalisation process:

- by accompanying the facets of the brand identity with a comparison, saying what the brand is and what it is not;

- by accompanying the words with images (brand concept board);

- by reinforcing the facets through training initiatives and creating local brand relays (keepers of the flame);

- by not delegating strategic implementation (such as advertising and the Web) to the local level.

At this point, it is important to distinguish between exported brands and global brands in the strict sense of the term. Jaguar, Porsche and BMW are exported brands – Jaguar's brand values have not been redefined for globalisation, while BMW and Porsche certainly incorporate the characteristics of the global market (in fact the US market) in order to define the specifications of their future products. The Porsche 928 was designed for the United States, its broad highways and style of driving, and the design of the latest BMW Series 5 was developed entirely with the United States in mind. But what you are buying is Coventry, Stuttgart or Munich – the brands have not changed in the slightest in respect of their identity and core values. The same is true of Chanel. These are brands exported worldwide.

The brand to be globalised must think about its identity. Will the identity that has ensured success in its country of origin guar-antee success in the rest of the world, or at least the key countries in which it is to be marketed? There is therefore an interaction between the first (defining brand identity) and second (choosing regions and countries) phases of brand globalisation. When a brand is exported, it immediately acquires the added values associated with its international perception, and it enjoys the 'spill-over effects of international perception'. Absolut is not highly rated in Sweden, but in the United States – where it is perceived as an imported vodka, while Smirnoff (the local leader) is produced in the United States – it has created the premium segment.

Separate the domestic and the international positioning

When it leaves its country of origin, a brand is transformed, and changes its nature. For example, Barilla in Italy is a popular 'main-stream' pasta brand that offers good value for money and inspires confidence. As shown by Table 16.7, in other countries it is positioned as the ultimate Italian 'must have', top quality, traditional and fashionable, but loses its 'value for money' and 'confidence' – it takes time to build up confidence.

Generally speaking, exported brands must be positioned at the top of the range since they have to support transport costs and customs duties. Furthermore, it is an opportunity to take advantage of the spill-over effects of perceived brand globalness.(PBG). In this way, the Swedish vodka Absolut created

Table 16.7   Barilla's international and domestic image

Percentage perceiving the brand to be:	Italy	France	Germany
High quality	34.9	56.9	40.6
Trustworthy	56.6	44.8	17.4
Good quality/price	33.8	26.8	17.2
Fashionable	11.0	19.6	26.1
Authentic	8.9	16.0	13.7

Source: Kapferer and Schuiling (2004)

the top-of-the-range (premium) segment in the United States, where it is sold for 20 per cent more than the local market leader (Smirnoff), which has factories scattered throughout the region.

Choosing regions and countries

An examination of the so-called global brands reveals that they are far from being as widely distributed throughout the world as we are led to believe. Of course, this could be because conquering world markets is a gradual process and a company must first of all establish itself as the leader on its domestic market. For example, the first Wal-Mart was not established outside the United States until 1991, 30 years after the creation of the first store in this famous US chain, while McDonald's accessed other markets gradually, one by one.

However, there is another explanation – not all countries are potential customers for the brand in question. For example, dairy products are not part of Asian culture, which is a handicap for Danone. Similarly, yoghurt is not a part of US culture and this is a handicap for Dannon USA which, although created in 1942, has not managed to impose itself as a major brand. The Japanese do not like their perfume to impinge on others, which is a handicap for all brands of strong perfume. This is why brands such as Paloma Picasso, with its characteristically Spanish values and strong essences, sell better in Texas, California and of course southern Europe, but also in countries (such as Germany) whose tourists visit southern Europe.

At this stage a strategic analysis should be carried out to assess the potentials of each country and the barriers to accessing their markets. This analysis should incorporate:

- the size of the existing market;

- indicators of growth and/or the latent potentials of this market, and its 'segmentability' – sociocultural develop-

ments and the growth of purchasing power;

- consumer insights on their prospects for rapid development;

- the nature of any competition and its ability to react – does the brand in question have the potential for strong differentiation, or a 'plus value'?

- the existence of a rudimentary brand equity in the country or region (via tourism or the international media which transmit brand images into homes throughout the world);

- the existence of adequate distribution channels likely to promote the brand concept;

- the existence of a media network;

- the existence of adequate commercial partners at local level;

- the non-existence of barriers to market access – customs, formal and informal regulations;

- the potential for registering or buying the brand name (a check that it is not already owned locally).

The presence of trade barriers was why countries like India, fearing a sort of neo-colonialism through the intermediary of companies, for a long time remained closed to imports. It would have been theoretically possible, for example, to manufacture a major brand of car in that country, but this would require all the subcontractors who are a necessary part of the production process to do the same thing. In the absence of subcontractors and adequate partners, there is a risk of departing from the brand contract in that particular country – its cars will sell but will be of inferior quality. This was also a problem in Brazil for a long time.

As has already been stated, the key issue in brand naming is the globalisation of product platforms – for example, Unilever defined five platforms for margarine. It is not a major problem that one of these platforms is Becel in Portugal and ProActiv elsewhere – since global economies and synergies must first of all be achieved at production and concept/positioning level, the name becomes a secondary problem. As the focus of media attention, a name that is the same everywhere is of course desirable, but it is not the central issue because it is not the principal source of increased profitability.

The result of the strategic analysis of the countries in question sometimes explains the distribution of sales of international brands. Thus, the three key countries for The Laughing Cow brand are of course its country of origin but also Germany and Saudi Arabia, where temperatures are so high that processed cheese is the only way to provide the daily milk intake for both adults and children. The creation of factories in Morocco and Egypt has also reduced the problem of customs barriers.

Within the context of globalisation, the order in which countries, regions and continents are 'conquered' is also a strategic issue. For example, Amore Pacific is the international flagship brand of the Korean company of the same name – it embodies its know-how, values and ethics. It is also a modern brand that seeks to ally itself with the concept of western beauty without rejecting its Asiatic origins. In 2003 the question arose as to which it should penetrate first, the US or European market. Apart from the issues addressed above, the company was concerned whether it was in its best interest to advertise success in Europe in the United States, or vice versa. Given that perceived brand globalness is not a driver of preference in the United States, or at least less so than in Europe (Holt, Quelch and Taylor, 2003), it was decided to penetrate the US market first. In addition, the United States seem geographically, socially and culturally much closer to Korea than Europe, which is not only distant and fragmented, but also has strong well-established brands.

It will come as no surprise that, today, all western brands are looking towards the East:

▮ Eastern Europe and Russia are two of the long-awaited growth regions for brands battling it out on saturated western markets. They also offer a competitive advantage for Scandinavian brands that have long-established ties with these regions, and for Germany whose area of influence has always historically been Eastern Europe. But given the present low purchasing power, it is also an area of expansion for brands positioned according to price, such as the Korean brands LG, Samsung, Daewoo and Khia, and the Turkish brands targeting Romania, Bulgaria and Albania.

▮ China is another growth region – today, one-third of its billion inhabitants are creditworthy. It is significant that barely two years ago, l'Oréal was achieving 49 per cent of its turnover in Western Europe, 32 per cent in the United States and only 19 per cent in the rest of the world. Given the considerable needs of Asia in general, due to the size of its population and its improving standard of living, it is easy to understand that l'Oréal's priorities now lie in this direction. This is reflected by the fact that one of the group's basic international research centres was established in Japan, and also by the group's acquisition of Japanese brands. Gone are the days when Chinese women only looked at western brands. Today they are very much aware of their Asiatic origins and are now turning to luxury and top-of-the-range Japanese and Korean brands – as evidenced by the success of the Korean brand, La Neige, in the department stores of Hong Kong and Shanghai. This is why l'Oréal bought the Japanese brand Sue Uemura, whose global brand portfolio reflects cultural diversity. Finally, the 11 global brands in the l'Oréal portfolio are to be launched in China.

India, which is slowly emerging from a protectionist phase in respect of its identity and the desire to preserve its independence, will be the other growth region of the future. The competitive positions are already being taken up. The same applies to Brazil.

Accessing the markets

A brand is not a simply a name on a particular range of products – it is what distinguishes those products, and a source of added value in the eyes of the target market. A brand is established over a period of time, and nothing is more important than a brand's first initiatives in a country, since these are what determine its long-term representation. The mainstay or basis of this representation is the 'prototype'. It should be remembered that this key notion was identified by the psychology of abstract concepts (see page 115) – the prototype is the 'best exemplar' which embodies the brand identity.

Today, in response to the demands of rationalisation and efficiency, many brands have two levels of branding – the parent brand and the daughter brand. A typical brand architecture is that of the source brand, a branded house with two levels. Frito Lay, Garnier, Dannon, Müeller, Campina, Ford, Toyota and Renault are all typical source brands. The brand can only be globalised via its daughter brands, which themselves cover a range of products. The key to globalising these parent brands is therefore a good daughter brand.

It is significant that Garnier was able to begin its globalisation in 2001 when it realised that that it finally had a suitable prototype, one that could embody the brand's modern values (see page 306). This prototype – Fructis Style, created in 2000 – was the most recent of all the Garnier daughter brands, but it was the one that enabled Garnier to be launched in the United States, the Republic of South Africa, Brazil and China. It is now the segment leader in all these countries.

Globally speaking, there are two major strategies for accessing national markets, by creating a new category or segmenting an existing category.

Creating a new category

Garnier is a typical example of this. The parent brand establishes itself by launching a daughter brand that becomes the reference, the pioneer of a new category which has the benefit of the 'first mover advantage', little or no competition and easier negotiations with distributors who are eager for creative innovations and value rather than a mere change of brands between competitors. The downside of this strategy is that it requires a greater investment in marketing and advertising. Its success also establishes the meaning of the parent brand, which enables it to launch its other daughter brands at a later date.

Nivea uses the same strategy even though it has an 'umbrella brand' architecture. It launches Nivea Cream before the lines that establish its competence in the facial and body care sector, the keys to creating a long-term bond of confidence.

Segmenting an existing category

The alternative strategy involves the immediate creation of a significant volume of business by launching a differentiated product, based on the brand values, but in a large-volume local category. For example, in Lebanon Yoplait began by launching two traditional local dairy products, Laban and Labneh. The aim was to quickly become the referent for traditional fresh dairy products by giving the country what a large industrial company can give – superior and consistent quality, more hygienic products, a more subtle taste, products with a longer shelf life, and more practical packaging.

Lactalis, an international giant of the cheese industry, globalised its umbrella brand Président in the same way. The Président business model is the segmentation of generic categories. Created in 1968, it became the leading brand of France's leading cheese (Camembert) and then the leading brand of butter, before extending to other products such as Brie and Emmental. By segmenting the generic category, Président introduces modern quality, practicality, adaptability to new uses and so on. The mistake would be to try to globalise Président by exporting Camembert – for example, why would the Spanish, Russians or Kazakhs want to eat Camembert? At best it would appeal to a tiny minority (a niche). This is not how a leading brand is recreated – and this is the key issue.

It is the business model of the brand that has to be globalised. For Président, this involves recreating – in Russia, Kazakhstan, Spain or any other country – the initiative used to successfully create the original brand, by segmenting a large-volume traditional local category.

It is worth noting that Danone, unable to create a new category of dairy products in Asia, decided to establish itself by segmenting an existing category to embody its key value, health. Throughout the world, Danone is famous for its yoghurts and mineral water. In Asia it puts its name to biscuits – that promise health (growth and vitamins) to parents and children – via global daughter brands such as Prince and Pepito, or by endorsing an ultra-popular, leading local brand such as Jacob's in Indonesia, Thailand and Singapore, and Tiger in China.

Choosing the brand architecture

Should the brand architecture be the same in all countries? Maybe it 'should' but can it in fact be the same? The gradual globalisation of a brand with two levels of branding (including a source brand or endorsing brand) automatically raises this type of question. Also, adaptation is governed by practical considerations – it is impossible to recreate what was achieved without the pressures of time and profitability in other markets, including the country of origin. Depending on the country, the type of brand architecture used will be the 'horizontal crunch' and/or the 'vertical crunch'.

The 'horizontal crunch' involves reducing the horizontal range of brands and 'nicheing' certain brands below others. Thus, in the United States, it is possible to find a Mini Babybel cheese with a taste of Bonbel, the whole being endorsed by The Laughing Cow, whereas in France and Germany these three names correspond to three different brands. But when a company moves into the United States, the problem is not so much ensuring greater market coverage with a portfolio containing a range of speciality products as surviving by capitalising. What was an independent brand becomes a daughter brand or an additional item under the same brand name (line extension).

The 'vertical crunch' has the reverse effect – vertical brand architectures with three levels of branding are reduced to two levels for reasons of efficiency and practicality. This type of crunch is subdivided into the 'top-down crunch' and the 'bottom-up crunch'.

The 'bottom up crunch' helps to reduce the number of levels by suppressing the one in the middle and raising the one at the bottom. In Europe, l'Oréal Paris is represented in the shampoo market by the Elsève brand, whose products have names (such as Color Vive) that describe the function of the product. They are therefore referred to as Elsève Color Vive by l'Oréal. The driver (what the consumer actually buys) is Elsève, while l'Oréal Paris acts as an endorsement.

In the United States, it was decided to do away with Elsève but to give all the products in the range the suffix 'Vive': Nutri Vive, Vita Vive, Color Vive, Curl Vive, Hydra Vive, Body Vive. This makes the relationship between l'Oréal and its products much stronger and more direct, which in turn promotes a reciprocal regeneration. The brand now has a co-driver since US consumers are not buying l'Oréal shampoo or Color Vive, but a combination of the two – l'Oréal Color Vive. This also avoids the fragmentation of publicity in a country where media costs are extremely high.

The 'top-down crunch' occurs when an endorsing brand becomes a driver and relegates the daughter brand to the role of descriptor. It is significant that in Europe, the European brand of biscuits Lu is sold by speciality brands. According to the packaging, Lu comes under the aegis of its daughter brands Prince, Pim's and Mikado. Below the names, each specific product may even be described as an 'energy added' biscuit, for example.

In the countries to be 'conquered' by the brand (like the United States), Lu has been upgraded from an endorsing brand to a range brand, while the other names are less prominent on the packaging and become descriptors.

Choosing products adapted to the markets

Managing the growth of business and the establishment of the brand simultaneously means constantly adapting the marketing – and therefore the product ranges – to the market, but within the framework of a well-defined and coherent strategy. As has already been stated, the 'prototypes' must be chosen as a function of the image to be created. Gone are the days when importers decided which products would be allowed into a country on the basis of purely short-term requirements. These importers were merchants and intermediaries, not shareholders in the company, and therefore had no long-term objectives. This was why many brands were launched via different products in countries that were in fact quite close to the country of origin. Within the space of a few years, this led to discrepancies in the product image and therefore to significant discrepancies in the price premium.

Products must be a source of rapid growth and yet comply with the sphere of influence that the brand wants to establish over a period of time. Product campaigns, especially in the initial stages, can help to achieve this. The different ways in which products are adapted to suit different countries, areas and regions were examined earlier as part of the localisation-globalisation dilemma.

Constructing global campaigns

Not all brands want to globalise their communication. Japanese companies typically allow their subsidiaries, in all their branches, a great deal of freedom at local level. Of course, this creates an impression of disunity since the images projected by the various branches within the same country tend to be very different. But from a cultural point of view, large Japanese – and more recently Korean – groups seem to want to offset the extreme standardisation of their global products (the source of economies of scale) by allowing this freedom at local level. These local subsidiaries are mainly sales subsidiaries whose purpose is to optimise the sales of global products in a particular country. Their local managers are judged on these results, not on the attendant creation of brand equity. Their marketing structures are essentially operational marketing structures, with the exception of Sony, which has developed its brand concept in other countries, and Toyota in the United States.

Another brand that favours a local approach is Bonduelle, a leading company on the European vegetable market, where it has to confront an amazing diversity of situations. In Spain, for example, the brand had to access the market via the frozen foods sector, in Russia via tinned sweetcorn. Peas, its flagship product, vary greatly from country to country. The Germans and Dutch like large, green peas, while the French prefer small, sweet, extra fine peas. In Italy, Germany and the Netherlands, peas are mainly used for decoration (as in a salad), which gave rise to the launch of Bonduelle's 'Crea Salad'. Faced with such diversity, the company has centred its globalisation initiatives around internal values and company dialogue. Furthermore, the name, logo and packaging are the same for all products, although advertising remains very local.

An increasing number of brands want to control their global image. While it is important to start by creating a brand identity platform, this serves no purpose unless it is presented coherently throughout the world. So, if a brand has decided to conduct a voluntarist policy of globalisation, it needs to develop its own procedures for constructing its global campaigns. The most typical are outlined below.

Globalising communications: processes and problems

Today, brands want to globalise their advertising, although this may not be possible in certain situations for practical reasons. There is no shortage of questions on this score. How do brands construct global campaigns without damaging promotional creativity? How do they avoid demotivating the countries concerned? How do they inject a positive spiral into the company, throughout the countries concerned, to destroy the not-invented-here (NIH) syndrome? The great progress made in this field provides benchmarks from which lessons can be learnt. In the following analysis, it will be noted that, first and foremost, these campaigns identify what unites the brand, which is what it wants to globalise:

▮ the brand spirit, the parameters of brand identity;

▮ the brand's visual identity;

▮ the strategic product (prototype);

▮ the executional codes of the campaign.

These must be identified before moving any closer towards an identical copy strategy, a common creative concept or even a global campaign. Companies also vary depending on whether they impose a certain discipline or encourage the search for standardisation.

Contrary to appearances, McDonald's is not particularly prescriptive when it comes to brand advertising. Of course the marketing is global, like the product. With a few exceptions and adaptations (which are the focus of media attention), the concept is strong because it is standardised the world over – even though McDonald's is organised according to national subsidiaries that are virtually independent. With regard to advertising, the company's corporate headquarters run the Ronald McDonald films and charity initiatives, and offer guidelines without seeking to impose any form of obligation or control. This is explained by the McDonald's business model – the form of the advertising cannot be imposed upon those who pay for it, the franchisees in each country who pay 4 per cent of their turnover for the franchise. Once a month, a vote is taken at the country's executive headquarters in respect of future campaigns.

Even so, an incredible impression of 'commonness' emerges from the television ads in all the franchise countries. But this is not the result of any form of constraint – at McDonald's, informality is the unifying principle. It is due to the high level of understanding and sharing, by the group's advertising managers worldwide, of the following elements:

▮ the state of mind of the brand, its concept (food, family and fun, simple human truths) and the essence of the brand (the child within us);

▮ the brand promise expressed according to a traditional 'laddering' (features, functions, rewards, values, personality);

▮ the golden rules of advertising (tenets of Great McDonald's Advertising), such as 'every McDonald's ad is a brand ad' or 'show human relationships', 'stay current: understand me, the client' or 'woven into the fabric of local, everyday life', or 'always put emotion into it'.

As a result, the baselines vary greatly depending on the country, but they all represent the same source, the same identity, whether it is 'Mac your day' (Australia), 'Every time a good time' (Germany), 'Smile' (South America), or 'You know our products from the cradle' (Poland).

To promote even greater standardisation, without damaging the McDonald's business model, advertising films from all over the world are shown at the Creative Brand Seminars held on a regular basis. This encourages countries to use very creative films that, although produced in other countries, are still extremely relevant. The 'best practices' are posted on the Intranet and discussed at McDonald's Hamburger University. Finally, incentives are offered for using other countries' films. Today, 50 per cent of McDonald's television advertising is based on the sharing and use of these 'best practices'.

The car manufacturing group Volkswagen is extremely centralised in respect of marketing, but when it comes to advertising, allows great freedom of expression within a strong brand framework. For example, each country can produce a different film (based on the same strategic and creative brief) for the market's most popular models, because creative advertising is not centralised. However, for less 'mainstream' products such as the 4 x 4 Touareg or the Phayton, a single film is produced by the German group's corporate headquarters.

The new Polo provides a good example of the creative process. It is based on the very strong Volkswagen brand platform. In the past, the brand concept was centred around reliability and the tone characterised by an implicit understanding (humour) with the consumer. Today, due to the presence of the

Skoda and Seat brands, the brand concept has evolved – it is now based on the democratisation of excellence. Then there is the platform of the daughter brand, the framework of the positioning of the model and the consideration of all the models in the 'Tone and Style of VW Advertising' framework. This framework is reminiscent of the principles used by the Tribal DDB advertising agency since 1960, which have created the exceptional distinctiveness of VW advertising and invested the brand with its unique personality. It includes such principles as: 'Do not exaggerate: call a spade a spade', ' Don't shout, he can hear you especially if you talk sense', 'Be authentic, honest, human, open, accessible', 'Make people think and smile', 'Be teasing, elliptic: one should understand only at the point of revelation' and finally and most importantly 'Be original'. In DDB ads, Volkswagen cars rarely move.

The positioning of the Polo that provided a worldwide framework was 'Polo inspires self confidence because you can feel it is the only car in its class that is built without compromise'. Then a creative brief was produced that summarised the advertising objectives, the advertising target and the consumer insight ('I feel I can take on the world'), the product range and the reason to believe. Using this brief, local DDB agencies set to work and came up with the creative idea that was finally used: 'Tough new Polo, careful it doesn't go to your head'. Then the films based on this creative concept were produced by the local teams in each country.

Philips was recently restructured as a centralised organisation for a global brand, with its headquarters in the Netherlands. The new 'unique' brand concept was established – 'A unique experience' – valid for all three market segments (home entertainment, personal expression and professional business products). The company's senior management now decides on the choice of transnational products that will form the basis of the brand's publicity. It centralises briefings and develops the advertising campaigns with local design teams. The pre-test procedure is centralised, as is production, with additional items built in at the filming stage of the ad, to reduce the cost of line extensions.

Nivea uses a similar model, with very explicit guidelines on the brand identity, the personality of each sub-brand, and the strict provisos for handling the publicity that create the 'Niveaness' so typical of all the brand ads, in spite of their diversity. The director of Nivea's Worldwide Marketing, based in Hamburg, appoints three local marketing directors to work on a project, in partnership with the TBWA Hamburg advertising agency. They are chosen from countries throughout the world and their task is to define the creative platform. This is then sent to the local TBWA agencies of the three marketing directors which produce creative ideas and then campaigns. The campaign chosen is then imposed in all countries unless it has to be customised. This happened in the case of the campaign to relaunch Nivea Soft, for which the creative idea was 'soft as the morning rain'. But this had to be adapted for three countries – the UK, where it rains a lot, Saudi Arabia, where it hardly rains at all, and Indonesia, where rain is associated with the devastation caused by monsoons. The adapted ideas for each of these countries were:

- so light, soft sensation for beautiful skin (UK and Australia);

- it feels like under the trees (Indonesia);

- it feels like the summer rain (Saudi Arabia).

These case studies illustrate the typical processes of groups wanting to globalise their advertising. But it should be remembered that globalisation must be pragmatic and take account of strong regional differences (different competitors, different consumer needs). It is therefore advisable to:

- Start by globalising at regional level. For example, start in Asia and then incorporate the United States and Europe, or vice versa.

- Establish common brand platforms (identity) and share the spirit of the brand to create an implicit sense of affinity.

- Establish guidelines for the handling of advertising, which are either limited to using common symbols of recognition or go much further in order to bring out the personality of the brand.

- If necessary, admit that the angle of attack cannot be the same for all markets (positioning versus competitors, the unique compelling competitive advantage), depending on regions and/or continents.

- Remember that, while a single advertisement is of course economically justifiable in the pursuit of this objective, the objective of branding is not to save money but to boost business. Working at international level is expensive since it requires the creation of an international structure, the organisation of lots of meetings, and so on.

- Possibly be more prescriptive with regard to common strategic products than local tactical products.

In conclusion, it is important to define the relationship to be established with the countries concerned – is it a logic of supplier and customer or one of authority, between decision maker and subordinate? Depending on the possibilities, there is a choice between decentralised or centralised management. There are six types of relationship or different managerial functions, as summarised in Figure 16.1, that can be applied to all elements of brand marketing. The globalisation process of each company can be represented on this grid by marking (with a cross) the point of intersection between an element of the marketing mix and the type of relationship with the countries concerned, in respect of this particular element.

Function / Brand mix	Ignore	Inform	Persuade	Approve	Decide	Oblige
Product Concept Positioning Price Distribution CRM Web activity Activation Promotion Advertising – creative concept – executional guides – production						
	Decentralised			Centralised		

Source: TBWA

Figure 16.1   Managing the globalization process

Making local brands converge

A classic strategy for globalisation consists of unifying the local brands inherited during the growth of the groups. Big groups have, historically speaking, often chosen a strategy of external growth through the buying up of strong local brands. The industrial sector typically uses this strategy: Schneider has never stopped purchasing local leading brands of electronics, for instance. In buying these well-established reputations, these companies were able to smooth their way through local markets. This approach also involves fast-moving consumer goods. The former BSN took over the famous Belgian biscuit brand, Beukelaer, the local equivalent of Lu. The Swedish group Molnycke bought Nana in France, which then joined the Scandinavian brand of sanitary protection, Libresse.

Given this patchwork type of situation where there is not much standardisation in the brand portfolio, companies proceed to regroup brands around the same positioning.

Two scenarios are then possible:

▍ The company changes the names of the local brands by substituting the name of its own brand.

▍ In the second scenario, the company decides to keep the local brand equities connected to the brand names. General Motor's branch in Europe is called Opel while in the UK it is known as Vauxhall. However, these brands do need to converge.

The harmonising process of a brand portfolio is quite tricky and should always be conducted on a voluntary basis, since the initial situations of each separate brand name are never the same. A systematic programme of unification according to the style, but above all according to the product basis, must be implemented. The example of Mölnycke is interesting from this point of view. In the female hygiene market, the intimate relationship which has slowly been built up with the client is a key factor in the capital of the brand, of course, there is the product benefit, but there is also the climate of a relationship within the brand identity. This relationship must be maintained. Having judged it necessary to preserve the brand capital attached to Nana in Southern Europe and to Libresse in Northern Europe, at the same time as Procter & Gamble was entering the market with Always, the Mölnycke group progressed in three steps.

The first step consisted of determining together what the unique positioning of these two brands could be. The positioning revolved around the concept of what is 'natural'. Deeper examination revealed that this concept gave rise to different readings, according to the country under examination. In Scandinavian countries, the home territory for Libresse, nature in its strictest sense was evoked, whereas in the home countries of Nana nature connoted spontaneity. The second step consisted of bringing the brand image of Libresse and Nana closer together as they were quite different to start with. Libresse had to develop a more feminine image and more humour, going so far as to include a man in the advertisement for the first time. As for the Nana woman, she had to evolve in her commercials, become more natural with less frivolity, more pared down to the essential, more thoughtful.

This second step was brought about by specific communications, but then having achieved a single concept for the brand, the third step consisted of launching new products shared by both brands with the same commercial.

In conclusion, analysis of this internationalisation strategy enables the definition of the typical pathway to follow in all countries with similar constraints. The process is made up of seven basic steps (see Table 16.8). A consensus of opinion about the kernel of the brand, the deep identity to which all subsidiaries must adhere, is the essential starting point of these seven steps. This adhesion is revealed through visible signs such as logos, codes, tone and style. The ultimate phase is the quest for commercials that resemble each other more and more, until a single commercial is possible for all.

The reader will have understood by now that whether or not to have common advertising is not the important issue. One cannot reduce the question of globalisation to knowing whether it is possible to produce a standard commercial.

Of much greater importance are the existence of one common invisible kernel and competitive positioning and economies of scale at the production level.

Table 16.8 How to make local brands converge

Step 1	Is internationalisation necessary?
	Pertinence of globalisation for the brand or brands?
Step 2	Which brand facets should be internationalised?
	Which ones should not?
Step 3	Agreed-upon description for the network of the common kernel, brand platform, identity prism and positioning
Step 4	Definition of the common visible facets, of the graphic charters, packaging charters, charters of advertising expression
Step 5	Definition of the common copy strategy
Step 6	Definition of the common advertising execution
Step 7	Global launching of common products

Source: Adapted from F. Bonnal/DDB

Part Four

Brand valuation

17

Financial valuation and accounting for brands

Financial evaluation and accounting procedures for brands have become subjects of considerable debate, as can be seen by the numerous articles that have been published on the subject, and also by the number of *ad hoc* committees that have been set up nearly everywhere by national accounting institutions. This intense interest in the subject has several technical, economic and fiscal aspects but especially reflects the discovery of the importance of intangible investments in modern companies and of the growth that a brand can generate in certain cases. The debates are becoming international as they concern the financial information of large multinational corporations holding brands that are strong or presumed to be. However, from one country to another differences exist between accounting procedures for brands and their place on the balance sheet. This could greatly affect the interpretation of the health of these companies. On top of this within the same country, the accounting text and regulations may be contradictory, thus creating certain possibilities which may be seized by certain innovating companies. In this instance the practice was ahead of the

rules and indeed shaped the accounting regulations.

The reason for the sudden interest in this subject – it was hardly mentioned before 1985 – is the large increase in the number of takeover bids for companies with brands. The financial and tax implications of the new problems posed by goodwill were considerable.

When one company is bought by another, there is often a huge difference between the book value of the company assets and the price paid, especially if there are strong brands and positive forecasts of growth. This difference is called goodwill: it is actually a measure of the financial markets' positive attitude to the future of the company. For accounting purposes, the payment by the acquiring company must lead to the inclusion in its balance sheet of what has effectively been bought (assets minus debts) so as to get a perfect match between these elements and the price paid (see Figure 17.1).

In all modern accounting systems and norms, goodwill must be allocated to the specific items that have created it. Brands are one of these, as well as patents, know-how and databases. Hence, it can be said that the question of brand valuation has stemmed from the necessity to account for sometimes huge goodwill payments when major corporations were sold. There are other situations where brands need to be evaluated. For instance, when a brand is purchased, the value of this asset must be made explicit.

Accounting is governed by the principle of prudence. Its evaluations must be shown to be valid, coherent and reproduceable. This is why, paradoxically, only the brands that have been bought individually, or that were included in the price paid for a company, can be posted in the balance sheet of the acquiring company. The overall price paid gives an upper limit to their value. So far, all over the world, the principle of prudence has led national and international accounting norms and standards to forbid the posting in the balance sheet of internally grown brands. It is of course possible to propose brand valuations, but as long as the brands have not been bought and sold, there is too much doubt about the validity of these estimates. Brands acquire value through the market.

Accounting for brands: the debate

The debate on the inclusion of all of the brands, whether they be purchased or created, raises basic questions about the very essence of accounting. Why do balance sheets and company accounts exist? Is it to give an estimation of the true financial value of the company (which of course is very subjective) or, following the accounting prudence principle, to include only objective data and to assess only past and recorded transactions? Until now the second idea has been chosen in all countries: therefore only transactions involving external brands are recorded. If the internal brands were to be noted, the principle of reality would be respected at the expense of reliability and of the consistency of accounting. In fact, what would we think of a balance sheet which was based on non-uniform and sometimes subjective methods of evaluation? The inclusion of an acquired brand does not violate the principle of book-keeping at historical costs, which is a fundamental accounting principle. How then can internal brands be valued? As we will see later

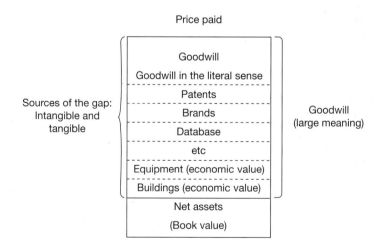

Figure 17.1 The issue of fair valuation of brands

on, the valuation methods, which are based on historical costs or replacement costs, are not good enough. The best methods are those based on projections of future income, which are highly subjective. A certain amount of uncertainty and heterogeneity, which are against the rules of caution, would be created if these were included in the balance sheet.

But one may contend that the function of accounting is to present a framework to identify and deal with a company's commercial expenses which are accumulated in the form of intangible assets that are developed internally. For the moment, these outlays are treated as expenses and are deducted from the company's income for the year in question; this in turn reduces the amount of tax that the company has to pay. However, some tax authorities are beginning to clamp down on the payment of back taxes. For example, they now consider that the money spent to produce advertising commercials can no longer be classified as expenses but are rather investments and thus are no longer exempt from tax.

Accountancy, just like taxation, is interested in the recording of costs (as expenses or as investments). Financial analysis estimates the discounted value of certain assets as a function of the probability of the future income that they are supposed to generate. Thus, there will not be only one value of the brand because valuation methods depend on the goals of the valuation. The accounting principles already exist and can integrate with some reservations the costs accrued during the creation of a brand. It is for the finance people to estimate the market value of these assets according to their own methods. This reasoning already exists for buildings and thus can also be applied to brands.

Here, a first conclusion is taking shape concerning the monetary value of brands: ideally for a valuation method to be acceptable it should be possible to apply it equally well to brands which are to be bought and to brands that already exist within the

company, with a financial aim as well as an accounting aim. However, this is not possible.

The notion of value is highly dependent on your position. Rowntree was worth £1 billion for its shareholders and £2.4 billion for Nestlé! For Midland Bank, Lanvin was worth £400 million; for Henri Racamier and L'Oréal it was worth £500 million. On top of this, accountancy is controlled by a principle of prudence, objectivity and coherence through time. By definition, in its own evaluation, a raider thinks and acts differently. He does not want to be prudent and is rather subjective. The valuation of brands in the context of mergers and acquisitions is a one-off operation: it aims to fix a price at the start given the intentions and synergies that can be expected by the potential buyer. Accounting for brands should obey different norms since their value derives from a different point of view. When there is no transaction involved, the internal brand is valued either as a function of accrued costs or as a function of its everyday usage (and not what another party could do with it). Therefore, there will definitely be a gap between the value of the brand which is bought and of the brand which is created. Moreover, the need to constantly revalue brand values either up or down, in a subjective manner, if they are legitimately noted in the balance sheet introduces fluctuations which undermine the reliability of company accounts. We can reply that the value of the inventory which, in Europe, is indicated annually in the notes to the accounts does not have this effect. It is understandable why the accounting experts at the London Business School who were studying the case for the inclusion of all brands on the balance sheet gave an unfavourable opinion (Barwise, 1989) concerning home-grown brands.

It is a paradox that those who support the most the argument of posting brand values are the marketing people. Perhaps they are hoping to find a method accepted by accountants and financiers of valuing the long-term effects of marketing decisions. However, even though everybody agrees orally that, for example, advertising has both short- and long-term effects, controllers analyse brand performance within a short span of time. Product or brand managers have to produce positive annual operating accounts, positive profit and loss accounts. Thus, evaluation and control are done on an annual basis. This type of behaviour encourages all decisions which are profitable in the short-term. Marketing people would like to have a way to counterbalance this short-term bias, which has the effect of ballooning annual earnings but of eventually undermining brand equity through rapid promotions and brand extensions which are too far from the core activity. On the other hand, looking for gains in awareness at any price may not always add to the marginal increase in brand equity and thus should be halted, with the money put to better use.

More generally, the value of a brand can be measured if the sources of this value can be located, in other words to measure is to understand. Therefore the resulting figure does not interest marketing as much as the process by which it is acquired, that is, the understanding of how a brand works, of its growth, of its increase or loss in value. This understanding is a learning experience and introduces logical and analytical elements to areas where magical beliefs dominated. It also supplies the means for a real communication between people working in marketing, accounting, finance, tax and law. Finally, even if, for reasons linked to tax or respect for the principle of objectivity and accounting coherence, the inclusion of internal brands on the balance sheet is still not recommended and should not be practised by the company, brand valuation remains a worthy exercise to be carried out internally, for all the above mentioned reasons. Mergers and acquisitions are in the end exceptional events even though they do catch the media's attention. The valuation of brands should not be restricted simply to mergers and acquisitions, it is also needed for the benefits that can be obtained from the point of view of management: for help in the decision-making process, for management control, for information systems, for marketing training and for education of product and brand managers. At this time when much is being said about the decline of brands, it is healthy to wonder what the real value of their awareness, image and public esteem is. Brand equity is based on psychological indicators, which are measured from the consumers' point of view, and is only worth something if it results in extra profits. The demands which arise from the presentation of company accounts and from shareholder and investor information are one thing, those arising from a management control system are another. The two should not be mixed up because they do not have the same objectives nor are they faced with the same constraints.

The notion of value is ambiguous and a source of several misunderstandings. It is important to understand that there is no single value for a brand; in fact, there are several because the valuation will be different depending on its aims:

- the value of liquidity in the case of a forced sale;
- the book value for company accounts;
- the value needed in order to encourage banks to lend the company money;
- the value of losses or damage to the worth of the brand;
- the value in order to estimate the price of licences;
- the value for management control, which depends on the behaviour encouraged in managers;
- the value for the partial sale of assets;
- the value in case of a takeover or of a merger and acquisition.

For the last case the buyer only asks one question: by how much will actual income rise due to the acquisition of a company with a strong brand? In order to reply to this question the company will evaluate any possible synergies that may exist between the two companies, any resulting cost savings (due to production, logistics, distribution, marketing), any extra capacity to impose one's decisions on distributors or the possibility of brand extensions or internationalisation. The proposed price for buying the company will be shaped by these questions. However, none of these questions will have any influence on the book value of the company's brands.

What conclusions should be drawn at this stage? Financial valuation of brands allows for the multi-disciplinary meeting of all the company's departments: marketing, audit, finance, production, tax, etc. A capitalistic perspective is introduced in the long run, counterbalancing the logic of annual valuation perspectives. It acts as a reminder of the fact that a company's wealth no longer comes solely from the land, plant and equipment but also from its intangible assets (know-how, patents, brands, etc).

The debate on the value of brands and the way to account for them as assets is essentially an accounting one. This is not the essential benefit, but rather the integration of brand value in evaluating marketing and advertising decisions, which have been up to now subject to one single criterion: the preservation of the annual operating statement of the brand. Before we start to talk about the different valuation techniques, it is important to remember that the real objective of a valuation (for an acquisition or for the presentation of company accounts or for management) modifies the criteria of valuation for these methods. Depending on this objective we will have to choose between these demands which are, unfortunately, not very compatible: more validity or more reliability? more subjectivity or more objectivity? more present value or more historical costs?

What is financial brand equity?

The 1990s witnessed the flourishing of the concept of brand equity (Aaker, 1990). The act of combining a financial concept (equity) with a manifestly marketing-based notion (the brand) is symptomatic of a growing awareness of the financial value of brands, which has emerged from the exclusive world of advertising and marketing to become a very serious factor which – given the importance of equity – has a major impact on overall management.

It is worth mentioning again what is meant by 'equity' in financial terms, and thus what connotations emerge from the combination of the terms 'brand' and 'equity'. Literally, equity is 'the owner's claim on the business'. It represents an ownership interest in an enterprise. This equity (called equity securities) is opposed to debt securities, although both are sources of funds, hence liabilities in the balance sheet. The use of the term 'equity' when attached to a brand refers in fact not to a liability but to an asset, built over time thanks to the investment of the business in it. For the sake of precision one should speak in fact of brand assets, not of brand equity.

Curiously enough, although the term 'brand equity' represents an invitation to combine the marketing perspective with the economic and financial perspective, subsequent events have revealed a disagreement within the community of experts. When it came to measuring this brand equity and discussing what makes a strong brand, there was a split between what some called 'consumer-based brand equity' and others referred to as 'financial brand equity'.

The former school of thought (consumer-based brand equity) approaches the question of brand value by taking the customer's point of view. This in turn leads to several different theories. Some believe that brand value exists wherever the preferences expressed for a brand are greater than a simple assessment of the utility of the product or service's attributes would have suggested. We can see that this approach considers the brand as a surplus, a preference that cannot be accounted for by the product alone. It is measured as a residual:

BE = Declared preference – preference predicted by product utilities

As we can see, this theory sees the brand as the degree of influence that exists over and above the product itself: the brand is thus restricted entirely to an intangible, emotional dimension. However, BMW – one of the world's strongest brands – owes its strength and attraction as much to a product with special, unique performance as it does to the image of its owners that the brand conveys.

Others (Aaker, 1990) maintain that brand value incorporates all of the following variables: recognition, perceived quality, imagery, loyalty and patent quality. Note that according to this definition – and in contrast to the previous definition – the product is included in brand equity because of the patents that make it different or even superior.

Still others, taking a highly cognitive approach (Keller, 1998), see the brand as a collection of memory associations that generate a different reaction to the brand. Keller, for example, speaks of positive customer-based brand equity if identification of the brand produces a more favourable reaction than if the brand is not identified. However, he also defines negative customer-based brand equity as a situation in which such identification leads to a less favourable reaction. Note that in the financial context which produced the notion of equity, there is no such thing as negative equity. The latter school of thought is populated by financial analysts whose role it is to evaluate assets (which can sometimes include intangible assets, and thus brands). From their economic perspective, brand equity is the value today of profits imputable to the brand in the future.

An economic analysis of brand equity requires us to look more closely at the word 'imputable'. The question is, imputable by whom? In contrast to the consumer-based approaches, the economic analysis prompts a simple yet fundamental observation: the brand is a conditional asset (Nussenbaum, 2003). After all, without a product (or service) there is no brand. In order to produce a profit or EVA (economic value added), there must already be sales, and thus a tangible base for the brand and its distribution. Here, 'already' means in advance: spending and paying come before receiving. This gives us the basic equation:

$$\text{Value} = -I + R$$

This equation is exactly the same as the following, more fully developed, version giving the value of any asset. Since an asset is a factor with inherent future values, its value appreciates by the present sum of its future expected profits once the initial investment has been deducted.

$$V = -I + \sum_{t=1}^{n} \frac{(R_i - D_i)}{(1+r)^i}$$

Imputation of added value to the conditional asset that is the brand presupposes the following:

1. That a value already exists to be shared.

2. That the tangible and intangible factors required for its production have been factored in.

3. That a residual or excess profit remains after paying for these advance assets, which make production and distribution possible.

We believe it is time to bring the two approaches to the concept of brand equity together. After all, the brand is a tool for increasing business: its value is linked to, and dependent on, this objective.

Economic analysis tells us that, irrespective of a brand's reputation, image, preference factors and loyalty, the brand has no value if the company does not produce an excess profit capable of paying off the existing assets (tangible and intangible). Reputation and image do not constitute value in themselves if they do not translate into a profitable product or service.

Seen in this way, it is an illusion to believe that a brand has value simply because it has 'magic'. Many entrepreneurs have bought brands on this basis, but have never been able to convert this value into a hard profit. A brand is only worth anything if a profitable economic formula can be built around it; which is something of a paradox, given that this is an entirely consumer-based concept. However, the economic realities are clear: even if a name has an attraction for consumers, it does not guarantee future profits.

This can be illustrated by an example. The now-defunct Ribourel (property development) brand was the subject of a debate on the exact theme of this chapter. How much was it worth? It was shown that it was worth nothing: the brand's image was associated with value for money, but there was no way of turning this into a profit margin. The Ribourel concept was founded on an idea that was strong and attractive, but economically unachievable. The brand had no economic value under such circumstances.

The reader may remember the terse, shocking statement issued by Daewoo in offering to buy Thomson for the symbolic price of one euro. The point being made was that the brand had no value. One might retort that quite the reverse was shown to be true under the management of CEO Thierry Breton; but in fact, what Thierry Breton did was to bring about a change in the business model in order to return the company to added value.

Using the same logic, if a brand can induce the consumer to pay a price differential but the cost of creating the brand is greater than the price increase, the brand has no value.

We should therefore put forward a unifying definition of a brand that has value (strong brand equity): *a strong brand is a name that influences buyers through the value it offers and is backed by a profitable economic formula.*

In this definition, several points should be noted:

▌ Modern competition revolves around concepts and ideas. A name is associated with an attractive, unique value that provides the source of its purchasing influence.

▌ Strength can also refer to the number of people who associate the brand with this idea. A brand is a strong shared idea; for example, everyone says that BMWs are the best cars.

▌ This must be turned into an economically profitable reality.

We can clearly see both the connection and the ambiguity between the purely consumer-based and purely economic approaches. It all hangs on the use of one common word 'value', which takes on two different meanings. From the point of view of the marketer, taking his cue from the work of the psychologist M Rokeach, a value is an ideal to be attained, mobilising our energies and directing our choices. For the economist, however, it is a balance: $V = -I + R$.

A strong brand thus focuses its efforts on attaining a value through the consumption of a product or service which is given its meaning by marketing and advertising. However, this same brand has no economic value if this approach does not result in EVA: it is useless.

An economic formula for the brand does exist: this is one of the two keys to its value.

From economic value added to the brand

Over the last 10 years, intense accounting debates have raged in the United States, mainland Europe and Great Britain over the evaluation of brands. These debates centre around questions with significant repercussions for companies and their profit-and-loss accounts:

▌ When can a brand be activated and recorded on the balance sheet? Does it have to have been bought? If so, this excludes home-grown brands.

▌ Should brands be depreciated? If so, over what period?

▌ How do you reliably assess the value of a brand?

These issues should not be perceived as being of academic interest only: in fact, they ask important questions as to the very nature of brands and their impact on the added value created by the company over the lifespan of the brand. This last point thus prompts the following question: do brands have a life cycle? We know that in retrospect, we can reconstruct the life cycle of a product, with its typical launch, growth, maturity and decline phases. We say 'in retrospect' because during the life of a product, it is always possible to maintain that the situation we know as the mature stage simply points to insufficient effort (too few line extensions, too little international expansion, and so on).

Now, by feeding on new products that replace the old, the brand 'surfs' product life cycles and acquires from them an apparently indefinite lifespan. Nevertheless, the debate on the depreciation of brands leads to very different conclusions depending on whether one believes that brands have a life cycle (and should thus be depreciated), or that they do not. If a brand's lifespan cannot be determined in advance, there is no justification for depreciation.

However, we should start at the beginning, with the question of the nature of brands. Remember that a brand cannot exist without a product (or service): a product or service is needed before the brand can perform its economic role, which is to add value through the differentiation it creates and the added values it promises. In this respect, a brand is a true conditional asset. Its value can take a tangible form only if the company has already made a capital investment in producing and deploying the brand platform – its products or services. The consequences of this point are crucial: the brand is an added value, and thus if we are to take financial advantage of it, we must have profits, but only once we have allowed (at a given rate, t) for the capital required for its production (Nussenbaum, 2003). The company must therefore already have produced EVA. Remember the EVA equation:

EVA = nett EBIT after tax − t (Tangible Assets + Working Capital Requirement)

Still following the basic theory which dictates that the brand is a conditional asset, we should also factor in the cost of other intangible assets that have contributed to the business; for example, patents (which are crucial in the high-tech or medical marketing industries). Once these directly evaluable assets have been factored in, the residual thus derived will create the envelope within which we find the economic value of the brand and of other intangibles that cannot easily be evaluated directly.

This once again raises the question of identifying these other sources of added value. It stems from an assumption which forms the basis of economic and accounting practice worldwide – that a brand has no value unless it is able to produce excess profit even after taking into account the factors that enable the production and distribution of the products and services, regardless of whether these factors are physical and tangible or non-physical and intangible.

This theory of conditional assets accounts for the progressive, steady process of evaluating brands by means of allocating successive residual balances: EBIT, nett EBIT (after the imposition of company tax), EVA, and EVA after the direct identification of certain intangible assets.

Theoretically speaking, then, the brand evaluation process is simple (it consists of a series of successive residual balance allocations). However, for reasons related not so much to methodology as to the company's information system, it is tricky to implement in practice. To put a value on a brand, we have to be able to identify its profits – yet a brand can span many markets governed by a variety of different economic mechanisms, or markets in which factors such as the relative value of the brand in comparison to other assets might not be the same. For example, the relative importance of the brand in sales of a hair products brand is not the same in all distribution channels: it is important in the modern channel (supermarkets and hypermarkets), but very weak when the same product is sold directly by hairdressers, on account of the strong influence of the hairdresser's recommendation to the customer. To develop this idea further: for any given brand in any given channel, the degree to which this brand influences the customer's purchasing decision will vary depending on whether the product is a shampoo or a hair colouring product. Analyses must therefore be conducted individually at the relevant level, not collectively at the overall level. The question thus becomes: do we have the appropriate reporting data that such an analysis requires?

The brand: an identifiable asset?

We know that according to standard accounting practices, an asset can only be entered in the accounts if it can be identified and clear future economic benefits can be attributed to it. Inter-country debate currently rages on the criteria for such identifiability.

Some countries implement a tough criterion: transferability. It is a tough condition because before an asset can be transferable, legal rights for this asset must be held; not only this, but a market must also exist. An alternative criterion has a more economic basis: it is sufficient to be able to trace specific revenue back to this asset. How is this viewed in worldwide terms?

Under current international accounting standards (IAS), an asset is deemed to be identifiable if we hold rights over it: in other words, if these rights can be protected. Logically, therefore, according to this concept, the company can exercise no legal rights over market share or a client base. From the IAS standpoint, an intangible asset can be recorded if:

▓ the recorder controls, holds the aforementioned legal rights;

▓ it is transferable (separable);

▓ it is the source of specific future revenue extending beyond the yearly accounting period.

In other countries such as France, market share can be activated and posted in the balance sheet.

The US position is a pragmatic one: what conditions must be met here before an intangible asset can be entered separately into the consolidated accounts once a company has been absorbed or bought out? They are twofold: separability (it can be transferred independently of the rest of the company) and the unambiguous allocation of specific revenues.

Pragmatically, to avoid ambiguity, the US standard supplies a list of intangible assets. In the Statement of Financial Accounting Standards no 141, FASB), this list specifies exactly what can be allocated: no reference is made to market share. Nor is know-how included, as this is an abstract concept (except in the form of computer software). However, it does include the valuation of a customer database. The US position thus concerns itself less with legal property, instead taking a more economic approach.

The new draft IAS, which will become prevalent in stock-exchange-listed companies throughout the world, is similar in design to the US model.

However, a case does exist where the brand is, and remains, unrecordable: when it is an 'internal' brand, that is, one created by the company itself and thus not bought, or one found in a company that has been bought by or merged with the company. Accounting is subject to the principle of prudence: what is a brand worth? The price paid by a party buying the company already offers an indication in the form of an upper threshold, once all other assets within the company have been deducted at their economic value. When there is a market transaction, then, the value acquires a physical form. Until that time, it is merely a virtual, potential value. In all countries, recording unreliable information in the accounts is perceived as a much greater evil than that of failing to take an economic value (the brand) into consideration.

Value depends on the evaluation goals

Incongruous though it may seem, the brand contains not one value but many: everything depends on the evaluation goals. Thus, if the goal is to assess a contribution containing an intangible asset, to be checked by an auditor, a prudent approach should be taken.

Similarly, it is an universal truth that value is in the eye of the beholder. For example, only Coca-Cola could offer US $1 billion to buy the little round Orangina bottle. With its network of bottlers in all countries worldwide, it would instantly be able to multiply sales of the product – which was based on the same business model as Coke (selling syrup to bottlers) – tenfold. Pepsi-Cola offered less, as did Schweppes: hardly surprisingly, since their brand development plan was simply not on the same scale as Coca-Cola's.

Lastly, we are bound to get different figures when evaluating for estimation purposes than when evaluating for balance sheet recording

purposes. In producing an estimate, it is permissible to include future plans, new production factories and shops that may be opened, or brand extensions into other categories. This makes the brand's future potential look even brighter. However, when it comes to recording for accounting purposes, prudence is required. It is not possible to make use of such predictions, since the projected factories, stores and extensions do not actually exist, and therefore cannot be included. Under European accounting law, no allowance can be made for that which does not exist. However, under IAS such possibilities could be taken into account, taking their cue from the more flexible US standards.

In the Coca-Cola/Orangina case, we therefore find ourselves in an odd situation: the value of the brand appears to differ depending on which company perspective we consider the question from. In the consolidated accounts of Coca-Cola in the United States, the value recorded for the Orangina brand would have taken into consideration the expansion potential from its new distribution. In the accounts of Pernod-Ricard, the company originally holding the Orangina brand, it would have had a different value as part of a transfer operation.

Evaluating brand valuation methods

A number of methods have been proposed to define the value posted in the balance sheet when a brand is part of the assets of an acquired company, or any other instance when this valuation is needed. They can be positioned on a two-dimensional mapping. The horizontal axis refers to time (but do we base the analysis on the past, the present or the future?). This axis discriminates between valuations based on historical costs (those that helped build the brand), valuations based on present earnings, on market price, and those which rely on a business plan: that is to say, a forecast. The vertical axis is a real/virtual dimension. Some analysts rely on hard facts (historical accounts are facts, as well as present earnings). However, some methods rely more on estimates about the present (the replacement method), or about the future (the discounted cash-flow method). We now analyse these methods in turn.

Valuation by historical costs

The brand is an asset whose value comes from investments over a period of time (even though accountants do not strictly regard this as a true form of investment). The logical approach would therefore be to add together all the costs associated with a particular period: development costs, marketing costs, advertising and communication costs, etc. These costs can be determined objectively, and will have been in past income statements.

As we can see, this approach allows us to overcome the tricky problem of separability, by isolating the direct costs associated with the brand and also by attributing to it the indirect costs such as the sales force and general expenses. Even though this method is simple and logical, it nevertheless raises the following practical difficulties, which reintroduce a certain subjectivity:

- Over what period should costs be accounted for? Numerous brands are very old as we have seen: Coca-Cola dates back to 1887, Danone to 1919, Lacoste to 1933, Yves Saint Laurent to 1958, Dim to 1965. Should we include costs right from their beginnings? Everyone knows of old brands that no longer exist. Companies must go back in time and ask themselves if past advertising still has an effect today.

- Which costs should be taken into account? Investment in advertising has a dual marketing role: one part generates extra sales, which can be measured immediately, while the other part builds brand awareness and image which facilitates future sales. The practical difficulty is in estimating year by year the weight that should be attributed to each part. Also, how far ahead

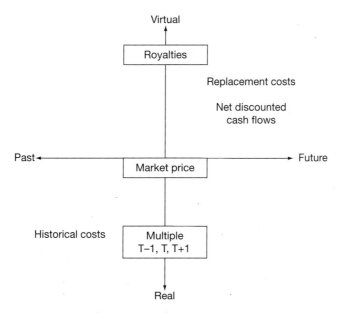

Figure 17.2   Positioning brand valuation methods

are we looking when talking about future sales? On top of this we have to look at the advertising wear-out curves over a given time period. If, as has been shown in studies on the persistence of attitude changes, such effects decrease in a linear manner over, for example, five years, it may be that expenses arising over this period, including only 20 per cent of those for year $n-5$, can be posted.

▌ It is not simply a question of adding up the costs, you also have to take into account an appropriate discount rate which has to be calculated.

On top of the subjective nature of the answers to the above questions, valuation by costs causes several basic problems which are linked directly to a partial understanding of the brand:

▌ When creating a brand, a large part of the long-term investment does not involve a cash outlay, and therefore cannot be posted to the accounts. These include stringent quality controls, accumulated know-how, specific expertise, involvement of personnel, etc. All of these are essential for encouraging repurchase, for the brand's long-term reputation and for word-of-mouth. There would be no trace in the accounts of brands like Rolls Royce because there were no advertisements for it.

▌ One of the major strategies to create a strong brand consists of choosing a competitive launch price, which may be the same as that of competitors even though the product is upgraded. Swatch is an ideal example of this. They could have opted for a slight price differential, or a price premium, to cover the costs of innovation and of upgrading the product. They decided, however, to set an aggressive price that was equal to that of their competitors, thus maximising the brand's price/quality ratio and enhancing its attractiveness. This

is one of its key success factors. Unfortunately, this non-cash investment would not appear in a system where only cash expenditures are registered.

▌ The method therefore favours brands whose value only comes from advertising and marketing and which have a significant price premium. It would not apply to brands such as Rolls-Royce or St Michael (Marks & Spencer's brand) which advertise very little. It could also be said that past expenditure is not a guarantee of present value. There are several brands that are heavily advertised but of little value and are coming to the end of their life.

▌ This method is favourable to recent brands and *a fortiori* to internal brands that are in the process of being created, as we have already seen.

Valuation by replacement costs

To overcome the difficulties arising from the historical costs approach, it might be better to place oneself in the present and to confront the problem by resorting to the classic alternative – as we cannot buy this brand, how much would it cost to recreate it? By taking its various characteristics into account (awareness, percentage of trial purchases and repurchases, absolute and relative market share, distribution network, image, leadership, quality of the legal deposition and presence in how many countries), how much would we have to spend, and over what period, in order to create an equivalent brand?

Is it possible to remake Coca-Cola, Schweppes, Mars, Buitoni or Martell? Probably not. How about Benetton, Bang & Olufsen, Saab or Epson? More than likely. For a certain number of brands, the question no longer arises since it is impossible to recreate them. The context has changed too much:

▌ They were created in an era when advertising expenditure was negligible and the brand was nurtured over time by word-of-mouth. Today, it costs so much for a 1 per cent share of voice that it has become impossible to create a leading brand through unaided awareness. In any case unaided awareness is a restricted area and to gain access a competing brand must leave. This is because of memory blocks. There is no reason why today's well-known brands should allow themselves to be thrown out.

- It is difficult to imitate the performance level of brand leaders. Backed by research and development and an intangible but very real know-how, they enjoy a long-lasting competitive advantage and a resulting image of stability. Any challenger is taking a risk. Unless they have access to the necessary technology, their chances of encouraging repurchasing and loyalty are virtually zero.

- Major retailers have now become exacting gate-keepers. They give pride of place to their own brands, only selling one or two national brands that tomorrow will be international.

- Finally, considering the high failure rate of new product launches, it is easy to understand the uncertainty of the return on the large amount of money that has to be invested in the long term. If you are going to pay a lot you might as well buy certainty. Hence, the clutter of takeover bids, raids, mergers and acquisitions of firms with strong brands that are already market leaders.

On the other hand, when these factors which hinder market entry are no longer present, the market is more accessible. The possibility of creating tomorrow's brand leaders from scratch ceases to be theoretical, even though uncertainty and the necessary time element may still exist. Therefore, future Benettons will probably be created. Franchising allows wider market penetration without admitting defeat at the hands of major retailers. What is more, the fashion industry is open to new ideas. In this domain, style is more important than technology. Computer services and the high-tech world in general are also open to innovation. Generally speaking, the future will see the emergence of new international brands, each positioned in its own particular niche. They will thus no longer seek global awareness but will aspire to be leaders in particular market segments.

Brand valuation by replacement costs nevertheless remains very subjective. It requires the combined opinions of experts and ambiguous procedures. On top of this it should be remembered that the aim of the valuation process is not, in itself, to arrive at a value but to get an idea of the economic value of the asset in question – in this case the brand. Cost methods focus on the inputs, whereas the economic value is based on the outputs – what the brand produces and not what it consumes. Profit is not generated through investments but through market domination and leadership.

Valuation by market price

When valuing a brand why not start with the value of similar brands on the market? This is how property or secondhand cars are valued. Each apartment or car is inspected and given a price that is above, equal to or below the average market price of similar goods.

Even though this method is very appealing, it raises two major problems when applied to brands. First, the market doesn't exist. Although such transactions are often cited in the financial pages, acquisitions and brand sales are relatively few. Brands are not bought to be sold again. In spite of this, we can get an idea of the multiples applicable to each sector of activity (from 25 to 30) thanks to the number of transactions that have taken place since 1983. Thus, such an approach could tempt some wishing to value a brand.

However, there is a major difference between the real estate market and the market for brands, which is relatively small. On the real estate market the buyer is a price-taker, that is, the price is fixed by the market. Irrespective of the use that he or she will make of the property, the price remains the same. For brands, the buyer is a price-setter, that is, he or she sets the price of the brand. Each buyer bases his/her valuation on his/her own views, on potential synergies and on his/her future strategy. Why did Unilever pay 100 million euros for Boursin, the well-known brand of cheese? It can be explained by the pressing need of this group to acquire shelf space in major supermarkets in which it had previously been absent. Having at its disposal a compulsory brand, they saw a way of opening the door to other speciality products. In April 1990 Jean-Louis Sherrer was bought for three times less than the price that Mr Chevalier paid for Balmain two months earlier. For Mr Chevalier, Balmain was a means of entry – or rather re-entry – into the luxury market. Hermès, which was already present on this market, didn't need to pay this price (Melin, 1990).

In abstract terms the purchase price is not the price paid for the brand but is the inter-action between brand and purchaser. To use the price paid for a similar brand as a reference, without knowing the specific reasons behind that brand's purchase, ignores the fact that an essential part of the price probably included the synergies and the specific objectives of the buyer in question. Each buyer has his/her own intentions and ideas. The value cannot be determined by proxy.

This is what distinguishes fundamentally the market for brands from that for real estate, or for example for advertising agencies. In the case of the latter, norms and standards exist that are not dependent on the buyers' intentions (50 to 70 per cent of the gross margin on top of the net assets). Despite this, valuations in the luxury market frequently take into account recent transactions and use a

multiple of the sales (1.5 for Yves Saint Laurent, 2 for Lanvin and for Balmain, 2.9 for Martell, 2 for Bénédictine).

Considering the difficulties which are inherent in the cost-based methods or in the referential methods on a hypothetical market, prospective buyers tend rather to look at the expected profits from brand ownership. Since the third type of approach relies on two major philosophies, we are devoting a special section to it.

Valuation by royalties

What annual royalties could the company hope to receive if it licensed the rights to use the brand? The answer to this question would form a means of directly measuring the brand's financial contribution and would also solve the problem of separability. The figure obtained could subsequently be used to calculate the discounted cash flows over several years. The difficulty is that this is not a very common practice in most markets. They are found in the luxury and textile markets.

From a conceptual point of view, it is not certain that this method properly separates just the value of the brand (Barwise, 1989). In fact, companies often use licences to reach countries where their brand is not present. However, the royalty fee does not include solely the use of the brand. The brand owner also undertakes to supply a package of basic materials, know-how and services, which allow the licensee to maintain the brand's appropriate quality level.

Valuation by future earnings

Since the brand aspires to become an asset, it is best to begin by a reminder of what an asset is. It is an element which will generate future profits with reasonable certainty. Valuation methods have been developed on the basis of expected returns of brand ownership. Naturally, these tie in fully with the purchaser's intentions. If he/she wishes to internationalise the brand, it will be of more value to him/her than to a buyer wishing to keep it as a local brand. The value measured by expected profits cannot be separated from the characteristics of the future buyer and from his/her strategies for the brand. This explains why the stock market value compared to a predator's value of a branded company will always be structurally lower. The former valuation is related to the existing business, taking into account current facts and figures provided by the firm. The latter comes from the over-valuation created by the prospect of synergies, complementary marketing processes and the attainment of strategic market positions.

The process of valuing the expected profits of the brand can be divided into three independent stages (see Figure 17.3):

1. The first step involves separating and isolating the net income associated with the brand (and not with the company for example).

2. The second step is to estimate the future cash flows. This requires a strategic analysis of the brand in its market or markets.

3. The third step involves choosing, by using a classic financial method, a discount rate and period.

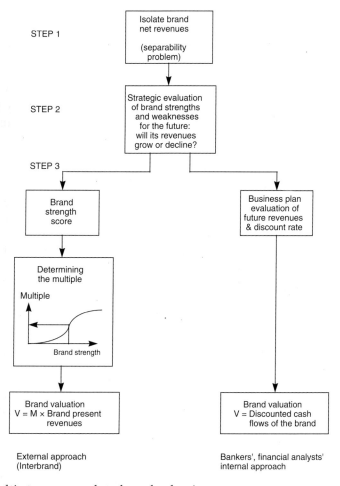

Figure 17.3   A multi-step approach to brand valuation

This is the classic method of valuing all investments, whether tangible or intangible. The analyst calculates the anticipated annual income attributable to the brand over a 5- or 10-year period. The discount rate used is the weighted average cost of capital, which if necessary is increased to take account of the risks arising from a weak brand (that is to reduce the weight of future revenues in the calculation of the present value). Beyond this period, the residual value is calculated by assuming that the income is constant or growing at a constant rate for infinity (Nussenbaum, 1990). The following formula is used:

$$\text{Value of the brand} = \sum_{t=1}^{N} \frac{RB_t}{(1+r)^t} + \frac{\text{Residual value}}{(1+r)^N}$$

where:

RB_t = Anticipated revenue in year t, attributable to the brand

r = Discounting rate

$$\text{Residual value after year } N = \frac{RB_n}{r} \text{ or } \frac{RB_N}{r-g}$$

where:

g = rate of revenue growth

This is the classic model for valuation by the discounted cash flow method, even though analysts offer numerous variations of it (Mauguère, 1990; Melin, 1990). This method was used to value Cognac Hennessy at 6.9 billion francs, based on a capitalisation of its net revenue over 25 years at a rate of 6.5 per cent (Blanc and Hoffstetter, 1990).

This method was also used to value the Candia milk brand as part of a restructuring programme. The final figure, which was around 1.8 billion francs, was the result of a business plan within which two questions were discussed:

▌ Knowing that milk is a commodity, what percentage of Candia's future sales will be generated by products which are heavily marketed, differentiated and have a strong identity which justifies a price premium?

▌ At how much do we estimate the price premium that Candia can demand over more ordinary products? In such markets, even a tiny difference may amount to huge profits.

Sceptics of this method (Murphy, 1990; Ward, 1989) object to its three sources of uncertainty: the anticipation of cash flows, the choice of period and the discount rate:

▌ By definition any forecast is uncertain. This does not apply only to brands, but to any investment evaluation – tangible or intangible – which is calculated by the above method. For brands, cash flow forecasts could be ruined if a competitor launched a superior product which was not accounted for in the calculations. This argument overlooks the fact that these forecasts were made after an in-depth analysis of the brand's strengths and weaknesses (on the basis of the criteria presented earlier). It can be assumed that these were included when the anticipated cash flows were calculated. In any case the discounting rate takes into account the anticipated risk factor.

▌ A second criticism lies in the subjective nature of the choice of a discounting rate. However, on the one hand analysts test the sensitivity of their findings against variations in this rate, and on the other hand, this rate is fixed by taking into account stable company data, such as its average cost of capital. The only subjective factors are the risk premium and the future rate of inflation. Furthermore, very often the risk is zero from the purchaser's point of view as he or she feels that success is a certainty.

▌ Finally, there are those who criticise the choice of period for calculating cash flows. Why 10 years and not 15? What is the value of forecasts made so far ahead? On the one hand, the brand may disappear after only a few years and on the other, in certain volatile sectors three years is already a long time (eg laptop computers).

This is where the view of certain UK valuers comes from. They believe that brand value should be based on that which is certain, ie the net income of the brand at the moment. This is the basis of the multiple method. Brand value is calculated by applying a multiple to the current profits of the brand, measured over three years (t–2, t–1, t). This approach does not need internal data.

Valuation by present earnings

Who can predict the future? How can one be sure that the forecasts of a business plan will be matched? In fact, one of the reasons so many Internet brands have been heavily over-valued is that they made no profit whatsoever (eBay excepted). The brand valuation process relied exclusively on forecasts and business plans which were created just to attract new investors, so the founders could resell before the collapse of the illusion.

Interbrand, a major brand valuation company, has promoted a specific approach to circumvent this problem. No business, no brand. Interbrand valuations rely exclusively on three years: last year, this year and next year. After partitioning each year's revenue to pay for the invested capital which made the business possible and other direct intangible assets, one is left with a global residue, made of a weighted average of the residues of each of these three years. This residue should be then multiplied by a figure called 'the multiple', hence the name of the Interbrand proprietary method: the multiple method. Although Interbrand seems to have moved now to the most orthodox method (discounted cash flow), we analyse this former approach on which many brand valuations have been based.

In the financial valuation of companies, it is typical to examine what is known as the price/earnings ratio (P/E). This ratio links the market capitalisation of a firm to its net profits. A high ratio is a signal of high investor confidence and optimism in the growth of future profits. Even though the brand is not the company, the same reasoning can be applied:

$$\text{Firm}:P/E \quad = \frac{\text{Market value of equity}}{\text{Known profits}}$$

$$\text{Brand}:\text{Multiple} \quad = \frac{\text{Value to be calculated}}{\text{Net profits of brand}}$$

The only difference lies in the fact that for a brand there are no data on its market capitalisation because it doesn't exist, therefore it is this that we are trying to calculate. This notional market value of equity is the price to be paid for the brand (before the effect of overbidding). In order to calculate this, it is necessary to determine M, the multiple which is equivalent to the P/E ratio specific to the brand.

There are four stages to this method:

1. **Calculating the applicable net profit.** Interbrand uses the profits for the last three years (t–2, t–1, t), thus avoiding a possibly atypical evaluation based upon a single year. These profits are discounted to take account of inflation. A weighted average of these three figures is calculated in accordance with what we consider to be the most and least important years. This weighted average after-tax net profit which is attributable to the brand forms the basis of all calculations.

2. **Assessing the brand's strength.** This method uses a set of marketing and strategic criteria to give the brand an overall mark. Interbrand uses only seven of these factors and takes a weighted sum of the individual marks for each factor in order to calculate the overall mark, as can be seen in Table 17.1 (Penrose, 1989).

3. **Estimating the multiple.** A relationship necessarily exists between the multiple (an indicator of confidence about the future) and this score for brand strength. If this relationship was known precisely, the multiple would then be predicted by the brand strength score. For this,

Table 17.1   A method of valuing brand strength

Factor of valuation	Maximum score	Brand A	Brand B	Brand C
Leadership	25	19	19	10
Stability	15	12	9	7
Market	10	7	6	8
Internationality	25	18	5	2
Trend	10	7	5	7
Support	10	8	7	8
Protection	5	5	3	4
Brand strength	100	76	54	46

Source: Penrose/Interbrand (1990)

Interbrand developed a model known as the 'S-curve' which plots the multiple against brand strength.

The model is based on Interbrand's examination of the multiples involved in numerous brand negotiations over recent periods – in sectors close to the one being studied. The P/E of the companies with the closest comparable brands are used. Interbrand then reconstructed the company's profile and brand strength. Plotting the multiples (P/E) against the reconstructed scores results in an S-shaped curve (see Figure 17.4).

4. **Calculating brand value**. This is calculated by multiplying the applicable net brand profit by the relevant multiple.

We can illustrate this method by an actual case. In 1988 Reckitt & Colman valued its brands in this way. They valued household and hygienic goods where they were market leaders, as well as food products (condiments) where they were also a leader, and finally pharmaceutical goods where they had an average position.

The specific situation enjoyed by those brands in the first group is as follows:

▨ world leadership;

▨ growing markets, with few new entrants except for distributors' own-brands;

▨ unaided brand awareness (eg Airwick) high in the UK and in Anglo-Saxon countries but less so in France;

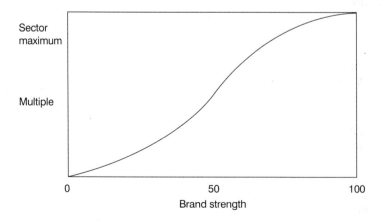

Figure 17.4   The Interbrand S-curve – relation between brand strength and multiple

▮ customers' brand loyalty;

▮ strong brand image and assurance of quality;

▮ for each of its brands, little possibility for diversification.

Reckitt & Colman estimated that 5 per cent of profits on these brands came from sales under distributors' own-brands. Interbrand considered that the remaining 95 per cent was the brand's gross profit. The income generated by the brand can be calculated by subtracting the expected return on investment from net assets. The net revenue was weighted according to the importance of each brand and discounted for the previous three years. The following results were obtained for each category:

▮ household and hygienic products: £53.8 million;

▮ food products: £24.7 million;

▮ pharmaceutical goods: £17.1 million.

What multiple should be applied? For the first group, the multiple used by Reckitt & Colman in 1985 when buying Airwick was applied. A multiple of 17 was used for food products and was based on recent transactions in the sector during the last few years, for example the BSN–Nabisco takeover bid. Finally, a multiple of 20 was used for the pharmaceutical group. In fact, recent transactions in the pharmaceutical industry had been using multiples which were closer to 30. A lower multiple was chosen in this case because of Reckitt & Colman's relatively weak position in the sector. By applying these figures to the net revenue in each category, the following brand values were estimated:

▮ household and hygienic products: 53.8 × 20 = £1,076 million;

▮ food products: 24.7 × 17 = £420 million;

▮ pharmaceutical goods: 17.1 × 20 = £342 million.

Comparison of the cash flow and multiple method

The multiple method, which was developed in the UK, is becoming a classic. It was, in fact, used by such companies as Rank Hovis McDougall and Grand Metropolitan whose decisions to post brand values to their balance sheets caused a controversy which is still not settled. It is also the method which communicates the most through books, articles and seminars. The simplicity of the method used is such that it is uncharacteristic of the stringent world of financial analysis. All this said, is it valid?

First, the multiple method is not all that different from the classic method of discounted cash flow. It is a particular example of it.

When a constant and infinite annual cashflow is expected, the present value of the brand is defined thus:

As we can see, the multiple is none other than

$$\text{Brand value} = \frac{RB}{(1+r)} + \frac{RB}{(1+r)^2} + \frac{RB}{(1+r)^3} + \dots + \frac{RB}{(1+r)^\infty} = \frac{RB}{r}$$

the inverse of the cost of capital adjusted for risk ($1/r$). If a constant growth rate (g) of annual income is expected, the multiple is:

Equations aside, the point to remember is that

$$B = \frac{1}{r-g}$$

we cannot reproach the method of discounted cash flows for making certain hypotheses, since the multiple approach is itself a particular hypothesis, which is equally as questionable but not explicit. It draws its apparent validity from the fact that all its calculations are based upon:

▮ net known profits attributable to the brand over the previous three years;

▌ marketing data and the subjective opinions of managers regarding brand strength;

▌ multiples based on recent transactions by similar companies;

▌ an S-curve, using information from a database to plot these multiples (or P/E ratios) against brand strength scores.

However, face validity (or appearance) does not mean validity *per se*. In its present form, Interbrand's method poses various problems:

1. Market multiples, which were used as parameters for the S-curve, are not valid indicators of the strength of the brands even though they were the mainstay of these transactions. In fact the final transaction price includes both the estimated value of the brand and a certain amount which is due to overbidding. For example, in the fight between Jacob Suchard and Nestlé, the initial bid was 630 pence and the final bid was, 1,075 pence! Market prices include the effect of this overbidding and thus overvalue the brand. It is therefore rather curious that we are trying to link market multiples to a value for brand strength as this value ignores the effect of overbidding. For this reason a certain doubt arises about the applicability of this method to value and post to the balance sheet unacquired, internally created brands. The value attributed to the asset will be greater than the value of the brand as it will include an unspecified amount which is a result of overbidding! The fact that companies may nevertheless have used this method to represent their brands as assets in no way validates this approach.

2. Even in a market where there is no overbidding, the stated multiple measures the value of the brand from the point of view of the potential buyer. It expresses his vision, his strategies and any synergies that he may expect. The fact that in 1985

BSN did not buy Buitoni despite it being reasonably priced does not mean that Buitoni was worth less but means that it was worth less in the eyes of BSN. In 1988 Nestlé valued it at several billion Swiss francs. It again seems strange to try to relate market multiples, which are closely linked to the buyer, to the scores for brand strength, which are calculated by an outsider and do not include the synergistic benefits. This poses a problem when internally created brands are posted to the balance sheet. They are valued in the context of a 'going concern' according to their current benefit to the companies who own them. On the other hand, multiples supplied by the market are calculated with the idea of using them for a totally different reason.

3. For the moment, no illustrations of the S-curve showing the variance around the curve have been published. This variance is a measure of the quality of the empirical relationship between the two variables. As it is, the curve would have us believe that there is zero variance, which is impossible. A single brand strength score probably corresponds to several multiples or at least to a range of values (within which the S-curve is found). Such uncertainty causes problems as in reality the financial value of a brand is very sensitive to even a slight change in the multiple. Going back to the Reckitt & Colman's household and hygiene brands, we see that a one point variation in the multiple results in either a £53.8 million increase or decrease in the value of the brand. This is a far cry from the principles of prudence, reliability and rational certainty which govern accounting practice and information.

4. The very validity of the S-curve is questionable. Interbrand uses the following argument: a new brand grows slowly during its early stages. Then, once it

moves from being a national brand to being an international one, its growth is exponential. Finally, as it moves from the international to the worldwide arena, its growth slows once more. For example, the difference between Buitoni's purchase and resale price signalled the transition of a national brand to a European wide one.

Experience shows that brands are susceptible to large threshold effects. Their strength with customers and retailers is developed in stages. Thus, today, a moderately known brand may be worth virtually the same as a little known one. However, beyond a certain threshold, it grows in value. Research on brand awareness has shown that, in markets with intensive communication, it is only once a brand has reached a certain level of aided awareness that its unaided awareness will start to increase. This is due to a memory block. Likewise, major retailers are replacing middle-of-the-range brands with their own products. These brands rely more on supply than on demand and they would cease to be sold if the retailers replaced them with their own brands. Thus their future is very unstable. This would lead us to believe that the relationship between brand strength and the multiple – provided that both are assessed by the same potential buyer – is better illustrated by a stepped graph (See Figure 17.5).

In conclusion, the widespread use of the multiple method is not proof of validity, as we have just seen, but testifies to its simplicity and handiness for non-specialists, and therefore its internal educational value. A small variation in the chosen multiple leads to important differences in the value of the brand. The present method of choosing the multiple is unsatisfactory from the point of view of reference multiples and of the brand strength scores. What can we make of a total score which is obtained after subjective weightings of factors which are sometimes redundant or in any case correlated? This wish for simplicity is to the detriment of the method's validity. Despite its claim to be accurate, the multiple method in its present form is just as subjective as that of discounted cash flows. To use a hundred or so criteria instead of seven would change nothing. By doing this, we introduce a certain amount of redundancy between the criteria, which results in more weight being given to some factors. As long as the method is subjective, it should remain transparent. The multi-criteria method gains nothing from being summarised in a single score since there are many implicit hypotheses in the weightings.

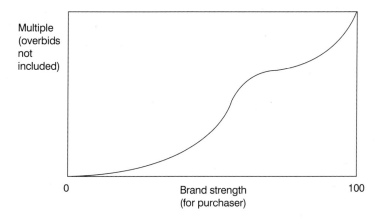

Figure 17.5   Stepped graph showing relationship between brand strength and multiple

The brand profile should be used instead to make a realistic, valid business plan, materialising in discounted cash flows.

Last but not least, the multiple method is too sensitive to small variations of the multiple itself. Multiplying 800 million by seven or eight makes a lot of a difference. Such sensitivity is at odds with the principle of prudence. Brand valuation is not an exact science. It is not acceptable to obtain outputs that can vary by million pounds just by changing the multiple by 1 unit. This is probably why recently Interbrand moved unobtrusively towards the classic financial methodology, the discounted cash-flow approach.

The nine steps to brand valuation

How do we evaluate the brand in practice using the discounted cash-flow method? During a company acquisition, as soon as the target company has been taken over by its buyer, it becomes necessary to record its assets *at their true value* in the consolidated accounts of the buyer company or group. These assets include tangible and intangible assets; the brand falls into the latter category.

Given that the purchase price for the company is generally well above its nett accounting value, the difference (or gap) is known the first consolidation difference, or goodwill in the wider sense of the term. It must be allocated to its various components, the company assets, evaluated at their 'fair value'. The non-allocated residual balance will be referred to as goodwill in the strict sense. How then do we determine the value of each asset and, in particular, the value of a brand? This takes the form of a nine-stage procedure:

1. The first key stage is to segment the brand into strategic units. In order to be able to isolate the share of added value imputable to the brand, we need to work from the bottom up, starting with the factors that produce the sales and profits: the 'cash-generating units' and 'reporting units'. We must identify the excess profit of each of these strategic units, which then allows us to establish what share of this excess profit is imputable to the brand, remembering that this share can vary from one unit to another. Furthermore, the individual profitability structures and growth potential for each unit may be very different.

    Thus, for a hygiene and beauty brand, the relevant unit would operate at product level for each distribution channel. Each product has its own individual profitability structure; and furthermore, the relative weight of the brand in the consumer's decision-making process varies from product to product. Lastly, sales and growth potential also vary from product to product and from channel to channel.

2. The second stage will be to build the forecasted profit accounts using the business plan. Like any asset, the brand has no value apart from the potential for future profit derived from its use. What will this use be? What sales do we expect? At what price? With what sales and marketing expenditure?

    This second stage aims to define the overall share imputable to intangible assets in the financial results forecasted for each of these units, and is known as the EVA (economic value added). This is obtained by taking the product or business's trading profit and subtracting company tax (which gives nett EBIT), then allowing for permanent invested capital and working capital requirement (which gives the EVA). Invested capital is entered at a 'normal' rate (t), the average cost of the capital. This produces the following sequence of residual balances:

    EBIT – Taxes = t (Tangible Assets + WCR) + t' (Intangible Assets)

Nett EBIT – t (Tangible Assets +WCR) = EVA = t' (Intangible Assets)

Remember that these calculations are based on a business plan: they are forecasts for future profits under a specific growth hypothesis.

3. The third stage is where we deduct from this EVA the contributions of other intangible assets once they become directly evaluable: for example, assigning a value to patents based on the usual rates applied in this area, or the virtual allowance made for a portfolio of customers or subscribers, a function of market practices. We should add that if the brand operated exclusively through licences (as is the case with certain luxury brands), its contribution could then be evaluated directly. This deduction, made in order to account for other intangible assets required for business, reminds us that the brand is indeed a conditional asset.

4. So is this residual balance the share of the profit attributable to the brand? Not necessarily: this is where the allocations to the brand and to other potential candidates stage comes in. Here, we should ask ourselves what weight the brand carries in the customer's purchasing decision for each analysis unit (that is, each product in its distribution channel). This is a question for an expert jury to answer. Other methods exist. The customers themselves could be interviewed. A typical study consists first of identifying all the product choice criteria, then measuring the influence each one has in the customer's decision, and lastly evaluating the brand's share in the perception associated with each criterion. For example, we know that the brand has a strong influence on the perception of taste: in blind testings, consumers preferred Pepsi to Coca-Cola, but as soon as the brand is identified, they claim to have preferred the glass of Coca-Cola. Conversely, recognition of the brand has no influence on the perception of its presence in stores. By adding together the respective influence of each of these criteria and balancing these against the role played by the brand in evaluating each of them, we obtain an overall percentage which measures the brand's total influence in the purchase. A typical service station brand will score a 30 per cent rating, whereas a soft drink brand will be of the order of 70 per cent.

5. Once armed with this percentage, we can then calculate year by year, in the business plan, the share of excess profit attributable to the brand for each cash-generating unit or reporting unit.

6. Given that the ultimate goal is to produce a discounted sum of these revenues specifically attributable to the brand, we must first fix on the discount rate to be used. It will depend on our understanding of risks: in other words, are the brand's levers of added value durable in the long term? How is the market growing? Is it open to competition? Is it becoming commoditized? Is it becoming sensitive to price, and thus to distributor's brands? What is its state of innovation? What is its R&D potential, and so on?

7. The purpose of this seventh stage is to conduct a strategic audit of the brand and a 'risks and opportunities' audit, by examining (see Table 17.2):

   – the risks associated with the market;
   – the risks associated with the brand and the long-term status of its differentiating features;
   – the risks associated with the product itself;
   – the risks associated with the company, its staff and its finances for developing the brand;
   – the opportunities for geographical expansion;
   – the opportunities for brand extension into other product categories.

This strategic analysis produces a risk evaluation, and thus a discounting rate for future use.

8. This stage is that of the discounted sum of profits attributable to the brand, based on the discount rate identified above, after the strategic audit of the brand. It produces the brand's value, which will in theory be taken as a deduction from goodwill and recorded on the balance sheet as such. It is a good idea at this stage to check whether the value obtained is especially sensitive to the discount rate used.

9. Finally, an evaluation should not be confined to one single method. The goal of reliable accounts and fair value evaluation demands cross-checking against other evaluation sources. It is true that only the discounted cash-flow method is economically valid and accepted by official accounting and auditing bodies.

But it is also true that other methods exist; these may not be accepted to the same degree, but they can be used for cross-checking results. Fair value has to be obtained through a narrowing-down process; it cannot be calculated directly.

For this reason, it is common to cross-check results obtained from the discounted sum of revenues imputable to the brand with an evaluation based on the royalties method. To do this, we calculate which royalty rate would, when applied to forecasted turnover, give the same overall current royalty value after discounting. It is reassuring if this rate matches standard figures for the sector. For example, in the hair-care products sector, l'Oréal would pay Jacques Dessange 3 per cent of its turnover for products sold under its licence name.

If the gap between the results produced by these two approaches is too wide, a

Table 17.2 Assessing brand strength: strategic diagnosis

Risks associated with the future market	Growth of the market
	Profitability of the market
	Importance of competitor and retailer brands
	Expected technological innovations
	Changes in customer expectations
	Strength of barriers to entry
Risks associated with the sources of brand value	Quality of past advertising support
	Image and reputation
	Quality of trade marks and their registration
	Customer loyalty
	Distributor attitudes and loyalty
	Attitudes of opinion leaders
	Relative position in the market
Risks associated with the product	Life of patents
	Existence of 'me too' brands and product copiability
	R&D perspectives
Risks associated with the business	Financial support
	Strategic coherence
Potential	Potential for geographical extension
	Licensing potential
	Potential for extension into other product categories

complete rethink is necessary in order to identify the sources of the discrepancy and, if appropriate, to correct them. For example, in an evaluation, the value of non-directly-calculated intangibles works out at a royalty rate of nearly 30 per cent. This is impossible. After analysis, it is decided to impute one-third of the value to the brand and two-thirds to the market share (an asset that can be recorded on the balance sheet in some countries).

An alternative version of the above procedure exists. It consists of taking (during Stage 4) the discounted sum of the combined value of all intangible assets; that is to say, the EVA taken as a whole – after having used the strategic audit matrix to establish the discount rate to be used, of course. This overall intangible asset value is thus distributed between each of them afterwards. As we can see, this variation assumes that the basis for distribution remains more or less the same regardless of which cash-generating units and products are involved.

The evaluation of complex cases

The above method works well for most brands, and is the standard approach. However, there are cases where, in order to evaluate certain brands – or brands in unusual market situations – we have to use one of the other methods examined above.

The case of loss-making companies

The above procedure is based on the theory that the brand is a conditional asset, and hence its value is obtained after the deduction of an allowance for the capital invested in production. This poses the problem of how to value brands owned by loss-making companies.

According to the above approach – which assumes a profitable balance – if there are no profits then the brand has no economic value in its current sphere of activity. It acquires value only if a new business plan, with very different cost structures, can demonstrate not only that the company can generate a profit, but also that there will be excess profits even after an allowance has been made for the tangible and intangible assets required for the production and distribution of the product or service.

Financial valuation thus dispels any mirages surrounding the brand: regardless of its reputation and image, a brand acquires value only if it is backed by a profit-making business plan. The term 'mirage' is an apposite one, as many buyers allow themselves to be seduced by brand awareness and image statistics. The economic approach reminds us that reputation and image are worth nothing unless they produce profit – with the help of other assets, which have to be factored in.

The case of abandoned and subsequently resold brands

Companies regularly kill off brands; in order for mega-brands to be created, business operations have to be contracted to just a handful of brands, and many must thus be disposed of. For example, Nestlé abandoned Chambourcy, and PSA abandoned Talbot. Nevertheless, brands can be sold on after several years of inactivity. How can we use the multi-stage approach shown above if there has been no economic activity, and therefore no profit or loss figures? How, for example, can we estimate the value of a brand which has lain dormant for years, such as Talbot, Simca, Studebaker or Plymouth? According to the successive residuals approach, we should assess it as part of the new business plan incorporating this revitalised brand; or in any event, this is what the buyer should do before buying.

Another evaluation method consists of measuring the additional price and margin that the use of the hitherto defunct brand would enable its new user to command.

We have to consider this in terms of the differential margin: although the brand might make it possible to charge a higher public price at the retail level, the retailer might well keep the majority of this increase and hand over only a modest proportion to the end-purchaser. In fact, this is often what actually happens: when the brand is weak, and returns to the market place after a long absence, retailers take advantage of the fact to increase the size of their cut.

It is in the interests of the seller to use a different valuation method. A good candidate is the replacement cost method (the amount that has to be spent now to rebuild the brand and its residual reputation, along with all of its copyright registrations worldwide, for example). As a last resort, there is always sale by auction.

How can weak brands be evaluated?

Some brands remain brands only in the legal sense: they have become mere names, and no longer influence buyers. How are these to be evaluated? This is a common scenario. Given that money was paid for these brands, the replacement cost method is advisable. For example, how much would need to be spent today to:

▌ create a brand in this sector: name research, name tests and so on;

▌ trade mark it in all relevant countries;

▌ devise a graphic theme for a new logo and so on?

How can young brands be evaluated?

This case is similar to the previous one. Once a young brand has proven that it can be profitable (for example, in the fashion market), the commodity being sold is in fact the time and money saved in establishing the legal and image foundations of the brand (its name and visual identity). Going beyond this means indulging in the same sort of risks taken by all investors in the dot.com brands, often to their cost. Unlike our fashion example, these brands had provided no proof that they could one day make money. Without a business, and in any case without profits, they could not be evaluated in any reliable way. This was the cause of the Internet boom: five-year business plans produced estimated revenues which, when multiplied by a factor of between three and seven, resulted in exorbitant valuations.

How can parent brands be evaluated?

Today, brand theory dictates a two-level architecture with a parent brand and daughter brands. For example, Garnier is a parent brand, while Fructis, Ambre Solaire, Feria and Graphic are daughter brands. So how can we calculate the value of parent brands such as Garnier and l'Oréal Paris?

Remember that the first essential stage in the process is segmentation into strategic units: cash reporting units.

It is this requirement that the analysis be conducted at the level of reporting units and cash generating units that provides an explanation of how to evaluate parent brands that contain several daughter brands. Typical examples are Chanel and Dior. For example, there is no such thing as a Chanel perfume; rather, there are products with brands such as Chanel No 5, and Chanel No 18. These are daughter brands. The same is true with Dior Parfum: the reason it has created a Fahrenheit unit, producing profit and loss accounts, is that value is being created at this point. By adding up our evaluations of individual daughter brands, we arrive at an overall cumulative value for them. The value of Dior itself, separated from its daughter brands, is thus a residual one.

What about the brand values published annually in the press?

Given the rigour and hard work required in an evaluation of intangible assets conducted by the company itself, which has full access to all relevant information, what should we make of the annual 'hit parade' charts which appear in the economics press, giving new values for the top worldwide brands (see page 19)? What methodology is used for this?

The Interbrand research company, which is overwhelmingly the main producer of such data, has used two methods over time. Historically, it has attempted to derive values for brand EVA from public information in the annual reports of stock-exchange-listed companies and a variety of other public sources. Not being able to work with a business plan, given the confidentiality of company plans, Interbrand instead analysed data from the last two years. So how does it make the leap from EVA to brand value? It used an estimation of the share of EVA attributable to the brand, multiplied by a figure (the 'multiple'), itself derived from a statistical model based on the analysis of the price/earnings ratio (p/e) for stock-exchange-listed companies such as Gillette. The price/earnings ratio is actually a multiple itself. It compares the stock value with the profits associated with that stock: this will indicate, say, that a stock is worth 10 times its dividend price.

Interbrand configured its statistical model using stock-exchange-listed companies. Knowing the multiple (p/e) for each company, it performed a strategic analysis of its brands, following a method similar to the one we have described for our strategic audit of the brand. The end result of Interbrand's strategic evaluation of the brand is an overall score for the brand, measuring the strength of the brand (the 'brand strength index'). This is the sum of the partial scores obtained from each of the individual audit criteria (see page 466, Table 17.2). The criteria are leadership, stability and so on. It is then easy to identify the statistical relationship between the recalculated strength of the brands and the virtual multiple approximated by the price/earnings ratio (p/e) on the stock exchange. This statis-tical relationship has never been published, but has been represented as shown in Figure 17.4.

Having produced an external estimate of the EVA for each brand, it was then easy for Interbrand to calculate the brand strength index which, when factored into the statistical model, identifies the virtual multiple. All that remained at this point was to measure this virtual multiple as the share of estimated EVA allocated to the brand.

Several remarks can be made about this external procedure, which is used to produce the published 'league tables' of global brand value.

The tables are based on this logic, except that they are not in possession of all of the relevant information (as opposed to, say, an auditor appointed by the company to value its brands). They are thus obliged to obtain an external estimation based on the accounts published by stock-exchange-listed companies, and the figures are subject to a wide margin of error. Furthermore, these league tables cannot measure the value of brands belonging to family-run companies such as Mars, Levi's and Lacoste, which do not release public figures. Nor can they include brands belonging to companies producing consolidated accounts that are not broken down by brand. Lastly, they exclude cases in which sales may be attributable to factors other than pure demand. Consider air transport, for example, where the policy of alliances means that it is possible to end up flying with Delta Airlines after having bought an Air France ticket. Also, a significant part of demand is influenced by exit barriers such as frequent flyer cards: this is not pure demand driven by customer preference.

Other critical remarks may be made about this approach, as we have already seen, including sensitivity to variations in the multiple, and the validity of the graph.

Recently, Interbrand seems to have changed its method of producing its 'global brand value' league tables, moving towards a more conventional financial and economic approach. Although its methodology has not been explicitly published, reference has been made to 'net present value of future brand earnings', which would be more in line with our recommended nine-step process. However, questions must be asked as to the validity of estimating these future brand earnings, without internal access to the company in question, by 'experts' with no knowledge of the actual business plan or the real financial data. Yet it is on such fragile estimates that the annual brand table published by *Business Week* – and faithfully reproduced by the world's economic press – is based.

Bibliography

Aaker, D (1990) Brand extensions: the good, the bad and the ugly, *Sloan Management Review*, Summer, pp 47–56

Aaker, D (1991) *Managing Brand Equity*, Free Press, New York

Aaker, J (1997) Dimensions of brand personality, *Journal of Marketing Research*, **24**, Aug, pp 347–56

Aaker, D (1996) *Building Strong Brands*, Free Press, New York

Aaker, J (1995) Conceptualizing and measuring brand personality, Working Paper no 255, Anderson Graduate School of Management, UCLA

Aaker, D and Biel, A (1993) *Brand Equity and Advertising*, Lawrence Erlbaum, Hillsdale, New Jersey

Aaker, D and Joachimstahler E (2000) *Brand Leadership*, Free Press, New York

Aaker, D and Keller, K L (1990) Consumer evaluations of brand extensions, *Journal of Marketing*, Jan, **54** (1), pp 27–41

Abric, J-C (1994) Pratiques sociales et représentations, Presses Universitaires de France, Paris

Advertising Research Foundation (1995) *Exploring Brand Equity*, Advertising Research Foundation, New York

Agefi (1990) Le goodwill, objet de controversé en Europe, *Agefi*, 1 Feb

AhluWalia, R (2000) Examination of psychological processes underlying resistance to persuasion, *Journal of Consumer Research*, **27** (2), Sep, pp 217–32

Ailawadi, K and Harlam, B (2004) The determinants of retail margins: the role of store brand share, *Journal of Marketing*, **68** (1), Jan, pp 147–65

Ailawadi, K, Lehmann, D and Neslin, S (2003) Revenue premium as an outcome measure of brand equity, *Journal of Marketing*, **67** (4), Oct, pp 1–17

Alba, J W and Chattopadhyay, A (1986) Salience effects in brand recall, *Journal of Marketing Research*, **23**, p 369

Alden, D, Steenkamp, and Batra, R (1999) Brand positioning through advertising in a global consumer culture, *Journal of Marketing*, 63

Alden, D, Steenkamp, J-B and Smith, R E (1999) Brand positioning in Asia, North America and Europe, *Journal of Marketing*, **63** (1), pp 75–87

Ambler, T and Styles, C (1996) Brand development versus new product development, *Marketing Intelligence and Planning*, **14** (7), pp 10–19

Arnault, B (2000) *La Passion Creative*, Plon: Pocket, Paris

Arnold, T (1989) Accounting for the value of brands, *Accountant's Magazine*, Feb, p 12

Azoulay, A and Kapferer, J-N (2003) Do brand personality scales really measure brand personality?, *Journal of Brand Management,* **11** (2), Nov, pp 143–55

Baillot, J (1990) La marque et l'automobile, *Humanisme et Entreprise*, **181**, June, pp 5–8

Balachander, S (2003)

Balachander, S and Ghose, S (2003) Reciprocal spillover effects: a strategic benefit of brand extensions, *Journal of Marketing*, **67** (1), Jan, pp 4–14

Baldinger, A (1992) What CEOs are saying about brand equity, *Journal of Advertising Research*, Jul/Aug, **32** (4), pp 6–12

Barwise, P (1989) *Accounting for Brands*, London Business School

Barwise, P (1993) Brand equity: snark or boojum, *International Journal of Research in Marketing*, **10** (2), pp 93–104

Batra, R (2002) How brand reputation affects the relationship of advertising and brand equity outcomes, *Journal of Advertising Research*

Bedbury, S (2002) *A New Brand World*, Viking, New York

Bell, D, Lal, R and Salmon, W (2003) Globalization of retailing, Globalization of Markets Colloquium, Harvard Business School, May

Berard, C (1990) La marque: élément du patrimoine de l'entreprise, *Revue de l'ENA*, 202, May, pp 24–25

Berry, N C (l988) Revitalizing brands, *Journal of Consumer Marketing*, **5** (Summer), pp l5–20

Birkigt, K and Stadler, M M (1980) *Corporate Identity: Grundlagen, Funktionen, Fallbeispiele*, Verlag Moderne Industrie, Munich

Birol, J and Kapferer, J-N (1991) Les campagnes collectives, Internal document, Agence Sicquier-Courcelles/HEC

Blackett, T (1985) The role of brand valuation in marketing strategy, *Marketing and Research Today*, Nov, pp 245–47

Blackston, M (1992) Building brand equity by managing the brand's relationships, *Journal of Advertising Research*, May/Jun, **32** (3), pp 79–83

Blanc, C and Hoffstetter, P (1990) L'évaluation des marques, HEC Research paper, under the direction of J-N Kapferer, June, Jouy-en-Josas

Boddewyn, J, Soehl, R and Picard, J (1986) 'Standardization in international marketing: is Ted Levitt in fact right?, *Business Horizons*, pp 69–75

Bon, J, Michon, C and Ollivier, A (1981) Etude empirique de la demographie des marques: le rôle de la publicité, Fondation Jours de France pour la recherche en publicité, Paris

Bontemps, A and Lehu, J-M (2002) *Lifting de marque*, Editions d'Organisation, Paris

Bottomley, P P and Holden, S (2001) Do we really know how consumers evaluate brand extensions?, *Journal of Marketing Research*, **38**, Nov, pp 494–501

Botton, M and Cegarra, J J (1990) *Le nom de marque*, McGraw-Hill, Paris

Boush, D (1993) Brands as categories, in *Brand Equity and Advertising*, ed D Aaker and A Biel, Lawrence Erlbaum, Hillsdale, NJ, pp 299–312

Brandenburger, A and Nalebuff, B (1996) *Coopetition*, Doubleday, New York

Broadbent, S (1983) *Advertising Works 2*, Holt, Rinehart and Winston, London

Brodbeck, D and Mongibeaux, J F (1990) *Chic et Toc: le vrai livre des contrefaçons*, Balland, Paris

Broniarczyk, S and Alba, J (1994) The importance of the brand in brand extension, *Journal of Marketing Research*, **31**, May, pp 214–28

Brown, S, Kozinets, R and Sherry, J F (2003) Teaching old brands new tricks, *Journal of Marketing*, **67** (3), Jul, pp 19–33

Brown, T and Dacin, P (1997) The company and the product: corporate associations and consumer product responses, *Journal of Marketing*, **61** (1), Jan, pp 68–84

Buchan, E and Brown, A (1989) Mergers and acquisitions, in *Brand Valuation*, ed J Murphy, Hutchinson Business Books, London, pp 81–94

Buchanan, W, Simmons, R and Bickart, S (1999) Brand equity dilution: retailer display and context brand effects, *Journal of Marketing Research*, Aug, **36**, pp 345–55

Buck, S (1997) The continuing grocery revolution, *Journal of Brand Management*, **4** (4), pp 227–38

Burgaud, D and Mourier, P (1989) Europe: développement d'une marque, *MOCI*, **889**, pp 125–28

Buzzell, R D (1968) Can you standardize multinational marketing?, *Harvard Business Review*, Nov–Dec

Buzzell, R D and Gale, B T (1987) *The PIMS Principles*, Free Press, New York

Buzzell, R D, Gale, B T and Sultan, R G (1975) Market share – a key to profitability, *Harvard Business Review*, Jan–Feb, pp 97–106

Buzzell, R D and Quelch, J A (1988) *Multinational Marketing Management*, Addison Wesley, New York

Buzzell, R D and Quelch, J A (1990) *The Marketing Challenge of 1992*, Addison Wesley, New York

Cabat, O (1989) Archéologie de la marque moderne, in *La marque*, ed J-N Kapferer and J C Thoenig, McGraw-Hill, Paris

Carpenter, G and Nakamoto, K (1990) Competitive strategies for late entry into market with a dominant brand, *Management Science*

Carratu, V (1987) Commercial counterfeiting, in *Branding: A key marketing tool*, ed J Murphy, McGraw-Hill, London

Carroll, J M (1985) *What's in a Name?* Freeman, New York

Cauzard, D, Perret, J and Ronin, Y (1989) *Image de marque et marque d'image*, Ramsay, Paris

Chan, C and Mauborne, R (2000) Value innovation, *Harvard Business Review*

Channon, C (1987) *Advertising Works 4*, Cassell, London

Chanterac, V (1989) La marque a travers le droit, in *La marque*, ed J-N Kapferer and J C Thoenig, McGraw-Hill, Paris

Charbonnier, C and Lombard, E (1998) Can multi-product brands support various personalities? Esomar Annual Conference Proceedings, Vienna

Chateau, J (1972) *Les sources de l'imaginaire*, Editions Universitaires, Paris

Chaudhuri, A (2002) How brand reputation affects the advertising brand equity link, *Journal of Advertising Research*, May-June

Chevalier, M (2003) *Pro Logo*, Editions d'Organisation, Paris

Chinardet, C (1994) *Trade-Marketing*, Editions d'Organisation, Paris

Chip, H, Bell, C and Sternberg, E (2001) Emotional selection in memes: the case of urban legends, *Journal of Personality and Social Psychology*, **81**, Dec, pp 1028–41

Christensen, C (1997) *The Innovator's Dilemma*, Harvard Business School Press, Cambridge, MA

Clarke, D G (1976) Econometric measurement of the duration of advertising effect on sales, *Journal of Marketing Research*, **13**, Nov, pp 345–50

Claycamp, H and Liddy, L (1969) Prediction of new product performance, *Journal of Marketing Research*, **6** (3), Nov, pp 414–20

Cohen, M, Eliashberg, J and Ho, T (1997) An anatomy of a decision support system for developing and launching line extensions, *Journal of Marketing Research*, **34** (1), Feb, pp 117–29

Collins, J and Porras, J (1994) *Built to Last*, Harper Business, London

Conseil National de la Comptabilité (1989) La formation du capital commercial dans l'entreprise, 27.A.89.16, Sep

Cooper, M (1989a) The basis of brand evaluation, *Accountancy*, Mar, p 32

Cooper, M (1989b) Brand valuation in the balance, *Accountancy*, Jul, p 28

Corstjens M and Lal, R (2000) Building store loyalty through store brands, *Journal of Marketing Research*, **37** (3)

Corstjens, J and Corstjens, M (1995) *Store Wars: The battle for mindspace and shelfspace*, Wiley, London

Corstjens, M (1999) *Store Wars*, Wiley, Chichester

Crimmins, J (1992) Better measurement and management of brand value, *Journal of Advertising Research*, Jul/Aug, **32** (4), pp 11–19

Cross, R and Smith, J (1994) *Customer Bonding*, NTC Business Books

Crozier, M (1989) *L'Entreprise à l'Ecoute: apprendre le management post-industriel*, InterEditions, Paris

Dacin, P and Smith, D (1994) The effect of brand portfolio characteristics on consumer evaluations of brand extensions, *Journal of Marketing Research*, **31**, May, pp 229–42

Darby, M and Kami, E (1973) Free competition and the optimal amount of fraud, *Journal of Law and Economics*, **16** (1), pp 67–88

Davidson, J H (1987) *Offensive Marketing*, Gower Press, London

Davis, S (2000) *Brand Asset Management*, Jossey-Bass, San Francisco, CA

Dawar, N (2002) How brand reputation affects the relationship of advertising and brand equity outcomes, *Journal of Advertising Research*

Dawar, N and Anderson, P (1992) Determining the order and direction of multiple brand extensions, Working Paper no 92/36/MKT, INSEAD

De Chernatony, L (1996) Integrated brand building using brand taxonomies, *Marketing Intelligence and Planning*, **14** (7), pp 40–45

De Chernatony, L and McDonald, M (1994) *Creating Powerful Brands*, Butterworth-Heinemann, Oxford

Defever, P (1989) L'utilisation de la communication électronique sur les lieux de vente, *Revue francaise du marketing*, **123** (3), pp 5–15

Degon, R (l994) La marque et le prix, *Journée IREP La Marque*, Sep, pp 28–38

Dhalla, N K (1978) Assessing the long term value of advertising, *Business Review*, **56**, Jan–Feb, pp 87–95

Diefenbach, J (1987) The corporate identity as the brand, in *Branding: A key marketing tool*, ed J Murphy, McGraw-Hill, London

Dru, J-M (1996) *Disruption*, Wiley, New York

Dru, J-M (2002) *Beyond Disruption*, Wiley, New York

Dubois, B and Paternault, C (1995) Understanding the world of international luxury brands, *Journal of Advertising Research*, **35** (4), Jul–Aug, pp 69–76

Durand, G (1964) *L'imagination symbolique*, PUP, Paris

Durand, G (1969) *Les Structures Anthropologiques de l'Imaginaire*, Bordas, Paris

Duvillier, J P (1987) L'absence d'enregistrement à 1'actif du fonds de commerce, *Revue française de comptabilité*, October, **183**, p 36

Dyson, P, Farr, A and Hollis, N (1996) Understanding, measuring and using brand equity, *Journal of Advertising Research*, **36** (6), Nov–Dec, pp 9–21

East, R and Hammund, K (1996) The erosion of repeat-purchase loyalty, *Marketing Letters*, **7** (2), pp l63–71

Ehrenberg, A (1972) *Repeat Buying*, Edward Arnold, London

Ehrenberg, A, Barnard, N, Kennedy, R and Bloom, H (2002) Brand advertising as creative publicity, *Journal of Advertising Research*, **42** (4), Jul/Aug, pp 7–18

Eiglier, P and Langeard, E (1990) *Servuction*, Editions d'Organisation

Eliade, M (1952) *Images et Symboles*, Gallimard, Paris

Erdem, T, Zhao, Y and Valenzuela, A (2004) Performance of store brands: a cross country analysis of consumer store brand preferences, perceptions and risk, *Journal of Marketing Research*, **41**, pp 86–100

Farquhar, P H (1989) Managing brand equity, *Marketing Research*, Sep, **1** (3), pp 24–33

Farquhar, P H (1994) Strategic challenges for branding, *Marketing Management*, **3** (2), pp 9–15

Farquhar, P H, Han, J, Herr, P and Ijiri, Y (1992) Strategies for leveraging master brands, *Marketing Research*, Sep, pp 32–39

Feldwick, P (1996) What is brand equity anyway and how do you measure it ?, *Journal of the Market Research Society*, **38**, pp 85–104

Feldwick, P and Bonnal, F (1995) Reports of the death of brands have been greatly exaggerated, *Marketing and Research Today*, **23** (2), May, pp 86–95

Feral, F (1989) Les signes de qualité en France à la veille du grand marché communautaire et à la lumière d'autres systèmes, *CERVAC*, Université d'Aix Marseille 3, October

Financial Times (1993) *Accounting for Brands*, London, FTBI Report

Firat, F and Dholakia, N (1998) *Consuming People*, Routledge, London

Folz, J-M (2003) Managing two brands for success: Peugeot and Citroen, in *Marken Management in der Automobilindustrie*, ed R Kalmbach and B Gottschalk, Auto Business Verlag, pp 341–62

Fombrun, C (2001) Corporate reputation, *Thexis*, **4**, pp 23–27

Fombrun, C, Gardberg, J and Sever, J (2000) The reputation quotient, a multi stakeholder measure of corporate reputation, *Journal of Brand Management* (7), pp 241–55

Fourcade, A and Cabat, (1981) *Anthropologie de la publicité*, Fondation Jours de France pour la recherche en publicité

Fournier, S (1998) Consumers and their brands, *Journal of Consumer Research*, **24** (4), Mar, pp 343–73

Frey, J B (1989) Measuring corporate reputation and its value, Marketing Science Conference, Duke University, NC, USA, 17 March

Fry, J N (1967) Family branding and consumer brand choice, *Journal of Marketing Research*, **4**, Aug, pp 237–47

Fry, J N, Shaw, D, Haehling, C and Dipchand, C (1973) Customer loyalty to banks: a longitudinal study, *Journal of Business*, **46**, pp 517–25

Gali, J (1993) Does consumer involvement impact evaluations of brand extensions?, unpublished doctoral dissertation, HEC Graduate School of Management

Gamble, T (1967) Brand extension, in *Plotting Marketing Strategy*, ed L Adler, Interpublic Press Books, New York

Garbett, T (1981) *Corporate Advertising*, McGraw-Hill, New York

Geary, M (1990) Fusions et acquisitions: le problème de goodwill, in *Seminaire: Le traitement du goodwill*, 1 February, PF Publications Conferences, Paris

Gelle, T (1990) La comptabilisation des marques, HEC research paper, under the direction of L Collins, May, Jouy-en-Josas

Glemer, F and Mira, R (1993) The brand leader's dilemma, *McKinsey Quarterly*, 2, pp 34–44

Greener, M (1989) The bomb in the balance sheet, *Accountancy*, August, p 30

Greig, I and Poynter, R (1994) Brand transfer: building the Whirlpool brand in Europe, *Esomar Conference Proceedings, 26–29 October, Building Successful Brands*, pp 65–78

Guest, L (1964) Brand loyalty revisited: a twenty years report, *Journal of Applied Psychology*, **48** (2), pp 93–97

Gürhan-Canli and Maheswaran (1998) The effects of extensions on brand name dilution enhancement, *Journal of Consumer Research*, **35**, Nov, pp 464–73

Hague, P and Jackson, P (1994) *The Power of Industrial Brands*, McGraw-Hill, London

Hallberg, G (1995) *All Consumers are not Created Equal*, Wiley, New York

Hamel, G and Prahalad, C (1985) Do you really have a global strategy?, *Harvard Business Review*, Jul–Aug

Hamel, G and Prahalad, C K (1994) *Competing for the Future*, Harvard Business School Press, Boston, MA

Heather, E (1958) What's in a brand name, *Management Review*, Jun, pp 33–35

Heilbrunn, B (2003) The drivers of brand attachment, Working paper, EM Lyon

Heller, R (1986) On the awareness effects of mere distribution, *Marketing Science*, **5**, Summer, p 273

Hem, L (2003) Context effects in brand extensions: implications for evaluations, *Annual EMAC Conference Proceedings*

Henderson, P and Cote, J (1998) Guidelines for selecting or modifying logos, *Journal of Marketing*, **62** (2), Apr, pp 14–30

Hill, S and Lederer, C (2001) *The Infinite Asset*, Harvard Business School Press, Boston, MA

Hirschmann, E and Holbrook, M (1982) Hedonic consumption, *Journal of Marketing*, **46** (2), pp 92–101

Hite, R and Fraser, C (1988) International advertising strategies of multinational corporations, *Journal of Advertising Research*, Aug/Sep, **28** (4), pp 9–17

Hoch, S (1996) How should national brands think about private labels?, *Sloan Management Review*, **37**, Winter, pp 89–102

Hoch, S and Banerji, S (1993) When do private labels succeed?, *Sloan Management Review*, Summer, pp 57–67

Holbrook M, Hirschmann E (1982) The experiential aspects of consumption, *Journal of Consumer Research*, **9**, 2, Sep, pp 132–40

Holt, D, Quelch, J and Taylor, E (2003) Managing the transnational brand: how global perceptions drive value, Globalization of Markets Colloquium, Harvard Business School

Hout, T, Porter, M and Rudder, E (1982) How global companies win out, *Harvard Business Review*, Sep–Oct

Hussey, R and Ong, A (1997) Accounting for goodwill and intangible assets, *Journal of Brand Management*, **4** (4), pp 239–47

Ind, N (2001) *Living the Brand*, Kogan Page, London

Interbrand (1997) *Brand Valuation*, Premier Books, London

Interbrand (1998) *Brands: The new wealth creators,* Macmillan Business, Basingstoke

IREP (1994) *La Marque*, Seminar on Branding, September, Institut de Recherches et d'Etudes Publicitaires, Paris

Jacobson, R and Aaker, D (1985) Is market share all that it's cracked up to be?, *Journal of Marketing*, **45** (4), Fall, pp 11–22

Jacoby, J and Chestnut, R (1978) *Brand Loyalty and Measurement*, Wiley, New York

Jaubert, M J (1985) *Slogan, mon Amour*, Bernard Barrault Editeur, Paris

Joachimsthaler, E and Aaker, D (1997) Building brands without mass media, *Harvard Business Review*, **75** (1), Jan–Feb, pp 39–52

Jones, J P (1986) *What's in a Name: Advertising and the concept of brands*, Lexington Books, Lexington, KY

Kapferer, J-N (1986) Beyond positioning, retailer's identity, *Esomar Seminar Proceedings, Brussels, 4–6 June*, pp l67–76

Kapferer, J-N (1991) *Rumors: Uses, interpretations and images*, Transactions, New Brunswick

Kapferer, J-N (1995a) Stealing brand equity: measuring perceptual confusion between national brands and copycat own-label products, *Marketing and Research Today*, **23** (2), May, pp 96–103

Kapferer, J-N (1995b) Brand confusion: empirical study of a legal concept, *Psychology and Marketing*, **12** (6), pp 551–68

Kapferer, J-N (1996) Alternative methods for measuring brand confusion created by retailers imitation, HEC Research Report

Kapferer, J-N (1998) The role of branding in medical prescription, HEC Graduate School of Management, Research Paper Series

Kapferer, J-N (2001) *Reinventing the Brand*, Kogan Page, London

Kapferer, J-N (2003) Corporate and brand identity, in *Corporate and Organizational Identities*, ed B Moingeon, Routledge, London

Kapferer, J-N (2004) Building brands by rumors, in *Rumours as Medium: Facetten der medienkultur* (Vol 5), ed M Bruhn, V Kaufmann, W Wunderlich and A Haupt, Springer, Berlin

Kapferer, J-N and Laurent, G (1988) Consumers' brand sensitivity: a new concept for brand management, in *Defining, Measuring and Managing Brand Equity, Marketing Science Institute: A conference summary*, Report pp 88–104, MSI, Cambridge, MA

Kapferer, J-N and Laurent, G (1995) *La Sensibilité aux Marques*, Editions d'Organisation, Paris

Kapferer, J-N and Laurent, G (1996) How consumers build their perception of mega-brands, unpublished working paper, HEC Graduate School of Management

Kapferer, J-N and Laurent, G (2002) *Identifying Brand Prototypes*, HEC Research Report

Kapferer, J-N and Thoenig, J C (1989) *La Marque*, McGraw-Hill, Paris

Kapferer, J-N, Thoenig, J C *et al* (1991) Une analyse empirique des effets de l'imitation des marques par les contremarques: mesure des taux de confusion au tachystoscope, *Revue française du marketing*, Jan, 136, pp 53–68

Kapferer, J-N Thoenig, JC (1992) *La Confusion des Marques*, Prodimarques, Paris

Kapferer, P and Gaston Breton (2002) Lacoste: the legend, chen Church Ridir, Paris

Keller, K L (1992) Conceptualising, measuring and managing customer based brand equity, *Journal of Marketing*, Jan, pp 1–22

Keller, K L (1998) *Strategic Brand Management*, Prentice Hall

Keller, K (2003) Brand synthesis: the multidimensionality of brand knowledge, *Journal of Consumer Research*, **29** (4), pp 595–600

Keller, K L and Aaker, D (1992) The effects of sequential introduction of brand extensions, *Journal of Marketing Research*, **29** (1), Feb, pp 35–50

Keller, K, Heckler, S and Houston, M (1998) The effects of brand name suggestiveness on advertising recall, *Journal of Marketing*, **62** (1), pp 48–58

King, S (1973) *Developing New Brands*, Wiley, New York

Kirmani, A, Sood, S and Bridges, S (1999) The ownership effect in consumer responses to brand line stretches, *Journal of Marketing*, **63** (1), pp 88–101

Kleiber, G (1990) *La Semantique du Prototype*, Presses Universitaires de France, Paris

Klein, N (1999) *No Logo*, Picador, New York

Klink, R and Smith, D (2001) Threats to the external validity of extension research, *Journal of Marketing Research*, **38**, Aug, pp 326–35

Knox, S (1996) The death of brand deference, *Marketing Intelligence and Planning*, **14** (7), pp 35–39

Kotler, P (1973)

Kotler, P (2002) *Kotler on Marketing*, Paris: Village Mondial

Kotler, P and Dubois, B (1991) *Marketing Management*, Publi-Union, Paris

Kotler, P and Gertner, D (2002) Country as a brand, product and beyond, *Journal of Brand Management*, **9** (4–5), Apr, pp 249–61

Kozinets, R (2002) Tribalized marketing: the strategic implications of virtual communities of consumption, *European Management Journal*, 17, June, pp 252–64

Krief, Y (1986) L'entreprise, l'institution, la marque, *Revue française du marketing*, **109**, pp 77–96

Krief, Y and Barjansky, M (1981) La marque: nature et fonction, *Stratégies*, 261 and 262, pp 37–41, 32–36

Kripke, S (1980) *Naming and Necessity*, Harvard University Press, Cambridge, MA

Laforet, S and Saunders, J (1994) Managing brand portfolios: how the leaders do it, *Journal of Advertising Research*, **34** (5), pp 64–67

Lai, K and Zaichkowsky, J (1999) Brand imitation: do the Chinese have different views, *Asia Pacific Journal of Management*, **16** (2), pp 179–92

Lakoff, G (1987) *Women, Fire and Dangerous Things*, University of Chicago Press, Ill

Lane, V and Jacobson, R (1995) Stock market reactions to brand extension announcements, *Journal of Marketing*, **59** (1), pp 63–77

Laurent, G and Kapferer, J-N (1985) Measuring consumer involvement profiles, *Journal of Marketing Research*, **22**, pp 41–53

Laurent, G, Kapferer, J-N and Roussel, F (1987) Thresholds in brand awareness, *40th Esomar Marketing Research Congress Proceedings*, Montreux, Sep 13–17, pp 677–99

Laurent, G, Kapferer, J-N and Roussel, F (1995) The underlying structure of brand awareness scores, *Marketing Science*, **14** (3), pp 170–79

Leclerc, F, Schmitt, B H and Dube-Rioux, L (1989) Brand name à la francaise? Oui, but for the right product!, *Advances in Consumer Research*, **16**, pp 253–57

Leif Heim Egil (2002) Variables moderating consumers' reactions to brand extensions, Association for Consumer Research, European Conference Proceedings

Leuthesser, L (1988) Defining, measuring and managing brand equity, Marketing Science Institute, Report no 88–104, Cambridge, MA

Levitt, T (1967) Market stretching, in *Plotting Marketing Strategy*, ed L Adler, Interpublic Press Books, New York

Levitt, T (1969) The augmented product concept, in *The Marketing Mode: Pathways to corporate growth*, McGraw-Hill, New York

Levitt, T (1981) Marketing intangible products and product intangibles, *Harvard Business Review*, **59** (3), May/Jun, pp 94–102

Levitt, T (1983) The globalization of markets, *Harvard Business Review*, May/June

Levy, S (1999) *Brands, Consumers, Symbols and Research*, Sage, Thousand Oaks, CA

Lewi, C and Kapferer, J-N (1996) Consumers' preference for retailers' brands, *Esomar Conference Proceedings – The Big Brand Challenge*, Oct 9–11, pp 229–41

Lindsay, M (1990) Establish brand equity through advertising, *Marketing News*, 22 Jan, pp l6–17

Lindstrom, M (2003) *BRANDchild*, Kogan Page, London

Loden, D J (l992) *Mega Brands*, Irwin, Ill

Loken, B and Roedder John, D (1993) Diluting brand beliefs: when do brand extensions have a negative impact?, *Journal of Marketing*, **57**, July, pp 71–84

MacInnis, D J and Nakamoto, P K (1990) Examining factors that influence the perceived goodness of brand extensions, Working Paper no 54, University of Arizona

Macrae, C (1991) *World Class Brands*, Addison-Wesley, England

Macrae, C (1996) *The Brand Chartering Handbook*, Addison-Wesley, Harlow, UK

Maffesoli, M (1996) *The Time of the Tribes: The decline of individualism in mass societies*, Sage, Thousand Oaks, CA

Magrath, A J (1990) Brands can either grow old gracefully or become dinosaurs, *Marketing News*, 22 Jan, pp l6–17

Marconi, J (1994) *Beyond Branding*, Probus, Chicago

Margolis, S E (1989) Monopolistic competition and multiproduct brand names, *Journal of Business*, **62** (2), pp 199–210

Marketing Mix (1987) Monter une gamme: un problème majeur, *Marketing Mix*, **17**, Nov, pp 40–6

Marion, G (1989) *Les images de l'entreprise*, Les Editions d'Organisation

Martin, D N (1989) *Romancing the Brand*, American Management Association, New York

Mauguère, H (1990) *L'évaluation des entreprises non cotées*, Dunod Entreprise, Paris

Maurice, A (1989) Enquête sur les contremarques: les apprentis sorciers, *References*, May, pp l6–20

Mazanec, J A and Schweiger, G C (1981) Improved marketing efficiency through multiproduct brand names? *European Research*, Jan, pp 32–44

McAlexander, J H, Schouten, J W and Koenig, H F (2002) Building brand community, *Journal of Marketing*, **66** (1), Jan, pp 38–54

McKenna, R (1991) *Relationship Marketing*, Addison-Wesley, Reading, MA

McKinsey Corp (1990) *The Luxury Industry*, McKinsey, Paris

McWilliam, G (1989) Managing the brand manager, in *Brand Valuation*, ed J Murphy, Hutchinson Business Books, London, pp 154–65

Meffert, H and Bruhn, M (1984) *Marken Strategien in Wettbewerb Gabler*, Wiesbaden

Melin, B (1990) Comment evaluer les marques, Research paper, under the direction of J-N Kapferer, HEC, June, Jouy-en-Josas

Meyers-Levy, J (1989) Investigating dimensions of brand names that influence the perceived familiarity of brands, *Advances in Consumer Research*, **16**, pp 258–63

Miniard, Sirdeshmukh and Innis (1992) Peripheral persuasion and brand choice, *Journal of Consumer Research*, **19**, Sep, pp 226–39

Mischel, G (2000) *L'Extension de Marque*, Vuibert, Paris

Moingeon, B and Soenen, G (2003) *Corporate and organizational identities*, Routledge, London

Mongibeaux, J F (1990) Contrefaçons et contremarques, *Revue de l'ENA*, Sep–Oct

Moore, E, Wilkie, W and Lutz, R (2002) Passing the torch: intergenerational influences as sources of brand equity, *Journal of Marketing*, **66** (2), Apr, pp 17–37

Moorhouse, M (1989) Brand accounting, in *Brand Valuation*, ed J Murphy, Hutchinson Business Books, London, pp 143–53

Muller, M and Mainz, A (1989) Brands, bids and balance sheets: putting a price on protected products, *Acquisitions Monthly*, Apr, **24**, pp 26–27

Muniz, A and O'Guinn, T (2001) Brand community, *Journal of Consumer Research*, **27** (4), March, pp 412–32

Murphy, J (1989) *Brand Valuation*, Hutchinson Business Books, London

Murphy, J (1990) *Brand Strategy*, Director Books, London

Nedungadi, P and Hutchinson, J W (1985) The prototypicality of brands, in *Advances in Consumer Research*, 12, ed E Hirschman and M Holbrook, Association for Consumer Research, pp 498–503

Nelson, P (1970) Information and consumer behavior, *Journal of Political Economy*, **78** (2), pp 311–329

Neuhaus, C F and Taylor, J R (1972) Variables affecting sales of family-branded products, *Journal of Marketing Research*, **14**, Nov, pp 419–22

Neyrinck, J (2000) *Les paradoxes du marketing*, Editions d'Organisation, Paris

Nielsen, (1992) *Category Management*, NTC Business Books

Nohria, N and Hansen, M (2003) Organising multinational companies, Harvard Business School Globalization Conference Proceedings

Nussenbaum, M (1990) Comment évaluer les marques, *Option Finance*, 7 May, **113**, pp 20–2

Nussenbaum, M (2003) Juste valeur et actifs incorporels, *Revue d'Economie Financière*, 71, pp 71–86

Olins, W (1978) *The Corporate Personality*, Mayflower, New York

Olins, W (1989) *Corporate Identity*, Thames and Hudson, London

Oliver, T (1987) The wide world of branding, in *Branding: A key marketing tool*, ed J Murphy, McGraw-Hill, London

Parameswaran, M G (2001) *Brand Building Advertising*, Tata McGraw-Hill, New Delhi

Pariente, S (1989) *La concurrence dans les relations industrie–commerce*, Institut du commerce et de la consommation, Paris

Park, C W, Javorskey, B J and MacInnis, D J (1986) Strategic brand concept–image management, *Journal of Marketing*, **50** (Oct) pp 135–45

Park, C W, Milberg, S and Lawson, R (1991) Evaluation of brand extensions, *Journal of Consumer Research*, **18**, Sep, pp 185–93

Pastoureau, M (1992) *Dictionnaire des couleurs de notre temps*, Editions Bonneton

Pauwels, K and Srinivasan, S (2002) Who benefits from store brand entry, Working Paper, UCLA

Pearson, S (1996) *Building Brands Directly*, Macmillan, Basingstoke

Peckham, J O (1981) *The Wheel of Marketing*, Nielsen, Chicago

Pendergrast, M (1993) *For God, Country and Coca-Cola*, Maxwell MacMillan, New York

Penrose, N (1989) Valuation of brand names and trade marks, in *Brand Valuation*, ed J Murphy, Hutchinson Business Books, London, pp 32–45

Peppers, D and Rogers, M (1993) *The One to One Future*, Piatkus, London

Perrier, R (1989) Valuation and licensing, in *Brand Valuation*, ed J Murphy, Hutchinson Business Books, London, pp 104–12

Pettis, C (1995) *Technobrands*, Amacom, New York

Porter, M (1980) Choix stratégiques et concurrence, *Economica*, Paris

Pourquery, D (1987) Mais ou est donc passé Béatrice Foods? *Le monde affaires*, 7 November, pp 10–12

Publicis (1988) Advertising in Europe, *Publicis*, September, 1

Quelch, J and Harding, D (1996) Brands versus private labels, fighting to win, *Harvard Business Review*, Jan–Feb, **74** (1), pp 99–111

Quelch, J and Hoff, E (1986) Customizing global marketing, *Harvard Business Review*, May/Jun

Quelch, J and Kenny, D (1994) Extend profits, not product lines, *Harvard Business Review*, Sep–Oct, **72** (4), pp 153–64

Ramsay, W (1992) The decline and fall of manufacturer branding, *Esomar Conference Proceedings – The Challenge of Branding*, 28–30 October, pp 233–52

Rangaswamy, A, Burke, R and Oliva, T (1993) Brand equity and the extendibility of brand names, *International Journal of Research in Marketing*, **10** (1), pp 61–75

Rao, V R, Mahajan, V and Varaiya, N (1990) A balance model for evaluating firms for acquisition, Working Paper, Graduate School of Management, Cornell University, NY, Jan

Rapp, S and Collins, L (1994) *Beyond Maxi-Marketing*, McGraw-Hill

Rastoin, N (1981) Sortez vos griffes, *Coopération – distribution – consommation*, **5**, pp 26–35

Reddy, S, Holak, S and Bhat, S (1994) To extend or not to extend, *Journal of Marketing Research*, **31**, May, pp 243–62

Rege, P (1959) *A vos marques*, Favre, Lausanne

Regouby, C (1988) *La Communication globale*, Les Editions d'Organisation, Paris

Reichheld, F (1996) *The Loyalty Effect*, Harvard Business School Press, Boston, MA

Resnik, A, Turney, P and Mason, J (1979) Marketers turn to counter segmentation, *Harvard Business Review*, **57** (3), pp 115–29

Revue Française de Comptabilité (1989) Le débat sur les marques en Grande-Bretagne, *Revue Française de Comptabilité*, Oct, **205**, p 19

Revue Française de Comptabilité (1990) Incorporels identifiables: le projet australien, *Revue Française de Comptabilité*, Jan, **208**, p 11

Ridderstrale, J and Nordstrom, K (2000) *Funky Business*, FT Publishing, London

Ries, A (2000) *Advertising is Dead*, McGraw-Hill

Ries, A and Trout, J (1987) *Positioning*, McGraw-Hill, Paris

Ries, A and Trout, J (1990) *Bottom Up Marketing*, PLUME books

Riezebos, H (1994) *Brand-Added Value*, Eburon, Delft, Netherlands

Riezebos, H and Snellen, M (1993) *Brand Names Changes*, Erasmus, Management Report Series, no 149

Riezebos, R (2003) *Brand Management*, Prentice Hall, New York

Rijkenberg, J (2001) *Concepting*, Warc, New York

RISC (1991) *Brand Value and Management in the Luxury Industry*, Sep, International Research Institute on Social Charge, Paris

Roeder-John D, Loken, B and Joiner, C (1995) The negative impact of brand extensions: can you dilute flagship products, Research paper, University of Minnesota

Romaniuk, J and Ehrenberg, A (2003) Do brands lack personality?, Marketing Science Centre Research Report no 14, May, University of South Australia

Rosch, E (1978) Principles of categorization, in *Cognition and Categorization*, ed E Rosch and B Lloyd, Lawrence Erlbaum, Hillsdale, NJ, pp 27–48

Rosch, E and Lloyd, B (1978) *Cognition and Categorization*, Lawrence Erlbaum, Hillsdale, NJ

Rubinson, J (1992) Marketers need new research tools to manage the complex brand portfolios of the 90s, *Marketing Research*, **5** (3), pp 7–11

Russell, A (2002) Investigating the effectiveness of product placements in television shows: the role of modality and plot connection congruence on brand memory and attitude, *Journal of Consumer Research*, Dec, pp 306–18

Rutteman, P (1989) Mergers, acquisitions, brand and goodwill, *Accountancy*, September, p 27

Rutteman, P (1990) Boosting the profits of the brands industry, *Accountancy*, January, pp 26–27

Samways, A and Whittome, K (1994) UK brand strategies: facing the competitive challenge, a Financial Times Management Report, Financial Times, London

Santi, M (1996) The determinants of profitability among suppliers of distributors' own brands, unpublished working paper, HEC Graduate School of Management

Saporito, B (1986) Has been brands go back to work, *Fortune*, 28 Apr, pp 123–24

Sattler, H (1994) *Der Wert von Marken*, Research Paper no 341, Institut für Betriebswirtschaftslehre, Kiel University

Saunders, J and Guoqun, F (1996) Dual branding: how corporate names add value, *Marketing Intelligence and Planning*, **14** (7), pp 29–34

Saunders, J and Watters, R (1993) Branding financial services, *International Journal of Bank Marketing*, **11** (6), pp 32–38

Schechter, A (1993) Names changes increase, *Marketing News*, American Marketing Association, 1 March, p 1

Schlossberg, H (1990) Brand value can be worth more than physical assets, *Marketing News*, 5 Mar, p 6

Schmitt, B (1999) *Experiential Marketing*, Free Press, New York

Schmitt, B (2003) *Customer Experience Management*, Wiley, New York

Schmitt, B and Zhang, S (2001) Creating local brands in multi lingual international markets, *The Journal of Marketing Research*, **38** (3)

Schnaars, D (1995) *Imitation Strategies*, Free Press, New York

Schroiff, H-W and Arnold, D (2003) Managing the brand–product continuum in global markets, Globalization of Markets Colloquium, Harvard Business School, May

Schuiling, I and Kapferer, J-N (2004) How global brands really differ from local brands, paper under review, Université Catholique de Louvain, Belgium and HEC Paris, France

Schwebig, P (1985) *L'identité de l'entreprise*, McGraw Hill, Paris

Schwebig, P (1988) *Les communications de l'entreprise*, McGraw-Hill, Paris

Seguela, J (1982) *Hollywood Lave Plus Blanc*, Flammarion, Paris

Selame, E and Selame, J (1988) *The Company Image*, Wiley, New York

Sicard, M C (2003) *Luxe, mensonge et marketing*, Village Mondial, Paris

Silverstein, M and Fiske, N (2003) *Trading Up*, Portfolio Penguin

Simon, H (2000) *Hidden Champions*, Harvard Business School Press, Cambridge, MA

Simon, C J and Sullivan, M W (1989) The measurement and determinants of brand equity: a financial approach, Working Paper, Oct, University of Chicago

Smith, D and Park, C W (1992) The effects of brand extensions on market share and advertising efficiency, *Journal of Marketing Research*, **29**, Aug, pp 296–313

Steenkamp, J B, Batra, R and Alden, D (2002) How perceived globalness creates brand value, *Journal of International Business Studies*, **0**, pp 1–13

Stobart, P (1989) Brand valuation: a true and fair view, *Accountancy*, Oct, p 27

Stobart, P (1994) *Brand Power*, Macmillan, Basingstoke

Sudovar, B (1987) Branding in the pharmaceutical industry, in *Branding: A key marketing tool*, ed J Murphy, McGraw-Hill, London

Sullivan, M (1988) Measuring image spillovers in umbrella branded products, Working Paper, Graduate School of Business, University of Chicago

Sullivan, M (1991) Brand extension and order of entry, Marketing Science Institute, Report no 91–105, Cambridge, MA

Sullivan, M (1992) Brand extensions: when to use them, *Management Science*, **38**, Jun, pp 793–806

Swaminathan, V, Fox, R and Reddy, S (2001) The impact of brand extension introduction on choice, *Journal of Marketing*, **65** (4), pp 1–15

Swiners, J L (1979) Bilan critique du rôle de la copy–stratégie dans la pratique publicitaire actuelle, *IREP*, Jun, 19

Tauber, E (1988) Brand leverage: strategy for growth in a cost-control world, *Journal of Advertising Research*, Aug–Sep, **28** (4), pp 26–30

Taylor, R (1987) The branding of services, *in Branding: A key marketing tool*, ed J Murphy, McGraw-Hill, London

Tchakhotine, S (1952) *La Propagande Politique*, Gallimard, Paris

Thil, E and Baroux, C (1983) *Un Pave dans la Marque*, Flammarion, Paris

Thiolon, B (1990) La marque et la banque, *Humanisme et Entreprise*, **181**, June, pp 29–32

Thoenig, J C (1990) *Les performances économiques de l'industrie de produits de marque et de la distribution*, ILEC, Paris

Touche Ross Europe (1989) *Accounting for Europe Success by A D 2000*, Internal Report, Touche Ross Europe, London

Trout, J and Ries, A (1981) *Positioning: The battle for your mind*, McGraw Hill

Trout, J and Rivkin, S (2000) *Differentiate or die*, Wiley

Tuvee, L (1987) L'histoire du marketing global: bibliographic commentée, *Revue Française du Marketing*, **114** (4), pp 19–48

Sapolsky, H M (1986) *Consuming Fears: The politics of product risks*, Basic Books, New York

Sappington, D and Wernerfelt, B (1985) To brand or not to brand? *Journal of Business*, **58**, Jul, pp 279–93

University of Minnesota Consumer Behavior Seminar (1987) Affect generalization to similar and dissimilar brand extensions, *Psychology and Marketing*, **4** (Fall), pp 225–37

Upshaw, L (1995) *Building Brand Identity*, Wiley, New York

Valette Florence, P (2004) La personnalite de la marque, *Recherches et Applications en Marketing*

Van Gelder, S (2003) *Global Brand Strategy*, Kogan Page, London

Van Riel, C (2001) Corporate branding management, *Thexis*, **4**, pp 5–12

Veblen, T (1889) *The Theory of The Leisure Class*, Macmillan, New York

Viale, F (1994) Faut-il inscrire les marques an bilan? *Les Echos*, 11 Nov

Viale, F and Lafay, F (1990) Les marques: un nouvel enjeu pour les entreprises, *Revue Francaise de Comptabilité*, 216, Oct, pp 92–99

Ville, G (1986) Maîtriser et optimiser l'avenir d'une marque, *Esomar Congress Proceedings*, pp 527–41

Villemus, P (1996) *La Déroute des Marques*, Editions d'Organisation, Paris

Wansink, B and Ray, M (1996) Advertising strategies to increase usage frequency, *Journal of Marketing*, **60** (1), Jan, pp 31–47

Ward, K (1989) Can the cash flows of brands really be capitalized? in *Brand Valuation*, ed J Murphy, Hutchinson Business Books, London, pp 70–80

Warin, G and Tubiana, A (2003) *Marques sous licence*, Editions d'Organisation, Paris

Wathieu, L, Zaltman, G and Liu, Y (2003) Rooting marketing strategy in human universals, Globalization of Markets Colloquium, Harvard Business School

Watkins, T (1986) *The Economics of the Brands: A marketing analysis*, McGraw-Hill

Wentz, L (1989) How experts value brands, *Advertising Age*, 16 Jan, p 24

Wernerfelt, B (1988) Umbrella branding as a signal of new product quality, *Rand Journal of Economics*, **19** (Autumn), pp 458–66

Wernerfelt, B (1990) Advertising content when brand choice is a signal, *Journal of Business*, **63** (1), pp 91–98

Winram, S (1987) The opportunity for world brands, in *Branding: A key marketing tool*, ed J Murphy, McGraw-Hill, London

Yentis, A and Bond, J (1995) Andres comes out of the closet, *Marketing and Research Today*, **23** (2), May, pp l04–12

Yoshimori, M (1989) Concepts et stratégies de marque au Japon, in *La marque*, ed J-N Kapferer and J C Thoenig, McGraw-Hill, Paris

Young, R (1967) Multibrand entries, in *Plotting Marketing Strategy*, ed L Adler, Interpublic Press Books, New York

Young & Rubicam (1994) *Brand Asset Valuator*, Young & Rubicam, London

Yovovich, B G (1988) What is your brand really worth? *Adweek's Marketing Week*, 8 August, pp 18–24

Yovovich, B G (1995) *New Marketing Imperatives*, Prentice Hall, Englewood Cliffs, NJ

Zaichkowsky, J and Simpson, R (1996) The effect of experience with a brand imitator on the original brand, *Marketing Letters*, **7** (1), pp 31–39

Zareer, P (1987) De la valeur des marques de commerce, *CA Magazine*, Feb, p 72

Zhang, S and Schmitt, B (2001) Creating local brands in a multilingual international market, *Journal of Marketing Research*, **38**, Aug, pp 313–25

Zyman, S (1999) *The End of Marketing as We Know It*, Harper Business

Index

NB: page numbers in *italic* indicate figures or tables

Also published by Kogan Page

Beyond Branding: *How the new values of transparency and integrity are changing the world of brands*
Nicholas Ind

Brand Driven: *The route to integrated branding through great leadership*
F Joseph LePla, Susan Davis and Lynn M Parker

Brand Failures: *The truth about the 100 biggest branding mistakes of all time*
Matt Haig

Brand Management Checklist: *Proven tools and techniques for creating winning brands*
Brad van Auken

Brand New Brand Thinking: *Brought to life by 11 experts who do*
Edited by Merry Basking and Mark Earls

Brand Royalty: *How the world's top 100 brands thrive and survive*
Matt Haig

BRANDchild: *Remarkable insights into the minds of today's global kids and their relationships with brands*
Martin Lindstrom

The Essential Brand Book: *Over 100 techniques to increase brand value*
2nd edition, Iain Ellwood

Global Brand Strategy: *Unlocking brand potential across countries, cultures and markets*
Sicco van Gelder

If You're So Brilliant... How Come Your Brand isn't Working Hard Enough?: *The essential guide to brand management*
Peter Cheverton

Integrated Branding: *Becoming brand-driven through company-wide action*
F Joseph LePla and Lynn M Parker

Living the Brand: *How to transform every member of your organization into a brand champion*
2nd edition, Nicholas Ind

Marketing: *Essential principles, new realities*
Jonathan Groucutt, Peter Leadley and Patrick Forsyth

Marketing Communications: *An integrated approach*
4th edition, P R Smith and Jonathan Taylor

Media Monoliths: *How great brands thrive and survive*
Mark Tungate

The Philosophy of Branding: *Great philosophers think brands*
Thom Braun

Reinventing the Brand: *Can top brands survive the new market realities?*
Jean-Noël Kapferer

The above titles are available from all good bookshops. To obtain further information, please contact the publisher at the address below:

Kogan Page Limited
120 Pentonville Road
London N1 9JN
United Kingdom
Tel:+44 (0) 20 7278 0433
Fax:+44 (0) 20 7837 6348
www.kogan-page.co.uk